Social Problems For The Twenty-First Century

Social Problems For The Twenty-First Century

FIRST EDITION

J. John Palen

Virginia Commonwealth University

Boston   Burr Ridge, IL   Dubuque, IA   Madison, WI
New York   San Francisco   St. Louis
Bangkok   Bogotá   Caracas   Lisbon   London   Madrid   Mexico City
Milan   New Delhi   Seoul   Singapore   Sydney   Taipei   Toronto

McGraw-Hill Higher Education

A Division of The **McGraw-Hill** Companies

Social Problems for the Twenty-First Century

Published by McGraw-Hill, an imprint of The McGraw-Hill Companies, Inc. 1221 Avenue of the Americas, New York, NY, 10020. Copyright © 2001 by The McGraw-Hill Companies, Inc. All rights reserved. No part of this publication may be reproduced or distributed in any form or by any means, or stored in a database or retrieval system, without the prior written consent of The McGraw-Hill Companies, Inc., including, but not limited to, in any network or other electronic storage or transmission, or broadcast for distance learning.

Some ancillaries, including electronic and print components, may not be available to customers outside the United States.

This book is printed on acid-free paper.

2 3 4 5 6 7 8 9 0 WCK/WCK 0 9 8 7 6 5 4 3 2 1

ISBN   0-07-048141-5

Editorial director: *Philip A. Butcher*
Senior sponsoring editor: *Sally Constable*
Development editor: *Rosalind Sackoff*
Marketing manager: *Leslie Kraham*
Project manager: *Jim Labeots*
Production supervisor: *Michael McCormick*
Freelance design coordinator: *Pam Verros*
Senior photo research coordinator: *Keri Johnson*
Supplement coordinator: *Jason Greve*
New media: *Kimberly Stark*
Cover illustration: *Paul D. Turnbaugh*
Compositor: *Carlisle Communications, Ltd.*
Typeface: *10/12 Palatino*
Printer: *Quebecor Printing Book Group*

Library of Congress Cataloging-in-Publication Data

Palen, J. John.
    Social problems for the twenty-first century / J. John Palen.
        p. cm.
    Includes bibliographical references and indexes.
    ISBN 0-07-048141-5
    1. Social problems—United States. 2. United States—Social conditions—1980-
HN59.2 .P375 2000
361.1'0973—dc21
                                        00-022122

www.mhhe.com

Dedication

Dedication

for Karen

About the Author

J. John Palen

J. John Palen has authored twelve books on sociology and is a Professor of Sociology at Virginia Commonwealth University where he has received the College of Humanities and Sciences Distinguished Scholar Award. In 1997 he was designated a Fulbright Distinguished Scholar and has held the Fulbright Chair in North American Studies at the University of Calgary. He likes progressive jazz, hiking in the Blue Ridge Mountains, and exploring cities.

Preface

Social Problems for the Twenty-First Century is a text written for a new century and a new millennium. Although there are any number of social problems textbooks available, many of them were originally written during the 1970s or 1980s, before most of the students taking social problems now were even born. Social problems issues and knowledge have changed a great deal since Jimmy Carter was president.

This text makes two basic assumptions about social problems and how they should be presented. First, it assumes that scientific inquiry and research is the best means of understanding and predicting human behavior. Personal experiences and philosophical beliefs about the nature of human behavior can be both insightful and valuable; however, personal insights or common sense, even though sounding reasonable, should not be confused with empirical data.

Second, the text assumes that social facts never occur in a vacuum. Data rarely, if ever, "speak for themselves." How a person interprets particular facts depends on his or her orientation, beliefs, and theoretical perspective. For example, those who believe that there is a fundamental contradiction between the American ideology of competitive individualism on one hand and the constraints of a rigid social system on the other hand, will view data on crime in one fashion. Those holding a functionalist or labeling perspectives may interpret the same data very differently.

Social Problems for the Twenty-First Century presents data, scientific knowledge, and opinions as accurately and as fairly as possible. The goal is to build on students' natural interest in social problems and encourage them to develop both a sociological perspective and a sociological imagination that will allow them to examine social problems in a critical fashion. Instructors and students alike have a right to expect that they can rely on a text to present research data accurately and honestly. If this is done, the instructor need have no reservation about stressing or advocating a particular theoretical approach or course or action. I believe instructors have every right—and sometimes an obligation—to tell their students where they stand on the social issues under discussion. *Social Problems for the Twenty-First Century* provides the instructor with a trustworthy base from which she or he can feel free to elaborate, disagree, and discuss.

Social Problems for the Twenty-First Century encourages the student to think about significant policy and social implications. "Everything everywhere is getting worse" approaches are not only inaccurate, but they also imply nothing can be done and discourage students from attempts to improve the future. However, students need to be made aware that "solutions" to problems often involve contradictions and trade-offs, and that social problems are not necessarily the consequence of social disorganization and/or breakdown. For example, the anti-Semitism of Nazi Germany was a product of a highly organized and smoothly functioning system, not the product of a system that was suffering from major internal dissension.

Finally, a textbook also has to be honest about what it cannot do. It would be pompous to suggest that any social problems textbook has the answers to the nation's ills. While this text makes some suggestions with regard to specific issues, there are no guaranteed surefire solutions.

I confess to being optimistic about the future. As expressed by Martin Luther King, Jr., "I refuse to accept the view that mankind is so tragically bound to the starless midnight of racism and war that the bright daybreak of peace and brotherhood can never become reality. I believe that unarmed truth and unconditional love will have the final word."

Organization of the Text

Social Problems for the Twenty-First Century is divided into six parts. Part One, *Looking at Social Problems,* introduces students to the ways in which sociologists use their sociological imagination and research to define and address social problems. It also discusses the major theoretical approaches and ways to distinguish bogus facts and dubious facts from real data in our fact-clogged era.

Part Two, *Problems of Inequality,* begins the focus on specific social problems by discussing the most crucial social issues today—those involving inequality. Chapter 2, "To Have and Have Not," examines economic inequality and poverty. Chapter 3, "The Color Line," delves into America's most persistent and polarizing problem, the issues surrounding race. Chapter 4, "The Cracked Melting Pot," broadens the discussion to our increasingly multiethnic society and the consequences of being Hispanic, Asian American, or Native American today. Chapter 5, "The Gendered Order," examines gender inequality and the crucial role gender plays in defining social problems. This chapter was authored by Meg Wilkes Karraker.

Part Three, *Problems of the Global Setting,* examines social problems whose effects extend beyond national borders. Chapter 6, "The Question of People," looks closely at the consequences of population growth, both for the world and for the United States, and fully explores the problem of immigration reform and its consequences. Chapter 7, "Urban Life and Deviance," examines the city as the setting for most social problems and the role of city life in social problems. Chapter 8, "The Economy and the World of Work," explores the ways in which downsizing, restructuring, and other economic changes unthought of two decades ago have affected individuals, families, and communities.

Part Four, *Problems of the Life Cycle,* deals with social problems that affect individual and society differently at different life stages. Chapter 9, "Education under Stress," examines how America's educational system has failed to adapt to the educational requirements of the new century. Chapter 10, "Ties That Bind: The Changing Family," discusses the massive changes in marriage age, divorce rates, and out-of-wedlock births that are transforming the structure and definition of American families. Chapter 11, "Aging and Ageism," looks at these emerging social problems as we move into an era when both the numbers and percentage of the aged population is dramatically increasing.

Part Five, *Problems of Violating Social Norms,* examines how selected social problems affect individuals as well as society. Chapter 12, "Crime and Violence," discusses the social problem that opinion polls most commonly list as the nation's most serious social problem—crime. Considerable attention is given to white-collar crime, organized crime, and professional crime as well as the more commonly covered street crime. Chapter 13, "Substance Abuse: Legal and Otherwise," examines the social history and current status of alcohol abuse, drug usage, and cigarette smoking as well as how attitudes and policies have changed and are likely to change in the future. Chapter 14, "Problems of the Health System and Mental Disorders," discusses the increasing problems associated with the restructuring and cutbacks of both insurance and health services in delivering adequate health and mental health services, and especially the social problems associated with the AIDS epidemic. Chapter 15, "Society and Sexuality," discusses the social consequences of the sexual revolution over the past quarter-century, gender patterns, prostitution, and pornography.

Part Six, *Looking Ahead,* examines emerging social problems of the twenty-first century. Here the emphasis is on new social problems, especially the social consequences of environmental degradation and of war and terrorism.

Features of the Text

Chapter Opener and Outline. Each chapter opens with a vignette or quote that links to the chapter content. A detailed outline takes the reader through the chapter content.

Dubious Fact. Designed to sharpen the reader's awareness of accuracy and honest discussion, each chapter opens with an eyebrow-raising "fact" that on the surface appears to be accurate. It is followed by the actual reality.

Boxes. Each chapter has two boxes designed to spark student interest and discussion.

MAKING A DIFFERENCE shows how people who get involved in community and society can have an impact on helping to fix a societal ill.

ONGOING ISSUES are provocative discussions of topics that are in the forefront of the field. Critical thinking questions at the end of each box provide practical applications.

Theoretical Approaches. Before detailed presentation of data, each chapter provides an examination of the topic as seen from functionalist, conflict, and interactionist perspectives.

Ethnic Issues. Although we live in a multiethnic society and Hispanics will soon be the largest minority population in America, social problems texts commonly combine a brief discussion of ethnicity into a chapter on race.

Social Problems for the Twenty-First Century has two chapters on race; Chapter 3, "The Color Line", and Chapter 4, "The Cracked Melting Pot," which discusses Latinos, Asian Americans, Native Americans, and white ethnic populations.

Gender Issue. Because of the importance of gender, this text includes a specially commissioned chapter, The Gendered Order, written by Meg Wilkes Karraker, associate professor of Sociology at St. Thomas University in Minnesota. From her unique position as Executive Officer for Sociologists for Women in Society, Dr. Karraker is able to look at gender issues from an intellectually stimulating, yet practical, point of view.

Toward the Future. Each chapter concludes its coverage of a topic with a section that discusses future prospects and the most likely developments regarding a social problem over the next several decades.

Questions for Discussion. Each chapter ends with a series of thought-provoking questions that can be used to stimulate classroom discussion or, as student assignments.

Photos and Illustrative Material. An extensive photo program with captions that elaborate upon text material, illustrated and emphasizes important text concepts. Tables, figures, and graphs have been designed with the beginning student in mind.

Suggested Resources. At the end of each chapter is a list of suggested websites, videos and films, books, and articles to expand on material discussed in the chapter.

Internet Exercises. Two exercises at the end of each chapter take the student online to analyze carefully-chosen sites and social issues relevant to each chapter and to students' interests.

Glossary. A social problems text requires clear explanation of sociological terms. Key terms are defined in the margin of the text and there is a complete glossary at the end of the text.

Summary. A "bullet" summary helps students review the important themes of each chapter.

Methodological Appendix. A methods appendix provides an overview of the major ways of how to go about doing sociological research. This appendix can be used as an adjunct to Chapter 1 for instructors who wish to devote more time to "how we know what we know."

Supplements Package

As a full service publisher of quality educational products, McGraw-Hill does much more than just sell textbooks to students. We create and publish an extensive array of print, video, and digital supplements to support instruction on your campus. Orders of new (versus used) textbooks help us to defray the cost of developing such supplements, which is substantial. Please consult your local McGraw-Hill representative to learn about the availability of the supplements that accompany *Social Problems for the Twenty-First Century.*

Support for the Student

- **Making The Grade** CD-ROM packaged **free** with the text, provides students with an excellent resource that offers enrichment, review, and self-testing. The following components are included:
  - Internet Primer
  - Study Skills Primer
  - Guide to Electronic Research
  - Twenty multiple-choice questions per chapter that are graded automatically
  - Learning Styles Assessment
  - Link to the book's web-based Online Learning Center
- **Student's Online Learning Center** is a web-based, interactive study guide featuring URLs relevant to each topic, self-grading quizzes, overviews, learning objectives, key term flashcards and more for each chapter. Please visit at www.mhhe.com/Palen.
- **PowerWeb** is also packaged **free** with the text. PowerWeb is a password protected website developed by Dushkin/McGraw-Hill giving students:
  - Web links and articles
  - Study tools—quizzing, review forms, time management tools, web research
  - Interactive exercises
  - Weekly updates with assessment
  - Informative and timely world news
  - Material on how to conduct Web research
  - Daily news feed of topic specific news
  - Access to *Northern Lights Research Engine* (received multiple Editor's Choice awards for superior capabilities from *PC Magazine*)
- **Student Study Guide**

Support for the Instructor

- **Instructor's Manual,** prepared by John Mahoney, Virginia Commonwealth University, provides sociology instructors with detailed key terms, essay questions, additional lecture ideas, and much more.
- **Testbank,** also prepared by John Mahoney, Virginia Commonwealth University and fully coordinated with the Instructor's Manual and Student Study Guide.
- **Computerized Testbank,** easy-to-use computerized testing program for both Windows and Macintosh computers.

- **PowerPoint Slides,** complete chapter-by-chapter slideshows featuring tables, illustrations, photos and more (may be accessed on the web to use with PageOut for creating individual websites for the class). Instructor's are welcome to generate overhead transparencies from the slides if they wish to do so.

- **Instructor's Online Learning Center** contains a variety of resources, activities, and classroom tips. The text's Instructor's manual, PowerPoint slides and more may be accessed electronically on this site.

- **PageOut: The Course Website Development Center** is designed for the professor just beginning to explore Web options or the professor needing to save time and simplify this process. In less than an hour, even the most novice computer user can create a course website with a template provided by McGraw-Hill (no programming knowledge required). **PageOut** lets you offer your students instant access to your syllabus, lecture notes, and original material. Students can even check grades online. And, you can pull any of the McGraw-Hill content from the Palen Online Learning Center into your website. PageOut also provides a discussion board where you and your students can exchange questions and post announcements, as well as an area for students to build personal Web pages. To find out more about PageOut, ask your McGraw-Hill representative for details, or fill out the form at www.mhhe.com/pageout.

- **Presentation Manager** is a CD-ROM that includes the contents of the Instructor's Manual, Testbanks, PowerPoint slides and more for instructors' convenience in customizing multimedia lectures.

- **PowerWeb**—see description under Support for Students section above. For further information, visit the PowerWeb site at http://mhhe/NewMedia/dushkin/index.html#powerweb.

- **SocCity** is a veritable melting pot of sociology cybersources, information, and Internet activities for students and instructors alike. Just click on any of the four buttons on the left side of your screen and get started (www.mhhe.com/soscience/sociology).

- **Videos**—a wide variety of videos from the Films for Humanities and Sciences series as well as other sources is available to adopters of this text.

Acknowledgments

Although I take full responsiblity for any errors in the volume, either of omission or commission, it is clear that the strengths of *Social Problems for the Twenty-First Century* are due to the contributions of a number of people. The text benefited from the assistance and talent of colleagues, both in sociology and at McGraw-Hill. Dr. Meg Karraker especially merits credit for authoring a splendid gender chapter. Jeffery Will joined in initially formulating plans for developing the text. My colleague, John Mahoney deserves credit for writing the excellent Internet exercises. The text also has profited from the comments and suggestions of a number of colleagues in sociology who reviewed early drafts of my manuscript. My sincere thanks go to:

Sergio A. Banda, *Fullerton Community College*

Rita Duncan, *Tulsa Community College*

Kenneth Eslinger, *John Carroll University*

Timothy Evans, *Allegheny Community College*

Kurt Finsterbush, *University of Maryland at College Park*

Lee Frank, *Community College of Allegheny County*

Donald Green, *Oxnard College*

Mary Holley, *Montclair State University*

Janet Hope, *St. John's University*

Wanda Kaluza

Robert McNamara, *Furman University*

Stephen Muzzatti, *Clark College, Vancouver, Washington*

Ronald A. Penton, Sr., *Gulf Coast Community College*

Anne R. Peterson, *Columbus State Community College, Ohio*

Pamela Rountree, *University of Kentucky*

Jon A. Schlenker, *University of Maine, Augusta*

Dale Spady, *Northern Michigan University*

Edward G. Stockwell, *Bowling Green State*

Peter Vivisto, *Augustana College*

Jo Wayne, *Gordon College*

Nathan Zirl, *University of Texas, El Paso*

At McGraw-Hill I would especially like to thank my Development Editor, Roz Sackoff, whose judgement and professional skills I have come to rely upon. I will miss our regular e-mails. Inge King, with whom I have worked on other books, once again did a fine job as photo editor. I also owe major debts to Jill Gordon, my fine original Sponsoring Editor, and to Phil Butcher, McGraw-Hill's sociologically-knowledgeable Editorial Director and Publisher. Finally, very special thanks go to Sally Constable, Sponsoring Editor for Sociology, whose skill, energy, and encouragement, coupled with her sense of humor, saw the text through to completion.

J. John Palen

Brief Table of Contents

Table of Contents

Chapter 10
Ties That Bind: The Changing Family 266

Chapter 11
Aging and Ageism 298

Chapter 14
Problems of the Health
System and Mental
Disorders   392

Chapter 15
Society and Sexuality   428

List of Boxes

Visual Preview

Social Problems for the Twenty-First Century is an exciting and contemporary integrated learning package, reflecting the concerns and problems of the new century and the new millennium. J. John Palen presents the latest sociological data, knowledge, and opinions so that any instructor, regardless of his or her theoretical orientation, will have a trustworthy base from which to elaborate, disagree, or discuss. The text builds on students' natural interest in social problems and encourages them to develop both a sociological perspective and a sociological imagination that will allow them to examine social problems in a critical fashion.

Chapter Opener and Outline

Each chapter opens with a vignette or quote that links to the chapter content. A detailed outline takes the reader through the chapter content.

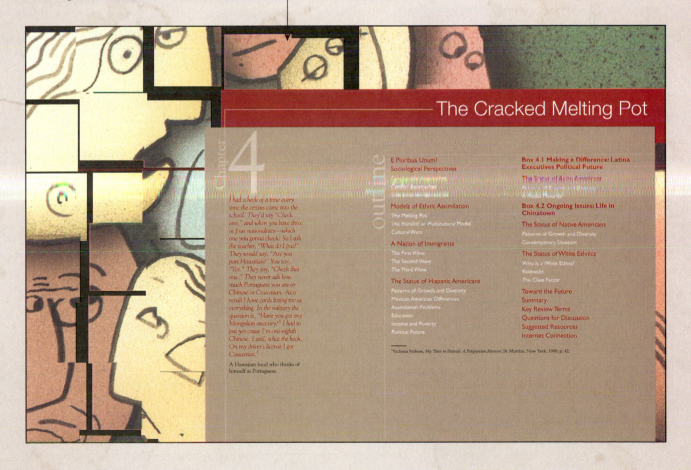

Table 5.2 shows, white women earned more than black women, who in turn earned more than Hispanic women. However, the median weekly earnings for white women were the same as those for black men, but higher than those of Hispanic men.[74]

The apparent inroads women have made in earnings relative to men are largely due to the erosion of men's real earnings over the same period.[75] Richard Hogan and Carolyn Perrucci have calculated that the declining gender gap in earnings is due not to women's progress toward achieving earnings equity, but rather to the fact that male earnings declined more rapidly in terms of constant dollars than did female earnings.[76] Furthermore, Hogan and Perrucci argue that any small decline in the gender gap has been at the expense of a marginal increase in the racial gap in earnings.[77]

The gap that persists between women's and men's earnings is largely due to industry, firm, and occupational segregation. According to Tomaskovic-Devey, women tend to be "ghettoized" rather than spread across industries, occupations, firms, and specialties.[78] U.S. Department of Labor statistics show that 40.1 percent of employed women work in technical, sales, and administrative support occupations, and 31.4 percent are employed in managerial and professional specialty occupations. One out of every five employed women works as a primary or secondary teacher, secretary, or cashier.[79]

Women now enter college in greater numbers than men and are entering certain high-paying fields in record numbers (e.g., by 1994 the percentages of women earning degrees in medicine, dentistry, and law had risen to 37.9, 38.5, and 43.0 percent respectively).[80] Occupational disparities in pay persist, however, even at the highest levels. The **glass ceiling** refers to barriers to women's upward mobility through the highest levels in organizations. Among Fortune 500 companies, only 11.2 percent of corporate officers are women, and just 3.8 percent of the individuals holding one of the highest executive titles (chairman, vice chairman, chief executive officer, president, senior vice president, executive vice president) are women.[81] A recent study of men and women in the corporate elite in southern California suggests that women are more likely than men to emphasize social networks and such strategies as obtaining advanced educational degrees or modifying behavior to break through the glass ceiling.[82]

glass ceiling
barriers to women's upward mobility through the highest levels in organizations

Poverty and Economic Opportunity

Married-couple families with employed wives have the highest median annual income of any family type. As shown in Table 5.3, married-couple families in which the wife was not employed had a median income just 60 percent of that of married-couple

[74]U.S. Department of Labor, Bureau of Labor Statistics, *Employment and Earnings, 2nd Quarter,* http://stats.bls.gov/news.release/wkyeng/t02.htm, 1999.
[75]Barbara F. Reskin and Patricia A. Roos, *Job Queues, Gender Queues: Explaining Women's Inroads into Male Occupations.* Temple University Press, Philadelphia, 1990, pp. 306–307.
[76]Richard Hogan and Carolyn C. Perrucci, "Producing and Reproducing Class and Status Differences: Racial and Gender Gaps in U.S. Employment and Retirement Income," *Social Problems* 45, 4 (November), 1998, pp. 528–549.
[77]Hogan and Perrucci, p. 530.
[78]Donald Tomaskovic-Devey, *Gender and Racial Inequality at Work: The Sources and Consequences of Job Segregation,* ILR, Ithaca, NY, 1993, pp. 122–123.
[79]U.S. Department of Labor Women's Bureau, 1999.
[80]U.S. Bureau of the Census, *Statistical Abstract of the United States,* U.S. Government Printing Office, Washington, DC, 1997.
[81]"Fact Sheet: 1998 Catalyst Census of Women Corporate Officers and Top Earners," www.catalyst-women.org, June 18, 1999, p. 1.
[82]Sally Ann Davies-Netzley, "Women above the Glass Ceiling: Perceptions on Corporate Mobility and Strategies for Success," *Gender and Society,* 12, 3 (June), 1998, pp. 339–355.

Key Terms and Definitions in Margin

Key terms are defined in the margin on the page where the term is first introduced, making it easier for the reader to study the material.

Dubious Fact

A chapter-opening, eyebrow-raising Dubious Fact is designed to sharpen the reader's awareness of accuracy and honest reporting. This "fact" appears to be accurate but the Dubious Fact is followed by the actual reality.

Dubious Fact

The most deadly drugs in America are cocaine and heroin.

Cocaine and heroin cause roughly 15,000 deaths a year in the United States. Legal drugs are far more deadly. Alcohol causes 90,000 deaths a year, while tobacco causes over 400,000. Worldwide, 3 million people a year die as a consequence of smoking tobacco.

Drugs as a Way of Life

Cramming for an exam, your roommate lights another cigarette and pours another cup of coffee. Writing an overdue term paper, you pop a pep pill to stay awake. Finishing several hours later, you both relax by having a beer. Two hours later, unable to fall asleep, you take a Sominex and an aspirin.

Extent of Usage

America has become a giant drugstore, where "better living through chemistry" seems to have become a national slogan. We accept that most people cannot get through a normal day without taking drugs of some sort. If you doubt this, go through your living quarters and count the number of drugs you find. Include all prescription and nonprescription "medicines," such as sedatives, tranquilizers, stimulants, and narcotic and alcoholic based cough syrups. Because alcohol is a drug, include beer and alcoholic beverages in your total. Be sure not to overlook the pack of cigarettes with its addictive nicotine. Then include milder drugs, such as caffeine in coffee or tea. All the above are legal drugs.

Name the problem, and there is a drug to solve it. Drugs are the answer to outbursts of temper, lack of energy, inability to sleep, constipation, and diarrhea. Psychoactive (mood-altering) drugs promise even more by providing shortcuts to self-awareness, inner peace, and euphoria, or by simply allowing one to forget or ignore all the complex and messy problems that come with being alive. There is Ritalin for hyperactive children and Prozac for everyone else. We even expect to cure drug problems with drugs (e.g., heroin dependence with methadone or buprenorphine). While reading this chapter, keep in mind that, while using drugs to solve problems or to make us feel better is imbedded in our culture, society makes sharp distinctions between using what are defined as legal drugs and those prohibited as illegal.

Social Definitions of Drugs

In the first chapter we discussed C. Wright Mills's distinction between private troubles and public issues. Drug abuse falls into the second category because it harms society and the problem can be resolved only with collective action. Today drug abuse is closely associated with crime. According to the National Institutes of Justice, the percentage of arrestees testing positive for illicit drug use ranged from 51 percent in San Jose to 80 percent in Chicago (based on urine samples of male arrestees in 23 cities).[1] In New York City, where three-

[1]Office of National Drug Control Policy, *Drug Data Summary,* Government Printing Office, Washington, DC, April 1999, p. 2.

Effective Tables

Easy-to-read tables present the latest findings and summarize important concepts.

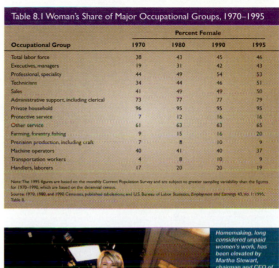

Table 8.1 Woman's Share of Major Occupational Groups, 1970–1995				
	Percent Female			
Occupational Group	1970	1980	1990	1995
Total labor force	38	43	45	46
Executives, managers	19	31	42	43
Professional, speciality	44	49	54	53
Technicians	34	44	46	51
Sales	41	49	49	50
Administrative support, including clerical	73	77	77	79
Private household	96	95	95	95
Protective service	7	12	16	16
Other service	61	63	63	65
Farming, forestry, fishing	9	15	16	20
Precision production, including craft	7	8	10	9
Machine operators	40	41	40	37
Transportation workers	4	8	10	9
Handlers, laborers	17	20	20	19

Note: The 1995 figures are based on the monthly Current Population Survey and are subject to greater sampling variability than the figures for 1970–1990, which are based on the decennial census.
Source: 1970, 1980, and 1990 Censuses, published tabulations, and U.S. Bureau of Labor Statistics, *Employment and Earnings* 43, no. 1: 1995, Table 8.

Homemaking, long considered unpaid women's work, has been elevated by Martha Stewart, chairman and CEO of Martha Stewart Omnimedia, into a multi-million dollar business.

Douglas Healey/AP/Wide World Photos

The Color Line

The Cracked Melting Pot

†Victoria Nelson, *My Time in Hawaii: A Polynesian Memoir*, St. Martins, New York, 1989, p. 37.

Ethnic Issues

In order to realistically treat an important issue for the twenty-first century, this text includes two chapters on Race: Chapter 3, "The Color Line," and Chapter 4, "The Cracked Melting Pot," which discuss Latinos, Asian Americans, Native Americans, and white ethnic populations.

Box 4.1   Making a Difference

Latina Executives

Latina women are beginning to enter the corporate executive suites. Among those making it is Gloria De Neochea, a long-time single mother who grew up in the poor southern California border town of Calexio and worked her way through school. She is currently Manager of the Mattel Foundation in California, where she oversees the corporation's grants, arts, and social welfare programs. De Neochea also directs the foundation's volunteer program. She started foundation work 10 years ago at the Carnegie Foundation.

According to De Neochea, working for a company foundation is better than just being part of the corporation. "It's the best of both worlds. You distribute the company's profits and give back to children. The other rewarding part is helping employees give back to the community. You have an opportunity to be a link."[a] She encourages young Latinas to be "strong, smart, and bold" and to "face every obstacle as a learning and growing opportunity."

De Neochea feels that Latinas have unique skills that they can contribute to corporations. "It's difficult to assess each corporate culture and find thoughtful ways you can contribute to the company's goals. But it is extremely rewarding to give our unique perspective as women and Latinas to management's knowledge base and help a company succeed. Companies succeed because of diversity."

[a]Jerry Berrios, "A Balancing Act," LATINA/Style, 3(2): 25–26, 1997.

Making a Difference

Designed to spark student interest and discussion, Making a Difference boxes show how people who get involved in community and society can have an impact on helping to address a societal ill. Critical thinking questions at the end of each box provide practical applications.

Ongoing Issues

Ongoing Issues boxes provide provocative discussions of topics that are in the forefront of the field. Critical thinking questions at the end of each box provide practical applications.

Box 10.1   Ongoing Issues

The Way We Never Were

In her books, *The Way We Never Were: American Families and the Nostalgia Trap* and *The Way We Really Are: Coming to Terms with the America's Changing Families* Stephanie Coontz argues that working mothers are here to stay. In *The Way We Really Are* Coontz says:

"One of the most common misconceptions about modern marriage is the notion that coprovider families are a new invention in human history. In fact, today's dual-earner family represents a return to older norms, after a very short interlude that people mistakenly identify as 'traditional.'

. . . Proponents of the modified male breadwinner family believe that if we could drastically reduce the number of single-mother households, raise wages for men, and convince families to get by on a little less, we might be able to get wives to quit work during their child raising years. . . . But a return to the norm of male breadwinner families is simply not feasible for most Americans.

It is not just a dollars-and-cents issue. Most women would not give up the satisfactions of their jobs even if they could afford to quit. They consistently tell interviewers they like the social respect, self-esteem, and friendship networks they gain from the job, despite the stress they may face finding acceptable child care and negotiating household chores with their husbands. . . . Another reason women do not want to quit work is that they are not willing to surrender the increased leverage it gives them in the family. The simple truth is that women who do not earn income have much less decision-making power in marital relations than women who do."[a]

[a]Stephanie Coontz, The Way We Really Are: Coming to Terms with America's Changing Families, Basic Books, New York, 1997.

Internet Connection www.mhhe.com/palen

1. A good resource to begin with is the U.S. Department of Education's home page, (*www.ed.gov/index.html*). Here, you will find links to many useful sites including, The Digest of Educational Statistics, The Encyclopedia of Educational Statistics, and The National Library of Education. Click on "Nations Report Card (NAPE)." NAPE stands for the National Assessment of Educational Progress, a congressionally mandated project that has been monitoring the academic performance of fourth, eighth, and twelfth graders since 1969. Click on "Science" and then go to "Findings" (*www.nces. ed.gov/nationsreport card/science/sci_findings.asp*).

   a. What does NAPE have to say about the performance of U.S. students in the sciences?

   b. Check their performance in other subjects.

   c. Does NAPE make any provision for international comparisons of U.S. students with their counterparts in other nations?

2. Visit the website of the National Education Association (NEA), "America's oldest and largest organization committed to advancing the cause of public education" (*www.nea.org/*). Click on the "Issues" button.

   a. What is the NEA's position on Bilingual Education?

   b. What are the reasons that it gives for taking this position?

   c. What other issues that the NEA is currently concerning itself with?

   d. Would you consider this to be a liberal or conservative organization? Why?

Internet Connection

Internet exercises in every chapter take students online to analyze carefully chosen sites and social issues relevant to each chapter and to students' interests.

Oprah Winfrey, one of America's most respected personalities, wearing her newly-presented special 50th Anniversary Gold Medal for her contributions to reading and books while holding her 1999 National Book Awards trophy.

Diane Bondareff/AP/Wide World Photos

Toward the Future

Each chapter concludes with a section entitled Toward the Future that discusses future prospects and the most likely developments to impact the social problem for the next decade.

Toward the Future

As the new century begins, the American dilemma with race continues to polarize the population. Racism persists but, compared to the last century, patterns of racial segregation are slowly declining and racial prejudice and discrimination are decreasing. During the twenty-first century, issues that the twentieth century defined as being racial questions will increasingly be redefined as issues of social class rather than color. The new century may see the African American population increasingly split between a middle-class segment growing in confidence and affluence and a truly disadvantaged segment isolated from the rest of the society. The success of the first group will further highlight the despair and desolation of the latter.

Paradoxically, the economic success of an African American suburban middle class raises the possibility that an African American heritage that survived 300 years of adversity could be weakened and undermined by economic success. This is what occurred with European and Asian immigrant populations. The common assumption, that the lives of blacks, because of race, will always be different than those of whites or Asian Americans, may not hold in the future. If the significance of race declines, African American heritage could come to have the same significance to future generations of middle-class suburbanites as Irish, German, or Italian heritage does now for European-background groups. In other words, having a black heritage would be something of interest but not something that strongly affects one's daily life. It would be equivalent to being Japanese American or Italian American today.

For poor blacks, future prospects are guarded, but the turn of the century showed some positive signs. The down side is that, while affirmative action programs have

80

A Wealth of Media Resources

Making the Grade

This CD-ROM, packaged free with the text, provides students with an excellent resource that offers enrichment, review, and self-testing.

PowerWeb

Offered free with the text, PowerWeb is a turnkey solution for adding the Internet to a course. A password-protected website developed by Dushkin/McGraw-Hill, PowerWeb offers instructors and students course-specific materials, web links and articles, student study tools, and more.

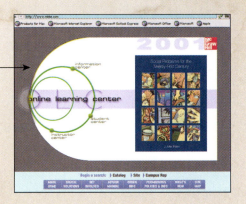

Online Learning Center

Online Learning Center is a text-specific website (www.mhhe.com/palen) that offers students and professors a variety of resources and activities. Material from this website can be used in creating the PageOut website.

PageOut: The Course Website Development Center

Designed for the instructor just beginning to explore web options, PageOut allows even the most novice computer user to create a course website with a template provided by McGraw-Hill.

Create a custom course Website with PageOut, free with every McGraw-Hill textbook.

To learn more, contact your McGraw-Hill publisher's representative or visit www.mhhe.com/solutions.

Social Problems For The Twenty-First Century

Chapter 1

*That the teaching of Sociology
has so heavily stressed
poverty, crime, divorce, and
other social disorders was
doubtlessly unavoidable . . . it
is nonetheless unfortunate.
That emphasis has a certain
morbid effect upon the minds
of young people, it makes
them imagine they ought to be
agitators, radicals, reformers,
philanthropists, or social
workers. It tends to fill their
heads with queer, half-baked
ideas.*

From the introduction to Ross L.
Finney, *Elementary Sociology*,
1923.

Social Problems and Sociology

When Is a Problem a Social Problem?

Most everybody thinks they know about social problems. After all, we all "know" obvious things, for example, that lower-class individuals commit more crime than members of the upper classes, that churchgoers are less racially prejudiced than people who don't go to church, that Catholics have fewer divorces than Protestants, and that far more husbands murder their wives than wives their husbands.

The problem is that *none* of these cases of "obvious" common sense is true. It turns out that, while the poor are more likely to engage in street crime (and more likely to get caught and punished), the middle class commits more white-collar crime. Moreover, for 30 years scientific surveys have shown that regular churchgoers are more likely to be racially prejudiced than those who do not attend, and for two decades now Catholics have had higher divorce rates than Protestants. Finally, while husbands are more likely to physically abuse wives, wives are slightly more likely to kill their husbands. (Applying deadly force with a Saturday night special requires no special strength.) The problem with commonsense knowledge is that, although it is common, it may or may not be accurate and reliable. What "everybody knows" is often erroneous. And if we don't have the correct information about social problems, our solutions may cause more harm than good.

As citizens, we are bombarded with contradictory interpretations of the social problems affecting our society. The media tell us that crime is rampant in the streets, the poor are stealing us blind through welfare fraud, and race relations are at their lowest point in decades. Are these things true? And if so, how should we react? We are confused. We want to be charitable to the poor panhandling on our streets, but are they really in need or just too lazy to look for a job? We hear that people are being downsized out of jobs because of unfair foreign competition, but why can't they find new jobs, given the abundance of entries in the local want ads? We know racial inequities persist but are told that affirmative action promotes reverse discrimination. We are upset over reports of vicious street crime and of lawyers tying up the courts and getting the guilty off on technicalities, but we wonder whether locking up even more people is the answer.

Even in the make-believe world of soap operas, life has become more complex. The synopsis of the soap *As The World Turns* for two days in February 1998 tells us that:

> Ben killed Teague then struggled to save Jack, who later underwent extensive surgery. Ben defended having to shoot Teague when quizzed by the district attorney. Lily was upset that Holden was found guilty of attacking Molly and burning down the church. With help from Matt, James took Holden hostage, then escaped when being transported to prison.[1]

We know there are problems everywhere, but what makes a problem a social problem? And are social problems really all that serious in America? Or is it largely media hype? Finally, what if anything can be done to address or solve social problems?

To begin our discussion let's look at how sociologists examine social problems from a sociological perspective. When reading this text, note how sociologists, as sociologists, try to look at problems analytically and structurally rather than emotionally; they examine not just how changes affect us personally but how changes influence society as a whole. Sociologists look at social problems from a sociological perspective that encourages the structural examination of issues within their societal context.

---

[1] "In Case You Missed . . .," *Richmond Times-Dispatch*, February 14, 1998, p. F55.

Not everyone is prospering from early twenty-first century economic affluence. Some still rely on food programs for a Christmas meal.

Kathy Willens/AP/Wide World Photos

Personal Problems versus Social Issues

Because Americans stress personal individualism, we commonly think of problems as individual rather than group issues. We are more likely to think in terms of the individual "deviant" and his or her problem rather than the social, economic, and historical circumstances that produced the problem. In discussing drug usage, for instance, the tendency is to focus on the deviant behavior of the drug user rather than on why some countries have major drug problems and others do not. If we focus only on deviant individuals, courses studying social problems become little more than talk shows focusing on "nuts, sluts, and perverts."[2]

While an approach that looks only at the individual can be insightful in explaining unique behaviors, sociologists believe that individual acts are best understood when placed in their sociological context. The famous American sociologist, C. Wright Mills, put it best when he wrote that if one or two people experience adversity, or "personal troubles," we may well question the effort or integrity of those persons. When, however, hundreds of thousands of individuals experience these troubles in much the same way, then we have a "societal issue."[3] Mills argued

[2]Alexander Liazos, *People First, An Introduction to Social Problems*, Allyn and Bacon, Boston, 1982.
[3]C. Wright Mills, *The Sociological Imagination*, Oxford University Press, New York, 1959.

5

that because personal problems are highlighted in America, there is little recognition that the causes of many personal problems are structural and thus can only be resolved by structural changes in the society.

> *Troubles* occur within the character of the individual. . . . Accordingly, the statement and the resolutions properly lie within the individual as a biographical entity and within the scope of his immediate milieu. . . . A trouble is a private matter: values cherished by the individual are felt to be threatened.
>
> *Issues* have to do with matters that transcend these local environments of the individual and the range of inner life. An issue is a public matter: some value cherished by the public is felt to be threatened.
>
> When in a city of 100,000 only one man is unemployed, that is his personal trouble, and for its relief we properly look to the character of the man. . . . But when in a nation of 50 million employees, 15 million men are unemployed, that is an *issue*, and we may not hope to find its solution within the range of opportunities open to any one individual.[4]

Government social programs are usually designed to deal with *individuals* and their troubles rather than to change the underlying social maladies causing such social problems as unemployment, family dissolution, poverty, and crime. Sociologists, by contrast, are concerned with social issues rather than individual problems. This is not to suggest that sociologists see people with problems simply as helpless victims of historical forces that defy intervention. Rather, while stressing structural explanations, sociologists are aware that the tension between social structure and personal responsibility is very real. Consequently, when sociologists examine social problems they are concerned with how personal troubles represent societal level concerns.

The Sociological Perspective

sociological perspective
focus on seeking general overall patterns rather than individual examples.

sociological imagination
allows us to develop a broad perspective as to how social norms and behaviors affect our lives.

The **sociological perspective** on social problems thus places its focus not on the behavior of specific individuals, but on seeking general social patterns.[5] Its emphasis is not on unique occurrences, but rather on patterns of common behavior. The sociological perspective looks to the group and the social determinants of behavior instead of the more common individualistic psychological perspective. Because sociologists are interested in how the social interaction among individuals affects and influences behavior, sociologists analyze variations between groups. We do this by gaining an understanding of the relationship between personal troubles and social issues.[6] We also try to develop a **sociological imagination** that allows us to go beyond our narrow individual view of the world to a broader perspective where we can see how societal patterns affect our personal lives. For instance, even a supposedly totally personal act such as suicide turns out to have major variations based on group membership.[7] Sociologists are interested not so much in why John Smith committed suicide as in why suicide *rates* are much higher among persons having certain characteristics (such as being white, male, older, Protestant, and affluent rather than poor).

Using a sociological perspective, the following pages will examine problems such as crime, poverty, racism, AIDS, population growth, family change, substance abuse, and host of other social problems found in American society.

---

[4]C. Wright Mills, *The Sociological Imagination*, Oxford University Press, New York, 1959, p. 8.

[5]Peter Berger, *An Invitation to Sociology*, Anchor Books, Garden City, NY, 1963.

[6]C. Wright Mills, *The Sociological Imagination*, Oxford University Press, New York, 1959.

[7]The classic study of the relationship between group membership and suicide was done a century ago in France by Émile Durkheim. It still remains an excellent example of solid research. Émile Durkheim, *Suicide*, (trans. John Spalding and George Simpson), Free Press, New York, 1951 (orig. publ. 1897).

We will be especially concerned not only with what has already occurred, but with how social problems are likely to impact our lives in the twenty-first century.

Recognizing Social Problems

Why do some social issues or concerns become recognized as social problems and others don't? Some contend that what becomes a social problem are those issues which are considered problems by much of the general public. That is, the problem must affect much of the society, not just those directly involved. That is the view taken by this text. Sometimes, though, issues are in transition. Gay rights issues are a case in point. Providing gays civil rights is increasingly being defined as a societywide problem rather than just the concern of those directly affected.

Some sociologists say that public recognition is not crucial for an issue to be a social problem. They say that social problems are the issues identified by social scientists as those about which people should be concerned. There are often wide differences between professionals and the public. Until the 1970s, for instance, environmental pollution and rapid population growth were not viewed by the general public as social problems. Today, both are seen by most Americans as social problems. However, both issues remain predominately middle-class crusades. Poor and minority peoples are more likely to be concerned with immediate needs, such as jobs and housing, rather than pollution or population growth. To someone at the bottom economically, an environmentalist may appear to be a rich person with a summer home who wants to keep trailers from moving in and spoiling the landscape.

Definitions concerning what is or is not a social problem thus tend to be subjective. The concern may vary over time and place. Is college drinking a social problem or just students having fun? How about using marijuana? Different age groups and those with different income levels and occupations differ in their views. There are even differences by regions of the country. Western states, for example, are likely to take a less punitive view of private marijuana usage. Also, those in power rank problems differently than those who are relatively powerless. For example, drug use would be high on the list of the powerful, while poverty and inequality would be high on the list of the powerless.

Having "professionals" such as sociologists decide what constitutes a social problem doesn't resolve the question, since sociologists differ as to whether or not social problems can be objectively identified. Some sociologists maintain that any selection of problems is subjective since all writers on social problems have moral and political values that taint their selection and presentation.[8] Others believe the process of identifying social problems can indeed be objective. Robert Nisbet, for instance, has suggested that most sociologists identify social problems based on two criteria: (1) those activities defined as social problems involve a mode of behavior that violates the norms and values widely held in the society; (2) the social problems selected are those upon which sociologists can meaningfully speak as the result of decades of scientific research.[9] The second criterion is more a practical explanation of why sociology books on social problems cover certain problems and not others.

This text takes the position that it is impossible to eliminate personal values and experiences and we invariably make value judgments about which social problems are most important and what should be done about them. Both professionals and

---

[8]See, for example, Jerome H. Skolnick and Elliot Currie, *Crisis in American Institutions*, 11th ed., Allyn and Bacon, New York, 2000, pp. 2–3.

[9]Robert Nisbet, "The Study of Social Problems," in Robert K. Merton and Robert Nisbet (eds.), *Contemporary Social Problems*, Harcourt Brace Jovanovich, New York, 1971, p. 2.

Box 1.1 Ongoing Issues

Body Type and Criminality

During the twentieth century, a number of unscientific explanations for human behavior entered, for a time, the scientific mainstream. Early in the century the famous Italian physician Cesare Lombroso (1835–1909), for example, described criminals as *atavistic types* or throwbacks to "the ferocious instincts of primitive humanity and inferior animals."[a] Such an atavistic individual had not only a smaller, undeveloped brain but a whole host of physical characteristics, such as small close-set eyes, large teeth, fleshy rodentlike pouches in the cheeks, ears lacking lobes, large amounts of body hair, and eyes of different colors.

Later, in 1939, Ernest Hooton, an anthropology professor at Harvard, published *Crime and the Man,* which (on the reported evaluation of 13,873 prison inmates) claimed to prove that criminals could be identified biologically.[b] Through questionable statistical manipulation, Hooton claimed to be able to distinguish biological differences not only between offenses but also by state of residence. In spite of poor sampling and biased presentation, this nonsense was widely accepted. Noted on page 9 (Figure 1.1) is Hooton's description of the typical Massachusetts criminal.

Another popular (and unsupported) physiological theory that found its way into virtually all the psychology and sociology texts published during the 1940s and 1950s was William H. Sheldon's descriptions of the relationship between body build, which he called *somatotypes,* and personality. Of the three body types—endomorphs, mesomorphs, and ectomorphs—Sheldon stated that the "jock" mesomorphs were the most likely to become criminals.[c] (Interestingly, Sheldon also found that the same body type that predominated among criminals was found among salesmen and politicians.) During the 1940s and 1950s, Sheldon was considered a responsible scientist, and colleges such as Harvard, Yale, Princeton, Vassar, and Wellesley allowed him to take nude photos of their incoming students as part of his studies of body shape and intelligence. In fact, nude photographs were taken of such later notables as George Bush, Bob Woodward, Meryl Streep, Diane Sawyer, and Hillary Rodham Clinton.[d]

The physiological theories of Lombroso, Hooton, and Sheldon linking appearance and behavior all suffer from inadequate sampling, misapplied statistics, and biased interpretation. Today they are discredited as having no scientific validity. However, newer theories arguing that biology determines behavior can be found in bestsellers like *The Bell Curve* (1994), which argues that genetics determines intelligence.[e]

[a]Cesare Lombroso's "Introduction," in Gina Lombroso-Ferrero, Criminal Man According to the Classification of Ceasare Lombroso, *Patterson Smith, Montclair, NJ, reprinted 1972, p. xiv.*
[b]Ernest A. Hooton, Crime and the Man, *Harvard University Press, Cambridge, MA, 1939.*
[c]William H. Sheldon, Varieties of Delinquent Youth, *Harper, New York, 1949.*
[d]Ron Rosenblam, "The Great Ivy League Nude Photo Scandal," *New York Times Magazine, January 15, 1995, pp. 26–31,40, 46, 55, 56.*

nonprofessionals alike make subjective judgments on how social problems should be solved. Everyone has biases, but sociologists make a conscious effort to try to take their own biases into consideration. Others discussing social problems aren't always as careful. For example, solutions suggested by the major media commonly reflect the current views of those in power, and the biases of those in power favor the status quo. In fact, the media play an increasing role in defining what our social problems are.

Popular beliefs about the causes and cures of social problems fluctuate from decade to decade. For example, while crimes against persons consistently rank near the top in opinion polls as the nation's most pressing social problem, over the years popular beliefs as to the "causes" of crime have varied widely. Early in the twentieth century, crime was commonly viewed as an inherited biological trait, and criminality, like hair color, was believed to be passed through the genes (see Box 1.1). Criminals were said to have physical features such as small beady eyes. Others viewing crime from within a traditional religious framework, saw crime as being a moral failing. "Defective" classes were deficient in moral character, and thus the goal of punishment was to reform the moral char-

Figure 1.1 Old American Criminals: Mosaic of Cranial, Facial, Metric and Morphological Features: Massachusetts

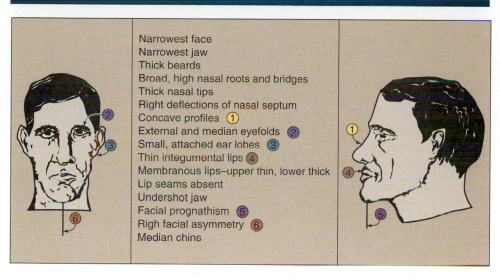

Narrowest face
Narrowest jaw
Thick beards
Broad, high nasal roots and bridges
Thick nasal tips
Right deflections of nasal septum
Concave profiles ①
External and median eyefolds ②
Small, attached ear lobes ③
Thin integumental lips ④
Membranous lips—upper thin, lower thick
Lip seams absent
Undershot jaw
Facial prognathism ⑤
Righ facial asymmetry ⑥
Median chins

From: Ernest A. Hooton, *Crime and the Man*, Harvard University Press, Cambridge, MA, 1989, p. 57.

acter of the offender. Using either the biological or moral explanations of criminality, social problems such as crime and alcoholism were said to be caused by "bad" people who broke the rules of society that "good" people knew had to be followed.

By the middle of the twentieth century, these views had largely been replaced by the so-called "modern" social work view that crime was not caused by bad individuals but rather was a consequence of social disorganization brought on by urbanization and modernization. Crime was thus a result of social strain and improper socialization of some individuals. Blame had been shifted from the individual to the social system itself. Delinquency, in this view, was not so much criminality as a form of social maladjustment and "acting out" as a means of achieving attention. The counterculture era of the late 1960s and early 1970s went further by redefining some crimes as legitimate political statements against an unjust and oppressive capitalistic state. In this view, those who violently opposed the system were not social offenders but revolutionaries in the vanguard of the struggle. Today, the wheel has turned in a more conservative direction, and law violators are likely to be viewed not as revolutionaries but as antisocial predators.

Sociologists also are concerned with how our perception of a problem affects our ability to deal with it. As early sociologist W. I. Thomas noted, in what has become known as the **Thomas theorem**, "If men define situations as real, they are real in their consequences."[10] In other words, what people believe about reality is more important than the reality itself since we act on our beliefs. If people believe the sky is falling, they will act on that belief (perhaps by building bomb shelters, as Americans did during the Cold War). Sociologists recognize that beliefs about what is "true" often have more important consequences than the actual social reality.

Thomas theorem
situations defined as real are real in their consequences.

---

[10]For a detailed discussion of how this theorem, perhaps the most influential in sociology, has been both misquoted and misattributed, see Robert K. Merton, "The Thomas Theorem and the Matthew Effect," *Social Forces*, 74:379–424, December 1995.

Problems That Can Be Fixed

Social problems must be capable of being "fixed" in some way. If something is fatalistically viewed as inevitable, it is a social condition, not a social problem. To become a social problem, private problems *must* become public issues. For example, poverty and inequality throughout most of history have been regarded not as social problems but as social conditions that had to be fatalistically accepted. Historically, poverty was regarded in the same way as a hailstorm that destroyed crops. Both were unfortunate or even tragic but not something that society could change. If "that's just the way things are," or "the poor you have are always with you," is the assumption, then poverty is an individual misfortune like a bad crop, not a social problem caused by an unjust social system. The view of poverty as an unchangeable social condition is succinctly stated in the nineteenth-century Anglican Church hymn:

> The rich man in his castle,
> The poor man at his gate,
> God made them, high or lowly,
> And ordered their estate.

The history of the twentieth century was one of social conditions or personal problems—such as poverty, child labor, racial segregation, or the exploitation of women—being moved from the category of natural or inevitable misfortunes and placed in the category of social problems. This is a critical transfer, for only once a condition is defined as a changeable situation can it be rationally and practically addressed as a social problem. For example, while women for centuries have sought equal rights and opportunities, only during the past 30 years or so has women's traditional secondary social position been redefined as a social problem about which a majority of the population believed something had to be done. (As recently as the 1970s, states such as Texas did not allow a woman to have her own credit cards without her husband's permission.)

Definition

For our purposes, social problems are issues that are *socially recognized and shared,* and recognition as a problem is critical. **Social problems are issues that substantial numbers of the society view as violations of society's social norms or expectations, and about which people believe something can and should be done.**[11] It takes both social recognition and the belief that the situation can (and should) be changed to turn a social condition into a social problem. For an issue to become defined as a social problem, the hope of social change is extremely important. Also implicit in our definition of a social problem is the understanding that one society's social problems are not necessarily the same as another's. India has serious population problems, Ireland does not; the United States has a serious problem with handguns used in violent urban crime, Canada does not.

As Table 1.1 indicates social problems don't just spring full-blown upon a society; they have a history of development.

---

[11]A careful reader will note that this definition, while having the virtue of simplicity, begs a number of questions. For instance, what constitutes a substantial number of persons? Is it 9, 90,000, or 90 million? When the nine justices of the Supreme Court decided in 1954 in *Brown v. Topeka Board of Education* that segregated schools are inherently unequal and constitute a social problem, their views, in practical terms, were more important than the majority of the public's. Opinion polls taken at the time clearly showed the courts far ahead of the general population in viewing separate racial facilities as a social problem.

Table 1.1 History of a Social Problem

The identification and defining of social problems is an ongoing process. Most (but not all) social problems go through a series of recurrent stages.

Stage 1   *Defining the Problem.* Advocates and activists promote the idea that an existing social condition is detrimental to society and something needs to be done about it (e.g., racial discrimination, rape, AIDS). Protest groups are formed to lobby and pressure for governmental change.

Stage 2   *Acceptance and Legitimacy.* The social condition becomes "officially" defined as a social problem and programs are initiated. Government agencies may even be organized to address the problem. Policies are formulated and funded programs implemented to provide solutions.

Stage 3   *Disillusionment and New Demands.* Activists become dissatisfied and disillusioned with the government and with private policies and agencies, often accusing them of making too many compromises and being too bureaucratic.

Stage 4   *Rejection and Reformulation.* More radical members of the original protest group and strong advocates decide that existing programs are inadequate and have lost sight of the original goals. To restate and reinvigorate their issue, they may again turn to public protest to state their beliefs. They may also develop counter organizations that openly contest the approach taken by governmental agencies and semiofficial nongovernmental organizations.

Adapted from the model of social problems stages formulated by Malcolm Spector and John Kituse in *Constructing Social Problems*, Aldine deGruyter, New York, 1987.

Views of Human Nature

Our views of social problems and their possible solutions also reflect our philosophical views about human nature. Philosophical views about human nature run the gamut from outright superstition on one hand to blind faith in science on the other. A few perspectives, however, recur consistently throughout history. Keep in mind that these are not scientific theories based on research but philosophic views on the nature and meaning of life. Which of the following comes closest to your beliefs?

Humanity as Depraved

One of the oldest Western philosophical approaches to social problems is based on the seventeenth-century philosopher Thomas Hobbes's view of human nature: Every person seeks his own advantage, often against the other. In this view, most humans left to their own desires are destined to live out a life that is "nasty, brutish, and short."[12] Hobbesian approaches, and similar religious doctrines that view people as "naturally sinful," see social problems as inherent in human nature. Solutions are not really possible because social problems are caused by forces within individuals—"evil causes evil"—rather than within the system. Thus, alcoholism is seen not as an illness but rather as a sin or personal weakness, and drug users are judged as morally depraved.

---

[12]Thomas Hobbes (1588–1679) was an English social philosopher whose pessimistic view of human nature was presented in *The Leviathan*, originally published in 1651.

As this eighteenth century painting by Hogarth indicates poverty, viciousness, crime, drunkenness, and depravity are not twenty-first century inventions.

"The Chairing of the Member" courtesy of the Trustees of Sir John Soane's Museum

It follows that if social problems are the fault of mean, sinful, or vicious human beings, then the only way to solve problems is by dealing harshly with such individuals. Since people cause problems, a strict retributive justice would thus be the best means of controlling social problems and maintaining a civil society. In this Hobbesian view, society should be governed by the law of "an eye for an eye." This, in fact, has been the governing philosophy and practice of most nations throughout history, and it can still be found within some societies (and segments within our own society) today. A contemporary application of the Hobbesian view would advocate a widening of capital punishment offenses and a "lock them up and throw away the key" approach to other offenses.

Humanity as Perfectible

Strongly opposed to the view of human nature as in need of restraint is the perspective of the social philosopher Jean Jacques Rousseau, who regarded humanity as ultimately perfectible.[13] Those holding such optimistic views believe that social prob-

---

[13]Jean Jacques Rousseau (1712–1778) was a French social philosopher and writer of the enlightenment who discussed the good society in *The Social Contract,* 1762.

lems are not inherent in human nature, because people in their natural state are basically good. Rather, the viper in the garden is a corrupt social system that perverts benign human nature. Society makes victims of people rather than the other way around.

From this philosophical perspective, the obvious solution to social problems would be to liberate people from the repressive effects of a society that deprives them of their humanity. In this view the poor are seen not as a lazy and perhaps criminal class that deserves what they get, but rather as victims of a fundamentally unjust and exploitative system. The 1960s saw America make a brief return to Rousseauian beliefs, especially among political activists who believed that social revolution and a new social order would end repression.

Humanity as Moderately Perfectible

In modern Western societies, conservative political parties of the right have generally endorsed the pessimistic Hobbesian view of mankind, whereas liberals on the left have more or less followed the optimistic Rousseauian tradition. Most Americans vacillate between these views, and are influenced by the media's current view of the world. Nor are people always consistent in their views. Americans believe in a democratic government and the basic civil liberties of freedom of press, speech, and assembly, yet they waiver in supporting these basic rights when addressing some of the most pertinent social problems of the day. For instance, almost all Americans support the basic Constitutional rights of protection from illegal search and seizure, yet oppose such protections when they are applied to "hardened" criminals in minority urban areas. Americans tend to be middle-of-the-roaders, defining those outside the mainstream with negative terms such as the "radical left" or the "radical right." Government programs largely reflect a middle-of-the-road (and middle-class) consensus.

How Sociologists View Social Problems: Three Perspectives

Sociologists, going beyond philosophical positions, have developed theories of society to help explain why social problems occur. These theories are tied to research data. While data or facts are essential for science, however, data alone are not enough. To be scientifically useful, facts must be organized so that regular patterns or generalizations emerge, enabling us to explain or predict. A **theory** is a generalization that organizes concepts and data in a meaningful way. Theories give meaning to facts. Theories predict what will occur and also offer a systematic explanation of why it occurs. Good research tests existing theories and leads to their refinement or rejection. To be scientifically useful, a theory must be cast in a form in which it can be empirically supported or refuted. A theory, in short, must be testable, which means it must be formulated in such a manner that it can be disproved.

Sociological attempts to explain scientifically the "why" of social problems have in recent years fallen under one of three important theoretical perspectives. These are the **structural/functional, conflict,** and **interactionist** approaches. The first two of these are *macro* perspectives insofar as they focus on the behavior of groups or the society at large. The interactionist approach, by contrast, focuses on the *micro* or small group level. Within these general perspectives, sociologists

theory
a statement that organizes and relates facts in a way that explains the relationships among them.

Table 1.2 Simplified View of the Three Major Sociological Perspectives

	Functional	Conflict	Interaction
Level of Examination	Macro	Macro	Micro
Image of Society	Society is a system of interactive and independent groups. An existing, relatively stable system provides for the operations of society (not necessarily the best operation).	Society is composed of groups that are in conflict with one another over power and scarce resources. Conflict has a more important role than do shared interests in society.	Society consists of individuals who constantly interact. They use symbols to communicate values and thereby create social consensus.
Consequences of Social Problems	Social problems can produce dysfunction and disrupt the social system, resulting in social disorganization.	Conflict is inevitable between competing class, race, ethnic, and gender interest groups.	Perceptions of reality differ. How an action is defined affects reactions. Social problems are learned from others through social interaction.
Consequences for Society	Social problems disrupt the social order, so the system must be adjusted and dysfunctional elements reformed.	Only by struggle and conflict with those holding disproportionate resources can disadvantaged groups gain benefits.	Those who do not meet the shared consensus are stigmatized or labeled as deviant.
Example	Unequal economic rewards act to ensure that major social needs are met. Talented people are encouraged to fill functionally necessary positions.	Economic inequality is the result of a social system designed to keep some rich and many not. The system is designed to maintain the status quo rather than use the best people.	Socialization affects life chances. The rich are socialized to assume success. The poor are socialized to expect failure.

have developed more specific theories.[14] (Feminist theory will be discussed in detail in Chapter 5.) Keep in mind that because this is a social problems text, and not a book on sociological theory, what follows are generalized statements that do not contain all the nuances and subtleties of these approaches. Many differences within conflict, functionalist, and interactionist perspectives are not discussed here. Also, while these perspectives are presented here as self-contained theories, they often are not so neatly contained in reality. Table 1.2 summarizes the functional, conflict, and interactionist perspectives.

Functionalist Approaches

functionalist approaches

theories that view society as an integrated whole where the parts of the society have functions, or practices and patterns, that act to maintain society.

Functionalists approaches hold that society is a complex of major social institutions and that certain social functions or positive effects must be met for society to survive; social patterns, therefore, are best understood in terms of their conse-

---

[14]For a detailed discussion of these perspectives see Earl Rubington and Martin Weinberg, *The Study of Social Problems*, Oxford University Press, New York, 1971; and Richie P. Lowry, *Social Problems*, D. C. Heath, Lexington, MA, 1973.

quences or *functions* for the society. Major social institutions, such as the family, the legal system of police and courts, and the economic system, have functions that must be carried out if a society is to work properly. One function of education, for instance, is to socialize the next generation in the values of society. Society's parts are seen as interrelated and social problems disrupt the system.

Functionalist theories emphasize society and the interrelations of its institutions. The early theorist most often associated with the development of functionalism is Émile Durkheim.[15] The question he and later functionalists asked is: How does society meet its needs and maintain itself? Functionalists say that although conflict invariably occurs, social life persists because the society has structures which fulfill social needs or functions. Not all parts of society are necessary to its functioning well, but the existing structure of

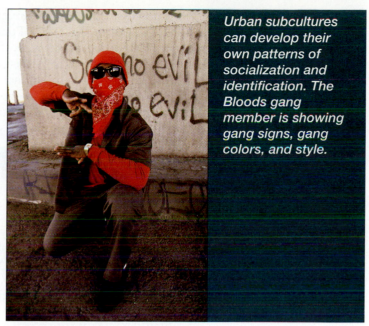

Urban subcultures can develop their own patterns of socialization and identification. The Bloods gang member is showing gang signs, gang colors, and style.

© Steve Starr/Stock, Boston

an ongoing social system does perform the necessary functions to keep itself going. Social problems, thus, are seen not as aberrations of the social system but as normal and inevitable occurrences or *dysfunctions* (that is, effects that lessen the effectiveness or adaptation of the system). Functionalists thus look at the way social institutions like the family or schools actually operate.

Functionalist approaches focus on problems arising as a consequence of cultural conflict where traditional roles, rules, and social structures break down and become dysfunctional. The result is social disorganization and deviance. The assumption is that social structures fail and disruptions of the social system occur to the point where institutional goals cannot be adequately met or where goals are actually in conflict. This is most likely to occur during periods of rapid change, such as urbanization and industrialization. At such times socialization based on agreed-upon and stable rules of behavior breaks down, causing confusion and social disorganization. Society is always changing, and failure to adapt effectively can lead to social problems. For example, because the family has lost many of its functions, the socialization it provides young people is both less complete and less uniform than in the past. Thus, problems of delinquency, drugs, or deviant behavior may develop. If the educational system breaks down in slums, residents are not sufficiently trained for jobs and thus remain unemployed and impoverished. To functionalists, the result is the breakdown of traditional institutions, increasing alienation, and a whole host of social ills. With the decline of traditional values and the disruption of socializing institutions—home, school, church—society's basic values are less adequately and less fully transmitted.

A functionalist framework directs attention away from the individual to the larger societal system. Functionalism concentrates attention on social structure and ascribes the faults, conflicts, and inadequacies that create social problems to the social system. Consequently, social problems cannot be solved simply by retraining or resocializing the disorganized individuals (although treatment of individual problems such as drug addiction is advocated). Their solution, rather, requires reorganizing the social system and rebuilding social structures. The good society implicitly is the society that works well and remains in balance.

---

[15]Émile Durkheim, *The Division of Labor in Society* (trans. George Simpson), Free Press, Glencoe, IL, 1964.

Functionalism was the dominant theoretical model until the major challenge of conflict theories in the 1970s. Functional approaches are criticized for ignoring process and treating the social system as static and unchangeable rather than dynamic. Functionalism is also accused of political conservativism—tending to accept the prevailing system as functional or natural, and thus supporting the status quo. Although functionalist oriented sociologists have generally been reformers, functionalists sometimes appear to view change as disruptive and disorganizing and to see a lack of consensus as dysfunctional for the society.

Conflict Approaches

conflict approaches
theoretical models of society that focus on struggle, competition, and change.

Conflict approaches focus on the social processes of competition, change, and conflict. They are concerned primarily with inequality. Conflict approaches have become perhaps the major contemporary paradigm or model. Unlike functionalist models, this perspective does not view societies as organized in orderly systems having shared values and beliefs. Rather, the conflict paradigm (or model of analysis) sees conflicting groups struggling for dominance. Conflict approaches reject the idea that social institutions can be reformed to work well. Conflict theories begin with the observation that society is held together in spite of variant groups having conflicting interests regarding scarce resources.

Controlling groups, through their dominance of the political system and social institutions, use their power to impose their worldview on others. Society, therefore, is held together—and we have some semblance of order within society, in spite of these conflicting interests—by the exercise of power by the dominant class over the less powerful lower classes. The crucial question is: Who has the power to enforce his or her will on others? While functionalists tend to see change as socially disruptive, conflict theorists see it as both inevitable and a means of producing desirable social change and reducing inequality. Lewis Coser has argued that conflict, rather than tearing apart the social fabric, may actually strengthen the group-binding and group-preserving cohesiveness of groups competing with one another.[16]

Conflict theorists examine how a dominant group, or class, comprising people with shared interests, bands together to exercise power and control the distribution of scarce resources. Conflict theorists generally see this conflict between competing interests within society as the root of our social problems, whether or not this conflict is detected by the have-nots. Conflict theorists traditionally have stressed class conflict, but racial, ethnic, or gender conflict are increasingly emphasized. The struggle for power among different income, religious, racial, ethnic, and gender groups is seen as inevitable. In such conflicts the powerful usually win.

Conflict theorists, along with functionalists, hold that the tendency for our society to see social problems as individual concerns limits our ability to see the structural arrangements within society. While conflict theory is sometimes portrayed as a response to functionalist theory, conflict theory traces its roots much earlier to Karl Marx (1818–1883), the 19th-century German economist and social theorist. Many conflict theorists are not Marxists, but most do share some of the central concerns raised by Marx.[17] **Marxists** emphasize class conflict and the central role played by economic structure in shaping the society.

Marxist theory
the explaining of a society's political and social behavior based upon its economic system.

Marx, with his cowriter Friedrich Engels, held a view of history in which society went through a set of stages from feudalism to capitalism to socialism to

---

[16]Lewis Coser, *The Functions of Social Conflict*, Free Press, New York, 1956.

[17]For a detailed discussion of the rise of conflict theory, see George Ritzer, *Sociological Theory*, 3rd ed., McGraw Hill, 1992, Chapter 7.

communism.[18] In each stage the economy determines the social characteristics of the society. Everything else—religion, politics, education, family form, and so on—can sometimes influence economic activities, but the shape of the society is ultimately determined by economic forces. Inequality thus is a direct result of a social structure designed to keep those at the top in power by the exploitation of the poor and powerless. The classic Marxist version proposes a zero-sum game in which the rich can only get richer by the poor getting poorer. In spite of their power advantage in controlling the superstructure of the state, however, the dominant group eventually causes such misery among the proletariat that the proletariat develop a class consciousness and overthrow their bourgeois oppressors. The capitalist state, by pushing the advantage of those at the top to an extreme, carries the seeds of its own destruction and hence of social change. Classic Marxists tend to be critical of proposals to reform social institutions since they say no real change can come until the capitalist economic system is replaced.

Non-Marxist conflict theorists say that conflict is indeed inevitable but that it usually has not played itself out the way Marx suggested. The history of the past century has not shown polarization into two hostile conflicting classes; instead it has shown the dramatic development of the urban middle class. This is an outcome Marx did not foresee. Nor did he foresee that the development of corporations as separate legal entities would allow the ownership of the means of production to be separate from operation of the means of production.

Conflict doesn't have to be over economic power but can also occur over values. In fact, today ethnic and gender conflict are often emphasized more than class conflict. Much of **feminist theory,** for instance, stresses the role of a patriarchal social order in suppressing and exploiting women (see Chapter 5). Conflict theorists, such as Ralf Dahrendorf, stress that today authority and power within systems is more important than ownership of property.[19] Thus, doing away with capitalism would not do away with conflicts. Different authority systems (economic, educational, religious, political, etc.) still have conflicting interests, and conflict between competing authority systems is part of modern life. However, this conflict largely has come to be institutionalized and controlled. Businesses and labor unions, for instance, have come to institutionalize sets of rules by which disputes are resolved without resorting to class violence. Thus, conflict is inevitable, but it is more likely to lead to disruption than to revolution. While functionalists have been criticized for being too conservative, conflict theorists have been attacked for being too radical in stressing the importance of conflict over order. Critics of conflict theory say that if there were as many contradictions and conflicts in society as conflict theorists say, modern society would not be able to maintain itself.

feminist theory
a theoretical approach for understanding society that focuses on the role of gender and the unequal treatment of women.

Interactionist Approaches

While functionalist and conflict approaches focus on the societal level, **interactionist approaches** look at social problems from the perspective of persons acting within a social world. Unlike macro-level functionalist or conflict theories, interactionists focus on the social psychology of everyday actions rather than on large aggregate units such as society or the economy. They are micro rather than macro oriented, looking at the process whereby people take the values and norms of a group and how groups construct and label their own social reality. They focus on how people interact in actual specific situations.

interactionist approaches
theories that focus on how people in society define themselves and their social relationships, and respond to social interactions.

---

[18]Karl Marx and Fredrich Engels, *Capital: A Critique of Political Economy,* International Publishers, New York, 1967 (orig. publ. 1867).
[19]Ralf Dahrendorf, *Class and Class Conflict in Industrial Society,* Stanford University Press, 1959.

Interactionists also are interested in how people communicate values using symbols (symbolic interaction). Interactionist theories are symbolic or social psychological in nature. Symbolic-Interactionists look at how everday interactions shape society, how people act toward one another and respond to one another using symbols. As George Herbert Mead explained early in the twentieth century, we build our personalities from our social experiences.[20] How do people become part of situations defined as social problems? Why do some individuals behave in one way and some in another?

Interactionists deal not so much with actions themselves, but with what the actions mean to other people and how they are communicated. Interactionists look at the way people take on the values of a larger group and construct their lives. Interactionists concern themselves with how we come to define ourselves (develop a self-concept) and how we define the social world (define the situation). Both of these definitions are learned through social interaction. Interactionists remind us that society is not just a concept but consists of people interacting. They stress the importance of peer groups such as friends in teaching behaviors and values and emphasize the significance of labeling. An interactionist looking at delinquency would be interested in how that person learns what the larger society defines as criminal norms, how he or she comes to define himself or herself as delinquent, and how being so defined (or labeled) by others affects their behavior. Symbolic interactionists focus their attention less on the objective situation or action and more on the subjective meaning for participants. As noted earlier, how a situation is defined affects what actions are then taken.

Using Theoretical Models

The above theoretical approaches are sometimes presented in textbooks as if they were mutually exclusive, watertight compartments. Actually, conflict theorists are aware of the importance of social integration, and functionalists recognize the role played by conflict; it is the degree of importance given to factors that distinguishes these models. In doing research, most sociologists pragmatically borrow from various models. A conflict perspective, for instance, seems suited for explaining poverty, whereas an interactionist perspective provides essential insights into understanding alcoholism. There also is considerable overlap. Conflict-oriented theorists often explain changing family patterns in a manner similar to that used by functionalists.

Now we turn to research—how sociologists meld theory and data in investigating social problems.

Theory and Research in Action:
How We Know What We Know

Theories are scientifically confirmed or contradicted by research, but everyday discussions of social problems are usually based on common sense and accumulated social beliefs. Common sense provides a rich lode of insights, but these frequently are contradictory. For example, the commonsense sayings "Nothing ventured nothing gained" and "A bird in the hand is worth two in the bush" convey opposite messages. Similarly, we are told of romantic attachments, "Absence makes the heart grow

---

[20]George Herbert Mead, *Mind, Self and Society*, University of Chicago Press, Chicago, 1964 (orig. publ. 1934).

fonder" and "Out of sight, out of mind." In fact, common sense can be employed to support *any* argument. Common sense is no substitute for solid empirical data.

In their research, sociologists, like other social and physical scientists, look for relationships or **correlation** between traits or characteristics, which are called **variables** because they can change from case to case or time to time. Commonly used sociological variables are age, race, gender, income, education, or occupation. Most of the best-known sociological studies use **quantitative methods** relying on statistical analysis for their interpretation of social problems. Government data, census information, and surveys are among the most commonly used sources of quantitative data. On the other hand, **qualitative studies** use micro or small group level analysis to better understand the meaning of social issues. Qualitative research uses **field study** or **participant observation** to focus not only on what occurs but on how participants interpret what has occurred. (Participant observation is an unstructured technique in which hypotheses are formulated and verified through direct field obervation.) Thus, while a quantitative study of deliquency might examine changes in national patterns of delinquency, a qualitative study might involve directly observing a street gang for two years. (See the "Methodological Appendix" for a discussion of sociological methods.)

This text makes every attempt to present the results of sociological research accurately. Where the facts are contested, that is noted. Keep in mind, though, that the facts are only the beginning, not the end of discussion and debate. Readers of this text will differ and disagree, sometimes vehemently, about the implications of the data for policy decisions. This is as it should be in a democratic society. Advocates of the three perspectives described in the last section often interpret the meaning and policy consequences of the same facts quite differently.

Dubious Facts

Before going any further, let us say a bit more about "facts." We are all familiar with the commonsense saying, "Facts speak for themselves." Unfortunately, not only do facts *not* generally speak for themselves, but sometimes widely held "facts" turn out to be anything but factual. We are a society that likes to accumulate bits of interesting information and trivia. The problem is that not all these facts are accurate. Sometimes "facts" that show up in media stories are supplied by individuals or organizations trying to make a point or lobby a position. The fact that a survey or other data comes from an interest group does not mean that it is inaccurate or misleading, but it does mean that questions about who did the study, how it was carried out, and who paid the bills should be asked.

Dubious or fake facts, when discovered, tend to undermine the seriousness of the problem discussed. Each chapter of this text opens with a "dubious fact." Among the commonly accepted "facts" in *Time*, in *Newsweek,* and on TV that are demonstrably untrue are the following examples. (Don't feel too bad if you find you have believed some of these nonfactual "facts"; in several cases, so initially did the author of this book.)

1. "Drug abuse, alcohol abuse, and pregnancy are the biggest problems in public schools today, compared to talking in the halls, chewing gum, and making noise in the 1940s." This much-repeated nonfact fits the common impression of the deterioration of American public schools. The problem is that there is no survey to support this statement. In reality, the list was made up in 1982 by T. Cullen Davis, a born-again evangelical Christian preacher, as his way of indicating slippage from the good old days.

2. "Domestic violence increases 40 percent on Super Bowl Sunday." This "fact," widely publicized by the National Organization for Women (NOW) in 1994, resulted

correlation
measure of strength of a relationship between two or more variables that systematically change together.

variable
characteristic that can change or differ from case to case.

quantitative studies
research based on numerical data and statistical analysis.

qualitative studies
research based on observational rather than numerical data.

field study
research done in real-life settings; participant observation is one variant.

participant observation
method in which the researcher participates in the activities of the group under study.

19

in NBC agreeing to run antiviolence public service announcements on Super Bowl Sunday. However, despite all the media hype about increases in aggression against spouses and girlfriends, the reality is that an examination of arrest data shows no increase in domestic violence on Super Bowl Sundays. In fact, given the dull nature of many Super Bowls, one could hypothesize that watching the game, far from making a male fan violent, is more likely to put him to sleep in front of the TV set.

3. "Drinking milk can cause diabetes." This alarmist claim was made by the Physician's Committee for Responsible Medicine, which sounds impressive. However, most medical researchers dismiss these claims as totally without foundation. Not generally known is that the Physician's Committee is a vegan advocacy group and against the exploitation of animals by using any of their products, including milk.

4. "One million elderly are victims of abuse each year." As best as can be determined, this scary statistic is apparently a projection of a poor-quality 1982 Washington, D.C., survey of 433 senior citizens, of whom only 74 responded. Three of these respondents said they had been abused. These three responses were then illegitimately projected to the nation, producing the totally unsupported claim that 1 million senior citizens a year are abused.

5. "Seventy percent of wives cheat on their spouses." This dramatic figure comes from Shere Hite's popular 1987 book, *The Hite Report: Women and Love: A Cultural Revolution in Progress.* However, Hite's questionnaires were not distributed using accepted random sampling techniques; they were distributed mostly to women's advocacy groups and selected counseling centers. The 70 percent figure received lots of exposure on daytime talk shows, but it is wildly out of line with the 11.5 percent figure of the 1991–1993 General Social Survey provided by the highly respected National Opinion Research Center at the University of Chicago. The National Opinion Research Center uses scientifically accepted sampling techniques to prevent bias. The 70 percent figure is wildly inaccurate hype.

6. "Postal workers are especially likely to be the perpetrators or victims of workplace violence." A spate of attacks by and on postal workers spawned several media interpretations of why postal work is especially alienating and why postal workplaces are thus violence prone. The phrase "going postal" has even come to mean acting crazy and violent. This, however, is another case of elaborate explanations for something that is not so. Actually, postal workers as a group are less, not more, likely to commit or suffer violence (except from dogs) than the average blue-collar worker. What is true is that anytime a postal worker commits violence anywhere, or anyone becomes violent in a post office, it makes national news. The same is not true of violence occurring within other groups. Truck drivers, for instance, are far more likely to be involved in violence than postal workers, but over the past six months how many front-page stories have you read about violence inflicted by truck drivers?

Do these examples mean that all statistics are suspect? No, not at all. But it does mean that before automatically accepting survey or other findings, especially those that seem unusually dramatic or shocking, you should ask yourself a few questions—especially if the dramatic findings support your own position. Often we are inclined to give data that seem to support our views less scrutiny than findings that challenge our beliefs. Readers should be cautious of "facts" that are not accompanied by information about who created the survey, whether the respondents were randomly selected, and what the response rate was. It is also useful to know who paid for the study and where it was published. Studies published in professional journals must pass through a rigorous peer review process before being accepted for publication. The same standards are not applied by popular magazines. Be especially careful about findings or statistics announced by an advocacy group at a press conference or by an author trying to hype sales of a new book on a talk show.

Box 1.2 Making a Difference

Basing Policy Decisions on Bad Research

At midcentury Sir Cyril Burt was the most famous psychologist in Great Britain and possibly in the world. His study of 53 pairs of identical twins who grew up apart was world famous, and he was the first psychologist ever to be knighted for his work. Burt claimed that his research proved that intelligence was genetically transmitted.[a] Converting his beliefs about intelligence into social policy, Burt played a crucial role in designing a national examination system that determined children's academic and career futures at ages 11–12, based on what came to be called the "eleven-plus exams." Since it was assumed that performance reflected intelligence, the system clearly favored upper- and upper-middle-class youths who were well prepared by expensive private schools.

The problem was that all of Burt's data on the inheritance of intelligence had been fudged.[b] Possibly because Burt's "data" supported the status quo beliefs of those who held that intelligence was higher among the upper classes, they didn't bother to note that all of Burt's twin cases had an identical correlation. Even Burt's colleague, a Mrs. Conway, turned out to be invented.

In 1985, Lenore Weitzman became famous for *The Divorce Revolution,* a groundbreaking study of California's no-fault divorce system.[c] Weitzman reported that after divorce women's households showed a dramatic 73 percent drop in income, whereas men's households showed a 42 percent increase. This was a radically larger gap than reported by earlier studies and suggested that middle-class women became impoverished by no-fault divorce, while men sharply improved their economic standard of living. This study continues to be widely cited in introductory textbooks; it has even been cited in court rulings.

From the first, however, there were questions raised about the study. Greg Duncan and Saul Hoffman, two long-term scholars in the area, found that although Weitzman claimed to use their methodology, her findings differed substantially from theirs. Their studies showed that both no-fault and fault divorce caused about a 30 percent drop in women's economic status and a 10 percent rise in men's.[d] A special Census Bureau study by Suzanne Bianchi, specifically conducted to test Weitzman's findings, also came up with findings similar to those of Duncan and Hoffman.[e] Weitzman's response to her critics was, "They are just wrong."[f] Complicating the dispute was Weitzman's refusal to follow the usual scientific custom of releasing her data so they could be examined by others.

The question is now resolved. The National Science Foundation, which had funded Weitzman's study, strongly pressured her to release her data, and Richard R. Peterson did a complete reanalysis of the data using Weitzman's original records. He found the actual figures using her data were not a 73 percent decline for a woman's standard of living and a 42 percent increase for men, but a 27 percent decline in women's postdivorce standard of living and a 10 percent increase in men's.[g] These figures are similar to what others have found. A 27 percent income decline is bad enough, but it is far from the catastrophic 73 percent decline that was quoted by texts and media for a decade—and which still shows up in many books.

Weitzman now concedes that her figures were wrong and blames the error on the loss of her original computer data or a weighting error or mistakes made by her research assistant.[h] Reference to the original records, however, indicates that Weitzman's claims of programming errors are not accurate.[i] The reasons for Weitzman's publishing erroneous data continue to be debated, but what occurred is that her data received rapid public acceptance while contradictory findings by major scholars did not.

There are lessons to be learned from the Burt and the Weitzman cases: (1) We all tend to look much more critically at studies that question our beliefs than at studies that support our positions. Supporters often don't ask what later seem to be obvious questions. (2) While erroneous data initially received widespread acceptance, other researchers eventually exposed the errors. In other words, the scientific method worked. Peer review is not perfect, but it does have built-in self-correcting mechanisms. Over time, the system of scientific review and replication does act to eliminate error, fraud, and sloppy work.

[a]Cyril Burt, "Is Intelligence Distributed Normally?" *British Journal of Statistical Psychology,* 16:175–190, 1963.
[b]Stephan Jay Gould, The Mismeasure of Man, *W.W. Norton, New York, 1981.*
[c]Lenore J. Weitzman, The Divorce Revolution: The Unexpected Social and Economic Consequences for Women and Children in America, *Free Press, New York, 1985.*
[d]Greg J. Duncan and Saul F. Hoffman, "What Are the Economic Consequences of Divorce?" *Demography,* 25:641, November 1988.
[e]Suzanne Bianchi, "Family Disruption and Economic Hardship," Current Population Reports, *Series P–70:23, March 1991.*
[f]Quoted in Susan Faludi, Backlash: The Undeclared War against American Women, *Anchor, New York, 1991, p. 22.*
[g]Richard R. Peterson, "A Re-Evaluation of the Economic Consequences of Divorce," *American Sociological Review,* 61:528–536, June 1996.
[h]Lenore J. Weitzman, "The Economic Consequences of Divorce Are Still Unequal," *American Sociological Review,* 61:537–538, June 1996.
[i]Richard R. Peterson, "Statistical Errors, Faulty Conclusions, Misguided Policy: Reply to Weitzman," *American Sociological Review,* 61:539–540, June 1996.

Evil-Causes-Evil Fallacy

evil-causes-evil fallacy

belief that if an act is bad it is caused by evil circumstances.

Finally, when examining the social problems in the following chapters, try not to fall into the **evil-causes-evil fallacy,** the belief that if an act or result is bad (e.g., alcoholism), then both its perpetrator and its "cause" must be equally bad. Some public figures speaking on social problems commit the fallacy of assuming that all social problems are caused by adverse circumstances.

A common example of this fallacy is attributing all crime to poverty, a cliché repeated by politicians and the general public. It fits the stereotype that crime is an act committed overwhelmingly by the poor. The trouble is that much crime is committed not by the poor but by the nonpoor. Whole categories of crime, such as white-collar crime or organized crime, are committed by the relatively wealthy. Even violent crimes, such as murder, often don't fit the "poverty causes crime" thesis, because many murders are emotional acts against a known person rather than actions directed toward getting money or goods. This is not to say that poverty and crime are unrelated. There is a connection, but it is not a simple or automatic one.

Can All Social Problems Be Solved?

Guest "experts" on popular talk shows frequently promulgate the view that to solve a particular social problem all that is required is to follow the author's sure-fire prescription and all will be fine. Easy policy answers to social problems, whether in the form of a simple version of welfare reform, redoing the school curriculum, or heavier penalties for offenders, rarely accomplish all their advocates promise. Unfortunately, there are no quick panaceas or simple solutions to complex questions. If there were, the problems would have long ago been resolved and ceased being problems. For any text to suggest that there are simple answers known only to the author would be the height of hubris, and insulting to those who have been working for decades on specific problems. Social problems are intertwined with the basic structure of modern post-industrial society, and "solving" such problems often involves weighing complex tradeoffs of benefits and losses (e.g., crime control versus personal liberty).

The real question isn't whether social problems can be reduced, but how and at what costs can they be reduced. We should ask ourselves not only how high is the cost but who pays the cost? Tightly controlled authoritarian societies, for instance, often have low levels of street crime. Most street crime is committed by young urban males, so if police can remove young males from the streets, crime decreases. A harshly enforced 9 P.M. curfew covering all males under age 25 could reduce crime. (Former President Clinton, during his 1996 presidential campaign, actually proposed a curfew for those under 18, but it has not been heard of since.) Keeping males under 25 off the streets at night would doubtless reduce crime. However, it would also violate their Constitutional rights as citizens. The question is not whether street crime rates can be sharply reduced, but what are the other consequences. Are lower crime rates worth some citizens losing Constitutional rights and individual liberty?

Some solutions to social problems are simply not going to be implemented because the solutions conflict with current social beliefs and practices. For example, legalizing drugs the same way we legalized alcohol would eliminate most of the problem of drug dealers and the use of violence to obtain money for drugs. Nonetheless, legalization is simply not going to occur, given the current attitudes of the majority of Americans. There is practically no chance that street drugs will be legalized and taxed by the government in the same way that it legalized and taxed alcohol.

The point here is not that our policies toward drugs, crime, or other problems should be changed, but that social policies invariably have unanticipated as well as anticipated consequences. If drug dealing is suppressed, for example, will the dis-

Some social programs are quite successful. Debbie Frazier now drives construction trucks, a job skill she learned through New Mexico's welfare-to-work program.

Alfred J. Hernandez/AP/Wide World Photos

placed dealers then turn to street robbery and burglary? We don't know for certain, but what we do know is that policies have consequences, and all of the consequences may not be clear, obvious, or desirable. Resolving one problem may, in fact, exacerbate another (e.g., cutting off illegal immigration raises the cost of middle-class goods and services). None of this means that social intervention should be abandoned. What it means is that informed social activism is more likely to be effective social activism. A goal of this book is to help educate student-citizens so that they will be able to make more informed choices about competing policy alternatives. The alternative is to have social policy choices made only by vested special interests.

Summary

Social problems are issues that substantial numbers of the society view as violations of the society's social norms and about which people believe something can and should be done. This chapter examines the different ways to view social problems and the three sociological approaches to them.

- Americans tend to think of social problems as personal troubles, but sociologists hold that the causes of social problems lie largely within the structure of society.

- Some consider social problems to be those that are so defined by the general public, others suggest that professionals should define what is or is not a problem.

- Those who view humans as inherently evil stress the necessity of having strong laws to control individuals who "cause" social problems. Those who see people as essentially perfectible believe that social problems arise from the antihumanitarian way society is organized.

- The **functionalist approach** concentrates attention not on individuals but on social structures at the macro or societal level. This approach emphasizes how societies share common interests and how social problems prevent the society from fulfilling its basic functions.

- The **conflict approach** also focuses on the macro level but stresses that conflict between competing interests within society is the root of social problems. The conflict approach asks the questions "Who benefits?" by the social structures underlying social problems and "In whose interests?" are social policies developed.
- The most famous conflict theory is **Marxism,** which views social problems as being caused by the capitalistic economic system.
- **Interactionist approaches,** more "micro" level and social psychological, look less at the society and more at the symbolic meaning of actions to individual social actors.
- In examining social problems, it is important to avoid the **evil-causes-evil fallacy,** the belief that if a result is bad then its cause must be equally bad, for example, attributing crime to poverty.
- Solving social problems in the real world involves social and economic costs; the solution to one problem may produce problems elsewhere.

☞Key Review Terms

conflict approaches
correlation
definition of the situation
empirical research
evil-causes-evil fallacy
feminist theory
field study
functionalist approaches

interactionist approaches
Marxist theory
participant observation
personal problems
qualitative studies
quantitative studies
social issues
social problem

sociological perspective
sociological imagination
symbolic interaction
theory
Thomas theorem
validity
variable

❓ Questions for Discussion

1. What is your instructor's sociological perspective? Do you agree with this perspective or not? Why?
2. How does your race, gender, age, and social class affect how you interpret data? Give examples.
3. What effect do the media have on defining social problems? Is this effect good or bad?
4. Can social problems be discussed objectively? Why or why not?
5. What do you think is the most important social problem facing the nation? Why?
6. In examining crime, what are the differences between personal problems and social issues?
7. How does commonsense knowledge about social problems differ from scientific knowledge? How can you distinguish between them?
8. Give examples of the evil-causes-evil fallacy in everyday life.
9. Is it worthwhile to try to solve social problems, or will that just make things worse?
10. What are the basic assumptions that functionalists and conflict theorists make about the organization and structure of society?

☛ Suggested Resources

Earl R. Babbie, *The Practice of Social Research*, 6th ed., Wadsworth, Belmont, CA, 1992. How to do sociological research, and the assumptions and logic underlying the various methodologies.

Edgar F. Borgatta and Marie L. Borgatta, eds., *Encyclopedia of Sociology*, Macmillian, New York, 1992. All you ever wanted to know about sociology in over 350 essays on diverse topics written by experts in the field.

Robert Bullah, Richard Madsen, William Sullivan, Ann Swindler, and Steven Tipton, *The Good Society*, Knopf, New York, 1991. An examination of American society and how to change it for the better.

Randall Collins, *Sociological Insights*, 2nd ed., Oxford University Press, New York, 1992. Collins uses C. Wright Mill's sociological imagination to provide insights into contemporary society.

Rick Schaefer, *Sociology*, 7th ed., McGraw-Hill, New York, 2001. A good basic introduction to the field of sociology.

William F. Whyte, *Participant Observation: An Autobiography*, ILR Press, Ithaca, NY, 1994. A view into sociology and participant observation by a master of the craft.

Internet Connection 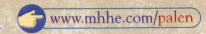 www.mhhe.com/palen

1. Visit the Society for the Study of Social Problems on the Web. (*www.itc.utk.edu/sssp/default.html*)
   a. What is the purpose of this organization and what resources does it have to offer to the study of social problems?
   b. Take some time to look at the many links that it provides to related websites.
2. What are the issues that concern the public the most? One way to find out is to visit the National Opinion Research Center at (*www.norc.uchicago.edu/homepage.htm*) Click on "General Social Survey" to learn more about this ongoing survey of U.S. households that has been conducted almost annually since 1972.
   a. Now go to the General Social Survey's Data and Information Retrieval System (GSSDIRS) by clicking on it. (*www.icpsr.umich.edu/gss/*) To use the GSS Search Engine to determine respondent's attitudes on a variety of social issues click on the GSS Search Engine (*www.icpsr.umich.edu/gss/search.htm*) and then click the subject index. You will see a long list of topics. Scroll down the list until you find "Problems (Cities, Crime, Drugs,. . . .)". To the right you will see a list of variable names. Click on any one of them to find out what NORC's respondents have reported about that particular problem. For example, regarding crime: In 1994, 1,138 respondents felt that the United States was spending too little money on halting the rising crime rate. A much smaller number (93) felt that the country was spending too much money.
   b. Examine some of the other issues and see what you come up with.

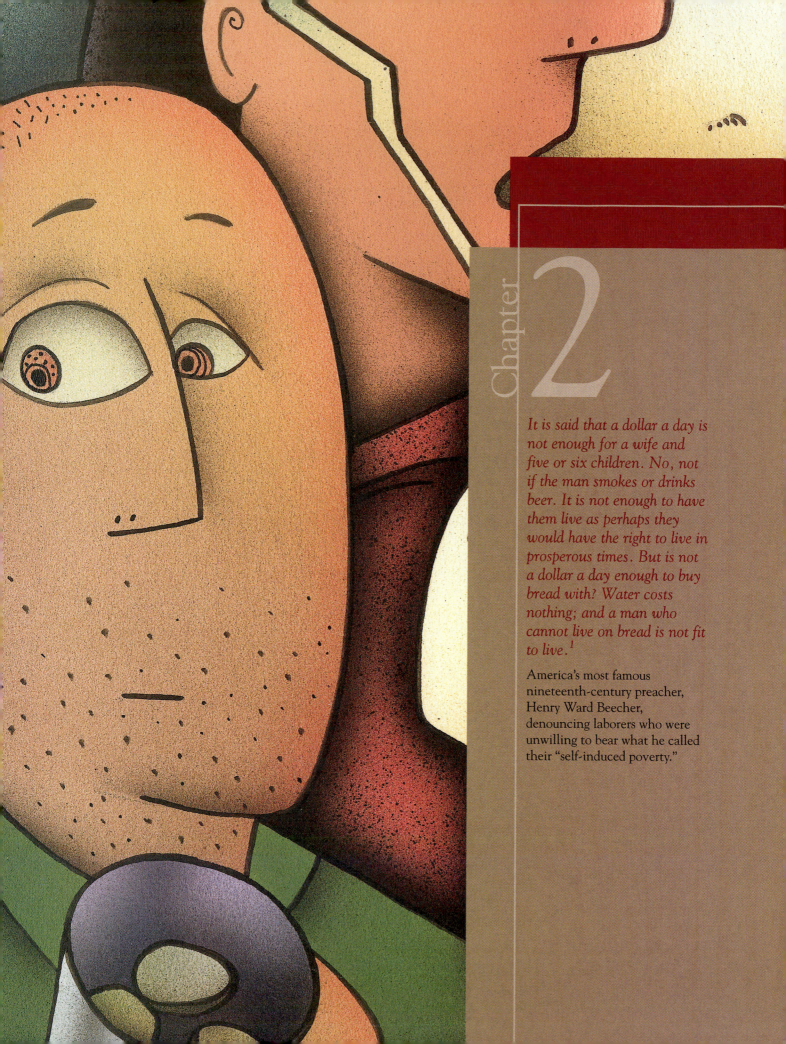

It is said that a dollar a day is not enough for a wife and five or six children. No, not if the man smokes or drinks beer. It is not enough to have them live as perhaps they would have the right to live in prosperous times. But is not a dollar a day enough to buy bread with? Water costs nothing; and a man who cannot live on bread is not fit to live.[1]

America's most famous nineteenth-century preacher, Henry Ward Beecher, denouncing laborers who were unwilling to bear what he called their "self-induced poverty."

To Have and to Havenot

[1]Henry F. May, *Protestant Churches and Industrial America*, Harper & Brothers, New York, 1939, p. 94.

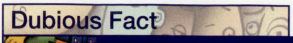
Inequality: Attitudes and Reality

Inequality refers to members of a society having different amounts of income, prestige, and power. Although the Declaration of Independence asserts that all people are "created equal," this statement refers to political equality rather than social or economic equality. From the time of birth, we never actually live together as equals. Social scientists note that inequality has characterized all human societies. All modern societies have systems of social and economic hierarchy, with some members being "more equal" and some "less equal." Sharp economic inequality has long been viewed as a social problem. As the ancient Greek philosopher Plutarch observed, "An imbalance between rich and poor is the oldest and most fatal ailment of all republics." Or as President John F. Kennedy put it: "If a free society cannot help the many who are poor, it cannot save the few who are rich." Both Plutarch and Kennedy recognized that sharp economic inequality undermines democratic society.

In this chapter we will see that the history of inequality in this country, and the history of social programs to deal with poverty and associated social ills, is a complicated blend of myth, politics, and special interests. We also will examine how the economic system increasingly is loaded against those at the bottom.

The American ideology of free enterprise says differences in economic rewards are both just and necessary. This view is especially held by members of the middle and upper classes, who concur that economic competition is the best way of distributing rewards and that people generally get what they deserve. The poor are far less likely to hold this view, seeing society holding them down. American society is divided between those who believe that success or failure is the result mostly of individual effort and those who hold it as a consequence of how society is organized.

Sociological Perspectives

We will discuss three societal or macro-level approaches or theories that explain this inequality: (1) functional theories, (2) conflict theories, and (3) theories of inherited biological differences. We will also examine interactionist theoretical approaches, which focus on the micro-level social-psychological consequences of poverty. Note that each theoretical approach leads to far different interpretations of social inequality.

Functionalist Approaches

As we saw in Chapter 1, functionalists generally stress the mechanisms that society uses to maintain stability, equilibrium, and order.[2] Functionalist approaches tend to assume that most existing social institutions and patterns serve a useful purpose—that they function as an integral part of a total social system. Functionalist approaches suggest that social stratification is crucial for a society's survival. By offering unequal rewards, a system of stratification attracts the most suitable people to society's most important positions. Kinsley Davis and Wilbert Moore put it this way: "If the rights and prerequisites of different positions in society must be unequal, then the society must be stratified, for that is what stratification means."[3]

Unequal rewards thus are seen as a means of ensuring that major societal positions are filled and needs met. To become a physician, for example, a medical student must endure at least six years beyond college of high tuition costs, grueling study, and a minimal social life. Without major financial and prestige incentives, few would undertake such an ordeal. Some functionalists would suggest that societies provide rewards of income, power, honor, or prestige to fill its important positions. Functionalists assume that societies become more efficient the more closely they approach a meritocracy in which reward is based upon individual merit, and that major structural changes in markets, corporations, and work patterns cause conflicts or dysfunctions which produce poverty.

Critics of functionalism say it tends toward an implicit conservative bias by suggesting that what exists does so because it works. They say this is circular reasoning insofar as functionalists assume that the most highly rewarded positions are also those most crucial to society's survival, and this is clearly not always the case. Functionalists concede that rewards often seem wildly out of proportion to society's needs. For example, dozens of baseball players make over $10 million a year, and the *average* major league baseball player makes over $ 1 million a year, while professional basketball players average over $3 million. It is difficult to see how the size of their financial rewards corresponds to their importance to the existence of society.

Critics also question whether the professions and managerial positions thought to be most functionally important actually do recruit the most competent people. Corporate officers who make the highest salaries often are not running businesses making the most profits.[4] There also is the question of what degree of difference in rewards is necessary. In 1960, when United States businesses dominated the world, the average after-taxes compensation of a chief executive at the largest U.S. corporations was 12 times that of the average worker. By the late 1990s the average yearly compensation for CEOs at the 500 biggest firms in the country had ballooned to almost 200 times that of the average worker.[5] In 1998 this amounted to annual compensation of $10.6 million.[6] (This huge difference is an American phenomenon. CEOs in Europe or Japan do not enjoy this degree of differential in salary.)

Functionalists say that such disproportionate rewards represent social dysfunctions. Functionalists stress the importance of pulling the poor into the national

---

[2]Talcott Parsons and Edward Shills (eds.), *Toward a General Theory of Action,* Harvard University Press, Cambridge, 1951.

[3]Kinsley Davis and Wilbert Moore, "Some Principles of Stratification," *American Sociological Review,* 10:243, 1945.

[4]"The State of Greed," *U.S. News and World Report,* June 17, 1996, p. 63.

[5]"Ibid., p. 63.

[6]"Wall Street Follies," *The New Yorker,* September 13, 1999, p. 32.

A hundred years ago John D. Rockefeller, Sr. built a huge fortune by ruthlessly crushing all competitors. Bill Gates has been charged with similar tactics. Both spent the second half of their careers trying to improve their public image by donating heavily to universities and education.

NYT Pictures

Barry Sweet/AP/Wide World Photos

economy, and the government is seen as having the prime role in encouraging those at the bottom to get schooling and job training. Functionalists, therefore, stress reforming the system to make it work more equitably and efficiently. Functionalists believe that unequal rewards motivate people to work harder and more efficiently and that the functional system is one that has enough inequality to encourage success, but not so much that it causes personal hardship or social disruption.

Conflict Approaches

Conflict theorists generally see inequality as the result of a social system designed to maximize profits by keeping costs and wages low. This exploits those at the bottom, with the result that there are a few rich and many poor. The problem is not the amount of wealth but its uneven distribution. Poverty for many ensures wealth for some. High unemployment can even be good for those at the top insofar as it keeps workers cowed and unlikely to join unions or agitate for improvement. Charity is used largely for social control rather than to alleviate problems.

According to Marxian theory, stratification systems are developed and used by the propertied classes to support their ends. These systems do not serve to fill functionally important positions with the best people; rather, they are used mainly to keep the lower class suppressed. Marx believed that the extent of this suppression would ultimately cause such misery among the proletariat that they would develop class consciousness, come to see the bourgeoisie as their oppressor, and overthrow them.

Non-Marxian conflict theorists also focus on what they see as the inevitability of conflict. However, non-Marxian conflict theorists argue that Marx's predictions have not been borne out; that is, there has been no sharp polarization of society into two conflicting classes. Instead, during the past century, the middle class has grown. Also, conflict has positive aspects. As Lewis Coser stated it, "Conflict between and within groups in a society can prevent accommodations and habitual relations from progressively impoverishing creativity."[7] Conflict theories have been criticized for a one-sided view of human life which ignores cooperation, but conflict theory has had a profound effect on sociology, not only in the examination of issues, but also in redefining which issues should be examined.

Biologically Based Approaches

Theories of stratification supposedly based on genetics have little scientific support, but they are discussed here since they continue to be widely held by the general public. One of the earliest and most influential of these theories, **Social Darwinism**, misapplied Charles Darwin's evolutionary theory to human beings using a sociobiological determinism. Social Darwinism with its suggestion of "survival of the fittest" was the dominant social theory of the late nineteenth and early twentieth centuries. Inequality, it claims, is natural—those who prove themselves superior in the competitive struggle are superior from birth and their strength lies in their genes. Social Darwinism is no longer taken seriously among scholars, but the concept of "survival of the fittest" still enjoys popular support as a commonsense theory of society and a justification for social inequality. (For a contemporary genetic theory of social behavior, see the discussion of *The Bell Curve* in Chapter 9.)

If large parts of individual behavior are determined by genetic structure, the consequences for social policy are profound. Some people would indeed be "born to lose," others to win. According to this view, aiding the weak and idle and providing welfare for the poor interferes with the laws of nature. Herbert Spencer, the major Social Darwinist philosopher of nineteenth-century England, put it this way:

> Blind to the fact, that under the natural order of things society is constantly excreting its unhealthy, imbecile, slow, vacillating, faithless members, these unthinking, though well-meaning, men advocate an interference which not only stops the purifying process, but even increases the vitiation. . . . And thus, in their eagerness to prevent the really salutary sufferings that surround us, these sigh-wise and groan-foolish people bequeath to posterity a continually increasing curse.[8]

Contemporary versions of this position can be heard in the United States Congress. According to such views, those who fail do so because they are innately inferior, because they just "don't have it." Both winners and losers are seen as basically deserving of their fate. Part of the attraction of such beliefs is that if the status of the poor is their own fault, then we as a society are absolved of any responsibility to eliminate poverty.

Social Darwinism
application of the "survival of the fittest" concept to social life in society.

---

[7]Lewis A. Coser, *The Functions of Social Conflict*, Free Press, Glencoe, IL, 1956, p. 153.
[8]Herbert Spencer, "Poverty Purifies Society," in *Social Statics*, D. Appleton and Co., New York, 1880 (orig. publ. 1851), pp. 353–354.

Sociobiology is a contemporary genetic theory of behavior that enjoys support in the natural sciences.[9] In the social sciences sociobiology receives less support because of some of its ethical, racial, gender, and cultural implications, particularly its assertion that much of social behavior is a process of biological evolution rather than cultural learning. Sociobiology suggests, for example, that males are less likely to be faithful mates than females because males are genetically programmed to seek to maximize the survival of their genes, a goal that is best accomplished through impregnating as many females as possible. Females, by contrast, are said to be programmed to seek permanent and secure environments for their offspring and thus are attracted to stable and powerful males.

Interactionist Approaches

While the preceding approaches all take a macro- or societal-level view of inequality, interactionist, or social psychological, approaches look at inequality at the individual level. They examine how inequality, and especially poverty, traps the poor, emotionally as well as economically. People are brought up and socialized into poverty as a way of life. Middle-class schools, the media, and society constantly tell the poor that they are less talented and less worthy. Interactionists study how the poor in an affluent society respond to their poverty: how they manage when everything around them encourages them to see themselves as failures unable to control their own destinies. Poor, single-parent families often are not only economically marginal but socially and educationally isolated. Such isolation reproduces poverty in the next generation. The "culture of poverty" thesis suggests that, in addition to low incomes, the norms and values into which the poor are socialized isolate them from the rest of the society. The social environment of the poor, with its low awareness of opportunities, low self-esteem, and emphasis on short-term gratification rather than a commitment to long-range goals, perpetuates intergenerational poverty. (For elaboration, see the section on "Culture of Poverty" later in this chapter.)

America's Rags-to-Riches Myth

America has a long-standing myth of itself as a land of opportunity where anyone can make good. In America, with its apparently limitless opportunity, open land, and streets said to be paved with gold, immigrants saw poverty as a temporary and correctable condition rather than an inevitable state. Newcomers coming to America's shores were told they were in a land where enterprise, hard work, and a bit of luck could lift them into the middle class, and maybe even make them rich. Though only a handful, such as Andrew Carnegie and Henry Ford, actually went from rags to riches, these few served as models of individual mobility for all the rest. The implicit message was that if you didn't make it, the fault was yours.

While the wealthy have long drawn the envy of the middle class, the poor are more likely to arouse hostility. Linking poverty to moral failure, Americans tend to scorn those who remain poor. (In part because of this belief, the United States was the last major industrial nation to adopt social welfare programs.) Continued poverty challenges the belief that individuals can control their own destinies. If the poor are not to blame for their own predicament—through laziness, lack of ambition, or the like—it would follow logically that the nonpoor are equally not re-

---

[9]Arthur Fisher, "Sociobiology Special Report: A New Synthesis Comes of Age," *Mosaic,* National Science Foundation, 22:2–17, 1991.

sponsible for their success. This conflicts with an important American belief—that success is the result of individual effort and work.

Attitudes toward poverty vary somewhat with the condition of the economy. During the Depression of the 1930s, attitudes toward those out of work were sympathetic. President Franklin D. Roosevelt stated the common belief when he said, "The test of our progress is not whether we add more to the abundance of those who have much; it is whether we provide enough for those who have little." Recent decades have seen public attitudes toward the poor, and government programs to aid them, become more conservative; the 1996 Welfare Reform Law, for example, ended entitlement programs that had been part of America's social welfare net since the 1930s. By contrast, the nation's two largest middle-class income transfer programs, Social Security and Medicare, together form the most expensive item in the federal budget, but they remain politically untouchable. (We will explore this issue in Chapter 11.)

The Widening Gap

Many Americans fear that even in periods of prosperity the good life is somehow slipping through their fingers. They worry that the gulf between rich and poor is widening—and that they are on the "have not" side. They have reason to be worried. For 20 years the income disparity between rich and poor has been increasing.[10] Federal data show that between 1970 and the late 1990s, the rich got richer, the poor got poorer, and the middle class (as defined as the middle 60 percent) treaded water. Looking at five different indicators, the Census Bureau says that all show a pronounced increase in the gap between the incomes of the well-to-do and those of the poor and the working class.[11] Even during the economic expansion of the 1990's inequality increased.[12] Most of the middle class have stayed in roughly the same place. The Census Bureau reported in 1999 that, in spite of the strongest economy and lowest unemployment in 30 years, the gap between rich and middle-income Americans has failed to narrow.[13] The biggest proportionate income losses during the 1980s and 1990s were suffered by nonunion, high-school-educated whites. Their median wage is still 10 percent below where it was in the 1990 census. Who is in power politically doesn't appear to have much impact. Income disparities widened during the Republican Reagan years of the 1980s, but they increased even further under the Democratic Clinton administrations of the 1990s. When taxes were cut in the 1980s, the rich got richer; when some upper-income taxes were increased in the mid 1990s, the rich got richer still.

Income

In 1935, during the height of the Depression, the poorest fifth of American families received only 4 percent of the national income (yearly wages, salary, or income from investments). By 1944, World War II, with its full employment and long hours of overtime, had raised the bottom fifth to 5 percent of the national income. Recent

---

[10]Douglas S. Massey, "The Age of Extremes: Concentrated Affluence and Poverty in the Twenty-First Century," *Demography* 33:4, 1996, p. 395.

[11]Steven Holmes, "Income Disparity between Poorest and Richest Rises," *New York Times,* June 20, 1996, p. A1.

[12]Frank Levy, *The New Dollars and Dreams: American Incomes and Economic Change,* Russell Sage, New York, 1998.

[13]"Rising Incomes Lift 1.1 Million Out of Poverty," *New York Times on the Web,* October 1, 1999.

years have eroded these modest gains, and the Bureau of the Census reports that the gap is wider than at any time since World War II.[14] The poorest fifth of American households now receive only *3.7 percent* of all income, while the top 20 percent's share has climbed to *49 percent* of all income.[15] Those in the *middle 60 percent* of the income distribution ($14,401 to $65,124 in 1995) have seen their income share decline from 52 percent of all income in 1967 to 47 percent in 1995. The way this works out in dollar terms is that as of 1998 the average income of the bottom 20 percent of families was $12,990, while the average figure for the top 20 percent was 11 times higher at *$137,480.*[16] The top 5 percent receive an average family income of *$183,000.*[17] Compared to other developed nations, America's rich do better and its poor do worse.

Wealth

Income data understate real economic differences since census figures measure only yearly salary or wage earnings rather than **wealth,** which includes total economic assets. Such assets include real estate, stocks, bonds, cash, and personal property and valuables. The most common way to achieve great wealth is to inherit it. In the United States today, *the bottom 20 percent of the population has negative wealth* (they owe more than they own), while *the top 20 percent hold 80 percent of all wealth.* The *top 1 percent owns 40 percent.* Over three decades ago, the economist Paul Samuelson described the situation quite graphically when he suggested that if we made an income pyramid out of a child's blocks, with each block standing for $1,000 of income, the peak would be far higher than the Eiffel Tower—but most people would be within a yard of the ground. The three richest people on earth have more financial resources than the 48 poorest countries.

The 1990 census recorded some 1.3 million millionaires in the country. By 2000 this figure had increased to 4.1 million. As of 2000 some 16 new millionaires were being created daily in California's Silicon Valley. In 1998 there were 189 billionaires in the United States.[18] Five of the top six billionaires have made their money in computers and software; Microsoft's Bill Gates's wealth as of 2000 was estimated to be $83 billion. (Gates's wealth is equal to that of the 110 million poorest Americans.) Of the 400 richest Americans, only 60 were women. The only African American woman among the richest Americans was Oprah Winfrey, who was worth $675 million. The overall pattern is that the middle class is getting squeezed, the rich are getting richer, and the working poor as well as the welfare poor are dropping even further behind.

Structural Mobility

During the twentieth century, most upward economic mobility in the United States has not been the result of individual efforts but rather **structural mobility.**

---

[14]U.S. Bureau of the Census, *Population Profile of the United States 1995,* Current Population Reports, P23–189, p. 41.

[15]U.S. Census Bureau, *Press Conference Speech on "Income, Poverty, and Health Insurance Estimates,"* September 26, 1996.

[16]Economic and Policy Institute and the Center on Budget and Policy Priorities, Study Release, Jan. 18, 2000.

[17]Elia Kacapyr, "Are You Middle Class?" *American Demographics,* October, 1996, p. 32.

[18]"Stock Dive Thins Billionaires' Club," *Associated Press News Service,* September 28, 1998.

That is mobility due to upward changes in the labor force. Massive economic shifts during the first three-quarters of the twentieth century shifted most people from working at relatively low-paying blue-collar and agricultural jobs to employment in better-paying white-collar positions. Roughly 80 percent of sons showed some mobility in relation to their fathers.[19] The so-called rising tide of prosperity lifted all boats. An exception for much of the century was African Americans, who were held back by segregation laws and customs that restricted access to education and jobs. Those in the majority population who failed to move up were, it was felt, simply unwilling to make the necessary effort.

The Middle-Class Squeeze

The long-held assumption that economic expansion automatically improves wages and living conditions has been undermined in the last two decades by factors such as deindustrialization, the job shift to cheaper labor overseas, and corporate employee downsizing. The middle-class worker can no longer count on upward structural mobility; the fear is downward structural mobility. For the blue-collar worker, the changes have been particularly severe, with industrial jobs being replaced with low-paying service jobs. Young male workers aged 25 to 34 have been hit the hardest. Their real after-inflation adjusted wages *dropped 25 percent* between the mid-1970s and the end of the century. Corporate downsizing and cutbacks have also hit college-educated middle managers. In 1996, for example, AT&T, part of the once secure "Ma Bell" corporate culture that "guaranteed" lifetime employment to good workers, announced cuts of 40,000 mostly middle-management jobs.

The result has been a **middle-class squeeze** in which younger generations no longer assume they will do better than their parents. Rather than anticipating upward mobility, they fear falling.[20] A college education is no longer a safety net. New male college graduates in 1996 actually made less than did 1990 graduates in real dollars. The bright spot was women's wages. During the same period, women's overall wages made small real dollar gains and college-educated women's salaries went up 10 percent.

One way of illustrating the extent to which the economic situation has changed for the middle class is to compare the experiences of young adults in the postwar generation with the experience of their children. In the mid-1950s, the average 30-year-old male worker could carry a mortgage on a median-priced home for 14 percent of his gross earnings. Thirty years later, it took a full 44 percent of his gross earnings to make the monthly payments on a median-priced home.[21] Housing costs today in real dollars are three times those of 1970, while middle-class incomes in real dollars are not much higher than 30 years ago. Today both husband and wife must work to purchase a house that as of 1970 could be bought with only one income. Even with low interest rates and a strong economy, it still takes two incomes for most families to purchase a home. Buying a home also often means other adjustments, such as working two jobs, delaying childbearing, or deciding not to have more children.

> **middle-class squeeze**
> the fear of the middle class that their position is worsening and their children will not do as well.

---

[19]David L. Featherman and Robert M. Hauser, *Opportunity and Change,* Academic Press, New York, 1978.
[20]Barbara Ehrenreich, *Fear of Falling,* Harper Perennial, New York, 1990.
[21]Frank Levy, *Dollars and Dreams: The Changing American Distribution,* Russell Sage, New York, 1987.

Half a century ago this steel mill in Youngstown, Ohio represented the industrial age in America. Now it is abandoned and its workers are gone.

Mark C. Burnett/Stock, Boston

Cyclical versus Structural Unemployment

Unemployment often has more to do with changes in the overall economy than with the activities of individuals. For much of this century, workers who were victims of the business cycle lost their jobs when the economy slowed down. Such unemployment is called **cyclical unemployment.** Workers laid off as a result of the vagaries of the economy could hope to get work when things picked up again. The Great Depression of the 1930s is a prime example of cyclical unemployment.

However, the structure of the U.S. economy has changed profoundly in the last 25 years. Manufacturers needing low-cost labor have largely gone abroad, and more and more of the remaining manufacturing is replacing people with machines. Similarly, many middle-management positions are being eliminated. This causes **structural unemployment** due to long-term changes in the economic system. For example, where a local bank loan officer once made mortgage loan decisions, the bank's computer program now commonly decides whether a loan applicant meets the "loan profile" and thus gets the loan.

With *structural unemployment,* cycles of economic growth or recession don't necessarily affect job opportunities. Technological change means unemployment often is more of a permanent condition than a temporary phase. For workers with limited education and few marketable skills, especially those trapped in the inner cities, structural unemployment, and thus poverty, is a way of life. The British term for the structurally unemployed is that they are "redundant," a term suggesting that they are economically unnecessary in a postindustrial labor force.

Deindustrialization is the loss of manufacturing industries and jobs. Good-paying blue-collar jobs began drying up in American cities in the 1970s. As the central city lost more and more jobs, and as the middle class (both black and white) began fleeing inner-city neighborhoods, those left behind found themselves living in areas without either employment or job contacts. Without jobs, or the hope of such, young inner-city males ceased being suitable stable marriage partners, and fatherless families became the norm.[22] The consequence has been children growing up in poverty, fatherless families without the guidance of responsible adult males. That so many young males living in such areas fall into crime and drug usage

cyclical unemployment
unemployment tied to the rise and fall of the business cycle.

structural unemployment
unemployment due to long-term changes in the economic system.

deindustrialization
shutting down of factories due to movement from a manufacturing to a service economy.

---

[22]William Julius Wilson, *When Work Disappears,* Knopf, New York, 1996.

should not be surprising to anyone. On the other hand, there is clear evidence that inner-city males who are employed behave in a responsible manner.[23] The difference between responsible and irresponsible behavior is often simply having a good job. Employed males, for example, are twice as likely as unemployed males to marry the mother of their first child.[24]

Who Has What

To understand poverty, it helps to know how inequality is built into the American system of social stratification. Societies can be economically divided in a variety of ways (Karl Marx, for example, used two categories: owners and workers). Here we will cut the pie using a four-class system: wealthy, middle class, working class, and lower class. We will then examine further divisions within these broad categories.

The Wealthy

We begin our examination of income distribution with the wealthy, which includes both the established wealthy and the nouveau riche. In the United States the wealthy are very rich indeed. The rich not only make more, they keep more. The tax code is structured so as to allow them to keep their assets. When middle-class investors sell assets such as stocks, mutual funds, or commercial properties, they have to pay a capital gains tax. For the very wealthy, however, Wall Street bankers have devised complicated tax schemes that allow rich investors to use the tax code in unanticipated ways to sell their stocks without paying any capital gains taxes.[25]

The Establishment William Domhoff suggests that the established upper class makes up only 0.5 percent of the United States population.[26] In social terms the upper-class establishment, sometimes referred to as the "old guard," includes only those families that have enjoyed wealth for several generations. The old rich have real class boundaries and a strong in-group solidarity.[27] As expressed in the old Boston doggerel:

Here in to Boston,
The home of the bean and the cod.
Where the Cabots speak only to Lowells,
And Lowells speak only to God.

The personal advantages of established wealth go beyond the economic. According to a famous anecdote, F. Scott Fitzgerald once remarked to Ernest Hemingway,

---

[23]Mitchell Duneier, *Slim's Table: Race, Respectability, and Masculinity,* University of Chicago Press, Chicago, 1992.

[24]Mark Testa, Nan M. Astone, Marilyn Krough, and Kathryn M. Neckerman, "Employment and Marriage among Inner-City Fathers," *Annals,* 501:79–91, January, 1989.

[25]Diana Henriques, with Floly Norris, "Wealthy, Helped by Wall St., Find New Ways to Escape Tax on Profits," *New York Times,* December 1, 1996, p. A1.

[26]G. William Domhoff, *Who Rules America Now?* Prentice-Hall, Englewood Cliffs, NJ, 1983.

[27]For a discussion of the WASP establishment, see G. William Domhoff, *Who Rules America Now? A View for the 80s,* Prentice-Hall, Englewood Cliffs, NJ, 1983. The classic work is E. Digby Baltzell, *The Protestant Establishment,* Vintage Books, New York, 1966.

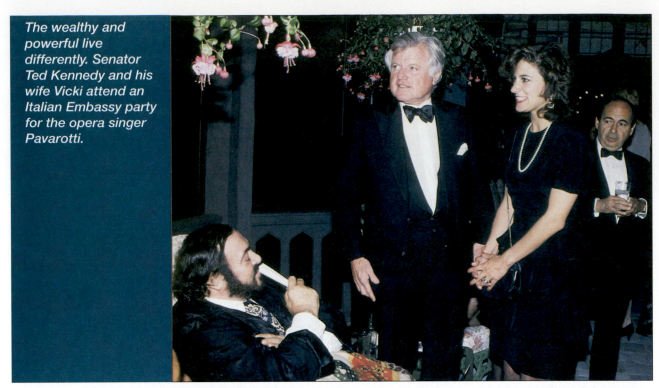

The wealthy and powerful live differently. Senator Ted Kennedy and his wife Vicki attend an Italian Embassy party for the opera singer Pavarotti.

© Vivian Ronay/Liaison Agency

"The rich are different." Hemingway's retort was, "Yes, they have more money." Hemingway was wrong; wealth can provide far more than luxurious estates, elegant yachts, expensive cars, and open-ended charge accounts. As Fitzgerald's novels show, having old wealth also involves a specific state of mind and attitudes. It would be absurd to suggest that all the rich think and act alike, but wealth—especially inherited wealth—does breed a unique culture. Psychiatrist Robert Coles refers to the way children of the rich are socialized as a sense of "entitlement." Wealthy children not only have more goods, more lessons, and more travel, but also a sense of themselves as entitled to what they receive. Coles says, "Wealth does not corrupt, nor does it ennoble. But wealth does govern the minds of privileged children, gives them a peculiar kind of identity which they never lose. . . . There is, I think, a message that virtually all quite well-off American families transmit to their children—an emotional expression of those familiar, class-bound prerogatives, money and power."[28] Until recently the established wealthy also controlled the nation politically and socially.

The majority of the old establishment wealthy still are white Anglo-Saxon Protestants (WASPs). Private schools often are where the old wealth and those on the way up first rub elbows. In order to help move his sons into the establishment, Joseph Kennedy, who had new money, sent his son John F. Kennedy and his brothers to prep school to speed their entry into the establishment. Private New England prep schools such as Choate, Groton, Hotchkiss, and St. Mark's both reinforce a sense of separateness and inculcate a sense of responsibility. Kennedy's "Ask not what your country can do for you, but what you can do for your country," is a reworking of the lessons he had been taught at Choate.

Politically, members of the establishment often are "Economic Republicans" rather than "Social Republicans." This means they are economically conservative

---

[28]Robert Coles, "The Children of Affluence," *Atlantic*, September, 1977, p. 54.

but socially moderate. They generally are uncomfortable with right-wing political-religious doctrines such as those espoused by Pat Robertson's Christian Coalition. Rather than being members of antiabortion groups, they are more likely to be board members of Planned Parenthood. The establishment wealthy, while still very powerful, no longer exercise the decisive economic or social dominance they once held. George Bush is the most recent President to have come from the WASP establishment. Bill Clinton, by contrast, was born into the lower middle class.

The Nouveau Riche Immediately below the established wealthy is a somewhat larger group (but still under 2 percent of the population) of new rich who actually are quite a bit richer than the old guard. Over the past 30 years the old WASP establishment has been substantially replaced (especially on the West Coast) by a new establishment based on performance. Highly selective universities, which once admitted on family background and "old boy" criteria, now largely admit based on intelligence, ability, and hard work. The new SAT or merit-based establishment, which includes those running new technology-based companies, places heavy emphasis on achievement and performance.

However, the old WASP establishment hasn't entirely faded from the scene. Inheritance and family still count. George W. Bush was admitted to Yale in spite of modest SATs, and then to the extremely competitive Harvard Business School in spite of his C+ average at Yale. Not everyone starts on an even playing field.

New wealthy tend to be much more ostentatious in displaying their affluence than do those with old money. The term **conspicious consumption** refers to their pattern of buying goods more for display than use.[29] As a group, the new rich are more inclined toward right-wing political beliefs than are the old wealthy. They tend to feel that they did it so others can also do it. As put by the sociologist Seymour M. Lipset:

> New wealth most often tends to have extremist ideologies, to believe in extreme conservative doctrines in economic matters. The man who makes money himself feels more insecure about keeping it than do people who possess inherited wealth. He feels more aggrieved about social reform measures which involve redistribution of the wealth, as compared with individuals, still wealthy, who have grown up in an old traditionalist background, which inculcates the values of tolerance.[30]

Aside from their money, what sets the more established rich apart from the nouveau riche is not so much what they do as the style in which they do it. Political figures born to wealth such as George Bush (senior and junior), Steve Forbes, or John Kennedy possessed a relaxed confidence which forever eluded rags-to-riches nouveau riche such as Lyndon Johnson, Richard Nixon, or Ross Perot.

The Middle Class

Given no specific categories from which to choose, over four out of five Americans simply say that they are "middle class." This label encompasses a wide range of incomes, occupations, and styles of life. Perhaps one way of demarcating the middle class is to say that this is the social class usually portrayed on television and the class at whom the lion's share of commercial advertising is directed. The middle class can be divided into upper-middle and lower-middle groups.

conspicious consumption
consumption designed to show ones status or position rather than consumption for actual use.

---

[29]Thorstein Veblen, *The Theory of the Leisure Class,* New American Library, New York, 1953 (orig. publ. 1899).
[30]Seymour Martin Lipset, "The Sources of the Radical Right," in Daniel Bell, ed., *The Radical Right,* Anchor Books, New York, 1963, p. 341.

Box 2.1 Ongoing Issues

The Power Elite

C. Wright Mills was arguably the most influential critical sociologist of mid-twentieth-century America. His writing on the military-industrial complex shaped the thinking of a generation of scholars and writers. The paragraphs below from *The Power Elite* give the flavor of his writing.[a]

"In the inner circles of the upper classes, the most impersonal problems of the largest and most important institutions are fused with the sentiments and worries of small, closed, intimate groups. This is one very important meaning of the upper-class family and of the upper-class school: 'background' is one way in which, on the basis of intimate association, the activities of an upper class may be tacitly coordinated. It is also important because in such circles, adolescent boys and girls are exposed to the table conversations of decision-makers, and thus have bred into them the informal skills and pretensions of decision-makers; in short, they imbibe what is called 'judgment.' Without conscious effort, they absorb the aspiration to be—if not the conviction that they are—The Ones Who Decide. . . ."

"The exclusive schools and clubs and resorts of the upper social classes are not exclusive merely because their members are snobs. Such locales and associations have a real part in building the upper-class character, and more than that, the connections to which they naturally lead help to link one higher circle with another."

"So the distinguished law student, after prep school and Harvard, is 'clerk' to a Supreme Court judge, then a corporation lawyer, then in the diplomatic service, then in the law firm again. In each of these spheres, he meets and knows men of his own kind, and, as a kind of continuum, there are the old family friends and the schoolboy chums, the dinners at the club, and each year of his life the summer resorts. In each of these circles in which he moves, he acquires and exercises a confidence in his own ability to judge, to decide, and in this confidence he is supported by his ready access to the experience and sensibility of those who are his social peers and who act with decision in each of the important institutions and areas of public life. One does not turn one's back on a man whose presence is accepted in such circles, even under the most trying circumstances. All over the top of the nation, he is 'in,' his appearance, a certificate of social position; his voice and manner, a badge of proper training; his associates, proof at once of their acceptance and of his stereotyped discernment."

[a]*C. Wright Mills*, The Power Elite, *Oxford University Press, New York, 1956, pp. 69–70.*

Upper-Middle Class The upper-middle class represents about 15 percent of the population and view themselves as the people who make society run. These are the professional, business, governmental, and educational people who manage the society. This also is the group in which most college students hope to find themselves. For members of the upper-middle class, one's career largely defines one's life. This is the group most likely to have advanced degrees and most likely to rely on their professional careers to support their comfortable homes and comfortable way of life. Active in civic groups and mainline churches, the upper-middle class also are the group most concerned that their children get into the "right" colleges and succeed. Education is correctly seen as the path to success.

Lower-Middle Class The lower-middle class comprises about a third of the population. This white-collar group shares many of the same attitudes and aspirations as the upper-middle class, but they have fewer resources to use in meeting their goals. Comprising groups such as small-business people, school teachers, and many government workers, the lower-middle class lacks the full educational and economic advantages of the upper-middle group. Perhaps because of their limited resources, small proprietors tend to be conservative in economic, political, social, and religious questions.

The Working Class

America's working-class population is shrinking. It was much larger than the lower-middle class 25 years ago, when most of the workforce was still manufacturing goods. Now, with deindustrialization, the working class is down to roughly 30 percent of the population. The working class differs from the lower-middle class in that its jobs are blue-collar manufacturing and service rather than white-collar. The working class includes both skilled and semiskilled workers. Education level is likely to be high school, with perhaps some additional trade school. From World War II until the 1970s, unionized blue-collar workers often made more than many white-collar workers. Some highly skilled members of the working class, such as master carpenters, plumbers, and mechanics, still do very well economically. However, as noted earlier, working-class workers as a group have seen their real wages considerably decline since the 1970s. Members of the working class tend to feel they are politically powerless and the school system is biased against their children. They are right.

The Lower Class

The lower class or poor comprise roughly the bottom 20 percent of the population. The poor can be divided into the working poor and the truly deprived or welfare poor (sometimes called the underclass). The line between the groups is not always sharp since some families move back and forth. Generally both groups have low educational levels, uneven work histories with high unemployment, and a high proportion of single-parent families.

Working Poor Largely overlooked in any discussion of wealth and poverty are the roughly 10 million working poor who hover about the poverty line. Regardless of what they do, the working poor are stuck on the bottom rung of the ladder of economic opportunity. Sometimes working two or more jobs just to get by, the working poor are finding that life is getting harder, not better. The working poor have seen their real income *drop* 10 percent since the late 1970s. According to Labor Department figures, the lowest-earning 10 percent of workers earned an average 1994 income of only $11,700, well below the official poverty line. For the working poor, any unexpected expense often pushes the family into debt. Stagnant wages and rising prices keep the working poor far from the American Dream, and more working-class families are slipping downward into this category. Two-thirds of the 40 million Americans with no health care live in families with full-time workers. Nearly three-quarters of the working poor are white, although black and Hispanic workers have a greater likelihood of being among the working poor.[31]

For inner-city workers who participate on the bottom level of the economy, the problem is economic survival. Many of the urban working poor are service-industry workers who perform tasks like making beds in hospitals and fixing food in fast-food restaurants. A detailed study of the working poor in New York City's Harlem found that, in spite of a strong commitment to the work ethic, many of the working poor in inner-city areas (especially if they are African

---

[31]Bureau of Labor Statistics, "A Profile of the Working Poor, 1996," U.S. Department of Labor, Washington, DC, Report 918, p. 1.

41

Even during a thriving economy structural poverty persists. Five-year-old Jeffery Johnson looking into his near empty refrigerator lives on the Navajo reservation in New Mexico.

Eric Draper/AP/Wide World Photos

American) have difficulty finding even minimum-wage jobs.[32] The problem is not the lack of a work ethic, but limited job opportunities, especially jobs paying a living wage.

In economic terms, the working poor may end up with less than those on public assistance. For a single-parent welfare mother with children, working a full-time job for minimum wage actually reduces both her cash and benefits. In their groundbreaking study of 379 mothers who receive welfare or work at low-paying jobs, Kathryn Edin and Laura Lein found that low-wage jobs frequently are not the path out of welfare.[33] Mothers with paying jobs had more income, but they spent twice as much as welfare mothers on expenses such as day care, transportation, medical costs, and housing. For the working poor, a work ethic provides few economic rewards. But, in spite of constant setbacks, the working poor keep struggling.

Truly Disadvantaged The truly disadvantaged or deprived have incomes under the official poverty level ($16,700 for a family of four in 1999). They also have negative wealth, owing more than they own. While the working poor may be on the bottom rung of the ladder of economic success, the truly disadvantaged aren't even on the ladder. Over half of this group haven't finished high school. The very poor also have high rates of social problems, such as drug usage, alcoholism, mental illness, and criminal arrest. This group is sometimes called the underclass, but some sociologists, like the author of this text, feel the term *underclass* has a class bias and prefer the term, *truly disadvantaged*.[34] Whatever they are called, the very poor disproportionately suffer the consequences of social problems. (Table 2.1 gives a brief summary of the U.S. class system.)

---

[32]Katherine S. Newman, "What Scholars Can Tell Politicians about the Poor," *Chronicle of Higher Education*, June, 23, 1995, pp. B1–B2.
[33]Kathryn Edin and Laura Lein, *Making Ends Meet: How Single Mothers Survive Welfare and Low-Wage Work*, Russell Sage Foundation, New York, 1997; and Kathryn Edin and Laura Lein, "Work, Welfare, and Single Mothers' Economic Strategies," *American Sociological Review*, 62:253–266, April 1997.
[34]Wilson, *The Truly Disadvantaged*.

Table 2.1 The Class System in America

Class	Portion of U.S. Population	Income	Wealth	Occupation	Education
Upper- (Old and New Rich)	2%	$180,000 up	Considerable, often inherited	Corporate heads, founders of technology firms, some doctors, lawyers	Elite colleges
Upper-middle	15%	$75,000–$180,000	Savings, property	Managers, professionals, executives	Graduate school
Lower-middle	33%	$30,000–$75,000	Some savings, home	Semiprofessional, teachers, small-business people	Some college or public college
Working	30%	$20,000–$55,000	Some savings	Skilled and semiskilled labor	High school
Lower (Working Poor and Truly Disadvantaged)	20%	$20,000 down—welfare	No savings	Unskilled	Illiterate to some high school

Source: Author.

Poverty: Definitions and Extent

It may seem easy to say what poverty is, but arguments over the term's meaning and definition abound. Many of the arguments center around the differences between two basic conceptual approaches: poverty as **absolute poverty** or as **relative poverty.** Acceptance of one of these definitions over the other represents more than merely a philosophical debate. At stake is how we regard (and deal with) the very nature of poverty in society.

Absolute Poverty

Absolute poverty is calculated from an objective preset standard of living, wherein a point is established below which persons are considered "poor." Absolute poverty definitions are usually based on objective criteria from which basic minimum need standards are set and to which individual situations are compared. The official U.S. government definition of poverty, first devised in 1965, uses an absolute measure of poverty by defining a minimal "market basket" of food and then

absolute poverty
absence of basic necessities of food, clothing, shelter, education, and health care.

relative poverty
feeling poor based on having less than others in the society, the emphasis is on inequality rather than an absolute level of need.

Box 2.2 Ongoing Issues

Advantages of Affluence

Money may or may not bring happiness; it certainly brings just about everything else. A number of commentators have looked at quality-of-life indicators and how they differ by class position. Not surprisingly, the rich and well-to-do have the best of everything; among their other advantages are the facts that they live longer, have fewer divorces, and are less likely to become overweight than the rest of us. (With regard to weight, just over half of low-income women have problems with obesity compared with four out of ten middle-income women and only one in eleven of those with high incomes.) Some interesting findings help illuminate these differences.

Longevity Middle- and upper-class people live longer because they live better, do safer work, and get better medical care than those who are less well off. Infants born into poor families are three times more likely to die during the first year of life.[a] Longer life expectancy is linked to higher income, education, and occupation. Among adult white males, those who never got as far as high school have a mortality rate half again as high as the college educated. Death rates for inner-city populations are staggering. A 15-year-old boy in New York's Harlem has less chance of surviving to age 45 than non-inner-city youths have of reaching age 65.[b]

Physical Health The poor have less access to health care and receive less adequate treatment. Only 4 percent of those with incomes above the average complain of fair or poor health, while almost a quarter of the poor do so.[c] In general, the higher a patient's social class, the better and more frequent the medical care he or she receives. However, the relationship is not linear. Nonunion working poor are the worst off because they have neither union health insurance nor a "green card" allowing free Medicaid medical care.

Calista Flockhart from *Ally McBeal* holds her 1999 Screen Actors Guild Award and reinforcing for young girls the belief that, "You can never be too rich or too thin."

Reed Saxon/AP/Wide World Photos

Mental Health

Generally, the lower the social class, the greater the incidence and severity of mental illness.[d]

The well-to-do benefit from earlier and better mental health care and also appear to suffer less stress than the poor.

Psychosis appears to be more prevalent in the lower classes; however, there is more treatment for neurosis in the middle and upper classes.

Family Stability

The lower the class, the earlier the age of marriage. The lower the class, the higher the rate of divorce, desertion, and family breakups due to the death of a parent.

Poor children are far more likely to grow up in homes with only one parent or no parent and to remain poor.

The overall pattern of the above selected factors is clear and unmistakable. Poverty may be a route to sainthood, but in every other respect wealth beats poverty hands down. Those who have written of the ennobling aspects of poverty have generally enjoyed lives free from malnutrition, slum living, and inferior schools.

[a]*Children's Defense Fund*, Child Poverty in America, *Washington, DC, 1991.*

[b]*Bob Herbert, "Death at an Early Age,"* New York Times, *December 2, 1996, p. A15.*

[c]*P. F. Adams and V. Benson, "Current Estimates from the National Health Interview Survey, 1989,"* Vital Health Statistics, *vol. 10, no. 176, U.S. National Center for Health Statistics, Washington, DC, 1990.*

[d]*A. B. Hollingshead and Fredrick Redlich,* Social Class and Mental Illness, *John Wiley & Sons, New York, 1958; and Leo Srole, et al.,* Mental Health in the Metropolis: The Midtown Manhattan Study, *McGraw-Hill, New York, 1962.*

multiplying by three and adjusting for inflation.[35] This index understates current poverty since housing costs have escalated faster than the market basket. Using absolute measures, if a minimum standard for the poor is set at, say, $16,700 (the 1999 level for a family of four), household incomes falling below that amount (i.e., $16,700 or less) are considered poor regardless of what other members of the society make. Those who make $16,700 or more are not poor, regardless of where they fall on the income hierarchy.

Because changes in definition produce different poverty levels, definitions are a political issue—a point to bear in mind when examining other social problems as well. In 1992 the U.S. Department of Commerce released a report detailing how poverty levels in the United States would look according to five different definitions of income: *money income* (the official definition); *private sector income,* which does not include cash transfers; *after-tax income; after-transfer income,* which includes the value of noncash government benefits (e.g., food stamps, housing subsidies, school lunches); and *inclusive income,* which includes equity on one's home. Estimates of the size of the poor population diverge sharply depending on the definition used to estimate poverty level. Keep in mind that all the definitions are arbitrary; their components are often influenced by political considerations since how poverty is defined affects the number of poor reported. Conservatives, for example, stress that the official figures overstate poverty by not taking into account noncash government benefits such as medical care, food stamps, and housing subsidies. Liberals, on the contrary, argue that the official figures understate poverty. Since the time the figures were developed, they say, housing costs have gone up faster than inflation; and most women didn't work outside the home in 1965, so the figures do not allow for childcare costs. Those who work with the poor agree that current poverty levels represent bare minimal levels. A living family wage which would provide a low, but adequate, level of life currently would be approximately $26,000 for a family of four.

Relative Poverty

Relative poverty as a concept is not based on particular income thresholds, but rather on how someone compares to the average person or family in the society at large. A variety of measures have been used to set a relative level of poverty. Perhaps the most often cited threshold is that of the National Bureau of Economic Research at Princeton, which sets the poverty line at one-half of the median household income for similar type families.

Measures of relative poverty focus not so much on poverty per se as on inequality. That is, the focus is not on whether a person has the minimum necessary to get by, but on how much that person has when compared to others. As the classic Thomas theorem discussed in Chapter 1 stated, "If men define situations as real, they are real in their consequences."[36] Thus, while the poor may objectively be better-off today, they often feel more deprived, more excluded from the "American way of life." Even the mass entertainment of the poor—television—constantly reminds them that they do not live like the people in the programs and the commercials. On television everyone seems, quite effortlessly, to enjoy an upper-middle class

Inequality *disparity in status or resources.*

---

[35]The original poverty line was developed by Mollie Orshansky of the Social Security Administration and was set at three times the cost of a minimal diet "market basket." This was based on the Agriculture Department finding that as of the mid-1960s the average family spent roughly a third of its income on food. See Mollie Orshansky, "Counting the Poor: Another Look at the Poverty Profile," *Social Security Bulletin,* 28:3–29, January 1965.

[36]Robert K. Merton, "The Thomas Theorem and the Matthew Effect," *Social Forces,* 74:379–424, December 1995.

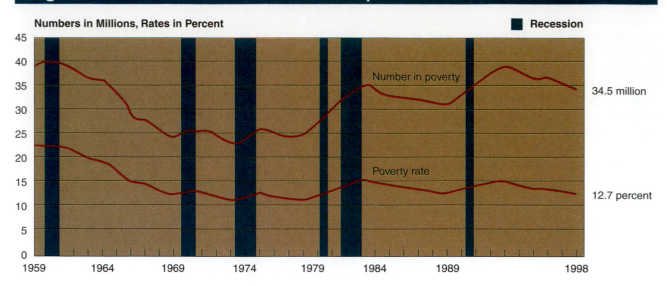

Figure 2.1 Number of Poor and Poverty Rate: 1959 to 1998

Numbers in Millions, Rates in Percent

■ Recession

Number in poverty — 34.5 million

Poverty rate — 12.7 percent

1959   1964   1969   1974   1979   1984   1989   1998

Note: The data points represent the midpoints of the respective years. The dark bars mark recession. The latest recession began in July of 1990 and ended in March 1991.

Source: U.S. Census Bureau, March 1960-March 1999 Current Population Survey.

lifestyle. Advertisements invariably feature a large ultramodern kitchen; there never is an old refrigerator, ancient gas stove, or worn out floor tiles. Absolute deprivation may be lower than it was in earlier periods, but relative deprivation is far greater. In cities where there are conspicuous displays of wealth and where it is clear that most others are better off, being on the bottom can lead to feelings of frustration, resentment, and anger.

The Extent of Poverty

The 1960 census reported a markedly more than one in five citizens (22 percent) below the poverty level. Because of this the federal War on Poverty was created in the mid-1960s, and its programs worked so well that by 1970 the overall poverty rate had dropped dramatically to 12.6 percent.[37] The poverty rate remained steady during the 1970s, but conservative social policies during the 1980s increased the poverty rate to over 15 percent by 1990. The Census Bureau reported in 1999 that a strong economy had decreased poverty rates to 12.7 percent.[38] This translates into 34.5 million American people living in poverty. We should keep in mind that, in spite of the recent declines in poverty rates, the levels are still higher than any year in the 1970s and higher than poverty levels in Canada or Western Europe. Figure 2.1 indicates changes in poverty rates since the 1960s.

Faces of the Poor

Who are the 34.5 million poor Americans? What do they look like? We constantly make commonsense assumptions about the poor, but only some of these assumptions are accurate. Today's poor are most likely to be children, people of color, and

---

[37]U.S. Bureau of the Census, *Statistical Abstract of the United States 1990,* Government Printing Office, Washington, DC, 1990, p. 458.

[38]"Rising Incomes Lift 1.1 Million Out of Poverty," *New York Times on the Web,* October 1, 1999.

As a group the elderly are doing better, but many older Americans spend their final years alone and in poverty.

© Jim Noelker/The Image Works

people living in female-headed families. However, contrary to common belief, more of the poor live in suburbs than in central city neighborhoods, and most of the working-age poor work and are not on welfare.

The Old and The Young When the War on Poverty programs took shape in the mid-1960s, the most vulnerable members of society were the elderly. In 1960, over 35 percent of those 65 and over fell below the poverty line. The next highest poverty group was children, with 27 percent poverty, so programs were also aimed at assisting families with small children (particularly through the Aid to Families with Dependent Children, or AFDC, program).

War on Poverty programs targeted the elderly (particularly through dramatic increases in Social Security payments) and between 1960 and 2000, the poverty rate for the elderly dropped from over 35 percent to under 11 percent. Although there still are many elderly poor, the elderly have gone from being those most likely to be poor to being the age group least likely to be poor (see Chapter 11). Since 1995 the poverty rate for the elderly has been lower than that for those of working age (18 to 64).[39]

Children have fared far worse. War on Poverty programs produced a dramatic drop of almost 50 percent in child poverty by 1970. After that date, however, poverty rates among children again began to grow, and by the early 1990s the poverty rate for children had reached 22 percent of all children—the highest rate of child poverty in 30 years. At the century's end economic growth had dropped child poverty rates to 19 percent, the first time the rate for children living in poverty had dropped below 20 percent since the 1970s.[40]

If instead of looking at what percentage of children are poor we look at what proportion of those who are poor are children, we see that a shockingly high 40 percent of all the poor are children. Another 10 percent of the poor are 65 or over. In terms of welfare reform, this means that half of those who are poor are either too young or too old to be in the labor force. Further sharp cutbacks in the number of poor receiving welfare means removing support funds from children and the aged.

---

[39]U.S. Census Bureau, "Press Briefing on *1995 Income, Poverty, and Health Insurance Estimates*," September 26, 1996.
[40]U.S. Census Bureau, "Poverty in the United States: 1998," *Current Population Reports*, P60–207, September 1999, p. viii.

People of Color For many people, the issues of race and poverty are intertwined (the next chapter discusses this complex relationship). However, the general assumption that most of the poor are minorities is inaccurate. Roughly half of those below the poverty line (48 percent) are white. Although more whites than any other race are in poverty, the *proportion* of various ethnic populations in poverty is another matter. One's chances of living in poverty are much greater if one is darker skinned. In terms of proportions, African Americans are 2.5 times more likely to live in poverty than whites. A third of African American children live in poverty, down from 43 percent in 1990. As a consequence of years of economic expansion, minority poverty rates finally are coming down. For example, in 1998 African American poverty rates dropped to 26 percent—still high, but the lowest in the 40 years the government has collected such data.[41] Poverty rates have also dropped for Hispanics, who do only fractionally better, with 25 percent below the poverty line. The figures were 12 percent for Asians, and 8 percent for non-Hispanic whites.

Single-Parent Families Single-parent families, especially female-headed families in which the mother never married, have a high probability of being poor. While many female-headed families are not poor, such families are over five times more likely than married-couple families to be living in poverty. While only 10 percent of the children living in married-couple families are poor, half of those in female-headed families are poor.[42] For example, median 1996 income for two-parent families with children was $45,000, while that for female-headed families was $18,000.[43] Thus, living in a two-parent family of any race generally means living out of poverty, while living in a fatherless family increasingly means living in a poverty family. Female householder, no-husband-present families have become the archetypal poverty family.

Poverty and out-of-wedlock birth are tightly associated. In recent years there have been major increases in out-of-wedlock births among all ethnic and racial groups, and there was a 60 percent increase in the last decade alone.[44] This is a dramatic shift. As recently as 1960, only 5 percent of all births were to unmarried mothers. By 1993, however, 22 percent of white births, 33 percent of Hispanic births, and 68 percent of African American births were occurring to unwed mothers. Regardless of one's religious, social, or political views on having children out-of-wedlock, it usually is an economic disaster. If a woman is poor, the best way to ensure that she remains poor is to become an unwed mother. U.S. Census Bureau data indicate that within five years of a baby's birth, 72 percent of white unwed mothers and 84 percent of black unwed mothers are on welfare.[45]

A quarter of today's out-of-wedlock births occur among teenagers. Teenage mothers as a group are poorer, less educated, and more likely to end up on welfare than other mothers. Whether one views poor unwed mothers as social problems or as social victims, there is no dispute that their children begin life with major disadvantages.

Urban, Rural, and Suburban Poor In terms of where the poor live, myth and reality differ sharply. Note in Figure 2.2 that the nation's capital, which has one of the highest income levels of any American city, also has the highest per-

---

[41]U.S. Census Bureau, "Poverty in the United States: 1998," *Current Population Reports*, P60–207, September 1999, p. ix ; and "Rising Incomes Lift 1.1 Million Out of Poverty," *New York Times on the Web*, October 1, 1999.
[42]Federal Interagency Forum on Child and Family Statistics, *America's Children: Key National Indicators of Well-Being, 1998,* Government Printing Office, Washington, DC, 1998.
[43]U.S. Census Bureau, *Statistical Abstract of the United States, 1996,* Government Printing Office, Washington, DC, 1996.
[44]"Big Rise in Births Out of Wedlock," *New York Times*, July 14, 1993, p. A1.
[45]"Rise in Single Parenthood Reshaping America," *New York Times News Service*, October 5, 1992.

Figure 2.2 Three-Year Average Poverty Rates by State: 1996, 1997, and 1998

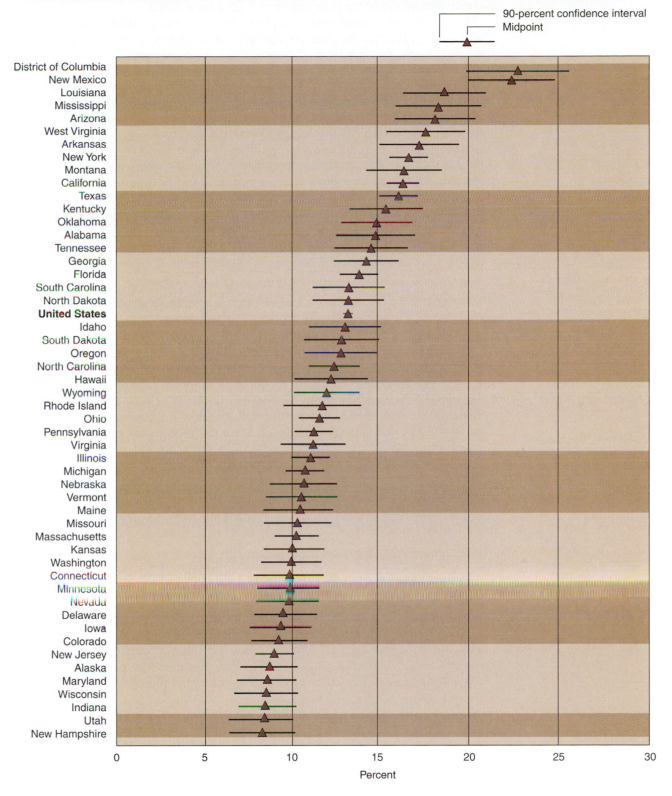

Source: U.S. Census Bureau, March 1997, 1998, and 1999 *Current Population Surveys.*

centage of its population in poverty. In Washington, D.C., the majority of the poor are urban African Americans, while in New Mexico, the state with the highest poverty rate, many of the poor are rural Native Americans.

The poor live in a greater variety of places than most people realize. We don't usually think of suburbs as housing poor people, but in fact over a third (36 percent) of the nation's poor live in suburbs.[46] Contrary to what most people believe, metropolitan areas actually have slightly lower poverty rates than rural areas. Rural poverty is less visible. While most people associate the inner city with poverty, it is important to keep in mind that less than half of all the poor live in cities (42 percent), and only a quarter of all the poor (23 percent) live in inner-city poverty areas. What these inner-city areas do have is the highest concentration of poor. In other words, most poor don't live there, but those who live there are more likely to be poor. Inner-city areas contain both the visible and the invisible poor. The *visible poor* are the young, the unemployed, the unskilled, and occasionally the criminal. The *invisible poor* are the aged, the disabled, and those who remain locked inside their residences because of the fear of violence outside. Especially for the aged, urban poverty is often more dehumanizing than rural poverty.

The Causes of Poverty: An Ongoing Debate

The dispute over whether the ills of poverty result from the faults of individuals or are caused by the society as a whole ultimately rests on one's view of human nature. Americans remain divided in their views. Roughly a third of the population believe that poverty is caused by lack of effort, a third believe it is caused by circumstances, and the remaining third believe it results from a combination of both. Overall, Democrats and those in lower income brackets are more likely to see poverty as a result of circumstances, while Republicans and the more affluent are more inclined to see poverty as the result of individual failure.

The "Culture of Poverty" Approach

The dominant academic view undergirding the 1960s War on Poverty was that the poor suffer from the liability of a *culture of poverty* more than simply from lack of funds. The culture of poverty was seen as a subcultural response in which—in reaction to their marginal position in society—the poor develop a unique set of norms and values.[47] Characteristics ascribed to the culture of poverty are low levels of aspiration, lack of planning, unstable marriage patterns, illegitimacy, and hostility toward authority. The poor in effect indirectly contribute to their own poverty. According to this view, the lives of the permanently poor are characterized by little rational calculation about things from planning meals to birth control. Their way of life is dominated by subsistence concerns.[48]

Implicit in the culture of poverty thesis is the belief that the poor have a value system different from that of the middle class, and that this value system—which

---

[46]William P. O'Hare, "U.S. Poverty Myths Explored," *Population Today,* October 1996, p. 2.
[47]The concept of the "cultural of poverty" originally came from anthropology. See Oscar Lewis, *LaVida: A Puerto Rican Family in a Culture of Poverty,* Random House, New York, 1966.
[48]David Zuccino, *Myth of the Welfare Queen,* Scribner's, New York, 1997.

Box 2.3 Making a Difference

A Place To Call Home

Rhonda Caldwell posed for a picture at the door to her room, said her goodbyes and dragged her belongings in boxes and plastic bags into a van waiting outside.[a] D.C. Village, the city's winter emergency shelter was closing its doors.

Caldwell's eight-month wait for new housing ended happily when her number was called. A place opened for her in a special city-financed apartment building for homeless families. . . .

Caldwell, 33, and her 4 year-old daughter, Tika, had arrived at D.C. Village in a police squad car back in November after Caldwell threatened a flophouse operator for forcing them out on the street.

. . . "This is your new home, Tika," Caldwell said as they walked to the front door. Inside they were escorted to Unit 2E, a one-bedroom unit with soiled carpets and threadbare furniture. It didn't seem like much at first. But then Caldwell noticed that for the first time in months, she was in a room that was quiet.

. . . "I guess I can smile now," she said. "I feel good. This place is not bad. It's really not bad. The walls are white. I'm just waiting to exhale. What I'm going to do from here, it's all up to me."

[a]Vernon Loeb, "After a D.C. Shelter, A Place to Call Home," *Washington Post*, April 2, 1997, pp. B1, B4.

---

emphasizes short-range gratification over **deferred gratification** and long-range goals—keeps the poor in poverty and isolates them from the rest of society. For example, long-term poverty in Appalachia has oriented people more toward anticipating failure rather than seeking success.[49] According to advocates, poverty results in the poor developing an autonomous culture of poverty that enables them to get by in a world not of their making.

War on Poverty programs for children were designed to give poor children an opportunity to achieve "cultural enrichment" that their parents could not provide and become middle class. Remaining examples of this approach are the Head Start school programs and the television series *Sesame Street*.

The culture of poverty thesis was sharply attacked during the 1970s and 1980s for stigmatizing and patronizing poor people and for blaming the victim. More recently, however, the perspective of seeing poverty as having cultural elements has been reintroduced by African American academics such as Elijah Anderson, who have researched how the isolated poor develop their own defensive culture.[50] (See the *Streetwise* boxed insert in Chapter 3.)

> **deferred gratification**
> *putting off short-term rewards for long-range goals.*

The "Lower-Class Culture" Approach

A far less generous version of the culture of poverty thesis is presented by Edward Banfield in his influential book *The Unheavenly City*.[51] Banfield paints a picture of the lower class as an unmotivated, uncontrolled, and potentially dangerous underclass of dropouts from society. After a quarter of a century, his controversial ideas are still hotly debated.[52] In Banfield's eyes, the bulk of the prob-

---

[49]Harry M. Caudill, *Night Comes to the Cumberlands*, Little, Brown, Boston, 1962.

[50]See, for example, Elijah Anderson, *Streetwise: Race, Class, and Change in an Urban Community*, University of Chicago Press, Chicago, 1990.

[51]Edward Banfield, *The Unheavenly City, Revisited*, Little, Brown, Boston, 1974.

[52]Banfield's ideas still stir controversy. The session "Colloquy: Banfield's Unheavenly City, Revisited—Redemption or Eternal Damnation?" was one of the best attended sessions at the Urban Affairs Association Meeting, Portland, OR, May 3–6, 1995.

lems of the poor largely result from their lack of an orientation toward the future that would allow them to meet long-range goals, along with their unwillingness or inability to control their base impulses. Banfield says the problem is not one of race but of personal attitude. "The lower-class forms of all problems are at bottom a single problem: the existence of an outlook and style of life which is radically present-oriented and which therefore attaches no value to work, sacrifice, self-improvement, or service to family, friends, or community."[53] In other words, unlike the middle class, the poor are not willing to practice deferred gratification.

Banfield defines the poor as a class not by using the usual measures of income, education, and occupation (all of which can be measured), but rather as "people who share 'a distinct patterning of attitudes, values, and modes of behavior.' "[54] Since one is the master of one's fate, the captain of one's soul, Banfield provides a rationale for those politicians who feel that the best answer to urban problems is benign neglect.

The "Blaming the Victim" Response

The late William Ryan's *Blaming the Victim* provides the opposing view—that social problems are caused not by individuals but by society and that lower-class people are not offenders but rather the victims and scapegoats.[55] Ryan says the generic process of blaming the victim is applied to almost every American problem:

> The "multi-problem" poor, it is claimed, suffer the psychological effects of impoverishment, the "culture of poverty," and the deviant value system of the lower classes; consequently, though unwittingly, they cause their own troubles.[56]

The whole process of blaming the victim occurs so easily, Ryan states, that it seems entirely rational and is barely noticed: First, a social problem is identified. Then, those affected by the problem are studied to see how, as a consequence of being deprived, they differ from the rest of us. Next, the difference is identified and defined as the cause of the problem. Finally, a humanitarian government program is established to reduce the differences. Humanitarians can have it both ways: They can, all at the same time, focus charitable interest on the defects of the victim, condemn the vague social and environmental stresses that produced the defect (some time ago), and ignore the continuing effect of victimizing social forces (right now). It is a brilliant ideology, says Ryan, for justifying a perverse form of social action designed to change, not society, but rather society's victim.

For Ryan, attempts to change the poor into the nonpoor without first remaking society are futile—Ryan denies that a problem-causing lower class exists, and that the poor are in any way responsible for their situation. Ryan further argues that the very fact of income inequality is both immoral and excessive, and everyone has a right to a fair share of reasonable necessities.[57]

---

[53]Banfield, *Unheavenly City, Revisited*, p. 235.
[54]Ibid., p. 56.
[55]William Ryan, *Blaming the Victim*, Vintage Books Random House, New York, 1971.
[56]Ibid., p. 5.
[57]William Ryan, *Inequality*, Pantheon, New York, 1981.

Welfare and Welfare Reform

Although the poor are influenced by the larger culture around them, they are never granted full membership in it. The poor, as noted earlier, are caught up in dual expectation networks. On the one hand, they hold most middle-class values, while at the same time they lack the means to live reasonable and secure lives.[58]

Changing Rules

The 1996 Welfare Reform Act (officially, the Personal Responsibility and Work Opportunity Responsibility Act of 1996) scrapped the nation's 61-year-old commitment to public assistance entitlement. Aid to Families with Dependent Children (AFDC) was replaced by a block grant program to states called Temporary Assistance to Needy Families (TANF). The assumption underlying the TANF program was that, in order to avoid a long-term welfare class, all jobless people should work, whether or not they have children. In line with this view, public assistance was changed from a form of support for family welfare to a temporary means of helping people until they become part of the labor force. Federal guidelines generally limit cash benefits to two years at a time and a total of five years in a lifetime for adults. Additionally, at least 50 percent of all single parents have to work by at least 2002. States have the option of exempting up to 20 percent of their recipients from these requirements and time limits.

Healthy adults without dependent children under age 6 lose welfare benefits once their two-year time limit is reached. Also, in order to get food stamps after the first three months, able-bodied recipients without dependents who are under age 50 must work at least 20 hours a week. Families leaving welfare keep Medicaid (health care) for a year.

TANF block grants allows states, within limits, to set their own eligibility rules and amounts paid. Following the federal lead, California in 1997 rescinded its decades-old mandate requiring counties to provide for the poor.[59] Wisconsin's "workfare" is the best-known program. It ended all cash welfare programs in 1996 and replaced them with wage subsidies. The Wisconsin program caps welfare payments at two years for any one period and has a five-year lifetime maximum. However, unlike most other state's programs, Wisconsin's workfare provides for job training, child care payments, health care, and public service jobs if employment is not available in the private sector.

Welfare Declines

The goal of the 1996 Welfare Reform Act was to move long-term welfare recipients into the workforce. The long-term consequences aren't yet known, but the nation's welfare roles are falling dramatically. Current numbers on welfare are at the lowest

---

[58]William Julius Wilson, *When Work Disappears: The World of the New Urban Poor,* Knopf, New York, 1996.
[59]Virginia Ellis and Dave Lesher, "Wilson Seeks to End Mandate on County Aid to Poor," *Los Angeles Times,* January 9, 1997, p. A1.

rates in over a quarter of a century. As of 1999, welfare recipients were down *46 percent* (14.1 million to 7.6 million) compared to 6 years earlier.[60] The rolls were the lowest they had been since 1969. Lower welfare rolls saved the federal government $55 billion over five years.[61] It also has left some of the very poor without a safety net.

Ending welfare entitlements has been strongly aided by the end of the century's healthy economy. The President's Council of Economic Advisors says that more than 40 percent of the decline is due to growth of the economy, while more than 30 percent is due to changes in state welfare laws.[62] The rest is due to other factors, such as more aggressive collection of child support. The new programs have been moving previous welfare recipients into the workplace. Some states have also encouraged recipients of assistance to upgrade their skills by attending trade schools or college. These programs have been more successful than anticipated, particularly in moving women off welfare.

The long-term success of welfare reform depends largely on whether the economy can create enough jobs to employ those with limited skills. Initially, a strong economy helped decrease welfare roles. However, as the numbers of those on welfare declines, further decreases become increasingly difficult since remaining long-term welfare recipients often have marginal educations, poor work habits, and no work skills. In our increasingly technological economy, there isn't a need for great numbers of minimally trained workers. For the hard-core unemployed, continued government tax write-offs may be necessary to encourage private employers to provide employment. Job placement programs also are essential to move people without work experience into the workforce.

As we begin the twenty-first century, the number of jobs available to the unskilled that pay a living wage is declining. For those barely possessing functional literacy and who lack the skills to compete in an increasingly computer-driven society, technological advances merely exile them to the economic margins of the society. We have two alternatives. We either ensure that everyone stays in school and actually learns employable skills, or we continue to marginally maintain the disadvantaged in a netherworld that offers them neither current satisfaction nor the hope of a better tomorrow.

Toward the Future

As the new century opens, America evidences both declining welfare roles and increases in economic inequality. There are increasing fears of downward mobility or at best stagnation among the middle class and increasingly real deprivation among the working poor. The new century starts as an excellent one for the upper class, a good one for the upper middle class, and a hard one for those at or near the bottom. The truly disadvantaged have lost much of the safety net provided by welfare programs, while most the jobs they hold pay less than a living family wage. Low-wage jobs also rarely provide health insurance.

Growing numbers of working poor are working harder than ever before and receiving comparatively less in compensation. Current trends suggest their lives are going to get harder and their economic situation more marginal. The likelihood is that, without major changes in federal legislation (such as tax codes), their real wages will slip ever further behind. However, there is little congressional concern

---

[60]"Welfare Rolls Lowest Since 1969," *New York Times*, April 11, 1999, p. 6.
[61]Charles Dervarics, "Is Welfare Reform Reforming Welfare?" *Population Today*, October 1998, p. 1.
[62]"Total on Welfare Is Lowest Since 1971," *New York Times News Service*, January 21, 1998.

about the fate of the working poor. Further decreases in capital gains taxes have more congressional support than tax relief for the working poor. If inequality is not to increase, the working poor have to have their incomes supplemented—by higher minimum wages, expanded earned-income tax credits, or other means—so that parents who work full time actually can earn a living wage and can support their families.

For most white-collar workers, the middle-class squeeze will continue. Most salaried white-collar workers will struggle to stay where they are. For much of the middle class, the problem increasingly will be real-wage stagnation. By contrast, managers and upper-middle-class professionals should do very well, and the gap will continue to grow between them and other white-collar workers. Not only in the United States but worldwide, managers and professionals are doing well. Finally, unless trends change, the rich will become far richer even than they did in the 1990s. The twenty-first century is opening as an era of increasing economic extremes.

For those at the bottom, the issue will be survival. Structural changes in the economy mean there is a decreasing need for unskilled labor. Muscle power can no longer be sold, and those with less than a high school education are essentially unemployable at decent wages. Market forces currently are pressing for greater inequality. For this not to happen, major changes in the educational system will be necessary. Unless we ensure that everyone receives a solid education, economic divisions will increase. If this does not occur, political and social stability may require welfare subsidies for those who are de facto unemployable. Alternatives are for government either to act as an employer of last resort by providing jobs or to provide government subsidies for businesses hiring the most marginal workers.

The societal and economic costs of doing nothing will be far higher. Without access to jobs that pay a living wage, the anger of those excluded will increase and crime rates and violence will accelerate. As relative deprivation increases, tensions are likely to grow between the haves and have-nots. Growing concentration both of poverty and of privilege will be the pattern unless government policies are set to rebalance the scales. If the new century is not to be one of an increasingly social and economic polarization between the haves and the have-nots, the problem of economic inequality has to be resolved. If it isn't the nation will pay a steep price.

Summary

Societies generally accept **inequality** as an inevitable condition, and U.S. government data indicate that the gap between the well-to-do and the poor has increased during the last two decades. Economic inequality often leads to social inequality.

- There are many different views on the division of wealth. The **functional theory** suggests that stratification is necessary to attract the most suitable persons to important societal positions. **Conflict theories,** especially **Marxist,** say that inequality is the result of a social structure designed to keep those at the top in power. Non-Marxist conflict theories, while agreeing on the inevitability of conflict, deny that conflict leads to an inevitable polarization of classes. Inherited-biology-based theories such as **Social Darwinism** or **sociobiology** assert that behavior is biologically determined by one's genes, a belief which encourages the assumption that those who are unsuccessful are innately inferior.

- We divide the population economically into four groups: **wealthy, middle class, working class,** and **lower class:** The wealthiest fifth of the population receives 46% of all national income; the middle class is treading water; the blue-collar workers have lost income for a quarter of a century; the poorest fifth of the nation is doing even worse, earning only 4% of the national income.

- There are fewer and fewer family-wage job opportunities for those with minimal education and skill levels.

- Chances of being a victim of **poverty** are considerably increased if one is young, belongs to a minority group, or lives in a female headed family.

- Contemporary poverty is increasingly structural; it is the result of the changing nature of a labor market in which technology increasingly replaces people.

- The **War on Poverty** assumed that the poor suffered not only from lack of money but also from a unique set of norms and values, called the **culture of poverty,** that cut them off from the rest of society.

- Characteristics of the culture of poverty were said to be low levels of aspiration, lack of planning, and hostility toward authority. Critics of this theory call this **blaming the victim** by attributing the liabilities of being poor to the poor themselves.

- Welfare reform has substantially reduced welfare roles, but future successes depend heavily on the availability of jobs paying a living wage.

- In addition to those in poverty, there are approximately 10 million working poor who are barely getting by.

☞Key Review Terms

absolute poverty
biologically based
  approaches
blaming the victim
class system
conflict approaches
conspicuous consumption
culture of poverty
cyclical unemployment
deferred gratification
deindustrialization
functional approaches
income

invisible poor
middle class
middle-class squeeze
lower class
nouveau riche
relative poverty
Social Darwinism
social inequality
social mobility
social stratification
socioeconomic status
structural unemployment
Marxist theory

poverty definition
relative poverty
structural mobility
structural unemployment
truly disadvantaged
underclass
upper class
visible poor
wealth
white collar
working class
working poor

? Questions for Discussion

1. Discuss public attitudes toward the poor. How have these attitudes changed over time?

2. How have the income differences between social classes been changing in America? What are the social and political consequences of these disparities?

3. Contrast the differences between income and wealth. Which is more important in the upper class and why?

4. Most Americans say they are middle class. Are they? What does it mean to be middle class in American society?

5. The chapter states that there are roughly 10 million working poor. What is life like for them? What does the future hold?

6. What is meant by the term "American Dream"? Has it changed? Is it a reasonable expectation in contemporary America?

7. Discuss structural mobility in America. Is it increasing or decreasing?

8. Millions of immigrants have come to America hoping to make their fortune. Is it possible today? What field(s) would you recommend to someone seeking economic success?

9. How does the government calculate poverty? Who are the poor? As a group what are the characteristics of the poor?

10. Welfare reform has become a major political topic. Why is this? What changes in welfare programs are occurring nationally and in your state?

☞ Suggested Resources

Derek Bok, *The Cost of Talent: How Executives and Professionals are Paid and How it Affects America*, Free Press, New York, 1993. An argument against the distortion of rates of compensation, written by one of those at the top.

G. William Domhoff, *The Power Elite and the State: How Policy is Made in America*, Aldine de Gruyter, New York, 1990. Looks at the power elite that he says makes major economic and social decisions in the United States and the world.

Barbara Ehrenreich, *Fear of Falling: The Inner Life of the Middle Class*, Harper Perennial, New York, 1990. Why the middle class are worried even in supposed good times.

Harold R. Kebo, *Social Stratification and Inequality: Class Conflict in Historical and Comparative Perspective*, 2nd ed., McGraw-Hill, New York, 1991. A good solid text on all aspects of social stratification.

Alex Kotowitz, *There Are No Children Here: The Story of Two Boys Growing Up in the Other America*, Anchor, New York, 1991. Seen through their own eyes what it means to grow up without hope in the Chicago housing projects.

Elliot Liebow, *Tell Them Who I Am*, Free Press, New York, 1993. A remarkable look at homeless women and how they got there by the late Elliot Liebow, a master of participant observation.

Francis Fox Piven and Richard Cloward, *Regulating the Poor: The Functions of Public Welfare*, Pantheon, New York, 1993. An update of the classic work on how welfare is designed to keep the poor poor.

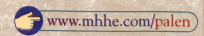

1. The U.S. Census Bureau website is an excellent source of information about poverty and wealth. It can be found at (*www.census.gov/*). For example, if you click on "Poverty" which is found under the heading, "People" you will find a broad array of reports and resources available to you online. Under the section titled, *POVERTY DEFINITIONS, THRESHOLDS, AND GUIDELINES* there are three buttons: "How the Census Bureau Measures Poverty"; "Poverty Thresholds"; and "HHS (Health and Human Services) Poverty Guidelines".

   a. What are the differences between "Poverty Thresholds" and "Poverty Guidelines"? (Note that in this chapter, we used the HHS Guideline figure of $16,700 for a family of four in 1999.)

   b. Why do you suppose that The Department of Health and Human Services has set the poverty guidelines higher for Alaska and Hawaii than for the rest of the contiguous United States?

   You will also find a comprehensive report on poverty in the United States under the section titled *CURRENT POPULATION SURVEY* [Click on "Poverty in the United States: 1998 (P60-207)"]. Other scholarly resources on the subject of poverty are The Institute for Research on Poverty at the University of Wisconsin at Madison (*www.ssc.wisc.edu/irp/*) and The Joint Center for Poverty Research of Northwestern University and the University of Chicago (*www.jcpr.org/*).

2. It is no surprise that conservatives and liberals have widely differing opinions on the extent of poverty and wealth in the United States. To look at a conservative side of the issue, visit the Heritage Foundation's website at (*www.heritage.org/*). In the Search Box at the top right corner of the screen, type in "poverty." You will see that the Heritage Foundation has created over 550 documents that relate to poverty in one way or another. Look at the one titled "The Myth of Widespread American Poverty" (*www.heritage.org/library/backgrounder/ bg1221.html*). On the other side of the issue, visit "Turn Left—the Home of Liberalism on the Web" at (*www.turnleft.com/liberal.html*). Click on "The Issues" and you will be taken to 15 basic issue groups. Click on "Economic Issues" and then again on "Share the Wealth." You will see a series of articles. Look at the one titled, "Divided Decade: Economic Disparity at the Century's Turn."

   a. Why is it, that conservatives and liberals view what is supposed to be objective data gathered by an impartial government agency so differently?

3

I am an invisible man. No, I am not a spook like those who haunted Edgar Allan Poe; nor am I one of your Hollywood-movie ectoplasms. I am a man of substance, of flesh and bone, fiber and liquids—and I might even be said to possess a mind. I am invisible, understand, simply because people refuse to see me. Like the bodiless heads you see sometimes in circus sideshows, it is as though I have been surrounded by mirrors of hard, distorting glass. When they approach me they see only my surroundings, themselves, or figments of their imagination— indeed, everything and anything except me.

Prologue to Ralph Ellison's *Invisible Man* (Random House, New York, 1952), perhaps the most famous book ever written about what it means to be African American.

The Color Line

Race in America

minority groups
category of people treated negatively because of appearance or cultural differences.

Approaching a century and a half after slavery ended, and three decades after the landmark civil rights legislation of the 1960s, race remains the great American Dilemma.[1] Racial issues still divide and polarize. This chapter will focus on African Americans, the next chapter on the discussion of Hispanics, Asian Americans, and Native Americans. In all cases we are discussing **minority groups,** that is, a category of people that is a subordinate segment of the society and lacks power. What makes a minority group a minority is not its size but its subordination.

Race as a Social Definition

The irony of all the discussion surrounding race is that *no* consensus exists on the question of what race is. Historically, race is a cultural invention that has been used in an astonishingly wide variety of ways.[2] At various times the term has been applied to nation-states (e.g., the Irish race), tribal groups (the Iroquois), language groups (Latins), religious and cultural minorities (Jews), and supposedly biological groups (Caucasoids). Until a generation ago, race was defined in most texts as shared biologically transmitted characteristics (and it still is in some sociology texts), but today scientists hold that racial classifications are more myth than science.[3] While racial categories are far too broad to be genetically meaningful, racial categories remain in common use and have profound social consequences. (See Box 3.1)

race
a group that is assumed to share common genetic traits that society sees as socially significant.

In sociological terms, **race** is a socially defined category of people who are thought to share biologically distinctive traits. Race is a social construct in which the social definitions are most important. As shown in Chapter 1, situations that are perceived to be real have real consequences. Thus, a person who is perceived as white *is* white, no matter what his or her genetic background is. While this makes no sense biologically, it does reflect social reality. We identify people as be-

---

[1]The concept of an American dilemma was developed by Gunnar Myrdal, *An American Dilemma,* Harper and Row, New York, 1944.

[2]Audrey Smedley, *Race in North America: Origin and Evolution of a Worldview,* Westview Press, Boulder, CO, 1998.

[3]See Ivan Hannaford, "The Idiocy of Race," *Wilson Quarterly,* Spring, 1994, pp. 8–35; and David L. Wheeler, "A Growing Number of Scientists Reject the Concept of Race," *Chronicle of Higher Education,* February 17, 1995, pp. A8, A9, A15.

longing to one race or another because we are socially taught or programmed to focus on particular physical characteristics. While in America we identify people racially largely by skin color, we could just as easily create biological races by using other criteria. Why not races based on hair color (new races: blond, brown, black, bald, dyed?). We could also have races based on eye color (new races: brown, blue, hazel, tinted contacts?).[4]

Race becomes important sociologically when individuals or groups are identified and responded to by others—either positively or negatively—on the basis of ascribed racial membership. Race becomes a social problem when it is used as a basis to discriminate. **Ethnicity,** in contrast to race, refers to groups sharing cultural features such as language, religion, national origin, and a common social heritage. Ethnicity will be discussed in the next chapter.

ethnicity
shared cultural heritage.

Constructions of Race

According to George Simpson and Milton Yinger, the term *race* is commonly used in three different ways: as a biological construct, a political construct, and an administrative construct.[5]

Race as a Biological Construct

In the biological construction of race, people belonging to a given race are said to share distinctive gene characteristics that produce specific physical traits. People are defined as either Caucasoid, Negroid, or Mongoloid (Asian) on the basis of skin color, nasal index, hair texture, hair color, eye color, head form, lip form, facial index, stature, and blood group. Sometimes even intellectual characteristics were claimed to vary by race.[6] Scientifically, however, the idea of a pure race is nonsense because the world's gene pools are mixed to the point where only general groupings can be distinguished. Moreover, differences within a supposed race sometimes are greater than those between races. Many residents of south India, for example, have darker skin pigment than most African Americans. In the United States we often speak as if whites and blacks belong to distinct genetic groups, but virtually all African Americans have some white ancestry, and just under a tenth of "whites" have some African American ancestry.

Race as a Political Construct

The political construction of racial categories stems from the placing of one race in a superior position over another. The defined races are often largely mythical in nature, such as the "Anglo-Saxon" or the "Aryan" race. In his political manifesto *Mein Kampf,* Adolf Hitler espoused the most notorious version of the myth of the

---

[4]Thanks to Timothy Evans for suggesting this idea.
[5]George Eaton Simpson and J. Milton Yinger, *Racial and Cultural Minorities,* 5th ed., Plenum, New York, 1985.
[6]See, for example, Carlton Putnam, *Race and Reality,* Public Affairs Press, Washington, DC, 1967; and Richard J. Herrnstein and Charles Murray, *The Bell Curve: Intelligence and Class Structure in American Life,* Free Press, New York, 1994.

Box 3.1 Ongoing Issues

Racial Identity as Defined by Law

Racial categories in the pre–Civil War South are commonly thought of as being rigidly fixed. Actually, early nineteenth-century racial definitions showed far more flexibility than definitions during much of the twentieth century. Virginia's racial definitions, for instance, were far more rigid in the 1930s than they had been a hundred years earlier.[a] In the 1830s there even was enough flexibility to allow some Negroes to legally change from black to white. However, by 1930 racial definitions hardened to where the "single drop rule" meant that any ascertainable trace of "Negro blood" meant someone was defined as Negro. Note how the laws became increasingly rigid. Following are portions of the Virginia state statutes:

1833. Chapter 80. "A court upon satisfactory proof, by a white person of the fact, may grant any free person of mixed blood a certificate that he is not a Negro, which certificate shall protect such person against the penalties and disabilities to which free Negroes are subject."

1833. Chapter 243. "Certain parties . . . who heretofore were held in slavery and acquired their freedom since 1806 are not Negroes or Mulattoes but white persons, although remotely descended from a colored woman, and are hearby released from all penalties whatever. . . ."

1866. Chapter 17. "Every person having one-fourth or more Negro blood shall be deemed a colored person. . . ."

1910. Chapter 357. "Every person having one-sixteenth or more Negro blood shall be deemed a colored person. . . ."

1930. Chapter 85. "Every person in whom there is ascertainable any Negro blood should be deemed a colored person. . . ."

[a]For further details on changing racial definitions, see John S. Mahoney, Jr., and Paul G. Koostra, "Policing the Races: Structural Factors Enforcing Racial Purity in Virginia (1630–1930)," paper presented at American Sociological Association, Washington, DC, August 23, 1995.

innate superiority of the "Aryan" race: "If we divide the human race into three categories—founders, maintainers, and destroyers of culture—the Aryan stock alone can be considered as representing the first category."[7] In North America neo-Nazi groups, such as the Aryan Brotherhood, and racist groups, such as the Ku Klux Klan (KKK), still espouse this view.

Race as an Administrative Construct

Administratively, races are established by either legislative act or bureaucratic practice. While supposedly based on biology, administrative definitions often change. For example, U.S. censuses of the early twentieth century defined anyone having "any trace" of African American blood as Negro. Obviously, such a racial definition is both impossible and meaningless. Today, the census reports race on the basis of self-identification by respondents. You are what you say you are. Self-identification emphasizes the *social* reality of race. Of course, biologically speaking, such self-choice of racial identity makes no sense.

Even in explicitly racist societies, administrative or political definitions of race sometimes give way to political and economic considerations. It is usually forgot-

---

[7]Quoted in Simpson and Yinger, *Racial and Cultural Minorities*, p. 34.

© Hulton-Deutsch Collections/CORBIS

Adolf Hitler was not above redefining his supposedly "fixed" racial groups to meet his political needs. Thus, German Jews were exterminated while his Japanese allies were proclaimed "Honorary Aryans."

ten that Adolf Hitler, while exterminating European Jews, declared his Japanese allies to be "Honorary Aryans." Similarly, in South Africa, under its pre-1990s system of racial **apartheid** (separateness), Chinese, Indonesians, and those from India were classified as Asians, while Japanese were classified as white. The South African government overruled the supposed biological foundation of their apartheid system to put the Japanese, a major trading power, in the "superior" white category. Even for racists, **social labeling** is far more important than biological criteria.

There are also U.S. examples. During World War II, for example, all Japanese Americans living on the West Coast were moved into interment camps. In spite of this, most of the young men intered volunteered for military service. One unit of Japanese-American soldiers, the 442nd Combat Infantry, was sent for advanced training to Fort Shelby in Mississippi, a state that was rigidly segregated between "whites" and "coloreds."[8] The governor had to decide whether the Japanese Americans were white or colored. He decided that as long as they were in uniform, they were white.

The Multiracial Controversy

The administrative racial categories used in the United States are relatively new. They were created in 1977 by the Office of Management and Budget (OMB) in order to gather racial data by placing everyone into one of four racial categories: (1) White, (2) African American, (3) American Indian, Eskimo, or Aleut, or (4) Asian or Pacific Islander (the additional category of Hispanic is defined as an "ethnic" category). These categories become confused as America becomes increasingly multiracial and multiethnic. The number of black-white marriages has quadrupled

apartheid
legally mandated racial separation.

social labeling
assigning group characteristics.

---

[8]The 442nd went on to become famous as the most decorated military unit in World War II. It was known as the "Christmas tree" outfit because of all the medals earned by its soldiers. The 442nd also had one of the highest casualty rates. Its battle cry, "Go for Broke!" has become part of the American language.

Tiger Woods, the most successful young golfer in history, holds his trophy after winning the National Pro-Am in Pebble Beach on February 7, 2000.

Bob Galbraith/AP/Wide World Photos

since 1970, and the 1990 census reported some 1.5 million interracial couples having some 2 million children.[9] Some children fit into two or three of the OMB racial categories. In California interracial babies are now the third largest category of births—after Latinos and whites, but ahead of Asians and African Americans (Figure 3.1).[10]

But while the world has changed, the categories have not. Susan Graham, executive director of Project RACE (Reclassify All Children Equally), points out that her son is classified as "white by the census, black at school, and biracial at home."[11] Similarly, the young golfer Tiger Woods has objected to being pigeonholed into a single racial classification. He points out that his mother is half Thai and half Chinese, and his father is a mixture of black, American Indian, and white. As he expresses it, "I'm just who I am."[12]

A *Newsweek* poll found that half of all African Americans (49 percent) and over a third of whites (36 percent) think there should be a multiracial category in the census.[13] Seven states already mandate the use of a multiracial category on state forms. Advocates of a multiracial category say that the "browning of America" is a reality and continued use of single-race categories smacks of the old racist idea

[9]Susan Kalish, "Multiracial Births Increase as U.S. Ponders Racial Definitions," *Population Today,* 23:2, April 1995.
[10]Kelvin M. Pollard and William P. O'Hare, "America's Ethnic and Racial Minorities," *Population Bulletin,* Population Reference Bureau, Washington, DC, 1999, p. 13.
[11]Linda Mathews, "More than Identity Rides on a New Racial Category," *New York Times,* July 6, 1996, p. 7.
[12]Jack E. White, "I'm Just Who I Am," *Time,* May 5, 1997, pp. 33–36.
[13]*Newsweek,* February 13, 1995.

Figure 3.1 U.S. Population by Race and Ethnicity, 1995 and 2020

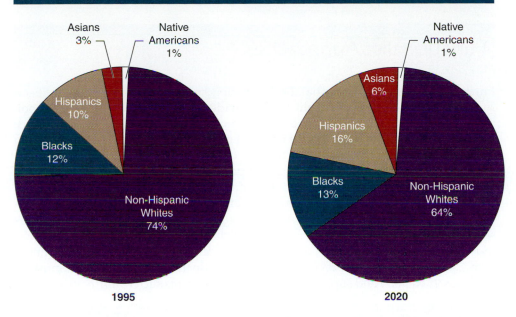

1995

2020

Source: U.S. Bureau of the Census, *Current Population Reports*, P25-1104: middle series projections. Washington, DC.

that "a single drop" of black blood automatically defines a person as black. Single categories also imply that race is unchangeable and absolute. Single exclusive categories don't reflect that as a people we are becoming more multicultural and multiracial.

Opposition to a multiracial category comes primarily from organizations such as La Raza and the National Association for the Advancement of Colored People (NAACP), who fear that a multiracial category will lower their numbers.[14] As the well-known Washington adage states, "The numbers drive the dollars." These organizations also are concerned that a multiracial category will make it harder to monitor and enforce civil-rights legislation. Gary Flowers, the spokesman for those opposed to a new category says, "This multiracial hocus-pocus pleases only a relatively few individuals, and for everyone else it's dangerous. . . . Behind it is an attempt to say that America is a melting pot and a color-blind society."[15] Note, however, that both sides define race using administratively defined criteria, not genetic differences.

In 1997 the Clinton administration rejected the creation of a multiethnic category.[16] However, as a concession, anyone who wants to can now check more than one of the racial categories. Some would go further and simply drop all racial categories. Roughly half of all blacks and whites (48 percent and 47 percent, respectively) think the census and government should stop collecting any information on race or ethnicity.[17]

---

[14]Lawrence Wright, "One Drop of Blood," *New Yorker*, July 25, 1994, pp. 46–55.

[15]Linda Mathews, "More Than Identity Rides on a New Racial Category," *New York Times*, July 6, 1996, p. 7.

[16]"Panel Rejects Multiracial Box for Forms," *Associated Press*, July 9, 1997.

[17]*Newsweek*, February 13, 1995.

Functionalist Approaches

Functionalists suggest that racial discrimination has persisted because it has been functional for whites. The wealthy were provided a cheap, exploitable labor pool. The middle class benefited from having a group at the bottom to do the dirty work of society—that is, the dirty menial jobs that no one else wants.[18] Poor whites also benefited by having a group below them in the social hierarchy. Such exploitation was often rationalized in terms of racial superiority.

Functionalists say that racial discrimination is socially and economically dysfunctional. It wastes valuable human resources. In an increasingly competitive global economy, the costs of not using all citizens are too high. Racial discrimination also creates severe social tensions, antagonisms, and conflicts that disrupt society. Functionalists thus argue that it is essential to reduce discrimination in order to increase commitment to the system among those previously excluded. To do this, social institutions must actively foster equality and support compensatory programs such as affirmative action.

Conflict Approaches

From a conflict perspective, those in power continue to benefit, as they did in the past, by playing on racial antagonisms. Race is a way for the economic elite to divide and conquer by diverting the working population from seeking higher wages and better working conditions. For example, by claiming that unions encourage black dominance over whites, poor whites can be kept nonunionized and low paid. Traditionally, politicians also profited from racial hostility and race baiting, according to the conflict oriented. This was a common election technique in the segregated South, and occasionally still surfaces today. Senator Jesse Helms of North Carolina won 1990 and 1996 elections over his black opponent, Harvey Gantt, by running TV ads suggesting that with a black Senator pushing affirmative action, whites would lose jobs.

Conflict theorists tend to view racial relationships essentially as power relationships, with power seen as a zero-sum game—that is, one group can only improve its status if others lose. Thus, when subordinate minorities try to change the balance of power, conflict ensues. To improve their status economically and socially, those at the bottom must organize politically. Only through demonstrating power, either through elections, strikes, or civil disruptions, can minorities make progress. Thus, group violence or the threat of violence is a legitimate political tool. Race is seen as a smokescreen the capitalist elites use to divide the working class. Only when whites and blacks come to see that they are jointly oppressed by the economic system will racism end.

Interactionist Approaches

Interactionists study how symbols are used socially to classify people into different groups. Interactionists also focus on the way prejudice and discrimination af-

---

[18]Herbert Gans, "The Uses of Poverty," *Social Policy,* July/August 1971, pp. 20–24.

Box 3.2 Making a Difference

The Color of Water

James McBride, in his much praised book, *The Color of Water: A Black Man's Tribute to His White Mother,* tells how his mother raised 12 children (all of whom became successful). The title of the book comes from when young James asked his mother, "What color is God's spirit?" His mother replied, "God is the color of water. Water doesn't have a color."[a] The following excerpt is from a conversation between young James and his mother.

"One afternoon I came home from school and cornered Mommy while she was cooking dinner. 'Ma, what is a tragic mulatto?' I asked.

"Anger flashed across her face like lightning and her nose, which tends to redden and swell in anger, blew up like a balloon. 'Where'd you hear that?' she asked.

" 'I read it in a book.'

" 'For God's sake you're no tragic mul—What book is this?'

" 'Just a book I read.'

" 'Don't read that book anymore.' She sucked her teeth. 'Tragic mulatto. What a stupid thing to call somebody! Somebody call you that?'

" 'No.'

" 'Don't ever use that term.'

" 'Am I black or white?'

" 'You're a human being,' she snapped. 'Educate yourself or you'll be a nobody!'

" 'Will I be a black nobody or just a nobody?'

" 'If you're a nobody,' she said dryly, 'it doesn't matter what color you are.'

" 'That doesn't make sense,' I said.

"She sighed and sat down. 'I bet you never heard the joke about the teacher and the beans,' she said. I shook my head. 'The teacher says to the class, "Tell us about the different kinds of beans,"

" 'The first little boy says, "There's pinto beans."

" ' "Correct," says the teacher.

" 'Another boy raises his hand. "There's lima beans."

" ' "Very good," says the teacher.

" 'Then a little girl in the back raises her hand and says, "We're all *human* beans!" '

"She laughed. 'That's what you are, a *human* bean! And a *fartbuster* to boot!' She got up and went back to cooking, while I wandered away, bewildered."

[a]*James McBride,* The Color of Water: A Black Man's Tribute to His White Mother, *Berkeley Publishing Group, New York, 1996,*

fect members of racial groups. Minority groups are constantly bombarded by subtle, and not so subtle, racial stereotypes. **Stereotypes** are fixed, usually unfavorable, beliefs about categories of people. Fixed mental images, such as intelligence, moneygrubbing, or criminality, are exaggerated and applied to all members of a group. Such stereotypes influence the thoughts and behaviors of both minority and majority populations. Suggestions that members of a group are less intelligent, more violent, or generally less human are bound to have social consequences. Stereotyped minority members may develop reactions that are turned inward as self-doubt, alcoholism, and drug usage, or reactions may be turned outward as aggression, crime, and violence. Stereotyped labels may thus result in self-fulfilling prophecies. But since racial stereotypes are learned behavior, say interactionists, they also can be unlearned or never taught. Children, for instance, can be taught to classify others not by race but by similarity of interests and concerns.

> **stereotype**
> *attributing fixed characteristics, usually negative, to all members of a group.*

Prejudice and Discrimination

The concepts of prejudice and discrimination are often treated as synonyms in everyday speech, but they are quite distinct. *Prejudice refers to attitudes,* and *discrimination reflects behavior.* The distinction between attitude and action is a crucial one.

Prejudice

Prejudice is a rigid predisposition to respond to a given group in a particular way. Prejudice is a prejudgment in which only selected "facts" are emphasized while others are ignored or de-emphasized. Implicitly, prejudice assumes the superiority of some and the inferiority of others. Prejudice can take the form of stereotyping, in which everyone in a group is given the same characteristics (e.g., all Italians are musical and Mafia connected). People who are prejudiced cling to their stereotypes emotionally and inflexibly; they are unlikely to be open to new information. Stereotypes of Jews as greedy and conniving, blacks as lazy and violent, and English as cold and aloof are rarely affected by evidence. Stereotypes sometimes carry mutually contradictory elements, as when the nation's ills are blamed on "Communist Jewish Wall Street Bankers."

Survey data consistently show that over recent decades the level of racial prejudice has markedly declined.[19] Some of this decline may be due to the greater sophistication of survey participants in avoiding "racist" responses, but most of it appears to reflect real changes. However, incidents of prejudice still occur on college campuses. This phenomenon may reflect divisions over the legitimacy of universities' use of affirmative action and the prospect of a highly competitive job market. (See the discussion of affirmative action in Chapter 9.)

Discrimination

Prejudice does not involve overt action, but discrimination does. As the classic definition by the sociologist Robin Williams states, "Discrimination may be said to exist to the degree that individuals of a given group who are otherwise formally qualified are not treated in conformity with these nominally universal institutionalized codes."[20] In other words, **discrimination** is unfavorable treatment of a group on arbitrary grounds.

Overt discrimination is far less evident today than 40 years ago, both because attitudes have become less prejudiced and because racial discrimination is now illegal. You don't have to first eliminate prejudice to end discrimination. Discrimination can be eliminated without first changing peoples hearts and minds. Legislation can stop discrimination, and when it does rates of prejudice usually drop as well.

Institutional discrimination or **institutional racism** refers to the established way social, political, and economic activities are structured by the society to keep minorities subordinated. Institutional discrimination is difficult to eliminate since it can occur without people being aware or their being bigots. Individuals who do not personally discriminate may accept institutional racism simply as an accepted and routine part of everyday life. For example, until 35 years ago, any whites visiting the South, regardless of their racial attitudes, discriminated by using restaurants, theaters, and public transportation facilities set aside for "white only." Another example of institutional discrimination would be hiring for a position solely on the basis of scores from tests that reflect white middle-class knowledge. Institutional discrimination is often difficult to root out because it is so embedded in the fabric of society. We must be careful not to uncritically accept the world around us simply because "that is the way things are."

---

[19]Glenn Firebaugh and Kenneth Davis, "Trends in Anti-Black Prejudice 1972–1984: Regional and Cohort Effects," *American Journal of Sociology*, 94:251–272, 1988.

[20]Robin Williams, Jr., "The Reduction of Intergroup Tensions," *Social Science Research Center*, 1947, p. 39.

Unlike other early immigrants almost all Africans came to America involuntarily in chains. Portrayed is a 1850s slave auction in Richmond, Virginia.

Bettmann/Corbis

Status of African Americans[21]

African Americans currently number 35 million people, or more than the population of Canada. African Americans are both the United States' largest minority group and the only one that has experienced massive out-and-out slavery.

The "Great Urban Migration"

Nineteenth-century black immigrants to northern industrial cities followed a settlement pattern similar to that of German, Irish, Polish, and Italian migrants. That is, blacks first settled in the poorest and most densely crowded older central areas

---

[21]There is no consensus on what term should be used when referring to black Americans. The May 1995 Current Population Survey by the Census Bureau did a special race/ethnic supplement which found that 44 percent of blacks preferred the term *black,* 28 percent favored *African American,* and 12 percent *Afro-American.* Census and government documents used *black* until 1997, and both *black* and *African American* since then. This text also uses both terms.

near the factories. Housing segregation was not extreme.[22] But while initial settlement patterns were similar to other groups, the way settlement developed was not. As members of white ethnic groups prospered, they or their children moved out of the inner-city ghettos into more dispersed neighborhoods of better quality and segregation decreased.[23] For whites, the melting pot generally worked, and ethnic identifications, particularly for western Europeans, have faded.[24] For African Americans racial identification has remained central.

Heavy black movement from the rural South to the cities of the North began with World War I (1914–1918). Northern industries, which depended upon a stream of European peasant immigrants for their laborers, suddenly found the supply of new workers cut off—and just at the time war-related orders were increasing. The largely untapped rural southern labor pool—both black and white—provided a solution. The South's harsh discriminatory Jim Crow laws (segregation laws) also encouraged out-migration. The five states of the Deep South—Alabama, South Carolina, Georgia, Mississippi, and Louisiana—lost 400,000 blacks through out-migration about the time of World War I, most being young people of working age.[25]

The North turned out not to be "the promised land," but despite discrimination and race riots, the cities of the North offered more opportunities than did the South. The tide of out-migrants from the South dramatically increased again during World War II, when the northern war industry was at full production, and it did not end until the late 1960s. During the twentieth century the Black population moved from being overwhelmingly rural to being more urban than the white population. Between 1940 and 1980, the African American population moved from one-quarter urban to four-fifths urban.

Moving South

African Americans today are moving not north but south to the sunbelt. During the 1990s, 65 percent of the nation's black population growth took place in the South, and 7 out of the 10 metropolitan areas gaining the most African Americans were in the South.[26] Black movement is especially heavy to the suburbs of southern metropolitan areas where many of those moving south are young college-educated blacks.[27] Such black urban professionals have been referred to by magazines such as *Ebony* as Buppies. The city of Atlanta not only has a black majority, but the Atlanta metropolitan region also holds half a million mostly middle-class black suburbanites.[28] The 1990 census indicated suburban African Americans have income levels 55 percent higher than blacks living in cities.[29]

[22]Reynolds Farley and William H. Frey, "Changes in the Segregation of Whites from Blacks during the 1980s: Small Steps toward a More Integrated Society," *American Sociological Review,* 52:24, 1994.

[23]Stanley Lieberson and Mary C. Waters, *From Many Strands: Ethnic and Racial Groups in Contemporary America,* Russell Sage Foundation, New York, 1988.

[24]Richard D. Alba, *The Transformation of White America,* Yale University Press, 1990.

[25]J. John Palen, *The Urban World,* 5th ed., McGraw-Hill, New York, 1997, p. 245.

[26]William H. Frey, "Black Movement to the South and Regional Concentrations of Races," Research Report, University of Michigan Population Studies Center, January 1998.

[27]Reynolds Farley and Walter Allen, *The Color Line and the Quality of Life in America,* Russell Sage Foundation, New York, 1987, p. 128.

[28]J. John Palen, *The Suburbs,* McGraw-Hill, New York, 1995, p. 117.

[29]William P. O'Hare and William H. Frey, "Booming, Suburban, and Black," *American Demographics,* September 1992, p. 32.

Not all those restricted to living in the historical black ghettoes were poor. Three of the founding members of The Northeasterners, an African American social organization, are seen walking on 127th Street in Harlem in 1930.

© Topham/The Image Works

Racial Segregation

Economic differences alone do not explain the segregation of African Americans from other U.S. citizens, for poor blacks do not live intermingled with poor whites, and middle-class whites are still more likely to live segregated from black upper- and middle-income households than from white lower-income households. The prime cause of residential segregation by race is discrimination—both public and private.

Housing Restrictions Until the Fair Housing Act of 1968, African Americans were restricted into specific black-only neighborhoods called "black belts."[30] Urban blacks, regardless of their income, education, or occupation, were restricted to living in ghettoes. Segregated housing patterns were reinforced by discriminatory actions by federal and municipal governments such as racial **restrictive covenants,** which were written into deeds and specified the groups that could not legally purchase the property. In the 1940s, for example, roughly 80 percent of the residential property in Chicago had restrictive covenants. Federal Housing Administration (FHA) manuals of the time urged the use of racial covenants and included a prepared racial covenant with a space left blank for the prohibited races and religions.[31] Although the Supreme Court ruled in 1948 that restrictive covenants could no longer be enforced through the courts, these covenants continued to have social force until they were declared illegal by the Fair Housing Act of 1968.

restrictive covenants *attachments to property deeds, especially those specifying ethnic-racial groups to whom the property cannot be transferred.*

---

[30]For a description of life in the old segregated ghettoes, see St. Clair Drake and Horace Clayton, *Black Metropolis,* Harcourt Brace, New York, 1945.
[31]Charles Abrams, *The City Is the Frontier,* Harper & Row, New York, 1965, p. 61.

In addition to legal restrictions, realtors would not show black purchasers housing in nonblack areas. For years the official code of ethics of the National Association of Real Estate Boards barred members from "introducing into a neighborhood members of any race or nationality, or any individual whose presence will clearly be detrimental to property values in the neighborhood."[32] Banks and other lending institutions also controlled residential patterns by not giving mortgages to members of minority groups unless they lived within areas of black occupancy. Areas that were undergoing racial transition were **redlined**— that is, a neighborhood was defined as a bad-risk area; therefore, few if any mortgage or home repair loans would be given by lending institutions. Redlining an area all but ensured a self-fulfilling prophecy of neighborhood decline whereby lending institutions, fearing property decline, almost ensured decline by their actions. Redlining is now against the law, but mortgage financing still shows patterns of racism.[33] Insurance companies may not provide coverage or offer only very high-priced coverage (in effect red lining) in some central city neighborhoods. Also still found are illegal activities such as **steering,** where potential black buyers are shown homes only in black or integrated areas.

Changing Patterns   We enter the new century as still a racially segregated society, but with declining levels of segregation. Indicators such as the Index of Dissimilarity (which statistically identifies the degree to which racial groups are distributed among city blocks) for decades have shown a pattern of slowly decreasing segregation levels. Research done by Reynolds Farley and William Frey looking at the 232 U.S. metropolitan areas with significant black populations, indicates that the highest current segregation levels are now found not in the South but in older northern smokestack cities.[34] Today, the lowest segregation levels are found in growing southern and southwestern cities with lots of new home building. Lower southern segregation definitely was not what was predicted 25 years ago. New areas are more likely to integrate while older neighborhoods stay segregated. Research by other scholars such as Douglas Massey and Nancy Denton also confirms declining, if still quite high, segregation levels.[35]

A Widening Gap: The Haves and Have Nots

Whatever socioeconomic measure is used, the gap between blacks and whites is considerable. Black infants have twice the infant mortality rates of whites; black children are three times as likely to live in poverty or in single-parent homes, and blacks are less likely to go to college than are whites. Black unemployment is double that of whites. A black American is six times as likely to die from a gunshot wound, and although blacks make up 12 percent of the population, half of all prison inmates are black. The median black family income level of $25,970 in 1995 was substantially below the all-household median of

[32]Charles Abrams, "The Housing Problem and the Negro," in Talcott Parsons and Kenneth Clark (eds.), *The Negro American,* Houghton Mifflin, Boston, 1966, pp. 512–524.

[33]"HUD Says Mortgage Policies Hurt Blacks, " *Washington Post,* March 2, 2000, p. A7.

[34]Reynolds Farley and William H. Frey, "Changes in Segregation of Whites from Blacks During the 1980's," *American Sociological Review,* 59:23–45, 1994. For the original 1960s study of segregation indices, see Karl E. Taeuber and Alma F. Taeuber, *Negroes in Cities: Residential Segregation and Neighborhood Change,* Aldine, Chicago, 1965.

[35]See Douglas Massey and Nancy Denton, "Trends in Residential Segregation of Blacks, Hispanics, and Asians, 1970–1980," *American Sociological Review,* 52:802–825, 1987; and Douglas Massey and Nancy Denton, *American Apartheid: Segregation and the Making of the Underclass,* Harvard University Press, 1993.

redlining
pattern of banks and financial institutions refusing to make any loans in inner-city areas defined as high risk.

steering
showing home buyers only homes in neighborhoods of their racial group.

Box 3.3 Making a Difference

"Letter from the Birmingham Jail"

Martin Luther King Jr. wrote the letter from which this is excerpted on April 16, 1963, after having been jailed for leading a civil rights demonstration in Birmingham, Alabama. "I have no fear about the outcome of our struggle in Birmingham, even if our motives are at present misunderstood. We will reach the goal of freedom in Birmingham, and all over the nation, because the goal of America is freedom. Abused and scorned though we may be, our destiny is tied up with America's destiny. Before the Pilgrims landed at Plymouth, we were here. Before the pen of Jefferson etched the majestic words of the Declaration of Independence across the pages of history, we were here. For more than two centuries our forebears labored in this country without wages; they made cotton king; they built the homes of their masters while suffering gross injustice and shameful humiliation—and yet out of a bottomless vitality they continued to thrive and develop. If the inexpressible cruelties of slavery could not stop us, the oppression we now face will surely fail. We will win our freedom because the sacred heritage of our nation and the eternal will of God are embodied in our echoing demands."

$34,076.[36] Some 26 percent of black families have income below the poverty level.[37] In the cities, members of the bottom, truly deprived population are often dark-skinned.

These data, all of which are accurate, nonetheless, presented alone give a misleading picture of the contemporary status of many African Americans. Presented without further elaboration or breakdown, the aggregate figures mask the increasing diversity of the African American population. There are now two black Americas: an increasingly affluent middle-class African American segment and an increasingly deprived inner-city population living in semipermanent poverty. Presenting just the statistical mean or median does not reflect the growing prosperity of the first, nor the increasing poverty and isolation of the latter. For while intact-family blacks are increasingly moving into the middle-class, the impoverished inner-city poor are becoming more isolated. To suggest that either is the total black experience denies the reality of the other. As expressed by the Harvard African American scholar, Henry Louis Gates, Jr.: "There are now two nations in America, and those two nations—one hopeless and one full of hope—are both black."[38] If we look at the first group, we reach the "obvious" conclusion that the system works; if one focuses on the second group, it equally "obviously" does not.

The Economically Successful There always has been a small black elite, little known to the white community, or even poor blacks, living in upper-class neighborhoods, having their children join Jack and Jill (the ultimate membership-by-invitation-only social club for black children), and sending their offspring to elite colleges and joining Links (an upper-class social association).[39] Established wealthy blacks lived a class apart. Today, social mobility into the upper reaches is more common.

---

[36]U.S. Bureau of the Census, *Current Population Reports, The Black Population in the United States: March 1996* (Update), P20–498, Washington, DC, 1997.

[37]U.S. Bureau of the Census, *Current Population Reports, The Black Population in the United States: March 1997* (Update), P20–508, Washington, DC, June 1998.

[38]Quoted in Michael Martin, "Harvard Black Scholar Laments Those Left Behind," *Richmond Times-Dispatch*, February 16, 1997, p. C1.

[39]Lawrence Otis Graham, *Our Kind of People: Inside America's Black Upper Class*, Harper-Collins, New York, 1999.

Suburban African Americans represent one of the most significant, and little noted, demographic trends of the early twenty-first century.

© Lawrence Migdale/Stock, Boston

Depending on what cutoff point is chosen, somewhere between one-third and three-fifths of African Americans are middle class. This means roughly 15 to 20 million people. Between the 1980 and 1990 censuses, the number of black managers, professionals, and officials had increased by more than half. Thirty years ago, less than half (45 percent) of young blacks age 25 to 29 had completed high school.[40] Now 86 percent of young blacks finish high school. To quote the Bureau of the Census: "In 1993, there was no statistical difference in the annual high school dropout rate of Blacks and Whites and of males and females. Blacks have thus closed the historical differential between their annual dropout rates and those of Whites."[41]

Other measures also document a similar pattern. As of 1993, the Bureau of the Census reported that among college-educated blacks, some 28 percent held executive, administrative, or managerial jobs, not statistically different from the 30 percent held by white men.[42] Most of the general public is still unaware that the census shows African American dropout rates and percentages of executives and managers equal to white males. Nor are they aware that the number of blacks earning professional degrees in law and medicine increased 35 percent over a decade earlier.[43]

[40]U.S. Bureau of the Census, *Current Population Reports, Educational Attainment in the United States: March 1987 and 1986,* P20–428, Washington, DC, 1988, Table 12.

[41]U.S. Bureau of the Census, Current Population Reports, *The Black Population in the United States: March 1994 and 1993,* P20–480, Washington, DC, 1995, p. 17.

[42]Ibid.

[43]William P. O'Hare et al., "African Americans in the 1990s," *Population Bulletin,* 46:28, 1991.

There are also variations within the African American community. West Indian blacks, for example, have higher levels of income, education, and occupation, as well as higher home ownership and proportion married.

More African Americans are going to college than ever before, partially due to sharply increased numbers of black women enrolled. A quarter of all African Americans aged 18–24 are currently enrolled.[44] According to the United Negro College Fund, between 1976 and 1994 there was a 20 percent increase in bachelor's degrees for black men, but a 55 percent increase for black women.[45] African American underrepresentation at institutions of higher learning increasingly reflects the disparity between the educational successes of black women and the lower enrollment of black men. African American women now are twice as likely to obtain a bachelor's or a master's degree as African American men. If African American males completed college at the same rate as African American females, most of the racial gap in college attendance would disappear. The college gender gap has social as well as economic consequences; the most profound being a sharp drop in the marriage rates of college-educated black women, due in part to the smaller numbers of equal-education marriageable males.

The median earnings of middle-class blacks remain below those of middle-class whites, although for the young the gap is narrowing. The 1990 census reported that families headed by younger (under 40) married college-educated blacks had 92 percent of the income of whites. This translated into an income of $54,400 for college-educated blacks as compared to $58,000 for college educated whites.[46] Add $20,000 to these figures to approximate current income figures.

The gap between better-educated whites and blacks is far greater when the comparison is not income but wealth. In terms of accumulated wealth and assets, the difference between blacks and whites is very large indeed. Even when education and experience are taken into account, African Americans control only about a quarter of the assets white Americans do.[47] Discrepancies in wealth, which is often inherited from previous generations, reflect the fact that, until this generation, blacks have had few assets to transfer. The first step toward wealth creation is often buying a home, and middle-class blacks have less equity in their homes. Young white couples often get a gift of money from their parents to put toward a down payment and thus pay fewer "points" or fees and lower interest rates. Young black couples are less likely to receive as much from parental resources.

The prospects for the future are mixed. For the well-educated, the old visible color bar is largely gone, and middle-class blacks are increasingly occupationally and economically similar to middle-class whites. African Americans can buy homes anywhere, and three-quarters of black population growth is occurring in the suburbs. Nonetheless, as Massey and Denton document, African Americans still remain more segregated than Hispanics or Asians.[48] For some middle-class blacks, upward mobility has not removed the long-term corrosive effect of accumulated insults, anxieties, and frustrations.[49] For some middle-class blacks, assimilation is both welcomed and feared because it raises the possibility that the next generation of middle-class suburban black children could lose much of their black identity.

---

[44]U.S. Bureau of the Census, *The Black Population of the United States: March 1996* (Update), P20–498, Washington, DC, 1997.

[45]"Black Women Fuel Advance" *Associated Press*, February 27, 1997.

[46]U.S. Bureau of the Census, *Current Population Reports, Money Income and Poverty Status in the United States: 1989*, P60–168, Washington, DC, 1990, Table 4.

[47]Melvin L. Oliver and Thomas M. Shapirio, *Black Wealth/White Wealth: A Perspective on Racial Inequality*, Routledge, New York, 1995.

[48]Massey and Denton, "Trends in Residential Segregation"; Massey and Denton, *American Apartheid*.

[49]Ellis Close, *The Rage of a Privileged Class*, Harper Collins, New York, 1993; and Joe R. Feagan and Melvin P. Sikes, *Living with Racism: The Black Middle-Class Experience*, Beacon, Boston, 1994.

The Disadvantaged

Ironically, improvements in the income and opportunity levels of middle-class African Americans have increased both the physical and psychological gap between black "haves" and "have nots." Until the Fair Housing Act of 1968, all urban blacks—regardless of their education, income, or occupation— were more or less in the same boat, and this shared adversity—like the commonly felt poverty of most Americans during the Depression—created a certain solidarity. Today that solidarity is being severely tested.

The ability of stable and better-educated families to move out of the old ghettos merely emphasizes the isolation and frustration of those left behind. A bitter and alienated underclass of outcasts often is the consequence. The welfare poor, both white and black, know they are being bypassed and ignored while others seem to be attaining the good life. Especially for poor people of color, few routes lead out of the bondage of the unstable slums. Without a stake in society or adequate educational training, often embittered by an environment of hopeless disadvantage, and poorly socialized into societal norms, the so-called urban **underclass** are America's "untouchable" caste.

The African American sociologist William J. Wilson argues that, "Race relations in America have undergone fundamental changes in recent years, so much so that now the life chances of individual blacks have more to do with their economic class position than with their day-to-day encounters with whites."[50] Most (but not all) research has supported this view.[51] Those trapped in inner-city slums have little in common with other city residents of any color. Poverty, crime, drug usage, and welfare dependency result in a condition that Wacquant and Wilson call **hyperghettoization.**[52] Their view is that the major causes for this hyperghettoization are low educational levels and lack of entry-level jobs more than raw job discrimination. As the demand for manufacturing workers declines and a rising premium is placed on skills appropriate to an advanced service-oriented economy, few inner-city youth receive schooling that provides them the educational or technical skills necessary to succeed in the contemporary workforce.

In *Streetwise* Elijah Anderson presents a 14-year participant observation study of life in two inner-city Philadelphia neighborhoods.[53] Anderson examines the effects of drugs on the area and how inner-city communities, cut off from outside opportunities, develop their own norms and behaviors regarding community, sexual, and family life. Lack of jobs and a pervasive racism against hiring young males keep these young men out of the workforce and on the streets. Young males learn to be "streetwise" through codes of street behavior designed to get and keep respect. Those who move successfully on the streets learn the "street wisdom" of how to communicate their intentions toward others through body language and facial expression. Without such knowledge, the street is dangerous because for otherwise powerless individuals every encounter is seen as a test of respect, respect for which one is willing to fight to the death. Violence under such a system becomes normative.

Disappearance of Work

How did such a situation develop? Are members of the so-called underclass just lazy, violent, immoral, and irresponsible? The data indicate that they generally share the values of the middle class. What they

---

underclass
the long-term poor who are in practice excluded from the social and economic life of society.

hyperghettoization
extreme racial segregation of very poorest inner city residents.

---

[50]William J. Wilson, *The Declining Significance of Race: Blacks and Changing American Institutions,* 2d ed., University of Chicago Press, Chicago, 1980, p. 1.

[51]See A. Silvia Cancio, T. David Evans, and David J. Maume, Jr., "Reconsidering the Declining Significance of Race: Racial Differences and Early Career Wages," *American Sociological Review,* 61:541–556, August 1966; and George Farkas and Keven Vicknair, "Appropriate Tests of Racial Wage Discrimination Require Controls for Cognitive Skill: Comment on Cancio, Evans, and Maume," *American Sociological Review,* 61:557–560, August, 1996.

[52]Loic J. D. Wacquant and William J. Wilson, "The Cost of Racial and Class Exclusion in the Inner City," *Annals of the American Academy of Political and Social Science,* 501:8–25, 1989.

[53]Elijah Anderson, *Streetwise: Race, Class, and Change in an Urban Community,* University of Chicago Press, Chicago, 1990.

lack is an opportunity to express those work and moral values. Poor inner-city persons of color are trapped in areas that have been abandoned by factories, businesses, and the middle class. Deindustrialization and industrial relocation have drained over half the well-paying blue-collar manufacturing jobs out of central cities. These jobs, often unionized, once provided enough in wages to marry and start a family. Now they are gone.

The plight of inner-city ghetto dwellers has been accelerated by the suburban flight of the upwardly mobile black population.[54] Working adult males in the past provided both knowledge of existing jobs and assistance in entering the workforce. The departure of working adults from inner-city neighborhoods also has undermined the churches, businesses, schools, and other institutions that provided neighborhood stability. A dearth of employed adults in the neighborhood weakens the belief that staying in school means being employed. Young ghetto males see no link between going to school and getting a job. In such an environment criminal activity such as drug dealing increasingly becomes a way of getting money. The Justice Department reported that in 1995 nearly one-third (32.2 percent) of all black men in their 20s were in jail, prison, on probation or parole—a sharp increase over the already high one-in-four proportion of five years earlier.[55] Since these aggregate figures also include the large majority of law-abiding urban and suburban males, this means in the majority of inner-city young males are involved with the criminal justice system. Part of the reason is that there are few legitimate job opportunities.

The problem of the inner city is not that a "welfare ethos" has taken over but that the economy has collapsed. This leads in turn to social collapse. As put by William J. Wilson's *When Work Disappears,* "For the first time in the 20th century most adults in many inner-city ghetto neighborhoods are not working in a typical week."[56] Wilson points out that as hard as life was in the post–World War II ghettoes, urban blacks at least had a reasonable hope of landing steady if low-paying work. Now, the collapse of the low-wage economy has turned once viable communities into crime-infested welfare-based slums. Adult unemployment rates in some of Chicago's poverty ghettoes have gone over 60 percent.[57] Without jobs, young men simply are not marriageable. As a consequence, female-headed families on public assistance become the norm. The dramatic drop in the number of young inner-city men with secure jobs has in turn led to a drop in marriage rates and increased births out of wedlock. These changes are comparatively recent. In 1960 two-thirds (65 percent) of black women aged 30 to 34 were married, but by 1990 this figure had reversed to where 61 percent were not married. In 1960 a quarter of all black births were out-of-wedlock; by 1994 the figure had increased to 68 percent.

Once the economy of an area collapses, the catastrophe of the inner city increasingly becomes one of economic isolation more than simply of race.[58] While racism as a pervasive social attitude explains why working-class blacks have been especially vulnerable to economic changes, understanding changes in the economy provides a fuller knowledge of the plight of the truly disadvantaged. Without access to jobs, welfare reforms are doomed to failure. If welfare reform fails, the result will be that the United States will further divide into two societies: one multiracial and reasonably prosperous; the other, disadvantaged and often dark skinned, living in semi-permanent poverty.

---

[54]William Julius Wilson, *The Truly Disadvantaged: The Inner City, the Underclass, and Public Policy,* University of Chicago Press, Chicago, 1987.

[55]"Black Offenders up Sharply," *Washington Post News Service,* October 5, 1995.

[56]William Julius Wilson, *When Work Disappears,* Knopf, New York, 1996, p. 1.

[57]Loic Wacquant and William J. Wilson, "Cost of Racial and Class Exclusion," p. 17.

[58]William Julius Wilson, *The Truly Disadvantaged.*

Oprah Winfrey, one of America's most respected personalities, wearing her newly-presented special 50th Anniversary Gold Medal for her contributions to reading and books while holding her 1999 National Book Awards trophy.

Diane Bondareff/AP/Wide World Photos

Toward the Future

As the new century begins, the American dilemma with race continues to polarize the population. Racism persists but, compared to the last century, patterns of racial segregation are slowly declining and racial prejudice and discrimination are decreasing. During the twenty-first century, issues that the twentieth century defined as being racial questions will increasingly be redefined as issues of social class rather than color. The new century may see the African American population increasingly split between a middle-class segment growing in confidence and affluence and a truly disadvantaged segment isolated from the rest of the society. The success of the first group will further highlight the despair and desolation of the latter.

Paradoxically, the economic success of an African American suburban middle class raises the possibility that an African American heritage that survived 300 years of adversity could be weakened and undermined by economic success. This is what occurred with European and Asian immigrant populations. The common assumption, that the lives of blacks, because of race, will always be different than those of whites or Asian Americans, may not hold in the future. If the significance of race declines, African American heritage could come to have the same significance to future generations of middle-class suburbanites as Irish, German, or Italian heritage does now for European-background groups. In other words, having a black heritage would be something of interest but not something that strongly affects one's daily life. It would be equivalent to being Japanese American or Italian American today.

For poor blacks, future prospects are guarded, but the turn of the century showed some positive signs. The down side is that, while affirmative action programs have aided in developing a growing African American middle class, they have had little impact on those in central city ghettoes. The more positive development is that the booming job market during the last few years is showing some unexpected gains for the most economically disadvantaged and socially alienated group in American society, young black males. Simply put, low unemployment areas have seen a sharp, and unexpected, movement of low education black males into the labor force. A major study of low-wage men in 322 metropolitan areas by Richard Freeman of Harvard and William Rogers of William and Mary shows that young black males with high school education or less—many saddled with prison records— are working in greater numbers, pulling in bigger paychecks, and committing fewer crimes.[59] The jobless rate of young black males is still twice that of young white males, but for the first time in 20 years the booming economy both pushed down young black male unemployment and pushed up entry-level wages by 15 percent.

The challenge of the new century will be to continue this pattern and bring even the most disadvantaged persons of color into the mainstream. At the most basic, this means access to entry-level jobs that pay a living wage. The problem is not the acceptance of middle-class work values, it is access to middle-class opportunities. Without access to decent jobs poor inner-city residents will revert to the status of an isolated semipermanent underclass. If everyone is to work, government programs may have to serve as the employer of last resort for the most poorly educated and trained who the private market can't economically absorb. This would be far less expensive both economically and socially than maintaining a permanent welfare class.

---

[59]Sylvia Nasar, "Booming Job Market Draws Young Black Men into Fold," *New York Times*, May 23, 1999, p. 1.

Summary

The term *race* has been applied to every imaginable entity, from nation-states to language groups to biological groups. Although biological definitions of race are out of date, race is popularly spoken of as if it were biological. In practice, race is a social variable with biological overtones (What matters is how people are defined.) Prejudice is a rigid predisposition to respond to people in a given way, whereas discrimination involves overt actions.

- Blacks are one of the most recent groups to migrate into urban areas; African Americans, while being four-fifths urban, are rapidly suburbanizing.

- Functionalists suggest that racist patterns and behaviors persist because they provide whites with cheap labor and someone to feel superior over.

- Conflict theorists generally see racism as a power issue, with those on top unwilling to share unless forced to do so.

- Social interactionists emphasize the influence of racism on the individual; racial stereotypes can make minority group members feel inferior or less intelligent.

- African American urban residents remain far more segregated than any other group because of discriminatory housing policies practiced by financial lending institutions and government agencies.

- Aggregate figures for all blacks do not accurately reflect the diversity of the African American community. For example, while blacks, as a group, are less advantaged than whites on virtually every economic and social measure, still at least a third of blacks are middle class, and increasingly the black middle class lives in the suburbs.

- Disadvantaged inner-city blacks are severely economically and socially isolated from both whites and middle-class blacks. Inner-city economic collapse has contributed to social collapse by leaving many unemployed and without role models.

- Currently the nation is divided into two societies: one reasonably comfortable and racially mixed, the other a disadvantaged underclass, often dark-skinned and living in poverty.

☞Key Review Terms

apartheid	labeling	redlining
affirmative action	multiracial	segregation
discrimination	prejudice	steering
great urban migration	race	stereotype
hyperghettoization	racism	
institutional racism	restrictive covenants	

? Questions for Discussion

1. What is race? How has the term been used? How do you and your friends use the term in everyday life?

2. The Census Bureau is considering adding a multiracial category. Discuss the pros and cons of such a change. Do you think this would be a good idea? Why or why not?

3. Discuss the difference between prejudice and discrimination. Can you have one and not the other? How prevalent is institutional racism?

4. Many of the Founding Fathers were slave owners, yet they fought for and believed in "equality." Discuss this dichotomy and how it has affected American thought and life.

5. Discuss the "great urban migration." How was this similar to immigration from Europe and how did it differ?

6. How have government policies affected residential racial segregation? How are patterns changing nationally? Are changes occurring in your locality?

7. A quotation by Henry Lewis Gates, Jr., states, "There are now two nations in America, and those two nations—one hopeless and one full of hope—are both black." Discuss this statement in line with current income, education, and occupation data regarding African Americans.

8. The author of this text states that the underclass shares the values of the middle-class. If this is so, why is life for the underclass so destitute, violent, and hopeless?

9. It has been suggested that middle-class suburban blacks differ little from their white neighbors. Will this result in race having less meaning for such populations? Why or why not?

10. Discuss how a social interactionist would say racial symbols and stereotypes are used. Does this occur in your college or university? How can it be changed?

Suggested Resources

Reynolds Farley, *The New American Reality*, Russel Sage, New York, 1996. Changing racial and other issues in America as seen by the demographer who has documented changing racial and segregation patterns for over 30 years.

Douglas S. Massey and Nancy A. Dunton, *American Apartheid: Segregation and the Making of the Underclass*, Harvard University Press, Cambridge MA. 1993. Black ghettoes are seen as consciously created and maintained today.

James McBride, *The Color of Water: A Black Man's Tribute to His White Mother*, Berkeley Publishing Group, New York, 1996. Acclaimed autobiography of growing up in Harlem in a large poor family with a white mother.

Studs Terkel, *Race: How Blacks and Whites Feel About the American Obsession*, New Press, New York, 1992. Terkel provides selections from candid tape recorded interviews with over 60 ordinary Americans on issues regarding race.

Cornel West, *Race Matters*, Beacon, Boston, 1993. A discussion of the continued importance of race in American life and a rebuttal of Wilson's thesis of the increasing importance of social class.

William Julius Wilson, *When Work Disappears*, Knopf, New York, 1996. Wilson's latest book on the limited future of the underclass in an America with fewer blue-collar entry-level jobs.

Malcom X, *The Autobiography of Malcom X*, Grove, New York, 1964. A must read. The famous black activist who was murdered because of his break with the Black Moslems details his progression from street hustler, to anti-white Nation of Islam spokesman, to his discovery of the religion of Islam.

Internet Connection 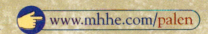 www.mhhe.com/palen

1. Search the website of The National Council of La Raza (*www.nclr.org/*) to see what you can find on the subject of the U.S. Census.
   a. What are the major concerns of La Raza regarding the U.S. Census? Compare these concerns with those of the National Congress of American Indians (*www.ncai.org/indianissues/census/census.htm*). Go to the U.S. Census Bureau Census 2000 home page (*www.census.gov/dmd/www/2khome.htm*). Click on "2000 Questionnaire," then click on "Informational Questionnaire" (*www. census.gov/dmd/www.infoquest.html*). Click on "Short Form" and you will see a sample of a census questionnaire.
   b. How does the Census plan to obtain information about a respondent's race?
   c. Does the questionnaire allow for the counting of people who consider themselves to be multiracial? Explain.
2. Go to the website of the National Association for the Advancement of Colored People (NAACP) (*www.naacp.org/*). Click on the button titled "About Us" to learn more about this organization and its objectives. Examine the current issues that it is involved in. You will notice that some are very symbolic in nature with broad appeal. Others are very specific to a particular circumstance or event.
   a. Which of these two kinds of issues do you feel is more effective in promoting the goals of the NAACP? Explain.

Chapter

4

I had a heck of a time every
time the census came into the
school. They'd say "Check
one," and when you have three
or four nationalities—which
one you gonna check? So I ask
the teacher, "What do I put?"
They would say, "Are you
part Hawaiian?" You say,
"Yes." They say, "Check that
one." They never ask how
much Portuguese you are or
Chinese or Caucasian. As a
result I have cards listing me as
everything. In the military the
question is, "Have you got any
Mongolian ancestry?" I had to
put yes cause I'm one-eighth
Chinese. I said, what the heck.
On my driver's license I got
Caucasian.[1]

A Hawaiian local who thinks of
himself as Portuguese.

The Cracked Melting Pot

[1]Victoria Nelson, *My Time in Hawaii: A Polynesian Memoir*, St. Martins, New York, 1989, p. 42.

E Pluribus Unum?

The United States is becoming a multiethnic society. In California one in three students in the public schools speaks a language other than English at home, and one of six was born outside the United States.[2] In Miami's Dade County, nearly 60 percent of the population speak a language other than English at home. One-third of New York City's population are immigrants and another 20 percent are their children.[3] Four of every 10 births (43 percent) in New York are to immigrants. The Census Bureau reports that 9.3 percent of the nation's population is foreign born, up from 7.9 percent in 1990.[4]

As the last chapter indicated, the concept of distinct races has no scientific validity. There remain, however, distinct ethnic differences. Members of **ethnic groups** share a cultural or social heritage that may include social customs, language, and religion. They feel bound together by common cultural ties. The German sociologist Max Weber defined an ethnic group as a collectivity based on the assumption of common origin.[5] Ethnic groups sometimes think of themselves as racially (i.e., biologically) distinctive, although they are not. For example, Serbs, Croats, and Bosnians often refer to themselves as "races," although they are in fact physically indistinguishable. What divides them is not biology but history and religion. Some of the ethnic minorities discussed in this chapter are new to America and others are the oldest immigrants. Though they possess different histories and cultures, what they have in common is a perception by the majority that they are somehow marginal to mainstream America.

Who is a member of an "ethnic minority"? What characteristics determine ethnicity? At what point does a person become so assimilated as to lose her or his ethnic identity? The answers to these questions are neither clear nor consistent. In one sense, all Americans are minorities since no one group accounts for over half the population. In practice, however, *minority status is defined largely in terms of low power and social disadvantage.* Ethnic status in the United States is closely tied to history, social rank, and political power. In 1977 the U.S. Office of Management and Budget (OMB) defined four "official" minority groups for statistical purposes—African Americans, Hispanics, Asian and Pacific Islanders, and American Indians

ethnic group
body of people seeing itself and seen by others as possessing a distinct culture.

---

[2]Paul Grey, "Teach Your Children Well," *Time,* Special Issue, Fall, 1993, p. 69.
[3]Celia W. Dugger, "Immigrant Influence Rises in New York City in 1990's," *New York Times,* January 9, 1997, p. A16.
[4]"In the U.S., Nearly 1 in 10 Is Foreign Born," *New York Times,* September 19, 1999, p. 27.
[5]Max Weber, "The Ethnic Group," in Talcott Parsons et al. (eds.), *Theories of Society,* vol. 1, Free Press, New York, 1961, p. 305. For a discussion of definitions, see Andrew M. Greeley, *Why Can't They Be Like Us?* Dutton, New York, 1971.

(including Alaskan Natives). Hispanic is considered an ethnic identity rather than a racial identity. The combined population of the four minority groups was 75 million in 1998.[6]

Sociological Perspectives

Functionalist Approaches

Because of their concern with social disorganization, functionalist approaches tend to emphasize shared values. Insofar as there is a consensus on values, functionalists believe, a common society is possible. Without a common core, differences can degenerate into ethnic conflict and violence. Seeing the necessity for common core values, functionalists also deplore ethnic prejudice, discrimination, and inequality as weakening core beliefs and institutions. Cultural differences are applauded as long as they do not undermine the nation's civil and political core. For functionalists, the goal is to integrate all ethnic groups into an American system that allows differences.

Conflict Approaches

Conflict theorists see the American system as one in which WASPs (White, Anglo-Saxon, Protestants) maintain their dominance by excluding others. Conflict theorists tend to see ethnic relations as a struggle for power in which one group can move ahead only if another gives ground. Historically, in order to maintain their position, those in control gradually and selectively shared power with older, largely assimilated ethnic groups such as the Germans or Irish. The same process continues today. Groups refusing to assimilate are excluded from power. Some ethnic-racial groups, such as African Americans, weren't even given the choice of assimilation.

While functionalists tend to see economic improvement of a group producing more political and social acceptance, conflict theorists tend to see economic improvement coming only as a result of political action. Thus conflict theorists advocate that ethnic groups organize themselves. Groups that are politically organized cannot only defend their own interests, but by using protests, demonstrations, civil disobedience, and violence or the threat of violence, they can change the rules by which the system operates. This kind of mobilization allows outsiders to gain an advantage. One example is the use of protests and civil disobedience by the civil rights movement in order to obtain equal treatment. Assuming that without conflict the excluded group cannot achieve equality, conflict theorists reject the concept of a national melting pot and support cultural differences. For conflict theorists, the goal is to gain economic and social equality while maintaining cultural uniqueness and separateness.

---

[6]Keven M. Pollary and William P. O'Hare, "America's Racial and Ethnic Minorities," *Population Bulletin*, Population Reference Bureau, Washington, DC, 1999, p. 10.

Interactionist Approaches

Interactionists look not to the societal macro level, but rather to how ethnicity affects the behaviors and attitudes of individuals. For instance, groups that look, dress, and speak differently are often stereotyped. Negative stereotypes can lead members of the discriminated groups to doubt their own worth and create self-fulfilling prophecies of negative behaviors. Social psychologists pay particular attention to how patterns of discrimination and prejudice are imparted by the dominant political-social group to lower-power ethnic groups. Alcohol and drug abuse have been one avenue of escape used by low-prestige groups to withdraw from what they see as an unfair and unequal contest.

Models of Ethnic Assimilation

The Melting Pot

melting pot model
belief that all ethnic groups upon coming to America should become part of one common American heritage.

During the first half of the twentieth century, the dominant American model for ethnic groups was that of the melting pot. The **melting pot model** assumed that the diverse traits of all heritages were to be merged and unified in a great American crucible or melting pot.[7] The result was said to be a new breed, an American. A statement of the melting pot creed, which assumes ethnic fusion, is inscribed on the base of the Statue of Liberty. However, rather than being a true mixture, the melting pot assumed that all ethnic groups would emerge from the crucible looking, speaking, and behaving like English speaking WASPs. In other words, rather than fusion, what would occur is the assimilation of each new group into the dominant group. As President Theodore Roosevelt bluntly put it, "We have no room for any people who do not act and vote simply as Americans and nothing else."[8] The extent of Anglo conformity can be seen in our schooling, where much of the early history and culture we are taught is English.

Richard Alba's research documents that there is increasing evidence that the melting pot analogy has validity for those coming from European backgrounds.[9] Some 50 million European immigrants came to these shores. Today, European groups have been assimilated. However, for those of non-European background,

---

[7]For a review of the concept of the melting pot, see Charles Hirshman, "America—Melting Pot Reconsidered," *Annual Review of Sociology,* Vol. 9, Annual Reviews, Palo Alto, CA, 1983, pp. 397–423.
[8]Quoted in Mark R. Levy and Michael S. Kramer, *The Ethnic Factor,* Simon and Schuster, New York, 1972, p. 12.
[9]Richard D. Alba, *Ethnic Identity: The Transformation of White America,* Yale University Press, New Haven, CT, 1990.

the distinction between European and non-European heritage remains a central societal division.[10] Blacks and (until after World War II) Asians, were automatically excluded from the melting-pot gene pool.

Behavioral Assimilation

Behavioral Assimilation Ethnic populations coming to America were and are expected to undergo **assimilation,** a process in which ethnic groups adopt the dominant culture's patterns and are absorbed into the cultural mainstream. Milton Gordon distinguished between behavioral (or cultural) assimilation and structural assimilation.[11] **Behavioral assimilation** takes place when groups are exposed to similar cultural influences (e.g., schools, television, and magazines), share the same political system, and do the same sort of jobs. This acceptance of diet, dress, and cultural behavior of the "host" society has historically taken place rapidly in the United States.

Structural Assimilation

Structural Assimilation By contrast, **structural assimilation** involves acceptance and assimilation into the primary social fabric of the dominant group. Structural assimilation is a gradual process—one that does not finish until substantial intermarriage has taken place and the subordinate group has joined the cliques, institutions, and primary groups of the dominant group. Structural assimilation essentially means the elimination of the minority group as a separate entity. Historically, in America those groups that are not structurally assimilated have been excluded from wielding real power in the society.

The Pluralist or Multicultural Model

During the last 25 years, the melting pot model has been replaced with the model or ideology of **cultural pluralism,** commonly referred to today as **multiculturalism.** In his 1997 book, *We Are All Multiculturalist Now,* Nathan Glazer argues that over the last two decades there has been a hard institutionalization of ethnic and racial differences such that multiculturalism has become institutionalized as an ideology.[12] Multiculturalism is the ideology favored by the majority of academics.[13] Cultural pluralism or multiculturalism maintains that American life benefits when each ethnic group retains its distinct cultural heritage—that is, American society remains a mosaic or salad bowl rather than becoming a melting pot.

Multiculturalism, as the term is commonly used, simply means being open to other cultures. However, political multiculturalism as an ideology assumes that racial and ethnic groups not only can but should remain distinct. Political multiculturalism means opposing the adoption of national cultural values.

assimilation
process by which a minority takes on the values of the dominant group and ceases to be a distinct entity.

behavioral assimilation
taking on the outward characteristics of the majority society, e.g., food, dress, behavior.

structural assimilation
full acceptance by the majority population, usually represented by intermarriage.

cultural pluralism
belief advocating that each group keep its distinct cultural characteristics, similar to multiculturalism.

multiculturalism
belief in the equality of all cultures and the value of diversity, similar to cultural pluralism.

---

[10]Stanley Lieberson and Mary C. Waters, *From Many Strands: Ethnic and Racial Groups in Contemporary America,* Russell Sage Foundation, New York, 1988.
[11]Milton M. Gordon, *Assimilation in American Life,* Oxford University Press, New York, 1964.
[12]Nathan Glazer, *We Are All Multiculturalist Now,* Harvard University Press, Cambridge, MA, 1997.
[13]Sean Wilentz, "Integrating Ethnicity into American Studies," *Chronicle of Higher Education,* November 29, 1996, p. A56.

Cultural Wars

The dispute between assimilationists arguing for an overarching national culture and political multiculturalists arguing for the greater importance of ethnic differences was part of the so-called "cultural wars" of the 1990s.[14] Recent examples include the battle over whether to tighten laws regarding legal and illegal immigration and the efforts to make English the official language of the country. Supporters of political multiculturalism denounce attempts to "Americanize" newcomers as "cultural genocide" and view the attempt to legislate English as the common language as the imposition of racist and elitist attitudes about the superiority of Anglo-American culture. Just because English customs and language were here first does not give them any special rights, political multiculturalists maintain. It is their contention that all languages and customs should be treated equally.

Those who advocate a national culture respond that immigrant groups traditionally came to America precisely to put ethnic and religious strife behind them and to become Americans. They argue that the failure to stress a common American culture will lead to ethnic and sectarian strife.[15] They worry that suggesting that a person's primary loyalty is to his or her ethnic, religious, or racial group rather than to the nation as a whole will result in narrow parochialism, encourage ghettos, and discourage people from entering the mainstream.[16] The historian Arthur Schlesinger reflects this view when he says that, when considering the nation's motto of *E Pluribus Unum* (from many, one), what is needed today is "less *pluribus* and more *unum*." (For a discussion of the fight over immigration policy, see Chapter 6.)

Some previous supporters of political multiculturalism are now questioning the consequences of elevating ethnic preservation and separatism to a position over national unity, given the civil wars and "ethnic cleansing" that occurred during the 1990s in once-functional nation-states such as Rwanda, Burundi, and Yugoslavia. In the name of ethnic cleansing, Serbs, for example, have murdered tens of thousands of their previous neighbors. In Rwanda and Burundi ethnic hatreds have led to over a million deaths.

Even in Canada, where multiculturalism is the official national policy, divisions between the English-speaking provinces and French-speaking Quebec have become bitter. The Quebec provincial government bans the use of English in government, business, and most public schooling. In 1995 Quebec voted by only 51 percent to 49 percent not to secede from Canada and form a separate French-speaking nation. Canadian political observers differ on whether Canada eventually will split along ethnic and language lines into two separate ethnic nation-states.

Pragmatists say that assimilation and multiculturalism should be viewed not as absolutes but as reciprocal aspects of group relationships. To accept one, you don't have to reject the other. Before comfortably becoming part of the social, political, and economic mainstream of a society, groups often must develop a pride in their group distinctiveness. American literature, for example, has benefited from a creative explosion of works of fiction and nonfiction discussing how various ethnic groups define the American experience (see, for example, Box 4.2 by Maxine Hong Kingston).

---

[14]For a recent critique of assimilation as racist, see Bill Ong Hing, *To Be An American: Cultural Pluralism and the Rhetoric of Assimilation*, New York University Press, New York, 1997; for a defense of assimilation, see Peter D. Salins, *Assimilation, American Style*, New Republic Books, New York, 1997.
[15]Benjamin Schwarz, "The Diversity Myth: America's Leading Export," *Atlantic*, May 1995, pp. 57–67.
[16]Martin E. Marty, *The One and the Many*, Harvard University Press, Cambridge, MA, 1997.

A Nation of Immigrants

How did America become a nation of immigrants? At the time the United States gained its independence in 1776, English, Scottish, and northern Irish (called Scotch-Irish) immigrants accounted for nine of every ten white settlers. Some still consider having colonial or Revolutionary War ancestors a special mark of distinction or "American-ness." However, long ancestry in the United States does not by itself assure high status; were this the case, Native Americans and African Americans would be at the top of the list.

The First Wave

The **first wave** of ethnic migrations following British settlement began in the 1820s and ran until roughly 1880. Many of the first-wave immigrants were Irish and German. Almost all were northern and western Europeans. In the late 1840s a million Irish fled Ireland because of a devastating potato famine that resulted in over a million people dying of starvation. Irish immigrants in America were discriminated against by the Protestant economic and social establishments. As the old Irish story goes, the immigrants discovered three things: first, the streets of America were not paved with gold; second, the streets weren't paved; and third, *they* were expected to do the paving. For them, getting on the road to success meant self-help by becoming one of the three *P*'s: priest, politician, or policeman. The Irish were closely followed by large numbers of Germans, who weren't welcomed either; the "Know Nothing" political party that dominated major cities such as Boston during the 1850s was founded as an anti-Catholic, anti-Irish, and anti-German political movement.

first wave
immigrants coming to the U.S. between 1820 and 1880, largely from the British Isles, Ireland, and Germany.

The Second Wave

The **second wave** of mass migration to the United States occurred between 1880 and the 1920s. While the first wave of immigrants had come from northern and western Europe, those who arrived after 1880 often came from eastern and southern Europe. For the first time, Italians, Greeks, Poles, and Russian Jews began arriving in significant numbers. During the 1860s (the decade of the American Civil War), under 2 percent of all immigrants were from southern and eastern Europe; by the decade of the 1890s, they were a majority (52 percent); and by the first decade of the twentieth century, they represented 71 percent.[17]

second wave
European immigrants to the U.S. between 1880 and 1920s, predominately from Southern and Eastern Europe, e.g., Slavs, Russians, Poles, Italians, Greeks.

The great number of immigrants—as many as a million a year during the first decade of the twentieth century—made rapid assimilation difficult. Major cultural differences between the newcomers and the older established groups further increased antagonism, as did the fact that many of the newcomers were Catholics or Jews. With the good farmlands already taken, the second wave of immigrants largely became urban industrial workers. The resulting concentration of immigrants in the central slums of the large industrial cities further emphasized their numbers.

By the turn of the twentieth century, nativist (then the term for those of British background) writers such as Josiah Strong were noting with alarm that over half the population of the larger cities of the Northeast and Midwest was foreign stock—

---

[17]Helen F. Eckerson, "Immigration and National Origins," *Annals of the American Academy of Political and Social Science*, 367:6, September 1966.

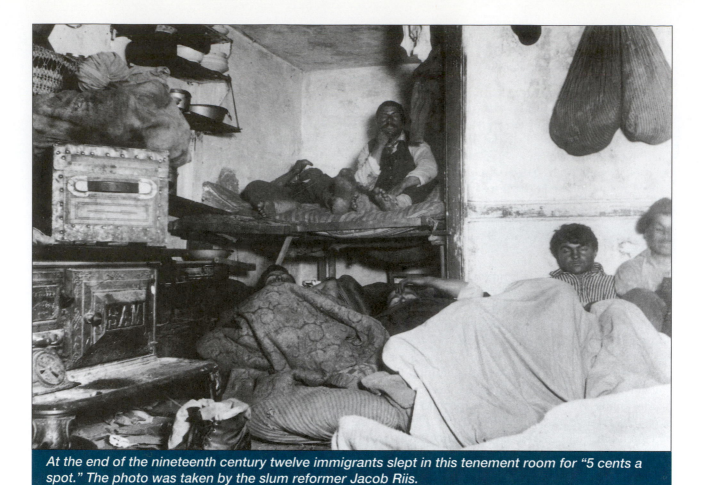

At the end of the nineteenth century twelve immigrants slept in this tenement room for "5 cents a spot." The photo was taken by the slum reformer Jacob Riis.

either foreign born or of foreign parentage.[18] In East Coast port cities such as New York and Boston, over three-quarters of the population was of foreign stock. Nativist writers applied arguments of racial inferiority against the southern and eastern Europeans. Their views propounded (1) ethnocentrism regarding the superiority of American ways and customs, (2) evolutionary views holding that American industrial society represented a higher stage of development than that of southern and eastern Europe, and (3) beliefs in the genetic superiority of nativists over new immigrants. Although the logic and weight given to each of these factors often differed, the conclusions were always similar. "Experts" agreed that the English settlers who had founded the nation, combined with Germans, Scandinavians, and other "first-wave immigrants" constituted a superior American fair-haired, blue-eyed race.

Nativist superiority was commonly assumed by academics during the early years of the twentieth century. The University of Wisconsin sociologist and liberal reformer E. A. Ross argued, for example, that southern and eastern European immigrants were racially inferior breeds whom no amount of schooling or "Ameri-

---

[18]One of the best known of the anti-immigrant books by the clergyman Josiah Strong sold three-quarters of a million copies; Josiah Strong, *Our Country*, Baker and Taylor, New York, 1891.

canization" could make equal to WASPs.[19] The common view was reflected in the writings of a prominent professor at Columbia University in 1909: "The southern and eastern Europeans are of a very different type from the north Europeans who preceded them. Illiterate, docile, lacking in self-reliance and initiative, and not possessing the AngloTeutonic conceptions of law, order, and government, their coming has served to dilute tremendously our national stock, and to corrupt our civic life."[20]

Since these supposed differences were regarded as fixed and unchangeable, the obvious answer was to exclude these groups from immigration to the country. Thus, immigration laws passed in the 1920s were designed to discriminate against southern and eastern Europeans; they set severe quota limits for those not having Anglo-Saxon, Irish, or Nordic-Germanic backgrounds. The National Origins Act of 1924 cut Italy's already reduced immigration quota down from 42,057 to 3,845 and Poland's from 30,977 to 5,981. This policy of deliberately discriminating among immigrants on the basis of preferred nationalities remained in force until 1968.[21]

Out of economic and social necessity, immigrants drew into their own protective, segregated urban communities. Older tenement areas surrounding the central business district became identified as Greek Town, Little Italy, Pole Town, and so on. One of the best-known sociological works, *Street Corner Society*, documents how young Italian background males became caught in the contradictions between the expectations of those in the ethnic community and the values of the larger society.[22]

The Third Wave

Today, all those of European background are usually thought of as having a common background, whereas **third wave** Hispanic and Asian newcomers are more likely to be viewed as "ethnic." Some 59 percent of Asians and 38 percent of Hispanics are foreign-born.[23] Only 3 percent of non-Hispanic whites are foreign-born. Ellis Island, where most European immigrants entered, is now a national museum. Los Angeles is the new immigrant port of entry. California alone houses half of all the country's immigrants, with large Vietnamese, Laotian, Philippine, Hong Kong, and other Asian immigrant communities, plus massive immigrant populations from Mexico and Central America. Census figures document these changes. Nationwide, while the non-Hispanic white population grew only 3 percent from 1990 to 1995 and the African American population increased 8 percent, the Hispanic population grew 20 percent and the Asian population 31 percent.[24] Figure 4.1 indicates the changing racial and ethnic distribution of the U.S. population over the twentieth century. Figure 4.1 also includes estimates for 2050, when only half the population will be non-Hispanic white.

third wave
current immigrants coming largely from Latin America and Asia.

---

[19]Edward Alsworth Ross, *The Old World in the New: The Significance of Past and Present Immigration to the American People,* Century, New York, 1913.
[20]Ellwood P. Cubberly, *Changing Conceptions of Education,* Mifflin, 1909, p. 15.
[21]For further details, see J. John Palen, *The Urban World,* 5th ed., McGraw-Hill, New York, 1997, Ch. 10.
[22]William Foote Whyte, *Street Corner Society,* University of Chicago Press, Chicago, 1943.
[23]Population Reference Bureau analysis of March 1998 *Current Population Survey.*
[24]Carol J. DeVita, "The United States at Mid-Decade," *Population Bulletin,* 50:19, March 1996.

Figure 4.1 U.S. Population by Race and Ethnicity, 1900 to 2050

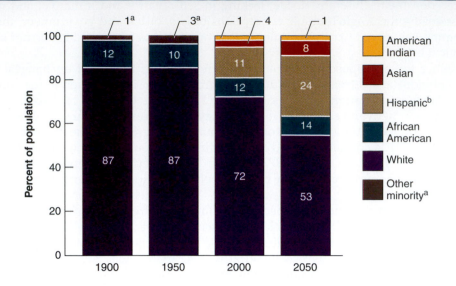

^aAmerican Indians, Asians, and Hispanics combined. These three groups combined made up less than 3 percent of the population in 1900 and 1950.

^bHispanics are excluded from American Indian, Asian, African American, and white categories. Hispanics may be of any race.

Source: Jeffrey S. Passel and Barry Edmondson, "Immigration and Recent Trends in Immigration to the United States," in Barry Edmondson and Jeffrey S. Passel (eds.), *Immigration and Ethnicity,* Urban Institute Press, 1994, Table 3; and U.S. Bureau of the Census, *Current Population Reports* P25–1130, Washington, DC, Tables I and J.

The Status of Hispanic Americans[25]

Within half a decade Latinos will outnumber African Americans as the nation's largest minority population.[26] The Hispanic-origin population in the United States now numbers 30 million persons or 11 percent of the national population.[27] This figure excludes the census estimate of an additional 4 million undocumented aliens. Hispanics, according to the census, are an ethnic group and can be of any race. The Urban Institute projects that the U.S. Hispanic population will number 39 million by the year 2010.[28]

---

[25]There is no agreement as to how the Hispanic-origin population should be addressed. Government documents use the term *Hispanic,* while academics (especially on the West Coast) mostly use the term *Latino.* The preferred term also differs from city to city. To try to resolve the name question, the Census Bureau ran a special race/ethnic group survey in the May 1995 *Current Population Survey.* It found 58 percent of the Hispanic-origin respondents favored *Hispanic,* 12 percent favored *Latino,* and 12 percent *Spanish origin.* Because group members prefer the term *Hispanic* over *Latino* by a five to one margin, it is the term most used in this chapter.

[26]U.S. Bureau of the Census, *Population Profile of the United States 1995, Current Population Reports,* P23–189, Washington, DC, 1995, p. 46.

[27]U.S. Bureau of the Census, "The Hispanic Population of the United States: March 1997 (Update)," *Current Population Reports,* P20–511, Washington, DC, July 1998.

[28]"The Future Immigrant Population of the United States," Program for Research on Immigration Policy, Urban Institute, Washington, DC, 1992.

Patterns of Growth and Diversity

The Hispanic American population is growing about four times faster than the population as a whole (Figure 4.2). Just between 1990 and 1998, it grew over 35 percent. Even if all legal and illegal immigration ceased tomorrow, the Hispanic population would continue to grow rapidly. This is due to two factors. First, the Hispanic population has a median age of 26.7 years, nine years younger than the non-Hispanic white median age of 35.5 years.[29] This means that far more of the Hispanic population is of childbearing age. Second, Hispanic women have higher than average birthrates. The fertility of California's Hispanics is changing the demographic makeup of the state. Since 1975, births in California to women of Hispanic origin have more than doubled (from 20 percent of the total to 44 percent), whereas births to non-Hispanic white women dropped from 68 percent to 38 percent.[30] Latinos constitute a full quarter (25.8 percent) of California's population. Indicative of the change is that in 1998 *Jose* replaced *Michael* as the most popular newborn boy's name in California and Texas.[31] California, which was taken from Mexico 150 years ago, may again have a Latino majority in a few decades.

More than half of all Latino Americans are found in two states: California and Texas. Most of these immigrants are from Mexico and Central America. New York has the nation's third largest Hispanic concentration; the majority are Puerto Ricans, some 2 million in the New York metropolitan area. Florida has a growing Cuban population, with the Miami metropolitan region approaching 1 million Hispanics. Some 64 percent of the U.S. Hispanic population is of Mexican origin, 11 percent are Puerto Rican, 5 percent are Cuban, 13 percent are Central or South American, and 7 percent are other.[32]

Hispanics come from a range of national origins and represent wide social-class differences, but overall, Latino populations are poorer than the white population. Rapid urbanization of Latino newcomers has resulted in crowding in the *barrios* or ghetto neighborhoods where some of the new arrivals settle. Barrios often are associated with high crime rates and membership in gangs. New immigrants (legal or otherwise) are often unfairly blamed for bringing with them drugs, crime, and other problems. Nonetheless, housing segregation has not been as severe for Hispanics as it has been for African Americans.[33] In Los Angeles, where immigration is heavy, levels of Latino segregation are increasing.[34] Outside a few major cities elsewhere in the country, however, patterns of segregation and discrimination are less institutionalized. Segregation is more by social class than by ethnicity.

---

[29]U.S. Bureau of the Census, *The Hispanic Population of the United States: March 1994, Current Population Reports*, P20–475, Washington, DC, 1994, p. 2.

[30]B. Meredith Burke, "Mexican Immigrants Shape California's Fertility, Future," *Population Today*, Population Reference Bureau, September, 1995, p. 4.

[31]Mireya Navarro, "Latinos Gain Visibility in Cultural Life of U.S.," *New York Times*, September 19, 1999, p. 18.

[32]U.S. Bureau of the Census, *Hispanic Population of the United States: March 1993*, Current Population Reports, P20-475, Washington, DC, 1994.

[33]Douglas Massey and Nancy Denton, *American Apartheid: Segregation and the Making of the Underclass*, Harvard University Press, Cambridge, MA, 1993.

[34]Fran D. Bean and Marta Tienda, *The Hispanic Population of the United States*, Russell Sage Foundation, New York, 1987.

Figure 4.2 Hispanic Population: 1930 to 2050 (Millions. Middle series projections)

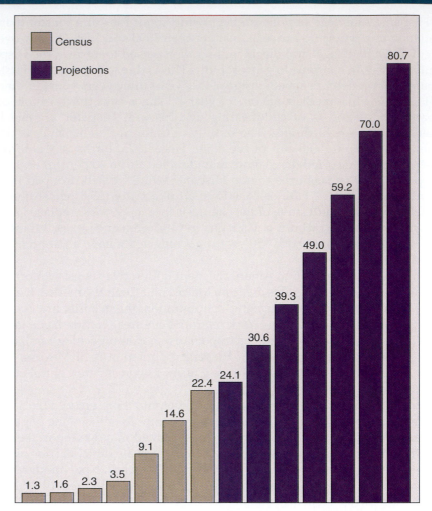

Note: Data for 1930 include only "Mexicans," data for 1940 include persons of "Spanish mother tongue," and data for 1950 and 1960 include persons of "Spanish surname."
Source: Population Reference Bureau.

Mexican American Differences

Two-thirds of Hispanics are Mexican Americans, but the label "Mexican American" covers a remarkably varied range of individuals. There is even considerable disagreement among Mexican Americans as to whether they are a racial group or a cultural group, and most middle-class Mexican Americans reject the label "minority group." Historically, the Mexican American population divided itself into three rough subcategories, a division that, over time, has come to be accepted by the non-Mexican or Anglo community. At the top of the pyramid were the "Spanish," those who had lived in California and New Mexico since before these areas became part of the United States. Following the Latin American pattern, this rel-

Cars play an important status role in Los Angeles communities, rich and poor. Here homeboys are displaying their award winning customized low rider.

© A. Ramey/Stock, Boston

atively small elite emphasized its Spanish heritage and "pure blood," which was supposedly untainted by Indian ancestry. Thus, the Spanish rancheros of early California are stereotyped as gracious rural grandees, as seen in the *Zorro* movies.

The second group, the U.S. native-born, constitute a middle layer that now often blends with the first group. Native-born Mexican Americans are often descendants of those who immigrated to the United States between the period of the Mexican revolutions of the early twentieth century and the 1970s. Overwhelmingly, the native-born group is made up of U.S. citizens, and an increasing number are middle-class. These middle-class citizens may, or may not, define themselves as Hispanic. Barrio-living, poor, American-born second-generation Latinos are known as *chicanos* in Texas and California. On the East Coast people often mistakenly think the term *chicano* refers to new illegal immigrants.

The third group, and by far the largest, comprises first-generation *mexicano* immigrants (legal and undocumented) and their children. This group is among the most poorly educated and least-skilled immigrant groups in the United States, often occupying low-paying service jobs.

In sociological terms, the distinction between the "aristocratic" Spanish and the "lowly" *mexicanos*, with differing class and racial overtones, serves a social purpose. It allows the "Spanish" to be socially accepted and to marry into Anglo society, while maintaining discrimination against *mexicanos*.

Assimilation Problems

For immigrant groups, assimilation into American values long has been thought of as a way of moving up, but Alejandro Portes and Min Zhou argue that for today's poor, nonwhite immigrants, who have little opportunity to join the middle class, assimilation into American ways can be dysfunctional. This is because in central-city neighborhoods assimilation means taking on the values and norms of the inner city, not those of the mainstream culture.[35] To assimilate into the street culture in high

---

[35]Alejandro Portes and Min Zhou, "The New Second Generation: Segmented Assimilation and its Variants," *Annals of the Americans of Political and Social Science* 530:74–90, 1993.

school may mean not studying and labeling anyone seeking to do well as being a "wannabe" or "acting white." Young Haitian immigrants in Miami or Mexican immigrants in Los Angeles are torn between following the "hard work brings success" orientation of their parents, or "becoming American" by identifying with the inner-city street values of their neighborhoods. Assimilation into local values locks one into poverty.

Education

According to 1998 Department of Education figures, four in ten of all adult Latinos have less than a high school education, and one-third of today's Hispanic students fail to finish high school.[36] Among Hispanic groups, the Mexican American rates are very low, with just under half (47 percent) of Mexican Americans aged 25–34 completing high school.[37] By comparison, the non-Hispanic white and black graduation rates are about 85 percent. More troublesome, the Hispanic dropout rate shows no sign of change. The Education Department says these rates cannot be explained by length of time in the United States, English proficiency, or social class. Today, those having less than a high school education can't effectively enter the job market.

American school systems have failed to reach and teach many Latino students. Border-region schools in particular have long discriminated against Mexican Americans, providing them with lower-quality educations than those offered to Anglo students. Schools have also failed to cope with the non-English speaking background of Mexican American children. A judge in Texas caused a controversy in 1995 by threatening to remove a child from his mother's household if English wasn't spoken at home. However, poor academic performance is not simply the result of not speaking English, since Cubans, the Hispanic population with the highest educational and income levels, are also the most likely to speak Spanish at home. The difference is that among young Cubans, Spanish is spoken as a second language, not the only language.

As of 2000, 12 percent of Latinos aged 25–44 have completed college, compared to 31 percent of non-Hispanic whites. Census Bureau figures indicate that as a group Hispanics are falling further behind non-Hispanics in college attendance.[38] However, these general figures mask substantial differences among Latino subgroups. Mexicans and Puerto Ricans have low educational levels, whereas Cubans are increasingly well educated, with a quarter of young adults now completing college. Cuban American college graduation rates as of 2000 equal those of non-Hispanic whites. A comparison of Hispanics with other groups can be seen in Figure 4.3.

Income and Poverty

As with education, general statements about Hispanic incomes cover a wide range of differences. As a group, Hispanics continue to suffer from higher than average poverty rates. Overall, Hispanic males make approximately two-thirds of what non-Hispanic white males make, whereas Hispanic females do somewhat better,

---

[36]"Study: 1/3 of Hispanics Fail to Finish School," *Richmond-Times Dispatch,* February 3, 1998, p. A2.
[37]U.S. Bureau of the Census, *Population Profile of the United States 1995,* p. 46.
[38]Carey Goldberg, "Hispanic Households Struggle as Poorest of Poor in U.S.," *New York Times,* January 30, 1997, p. A12.

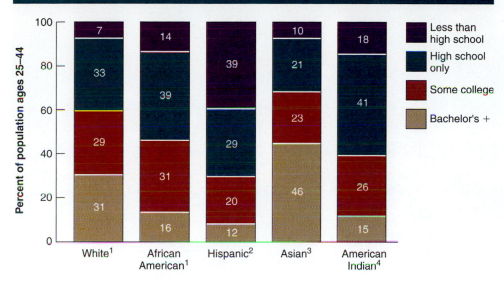

Figure 4.3 Educational Attainment of Adults Ages 25 to 44 by Race and Ethnicity, 1998

Percent of population ages 25–44

	White[1]	African American[1]	Hispanic[2]	Asian[3]	American Indian[4]
Less than high school	7	14	39	10	18
High school only	33	39	29	21	41
Some college	29	31	20	23	26
Bachelor's +	31	16	12	46	15

[1]Excludes Hispanics.
[2]Hispanics may be of any race.
[3]Includes Pacific Islanders and excludes Hispanics.
[4]Includes Eskimos and Aleuts and excludes Hispanics.
Source: Population Reference Bureau analysis of the March 1998 *Current Population Survey.*

making roughly four-fifths of the earnings of non-Hispanic white women.[39] Hispanic professional women are making strong economic gains. A strong work ethic has fueled the growth of a broad Latino middle class, with market researchers classifying about 75 percent of Hispanic households as middle class or higher.[40]

Overall, Latino income and poverty levels fall between those of non-Hispanic whites and African Americans.[41] However, Census Bureau data indicate that since 1995 Mexican American newcomers are *falling* rather than gaining in median income level.[42] Between 1995 and 1998 average Hispanic income levels briefly fell below those of African Americans.[43] However, overall rates mask wide variations by social class and nationality within the Hispanic population. Puerto Ricans, with a high proportion of female-headed households, and Mexican Americans are the poorest. On the other hand, Cuban Americans—many of whose families left Cuba with marketable skills—earn considerably more than other Hispanics. The rapid

---

[39]U.S. Bureau of the Census, *Population Profile of the United States 1995,* p. 47.

[40]Mireya Navarro, "Latinos Gain Visibility in Cultural Life of U.S." *New York Times,* September 19, 1999, p. 18.

[41]U.S. Bureau of the Census, "Poverty in the United States: 1998," *Current Population Reports,* P6–207, September 1999, p. ix.

[42]Carey Goldberg, "Hispanic Households Struggle as Poorest of Poor," *New York Times,* January 30, 1997, p. A1.

[43]U.S. Bureau of the Census and Bureau of Labor Statistics, compiled by the National Council of La Raza, July 1998.

Miami Beach, the center of Latino night life, is becoming increasingly concerned about raves attracting underage all-night partygoers and drugs.

Greg Smith/AP/Wide World Photos

growth of Cuban American income levels indicates their median income soon will equal or surpass the national median income level.

Contributing to the low resource base of Mexican Americans are birthrates higher than those for African Americans and three times higher than those for Anglos. The combination of larger families and low incomes results in a lower "investment" per child. Low educational levels, discrimination, and poor language skills tend to shunt Mexican Americans toward low-paying jobs with few opportunities for advancement. Other problems are that Mexican Americans are concentrated in industries that suffer cyclical unemployment, in service-sector jobs that pay poorly, and in manufacturing, which is declining in this country.

Political Future

Hispanics are underrepresented in the halls of power. Partially this is because two out of five Latinos 18 or over are not yet citizens and thus are ineligible to vote. However, Hispanics are increasing their voting numbers, and in the 1996 election Hispanic voters were almost as likely as other voters to vote. Nationally Hispanic voters account for only 5 percent of all voters, but they are concentrated in the important states of Texas, California, Florida, and New York. Latinos are 12 percent of the voters in Texas and 15 percent of California voters.[44] Orange County,

---

[44]B. Drummond Ayres, "The Expanding Hispanic Vote Shakes Republican Strongholds," *New York Times*, November 10, 1996, p. 27.

Box 4.1 Making a Difference

Latina Executives

Latina women are beginning to enter the corporate executive suites. Among those making it is Gloria De Neochea, a long-time single mother who grew up in the poor southern California border town of Calexio and worked her way through school. She is currently Manager of the Mattel Foundation in California, where she oversees the corporation's grants, arts, and social welfare programs. De Neochea also directs the foundation's volunteer program. She started foundation work 10 years ago at the Carnegie Foundation.

According to De Neochea, working for a company foundation is better than just being part of the corporation. "It's the best of both worlds. You distribute the company's profits and give back to children. The other rewarding part is helping employees give back to the community. You have an opportunity to be a link."[a] She encourages young Latinas to be "strong, smart, and bold" and to "face every obstacle as a learning and growing opportunity."

De Neochea feels that Latinas have unique skills that they can contribute to corporations. "It's difficult to assess each corporate culture and find thoughtful ways you can contribute to the company's goals. But it is extremely rewarding to give our unique perspective as women and Latinas to management's knowledge base and help a company succeed. Companies succeed because of diversity."

[a]Jerry Berrios, "A Balancing Act," LATINA/Style, 3(2): 25–26, 1997.

California—long considered one of the most conservative WASP bastions in the nation—is now 25 percent Latino. In 1996, Bob Dornan, an entrenched nine-term conservative Republican Congressman was defeated by Loretta Sanchez, a Latina Democrat.[45] He was again defeated in 1998.

The Hispanic vote is not monolithic, of course. Cubans vote overwhelmingly Republican, while Puerto Ricans and Mexican Americans largely vote Democratic. However, Latinos helped elect George W. Bush, Jr., a Republican, Governor of Texas in 1998 and his brother Jeb Bush, also Republican, Governor of Florida. In many respects Hispanics represent a new constituency, one that can swing future elections.

The Status of Asian Americans

Patterns of Growth and Diversity

The Asian population in the United States is growing dramatically, increasing more than 40 percent between 1990 and 2000. The American Asian population has surged from 3.5 million in 1980 to Census Bureau estimates of 12.1 million as of 2000.[46] It is estimated that there will be 17 million Asian Americans in the year 2010.[47] Currently,

---

[45]Ibid., p. 1.
[46]U.S. Bureau of the Census, *Population Profile of the United States 1995*, p. 48.
[47]J. John Palen, *The Suburbs*, McGraw-Hill, New York, 1995, p. 149.

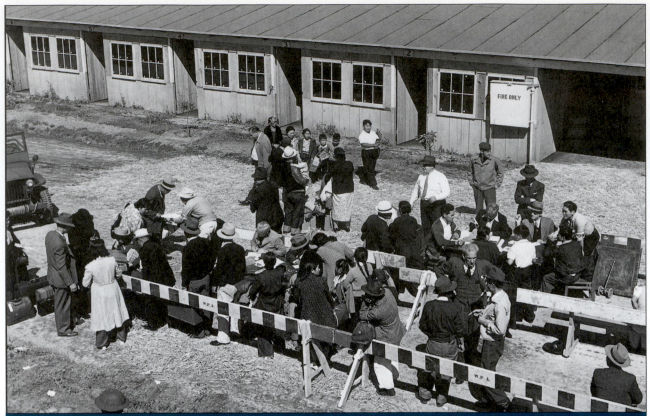

During World War II Executive Order 9066 authorized the removal of all Japanese Americans from the West Coast and their confinement under Army guard in inland internment camps. This shows Japanese Americans registering at the Santa Anita racetrack reception center. While awaiting relocation families were housed in the stables seen in the background.

most of the Asian population growth (86 percent) comes from immigration. Most American Asians are either immigrants or the children of immigrants. In fact foreign-born Asian Americans outnumber native-born Asian Americans.[48] Some of these new immigrants come with considerable educational and financial resources. Immigrants from Asia represent more than one-third of all legal immigrants to the U.S.[49]

Those of Asian background are the nation's most metropolitan population and reside almost entirely (94 percent) in metro areas. The Asian population in America is heavily concentrated on the West Coast, with four out of ten Asians living in California; more than 1 million Asian Americans live in the Los Angeles metropolitan area. Asians are less segregated than black or Hispanic populations.[50] Residential segregation is most likely to be self-segregation.

Although Asian Americans are often treated as a uniform group, they represent culturally and ethnically diverse populations. The largest Asian population group is Chinese (32 percent), followed by Filipinos (19 percent), Japanese (12 percent),

[48]"In the U.S. Nearly 1 in 10 Is Foreign Born," *New York Times,* September 19, 1999, p. 27.

[49]Sharon M. Lee, "Asian Americans: Diverse and Growing," *Population Bulletin,* 53:2, June 1998.

[50]U.S. Bureau of the Census, "Selected Social Characteristics of the Population, by Region and Race: March 1996," Government Printing Office, Washington, DC, 1997.

Figure 4.4 Median Household Income by Race and Ethnicity, 1997

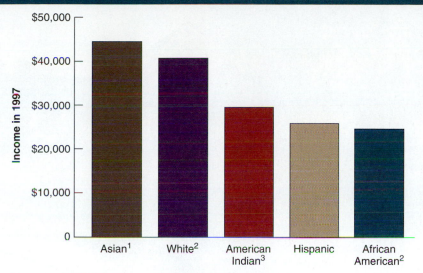

¹ Includes Pacific Islanders and excludes Hispanics.
² Excludes Hispanics.
³ Includes Eskimos and Aleuts and excludes Hispanics.

¹Includes Pacific Islanders and excludes Hispanics.
²Excludes Hispanics.
³Includes Eskimos and Aleuts and excludes Hispanics.
Source: Population Reference Bureau analysis of the March 1998 *Current Population Survey*.

and Koreans and Asian Indians (11 percent each). Asian populations generally have high school graduation rates that outstrip those of other minorities and the general population. Nearly nine out of ten Asian Americans 25 years of age and over have completed high school. More remarkably, Asian Americans have twice the proportion graduating from college as do whites.[51] Almost half of adult Asian American males (46 percent) and over a third of the females (37 percent) hold at least a college degree.

A Model Minority?

Economically, Asian Americans are doing well. The median Asian American family income is over $18,000 above the median for Hispanics and $20,000 above that for blacks (see Figure 4.4).[52] The Asian figure is bolstered by having a number of family members working in the household. High average incomes mask substantial populations of poor. As of 1998 some 14 percent of Asians were below the poverty line as compared to 13 percent of the overall population. Asian income

---

[51]Robert Gardner, Bryan Robley, and Peter Smith, "Asian Americans: Growth, Change, and Diversity," *Population Bulletin*, 40, October 1995.
[52]Sharon M. Lee, "Asian Americans: Diverse and Growing," p. 28.

Jacques Brinon/AP/Wide World Photos

differences reflect ethnic backgrounds, with Japanese Americans having the highest incomes and more recent immigrant Cambodians, Laotians, and Vietnamese the lowest. Asian American minority status is expected by some to erode and disappear in a couple of generations.

The relative economic success of Asian Americans can be linked to their success in using all family resources. For some, these resources include strong educational backgrounds, strong family systems, and family investment funds. Family support networks allow members to draw on capital from a household with several workers.[53] The pooling of wages provides funds for investment or education. For poor newcomers lacking these resources (and often not speaking English), the metropolitan ethnic enclave economy provides at least entry-level jobs.[54]

Ironically, doing well sometimes creates social problems. The open hostility directed against Asian immigrants during the first half of the twentieth century has sometimes been replaced with more subtle manifestations of prejudice. Being a so-called "model minority" has a price. Asian Americans may encounter a glass ceiling because they are seen as a "super minority." The hard work and success of Asian immigrants sometimes results in others who are less successful viewing the newcomers as unfair competitors.

---

[53]Sharon M. Lee and Barry Edmondson, "The Socioeconomic Status and Integration of Asian Immigrants in the 1980s," in James P. Smith and Barry Edmondson, (eds.), *The New Immigrants: Economic, Fiscal and Demographic Effects of Immigration,* National Academy Press, Washington, DC, 1997.

[54]Min Zhou and John Logan, "Return on Human Capital in Ethnic Enclaves: New York City Chinatown," *American Sociological Review,* 54:809–820, 1989.

Box 4.2 Ongoing Issues

Life in Chinatown

Maxine Hong Kingston is one of America's best-known writers. This excerpt from *The Woman Warrior: Memories of a Girlhood among Ghosts* discusses how Chinese immigrants transferred their traditional fear of government officials to life in California. The "ghosts" of the title reflect the Chinese term for white people.

"Occasionally the rumor went about that the United States immigration authorities had set up headquarters in the San Francisco or Sacramento Chinatown to urge wetbacks and stowaways, anybody here on fake papers, to come to the city and get their files straightened out. The immigrants discussed whether or not to turn themselves in. 'We might as well,' somebody would say. 'Then we'd have our citizenship for real.'

" 'Don't be a fool,' somebody else would say. 'It's a trap. You go in there saying you want to straighten out your papers, they'll deport you.'

" 'No they won't. They're promising that nobody is going to go to jail or get deported. They'll give you citizenship as a reward for turning yourself in, for your honesty.'

" 'Don't you believe it. So-and-so trusted them, and he was deported. They deported his children too.'

" 'Where can they send us now? Hong Kong? Taiwan? I've never been to Hong Kong or Taiwan. The Big Six? Where?' We don't belong anywhere since the Revolution. The old China has disappeared while we've been away.

" 'Don't tell,' advised my parents. 'Don't go to San Francisco until they leave.'

"Lie to Americans. . . . Don't report crimes; tell them we have no crimes and no poverty. Give a new name every time you get arrested; the ghosts won't recognize you. Pay the new immigrants twenty-five cents an hour and say we have no unemployment. And, of course, tell them we're against Communism. Ghosts have no memory anyway and poor eyesight. And the Han people won't be pinned down.

"Even the good things are unspeakable . . ."[a]

[a]*Maxine Hong Kingston*, The Woman Warrior: Memoirs of a Girlhood among Ghosts, *Vintage Books, New York, 1977, pp. 214–215.*

The Status of Native Americans

The North American indigenous population at the time of the 1607 English settlement at Jamestown probably was around 10 million.[55] That number was quickly reduced by smallpox, cholera, and other European diseases, as well as by conflict with European settlers. Sometimes there was intentional genocide, as when the British General Amherst (for whom the college is named) deliberately gave Indians blankets contaminated with smallpox during the colonial period. More frequently, there were simply pandemics of European diseases against which the American Indians had no resistance. By 1890, when the first federal census of Indians was taken, their numbers had been reduced to 250,000, and most of these were barely surviving on government reservations. In 1915 the Census Bureau predicted that "full-blooded" American Indians would eventually disappear.[56]

---

[55]Higher numbers occasionally have been published, but the higher figures are not supported by most scholars. See J. John Palen, *The Urban World,* 5th ed., McGraw-Hill, New York, 1997, p. 63.
[56]C. Matthew Snipp, "A Demographic Comeback for American Indians?" *Population Today,* November 1996, p. 4.

Patterns of Growth and Diversity

Today Native Americans are making a comeback, numbering over 2.3 million as of 1998.[57] In spite of increases in population, Native Americans still make up less than 1 percent of the total population. While more than 500 known tribes are listed, one half of all Native Americans belong to one of the eight largest tribes. Nonnative Americans tend to lump all Native Americans together, but in fact there is no single Indian culture. Even groups living in the same geographical area often have widely differing cultures and customs. The Pueblos and Navajos in the Southwest, for example, have fought over land and ways of life for centuries. In fact there is not even a common North American usage of the term Native American. In Canada native groups refer to themselves as Aboriginal Peoples or First Peoples.

The impact of the indigenous North American population on American civilization has always been out of proportion to its absolute numbers. From the colonial period onward, Europeans were fascinated by the concept of Native Americans as "noble savages" uncorrupted by urban vice. At the same time, they were horrified and repelled by the image of cruel and vicious barbarians: the savage attackers and scalpers of hard-working settlers and their innocent wives. (These notions parallel the Rosseauian and Hobbesian views of human nature discussed in Chapter 1.) The history of indigenous–white relations in the United States documents this ambivalent view: In paintings, "the noble red man" traits were highlighted; in literature, the savage ones. Motion pictures commonly portrayed Indians as loyal, childlike, cunning, excitable, and often cruel, while contemporary museums largely present the image of the Noble Savage.

The census reports a marked increase in those reporting themselves as "American Indian." Some non-Indians now claim Native American heritage, sometimes seeking financial gain. While the median income level for Native Americans remains very low, some nations or tribal groups have discovered natural resources on their land, and an increasing number of reservations now have gambling casinos. Treaties with Indian nations often specify that some state and federal regulations do not apply on reservation lands. Nor are cigarettes or gasoline sold on reservation lands subject to state sales taxes (this is being legally challenged by several states). Gambling casinos and tourism are creating new reservation-based businesses.[58]

Contemporary Situation

Today over half the Native American population is urban and only one-third still live on reservations. Four states have a Native American population of over 100,000—Oklahoma, California, Arizona, and New Mexico—and these states hold 42 percent of the American Indian population. The Native American population is young, with a median age of 26; four out of ten are under twenty years of age. In spite of the newfound prosperity of some tribal groups, Native Americans overall remain one of the nation's poorest groups.[59] Thirty percent of Native Americans are below the poverty level. As with other poor groups, the very poorest families tend to be single-parent households. Over a quarter (27 percent) of all Native American families are maintained by a female householder, and half of these

[57]U.S. Bureau of the Census, *Population Profile of the United States 1998,* Government Printing Office, Washington DC, 1999.

[58]Dan Frost, "American Indians in the 1990s," *American Demographics,* December 1991, pp. 26–34.

[59]C. Matthew Snipp, *American Indians: The First of This Land,* Russell Sage, New York, 1989.

Gambling has become the major industry of Native American tribes. Some 4,000 people waited in the cold rain for Harrah's Cherokee Casino in Cherokee, N.C. to open for the first time in 1997.

Chuck Burton/AP/Wide World Photos

single-parent families are poor. A few tribal groups have become prosperous from their casino earnings. Nationally, gambling is now the major reservation employer, providing jobs for as many as 300,000 Indians.[60]

Native American educational levels have improved significantly in recent years, with two-thirds (66 percent) of adults being high school graduates or better, and the figure rises to four-fifths for younger adults.[61] This puts Native Americans below blacks and whites but above Hispanics. Educational levels are highest among Native Americans living in cities and lowest on the reservations. There is also a wide variation in educational levels among reservations, with Blackfeet and Hopi having the highest proportion of high school graduates, and Navajo the lowest.[62]

[60]James Brooke, "On the Budget Talk from Washington, Indians See Cruelest Cuts of All," *New York Times*, October 15, 1995, p. 16.
[61]Kelvin M. Pollard and William P. O'Hare, "America's Racial and Ethnic Minorities," *Population Bulletin*, September 1999, p. 31.
[62]U.S. Bureau of the Census, *Population Profile of the United States 1995*, p. 51.

Finally, census data say nothing about those middle-class Native Americans who have assimilated and no longer identify themselves by their tribal association. This group makes up the majority of those having Native American ancestry. Such assimilated Native Americans usually are indistinguishable from their neighbors in behavior, attitudes, and lifestyle. Culturally assimilated middle-class Indians are sometimes referred to by reservation Indians as "apples—red on the outside but white on the inside." Roughly half of those who do identify themselves as American Indians marry non-Indians. Today there is a revival of Native American culture. Where there once was a stigma attached to Indian heritage, today it is a source of pride.

The Status of White Ethnics

Who Is a White Ethnic?

white ethnic
usually refers to working-class second- and third-generation Americans of eastern and southern European ancestry.

When one speaks of white ethnics today, the term no longer includes western or northern European groups such as Germans, Scandinavians, or Irish. Nor does it usually include largely assimilated immigrant groups such as European Jews. The term **white ethnic** is reserved for those second- and third-generation Americans of eastern and southern European ancestry. Until 1968 U.S. immigration policy treated these latter groups as being culturally and genetically inferior. White ethnics are concentrated geographically in the older frostbelt industrial centers of the Northeast and Midwest. As Michael Novak, an outspoken writer on ethnic membership, expresses it:

> I am born of PIGS—those Poles, Italians, Greeks, and Slavs, non-English-speaking immigrants, numbered so heavily among the workingmen of this nation. Not particularly liberal, nor radical, born into a history not white Anglo-Saxon and not Jewish–born outside what in America is considered the intellectual mainstream. And thus privy to neither power nor status nor intellectual voice.[63]

Contemporary sociology textbooks usually ignore the existence of white ethnic groups. Politicians in cities with large ethnic populations make no such mistake, understanding that many ethnic groups have a strong sense of ethnic pride. The late Mayor Richard J. Daley of Chicago, for instance, once snubbed the visiting King of Norway in order to show up at a Polish gathering wearing a "Polish Power" T-shirt. Mayor Daley could count; Chicago has far more Polish than Norwegian voters.

Rednecks

redneck
poor rural or working-class southern whites, often used in a derogatory sense.

Another cultural group, southern poor whites (derisively called **rednecks**), are treated as the southern rural or small town equivalent of white ethnics. The fact that southern poor whites are Ango-Saxon Protestants does not prevent them from being treated as powerless outsiders. Both the urban-white-ethnic group and the redneck group remind us that white skin is not enough to ensure prosperity or power.

---

[63]Michael Novak, *The Rise of the Unmeltable Ethnics*, Macmillan, New York, 1972.

Beginning as good-old-boy races on dirt tracks NASCAR-sponsored races have become a national sport while still retaining their southern roots. Unlike other sports where stars often remain aloof, drivers are expected to be friendly and available to fans.

© Dave Nagel/Liaison Agency

The Class Factor

Probably the most widely noted trait of both white ethnic and poor southern white populations is their comparatively heavy concentration in blue-collar or working-class occupations (although less than half of each group is actually blue-collar). The stereotypical media "angry white male" is either a working-class white ethnic male in the North or a "redneck" in the South. Ethnics and rednecks are aware of these stereotypes. Playing on working-class and regional features, the comic Jeff Foxworthy has made a career out of his "You're a redneck if . . ." jokes.

There is debate about the importance of ethnic factors as a predictor of behavior. Most social scientists would agree with the late Scott Greer's assertion: "Ethnic status is not a powerful differentiator among second and later generation whites from Europe."[64] Critics note that ethnic consciousness for third or later generations sometimes is a romantic sentimentalization of a past that never was. American Irish sing of an "Auld Sod" they have never seen, while "Saturday Italians," who do not speak Italian, drive into the city from their suburban homes on Saturdays to shop in Little Italy for ethnic foods. Critics of the ethnic factor also suggest that intermarriage has confused the question of ethnic identity. Many Americans have difficulty decoding their various ethnic backgrounds. For these, ethnicity has become a flexible category in which a person may have the choice of identifying oneself as either Italian, Puerto Rican, German, or Irish.

On the other hand, the sociologist Andrew Greeley takes the position that ethnicity remains a prime factor. He states:

---

[64]Scott Greer, "The Faces of Ethnicity," in J. John Palen (ed.), *City Scenes*, Little Brown, Boston, 1977, p. 156.

"among Western intellectuals there is an assumption that the only meaningful differences among human groups are social class differences—even black militancy and women's liberation are justified as class movements. In such a perspective, differences of language, religion, or national background are either irrational and ought not to be taken seriously or are a disguised attempt of the oppressor class to justify continuing oppression. A society divided along class lines and along lines of essentially economic political issues is an acceptable society, but there is no room there for divisions on issues that are primordial, ethnic, particularistic, and personal. Such issues and divisions are "irrational."[65]

Research by Richard Alba suggests that as groups become more middle class, ethnic differences fade into the background.[66] It does appear that much of the lifestyle attributed to ethnicity seems to be characteristic of blue-collar populations, regardless of their ethnic backgrounds.[67] Problems arising from alienation, urban crime, and business downsizing transcend ethnic lines. As a Boston woman put it, "Yes, you might call me an 'Italian-American,' but it doesn't do me much good when I have to face my kids taking drugs."[68]

There is, however, no logical reason why one has to vote only for class *or* ethnicity, excluding one or the other. Both class and ethnicity can operate simultaneously. For purposes of social research, however, ethnicity is not as strong a predictor of behavior as is social class.

Toward the Future

Ethnicity, an issue which seemed to be dying of disinterest 20 years ago, is now a major topic in North America and is likely to remain so in the early twenty-first century. The old concept of the melting pot has largely been supplanted by that of multiculturalism. The irony is that, at the same time, Americans are now more than ever exposed to a common mass media and to similar cultural influences. Thus, ethnic diversity receives increasing public approval at the same time real differences are declining. For those of European heritage, ethnic backgrounds appear to be blending into one general European ethnicity. The exceptions are some working-class white ethnics and some southern poor whites. The term *white ethnic*, like the term *redneck*, increasingly refers more to a social class than to any ethnic content.

By the year 2005, Hispanics will be the nation's largest minority ethnic group, and we are only beginning to discuss what changes will result from this growth. The common assumption is that the increasing number of Latinos will turn the nation more in the direction of Latin cultures and customs. However, this assumption may not prove accurate. Most middle-class Hispanics do not view themselves as unique. Rather, they see themselves as members of another American ethnic group rapidly assimilating into the general American culture. If this occurs, their future will be similar to that of most European-based ethnic groups. For the middle-class, being of Mexican or Cuban heritage a generation from now may mean little more than being of Irish or German heritage today. That is, their ethnicity is something of interest, but not something that affects their daily life. For the poor, however, ethnicity is more likely to remain an important identifier.

[65]Andrew M. Greeley, *Ethnicity in the United States: A Preliminary Reconnaissance,* Center for the Study of American Pluralism, National Opinion Research Center, Wiley, New York, pp. 22–23, 1974.
[66] Richard D. Alba, *Ethnic Identity: The Transformation of White America,* Yale University Press, New Haven, CT, 1990.
[67]See Arthur B. Shostak and William Gomber, *Blue-Collar World,* Prentice-Hall, Englewood Cliffs, NJ, 1968.
[68]Richard Sennett and Jonathan Cobb, *The Hidden Injuries of Class,* Vintage Books, Random House, New York, 1973, p. 16.

The assimilation of contemporary first-generation Asians into America is remarkable both for its speed and for its thoroughness. For better or worse, the second-generation Asian Americans are essentially American in customs, beliefs, and values. In the United States, Asians are increasingly treated as if they are just another white ethnic group.[69] White-Asian intermarriages have become the most common marriage pattern for American-born Asian American women. Four out of ten of all U.S.-born Asians had a spouse of a different race in 1990.[70] For some, this loss of a distinctive group identity is a serious concern. However, the reality is that maintaining a distinct Asian American population in the twenty-first century will depend heavily on the continuing immigration of newcomers. The twenty-first century will see Asian groups increasingly de facto defined as part of the general population.

Native Americans are actively rediscovering their identity. Census figures indicate that the number of people identifying themselves as American Indian exceeds what would be expected based on birthrates. Some of this identification may be based on attempts to assert tribal identification in order to share new-found gambling wealth, but most is based on increasing pride in having some Native American heritage.

---

[69]Sharon M. Lee, "Asian Americans: Diverse and Growing," p. 5.
[70]Ibid., p. 22.

Summary

- Minorities such as Hispanic Americans, Asian Americans, Native Americans, and white ethnics are often overlooked in the debate on minority groups in the United States.

- These groups have not structurally assimilated into the cliques, institutions, and primary groups of the dominant European group.

- The earlier ideology that encouraged the assimilation of immigrants has now been largely replaced by a belief in cultural pluralism or multiculturalism.

- Hispanics will be the nation's largest minority population in less than a decade, with a primarily urban population crowding into barrios, ghetto neighborhoods.

- The Mexican American population historically has been divided into three groups: a small elite emphasizing its Spanish heritage, a native-born working- and middle-class group, and a large bottom group of foreign-born *mexicanos*.

- Asian Americans are the fastest growing ethnic group in the United States, with the highest educational and income levels of any group in the United States.

- Native Americans have rapidly urbanized, but they remain the most rural of the minority groups discussed, with one-third still living on reservations. Education levels are rising but still lag behind those of the general population. Overall, the Native American population remains poor.

- In the North and East, the term *white ethnic* refers to second- and third-generation Americans of eastern and southern European ancestry, while in the South the equivalent (often derogatory) term is *redneck*. Northern white ethnics often are blue-collar workers who live in older central-city neighborhoods and older suburbs.

- White ethnics have a long history of discrimination imposed by older established WASP groups; at the turn of the century they were often characterized as racially inferior.

☞ Key Review Terms

Asian American
assimilation
behavioral assimilation
cultural assimilation
cultural pluralism
ethnic group
first wave

Hispanic
Latino
mass migration
melting pot
model minority
multiculturalism
Native American

pluralism
redneck
second wave
structural assimilation
third wave
WASP
white ethnic

❓ Questions for Discussion

1. Discuss the media's representation of minority groups. How are they presented? Are stereotypes used? How are media representations changing?

2. Should we keep or do away with census data by ethnic and racial groupings? How do we ethnically describe an American such as Tiger Woods?

3. How do immigrants today differ from those at the beginning of the century? How are they alike? What are the attitudes toward current immigration?

4. Define what is meant by multiculturalism. What are the positive and negative effects of multiculturalism?

5. The Hispanic American population is expanding about four times faster than the population as a whole. What are likely to be the consequences of this for American society?

6. Who are Hispanic Americans? How are Hispanic groups similar and how do they differ?

7. Asian Americans have sometimes been referred to as a super minority. What is meant by this? What are the consequences of being labeled a super minority?

8. Why is there a marked increase in those identifying themselves as Native American? How do Native Americans compare to other ethnic groups in the United States regarding income, education, and social status?

9. How have various ethnic groups used politics and the political system to gain power and influence? How successful have recent immigrant groups been in using this route to success?

10. How have American immigrant policies changed during this century? What is the current immigration policy? What should it be?

☞ Suggested Resources

Frank D. Bean and Marta Tienda, *The Hispanic Population of the United States,* Russell Sage, New York, 1987. Getting a bit dated but still an excellent compilation of data on the Hispanic population.

Sharon M. Lee, *Asian Americans Diverse and Growing,* Population Bulletin, Vol. 53, Population Reference Bureau, Washington, D.C., 1999. An up-to-date 40 page demographic description and analysis of the contemporary status of Asian Americans.

Kelvin M. Pollard and William P. O'Hare, *America's Racial and Ethnic Minorities,* Population Bulletin, Vol. 54, Population Reference Bureau, Washington, D.C., 1999. A solid 48-page demographic description and analysis of minorities in America.

Alejandro Portes and Alex Stepick, *City on the Edge: The Transformation of Miami,* University of California Press, Berkeley, 1993. How Cuban immigrants reinvented and reinvigorated a dying Miami as a bicultural city.

Ronald Takaki, *A Different Mirror: A History of Multicultural America,* Little Brown, Boston, 1993. Immigration as viewed by those directly involved from Massachusetts Indians to the 1992 East Los Angeles riot.

Internet Connection 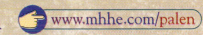 www.mhhe.com/palen

1. Imagine that you have a friend who is a foreign national desiring to seek political asylum in the United States. The U.S. Immigration and Naturalization Service's website is a good resource for you to begin with. It can be found at (*www.ins.usdoj.gov/graphics/index.htm*). First, you'll want to check to see what your friend must do to apply for immigration. Click on the "How Do I . . . ?" button. Questions and answers are listed alphabetically. Under "A" you'll find "Asylum" with several subheadings.
   a. What are the required criteria?
   b. What forms must be filled out? To look at all the forms available to immigrants, go back to the home page and click on the right side of the page under "INS Forms Now on Line." (Don't try to count them. It will take too long.) Finally, click on the section titled, "Statistical Reports". Click on any of the monthly statistical reports for information on a broad variety of topics ranging from border apprehensions to applications for asylum.
   c. How many southwest border apprehensions were reported for the Fiscal Year, 1999?
2. Should the United States enact legislation to make English the nation's official language? Concern over immigration to this country has prompted 25 states to enact such legislation. Here are two websites that support "official English":

   U.S. English, Inc.   *www.us-english.org/incindex.html*
   English First   *www.englishfirst.org/index.html*

   a. Visit them and list the primary reasons why "official English" proponents argue in favor of enacting such legislation.

      Now visit "James Crawford's Language Policy Website" at *www.ourworld.compuserve.com/homepages/JWCRAWFORD/.*

   b. Who are some of the major opponents of "official English" and why do they oppose such legislation?

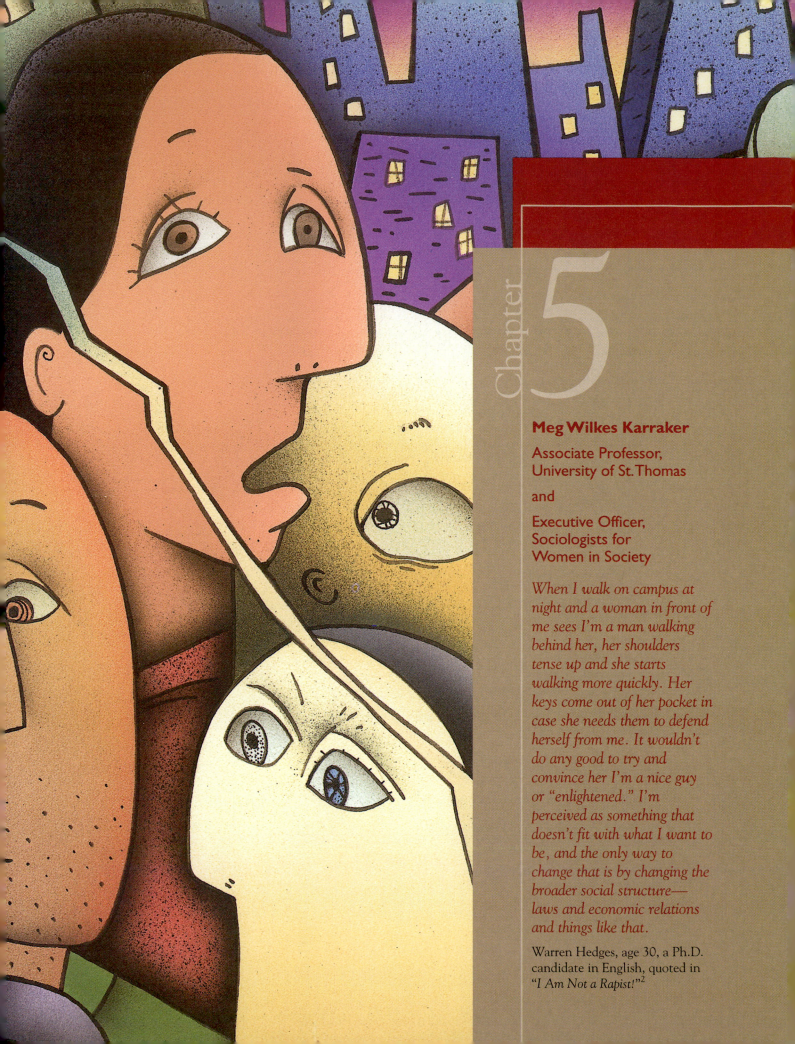

Chapter 5

Meg Wilkes Karraker

Associate Professor,
University of St. Thomas

and

Executive Officer,
Sociologists for
Women in Society

When I walk on campus at night and a woman in front of me sees I'm a man walking behind her, her shoulders tense up and she starts walking more quickly. Her keys come out of her pocket in case she needs them to defend herself from me. It wouldn't do any good to try and convince her I'm a nice guy or "enlightened." I'm perceived as something that doesn't fit with what I want to be, and the only way to change that is by changing the broader social structure—laws and economic relations and things like that.

Warren Hedges, age 30, a Ph.D. candidate in English, quoted in "*I Am Not a Rapist!*"[2]

The Gendered Order[1]

[1]Herbert W Wilkes, Jr. collaborated on the substantive, organizational, and editorial content of this chapter. Kate Gerundo identified audio-visual resources and Roz Sackoff suggested newsworthy illustrations. I thank them all for their contributions and support.

[2]John Stoltenberg, "I Am Not a Rapist!" in Steven P. Schacht and Doris W. Ewing (eds.), *Feminism and Men: Reconstructing Gender Relations*, New York University Press, New York, 1998, p. 92.

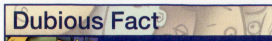

Gender at the Close of the Millennium: Still Problematic?

A special issue of the *New York Times Magazine* provides stunning testimony to the transformation of women's lives through the millennium.[3] An article in a special issue of *Scientific American* on men ("The Scientific Truth about Their Work, Play, Health, and Passion") credits a "feminist legacy" for the growth in programs that treat men who batter women. The Citadel, in Charleston, South Carolina, has graduated the first woman in its 156-year history as a state-supported military college.[4] Women's soccer came of age on July 10, 1999, as the team representing the United States beat the team from China in the Women's World Cup while a record 90,185 fans looked on in Pasadena, California.[5] In July 1999 Air Force Colonel Eileen Collins was the first woman to command a U.S. space flight, when the shuttle Columbia was used to launch the $1.5 billion Chandra X-ray Observatory.[6]

Given the dramatic evidence about shifting gender roles, and often our own experiences with gender in our personal lives, can we really continue to support the contention that gender remains a primary determinant of social problems today? This chapter begins with definitions of gender and gendered social order and considers some of the research on gender and biology; socialization and gender acquisition; and patriarchy, institutional sexism, and feminism. This chapter adds feminist theories to the three sociological theories applied throughout the book. The chapter then presents a discussion of some effects of gender in everyday life and explains how being female is associated with macrolevel social problems in three selected areas. Finally, the chapter closes with a discussion of social change and social movements, including third-wave feminism.

Social Constructions of Gender

Gender and the Gendered Social Order

gender
refers to both identity and statuses ascribed to men and women based on sociocultural distinctions

Gender refers to both identity and statuses ascribed to men and women based on sociocultural distinctions. Gender is inextricably bound with sex and sexual behavior (the subject of Chapter 15). Gender derives from roles built into social insti-

---

[3]"Women: The Shadow Story of the Millennium," Special Issue of the *New York Times Magazine*, May 16, 1999.
[4]"Citadel Graduates Its First Woman," *Star Tribune*, May 9, 1999, p. A26.
[5]"Flat-Out Fantastic," *Time*, July 19, 1999, pp. 58–67.
[6]"Third Try's a Charm," *Star Tribune*, July 23, 1999, p. A6.

tutions (economics, education, family, government, and religion), as well as relationships between women and men in everyday life. Lorber refers to this as the **gendered social order.**[7]

The social structure of an urban, capitalistic society determines how men and women participate and interact in society, as well as the kinds of social problems associated with gender inequality. The gap between women's and men's participation in some institutions narrowed considerably over the last half of the twentieth century. However, women continue to be underrepresented in higher status positions in economic, educational, government, religious, and other institutions. For example, women now constitute 46 percent of the American labor force. However, they continue to earn only 76 percent of what men earn in median weekly earnings for full-time workers. Meanwhile, to the detriment of wives' personal and marital happiness, employed wives continue to do a disproportionate share of the housework and care for children.[8]

Sexual harassment, not only in the workplace[9] but also in the schools[10] is pervasive, and a shocking proportion of women (by some estimates a quarter) report having been raped.[11] In some parts of the world, girls and women continue to be subjected to female genital mutilation (see Box 5.1), and rape continues to be a nasty accompaniment to war (see Box 5.2). In spite of changes in attitudes and behaviors surrounding gender in institutions, interactions, and everyday life, and some encouraging social policy initiatives, society remains a profoundly gendered social order.

gendered social order
the principle that gender roles are built into social institutions, as well as relationships between women and men in society

Gender as Biological and Social Construct

In 1953 Ashley Montagu published *The Natural Superiority of Women,* in which he argued that the biological, genetic, and physiological makeup of women make them not only equal but superior to men. In the fifth edition of his revolutionary book, anthropologist Montagu argues that the emotional and social qualities ascribed to and devalued in women are at the very core of a just social life.[12]

Others believe that gender differentiation and even the subordinate social status of women are rooted in biology. Wilson and other sociobiologists have claimed that biology and genetics limit the range of possible human behaviors, including those associated with gendered behaviors.[13] Fox and other sociologists who are sympathetic to sociobiology believe that beneath the wide variety of cultural differences lie common social structures and social institutions.[14] Human groups that

---

[7]Judith Lorber, *Feminist Theories and Politics,* Roxbury, Los Angeles, CA, 1998, p. 7.

[8]Arlie Russell Hochschild, *The Second Shift,* Avon, New York, 1989; Claudia Deane, "Husbands and Wives," *Washington Post,* March 25, 1998, p. A14; Karen S. Peterson, "Working Moms Like Family Life," *USA Today,* February 9, 1998, p. D1; Darlene L. Pina and Vern L. Bengtson, "The Division of Household Labor and Wives' Happiness: Ideology, Employment, and Perceptions of Support," *Journal of Marriage and the Family,* 55, 1993, pp. 901–912; J. Jill Sutor, "Marital Quality and Satisfaction with the Division of Household Labor across the Family Life Cycle," *Journal of Marriage and the Family,* 53, 1991, pp. 221–230.

[9]Elizabeth Kolbert, "Sexual Harassment at Work Is Pervasive Survey Says," *New York Times,* October 11, 1991, pp. A1, A11.

[10]U.S. Department of Education, "Sexual Harassment: It's Not Academic," www.edu.gov/offices/OCR/ocrshpam.html, July 18, 1999.

[11]Mary Koss, Christine A. Gidycz, and Nadine Wisniewski, "The Scope of Rape: Incidence and Prevalence of Sexual Aggression and Victimization in a National Sample of Higher Education Students," *Journal of Consulting Psychology,* 55, 1987, pp. 162–170.

[12]Ashley Montagu, *The Natural Superiority of Women,* 5th ed., Altamira, Thousand Oaks, CA, 1999.

[13]Edward O. Wilson, *Sociobiology: The New Synthesis,* Harvard University Press, Cambridge, MA, 1975.

[14]Robin Fox, "The Cultural Animal," *Encounter* 35, 1 (July), 1970, p. 33.

Middle class women's roles in society have radically changed from ornamental to practical. Lunch, once a leisurely social event is today more often a hurried task-oriented business activity.

Box 5.1 Making a Difference

Female Genital Mutilation

Clitoridectomy is a procedure in which the clitoris is cut from a female's body. *Infibulation* refers to an even more severe procedure in which a female's clitoris is excised and the sides of the labia are sewn together so that scar tissue forms over the opening to the vagina. Only a small hole is left open to permit urination and menstrual flow. This procedure is an important part of some female initiation rites. Female genital mutilation may function to secure cultural, gender, or religious identity, as well as to control female sexuality and reproduction. In some cultures, the practice is associated with hygiene, aesthetic, and health beliefs. In societies that practice some form of female genital mutilation, women who have not undergone the procedure are regarded as unmarriageable.

Some form of genital mutilation is experienced by almost all females in some societies (e.g., Ethiopia, Sierra Leone, and Somalia) and by the majority in others (e.g., Chad, Egypt, Kenya, and Nigeria). In 1996 the U.S. Centers for Disease Control estimated that 150,000 girls and women in families which had recently immigrated from Africa had had a clitoridectomy. Amnesty International considers female genital mutilation to be a violation of human rights. While a violation of criminal law if practiced in the United States, evidently some immigrant families send their daughters out of the United States for the procedure.[a]

Protest over the genital mutilation of girls and women has resulted in criminalization of the procedure in the United States. Furthermore, a recent provision of U.S. immigration law states that a woman fearing such a procedure could receive asylum and refugee status in the United States.[b]

Sensitized by feminist activists and health organizations by descriptions of the procedures (including the pain from lack of anesthesia and the infections, sterility, and even death that may follow), the World Health Organization and most African countries have moved to end these practices. Those seeking change have sometimes been accused, however, of ethnocentric insensitivity and colonial intrusion into the cultural practices of other societies.

In fact, in the mid-nineteenth century, clitoridectomy ("female circumcision") was an accepted treatment in the United States for masturbation, "nymphomania," or other behavior deemed by physicians (or husbands) to be inappropriate for females. Others point to the practice of hysterectomy (the second most common surgery in the United States, and one experienced by an estimated one-third of all women before the age of 60) as yet another way in which women's bodies and female sexuality are subordinated in male-centered culture.

[a]*Virginia Sapiro*, Women in American Society: An Introduction to Women's Studies, *4th ed., Mayfield, Mountain View, CA, 1999, pp. 178–79.*
[b]*Celia W. Dugger, "U.S. Grants Asylum to Woman Fleeing Genital Mutilation Rite," New York Times, February 17, 1997.*

could evolve cultural traditions that enabled them to adapt to changing environments (faster than genetics or biology) would be "naturally selected" to survive and flourish.

Fukayama believes that males and females have different reproductive strategies.[15] High-status males, he argues, are driven to have sex with many partners, thereby increasing the representation of their type in the genetic pool. Females, on the other hand, are compelled to secure alliances with males who can provide reliable security for them and their offspring.

While considering biological differences in such areas as physical strength and childbearing is important in shaping gender inequalities, sociologists view gender not as biologically determined but as socially constructed. **Anorexia nervosa** is a condition in which a person diets, and sometimes exercises, compulsively in an

anorexia nervosa
a condition in which a person diets and sometimes exercises compulsively in an effort to be thin, regardless of her measured weight

[15]Francis Fukayama, *The End of Order*, Social Market Foundation, 1999.

effort to be thin, regardless of her measured weight. **Bulimia nervosa** is a condition in which a person alternately engages in bingeing and purging, often with the aid of laxatives or other drugs and usually in secret. Such eating disorders, prevalent among American girls and women, are the result of the promotion of a cultural ideal of thinness and the social control of women.[16]

Studies of transgender individuals—people who seek surgical change from their biological sex—reveal something about the indeterminacy of gender. A study of 65 masculine-to-feminine persons demonstrates that individuals whose internalized sense of gender does not fit within a binary (feminine and masculine) framework are pressured to conform to the binary gender system, either by concealing their deviance or by transforming their presentations of self. Feminine men and masculine women are highly stigmatized social deviants, and fears for personal identity, economic security, and physical safety exert strong pressure on transgender individuals to conform to a binary system.[17]

Socialization and the Acquisition of Gender

The real differences between boys and girls, including those that may have a basis in biology, genetics, or physiology, are both more and less than believed to be.[18] Families are the first agents of gender acquisition. Studies conducted during the 1970s and 1980s—the period of early childhood for many readers of this book—indicate that parents treat female and male children differently from birth. In a typical study, parents perceived their daughters as softer and more delicate, while parents perceived sons as stronger and more alert.[19] Other studies find that parents treat daughters and sons differently, as indicated by toy selections, dressing preferences, and task assignments,[20] and that those parental differences have not changed significantly in over 15 years.[21]

Zern's study of child-rearing data from over 100 societies indicates that parental pressures toward achievement and independence in males is crosscultural.[22] However, gender role expectations vary in complex patterns among North Americans. For example, Latin cultures value virtue and modesty, often equating it with family honor, so Latin girls are strictly supervised.[23] However, studies indicate that not only do African American parents socialize daughters toward employment and independence,[24] but they encourage the development of more androgynous characteristics—blending expressive or emotional and instrumental or goal-

---

[16]Ruth A. Wallace and Alison Wolf, *Contemporary Sociological Theory: Expanding the Classical Tradition,* 5th ed., Prentice-Hall, Englewood Cliffs, NJ, 1999, pp. 380–381.

[17]Patricia Gagne and Richard Tewksbury, "Conformity Pressures and Gender Resistance among Transgendered Individuals," *Social Problems,* 45 (February), 1998, pp. 82, 86–99.

[18]Deborah Blum, "What's the Difference between Boys and Girls?" *Life,* July, 1999, p. 57.

[19]J. Rubin, F. Provenzano, and Z. Luria, "The Eye of the Beholder: Parents' Views on Sex of Newborns," *American Journal of Orthopsychiatry,* 44, 1974, pp. 512–519.

[20]Hugh Lytton and D. M. Romney, "Parents Differential Socialization of Boys and Girls: A Metaanalysis," *Psychological Bulletin,* 109, 2, 1991, pp. 267–296; Lynn K. White and David D. Brinkerhoff, "The Sexual Division of Labor: Evidence from Childhood," *Social Forces,* 60, 1981, pp. 170–181.

[21]A. Pomerleau, D. Bolduc, G. Malcuit, and L. Cossette, "Pink or Blue: Environmental Gender Stereotypes in the First Two Years of Life," *Sex Roles,* 22, 1990, pp. 359–367.

[22]D. S. Zern, "Relationships among Selected Child-Rearing Variables in a Cross-Cultural Sample of 110 Societies," *Developmental Psychology,* 20, 1984, pp. 683–690.

[23]Judith Ortiz Cofer, "The Myth of the Latin Woman: I Just Met a Girl Named Maria," in Estelle Disch (ed.), *Reconstructing Gender: A Multicultural Anthology,* 2d ed., Mayfield, Mountain View, CA, 2000, pp. 196–201.

[24]Beverly Greene, "African-American Women," in Lillian Comas-Diaz and Beverly Greene (eds.), *Women of Color: Integrating Ethnic and Gender Identities in Psychotherapy,* Guilford Press, Sluice Dock, NY, 1994, pp. 10–20; E. J. Smith, "The Black Female Adolescent: A Review of the Educational, Career, and Psychological Literature," *Psychology of Women Quarterly,* 6, 3, 1982, pp. 261–288.

oriented traits—in their daughters.[25] Asian American cultures that derive values and norms from Confucianism tend to regard women as secondary to men, yet Asian American women have strong traditions of political activism in the United States.[26] In contrast to stereotypic images of docility and subordination to men, Native American women fill leadership roles in their societies, both within tribal systems as chiefs and stretching across nationalistic concerns via organizations such as Women of All Red Nations (WARN).[27]

Gender socialization must be understood in racial, ethnic, religious, and other social contexts. However, generalizations about gender socialization are complicated by diversity within groups. For example, of the 3 percent of Americans who are of Asian background, some trace their family histories to Chinese workers who immigrated to the United States in the nineteenth century. More recently, in the last quarter of the twentieth century, Asian Americans came to the United States from culture areas in southeast Asia ranging from rural, community-oriented villages in Laos to urban, capitalist cities in Vietnam. These cultures differ not only in language but also in expectations for gender and other roles. Always, as in the case of Jewish American women who are targets of both scapegoating as women and anti-Semitism,[28] gender is but a part of the picture of identity development and differential treatment in society.

Other social scientists have studied the effects of the media on gender acquisition. Given that the average North American child spends more time watching television than engaging in any other activity,[29] the media, which includes time spent playing video games or watching movies as well as reading, is a pervasive source of gender stereotypes. Research indicates that males are considerably more likely than females to be depicted[30] and that women, when depicted, are more likely to be shown in gender stereotypical and subordinated roles.[31] Gender-typed media images are related to gender-stereotypical attitudes among children and youth.[32] Heavy television viewing is associated with an increase in gender-stereotypical preferences and sexist attitudes.[33]

[25]V. Binion, "Psychological Androgyny: A Black Female Perspective," *Sex Roles,* 22, 1990, pp. 487–507; Greene, 1994.

[26]Tracy Lai, "Asian American Women," in Estelle Disch (ed.), *Reconstructing Gender,* pp. 34–40.

[27]M. Annette Jaimes, with Theresa Halsey, "American Indian Women: At the Center of Indigenous Resistance in Contemporary North America," in Estelle Disch (ed.), *Reconstructing Gender,* pp. 217–224.

[28]Ruth Atkin and Adrienne Rich, " 'J.A.P.-Slapping': The Politics of Scapegoating," in Estelle Disch (ed.), *Reconstructing Gender,* pp. 56–59.

[29]C. Clark, "Race, Identification, and Television Violence," in G. A. Comstock, E. A. Rubenstein, and J. P. Murray, (eds.), *Television and Social Behavior: Volume 5: Television's Effects: Further Explorations,* U.S. Government Printing Office, Washington, DC, 1972.

[30]Francis Earle Barcus, *Commercial Children's Television on Weekends and Weekday Afternoons,* Action for Children's Television, Newtonville, MA, 1978; L. S. Long and R. J. Simon, "The Roles and Statuses of Women on Children's and Family Programs," *Journalism Quarterly,* 51, 1974, pp. 107–110; B. Lott, "The Devaluation of Women's Competence," *Social Forces,* 41, 1989, pp. 43–60; N. Signorelli, D. McLeod, and E. Healy, "Gender Stereotypes in MTV Commercials: The Beat Goes On," *Journal of Broadcasting and Electronic Media,* 38, 1, 1994, pp. 91–101.

[31]K. Durkin, "Television and Sex-Role Acquisition. I. Content." *British Journal of Social Psychology,* 24, 1985, pp. 101–113; D. W. Rajecki, J. A. Dame, K. J. Creek, P. J. Barrickman, et al., "Gender Casting in Television Toy Advertisements: Distributions, Message Content Analysis, and Evaluations," *Journal of Consumer Psychology,* 2, 3, 1993, pp. 307–327; S. H. Sternglanz and L. A. Serbin, "Sex-Role Stereotyping in Children's Television Programs," *Developmental Psychology,* 10, 1974, pp. 710–715.

[32]B. Eisenstock, "Sex Role Differences in Children's Identification with Counterstereotypic Televised Portrayals," *Sex Roles,* 10, 1984, pp. 417–430; P. E. McGhee and T. Frueh, "Television Viewing and the Learning of Sex-Role Stereotypes," *Sex Roles,* 6, 1980, pp. 179–188; Diana M. Zuckerman, Dorothy G. Singer, and Jerome L. Singer, "Children's Television Viewing, Race, and Sex-Role Attitudes," *Journal of Applied Social Psychology,* 10, 1980, pp. 281–294.

[33]N. J. Cobb, J. Stevens-Long, and S. Goldstein, "The Influence of Televised Models on Toy Preference in Children," *Sex Roles,* 8, 1982, pp. 1075–1080; M. Morgan, "Television and Adolescents' Sex Role Stereotypes: A Longitudinal Study," *Journal of Personality and Social Psychology,* 43, 1982, pp. 947–955; Suzanne Pingree, "The Effects of Nonsexist TV Commercials and Perceptions of Reality on Children's Attitudes about Women," *Psychology of Women Quarterly,* 2, 1978, pp. 262–277.

Patriarchy, Sexism, and Feminism

patriarchy
a system in which men are ascribed a disproportionate share of power and authority

sexism
the integrated cultural and social systems through which the disadvantages of gender are constructed, perpetuated, and enforced

feminism
advocates the equal treatment of women and men in society

Patriarchy refers to a system in which men and boys are ascribed a disproportionate share of power and authority. In patriarchal societies, girls' and women's place in society—roles and statuses—is not only circumscribed but disadvantaged.

Sexism refers to the integrated cultural and social systems through which the disadvantages of gender are constructed, perpetuated, and enforced. Sexism is integrated into the basic institutions of society—religion, government, family, education, and economics—so that every aspect of women's lives, from reproductive rights and physical well being through employment rights and material well being, is discriminatory.

Feminism addresses patriarchy and sexism by advocating the equal treatment of women and men in society. Feminism does not hold that *all* men oppress *all* women, but rather that sexism benefits a male status quo. In fact, recent work on men and feminism argues persuasively that sexism has negative effects on the quality of men's lives as well.[34]

Agents of socialization into a patriarchal system extend beyond those the individual encounters in early childhood and through the media. Family systems may serve as a microcosm of the larger society, socializing members for their respective roles as dominant and independent male or subordinate and dependent female. Families also provide everyday rehearsals for adult roles, including rights and responsibilities. Educational institutions formalize training for adult roles, while providing to men and withholding from women certain experiences and credentials needed for achieved status, including employment options.

Government institutions establish formal rules for social arrangements between men and women in civil and criminal life and penalties for violating these rules. English common law provided men with rights to use corporal punishment against their wives or their children. Until recently, in most states American women relinquished control of their property upon marriage. Yet only within the last generation have widows of farmers been liberated from the responsibility to pay inheritance taxes on the value of the farm when their husbands died.

Finally, through texts and teachings offered to the faithful as sacred and through organizations that provide a representation of the supernatural world on earth, religious institutions define the appropriate spheres of female and male, as well as women's and men's rights and responsibilities. Religions do this through teaching differently about female and male roles in sacred texts and through providing different opportunities for participation by women and men in areas of religious life.

Sociological Perspectives

Gender, along with age, is a basis for differentiation (and usually inequality) in all societies. While the social systems differ, other societies demonstrate both more and less equal treatment of men and women than we experience in American society. The consideration of inequality and its effects on the quality of life for women and men is both complex and changing.

Sociological theories differ in their consideration of the place of gender in society and the relation of gender to social problems. In this chapter we will again dis-

---

[34]See, for example, Steven P. Schacht and Doris W. Ewing (eds.), *Feminism and Men: Reconstructing Gender Relations,* New York University Press, New York, 1998.

cuss the contributions of two macrolevel theories, functionalist and conflict, as well as one microlevel theory, symbolic interactionist. In addition, we will consider the contributions of feminist theories to understanding the gender gap.

Functionalist Approaches

Functionalist theories seek to explain how institutions and other macrosocial arrangements shape common values, while achieving or failing to achieve consensus on gender. Talcott Parsons, whose body of work spanned the middle decades of the twentieth century, is considered the classic proponent of a functionalist theory of gender. Parsons argued that a gendered division of labor is functional for the survival of the social group. He suggested that families are best organized along clear gender lines, with men performing the instrumental tasks (i.e., those concerned with earning a living), while women perform the expressive tasks (i.e., those concerned with the well-being of the family, including maintaining the household, rearing the children, and supporting their husbands).[35]

Functionalist explanations of gender have been criticized for failing to address the inherently more powerful position such an arrangement gives men in society and in the family. Besides, some have argued that the theory is a justification for the family system and women's lower status, idealized in Parson's work. Further, some feminist scholars have argued that ascribing the expressive function to women puts them at a disadvantage in a patriarchal culture in which men's economic roles are more highly valued than women's nurturing roles.

Conflict Approaches

Conflict theories focus on the means through which social groups achieve their ends, including institutionalized patterns of inequality and the domination and oppression of women in a patriarchal system. Systems of gender inequality are devised and perpetuated by men for the advantage of males. According to this theory, women's generally lower status in terms of wealth, power, autonomy, and other resources originates in the larger size and greater strength of males and their strong drive for sexual gratification.[36]

For conflict theorists, the social problems surrounding gender domination and oppression arise from institutionalized practices in patriarchal societies. For conflict theorists the key to gender inequality is that women have less access to scarce and valued resources derived from participation in productive activities such as employment.[37] This causes gender stratification in such areas as women's wealth, power, prestige, and autonomy in the public sector.[38]

One criticism, leveled especially at Marxists, is the failure of conflict theory to recognize that not just class but gender can be a source of inequality. Marxist feminists have attempted to address this criticism by analyzing women's exploitation as producers of unpaid household labor. They view capitalists as

---

[35]Talcott Parsons and Robert Bales, *Family, Socialization, and Interaction Processes*, Free Press, New York, 1955.
[36]Randall Collins, *Conflict Sociology*, Academic Press, New York, 1975.
[37]Janet Salzman Chafetz, *Gender Equity: An Integrated Theory of Stability and Change*, Sage, Newbury Park, CA, 1990; Lise Vogel, *Marxism and the Oppression of Women*, Rutgers University Press, New Brunswick, NJ, 1983.
[38]Janet Saltzman Chafetz, *Sex and Advantage: A Comparative, Macro-Structural Theory of Sex Stratification*, Rowman and Allanheld, Totowa, NJ, 1984, p. 68.

exploiters of women's labor (both paid and unpaid), as well as men's paid labor.[39] From this analysis, women's status is higher in subsistence economies (where their role as economic producers is valued) than in surplus-producing economies.

Interactionist Approaches

Symbolic interactionists reveal the extent to which men and women define situations and reveal their selves through the creation and manipulation of symbols (such as language) in everyday life. Interactionists assert that gender is continually being socially constructed through social interaction.

Because symbolic interaction views human beings as creative and motivated by values,[40] the theory offers some optimism that humans can purposefully change patterns of interaction in society. For example, language can be used to symbolically validate subordinate or marginal status. The extent of gender bias in the written word has been reduced to the point where standards such as the Associated Press no longer use gender-specific occupational nouns (e.g., fire*man*) or courtesy titles (Mr., Mrs., Miss, Ms.) unless in a direct quote. The Associated Press also encourages writers to write in the plural to avoid gender specific pronouns (e.g., "they" instead of "he" or "she").[41]

Feminist Theories

Feminist theories are wide-ranging paradigms that ask questions about gender difference, inequality, and oppression from a woman-centered perspective. Feminist theory assumes that social phenomena, including social problems, are bound to gender and that women experience social life and society in different ways than do men. For feminist theorists the gendered status quo is produced by historical and sociocultural forces and is amenable to social change by humans. Feminist sociologists, therefore, see a central goal of sociology as social action to end gender inequalities. Sociologists for Women in Society (SWS) is an organization of more than 1,000 sociologists (faculty, graduate and undergraduate students, practitioners, and independent scholars) that exemplifies this goal.[42]

Among feminist theorists, Dorothy Smith's standpoint theory blends both macro- and micro-sociology to explore the systems of male domination that women experience every day (and every night) and how women think and feel about their experiences in subordinate positions.[43] Smith addresses the neglect of both women's worlds and women's perspectives. She advocates making women's lives central as subject matter for sociology and sees women's heretofore excluded point of view ("standpoint") as key to asking new research questions, challenging previously held assumptions, and creating a feminist paradigm for knowledge. True to feminist objectives, Smith's aim is to develop a sociology *for*, not just *about*, women.

---

[39]Beth Anne Shelton and Ben Agger, "Shotgun Wedding, Unhappy Marriage, No-Fault Divorce? Rethinking the Feminism-Marxism Relationship," in Paula England (ed.), *Theory on Gender*, pp. 25–26.
[40]Ruth A. Wallace and Alison Wolf, *Contemporary Sociological Theory: Expanding the Classical Tradition*, 5th ed., Prentice-Hall, Englewood Cliffs, NJ, 1999, p. 11.
[41]Norm Goldstein (ed.), *The Associated Press Stylebook and Libel Manual*, Perseus, New York, 1998.
[42]For information on this organization, e-mail *SWS@StThomas.edu* or write Sociologists for Women in Society, Mail #5058, 2115 Summit Avenue, St. Paul, MN 55105-1096.
[43]Dorothy E. Smith, *Texts, Facts, and Femininity: Exploring the Relations of Ruling*, Routledge, New York, 1990, pp. 1–2.

Even in nursery school many activities are gender-typed with boys and girls segregating into different activities.

Gender in Everyday Life

Research on conformity pressures and gender resistance demonstrates that gender is taken for granted as a natural aspect of everyday social life,[44] taken for granted, that is, until gender norms are violated or challenged.[45] As a system,

> Gender receives constant surveillance and is policed continually through social interactions that socialize new members and sanction those who violate the rules. Gender exists at both individual and group levels, where women and men "do gender" and others decode, interpret, and categorize individuals based upon presented gender cues. At the organizational level, gender exists to categorize individuals and assign them meanings and roles. At the institutional level, gender determines individuals' roles, statuses, rights, and responsibilities.[46]

Boys and Girls at Play: Gender and Childhood

Research has documented the extent to which the social life of children is highly gender-typed. Early gender-typing in the family persists into peer groups in childhood and reveals itself even in preschool experiences. Karin Martin has found a hidden curriculum—involving dressing up, permitting relaxed behaviors, requiring formal behaviors, controlling voices, instructing children about their bodies, and interacting among children—that turns children who are similar into boys and girls whose bodily practices differ by gender.[47]

---

[44]See, for example, Gagne and Tewksbury, "Conformity Pressures and Gender Resistence."

[45]Judith Lorber, *The Paradoxes of Gender,* Yale University Press, New Haven, CT, 1994.

[46]Gagne and Tewksbury, p. 81.

[47]Karin A. Martin, "Becoming a Gendered Body: Practices of Preschools," *American Sociological Review,* 63 (August), 1998, pp. 494–511.

Also, children segregate into same-sex play groups very early. Thorne's[48] research on boys and girls at play reveals how traditional gender roles and patterns of segregation are replicated and reinforced in children's games. She specifically cites the place of chasing, competitions, invasions, and pollution rituals (such as the fear of catching "cooties" from the other sex) in maintaining boundaries between boys' and girls' physical and social spaces. Thorne analyzes the powerful effects of childhood games (the one she observed was called "cootie tag"). She writes that aversion from girls or their possessions "is a powerful statement of social distance and claimed superiority. . . . Kids act out pollution beliefs in a spirit of playful teasing, but the whimsical frame of 'play' slides in and out of the serious, and some games of cooties clearly cause emotional pain."[49] Mary Berg, a mother of two, describes a game her son and his preschool friends play on the playground. In "Girl Trap," "a group of boys perch on the monkey bars like hungry raptors, peer down and select a target. . . . Once a girl is in their sights, they take aim with imaginary lasers and 'freeze' her. The 4- and 5-year old boys discuss tying her up, bashing her head, burying her in a pit."[50] The child's teacher agrees with Berg that the game is offensive and bans children from playing the game. Berg cautions, however, that in other schools every day such a game is viewed merely as "child's play" and tolerated as normal and acceptable behavior.

Gender Identity during Adolescence

The image of adolescence as an inherently stormy period has been successfully challenged by research.[51] Generally, adolescents gradually construct identities based on their circumstances and competencies, which results in increasing self-esteem for most during adolescence.[52]

Still, puberty and adolescence signal a dramatic shift in the social psychological life of females, as evidenced by changes in levels of some components of self-esteem, incidences of body-image disorders, and prevalences of risk-taking behaviors among some girls. The transition to junior high school may be particularly disturbing for some girls,[53] and a survey of 3,000 boys and girls aged 9 to 15 found that adolescent females have lower self-image, life expectations, and self-confidence than do adolescent males.[54] Another study found that adolescent girls are much more concerned about appearance, twice as likely to attempt suicide, and considerably more likely to experience high emotional stress than are boys.[55]

[48]Barrie Thorne, *Gender Play: Girls and Boys in School*, Rutgers University Press, New Brunswick, NJ, 1993.
[49]Thorne, p. 75.
[50]Mary Helen Berg, "Child's Play—Or Something More?" *Newsweek*, June 7, 1999, p. 13.
[51]Editha D. Notelmann, "Competence and Self-Esteem during Transition from Childhood to Adolescence," *Developmental Psychology*, 23, 1987, pp. 441–450; Morris Rosenberg, *Society and the Adolescent Self-Image*, rev. ed., Wesleyan University Press, Middletown, CT, 1989; Ruth C. Savin-Williams and David H. Demo, "Developmental Change and Stability in Adolescent Self-Concept," *Developmental Psychology*, 20, 1984, pp. 1100–1110.
[52]William A. Corsaro and Donna Eder, "Development and Socialization of Children and Adolescents," *Sociological Perspectives on Social Psychology*, Karen S. Cook, Gary Alan Fine, and James S. House (eds.), Allyn and Bacon, Boston, 1995.
[53]Roberta G. Simmons and Dale A. Blyth, *Moving into Adolescence: The Impact of Pubertal Change and School Context*, Aldine de Gruyter, New York, 1987.
[54]Peggy Orenstein, *Schoolgirls: Young Women, Self-Esteem, and the Confidence Gap*, Doubleday, New York, 1994.
[55]Linda Harris, Robert W. Blum, and Michael Resnick, "Teen Females in Minnesota: A Portrait of Quiet Disturbance," in *Women, Girls, and Psychotherapy: Reframing Resistance*, Carol Gilligan, Annie Rogers, and Deborah Tolman (eds.), Haworth Press, New York, 1991.

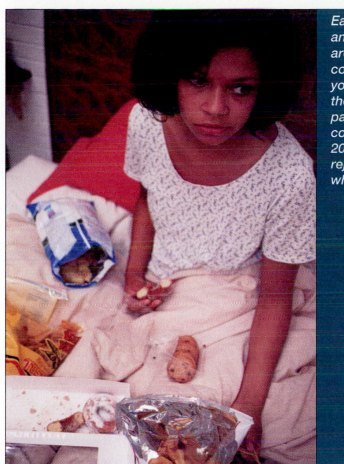

Eating disorders like anorexia and bulimia are becoming more common among young women. Even the Miss America pageant has become concerned. As of 2000 the pageant will reject candidates who are too thin.

PhotoDisc/Volume 25, Government and Social Issues

A recent survey of 1,932 adolescents 12 to 16 years old found that adolescent girls' self-reports of being overweight corresponded poorly with medical definitions of overweight. Fifty-two percent of girls (but only 25 percent of boys) who reported that they were overweight were in fact of normal weight by medical standards. White girls were significantly more likely than either black girls, black boys, or white boys to consider themselves overweight when in fact they were of normal weight. White girls were also significantly more likely to diet.[56]

Anorexia nervosa (self-starvation) and *bulimia nervosa* (binge eating, alternating with self-induced vomiting and fasting) are serious illnesses involving compulsive, life-threatening behaviors. An anorexic person considers herself fat and unattractive, regardless of her actual weight. Estimates of the number of women affected vary, but studies indicate that between 4 and 9 percent of female college students meet the clinical criteria for diagnosis.[57] Most individuals suffering from anorexia (85–95 percent) are women,[58] and 12 percent of

---

[56]Richard S. Strauss, "Self-Reported Weight Status and Dieting in a Cross-Sectional Sample of Young Adolescents," *Archives of Pediatric and Adolescent Medicine,* 153 (July), 1999, pp. 741–747.

[57]Sharlene Hesse-Biber, Margaret Marino, and Diane Watts-Roy, "A Longitudinal Study of Eating Disorders among College Women: Factors That Influence Recovery," *Gender and Society,* 13, 3 (June), 1999, pp. 385–408.

[58]American Psychiatric Association, *Diagnostic and Statistical Manual of Psychiatric Disorders,* 4th ed., 1994; Linda A. Jackson, *Physical Appearance and Gender: Sociobiological and Sociocultural Perspectives,* State University of New York Press, Albany, NY, 1992.

anorexics die.[59] African American women who are overweight seem to maintain a positive body image,[60] but Jackson notes that dieting using unhealthy methods and eating disorders are widespread and increasing among women of color.[61]

The high incidence of anorexia nervosa, bulimia nervosa, and other eating disorders is related to the high value placed on thinness and physical beauty in American society. The changing roles of women confronted during the transition from adolescence to adulthood are also a factor.[62]

Recently, some authors have suggested that adolescent males experience parallel shifts in self and identity, with different but also disturbing consequences for adjustment, health, and even mortality for some young men. Most American boys reach adulthood healthy. However, young men are more likely than young women to use alcohol and marijuana, to drive recklessly, to have several sexual partners, to contract sexually transmitted diseases, and to engage in physical violence, including homicide and suicide. (Rates of smoking are comparable between females and males, and females are also likely to contract certain sexually transmitted diseases.) Further, the death rate for males 15- to 19-years old is 112 per 100,000, more than 2.5 times the rate among females of the same age.[63]

The Second Shift and Gender Relations in Marriage

Attitudes about housework are certainly changing among women and men, especially among younger Americans. A recent study indicated that, among dual-income couples, men do about 45 percent, while women do about 55 percent, of the household chores.[64] However, men are more likely than women to over-report their contribution to housework, calling into question the true magnitude of changes in the division of household labor.[65]

Women continue to do more of the housework than do men, and the division of labor in household tasks remains sex typed. Men are more likely to make repairs, mow grass, remove trash, and shovel snow. Wives do more cleaning, cooking, shopping, laundry, and even bill paying than their husbands.[66]

Mothers are also more likely to be primarily responsible for the children. More than fathers, mothers arrange care for children, stay home with sick children, and

---

[59]Patrick F. Sullivan, "Mortality in Anorexia Nervosa," *American Journal of Psychiatry,* 152, July 1995, pp. 1073–1074.

[60]Shanette M. Harris, "Racial Differences in Predictors of College Women's Body Image Attitudes," *Women and Health,* 21, 4, 1994, pp. 89–104.

[61]Jackson, *Physical Appearance.*

[62]Richard Gordon, *Eating Disorders,* 2d ed., Blackwell, Oxford, UK, 1999.

[63]Frey Lund Sonnenstein, "Teenage American Males: Growing Up with Risks," *Scientific American* 10, 2 (Summer), 1999, pp. 86–99.

[64]Alice Lesch Kelly, "For Employed Moms, the Pinnacle of Stress Comes after Work Ends," *New York Times,* June 13, 1999, p. 18.

[65]Julie E. Press and Eleanor Townsley, "Wives' and Husbands' Housework Reporting: Gender, Class, and Social Desirability," *Gender and Society,* 12, 2 (April), 1998, pp. 188–218.

[66]Claudia Deane, "Husbands and Wives," *Washington Post,* March 25, 1998, p. A14.

Reprinted with special permission of King Features Syndicate.

coordinate transportation for children.[67] Joseph Pleck, who has studied male roles for over 25 years, reports that paternal availability (the amount of time fathers are near their children, either interacting or not) has increased to two-thirds of maternal availability.[68] Still, these changes are most evident in two-parent families, where gender equality and parental involvement are increasing.

A. R. Hochschild coined the term **second shift** to refer to the burden of housework that continues to fall primarily to women even when they work outside the home.[69] American women say they experience stress as a result of their overwhelming responsibilities for household duties along with paid employment.[70] They also say their dissatisfaction over the distribution of household labor has a negative impact on their marital satisfaction.[71] Therefore, Hochschild's recent finding that women experiencing this "time-bind" did not enthusiastically embrace workplace innovations that the corporation assumed would provide them with more creative work-family arrangements should not come as a surprise.[72]

second shift
the burden of housework which continues to fall primarily to women even when they work outside the home

Three Social Contexts of Gender

While the impact of gender on social problems throughout society is demonstrably wide-ranging, this chapter focuses on the examination of three macrolevel social problems: gender inequality in employment, poverty and economic opportunity, and sexual aggression.

[67]Deane; Kelley Hall, "Mom Has the Keys to the MiniVan: The Gendered Division of Child Transportation Work in Dual-Earner Married Families," paper presented at the Annual Meeting of the American Sociological Association, Chicago, IL, August 1999.
[68]Joseph H. Pleck, "Balancing Work and Family," *Scientific American* 10, 2 (Summer), 1999, pp. 38–43.
[69]Arlie Russell Hochschild, *The Second Shift*, Avon, New York, 1989.
[70]Karen Peterson, "Working Moms Like Family Life," *USA Today,* February 9, 1998.
[71]Darlene Pina and Vern Bengtson, "The Division of Household Labor and Wives' Happiness," *Journal of Marriage and the Family,* 55, 1993, pp. 901–912; J. Jill Suitor, "Marital Quality and Satisfaction with the Division of Household Labor across the Family Life Cycle," *Journal of Marriage and the Family,* 53, 1991, pp. 221–230.
[72]Arlie Russell Hochschild, *The Time Bind: When Work Becomes Home and Home Becomes Work,* Metropolitan, New York, 1997.

Table 5.1 Women's Labor Force Participation Rates by Race, Selected Years

Year	Race		
	Black	White	Hispanic
1980	53.1	51.2	47.4
1985	56.5	54.1	49.4
1990	57.8	57.5	53.0
1995	59.5	59.0	52.5
1998	62.8	59.4	55.6

Source: U.S. Department of Labor, Bureau of Labor Statistics, *Employment and Earnings*, January 1986, 1991, 1999, and *Handbook of Labor Statistics*, 1999.

Table 5.2 Median Weekly Earnings for Full-Time Wage and Salary Workers by Race and Sex, Second Quarter 1999

Race	Sex	
	Female	Male
White	$ 506	$ 689
Black	$ 419	$ 504
Hispanic	$ 363	$ 433
All races	$ 494	$ 665

Source: U.S. Department of Labor, Bureau of Labor Statistics, *Employment and Earnings*, Second Quarter 1999.
http://stats.bls.gov/news.release/wkyeng.t02.htm

Gender Inequality in Employment

Women constitute 46 percent of the labor force. The Women's Bureau of the United States Department of Labor reports that six out of every ten women ages 16 and over were in the labor force in 1998. Of women ages 20–54, approximately three-quarters are employed. White women's employment rates have changed little since 1994. However, African American and Hispanic women's rates have increased over the last two decades (Table 5.1). The higher a woman's level of education, the more likely she is to be employed. Furthermore, the presence of children is not a disincentive for most women to seek employment; even among women with children under age three, the majority are employed.[73]

The difference between men and women's earnings began to decline somewhat in the 1970s. Nevertheless, in 1999 women 25 years of age and older earned only 76 percent of what men earned for full-time wages and salaries. As

---

[73]U.S. Department of Labor Women's Bureau, "Facts about Working Women," www.dol.gov/dol/wb/public/wb_pubs/fact98.htm, 1999, pp. 1–2 and Tables 1 and 2.

Table 5.2 shows, white women earned more than black women, who in turn earned more than Hispanic women. However, the median weekly earnings for white women were the same as those for black men, but higher than those of Hispanic men.[74]

The apparent inroads women have made in earnings relative to men are largely due to the erosion of men's real earnings over the same period.[75] Richard Hogan and Carolyn Perrucci have calculated that the declining gender gap in earnings is due not to women's progress toward achieving earnings equity, but rather to the fact that male earnings declined more rapidly in terms of constant dollars than did female earnings.[76] Furthermore, Hogan and Perrucci argue that any small decline in the gender gap has been at the expense of a marginal increase in the racial gap in earnings.[77]

The gap that persists between women's and men's earnings is largely due to industry, firm, and occupational segregation. According to Tomaskovic-Devey, women tend to be "ghettoized" rather than spread across industries, occupations, firms, and specialties.[78] U.S. Department of Labor statistics show that 40.1 percent of employed women work in technical, sales, and administrative support occupations, and 31.4 percent are employed in managerial and professional specialty occupations. One out of every five employed women works as a primary or secondary teacher, secretary, or cashier.[79]

Women now enter college in greater numbers than men and are entering certain high-paying fields in record numbers (e.g., by 1994 the percentages of women earning degrees in medicine, dentistry, and law had risen to 37.9, 38.5, and 43.0 percent respectively).[80] Occupational disparities in pay persist, however, even at the highest levels. The **glass ceiling** refers to barriers to women's upward mobility through the highest levels in organizations. Among Fortune 500 companies, only 11.2 percent of corporate officers are women, and just 3.8 percent of the individuals holding one of the highest executive titles (chairman, vice chairman, chief executive officer, president, senior vice president, executive vice president) are women.[81] A recent study of men and women in the corporate elite in southern California suggests that women are more likely than men to emphasize social networks and such strategies as obtaining advanced educational degrees or modifying behavior to break through the glass ceiling.[82]

glass ceiling
barriers to women's upward mobility through the highest levels in organizations

Poverty and Economic Opportunity

Married-couple families with employed wives have the highest median annual income of any family type. As shown in Table 5.3, married-couple families in which the wife was not employed had a median income just 60 percent of that of married-couple

---

[74]U.S. Department of Labor, Bureau of Labor Statistics, *Employment and Earnings, 2nd Quarter,* http://stats.bls.gov/news.release/wkyeng/t02.htm, 1999.

[75]Barbara F. Reskin and Patricia A. Roos, *Job Queues, Gender Queues: Explaining Women's Inroads into Male Occupations.* Temple University Press, Philadelphia, 1990, pp. 306–307.

[76]Richard Hogan and Carolyn C. Perrucci, "Producing and Reproducing Class and Status Differences: Racial and Gender Gaps in U.S. Employment and Retirement Income," *Social Problems* 45, 4 (November), 1998, pp. 528–549.

[77]Hogan and Perrucci, p. 530.

[78]Donald Tomaskovic-Devey, *Gender and Racial Inequality at Work: The Sources and Consequences of Job Segregation,* ILR, Ithaca, NY, 1993, pp. 122–123.

[79]U.S. Department of Labor Women's Bureau, 1999.

[80]U.S. Bureau of the Census, *Statistical Abstract of the United States,* U.S. Government Printing Office, Washington, DC, 1997.

[81]"Fact Sheet: 1998 Catalyst Census of Women Corporate Officers and Top Earners," www.catalystwomen.org, June 18, 1999, p. 1.

[82]Sally Ann Davies-Netzley, "Women above the Glass Ceiling: Perceptions on Corporate Mobility and Strategies for Success," *Gender and Society,* 12, 3 (June), 1998, pp. 339–355.

Astronaut Eileen M. Collins, commander of a NASA shuttle mission.

NASA

Table 5.3 Median Annual Income of Families, by Family Type, 1997

Type of Family	Median Income
Married-couple family	$ 51,591
Wife in paid labor force	$ 60,669
Wife not in paid labor force	$ 36,027
Male householder, no wife	$ 32,960
Female householder, no husband	$ 21,023

Source: U.S. Bureau of the Census, *Money Income in the United States,* 1997.

families in which the wife was employed. Almost a quarter of all families with children were maintained by women with no husband present. Nearly a third of the families maintained by women with no husband present are living below the poverty level.[83]

Gender inequality is made more complex by the intersection of gender with class, race, and other social categories. For example, in case studies of the experience of Asian Americans in academic institutions and other organizations, Deborah Woo has examined the complicated and subtle intersections among gender, ethnicity, and institutional culture. She finds that even Chinese women (members of the "model minority") are restricted from advancing in today's labor mar-

---

[83]U.S. Department of Labor Women's Bureau, Table 6.

Sandra Hunt shares this small trailer with her daughter Carrie, twelve, and Hunt's four other children. Without a working car or job, Hunt and her five children became homeless in 1999 when the trailer park closed for the winter.

Brandy Baker/The Oakland Press/AP Wide World Photos

kets.[84] Recently the United Nations has begun to consider the linkages between gender and well-being and the implications for social policy at the international level.[85]

Social ambivalence toward women's economic independence can be viewed through the **feminization of poverty** and recent changes in welfare policies. The former refers to the observation that, increasingly, the poor in America are single, deserted, or divorced women and their children. The U.S. Bureau of the Census estimates that the poverty rate for families maintained by a female with no male present is almost six times the rate for married-couple families. While families maintained by a woman represent 18 percent of American families, they represent over half of the households living below the poverty level.

Recent changes in poverty programs have included distributing more funds directly to the states through block grants while attempting to eliminate long-term program dependence through workfare and program participation limits. However, the jobs for which program participants often qualify are at the bottom of the pay scale (often at wages too low to cover transportation, child care costs, and other basic needs).[86] These policies punish the chronically poor, including women and their dependent children, most severely. At least in their earliest forms, the newer policies neither reduced unemployment for single mothers nor raised families out of poverty.[87]

The decline in the number of welfare cases has indeed been more rapid than almost anyone would have predicted in 1996 when the *Personal Responsibility and Work Opportunity Reconciliation Act* was signed.[88] However, this decline has been in part due to the rapid growth in the American economy and the low inflation and unemployment rates. Women who remain on welfare after the implementation of these

feminization of poverty
the increasing trend for the poor in America to be single, deserted, and divorced women and their children

---

[84]Deborah Woo, *The New Face of Workplace Barriers*, Altamira, Thousand Oaks, CA, 1999.

[85]See, for example, Shahra Razavi, *Gendered Poverty and Well-Being*, Blackwell, Oxford, UK, 1999.

[86]Ellen Nakashima, "Va. Families Face Return in Poverty after Welfare," *Washington Post*, November 22, 1997, p. A1.

[87]Elaine McCrate and Joan Smith, "When Work Doesn't Work: The Failure of Current Welfare Reform," *Gender and Society* 12, 1 (February, 1998), pp. 61–80.

[88]Sheldon Danziger, "The Caseload Decline: A False Indicator?" *Is Welfare Reform Working? The Impact of Economic Growth and Policy Changes*, Congressional Briefing, March 12, 1999, p. 6.

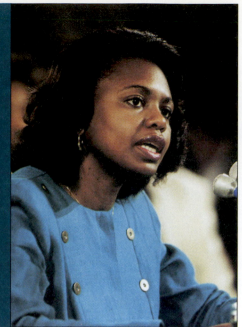

Anita Hill became famous for her accusing Supreme Court Justice Clarence Thomas of sexual harassment during his Senate Judiciary Committee confirmation hearings. The hearings emphasized the deep fault lines in American society, especially the divisions that can result when gender and racial issues conflict. Anita Hill was strongly supported as a victim by most women's organizations, and strongly criticized as an opportunist by the majority of black women. Over a decade later the division remains.

AP/Wide World

policy changes have the most personal problems (e.g., major depression, maternal or child health), the greatest labor market skill deficits, and are the least employable.[89]

Sexual Aggression: Sexual Harassment and Rape

From sexual harassment to rape, gender relations operate against a backdrop of violence fueled by men's dominance over women in the workplace, schools, and other institutional settings. **Sexual harassment** is unwelcome verbal or physical conduct of a sexual nature that affects the recipient's work conditions or contributes to a hostile environment. Although the precise incidence of sexual harassment is difficult to determine, one survey found that four out of ten women reported having encountered some form of sexual harassment and half of the men surveyed reported they had engaged in verbal or physical behavior that could be defined as sexual harassment.[90]

Studies in schools reveal higher levels of experience, with four out of five students experiencing sexual harassment at some time before high school graduation. While girls are only slightly more likely than boys to experience any sexual harassment, girls are more frequently harassed and report more negative emotional and learning effects.[91] Sexual harassment is illegal; Title IX of the Education Amendments of 1972 prohibits sex discrimination, including sexual harassment.

Victims of sexual aggression, including sexual harassment, are more likely to be female than male. **Rape**—sexual intercourse forced upon a person by either psy-

sexual harassment
unwelcome verbal or physical conduct of a sexual nature which affects the recipient's work conditions or contributes to a hostile environment

rape
sexual intercourse forced either by psychological coercion or physical force

---

[89]Danziger, p. 4.

[90]Elizabeth Kolbert, "Sexual Harassment at Work Is Pervasive Survey Suggests," *New York Times*, October 11, 1991, pp. A1, A11.

[91]American Association of University Women, *Hostile Hallways: The AAUW Survey on Sexual Harassment in America's Schools*, American Association of University Women Educational Foundation, Washington, DC, 1993.

chological coercion or physical force[92]—affects many more women than men. More than one in five women report that they have been forced to do something of a sexual nature.[93] Contrary to popular myth, rape is not a crime committed in dark alleys by sexually frustrated strangers. The vast majority of rapists—as many as three-quarters or more—are known to their victims. Almost half (47 percent) of college women who are victims of rape are raped by dates or romantic partners.[94]

Several studies have investigated the connection between gender inequality and sexual aggression. Cross-cultural research shows that the incidence of rape is highest in male-dominated, male-centered cultures. In those societies, sexual aggression is connected with male dominance and control of women.[95] A rape-supportive culture is one in which values and norms support the sexual objectification and exploitation of women. In the United States, cultural representations (e.g., advertisements, magazines, movies, music, television, and videos) depict women as sexually available and willing, even when the woman says "no." Likewise, cross-campus comparisons have shown that the highest incidences of rape are found at American colleges that emphasize male dominance and traditional masculine values (including heavy drinking). Campuses with less traditional masculine culture and where sexual aggression is treated seriously and punished severely are those with the lowest incidences of rape.[96]

Recent movements of men opposed to violence against women may indicate a cultural shift in some parts of society. Men Acting for Change (MAC) is a Duke University student organization whose members have been meeting since the early 1990s to share personal conversation, develop campus programs, and sponsor an annual conference around issues of gender, sexuality, sexual violence, and homophobia. In their meetings, the men recounted their socialization as males and the cumulative effects of that socialization as follows:

"In our culture, having a penis is supposed to be a package deal. You're supposed to have specific desires and pursue them in specific ways (aggressively and competitively). . . .[97] One student described the cumulative effect of his socialization as: "coming to the realization that I've never had a healthy relationship with a woman."[98]

During their meetings the men also expressed the growth in their sympathy for women (and men, sometimes themselves) who have been victims of sexual violence: "I probably know fifty survivors personally. . . . Being sensitive is not enough. . . . This sort of things was happening to women and it was going to change the way they reacted to all or most men. . . . And that prompted me to get involved with this program in Durham with men who batter their wives."[99]

---

[92]Bureau of Justice Statistics, "Rape Rates Showed No Change from 1996 to 1998," www.ojp.usdoj.gov/bjs/glance/rapenum, October, 1999.

[93]Mary Koss, Christine A. Gidycz, and Nadine Wisniewski, "The Scope of Rape: Incidence and Prevalence of Sexual Aggression and Victimization in a National Sample of Higher Education Students," *Journal of Consulting and Clinical Psychology*, 55, 1987, pp. 162–170; Edward O. Laumann, John H. Gagnon, Robert T. Michael, and Stuart Michaels, *The Social Organization of Sexuality: Sexual Practices in the United States*, University of Chicago Press, Chicago, IL, 1994; Robert T. Michael, John H. Gagnon, Edward O. Laumann, and Gina Kolata, *Sex in America*, Little-Brown, Boston, MA, 1994.

[94]*MS. Magazine* Campus Project on Sexual Assault, directed by psychologists Mary Koss, http://pubweb.ucdavis.edu/Documents/RPEP/Koss.num, October, 1999.

[95]Peggy Reeves Sanday, "Rape-Prone versus Rape-Free Campus Cultures," *Violence against Women*, 2, 1996, pp. 191–208.

[96]Patricia Yancey Martin and Robert A. Hummer, "Fraternities and Rape on Campus," in Alex Thio and Thomas C. Calhoun (eds.), *Readings in Deviant Behavior*, Harper Collins, New York, 1995; Michael Schwartz and Walter S. DeKeseredy, *Sexual Assault on the College Campus: The Role of Male Peer Support*, Sage, Thousand Oaks, CA, 1997.

[97]John Stoltenberg, " 'I Am Not a Rapist!' Why College Guys Are Confronting Sexual Violence," in Steven P. Schacht and Doris W. Ewing, (eds.) *Feminism and Men: Reconstructing Gender Relations*, New York University Press, New York, p. 92.

[98]Stoltenberg, p. 93.

[99]Stoltenberg, p. 95.

While Stoltenberg reports that *Playboy* magazine "ridiculed MAC as 'the pointy-headed, wet-behind-the-scrotum boys at Duke,' "[100] MAC is one of a small but growing number of men's groups in the movement against sexual violence and gender oppression. In *Feminism and Men: Reconstructing Gender Relations*, Schacht and Ewing profile a small sample of these groups, including a review of the history, principles, and membership of 10 organizations, along with contact information.[101]

Gender in the New Millennium

Both men and women are slow to question assumptions regarding the proper place of men and women in society. Institutions change even more slowly. However, not only do we see some evidence of change, albeit slow, in the quality of female and male relationships in everyday life and the relative statuses of men and women in organizations, the very nature of social movements surrounding gender is changing as well.

Social Change and Social Movements

In their various forms—revolutionary, reform, and even reactionary—social movements offer one prism through which to study social changes surrounding gender.[102] The imperialism that has bound traditional feminism is evident in discussions of issues that face women in developing societies. Well-intentioned American and Western European activists who seek to end practices such as genital mutilation (as described in Box 5.1) have been surprised by the sometimes cool reception they receive from indigenous groups, including women.

There is ample evidence of other dissent within the ranks of those who advocate equality for women. Germaine Greer, author of *The Female Eunuch*, which served as an angry polemic on sexual liberation, has recently published *The Whole Woman*. Greer charges that feminism has come to a "smug," "complacent" standstill and says, "It's time to get angry again."[103]

Gender and the Third Wave

Rebecca Walker encourages "whites to fight for minorities, heterosexuals to fight for gays and lesbians, and men to fight for feminists."[104] The direct actions of the organization have been modest (e.g., two "freedom rides" to promote voter registration and various charity events). Most recently this movement has been associated with the formation of the Third Wave Fund, an organization of affluent, influential activists which says it plans to fund grassroots activism, scholarships, and microenterprise.[105]

---

[100]Stoltenberg, pp. 89–90.

[101]Steven P. Schacht and Doris W. Ewing, "Profeminist Men's Groups Working toward Meaningful Change," in Schacht and Ewing (eds.), *Feminism and Men*, pp. 281–303.

[102]See, for example, two special issues of *Gender and Society:* Vol. 12, no. 6 (December), 1998 and Vol. 13, no. 1 (February), 1999.

[103]Elizabeth Gleick, "The Force Is with Her," *Time,* May 10, 1999.

[104]Jeri Derrig, "Author Rebecca Walker Speaks about Feminism and Racism," www.daily.iastate.edu/volumes/fall97/Oct-30-1997/fs1.html, July 11, 1999.

[105]"Third Wave," www.alt.culture.com/sentries/t/thirdxwave.html, 1999.

Box 5.2 Ongoing Issues

Rape in War

In her treatise on rape, Susan Brownmiller asserts that rape serves a critical function in society: "Rape is nothing more or less than a conscious process of intimidation by which *all men* keep *all women* in a state of fear."[a] She demonstrates the extent to which, throughout history, even during periods when warriors who rape were threatened with punishment and even death, rape has been a taken-for-granted activity during war. In other words, rape is an instrument of war.

While contending that "men who rape in war are ordinary Joes" themselves brutalized by war,[b] she provides extensive documentation of cases throughout history in which vanquished women were legitimated as victims of conquering soldiers. She also describes how accounts of rape by opposing armies have served as a tool of propaganda, as in accounts of the brutality of Nazis during World War II.[c]

Brownmiller's book also stimulates consideration of how sexual abuse provides a mechanism to corrupt the social structure of the vanquished. Rape victims are rejected and even expelled, as in the case of the women of Bangladesh who were raped during the fighting that followed Bengal's (East Pakistan's) declaration of independence from Pakistan in 1971. In a nine-month period, between 200,000 and 400,000 women were raped. Eighty percent of these women were Muslim. That culture enforces strict *purdah* (separation of women from men in all aspects of social life) and prohibits men from maintaining a relationship with a woman with whom another man has had sexual contact, even if that contact was involuntary on the woman's part.

Justification of the rape of women during war may accompany the systematic denigration and objectification of conquered peoples. While prohibited by the Uniform Code of Military Justice, first-person accounts during court martial and investigations revealed the extent to which American soldiers who raped Vietnamese girls and women referred to their victims as "gooks," "slopes," "slants," or "V.C. boom booms" (a reference to Vietnamese prostitutes).[d]

Rape has been a part of war during the twentieth century in Europe, Indonesia, Bangladesh, Rwanda, and Serbia. As a strategy of war, rape is used "to destroy national pride and honor." In Bosnia girls and women, primarily Muslims, were raped and made pregnant as part of a campaign of "ethnic cleansing" conducted by Serbs as part of the regular course of war but also as a systematic effort to erode the structure of family and community in the vanquished society. Even the Serbian Unity Congress (which disputes the claim that 20,000 Muslim women have been raped in Bosnia[e]) acknowledges that, during war, women suffer disproportionately.[f]

[a]*Susan Brownmiller, Against Our Will: Men, Women, and Rape,* Simon and Schuster, New York, 1975, p. 5.
[b]*Brownmiller, p. 25.*
[c]*Brownmiller, p. 39.*
[d]*Brownmiller, Chapter 2.*
[e]*Freda Adler, Gerhart O.W. Mueller, and William S. Laufer, Criminology, McGraw-Hill, New York, 1995.*
[f]*"Bosnia Rape," http://suc.suc.org/politics/rape/. 1999.*

Riot Grrls and Postmodern Feminism

According to postmodernists, technological progress and democratization movements have failed to deliver on promises of material well-being and real political participation. They hold that the old social theories no longer explain continually changing, often alienating, social organization. Postmodernists argue that contemporary society is, instead, increasingly dominated by mass-media images and rapid technological innovations.

In the early 1990s, the media was charged with attempting to exploit and trivialize riot grrrl as a cultural trend to be associated with popular music and fashion and not as a social movement concerned with radical politics and change. (Similar attempts to marginalize countercultural movements are common.) Riot grrrls instituted a moratorium on cooperation with mainstream journalists and reports of riot grrrl have all but disappeared from the popular media.[106]

Some scholars continue to investigate the place of riot grrrl in youth culture, feminism, and female development. Angela McRobbie is optimistic that girl-only subcultures, with their first commitment to the adolescent female group, signal a rejection of the ageism, homophobia, misogyny, racism, and violence that she says characterize the everyday lives of adolescent girls.[107] Others are less sanguine, asserting that the riot grrrl movement, like earlier feminist movements, is a white, middle-to-upper-middle-class movement which, while affirming homosocial bonding, has downplayed any lesbian connotations. In particular, some have criticized riot grrrls for failing to address the socioeconomic sources of their dissatisfaction, resulting in a sort of "dead-end elitism" of the already privileged.

Mary Celeste Kearney acknowledges that riot grrrls do have more education and access to camcorders, computers, and other means of postmodern cultural production, as well as the luxury of a longer period of adolescence before adulthood than their poor and working-class peers.[108] However, Kearney counters that much of the criticism of riot grrrls reflects a sexist bias, because male withdrawal is often viewed as consistent with male autonomy and independence, while female separatism is seen as elitism: "Riot grrrls are criticized for precisely those behaviors that run counter to the dominant construction of femininity, even while the traits to which they are adhering (independence, assertiveness, action, etc.) are highly privileged in our society."[109]

Movements like riot grrrl have not attracted large numbers of adolescent girls. Still, they articulate an ideology that emphasizes the vulnerability and power of female adolescence. Thus, they may have the potential not only to question the ageism, materialism, and sexism of postmodern society but also to "raise feminist consciousness on a large scale."[110] The next century will likely see an even greater variety of feminisms (e.g., ecofeminism) emerge, as well as greater attention to gender gaps around the world.[111]

Toward the Future

The last half of the twentieth century saw institutional changes in response to a variety of social problems around gender. The Equal Employment Opportunity Commission and affirmative action programs continue to draw attention to the causes of discrimination and inequity in the workplace. Title IX, the Education Amendment of 1972, has been credited with dramatically increasing athletic and

---

[106]Kearney, p. 162.
[107]Angela McRobbie, "Settling Accounts with Subcultures: A Feminist Critique," in S. Frith and A. Goodwin (eds.), *On Record: Rock, Pop, and the Written Word*, Pantheon, New York, 1990.
[108]Kearney, pp. 154–163.
[109]Kearney, p. 173.
[110]Kearney, p. 174.
[111]Donna Guy Mrinalini, and Angela Woollacott (eds.), *Feminisms and Internationalisms*, Blackwell, Oxford, UK, 1999.

other educational opportunities for girls and women. Both major political parties have seen credible candidates for President and the proportion of women in elected office continues to grow, albeit most noticeably at the local and state levels. More religious organizations now accept women into the ranks of the clergy and even those which do not (e.g., the Catholic church) continue to feel pressure to increase the participation of women at the highest levels. While the continuing extent of inequity should not be ignored, pressures for change are likely to continue.

On the microsocial level, the increasing participation of women in the labor force is likely to greatly affect the nature of gender relations in the public and the private sphere. More girls will expect to work when they become adults, although the path to satisfaction and respect in occupational activities is likely to continue to be plagued by a lack of consensus as men, women, and their employers determine how to construct an equitable, respectful labor force. If the past is an indication, the demand and opportunities for women laborers can be expected to reflect the larger employment situation. During times of low unemployment, such as in the late twentieth century, women can expect to find greater encouragement and support for labor-force involvement. This may translate into lower tolerance for sexual harassment and other discrimination on the job. During times of higher unemployment, women and other disenfranchised groups may find a less hospitable environment.

Few factors change the dynamics of intimate relationships more than a woman's employment. As women's contribution to their families' economic resources increases, so will their relative power in all areas of family life, from decisions about the timing of the birth of children to decisions about relocating for a job to questions about who will care for aging parents. The increasingly diverse options for intimacy, including delayed age at first marriage and gay and lesbian families, suggest that the impact of gender on such relationships will be increasingly diverse. Finally, sociologists and others studying the effects of gender in everyday life will need to be increasingly sensitive to the overlaying of age, ethnicity, race, religion, and other sources of cultural identification.

Summary

This chapter shows that gender continues to be a primary determinant of quality of everyday life, inequality in modern society, and problems in social arrangements. **Gender** derives from roles built into social institutions as well as relationships between women and men in everyday life, i.e., a **gendered social order.**

- While some argue that women are naturally superior and others believe the subordinate status of women is rooted in biology, studies reveal that gender is indeterminate and socially constructed: parents treat daughters and sons differently, different ethnic groups treat boys and girls differently, and the media serves as a pervasive source of gender stereotypes.

- **Feminism** addresses **patriarchy** and **sexism** by advocating that women and men in society be treated equally.

- Functionalist theory assumes that a gendered division of labor, in which men perform the instrumental tasks and women perform the expressive tasks, is functional for society.

- Symbolic interactionists assert that gender is continually being socially constructed through social interaction, as in the use of language to symbolically validate women's subordinate status.
- **Feminist theories** ask questions about gender difference, inequality, and oppression from a women-centered perspective. Feminist sociologists see the goal of sociology as social action to end gender inequalities.
- Gender is taken for granted as a natural aspect of everyday life, from childhood peer settings to adolescent self-images to household roles in marriages.
- Gender inequality persists in employment, with women earning only 76 percent of what men earn. Even among the corporate elite, women hit a **glass ceiling** that inhibits their movement into the highest levels in organizations.
- **Feminization of poverty** refers to the observation that the poor in America are increasingly single, deserted, or divorced women and their children and that over half of the households living below the poverty level are composed of women and their dependent children.
- **Sexual harassment** in schools and in the workplace and **rape** are most common where the culture emphasizes male dominance and control of women.
- During the first and second waves of feminism, women achieved suffrage with the passage of the Nineteenth Amendment and entered into reform politics and increasing assimilation of women into certain institutions.
- **Third-wave feminism** represents a reaction to criticisms of and an alternative to second-wave feminism. The next millennium will be characterized by the emergence of a variety of different feminisms.

☞ Key Review Terms

anorexia nervosa	gender	riot grrrl
bulimia nervosa	gendered social order	second shift
clitoridectomy	glass ceiling	sexism
feminism	infibulation	sexual harassment
feminist theories	patriarchy	third-wave feminism
feminization of poverty	rape	

? Questions for Discussion

1. In what ways are women today better off than women of their mother's generation? In what ways are they worse off? In what ways are men better off than men of their father's generation? In what ways are they worse off?

2. How do clitoridectomy, infibulation, and other forms of genital mutilation institutionalize women's place in the societies where these practices are followed?

3. In the 1970s Joan Acker characterized gender in terms of "cross-cutting cleavages." In what ways does gender continue to cut across class, race, and other statuses in American society?

4. If American culture is so "rape supportive," then why do not even more men rape?

5. Of the theoretical perspectives described in this chapter, which best address:
    a. The persistence of female/male bonds?
    b. Female hostility to other women?
    c. Satisfaction with one's gender in everyday life?
    d. The diversity of social arrangements around gender?

6. In what ways is patriarchy compatible with a market-oriented social structure? Would other gender arrangements be compatible with an urban, market-oriented society?

7. Outline the gender-specific hazards of growing up female. Of growing up male. Can you think of other hazards that were not raised in this chapter?

8. How do social forces during adolescence shape females and males in different ways?

9. Offer explanations for the persistence of occupational sex-typing and gender segregation into the twenty-first century. Of what significance is sex-typing and segregation in the workplace for the quality of men's and women's lives? Under what social structural conditions do you anticipate changes in the significance of gender in the workplace?

11. According to the U.S. Bureau of the Census, approximately half of all men and three-quarters of all women 65 years old and older have annual incomes below $15,000. Also, approximately three-quarters of men and one-quarter of women 75 years old and older are married (i.e., not single, widowed, or divorced). What do these generalizations demonstrate about the impact of gender in later life?

12. What kinds of social problems involving gender do you anticipate for the next millennium?

☛Suggested Resources

Publications

Abbott, Franklin (ed.), *Boyhood: Growing Up Male: A Multicultural Anthology*, University of Wisconsin Press, Madison, WI, 1998.

Atkin, Ruth, and Adrienne Rich. " 'J.A.P.-Slapping: The Politics of Scapegoating," in Estelle Disch (ed.), *Reconstructing Gender: A Multicultural Anthology*, 2d ed., Mayfield, Mountain View, CA, pp. 56–69.

Benedict, Jeffrey R., *Athletes and Acquaintance Rape*, Sage, Thousand Oaks, CA, 1998.

Blee, Kathleen M. (ed.), *No Middle Ground: Women and Radical Protest*, New York University Press, New York, 1998.

Bowker, Lee H. (ed.), *Masculinities and Violence*, Sage, Thousand Oaks, CA, 1998.

Brandwein, Ruth A. (ed.), *Battered Women, Children, and Welfare Reform: The Ties That Bind*, Sage, Thousand Oaks, CA, 1998.

Cofer, Judith Ortiz, "The Myth of the Latin Woman: I Just Met a Girl Named Maria," in Estelle Disch (ed.), *Reconstructing Gender: A Multicultural Anthology*, 2d ed., Mayfield, Mountain View, CA, pp. 196–201.

Dobash, Rebecca Emerson, and Russell P. Dobash (eds.), *Rethinking Violence against Women*, Sage, Thousand Oaks, CA, 1998.

Gordon, Richard, *Eating Disorders*, 2d ed., Blackwell, Oxford, UK, 1999.

Jaimes, M. Annette, with Theresa Halsey, "American Indian Women: At the Center of the Indigenous Resistance in Contemporary North America," in Estelle Disch (ed.), *Reconstructing Gender: A Multicultural Anthology*, 2d ed., Mayfield, Mountain View, CA, pp. 217–224.

Kimmel, Michael, "Saving the Males: Negotiating Gender and Difference at VMI and the Citadel," *Gender and Society*, forthcoming.

Lai, Tracy: "Asian American Women: Not for Sale," in Estelle Disch (ed.), *Reconstructing Gender: A Multicultural Anthology*, 2d ed., Mayfield, Mountain View, CA, pp. 34–41.

Ollenburger, Jane C., and Helen A. Moore, *A Sociology of Women: Intersections of Patriarchy, Capitalism, and Colonization*, 2d ed., Prentice-Hall, Upper Saddle River, NJ, 1998.

O'Toole, Laura L., and Jessica Schiffman (eds.), *Gender Violence: Interdisciplinary Perspectives*, New York University Press, New York, 1997.

Pollach, William, *Real Boys: Rescuing Our Sons from the Myths of Boyhood*, Henry Holt, New York, 1998.

Ray, Raka, *Fields of Protest: Women's Movements in India*, University of Minnesota Press, Minneapolis, 1999.

Razavi, Shahra, *Gendered Poverty and Well-Being*, Blackwell, Oxford, UK, 1999.

Ronai, Carol Rambo, Joe R. Feagin, and Barbara Z. Zsembik (eds.), *Everyday Sexism in the Third Millennium*, Routledge, New York, 1997.

Russell, Diana E.H., *Dangerous Relationships: Pornography, Misogyny, and Rape*, Sage, Thousand Oaks, CA, 1998.

Schacht, Steven P., and Doris W. Ewing (eds.), *Feminism and Men: Reconstructing Gender Relations*, New York University Press, New York, 1998.

Schander, Sara, *Ophelia Speaks: Adolescent Girls Write about Their Search for Self*, Harper, New York, 1999.

Sinha, Mrinalini, Donna Guy, and Angela Woollacott (eds.), *Feminisms and Internationalism*, Blackwell, Oxford, UK, 1999.

West, Traci C., *Wounds to the Spirit: Black Women, Violence, and Resistance Ethics*, New York University Press, New York, 1999.

Woo, Deborah: *The New Face of Workplace Barriers*, Altamira, Thousand Oaks, CA, 1999.

Audio-Visual Materials

Belly: Overcoming Bulimia, 1996, 22 minutes, Filmakers' Library. Chronicles the journey of one woman from bulimia to self-acceptance.

Beyond Beijing, 1996, 42 minutes, Women Make Movies. A personal document of the 1995 United Nations Fourth World Conference on Women.

Calling the Ghosts: A Story about Rape, War and Women, 1996, 63 minutes, Women Make Movies. Emmy award-winning documentary about female survivors in war-time Bosnia.

Date Rape, 1994, 52 minutes, Films for the Humanities and Sciences. Documentary-drama which follows professionals through the emotional and legal procedures involved in prosecuting a dramatized case of an acquaintance rape.

The Double Shift, 1996, 47 minutes, Films for the Humanities & Sciences. Uses cases and expert testimony, including an interview with a "househusband," to reveal the consequences of the "second shift."

Female Circumcision: Human Rites, 1998, 40 minutes, Films for the Humanities & Sciences. Documents the ritual and roots of female genital mutilation. Includes interviews with activists, medical personnel, and victims and discusses movements to ban the practice. (Note: Includes graphic scenes of female genital mutilation.)

Fifty Years of Silence, 1994, 52 minutes, First Run/Icarus Films. Award-winning film about an Australian woman who was taken prisoner by the Japanese during World War II and forced to submit to rape and beating in a military brothel.

Honorable Murder, 1998, 52 minutes, Films for the Humanities & Sciences. Scholars, judges, and clergy, as well as victims and their family members, discuss Middle Eastern cultural traditions that allow men to murder their female relatives who have eloped, been raped, or have otherwise dishonored the family.

I, Doll: The Unauthorized Biography of America's 11 1/2" Sweetheart, 1996, 57 Minutes, Women Make Movies. Links the history of Mattel's *Barbie* with culture, critics, and fans.

In the Name of God: Helping Circumcised Women, 1997, 29 minutes, Filmakers Library. Examines the traditional persistence of female genital mutilation and efforts to assist victims and change practices.

The Men's Movement, 1998, 30 minutes, Films for the Humanities & Sciences. Profiles the new "men's movement," including why men become involved and the implications for men and women in the twenty-first century.

Philomela Speaks, 1996, 19 minutes, Women Make Movies. One woman's story of acquaintance rape, examined through home movies, fairy tales, and feminist analysis to reveal gender and power relationships.

Postcards from the Future, 1996, 46 minutes, Films for the Humanities & Sciences. Features women throughout the world (including Algeria, Brazil, Chechnya, and New Guinea) who are gaining power and changing societies.

Rape: A Crime of War, 1996, 59 minutes, National Film Board of Canada. Relates the history and chronicles the first-ever international trial for rape as a war crime.

Ventre Livre: Freeing the Womb, 1995, 45 minutes, Women Make Movies. Using interviews, examines the poor state of health care for women in Brazil.

Websites

www.amnesty.org/ailb/intcam/femgen/fgm1.htm, *Amnesty International's* informational page on female genital mutilation.

www.cdds.vt.edu/feminism/, University of Vermont's website with links to feminist theory.

www.cs.utk.edu/~bartley/saInfoPage.html, Sexual assault information links.

www.dol.gov/dol/wb/welcome.htm, Homepage of the Women's Bureau of the U.S. Department of Labor.

www.embassy.org/wmn4wmn/, Homepage of the humanitarian organization Women for Women.

www.feminist.org, Homepage of the Feminist Majority Foundation.

www.hrw.org/about/projects/women.html, Homepage of the Women's Rights Division of Human Rights Watch.

www.law_lib.utoronto.ca/diana/sites.htm, Homepage of the University of Toronto's Women's Rights Database Group.

www.naral.org, Homepage of the National Abortion Rights Action League.

www.nau.edu/~wst/access/hotlist/fgmhot.html, Northern Arizona University's Cline Library information page on female genital mutilation.

www.now.org, Homepage of the National Organization for Women.

www.socrates.berkeley.edu/~annaleen/riot/online.html, Links for riot grrrls.

www.un.org/Conferences/Women/PubInfo/Status/Home.htm, Homepage of the United Nations and the Status of Women.

Internet Connection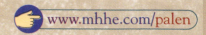

1. The U.S. Bureau of the Census (*www.census.gov/*), The U.S. Bureau of Labor Statistics (*www.stats.bls.gov/*), and FEDSTATS—Maintained by the Federal Interagency Council on Statistical Policy—(*www.fedstats.gov/*) are excellent sources of "official" information on women in the work place. The *Statistical Abstract of the United States* is available online, although it is somewhat awkward to use. To navigate to it from the Census home page, click on "Publications." Then, go to "General and Reference." At the bottom of the page you will find *The Statistical Abstract of the United States.* Click on "Document" and you will be taken to the Abstract. The page will contain both a table of contents and an index.

   a. See if you can find the table that compares men's and women's employment by occupation. (For example, it was Table 675 in the 1999 Statistical Abstract.) As you can see, women are underrepresented in most of the high-paying leadership positions.

2. The underrepresentation of women in powerful, high-paying jobs is evidence of the "glass ceiling." There are several excellent sites that address this subject. Begin by visiting the site of The Glass Ceiling Commission (Archived at Cornell University's Catherwood Library)—(*www.ilr.cornell.edu/library/e_archive/glassceiling/default.html*).

   a. What specific recommendations did the Glass Ceiling Commission make to foster upward mobility for women and minorities?

   Another excellent resource on the glass ceiling, and a forum for debate on the subject, is the Glass Ceiling website (*www.theglassceiling.com/Default.htm*). Finally, you may want to visit the site of the National Organization for Women (NOW) (*www.now.org/*) for information on a broad range of issues involving the movement for women's equality.

Morgan Luta came into the world two months ago, delivered on the dirt floor of a tin shack in a scabrous Nairobi, Kenya, slum. The fourth child of Rose, 28, and Benson, 32, arrived bawling and healthy. But with little likelihood of receiving medical care and nourishing food, the infant has a 1-in-10 chance of dying before his fifth birthday. The Lutas know little about birth control, making more unwanted pregnancies virtually inevitable, a prospect the couple dreads. Says Rose, as she breastfeeds her son: "This one was a mistake."

Michael Satchell, "Global Population: 6 Billion and Counting," *U.S. News & World Report*, October 11, 1999, p. 46.

The Question of People

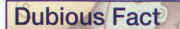
Population Growth

We rarely realize how much of our lives are tied to demographic (population) factors. Demography is not destiny, but it does have a major impact on individuals' (and nations') opportunities and behavior. As the old wisdom has it, the two most important factors determining our lives are our choice of parents and the year in which we were born. Some infants are fortunate enough to be born to well-off parents and grow up in an era of prosperity and peace. Others are born to poor parents and live in times of war and depression. Whether or not you get a good job when graduating depends not only on how many jobs are available but also on how many people are graduating that year. Demographic factors also are of great importance at the national level. We may be part of a "global economy" and live in a "global village," but some villages are far better off than others. Currently, the world's yearly population increase of 1.4 percent adds 84 million persons to the globe each year, or 230,000 new bodies every day.[1] *Ninety-seven percent of this growth is occurring in poorer developing countries.* Most of the world's growth is occurring in countries where the average wage is well below $2 a day.

Whether in Boston (as is the case here) or in Bangkok, increasing the number of people often increases the severity of other problems. More people means more traffic congestion, which means more wasted time, more wasted resources, and more pollution.

© Michael A. Dwyer/Stock, Boston

---

[1]Population Reference Bureau, *Population Today*, 28, 3, April 2000, p. 7.

Problems associated with the population explosion go well beyond simply providing enough food and jobs for everyone. Rapid population growth is also a major contributor to problems such as depletion of the rain forest, rising ozone levels, and global warming. More people mean more pollution and greater environmental destruction. We begin this chapter by examining world population growth and its consequences, and then discuss how population issues affect the United States, especially immigration.

Too Many People?

The present world population situation can be illustrated by the tale of the lily pads in the pond. If you start with one lily pad and the number doubles each day, you will have two pads on the second day, four on the third, and so on. If it takes 30 days before the pond is half full of lily pads, how long until the pond is totally full? The answer, of course, is one more day.

As far as world population is concerned, we are well on the way to filling up the pond. It took several million years from the time the first hominids walked on earth up until the Roman-Christian era before the world's population reached 250 million. Nineteen hundred years later at the beginning of the twentieth century the population of the globe had reached 1.6 billion. By 1960 this had increased to 3 billion, and we now number 6 billion. India alone each year adds almost as many people as in the entire population of Australia. By 2015 India will have a larger population than that of all the developed countries combined, including Russia.

The current estimated doubling time for the world population is 49 years.[2] An alarmist way to dramatize the magnitude of this increase is to point out that, at the current growth rate, it would take *only 250 years* to give the world a population of *over 200 billion persons*. The importance of this figure is that it is not going to happen. *Population growth is going to slow; it has to because our resources have limits.* The real question is *when and how* will it slow? Will this slowing be brought about by design (through worldwide control over fertility and hence lower birthrates), or by disaster (through widespread starvation and hence higher death rates)? In the past, population control always came through higher death rates.

The good news is that humans are increasingly taking control of their population growth. According to United Nations estimates, roughly half of all married women worldwide use contraceptives; this is double the proportion using them as recently as 1980. Another 120 million women would use modern family planning methods if accurate information and affordable services were available.[3] Because of the size of world population (6 billion), however, even with decreasing birthrates, we still will produce billions of new people. No one reading this book will ever live in a world that is not growing. The only question is whether during your lifetime the population will grow to 9 billion, or whether it will double to 12 billion. The most optimistic hope is that during the early decades of the twenty-first century growth rates in less-developed nations can be brought to where they approach those of developed nations today. Even a little difference in rates makes a huge difference in numbers of people. For example, based on slightly different fertility estimates, the United Nations projections show world population between

[2]*1999 World Population Data Sheet*, Population Reference Bureau, Washington, DC, 1999.
[3]International Conference on Population and Development, *Draft Programme of Action*, United Nations Fund for Population Activities, New York, 1994, p. 37.

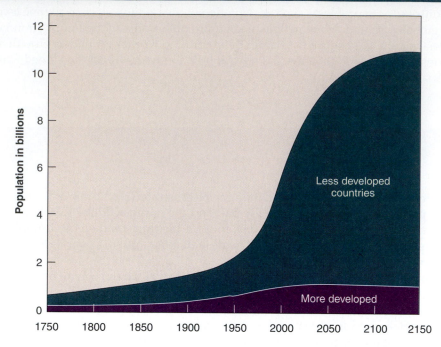

Figure 6.1 World Population Growth, 1750–2150

Less developed countries

More developed

Source: Before 1950—PRB estimates; 1950–2150—adapted from UN, *World Population Prospects: The 1994 Revision* (New York: UN, 1994): and long-range projections from the UN and the World Bank.

7.2 billion and 7.9 billion persons in just 20 years. These numbers may seem similar, but just the difference between the two projections equals the entire current population of Africa.

Sociological Perspectives

Functionalist Approaches

From a functionalist perspective, population growth is positive economically insofar as it expands markets and stimulates the demand for substitute materials and new technologies. Population growth is dysfunctional insofar as it increases the number of persons living at the subsistence level and causes serious environmental damage. The continued destruction of rain forests, the explosion in the size of Third World cities, the conversion of prime agricultural land to housing and other purposes, acid rain, and the destruction of the ozone layer are all seriously aggravated by population growth.

Functionalists see an immediate need to restore the balance between resources and population. Without population control, they see worldwide increases in hunger, disease, desperation, disorder, and despair. Thus, they advocate and support international birth control programs to bring down high birthrates.

Conflict Approaches

Conflict theorists tend to see population problems more as issues of resource control than of growth per se. Focusing more on the problem of resource distribution rather than simply on population growth, they note that food shortages in developing countries happen not because the world food supply is inadequate, but because those in power hinder and restrict its distribution. The problem is thus not low production but overconsumption by the wealthy in industrialized nations while poor nations and peoples struggle to survive. Some conflict theorists see the need for a mandated fair distribution of food and other resources.

Conflict approaches tend to frame immigration policies as a struggle between the rich "haves" and the poor "have-nots." Rich nations such as the United States strictly limit the number of poor people seeking a better life entering their countries. Similarly, conflict theory frames problems such as undocumented immigration within the context of the government policies practiced by rich nations. North American businesses, for example, exploit marginal immigrant workers, and U.S. citizens benefit from immigrant sweatshop exploitation in lower prices for clothing, shoes, and even cars.

Interactionist Approaches

Interactionist theorists are concerned with the ways that societies, especially developing nations, learn how to control their ability to reproduce. Throughout human existence, fertility has been paramount for group survival—a blessing as well as a sign of virility and prosperity. However, high death rates kept population size relatively stable. Only during the last half-century have death rates been dramatically reduced (causing populations to explode) in many developing countries, largely due to sanitary and public health measures imposed by governments. Interactionists might study whether a nation perceives or defines itself as having a population program, and the degree of it's need for action.

Looking to change individual fertility patterns, interactionists study how to change attitudes and behavior in a short time period. Among other policies, it has become evident that providing educational and nonhome employment opportunities for women does much to change traditional fertility values and practices.

The Demographic Transition

For most of the millions of years of human existence, the problem humans faced was not growth but survival. The earth had a small population because the high birthrates of humans were matched by equally high death rates. Malnutrition, famine, disease, plague, and war all kept death rates high and population increases minimal. How, then, did we get to the present situation?

World population was roughly 750 million in the year 1750. Then, western Europe, and countries such as the United States that were settled by Europeans, began experiencing a period of explosive growth (see Figure 6.1). This population surge was the result not of birthrates increasing but of death rates declining. During the past 250 years, developed nations experienced a population shift: from population stability based on high birthrates and death rates, through a period of rapid population growth due to death rates declining faster than birthrates, to a new period of stability based on low birthrates and death rates. This transformation is referred to as the **demographic transition.** The important thing to remember about the demographic transition in western Europe and its European-populated colonies is that growth occurred not because birthrates went up (they were already high), but because *death rates came down.*

A number of factors combined to produce the western European demographic transition declines in mortality. To put it in somewhat oversimplified form, roughly one-third of the decline in deaths was the result of increased agricultural productivity and stable government; another third resulted from the combination of environmental sanitation and personal hygiene, and the remaining third took place most recently as the result of modern medicine. The consequence of declining death rates was an explosive growth in population. By 1830 there were 1 billion living people. Much of the increased population migrated to the cities that were just beginning to undergo the technological and social transformation we call the Industrial Revolution. The demographic transition and the Industrial Revolution are closely linked, for without population growth there would not have been enough workers to run the new factories. Between 1830 and 1930 the world population doubled to 2 billion. Since then world population has increased to 6 billion.

The Western Population Boom

Declining European death rates during the eighteenth and nineteenth centuries gave Europe population increases that were double the world's rate. This occurred despite a net out-migration to America of at least 30 million people. Birthrates, by contrast, stayed high until the latter part of the nineteenth century. As middle-class parents in the new urban-industrial societies discovered that their children would survive, parents devoted more resources to each child. Middle-class parents also discovered that they could not profit from their children's labor. In economic terms, children in urban societies changed from being economic assets to being economic costs. Today the Department of Agriculture estimates the cost of rearing a child to age 18 is $183,000 for a family making the median income. (The upper-middle class figure is $218,000, and neither figure includes college education.)

By the 1930s birth and death rates were converging in developed urban industrial countries and the Western demographic transition was apparently completed. Thus, the "baby boom" (1946–1964) that occurred in the developed countries after World War II came as a considerable surprise to demographers. The American baby boom of 75 million births resulted in 10 percent more people born than had been predicted.[4] Contrary to popular belief, the baby boom was *not* caused by a return to large families but rather by a greater proportion of people marrying, along with an increase in families of two to four children. Moreover, the baby boom was the result of planned births. It is important to remember that planned fertility does not automatically have to mean lower fertility.

---

[4]Charles F Westoff, "The Populations of the Developed Countries," *Scientific American,* 231, 3, September 1974, p. 109.

Box 6.1 Making a Difference

Malthus's Theory of Population

The first to raise the specter of population growth as a problem was T. Robert Malthus (1766–1834). Malthus's main argument in his *Essay on the Principle of Population*, published in 1798, was that humans are part of the biological world and subject to the laws of nature just like other species. He set forth two basic postulates: (1) "food is necessary to the existence of man," and (2) "the passion between the sexes is necessary and will remain nearly in its present state."[a] Thus, unless there is some check, the size of a population will put pressure on the food supply, with the result that the masses of people will remain at a bare subsistence level of existence.

Malthus argued that increases in the food supply provide only temporary relief, for (temporarily) increasing food supplies above subsistence levels leads to decreasing death rates, more marriages, and higher infant survival rates, which again result in pressure on the food supply. "Population, when unchecked, increases in a geometrical ratio. Subsistence increases only in an arithmetical ratio."[b]

According to Malthus, there are only two ways in which population growth can be controlled: *preventive checks* and *positive checks*. Today, we would call preventive checks things that affect fertility and positive checks things that affect mortality. Malthus's preventive checks were "vice" and "moral restraint." By vice he meant things such as birth control, abortion, and infanticide. By moral restraint, he meant the postponement of marriage with no sexual activity.

Positive checks, which Malthus lumped under the general heading of "misery," included wars, famines, and disease, all of which increase mortality and thus maintain the balance between food and population. All was not totally dismal, however, for, in Malthus's words, "Evil exists in the world not to create despair but activity."[c] Thus, the tension between population and subsistence, which brought about vice and misery, also drove people, whom he saw as naturally indolent, to work harder. Malthus also condemned birth control, as much for economic as religious reasons. As he stated, "I should always particularly reprobate any artificial and unnatural modes of checking population, both on account of the immorality and their tendency to remove a necessary stimulus to industry."[d]

Marx and Engels denounced Malthus's work as "a blasphemy against man and nature," arguing that the status of the poor was due not to intemperate population growth but to class exploitation. Certainly, he underestimated the availability of new lands and the great advances in agricultural productivity. Malthus also slighted the importance of social change. By not acknowledging contraception—which was at that time in a prescientific state—he set up a direct relationship between passion and childbearing. Today, contraceptive knowledge inserts an additional variable of choice between sex and procreation.

[a]Thomas Robert Malthus, Population: The First Essay, *University of Michigan Press, Ann Arbor, 1959, p. 4.*
[b]*Ibid., p. 5.*
[c]*Ibid., p. 138.*

Growth in Developing Countries

All developed countries have low or no internal population growth. Developing countries, on the other hand, account for well over 9 out of 10 new people being added to the world's population. The poorer the country, the faster the population growth. All rich countries have small families, and the current population doubling time for developed countries is 583 years.[5] All poor countries have large numbers of children, and the average doubling time for developing countries (excluding China) is 40 years. Almost all of the 3 billion people projected to be added

---

[5]*1999 World Population Data Sheet*, Population Reference Bureau, Washington, DC, 1999.

Famines and starvation aren't a thing of the past. They exist in the world today. This near-dead mother and her ten-year-old daughter finally reached a Doctors Without Borders compound in southern Sudan. The Sudan relief operation of 1998 was the largest in the world to date, but tens of thousands still died. For two decades the fundamentalist Islamic Sudanese government has been trying to end a two-decade-old rebellion by largely African Christian southerners. In 2000 the government banned all relief agencies from southern Sudan.

Brennan Linsley/AP/Wide World Photos

to the world between now and 2030 will be added in developing countries , where the average yearly wage now is under $700.

Bad News Poorer developing countries are adding an annual increment of 84 million persons (of the world increase of 86 million) each year that must be fed and clothed just to maintain living standards, much less improve them. Funds needed for economic development and improving the quality of life are being consumed providing minimal subsistence to ever-increasing numbers of people. According to the United Nations Population Fund, some half-billion people are already unemployed or underemployed in such countries, and 30 million more enter the overcrowded job market each year. In an increasingly post-industrial world, large numbers of untrained workers is a national liability, not an asset.

Urban growth in the West was due more to the "pull" from the industrializing cities than to the "push" from rural areas. In developing countries, the pattern is reversed. People flood to the cities not because jobs are readily available there but because population pressure and agribusiness are pushing peasants from the farms. More people inevitably means more destruction of the environment, more elimination of rain forests, and more urban pollution. Third World cities are by far the most polluted on earth. Barring nuclear war, massive famine, or worldwide pestilence, any prognosis other than a larger population for developing countries is highly unrealistic. Therefore, any plans designed to help underdeveloped areas must build in the factor of substantial population growth.

Good News Fifteen years ago, all developing countries had fairly similar high fertility rates. Today, largely as a result of U.S. and U.N. funded family planning programs, roughly half of all couples in developing countries use contraceptives.[6] Many developing nations are replicating the demographic transition, doing in decades what took centuries in the West. For example, as of 1999 China's total fertility rate (number of children per woman) was 1.8 children.[7] (See Box 6.3.)

---

[6]Lori S. Ashford, "New Perspectives on Population: Lessons from Cairo," *Population Bulletin,* March 1995, p. 4.
[7]*1999 World Population Data Sheet.*

Worldwide, only Africa continues to have both high fertility and high mortality. The United Nations reports contraceptive usage in Africa is increasing, but it is still only roughly 15 percent.[8] As a consequence, the sub-Saharan African average still was 5.8 children per woman as of 1999. Niger has the world's highest fertility at 7.5 children per woman.[9] Africa currently is doubling its population every *25 years*.

Consequences For poor countries, rapid population increases mean more than just additional mouths to feed. As nations develop, they dramatically increase their energy usage, consumption of food and of consumer goods shoots up, and automobile pollution and resource destruction become major problems. The United Nations projects that by 2050 there will be twice as many people as now, but three times the amount of food and fibers will be consumed, and energy usage will increase fourfold. What this means for the globe is massively more destruction of rain forests, more strip mining, more pollution of air and water, more sewage and waste products, more environmental destruction and degradation, and an increasing problem with fresh water supplies. Currently, the richest 20 percent of the world's population consumes 86 percent of the world's goods and services. As more nations develop, the strain on the environment will sharply increase.

The Ticking Clock

An awareness of the time component is crucial to understanding what has been happening in high-fertility countries. In most Western nations birthrates did not begin to drop until death rates had been declining for over a century. Developing countries with already high populations cannot wait a century. However, slowing birthrates is more complex than reducing deaths—it depends on the individual decisions of millions of couples to limit the number of their children. Also, they must be able to get both the information and contraceptives needed to carry out their decisions.

The importation of modern sanitation, public health, and inoculations has resulted in rapid decreases in death rates in developing countries—often initially unaccompanied by other social or economic changes. In Sri Lanka (Ceylon), for example, malaria was largely eradicated in the 1950s by the decision to spray DDT from airplanes. In only two years Sri Lanka dropped its death rate by 40 percent. The transition to a drop in birthrates took several decades longer.

The Urban Explosion

Most of the world population increase is occurring in Third World cities. Urban areas are growing at least twice as fast as rural areas (Table 6.2). The World Bank estimates that as of 2000 there are 391 cities with over one million inhabitants. More than one-third of these cities first reached the one million mark in the 1990s. As recently as 1950 there were only two cities in developing countries with populations of over 5 million. Today there are 46 cities of over 5 million in developing countries. Some 284 of the 391 cities having over a million inhabitants are in developing countries. As a result there now are twice as many city residents in less-developed countries as in the cities of the

---

[8]International Conference on Population and Development, *Draft Programme of Action*, United Nations Fund for Population Activities, New York, 1994, p. 6.
[9]*1999 World Population Data Sheet*.

This street scene is of Bombay, India, but everywhere in the Third World city populations are exploding at unprecedented rates.

developed world. Of the 26 mega-cities with more than 10 million residents, 21 are located in developing countries. Booming Bombay, for example, is adding half a million new residents each year. It is difficult for us to keep up either intellectually or emotionally with these changes. It is important to remember that the problem of the population explosion is largely a problem of urban growth in developing countries.

The Debate over Growth

The consequences of current population growth remain heatedly debated. Among the better known advocates of growth restriction are the ecologist Paul Ehrlich and the Worldwatch Institute's Lester Brown. Paul Ehrlich's *The Population Bomb* popularized the possibility of unrestricted growth threatening world famine.[10] Lester Brown focuses on the environmental damage from population growth, such as global warming, depletion of the ozone layer, acid rain, and destruction of the rain forests.[11]

The most powerful advocate of population growth as an advantage was the economist Julian Simon, who died in 1998.[12] By stimulating a demand for goods,

---

[10]Paul R. Ehrlich, *The Population Bomb,* Ballantine Books, New York, 1968.
[11]Lester R. Brown, "Nature's Limits," in Lester R. Brown et al. (eds.), *State of the World, 1995,* W. W. Norton, Scranton, PA, 1995.
[12]Julian L. Simon, *The Ultimate Resource,* Pharos Books, 1981.

156

Figure 6.2 Urban and Rural Population Growth, 1950–2030s

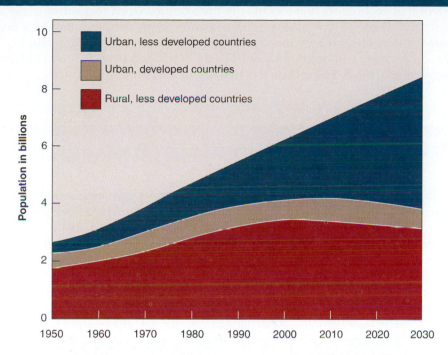

Source: U.N. World Urbanization Prospects: The 1996 Revision, (1997), tables A3–A6.

said Simon, population growth expands markets, leads to the discovery of substitute materials, and expands economic growth. Scarcities induce the search for solutions and technologies that leave us better off than if there had been no scarcity. Rather than forcing up the price of raw materials, population increases act to lower them by stimulating the search for substitutes. In Simon's words, "In the very long run, more people almost surely imply more available resources and a higher income for everyone."[13] Thus, increasing the world's population improves the world's standard of living. While Ehrlich's and Brown's views are similar to those of Al Gore, Simon's views provided support for the population policies of the Reagan and Bush administrations, which maintained there was no real population problem.

The opposing positions partially reflect the differences between the fields of *ecology* and *economics*. Economists tend to see growth as universally positive and the future as an extrapolation of the recent past. Technology, they believe, constantly pushes back and redefines any limits. Ecologists, on the other hand, study how living things relate to the environment and see all things living within a system that limits expansion. They see growing life in terms of S-shaped curves in which all biological growth processes are limited by carrying capacity. Thus, no species, be it algae in a petri dish, rabbits in the wild, or human beings, can indefinitely expand without damaging the natural system and its resources. This growth, especially in the Third

---

[13]Julian L. Simon, "More People, Greater Wealth, More Resources, Healthier Environment," in *Taking Sides*, Kirt Finsterbusch and George McKenna (eds.), Dushkin Publishing, Guilford, CO, 1994, p. 361.

World, inevitably leads to wholesale land degradation, deforestation, and huge increases in carbon pollution of air due to the increased burning of fossil fuels.

The economic growth that pleases the economists also piles up an environmental debt that economists don't include in their figures when measuring gross national product (GNP). It is not just an issue of how many people, but of how much ecological damage and how much extra pollution and sewage extra people produce. Ecologists point out that since 1970, the world has been stripped of forests equivalent to the size of the United States east of the Mississippi River.

Population Control Policies

Population growth is often discussed in emotional ways that suggest that the crisis is equally severe for all nations.[14] However, population growth is not a problem in the developed industrial and newly industrializing countries making up about one-quarter of the world's population. In fact, the population problem for most European nations and Japan is too few births. European population decline is being prevented only through immigration. Population policies in most economically advanced nations generally are designed to *increase* fertility. The governments of France and Sweden offer subsidies to encourage births, and the Israeli government, surrounded by faster-growing Arab populations, for years has sought to encourage fertility. Other nations—including Argentina, Greece, Japan, and Singapore—are also attempting to increase their respective populations. Attempts to encourage population growth reflect a host of economic, political, and nationalistic concerns. Among the most important is the perceived need to maintain a sufficiently large workforce to support existing social security and retirement systems.

The old Soviet Union maintained that there was no population problem and that under socialism's equal distribution of resources population problems would disappear. Family planning programs were criticized as Western imperialism, and poor nations were told that "development is the best birth control." Today the strongest supporters of population control programs are the developing nations, and four out of five developing countries now have active birth control programs. Even poverty-stricken Bangladesh, the most densely populated nation on earth, now has 45 percent of its women of childbearing age using some form of contraceptive. As a result, the number of children born to the average Bangladeshi woman has declined in 20 years from seven to four. Of course, this birthrate still doubles a population in just one generation. Currently, average childbearing in developing countries, excluding China, is four children per woman.[15] The boxed inserts on population policies in Singapore and China (Box 6.2 and Box 6.3) contrast two opposing policies and means of implementation.

Population Growth and World Hunger

No rich populations go hungry, only poor ones. Lester Brown warns that "the old formula of combining more and more fertilizer with ever-higher yielding varieties that helped almost triple the world grain harvest from 1950 to 1990 is no longer

---

[14]Paul Erlich and Anne H. Erlich, *Population, Resources, and Environment*, W. H Freeman, San Francisco, 1970.
[15]*1997 World Population Data Sheet*, Population Reference Bureau, Washington, DC, 1997.

Box 6.2 **Ongoing Issues**

Population Eugenics in Singapore

After decades running one of the world's most effective family planning programs, Prime Minister Lee Kuan Yew of Singapore announced in 1983 that the future of the nation now dictated that birthrates be *increased* among the better educated. The Prime Minister stated that "nature, or what is inherited, is the greater determinant of a person's performance than is nurture. . . . If we continue to reproduce ourselves in this lopsided way, we will be unable to maintain present standards. Levels of competence will decline. Our economy will falter; administration will suffer; and our society will decline."[a]

Singapore thus became the first nation since World War II to base its population policies openly on eugenic arguments, assuming that better-educated parents produced brighter children.[b] In spite of the fact that these eugenic arguments have largely been discredited scientifically, all family planning programs were shut down and in their place pro-fertility programs initiated. A controversial Graduate Mothers Program provided financial and other incentives to university women, and only university women, to transmit their supposedly superior genes, while a Sterilization Cash Incentive Scheme offered grants to poorly educated couples if the wife agreed to being sterilized. These early programs were modified as better-educated women expressed resentment at the government for viewing them as baby machines.

Currently, a government Social Development Unit (SDU) encourages marriages by bringing together single university graduates at dances, bowling clinics, computer workshops, holiday resort trips, and even cruises (dubbed "love boat cruises"

by Singaporeans). All these activities are government subsidized, as is a free computerized matchmaking service. Programs offer financial incentives to encourage those financially best off to have more children. (Affluent families worldwide tend to have the fewest children.) In practice, this emphasis on affordability ("Have Three or More If You Can Afford It") targets the same population as the earlier Graduate Mothers Program. As expressed by the SDU's deputy director, "If you want to produce geniuses, you have to get the graduate man to marry a graduate girl."[c] Benefits for better-off couples as of the late 1990s included tax rebates of $12,000 for third and fourth children, tax rebates for child care available for working mothers up to $12,000, priority in children's school selection, and priority in obtaining new housing. Delivery costs are also subsidized after the second birth. An additional tax rebate of $12,000 is offered if the mother has a second child before age 28.

The effects of Singapore's eugenics-based policies appear moderate. Singapore is a heavily consumption-oriented society, and Singapore's more better-educated and more-affluent couples are reluctant to trade any part of their high standard of living for larger families.

[a]*"Lop-Sided Birth Rate Drop; 80% Nature and 20% Nurture; Talent for the Future," Straits Times (Singapore), August 14, 1983.*
[b]*J. John Palen, "Fertility and Eugenics: Singapore's Population Policies," Population Research and Policy Review, 5, 1986, pp. 3–14.*
[c]*"How to Marry Up, and Avoid the Frogs and Nerds," New York Times, July 11, 1988.*

working well and there is no new formula."[16] We have lost our unbounded optimism and faith in technology characterized by President John F. Kennedy's 1963 statement: "We have the means—we need only the will." At that time, the food problem as perceived by most developed countries was how best to dispose of food surpluses. Today the problem isn't so much the production of enough food as the maldistribution between population and resources.

---

[16]Quoted in Paola Scommengna, "UN Food Summit Tries to Focus World Attention on Hunger," *Population Today,* November 1996, p. 2.

Box 6.3 Ongoing Issues

China's "One Child Only" Policy

China's population, 1.25 billion persons, is equal to the combined populations of the 21 nations of western Europe, all 35 nations of South America and the Caribbean, plus Mexico, Canada, and the United States. One of every four infants born in the world today is born in China. For over 25 years, China has followed a "one child only" program backed by massive propaganda campaigns, incentives, and strong sanctions. Those having only a single child may receive monthly bonuses, release time from work, increased ration card allotments, and "one-child glory certificates." In the cities, birth control through IUD insertion, sterilization, the pill, or condoms is an integral part of urban Chinese life. China's population control programs have lowered its rate of increase to only 1.1 percent a year (doubling time 66 years), which is half the rate of increase in other developing nations.

China's procedures used to enforce the one-child policy have drawn international criticism. There is strong pressure to have the wife sterilized at the first birth, and after a second birth the pressure is intense. Having a third child is "not permitted" and officially is to be "resolutely prevented" by abortion. The biggest obstacle to the one-child family is tradition. In spite of legal equality between the sexes (e.g., the Chinese slogan "Women hold up half the sky") and strong propaganda campaigns favoring female births, wives and husbands overwhelmingly still want a male child. Parents desire a boy for reasons of both prestige and practicality. Traditionally, the birth of a son is seen as a sign of good fortune. In the south Chinese dialect of Fukien the announcement of the birth of a son literally translates as "I am triumphant." Practically, sons work the family fields (daughters work the fields of their husband's family), and four out of five families still are agrarian based. Additionally, in China sons have the responsibility for caring for parents. Not to have a son, especially in rural areas, leaves parents without anyone to care for them in old age since there is no national pension system. (In the Western world, daughters traditionally have primary responsibility to care for aged parents.)

The Chinese government is fighting the re-emergence of the ancient custom of female infanticide. Although females live longer than males, China now has 40 million more males than females, and pregnancy tests to determine the sex of a fetus are increasingly being used to decide whether the fetus will be allowed to come to term. To reduce abortion rate of female fetuses, regulations now permit a couple to have a second child if they have a daughter, she is at least eight years old, and the mother is over 30 years of age. This exception to the "One Child Only" policy reflects a clear pro-male bias by allowing a couple having a girl to have a second chance.

The Chinese approach to lowering fertility rates is not being copied. Aside from ethical questions, it requires a degree of national commitment and a level of communal enforcement not found elsewhere. However, the consensus in China is that population growth must be brought under control by any means if China is not to again undergo the famines and disasters that characterized its past.

New Lands

From the days of the first farmer until about 1950, the major means of expanding food supplies was bringing new lands under cultivation. Now, because virtually all the available cropland is being used and some of the best cropland is being urbanized, additional yields must be obtained from existing cropland. Since the 1970s, improved crop yields have provided all of the increases in food output. There now is only one acre of cropland for each person. Attempts to add farmland often create greater problems. Over half the world's wetlands have been drained, rain forests have been cut down, and poor farming practices are turning existing soils into desert.

The Green Revolution

The so-called **Green Revolution** of the 1970s, with its "miracle" strains of wheat and rice, was expected to banish hunger from the globe. Before the Green Revolution, for example, the average rice yield per acre was between 0.6 and 1.4 tons an acre. Green Revolution seeds have more than doubled the potential to between 2.4 and 4 tons per acre. Moreover, Green Revolution rice strains produced three crops a year instead of the usual two. The down side, other than that the rice grown from the new seeds does not taste anywhere near as good, is that the new strains require not only irrigation but also increasing amounts of pesticides and fungicides.

Currently, the overall world food situation remains adequate but precarious; for the long run, it could be disastrous. Agricultural productivity, after rising by more than 2 percent a year for 40 years, grew barely 1 percent a year during the 1990s—well below the 1.5 percent per year increase in world population.[17] Africa's 1990s agricultural productivity was actually below that of the 1960s. Sub-Saharan Africa now imports one-fifth of its grain. For such a potentially productive area to rely so heavily on outside supplies is not only expensive, it is dangerous. Today, export grain is no longer given away as food aid but sold on the world market. Poorer nations have no free surplus grain upon which to draw.

Green Revolution
recent dramatic improvements in agricultural yields—especially in developing countries—due to the use of new genetically-engineered seeds.

Political Economy

In poor countries the major food problem often is not inadequate food production but the social organization of food production. The poorest countries often have the most unequal land distribution, with a handful of elite families and multinational agribusiness conglomerates controlling most of the productive land. Agribusiness farms produce cash crops for export rather than meeting local needs. Cash crops are exported, while local populations go hungry. The absence of stable governments and of adequate distribution systems also strongly contributes to local poverty and hunger. During the 1992 famine in Somalia, the major bottleneck was not the lack of food, but rather a nonexistent transport system complicated by political chaos resulting from the country being divided among competing warlords. Without a national government, food could not be moved to where it was needed. People starved while food rotted on ships for lack of any political agreement among competing clans.

Fish from the Ocean

The oceans have long been an abundant source of food, and worldwide fish consumption averages out to almost 40 pounds per person per year, well above beef consumption. Fish provide the main source of protein for the population of some 40 countries.[18] The problem is that the world fish catch reached a peak in 1970 and has been declining since. Sophisticated radar-guided huge net-fishing fleets and the floating fish-processing factories used by Japan, Russia, Taiwan, Spain, and others have resulted in overfishing to the point where the present catches of many kinds of table fish exceed the regenerative capacity of the species. Once-common

---

[17]"Population Surpassing Cropland Productivity," *World Population News Service Popline,* September–October 1997, p. 3.
[18]George Moffett, "The Population Question Revisited," *Wilson Quarterly,* Summer 1994, p. 75.

Members of the environmental organization Greenpeace hang a sign on a factory trawler protesting such industrial factory ships vacuuming the ocean clean and breaking the food chain for other species.

Greenspace/AP/Wide World Photos

varieties have become listed as endangered species. Cod, which for three centuries seemed unlimited in the North Atlantic, has now virtually disappeared. To save dwindling replacement stocks, in 1994 the U.S. Commerce Department and the Canadian government had to shut down all commercial fishing from the North Atlantic Georges Banks to southern New England waters.[19] Commercial fishing from Maine to Florida has declined dramatically because increased pollution runoff and the building of homes along the coastline have destroyed spawning habitats. This is particularly true of coastal shellfish cultures. For example, the once rich Chesapeake Bay now produces hardly any oysters. With increasing competition for the remaining species, world fish harvests are declining both in quality and quantity.

Still, the regulation of harvesting in international waters has been strongly resisted by some nations. Only a threatened boycott of Japanese goods in Europe resulted in Japan's agreements to temporarily cease the commercial killing of whales. Endangered fish species will have to have similar international protection if they are not to be harvested to extinction.

Aquaculture, the farming of fish or seafood in enclosed ponds or in ocean pens, is increasing. China already obtains 40 percent of its fish harvest from farmed fish ponds. Almost all catfish now sold in the United States are raised in fish ponds. Ocean fish pens also have been used for a number of years. Maine fish farmers first brought Atlantic salmon to market in 1988, and since that time annual production has gone to 13.5 million pounds, with a half-million pounds of trout thrown in for good measure.[20] It is virtually certain that the catfish, Atlantic salmon, or trout that you order at a Red Lobster or other chain restaurant came from a fish farm or ocean pen. The United Nations estimates world fish needs at 91 million metric tons a year.[21] Current commercial fishing harvests 57 metric tons. This means the remaining 34 million tons must come from aquaculture. This is over double the current tonnage.

---

[19]"Fisheries Closed in New England," *Boston Globe,* December 8, 1994, p. 1.
[20]Lawrence Latane III, "For Some Maine Farmers, Salmon Is a Bumper Crop," *Richmond Times-Dispatch,* November 15, 1995, p. A4.
[21]Ibid.

Changing Diets

Simplifying diets in rich nations can temporarily increase the food available to poorer nations. Protein is more expensive than carbohydrates, and animal protein is far more costly than vegetable protein. The average North American consumes—in the form of either grain or meat—roughly five times as much grain as a person in India. Many American pets eat better than poor children in the least developed countries. However, attempts to solve long-term food problems by simplistic "solutions" such as eating one less hamburger a week or doing away with all household pets are essentially useless as long as population growth exceeds agricultural growth. Some of the poorest countries are doubling their populations every 20–25 years. In such situations external assistance can stave off temporary disaster, but it cannot prevent eventual catastrophe.

Other Issues of Population Growth

Here we will examine several issues that are affected by population growth. Specifically, we will look at the effect of population growth on age structure, women and maternal health issues, and religious attitudes.

Age Structure

Developing countries have very youthful age structures (Figure 6.3). In 2000, 35 percent of the inhabitants of the developing world were under 15 years of age. By contrast, the figure for the developed regions was only 20 percent. In Kenya, Syria, and Yemen, half the population is under 15 years of age, while the figure is less than 20 percent in Germany, England, and France (the United States figure is 22 percent).[22] Developing countries are being hit twice: They not only have fewer resources, they also have age structures heavily loaded with dependent young people who must be fed, housed, educated, and otherwise provided for. Harvests may be enlarged and more schools built, but if these only just keep pace with population growth, they do nothing to improve the quality of life. Funds that are desperately needed for investment in nation-building are of necessity consumed supporting an ever larger number of dependent young. Developing nations also have a built-in growth momentum due to their increasing number of potential mothers. In terms of nations, it is clearly the case that "the rich get richer and the poor get children."

Women, Maternal Health, and Family Planning

Maternal Mortality Maternal death rates due to pregnancy are 15 to 50 times higher in developing countries than in developed countries. The United Nations estimates that at least half a million women die each year from complications arising from pregnancy and childbirth, and 99 percent of these deaths occur in developing countries. In some countries as many as half the maternal deaths occur as

---

[22]*1997 World Population Data Sheet*, Population Reference Bureau, Washington, DC, 1997.

Figure 6.3 Population Pyramids for Western Europe and Sub-Saharan Africa, 1995

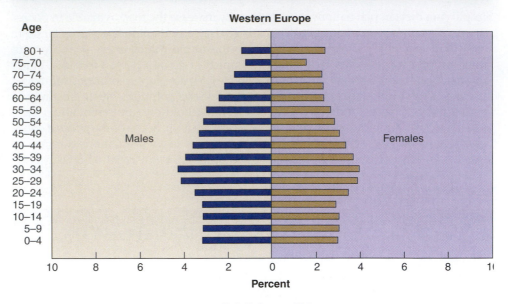

Western Europe

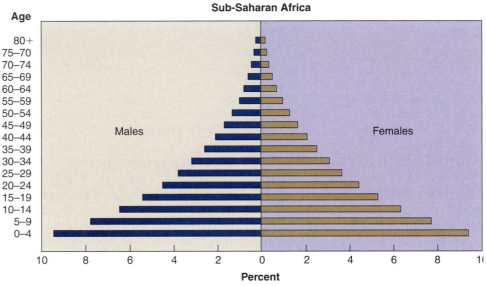

Sub-Saharan Africa

Source: U.N. The Sex and Age Distribution of the World Populations: *The 1992 Revisions*, (New York: UN, 1993).

a result of unsafe abortions. Large families also decrease the productivity of women and increase health costs. Over the last decades, great strides have been made in narrowing educational opportunities between males and females, but there are still 960 million illiterate adults in the world, and two-thirds of them are women. According to the United Nations, some 130 million children are still denied access even to basic primary education, and 90 million of these are girls.[23] The

---

[23]International Conference on Population and Development, *Draft Programme of Action*, p. 8.

1994 World Population Conference held in Cairo strongly endorsed increasing educational and job opportunities for women and giving all women the right to plan their own pregnancies and the right to birth control.

A Note on Abortion The World Health Organization estimates that each year 20 million abortions occur under unsafe conditions.[24] Some 95 percent of unsafe abortions take place in less-developed countries. In the United States, the 1973 *Roe v. Wade* Supreme Court decision outlawing state anti-abortion laws created a political and moral controversy which continues to rage today. The ethics of abortion is an issue on which the American public is still sharply divided, with "pro-choice" feminist groups vocal in defense of abortion and "right to life" groups—often with religious affiliations—strongly opposed to abortion. Positions on both sides are often so strongly held that real discussion of the topic is all but impossible.

However, within a few years public confrontations probably will become less common. It is also possible that public violence over abortion clinics will sharply decline. This will occur not because of agreement or exhaustion but rather because of changes in medical technology. Preven, the morning-after pill, is now available in drug stores, and the French-developed RU-486 abortion pill is now being manufactured in the United States. Use of such drugs, by eliminating most surgical abortions, will eliminate most surgical abortion clinics, probably within a decade. While beliefs about abortion are unlikely to change, the new drugs increasingly make any decision a private one between a woman and her physician.

Religious Attitudes

Contrary to popular belief, religious motives are not a major factor limiting the use of birth control. Jews and Protestants, except for a few fundamentalist sects, generally endorse modern contraceptive methods. Within the Islamic world, some fundamentalist clerics support high fertility, but governments overwhelmingly do not. Muslim countries—including Egypt, Turkey, Pakistan, and Bangladesh—all have active government-sponsored family planning programs. Even in Iran, where after the 1979 revolution the mullahs first opposed birth control, religious leaders have created an effective family planning program that even offers free vasectomies. What changed their mind was a doubling of the population in 15 years.

Similarly, Hindu, Buddhist, and other religious leaders generally advocate family planning. Population growth in most countries is far more related to the perpetuation of traditional social customs than to religion per se. The greatest hindrance to population control today is nations' limits on the social and economic roles permitted women—particularly outside major cities. Young girls' access to schools, and hence their knowledge of alternatives, is still severely restricted in some places.

The Roman Catholic Church is the only major religious body opposed to birth control. Pope Paul's 1968 encyclical *Humanae Vitae (On Human Life)* emphatically stated the position "that each and every matrimonial act must remain open to the transmission of life." There is a difference, however, between the official pronouncements of church leaders and the private behavior of believers. In the United States today there is virtually no difference in contraceptive attitudes and practice between Catholics and non-Catholics. Catholics, in fact, actually have somewhat smaller families than non-Catholics. Nominally Catholic

---

[24]World Health Organization, "Unsafe Abortion: Global and Regional Estimates of Incidence and Mortality Due to Unsafe Abortion," WHO, Geneva, Switzerland, 1998.

Italy, just outside the doors of the Vatican, has not only one of the world's highest abortion rates but also, with 1.2 children per woman, the lowest birthrate in the world.

Nor are Catholic church policies as uniform as sometimes portrayed. The French Catholic Bishops Conference in 1996 openly contradicted Vatican doctrine by putting the bishops on record as stating that under certain circumstances the use of condoms is not only permitted but "necessary" to keep AIDS from spreading.[25] In the United States, the Catholic Church has in practice, if not publicly, conceded that the debate over birth control is over. For the past two decades the American Catholic Church has turned its attention from birth control to eliminating abortion.

The major impact of religion on family planning comes from the political coalition of the Religious Right, Catholic Church officials, and socially conservative Republicans who have joined together to lobby the U.S. Congress to ban using any U.S. funds for United Nations family planning programs.

United States Population Issues

In a period spanning over 200 years, the United States population grew—through immigration and natural increase—from 3.5 million in 1776 to 273 million in 2000. Just since 1970 over 65 million persons have been added to the population of the United States. Here we will discuss two problems facing the United States: the aging of the population and the question of immigration.

Aging Baby Boomers

Because Chapter 11 will discuss in detail the consequences of aging and ageism, we here will discuss only the general problem of an aging population. At the crest of the baby boom in 1957, the total fertility rate was 3.8 children per woman. Today the figure is half that. America's problem is not too many dependent young but how to cope with a population that is rapidly growing elderly. At the beginning of the century only 4 percent of the United States population was over 65. Currently it is 12 percent, and by 2030, when almost all the baby boomers will have retired, it will shoot up to 25 percent. The result is a decreasing proportion of working-age taxpayers supporting a growing number of persons on Medicare and Social Security. The United States now has three workers to support every older person on Social Security, but that will decrease to only two workers for every retiree as the baby boomers retire. This is a serious issue for today's college students, who will be paying the bill. Whether or not Congress has the political will to pass necessary Social Security reforms remains to be decided. (See Chapter 11.)

Immigration: Pro and Con

America's most contentious current population issue is immigration (Figure 6.4). One hundred years ago steamers filled with European immigrants in steerage crowded New York harbor. Today's immigrants flood into California, coming from Asia through LAX or by land from Latin America. Today, as earlier, there are those

---

[25]"Bishops OK Condom Use in AIDS Fight," *Associated Press News Service*, February 13, 1996.

Figure 6.4 Immigration to the United States, 1890–1994

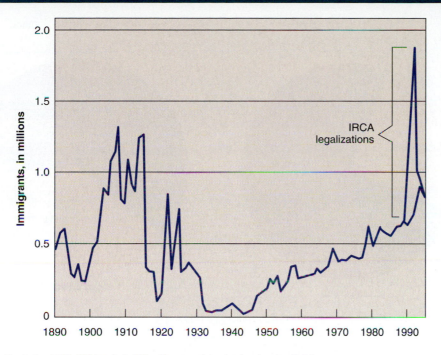

Note: Totals for 1989–1994 include 2.7 million residents legalized under IRCA.
Source: Immigration and Naturalization Service, *1993* and *1994 Statistical Yearbook*.

who believe immigration should be more controlled. Peter Brimelow, for instance, has made a career arguing that America's current immigration policies are a disaster because they encourage immigration of the less skilled who will be economic liabilities while transforming the ethnic and racial makeup of the country.[26] Certainly, after half a century of pro-immigration attitudes and legislation, the 1990s saw a strong resurgence of anti-immigrant sentiment. Voters in California, the nation's most multicultural state, in 1994 passed Proposition 187, banning illegal immigrants from using government-supported social services and nonemergency health care. At the national level, the 1996 Welfare Reform Act barred welfare service to all illegal, and also some legal immigrants (bans on welfare for legal immigrants were rescinded by Congress in 1998). Why did all these changes come about?

Changing Patterns The debate over immigration has become heated for three main reasons. First, the number of immigrants is increasing. The Immigration Act of 1990 increased legal immigration by 40 percent and legal immigration now is 900,000 a year, not counting asylum seekers. According to the Bureau of the Census, as of 1996 some 24.5 million people—nearly 1 of every 10 people living in the United States—was born in another country.[27] Thus, the proportion of immigrants in the population is at the highest level since 1910. In addition, Immigration and Naturalization Service (INS) data indicate there are 5 million undocumented

---

[26]Peter Brimelow, *Alien Nation: Common Sense about America's Immigration Disaster,* Random House, New York, 1995.

[27]William Branigin and Pamela Constable, "Floundering in a Wave of Immigrants," *Washington Post,* May 10, 1997, p. A1.

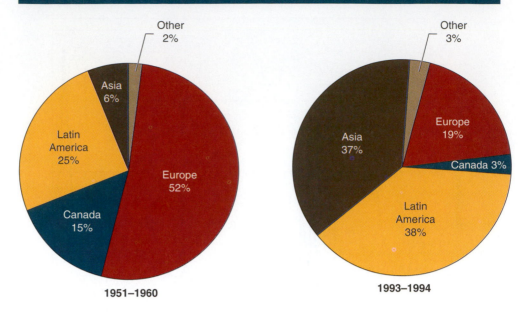

Figure 6.5 U.S. Immigrants by Region of Origin, 1950s and 1990s

1951–1960

- Other 2%
- Asia 6%
- Latin America 25%
- Europe 52%
- Canada 15%

1993–1994

- Other 3%
- Asia 37%
- Europe 19%
- Canada 3%
- Latin America 38%

Source: Immigration and Naturalization Service, *1994 Statistical Yearbook.*

immigrants living in the United States, and the permanent undocumented immigrant population is growing by 275,000 to 300,000 persons a year.[28] Using the most conservative estimates, this creates a net immigrant increase of 1.25 million persons a year.[29]

Most of the nation's population growth now comes from immigration or from the children born to immigrants. Native-born whites became a minority in California in 1998, and 42 percent of the children born in the state are now born to immigrants.[30] The Bureau of the Census estimates that by the year 2050 some 93 percent of U.S. population growth will be the result of immigration since 1990.[31]

Second, today's immigrants differ considerably in origin from immigrants of earlier times (Figure 6.5). Until 1968 most immigrants to the United States came from Europe. Now only 5 percent of U.S. immigration comes from northern and western Europe, while three quarters comes from Latin America and Asia. Ethnically and racially speaking, America has begun to look more and more like the rest of the world.

Third, immigration is being debated because there is uncertainty whether current immigrant groups will become part of America's economic and social struc-

[28]"Five Million Illegal Aliens Call the U.S. Home," *Associated Press News Service,* February 9, 1997.
[29]U.S. Bureau of the Census, "Population Projections of the United States by Age, Sex, Race, and Hispanic Origin, 1993 to 2050," *Current Population Reports,* P25–1104, Washington, DC, 1993; and Dolores Acevedo and Thomas Espenshade, "Implications of a North American Free Trade Agreement for Mexican Migration to the United States," *Population and Development Review,* 18, 4, December 1992, pp. 729–744.
[30]Philip Martin and Elizabeth Midley, "Immigration to the United States: Journey to an Uncertain Destination," *Population Bulletin,* 49, 2, September 1994, p. 8.
[31]William Branigin, "Immigration Issues Await New Congress," *Washington Post,* November 18, 1996, p. A12.

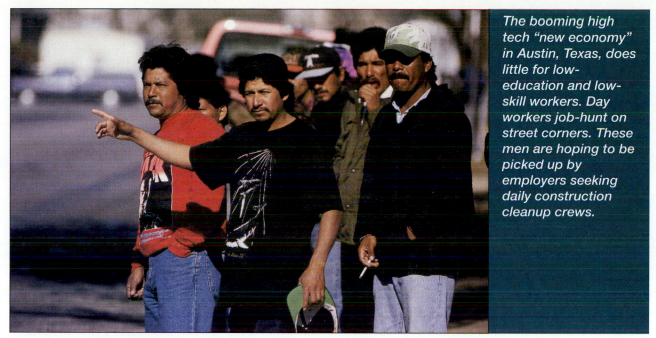

The booming high tech "new economy" in Austin, Texas, does little for low-education and low-skill workers. Day workers job-hunt on street corners. These men are hoping to be picked up by employers seeking daily construction cleanup crews.

© Bob Daemmrich/The Image Works

ture, as earlier groups did. There is concern that poorly educated immigrants are becoming a semi-permanent population of the economically marginal. Immigrants can be divided into two distinct camps: those with college degrees and specialized skills and those with virtually no education or job skills. Educated Asians and Latin Americans often arrive with advanced degrees, while poor Asian and Latin American immigrants often have marginal educations. More than one-third of all current immigrants do not have a high school diploma. Such low education levels mean immigrants have little chance to be other than marginal workers. Moreover, since 1970 the overall educational level of immigrants, especially those from Latin America, has been slipping. This is because current immigration law makes family reunification, not having skills or U.S. job needs, the primary criteria for admittance. Most legal immigrants are admitted because they are related to someone already here. "Chain migration," in which successive waves of immigrants bring in relatives, means migration disproportionately brings in those likely to need social services.

Immigration's impact falls particularly heavily on California, which currently houses one-third of the country's foreign-born population and half the nation's 5 million undocumented residents. This has put strains on the economic and social fabric of the state. As of 1995, services for undocumented immigrants cost over $3 billion a year, or nearly 10 percent of the state budget. Some two-thirds of the babies born in Los Angeles's four public hospitals were born to a parent who was an undocumented alien and whose medical and hospital costs were paid by public funds. Additionally, over 300,000 of the students in California's public schools and universities are undocumented residents. While some Californians are anti-immigrant, the major debate is the financial one of who should pay the costs. The issue is largely one of whether the federal government should aid states in providing federally mandated social, educational, and medical services.

Consequences for Economy Immigrants get blamed for taking jobs, crowding the schools, and filling welfare roles. But is this a fair picture? On the question of the economy, the answer is mixed. On the positive side, the 1997 comprehensive report of the National Academy of Sciences (NAS) concluded that immigrants contribute perhaps $10 billion to the nation's economy and those buying goods and services produced by immigrants also benefit by lower costs.[32] Immigrants also tend to be risk-takers and thus are more likely to be self-employed than native-born Americans, and this becomes more the case the longer the immigrant is in the country.[33] Regarding Social Security and welfare, immigrants with a high school education or better provide "instant adults" who pay more into the system than they take out.[34]

Affluent Americans generally benefit from immigration, poorer Americans lose economically.[35] The NAS study found that immigrants reduce the wages of low-skilled workers by 5 percent. Large-scale immigration of less-skilled workers lowers business costs and provides a work force for some businesses which otherwise could not exist. Immigration harms the economic opportunities of Americans without a high school education. Immigrant competition for middle-class jobs has been limited.

The 1997 NAS report concluded that immigrants "have a negative fiscal impact at the state and local level, but a larger positive impact at the Federal level."[36] Immigrant households are costly at first, mainly because of public education costs, but after 15 or 20 years immigrants produce fiscal benefits as they pay taxes. The difficulty is that the benefits are general to the entire nation, while the costs are concentrated in a few states. For example, the NAS found that while in New Jersey every native-born household pays only $232 a year to cover the net cost of services to immigrants, in California each native-born household pays $1,178 a year in taxes to support services for immigrants.[37]

The impact of immigrant workers is easiest to see in so-called "ethnic enclave" industries, where low-skill immigrant groups, because of their lower job turnover and their practice of filling vacancies with family members or others within the ethnic network, come to dominate the industry. This phenomenon has led to conflict in cities such as Miami, where African Americans and poor whites feel they have been excluded from certain job categories such as hotel work.

Research done by the demographer William Frey indicates in-migration of poor immigrants is beginning to result in the out-migration of poorer native-born Americans from states such as California and New York.[38] While poor groups traditionally have been "pulled" toward areas of economic development, they now are increasingly "pushed" by competition for jobs. "To oversimplify," says Frey, "for every Mexican who comes to Los Angeles, a white native-born leaves."[39] Since this movement is from states with higher welfare benefits (such as California) to states with lower benefits (such as Nevada), the native-born poor are not being drawn by higher welfare payments. Substantial substitution of immigrant labor for domestic labor also leads to greater racial polarization, because the poor out-movers are mostly white.

It is sometimes charged that African Americans are also being displaced by immigrant workers, but the NAS found no disproportionate effect on African Ameri-

[32]Robert Pear, "Academy's Report Says Immigration Benefits the U.S.," *New York Times*, May 18, 1997, p. A1.
[33]Dowell Myers, "The Changing Immigrants of Southern California," School of Urban and Regional Planning, University of Southern California, Los Angeles, 1996.
[34]Ben J. Wattenberg, "The Easy Solution to the Social Security Crisis," *New York Times Magazine*, June 22, 1997, pp. 30–31.
[35]Georg J. Borjas, "The New Economics of Immigration," *Atlantic Monthly*, November 1996, pp. 72–80.
[36]Robert, Pear, "Academy's Report," p. A24.
[37]Robert Pear, "Academy's Report," p. A24.
[38]38 William Frey, "The New White Flight," *American Demographics*, April 1994, pp. 40–48.
[39]Quoted in William Booth, "One Nation, Indivisible: Is It History?" *Washington Post*, February 22, 1998, p. A01.

cans. One area of future middle-class black versus immigrant conflict may be government employment. Government employment traditionally has been a major route to middle-class status for newcomer populations, from nineteenth-century Irish to African Americans during the last half of the twentieth century. In the major immigration city of Los Angeles, for example, African Americans are 11 percent of the population but hold 30 percent of all federal, state, and local government jobs.[40] In the Postal Service the figure is 63 percent. If economic times turn difficult and Latino and other newcomers demand a "fair share" of government jobs, political conflict is likely.

The most serious current concern, however, is the long-term earning capacity of poorly educated legal and illegal immigrants. Immigrants who arrived before 1970 initially made less than equally educated U.S.-born workers but after 15 to 20 years typically earned more than comparable American workers.[41] Those who arrived before 1970 also were less likely than the native born to have received public assistance. Such findings encouraged liberal immigration policies by suggesting that immigrants, through hard work, actually exceeded others in achieving the American Dream. Current arrivals are younger and less well educated. They are also more likely to be unemployed. Bureau of the Census data indicate that immigrants who arrived in this country since 1990 have rates of public assistance twice as high as rates for those born here.[42] Current legal immigrants are projected not to advance as fast as immigrants 20 years ago, and over their work careers to earn about 15 percent less than comparable whites. If this occurs, and the proportion of immigrant groups on welfare increases, there are likely to be political moves to further restrict immigration.[43] The crucial question is whether current low-education immigrants will remain stuck at lower skill and pay levels once they become familiar with the U.S. job market.

Toward the Future

The new century offers a mixed population picture. The economic split between economically advanced nations, (all of which have low birthrates) and poorer nations (all of which have higher birthrates) is increasing. The richest nations monopolize resources and consumer goods, while population growth in the poorest nations is absorbing both food production and economic development. In such nations malnutrition, misery, and possibly even starvation, are harsh realities. The fact that the world as a whole has sufficient food resources does not mean that life will improve in those poor nations with high birthrates. The picture is far brighter for newly industrialized countries (NICs). Although some of these countries were temporarily set back economically by the 1998 economic turndown, NICs such as Korea and Thailand now have recovered and have favorable long-term expectations. For developed European nations and Japan, the major population problem is not population growth but how to manage and support increasingly aging populations.

As the century opens, developed nations can help developing ones in temporary emergencies but for the long-run, developing nations must become more self-supporting. This means maintaining a balance between their resources (including

---

[40]Thomas Muller, "Immigrant Challenge," *The Wilson Quarterly,* Autumn 1994, p. 70.

[41]Barry Chiswick, "The Effects of Americanization on the Incomes of Foreign-Born Men," *Journal of Political Economy,* 86, October 1978, pp. 897–921.

[42]"Five Million Illegal Aliens Call the U.S. Home," *Associated Press News Service,* February 9, 1999.

[43]George J. Borjas, *Friends or Strangers: The Impact of Immigrants on the U.S. Economy,* Basic Books, New York, 1990.

food) and their populations. Otherwise, outside assistance can only postpone the eventual day of reckoning. Throughout most of history, the ecological balance between resources and human population growth has been maintained not by decreasing birthrates but by increasing death rates. However, the late twentieth century pattern was dropping death rates. Without sharp decreases in birthrates, the poorest countries will not develop. In 1992 the U.S. National Academy of Sciences in conjunction with the British Royal Academy of Sciences warned that "science and technology may not be able to prevent either irreversible degradation of the environment or continued poverty of much of the world. . . . Environmental changes may produce irreversible damage to the earth's capacity to sustain life." Their warning is even more relevant today. It is possible, of course, that the world's most prestigious scientists are wrong. If they are not, however, continuing the current population increases threatens the very existence of the globe. The hope for the new century is that the world will avoid catastrophe by increasing food production, controlling population growth, and making political and economic systems more responsive to the needs of their people.

In the United States questions concerning the effects of immigration may become both more heated and more political. Current immigration policies favor uneducated and unskilled immigrants who have a family member in the United States over the educated and the skilled. During good economic times, immigration questions remain largely theoretical, but questions about job effects and costs come to the fore when the economy turns sour. Affluent and middle-class Americans gain most from immigration. The negatives are most felt by less-educated workers. Class divisions over immigration are likely to widen. Ethnic-racial issues may also become more vocal because lower-paid minority workers feel most threatened by immigrants. As Chapter 1 noted, whether immigrants are taking jobs from others may not be as important in shaping policy as what people believe is happening.

Summary

The **population explosion** is a relatively new social problem. The earth has 6 billion people and we are adding another billion people to the globe every 12 years. Virtually all of this growth is occurring in developing nations. Of the 86 million persons added to the world every year, 84 million are born in developing countries.

- From a functionalist perspective, growth is functional insofar as it expands markets and stimulates demand. It is dysfunctional when the number of people living at subsistence levels increases and the environment is destroyed.

- Conflict theorists focus on the problem of unequal resource distribution. The problem is not underproduction of food and other resources but overconsumption by the industrialized nations.

- Interactionist social psychological approaches focus on the individual and how poorer, illiterate populations can be introduced to family planning measures.

- The **Western demographic transition** from high birth and death rates to low birth and death rates took roughly two centuries, with death rates dropping first and birthrates following as much as a century later.

- In developing countries, the importation during recent decades of modern sanitation, public health, and medicine have produced dramatic declines in mortality rates, while fertility rates have not similarly decreased from their traditional high levels. The consequence is a **population explosion** in Third World countries. Poor nations have as much as half their population under age 15. Religious beliefs are not a major factor in determining birth control usage.

- Scientists increasingly fear that continued population growth is leading to irreversible destruction and degradation of natural resources to the point where the earth's capacity to sustain life is being threatened.

- Historically, an overriding check on humanity's growth has been the food supply. The so-called **Green Revolution** has not banished hunger from the globe; rather, it has allowed more persons than ever before to survive.

- Current United States population growth is mostly attributable to immigration and the fertility of immigrants. The United States has two perceived population problems: the aging of the population and the integration of immigrants.

- Current legal immigrants from Mexico and Central America have educational and occupational levels below those of the native born and welfare rates above the native born. Debate rages over whether they will have the social mobility patterns typical of earlier immigrants.

☞ Key Review Terms

age structure	ecology	immigration
demographic transition	eugenics	Malthusianism
demography	fertility	mortality
developing countries	Green Revolution	population explosion

❓ Questions for Discussion

1. What is meant by the term "population explosion"? What are its effects?
2. Because the U.S. population is growing slowly, how does a world population program affect us?
3. What is the "urban explosion"? How is it related to the population explosion?
4. China and Singapore have unique population policies. Would their policies work elsewhere? Why or why not?
5. Do Malthus's views on population apply today? Why or why not?
6. What is the "Green Revolution"? Has it solved population problems?
7. How do European population policies differ from those of developing countries?
8. What effect does religion have on family planning and family size? Do different religions have different effects?
9. Is immigration today a benefit or problem for the United States?
10. If you had to come up with a population policy for the United States, what would it be?

Suggested Resources

Leon F. Bouvier and Lindsey Grant, *How Many Americans?*, Sierra Club Books, San Francisco, 1994. The Sierra Clubs view of population growth as threatening the nation's environment.

Peter Brimlaw, *Alien Nation: Common Sense about America's Immigration Disaster*, Random House, New York, 1995. The title says it all. Brimlaw argues with fire and brimstone that immigration needs to be further restricted.

Barry Edmonson and Jeffrey S. Passel, eds., *Immigration and Ethnicity: The Integration of America's Newest Arrivals*, Urban Institute, Washington, D.C., 1994. Expert articles discuss the impact of recent immigrants on the U.S. and the U.S. on recent immigrants.

Richard T. Gill, Nathan Glazer, Stephan A. Thernstrom, *Our Changing Population*, Prentice Hall, Englewood Cliffs, N.J., 1992. An economist, a sociologist, and a historian join forces to produce a readable demography text.

T. Robert Malthus, *Population: The First Essay*, University of Michigan Press, Ann Arbor, 1959 (original 1798). The original work on population and resources that started the debate.

Internet Connection 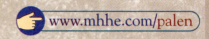 www.mhhe.com/palen

1. The U.S. Bureau of the Census (*www.census.gov/*) is the authoritative source of demographic data on the United States. Check out the population clocks for both the world and the United States on the home page. (At the time that this was written, the U.S. population was estimated to be 274,348,527.)

    The United Nations Population Information Network (*www.undp.org/popin/*) is another respected source of population data. Check out its information on world migration patterns by clicking on "World Population Trends," then hit the "Mortality and Migration" button. Select "International Migration Policies, 1995" and you'll see a picture of the publication. Click "continue" and then select "graphics."

    a. Look at each one of the graphic presentations. With regard to numbers, percentages and rates of migration, where does the United States stand in relation to other nations?

2. Population is a very political subject. Visit the website of the Population Research Institute (*www.pop.org/index.html*).

    a. What is the mission of this organization?

    b. What is its position on population growth?

    Many organizations, such as Negative Population Growth Inc. (*www.npg.org/index.htm*) and Zero Population Growth, Inc. (*www.zpg.org/*) are strong advocates of restricting or reversing population growth.

    c. Examine both sides of the debate over population growth using these websites. What is your conclusion?

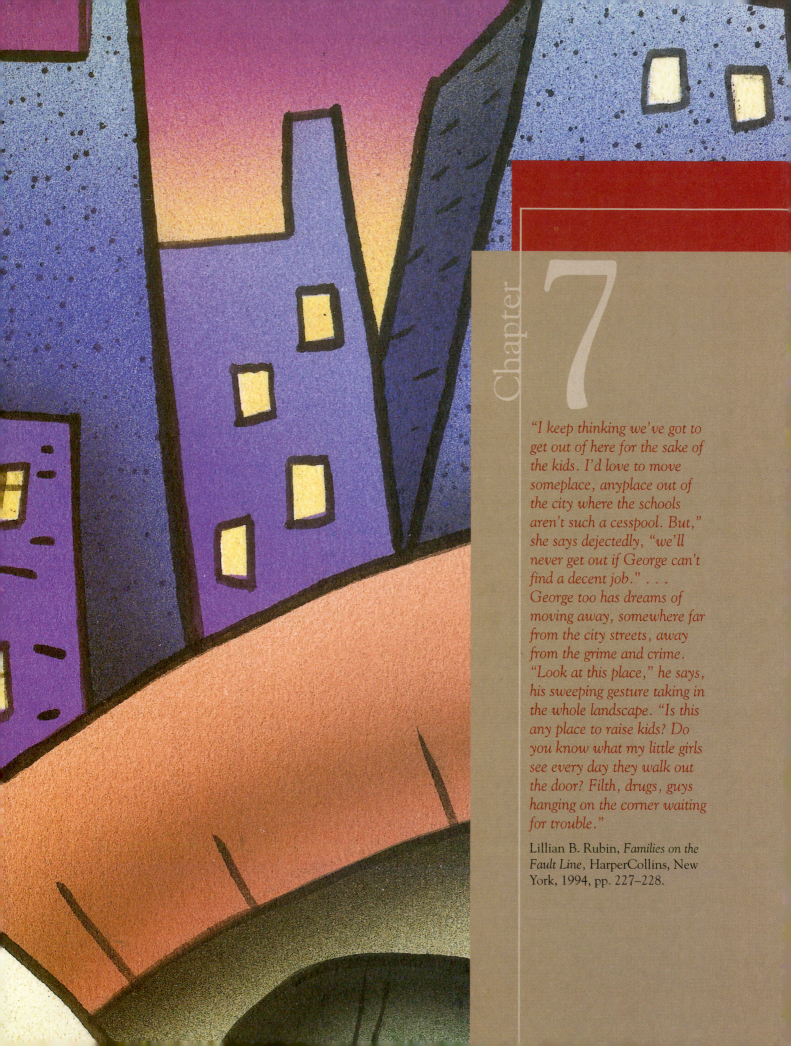

7

"I keep thinking we've got to get out of here for the sake of the kids. I'd love to move someplace, anyplace out of the city where the schools aren't such a cesspool. But," she says dejectedly, "we'll never get out if George can't find a decent job." . . . George too has dreams of moving away, somewhere far from the city streets, away from the grime and crime. "Look at this place," he says, his sweeping gesture taking in the whole landscape. "Is this any place to raise kids? Do you know what my little girls see every day they walk out the door? Filth, drugs, guys hanging on the corner waiting for trouble."

Lillian B. Rubin, *Families on the Fault Line*, HarperCollins, New York, 1994, pp. 227–228.

Urban Life and Deviance

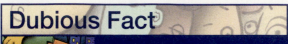
Urban Life

Only during the last century did any nation come to have the majority of its population living in urban places (Figure 7.1). One hundred years ago England was the only nation on earth that was more than half urban, and the United states didn't become urban until 1920. By midcentury only 30 percent of the world's population lived in urban places. Now that has changed. By the year 2005 for the first time in history, more than half the people on earth will live in urban places; by 2025, two-thirds of the world's population will live in urban places. Two hundred years ago, the world had no cities with 1 million inhabitants; now there are 391 such cities, 284 of them in developing countries. The population of the world's large cities is now growing by over a million people a week.

Whether we view rapid urban growth with pleasure or horror, whether we revel in urban variety or despise urban crowding, it is clear that massive urban growth is taking place worldwide. Large cities are generally viewed as having more wealth and more poverty, more crime and more culture, more divorce and more new family forms, more pollution and more industry, more crowding and more social mobility than rural places. Sociologists generally suggest that cities have more social problems because cities provide less social control and social integration. While in rural areas people live farther apart, they are often integrated into a common social network. People are more likely to know one another, at least by reputation, and being part of a social network acts to control some forms of deviance. Social problems don't exist only in cities, but urban areas are where the problems often are most intense. To the extent that high rates of social problems are associated with urban places, more urbanization means more social problems.

Targeting cities as the source of social ills has a long history. Early Christians, for example, felt that the city of Rome symbolized the degradation and debauchery of pagan life. (The graffiti on the walls of the public baths at Pompeii outdoes many of the scatological comments found in public lavatories today.) Contemporary Americans tend to see cities themselves as being a social problem. According to a Gallup Poll, only 19 percent of Americans consider city life to be the ideal. Suburbs (24 percent), small towns (34 percent), and rural areas (22 percent) are all rated higher by adult Americans.[1] However, while Americans may idealize small towns and farms, the majority of those reading this book actually live in metropolitan areas.

---

[1]Galloup Poll, *New York Times News Service*, October 8, 1989.

Figure 7.1 Percentage of Population Living in Urban Areas in 1994 and 2025

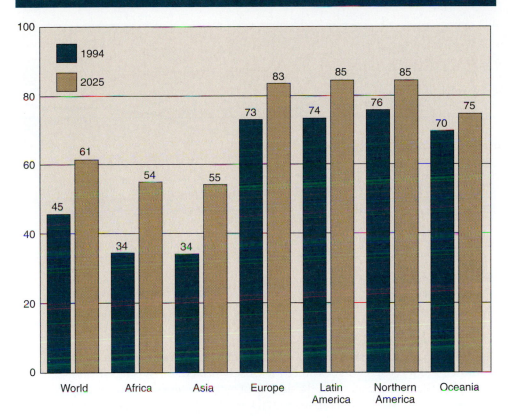

Source: United Nations, Department for Economic and Social Information and Policy Analysis, Population Dvision.

Urbanization and Urbanism

Four out of five Americans now live in metropolitan places (Figure 7.2). Thus, the United States has a high rate of **urbanization,** that is the proportion of people living in urban places. The United Nations estimates that by the year 2025 the rate will be 85 percent.[2] (Some urban researchers, including the author of this text, doubt that the rate of urban concentration will actually reach 85 percent, because new communication technologies permit population dispersion.) Recent American population trends suggest increasing deconcentration to outlying areas.[3]

Urbanism, in contrast to urbanization, refers to the *behaviors and ways of life* found in cities. Urbanization, or population concentration, is said to lead to the development of urbanism as a way of life, which in turn leads to social problems. In this view, the city is often seen not only as the setting for problems but also as the cause. Social problems policies are often implicitly based on the assumption that

urbanization
process of urban growth through the concentration of population in metropolitan places.

urbanism
behavioral aspects of urban life, the characteristics of urban life produced by city living.

[2]*Urban and Rural Areas 1994,* Population Division, United Nations, New York, 1995.
[3]Kenneth Johnson, "The Rural Rebound," *Reports on America,* Population Reference Bureau, Washington, DC, September 1999.

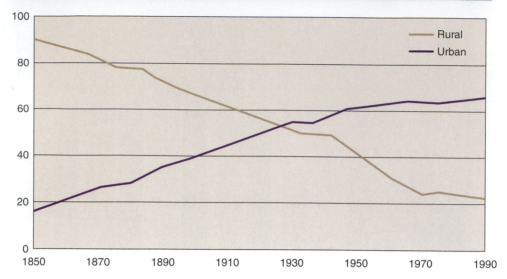

Figure 7.2 The Changing Landscape, U.S. Urban and Rural Residences, 1850–1990

Source: *1993 Statistical Abstracts.*

the amount of urbanism—that is, urban behaviors and ways of life—and the amount and kinds of social deviance are closely linked. Most times this association is simply taken for granted. As the author of a classic text on deviant behavior put it: "City living does not, of course, directly result in deviant behavior, but many of the conditions associated with city life are, to a preponderant degree, conducive to deviation."[4] Sociologically, the accuracy of this statement is not as important as is the fact that it is generally believed to be true. As noted in Chapter 1, situations that are perceived to be real are real in their consequences.

Sociological Perspectives

Functionalist Approaches

The Chicago School of Sociology, which dominated urban studies for the first half of the twentieth century, explained the city largely in terms of functionalist theory. Urban research focused on the dysfunctional aspects of urban change. Urbanization was seen as disruptive to the social fabric. Behavior patterns that are functional in a rural or small town setting are sometimes dysfunctional in the city. The increasing size, density, and heterogeneity of the city is seen as leading to the breakdown of primary groups, increases in crime, homelessness, and other signs of social disorganization, and the segregation of groups by race and class. The re-

---

[4]Marshall B. Clinard, *Sociology of Deviant Behavior,* 3d ed., Holt, Rinehart and Winston, New York, 1968, p. 88.

sulting urbanism as a way of life was viewed as economically productive but socially disruptive.

More recently, as American industrial cities have lost their manufacturing function, the social fabric of the inner city has collapsed. Functionalists would say that, in order to restore vitality to American cities, the city's zones or neighborhoods have to regain a functional purpose. This in turn can produce a social environment in which community can develop. Thus, cities need federal and state support to create new economic opportunities and functions for cities and their neighborhoods.

Conflict Approaches

Conflict theorists are less likely to see the decline of American central cities as a loss of urban function. Rather they see the decline of the central city as a direct consequence of conscious decisions by business elites to first invest, and then later disinvest, in the city. Early capitalism favored urbanization as a way of assembling cheap labor and ready markets. Today corporations benefit from economic dispersion, so they flee the city, possibly to the Third World.

Contemporary conflict-based political-economy theory focuses on how elites, following their own narrow economic interests, have profited by moving manufacturing and retailing from the city to the suburbs. Urban problems are viewed as a direct result of the operation of capitalistic markets in land and real estate.[5] Urban decay, thus, is seen not as the consequence of impersonal market forces but rather as the result of deliberate economic policies of capital flight. Urban problems reflect a struggle between the haves and the have-nots.

Conflict theorists suggest that an "urban growth machine" ideology influences governments to view cities not as places where people live, work, and have social relationships, but solely as places where "a good business climate" should be created. Elites view cities as urban growth machines where increasing the value of their commercial property comes ahead of community values or neighborhood needs. In the words of John Logan and Harvey Molotch, "Cities become organized enterprises devoted to the aggregate rent levels through the intensification of land use."[6] Local government is seen as largely being in the pocket of major economic interests, and revitalizing the city means downtown improvements for businesses rather than assistance to neighborhoods. Inner-city poverty is ignored unless it affects business interests.

According to conflict theorists, the only way such elite coalitions can be defeated and the cities made livable is through the organized political action of city residents. Only by organizing and taking control of the political structure can citizens stop the destruction of the city and defeat the elites who manipulate the urban growth machine for their own profit.

Interactionist Approaches

Interactionists looking at the social-psychological aspects of urban life focus on how cities affect individuals and how negative labels attached to urban places can result in negative public views of cities. Interactionists note that Americans have always been ambivalent about their cities, viewing them as more corrupt and socially disorganizing than small towns. Those in the tradition of theorists

---

[5]The two works that were the most crucial in spurring the conflict view of the city are David Harvey, *Social Justice and the City*, Arnold, London, 1973; and Manuel Castells, *The Urban Question: A Marxist Approach*, MIT Press, Cambridge, MA, 1997.
[6]John Logan and Harvey Molotch, *Urban Fortunes: The Political Economy of Place*, University of California Press, Berkeley, 1987, p. 13.

such as Georg Simmel and Louis Wirth suggest that social psychological problems of alienation, isolation, and social breakdown result from the city's disruption of primarily group relationships and the weakening of the traditional family bonds.

Others say that this is a considerable overstatement and that primary group relationships remain strong in urban places.[7] This is especially true of ethnic urban villagers who live in central city neighborhoods that are tightly knit and have a strong sense of group identity. Social psychologists note that the rebirth of urban neighborhoods and the development of community organizations can help tie urban dwellers to their neighborhoods. Although some inner-city areas have high levels of crime and social disorganization, this is by no means true of the city as a whole. Most city dwellers do know and help their neighbors.

Urban Patterns

We will start by looking at how social behavior and spacial characteristics are associated. For sociologists, distributional patterns of social problems are important because they shed light on the processes that cause the patterns. Why do some areas have high rates of social problems and others don't? A famous early model attempting to explain how cities are spatially and socially organized, was provided by Ernest Burgess, a member of the famous Chicago School of sociologists located at the University of Chicago.

concentric zonal hypothesis
theory of urban growth developed by Ernest Burgess suggesting that cities grow from the center to periphery through a series of concentric zones having distinct social and housing features.

Burgess's **concentric zonal hypothesis** suggested that cities grow from the center to the periphery through a series of circular zones.[8] Different land users—owners of single-family homes, apartment buildings, stores, factories, and warehouses—sort themselves out through the ecological processes of competition, segregation, invasion, and succession in such a way that similar-use zones arise. The zones reflect ecological competition, especially economic costs, rather than planning, zoning, or the efforts of government. Thus, downtown land usage went to the department stores and business offices that were most willing to pay the costs in terms of money, congestion, and pollution. Burgess and others also noted that each zone had distinctive social characteristics, with different kinds of social problems. Crime, mental illness, family breakdown, and other social problems were nonrandomly distributed throughout the metropolitan area. The Burgess hypothesis helps us understand why most American cities look so similar.

Newer Suburban Patterns

Metropolitan growth no longer moves out from the center zone by zone. Rather, since the 1960s, population growth has leapfrogged to outer suburban areas (and beyond), with retail trade and manufacturing increasingly located in the suburbs (Figure 7.3). (Edge cities are discussed later in the chapter.) Federally financed expressways meant factories no longer had to be located on railroad lines. The expansion of automobile ownership also meant that workers could live in the new suburbs, with mortgage costs underwritten by government loans, and drive to jobs that weren't on public transportation lines. As late as the 1940s most urban workers took public transportation to work; by the 1960s the vast majority were driving, increasingly

---

[7]Claude Fischer, "Toward a Subcultural Theory of Urbanism," *American Journal of Sociology,* 80:1319–1341, 1975.
[8]Ernest W. Burgess, "The Growth of the City: An Introduction to a Research Project," *Publications of the American Sociological Society,* 18:85–97, December 1924.

Figure 7.3 Concentric Zonal Growth Model

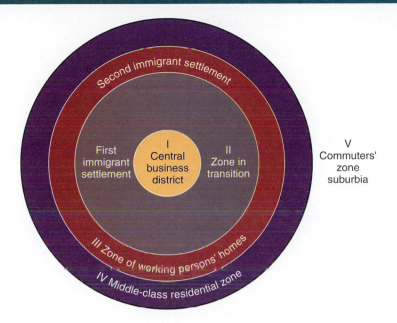

First immigrant settlement

I Central business district

II Zone in transition

Second immigrant settlement

III Zone of working persons' homes

IV Middle-class residential zone

V Commuters' zone suburbia

1.

2.

3.

Source: Ernest W. Burgess, "The Growth of the City: An Introduction to a Research Project," *Publication of the American Sociological Society*, 18:85–97, December 1924.

1. ©Vanessa Vick/Photo Researchers

2. American Destinations/Corbis CD

3. ©Thor Swift/Impact Visuals

from new suburban homes. As a result, metropolitan areas developed a complex polycentric form rather than just growing out from the old downtown (Figure 7.4).

As the spatial pattern of metropolitan areas has become more complex, so have social problems patterns. Crime, drug dealing, unemployment, welfare, and high levels of family disruption are no longer unique to inner-city zones. Actually, problems such as alcoholism, drug usage, and racism probably are more prevalent in the suburbs. White-collar criminals are heavily suburban residents.

Urbanism as a Way of Life

The classic sociological statement on how urbanization (urban growth) affects urban behavior patterns was developed 60 years ago by Louis Wirth. Building on earlier ideas of the social theorist Georg Simmel, Wirth suggested that three components of urbanization—size, density, and heterogeneity—create the distinct way of life called urbanism.[9] This urban way of life was implicitly contrasted with the more intimate and personal social structure and social relationships of small towns. Thus, Wirth argued that the city creates **urbanism as a way of life,** a unique culture of urbanism in which personal values are placed below impersonal calculation, where money is the universal standard of everything, and where the sheer size, noise, and complexity of the city create a pervading sense of impersonality and anonymity.[10] Such impersonality, with its dependence on impersonal and uncaring secondary groups, in turn leads to family disruption, crime, alcoholism, and

urbanism as a way of life

supposed consequences of urban living such as economic goal orientation and decreasing importance given to personal interaction and neighborhood values.

[9]Louis Wirth, "Urbanism as a Way of Life," *American Journal of Sociology* 44:1–24, July 1938.
[10]Some Chicago School classics describing the effects of urbanism as a way of life are William I. Thomas and Florian Znaniecki, *The Polish Peasant in Europe and America*, 5 vols., University of Chicago, 1918–1920; Louis Wirth, *The Ghetto*, University of Chicago Press, Chicago, 1928; Clifford R. Shaw, *The Jack Roller*, University of Chicago Press, Chicago, 1930; and Harvey W. Zorbaugh, *The Gold Coast and the Slum*, University of Chicago Press, Chicago, 1929.

Figure 7.4 The Polycentric Metropolis

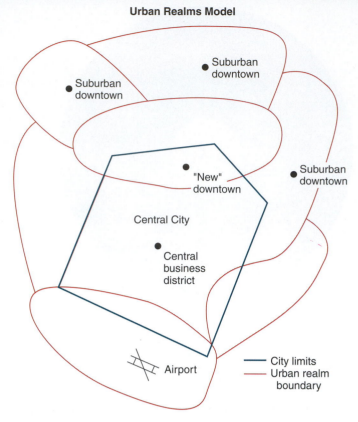

Urban Realms Model

- Suburban downtown
- Suburban downtown
- Suburban downtown
- "New" downtown
- Central City
- Central business district
- Airport

City limits
Urban realm boundary

Source: Truman A. Hartshorn and Peter O. Muller, "Suburban Downtowns and the Transformation of Metropolitan Atlanta's Business Landscape." Reprinted with permission from *Urban Geography*, Vol. 10, 1989, p. 378. Copyright V. H. Winston & Son, Inc., 360 South Ocean Blvd., Palm Beach, FL 33480. All rights reserved.

mental illness. The change from simple rural to complex urban was assumed to be both an inevitable and irreversible historical process.[11]

Much of today's writing about cities still suggests that urban behavior patterns, while often successful economically, produce disastrous social side effects, including personal alienation, social disorganization, breakdown of families, and all the ills often listed under the general heading of "crisis of the cities." (See Box 7.1.) Alvin Toffler, for example, in his best-seller *Future Shock* (1971), essentially restates Wirth's argument that urbanization creates anonymous and fragmented individuals:

> . . . we form limited involvement relationships with most of the people around us. Consciously or not, we define our relationships with most people in functional terms. So long as we do not become involved with the shoe salesman's problems at home, or his more general hopes, dreams and frustrations, he is, for us, fully interchangeable with any other salesman of equal competence. In effect, we have applied the modular principle to human relationships. We have created the disposable person: Moular Man.[12]

Fortunately, "Modular Man" is more fiction than fact. The image of a fast-paced, alienating, stimulating, and anonymous city life, which is then contrasted with the more romantic vision of the warm, personal, and well-adjusted though

---

[11]Georg Simmel, *The Sociology of Georg Simmel*, Kurt H. Wolff (trans.), Free Press, Glencoe, IL., 1950; Emile Durkheim, *The Division of Labor in Society*, George Simpson (trans.), Free Press, Glencoe, IL., 1960; and H. H. Gerth and C. Wright Mills (trans. and eds.), *From Max Weber: Essays in Sociology*, Oxford University Press, New York, 1946.

[12]Alvin Toffler, *Future Shock*, Bantam Books, New York, 1971, p. 97.

Box 7.1 Ongoing Issues

Geography of Vice

While sin seems to be randomly distributed throughout the population, commercial vice traditionally has had a distinct spatial pattern. Early in the twentieth century, every major city had a red-light district where the "sporting life" could be found. Red-light districts—with their saloons, brothels, and gambling places—were commonly situated at the edge of the central business district. Such locations offered easy access to both local residents and the traveling businessmen and conventioneers at downtown hotels. Among the most famous districts were Storyville in New Orleans, the Tenderloin in San Francisco, and the notorious First Ward or Levee in Chicago. This patterned distribution of commercial vice was clearly noted by the Chicago School sociologists during the 1920s.[a]

Established red-light districts were put out of business by a combination of economics and technology. Growing public pressure led to police payoff costs escalating beyond what the madams would pay, while at the same time the growing use of the telephone and auto were making it more convenient for a businessman to phone a "call girl" whom he could meet either at his hotel or at her apartment. With service just a phone call away, public visibility was no longer an asset. The technology of the telephone meant call girls could live anywhere. More recently, the technology of the VCR and the advent of X-rated cable TV channels has closed most of the central-city theaters specializing in X-rated films. Theaters are not necessary when X-rated videos can be picked up at the suburban video store, viewed on cable, or downloaded from X-rated websites.

Some cities still have semiofficial "adult entertainment districts" where one can find topless bars, massage parlors, adult bookstores, and "gentleman's clubs." However, cities that want to clean up such districts can legally do so. In 1999 the Supreme Court let stand New York City regulations that prohibit sex-oriented theaters, bookstores, massage parlors, and dance clubs from operating within 500 feet of homes, houses of worship, schools, or each other.[b]

Beginning in 1994, New York City began implementing a "zoning out" plan whose goal is to close most of the city's existing adult entertainment establishments. The effects clearly can be seen in New York's Times Square and 42nd Street. After decades as a center for sleazy businesses, the Times Square area has now undergone an economic and social revival. New businesses and theaters have opened, and even Disney has an entertainment center on 42nd Street.

[a]See, for example, Walter C. Reckless, "The Distribution of Commercialized Vice in the City: A Sociological Analysis," Publications of the American Sociological Society, 20:164–176, 1926.

duller rural life of the past is largely a stereotype. These images of city and rural life are part of our "common sense" culture—and they are mostly inaccurate. In fact, data indicate that most urbanites are anything but depersonalized and atomized members of modern society.[13] The idea that mental health is negatively affected by urban life also is unfounded.[14]

Subcultural Approach

Claude Fisher argues that urbanism does have an effect on people but does not produce social disorganization.[15] Fischer's **subcultural theory** suggests that, rather than destroying social and cultural groups as Wirth argued, urbanism creates and strengthens them. Fisher points out that only in the city can small groups reach a

subcultural theory
urban life increases social and cultural diversity.

---

[13]William Freudenburg, "The Density of Acquaintanceship: An Overlooked Variable of Community Research?" *American Journal of Sociology*, 92:27–63, 1986.

[14]Claude Fisher, To Dwell among Friends: Personal Networks in Town and City, University of Chicago Press, Chicago, 1982, p. 52.

[15]Claude Fischer, *The Urban Experience*, 2d ed, Harcourt Brace Jovanovich, San Diego, 1984, pp. 26, 35–39.

critical mass. Thus, the city contains sexual subgroups, model railroad subgroups, and even subgroups that get together every Sunday to play the tuba. And even when cities have serious problems, such as racial conflict, poverty, crime, and substance abuse, these problems are not confined just within the city boundaries.[16]

Are Cities Dying?

The cliché is that the American city is teetering on the brink of catastrophe. In this view, cities are places of deterioration, dirt, drugs, disorganization, and despair. The *New York Times,* in a 1996 front page article, for example, painted a picture of Camden, New Jersey, as being a dying city where only crime and corruption flourish.[17] The common wisdom suggests such cities hold only those lacking the option or energy to suburbanize. Those with means flee the city's high taxes and poor schools, while the level of urban poverty worsens. Descriptions of such cities often read like versions of Dante's *Inferno,* where the gate of hell bears the following inscription:

> Through me the way into the doleful city,
> Through me the way into eternal grief,
> Through me a people forsaken.
> (Canto III, Lines 1–3)

Certainly, the economic structural shift from manufacturing to service hit some older manufacturing cities hard. They have had to adjust to the loss of city blue-collar jobs and the departure to the suburbs or abroad of many manufacturing activities. Disinvestment and urban manufacturing plant closings have particularly hurt central city minority populations. During the last quarter of the twentieth century, New York City and Chicago lost over half their manufacturing jobs. Using the distinction made by C. Wright Mills in Chapter 1, personal troubles have become social problems.

The popular wisdom also is that older central cities have lost their capacity to serve as effective staging areas for newcomers and instead have become "sandboxes."[18] In such sandboxes, the poor occasionally get new toys (government programs) designed to keep them from becoming bothersome to the society. Those in the sandbox, however, stay there; the underclass doesn't get to enter the real world. This pessimistic view holds that unless the federal government provides funds to put the city on life-support systems, the downward slide to oblivion will continue. But is this an accurate picture? Are America's cities, particularly the larger ones, going down the drain? Do cities in general have a future?

More Optimistic Views

Fortunately, this dismal picture, while it fits a few cities, is a caricature of the larger American urban scene. There is a tendency simply to list city ills and overlook real urban strengths. American cities of the twenty-first century will have much more of a service and less of a manufacturing focus. While this means fewer blue-collar factory jobs, it also means more white-collar positions. The new office-based service economy has made the downtowns of cities such as Pittsburgh, Miami, and Los

---

[16]Herbert J. Gans, "Urbanism and Suburbanism as Ways of Life," in J. John Palen and Karl Fleming (eds.), *Urban America,* Holt, Rinehart and Winston, New York, 1972, pp. 184–200.
[17]Brett Pulley, "While a Dying City Languishes," *New York Times,* May 19, 1996, p. A1.
[18]George Sternlieb, "The City as Sandbox," *Public Interest,* Fall 1971, p. 4.

Crowds gather for the 1995 opening of the I. M. Pei-designed Rock and Roll Hall of Fame and Museum in Cleveland.

Angeles more vital than they were a decade or two ago. New York and Chicago increased their office space by over two-thirds between 1975 and 2000. Both cities have emerged as world financial and trade centers, as has Miami. Other cities, such as Dallas, Minneapolis, and Atlanta, have become regional financial centers. Cities, with their extensive fiber-optic-cable networks, are benefiting from their advanced telecommunications services. New York City, for instance, has its "Silicon Alley." Even Cleveland, oft-cited in the 1980s as a prime example of urban decline, now shows rebirth of downtown activity with its new baseball stadium and the Rock and Roll Hall of Fame. Pronounced dead a decade earlier, Cleveland by the late 1990s had become a tourist attraction. Most city downtowns have a secure economic base and consistently garner 20 percent of all new office construction.[19]

While the populations and economies of some old smokestack cities have declined, others have stabilized, and some are booming. New York, for instance, is seeing whole neighborhoods in Brooklyn and the Bronx revitalized by new immigrant groups, especially Asians and Jamaicans. Moreover, not all cities are old. Population growth has been strong in sunbelt cities, especially in the southwest, where fast-growing large cities include Phoenix and Dallas-Fort Worth. Las Vegas is the nation's fastest growing city. In spite of predictions of decline, and even a 1992 earthquake, Los Angeles is growing in terms of economic activity and cultural influence.

New hotels, with their dramatic atriums and public spaces, have also contributed to restoring some of the glitz and glamour of downtown. Major cities, such as New

[19]Bernard J. Frieden, "The Downtown Job Puzzle," *Public Interest,* Fall 1989, pp. 71–86.

York, Philadelphia, and Boston, that a decade or two ago were on the brink of bankruptcy are solvent today. Additionally, American cities present more vitality and liveliness than a decade ago. Festival marketplaces, beginning with Ghirardelli Square in San Francisco, Faneuil Hall in Boston, and Harbor Place in Baltimore, have remade old central areas. City restaurants and evening entertainment areas are expanding, not contracting. People may shop in the suburban malls, but for an evening out or dinner at other than a chain restaurant, the city is the place to go. Cities also serve to provide diversity, excitement, and nourishment for the soul. Young professionals are gentrifying some city neighborhoods, while new immigrant populations are bringing life to working-class neighborhoods that were all but written off a decade ago.

Local Variations

One of the reasons we have difficulty deciding whether the city is dying or blossoming, whether the city is a social problem or a social triumph, is that the city itself has become fragmented. There no longer is a "city" as such. Huge variations occur not only between city and suburbs, but within city areas. Cities are legal entities, but economically and socially there often is no unified city. Urban problems tend to be concentrated within specific localized areas of the metropolis. The city has become balkanized. While the new downtown of Los Angeles is rapidly moving into the twenty-first century, the south-central district slightly over a mile away is suffering from economic deindustrialization and welfare dependency. In the early twenty-first century these urban extremes are becoming more intense. The city increasingly juxtaposes privileges for the rich with deprivation for the poor.[20]

In many inner-city neighborhoods poverty remains and the social fabric continues to deteriorate, regardless of national economic trends. Federal government support for dealing with urban problems has dramatically decreased. President Ronald Reagan systematically dismantled established urban social programs during the 1980s, dropping direct federal aid to cities from $47 billion to $19.8 billion.[21] The 1990s saw President Bill Clinton providing good words, but little real funding, for urban problems. The only major new urban program during the 1990s was Empowerment (or Enterprise) Zones for economic development. Empowerment Zones with their tax breaks have wide bipartisan political support, but even many supporters concede that the programs are largely symbolic.[22] Because urban revenues are limited, city budgets often are balanced by cutting services to the poor. Unless federal or state governments provide new economic support (an unlikely possibility), the economic and social problems of central-city poverty areas can be expected to remain.

The urban pattern for the early twenty-first century may be the absence of any overall national pattern. Some localities are reforming, reorganizing, and renewing. Others are simply going through the motions. With cities now having to sink or survive on their own, some cities have lost economic vitality, while others, particularly in the sunbelt, are experiencing prosperity and expansion. Large older cities, such as New York, Philadelphia, and Chicago, are also economically stronger today than in 1990. Neither civic hand wringing nor civic boosterism is really useful in addressing real urban problems. Without federal support, successful local governments probably will be those that can reduce costs and increase community support—including community support through taxes.

---

[20]Douglas S. Massey, "The Age of Extremes: Concentrated Affluence and Poverty in the Twenty-First Century," *Demography*, 33:4, 395–412, 1996.

[21]David Ames et al., "Rethinking American Urban Policy," *Journal of Urban Affairs*, 14, 3/4, 1992, p. 209.

[22]Nicholas Lemann, "The Myth of Community Development," *New York Times Magazine*, January 9, 1994, pp. 27–28.

Problems and Changes in Urban Areas

As urbanism increasingly becomes the American way of life, the social and economic problems of urban places invariably become the nation's social problems. Of all the urban-based problems, probably the two most visible and grievous are racial polarization and homelessness.

Racial Divisions

For much of the twentieth century, whites and blacks in metropolitan areas have been distributed more or less like the hole and the doughnut: The hole represented central city blacks and other minorities, and the doughnut, suburban whites. Until World War I (1914–1918) the African American population was overwhelmingly rural and southern. Then, pushed by the increasingly severe racial climate and pulled by factory jobs in the North, some 5 million blacks moved to northern cities where there were job opportunities. By the time the migration had run its course in the 1960s, Chicago housed more blacks than the entire state of Mississippi, and the New York metropolitan area had more black residents than any state in the Old South.[23] In segregated industrial cities blacks were restricted to neighborhoods that were invariably densely packed with older and less desirable housing.

In 1968 the Open Housing Act permitted the black middle class to flee the ghettoes and join the white exodus to the suburbs. Major middle-class black suburbanization coincided with the deindustrialization of the central city. Many of the central-city factories, which had long provided entry to the world of work, were closing, and the result was inner-city population decline. In the decade following the Open Housing Act, New York's South Bronx lost 37 percent of its population, and the southside Chicago ghetto saw its population decline a similar amount. Once vital and vibrant city neighborhoods slumped, and the fabric of inner-city life seriously deteriorated.

As blue-collar jobs disappeared, many of the successful role models departed for the suburbs. Those left behind were deprived not only of jobs but also of access to informal job networks.[24] The result was their economic and social marginalization. Older working-class men continue to support a strong work ethic and respect for traditional values.[25] However, such older urban men are often viewed as anachronisms by the younger males who espouse the values of the "street."[26]

Today, the overall economic health of the city at large has only limited impact on job opportunities in the inner city. Even if there are increases in the number of downtown white-collar positions, such changes don't affect the lives of blue-collar job seekers. There is a mismatch between inner-city residents' job skills and the central-city jobs they can do.[27] Without access to jobs paying wages that will support a family, increases in unemployment, welfare dependency, and crime follow. It is impossi-

---

[23]Thomas F. Pettigrew, *Racially Separate or Together?* McGraw-Hill, New York, 1971, p. 3.

[24]William J. Wilson, *The Truly Disadvantaged: The Inner-City Underclass and Public Policy,* University of Chicago Press, Chicago, 1987.

[25]Mitchell Duneier, *Slim's Table: Race, Respectability, and Masculinity,* University of Chicago Press, Chicago, 1992.

[26]Elijah Anderson, *Streetwise: Race, Class, and Change in an Urban Community,* University of Chicago Press, Chicago, 1990.

[27]John Kasarda, "Urban Change and Minority Opportunities," in *The New Urban Reality,* Paul Peterson (ed.) Brookings Institution, Washington, DC, 1985, pp. 33–67.

Box 7.2 Ongoing Issues

Street Etiquette

In *Streetwise,* Elijah Anderson discusses the norms or rules of street conduct or street etiquette local people use to avoid conflict.[a] This excerpt discusses how adults living in the Philadelphia neighborhood he calls Village-Norton respond to young males.

"The residents of the area, including black men themselves, are likely to defer to unknown black males, who move convincingly through the area as though they 'run it,' exuding a sense of ownership. They are easily symbolically perceived as inserting themselves into any available social space, pressing against those who might challenge them. The young black males, the 'big winners' of these little competitions, seem to feel very comfortable as they swagger confidently along. Their looks, their easy smiles, and their spontaneous laughter, singing, cursing, and talk about the intimate details of their lives, which can be followed from across the street, all convey the impression of little concern for other pedestrians. The other pedestrians, however, are very concerned about them. . . .

"Because public interactions generally matter for only a few crucial seconds, people are conditioned to rapid scrutiny of the looks, speech, public behavior, gender, and color of those sharing the environment. . . . The central strategy in maintaining safety of the streets is to avoid strange black males. The public awareness is color-coded: white skin denotes civility, law abidingness, and trustworthiness, while black skin is strongly associated with poverty, crime, incivility, and distrust. Thus an unknown young black man must be readily deferred to. . . .

"Middle-income blacks in the Village, who also are among the 'haves,' often share a victim mentality with middle-income whites and appear just as distrustful of black strangers. Believing they are immune to the charge of racism, Village blacks make some of the same remarks as whites do, sometimes voicing even more incisive observations concerning 'street blacks' and black criminality. . . ."

[a]*Elijah Anderson,* Streetwise: Race, Class, and Change in an Urban Community, *University of Chicago Press, Chicago, 1990.*

ble to break this cycle without job opportunities. As William J. Wilson says, "Inner-city social dislocations . . . (joblessness, crime, female-headed families, and welfare dependence) should be analyzed not as cultural aberrations but as symptoms of racial-class inequality. It follows, therefore, that changes in the economic and social situation of the ghetto underclass will lead to changes in cultural norms and behavioral patterns."[28] (See Box 7.2.)

Urban Black Majorities?

African Americans constitute a majority of the population in the larger cities of Atlanta, Washington, D.C., Newark, Detroit, Baltimore, St. Louis, and New Orleans and in several medium-size cities, such as Richmond, Virginia (Table 7.1). However, the most important thing about this pattern is that it is self-limiting. Contrary to popular belief, most American cities are not "turning black." African American urban percentages actually are declining in most cities. The reason is largely demographic. African Americans constitute only one-eighth of the national population, and blacks are suburbanizing. So long as whites remain over four-fifths of the population, it is impossible for African Americans to become the majority population in more than a limited number of places. There are not enough African Americans to go around.

---

[28]William J. Wilson, *The Truly Disadvantaged,* p. 159.

Table 7.1 Metropolitan Areas with the Largest African American Populations, 1990

Metropolitan Area	African American Population	African Americans in Metropolitan Area (%)	African Americans in Central City (%)
New York	3,289,465	18.2	28.7
Chicago	1,547,725	19.2	39.1
Los Angeles	1,229,809	8.5	14.0
Philadelphia	1,100,347	18.7	39.9
Washington D.C.	1,041,934	26.6	65.8
Detroit	975,199	20.9	75.7
Atlanta	736,153	26.0	67.1
Houston	665,378	17.9	28.1
Baltimore	616,065	25.9	59.2
Miami	591,440	18.5	27.4

Source: Population Reference Bureau adaptation from U.S. Bureau of the Census.

Black Suburbanization

Within metropolitan areas, one of every three African Americans is a suburbanite.[29] This will approach one in two early in the twenty-first century. A decade ago the 1990 Census reported that even then over eight million African Americans were suburbanites, and some 40 metropolitan areas had African American suburban populations exceeding 50,000. Among the largest were suburban Washington, D.C., with 620,000 black suburbanites, Atlanta with 463,000, and Los Angeles with 401,000.[30] Flight to the suburbs today is increasingly not "white flight" but "black flight." Washington, D.C., for example, is experiencing substantial suburban flight, virtually all of it by middle-class African Americans. Between 1990 and 1996 alone, the nation's capital lost 10 percent of its population, and the largest group was long-term middle-class black residents.[31]

African American suburbanization is now the reality; the remaining question is whether African American suburbanization reflects housing integration, or merely the growth of all-black suburban enclaves. Until the 1980s African American suburbanization was substantially one of spillover from central cities into older inner-ring suburbs, that is, the classic **invasion-succession model** of one group supplanting another. The result, as expressed by John Logan, was that "the average black suburb is poor, fiscally stressed, and crime-ridden compared to other suburbs."[32]

This view of black spillover still is commonly expressed by the public (and some scholars), but the reality now is that an economic range of multiracial suburbs are

invasion-succession
process by which one activity or population displaces another in an ecological area.

---

[29]J. John Palen, *The Suburbs*, McGraw-Hill, NY, 1995, p. 116.
[30]Ibid., p. 117.
[31]D'Vera Cohn (reporting on a study done by George Grier), "D.C. Losing Longtime Residents to Suburbs, Study Finds," *Washington Post*, February 26, 1998, C1.
[32]John R. Logan, "Realities of Black Suburbanization," in Roland Warren and Larry Lyon (eds.), *New Perspectives on the American Community*, Dorsey Press, Chicago, 1988, p. 235.

parallel-growth model

simultaneous suburban growth of white and black populations, as opposed to invasion-succession.

more common.[33] The "spillover" pattern has been replaced by a "leapfrog" effect of blacks moving into newer subdivisions on the periphery. The last decade showed less racial replacement, and more **parallel growth** in suburbs for both blacks and whites.[34] While race remains the core variable in American society, for suburbanizing blacks, one's social class increasingly is more important in determining one's neighbors. Suburbs have the opportunity to achieve what the cities have largely failed to accomplish: establishing stable, economically viable, and racially and ethnically integrated communities.

Homelessness

homeless

poor urban residents who live full-time on the street.

Amount of Homelessness

Homelessness is among the most visible urban problems (New York also has unseen homeless communities that live in abandoned tunnels under the city[35]). Estimates of the number of homeless range from 250,000 to 2.2 million.[36] The numbers are subject to dispute, basically for two reasons. First, the homeless are a transient population and data are both difficult to obtain and often unreliable. Second, homelessness is a highly politicized issue. For example, a 1994 Clinton Administration report on homelessness said as many as 7 million Americans were homeless for some period in the late 1980s,[37] though scholars commonly cite much lower figures. Reviewing a number of studies, Jencks estimates the number of homeless at approximately 400,000.[38] In perhaps the best empirically grounded study, Rossi estimates the number of homeless on a given night at roughly half a million persons.[39] Another 4 to 7 million are so poor they could be pushed into the ranks of the homeless by an economic downturn.[40] Today, 400,000 to 500,000 homeless at any given time is the generally accepted figure.

Who is homeless has been changing. Three decades ago the inner-city homeless population was heavily made up of older, often alcoholic, skid-row men with acute personal problems.[41] The stereotype of the skid-row wino was then supplanted by that of the bag lady who had been deinstitutionalized from a psychiatric hospital and left to pick through refuse bins.[42] The 1990s version of the stereotype was more likely to be a disorganized, drug-taking, panhandler. Now a more complex picture is emerging.

---

[33]John M. Stahura, "Changing Patterns of Suburban Racial Composition," *Urban Affairs Quarterly,* 23:448–460, 1988; Nancy A. Denton and Douglas S. Massey, "Patterns of Neighborhood Transition in a Multiethnic World: U.S. Metropolitan Areas, 1970–1980," *Demography,* 28:41–63, 1991.

[34]Barrett A. Lee and Peter B. Wood, "Is Neighborhood Racial Succession Place Specific?" *Demography,* 28:21–40, 1991.

[35]Margaret Morton, *The Tunnel: The Underground Homeless of New York City,* Yale University Press, New Haven, CT, 1995.

[36]Jon Erickson and Charles Wilhelm (eds.), *Housing the Homeless,* Center for Urban Policy Research, Rutgers, New Brunswick, NJ, 1986, p. xix.

[37]Jason DeParle, "Draft Administration Report Sees Homelessness as a Vast Problem," *New York Times,* February 17, 1994, p. A1.

[38]Christopher Jencks, *The Homeless,* Harvard University Press, Cambridge, MA, 1994, p. 16.

[39]Peter H. Rossi, *Down and Out in America: The Origins of Homelessness,* University of Chicago Press, Chicago, 1989. Also see James D. Wright, *Address Unknown: The Homeless in America,* Aldine de Gruyter, Hawthorne, NY, 1989.

[40]For an example of the diversity of local area findings, see Jamshid A. Momenti (ed.), *Homelessness in the United States,* Vol. 1: *State Surveys,* Greenwood Press, New York, 1989; see particularly the introduction by Howard M. Bahr, pp. vi–xxv, and Chapter 11, "Homelessness in Tennessee," by Barrett A. Lee, pp. 181–203.

[41]See Donald J. Bogue, *Skid Row in American Cities,* University of Chicago, Community and Family Study Center, Chicago, 1963; and Carl I. Cohen and Jay Sokolovsky, *Old Men of the Bowery: Strategies for Survival among the Homeless,* Guilford Press, New York, 1989.

[42]For a review of deinstitutionalization and its consequences, see Michael J. Dear and Jennifer R. Wolch, *Landscapes of Despair: From Deinstitutionalization to Homelessness,* Polity Press, Oxford, 1987.

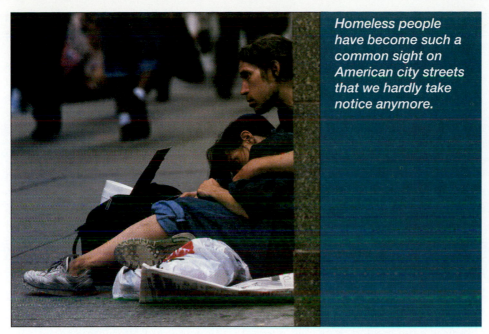

Homeless people have become such a common sight on American city streets that we hardly take notice anymore.

© Tom McKitterick/Impact Visuals

According to a new survey by HUD, 34 percent of homeless are familes and 66 percent are single. Two-thirds are male, 38 percent have less than a high school education, and 23 percent are veterans.[43] Most of the males on the street are white, whereas families on the street are more likely to be headed by black females. In the past, many of the economically marginal who were not in family units lived in single-room-occupancy (SRO) residential hotels. However, the number of SRO units has decreased by over 80 percent over the last two decades. At the same time, funds for low-cost housing were being severely decreased. Some of those on the street are there because we have been destroying cheap SRO housing without putting anything in its place (See Box 7.3).

Social Disabilities The problem, though, goes well beyond simply providing housing. There is a high level of social disabilities among the homeless. Homelessness frequently involves a whole series of pathologies such as alcoholism, drug addiction, mental illness, and criminal incarceration. It is accepted that roughly one-third of the homeless are mentally ill. Four of ten street people admit to having spent time in jail, and substance abuse is also admitted to by roughly half. Actual figures are assumed to be substantially higher. In terms of official records, more than four out of five homeless have been in a mental hospital or detoxification unit or have been convicted by the courts.[44] Thus, commonly made statements that the homeless resemble the rest of the population except for having had bad luck are inaccurate.

Those who end up on the streets typically have multiple personal problems. Most grew up in problem families or in foster care. Many have serious learning and physical health problems. Few have had success with marriage or other personal relationships. Many are social isolates, with six in ten never having married and most of the remainder being separated or divorced. Strained or minimal relations

---

[43]"Homelessness and the People They Serve." HUD, Government Printing Office, Washington, D.C., 1999.
[44]Peter H. Rossi and James D. Wright, "The Urban Homeless: A Portrait of Urban Dislocation," *Annals of the American Academy of Political and Social Science*, 501:137, January 1989.

with family and relatives is the usual pattern. Some shelter workers maintain that in an attempt to not "blame the victim" the seriousness of these personal problems is often overlooked or downplayed.[45]

What is not disputed is that the homeless are marginalized in a nation that has little interest in providing them broad-based (and often expensive) treatment and services. The homeless face an urban scene in which deindustrialization of the economy, downsizing of the welfare system, deinstitutionalization of the mentally ill, and destruction of marginal inexpensive housing make living a secure life far more problematic.

Public attitudes toward, and tolerance of, the homeless, and especially of panhandlers, has been hardening, with many citizens viewing the homeless not with pity but as a threat to public order. Even homeless shelters have had to develop strict policies to deal with major behavior problems like drug usage and fighting. Tough antivagrancy measures have been adopted in some of the previously most tolerant cities. New York has cracked down on aggressive subway panhandlers and car window washers, liberal Seattle has made it illegal to sit on downtown public sidewalks during business hours, and even tolerant San Francisco now arrests homeless people for urinating in public.[46]

Successful Approaches   There are a few signs of positive change. Some homeless have created their own alternative housing and alternative social communities.[47] A positive step is that cities such as New York are building or renovating new single-room-occupancy hotels.[48] These new SROs, known as supportive SROs, generally are run by nonprofit organizations that specialize in drug and alcohol treatment. The new SROs are constructed using a combination of state, federal, and private funds. The supportive SROs differ from the old SROs in that the goal is not simply to supply the homeless with a home but also to provide within the SRO a highly structured support system. The supportive SROs provide not only a clean room where no drug and alcohol use is tolerated but also services such as drug treatment centers, medical clinics, and job counselors. The new supportive SROs seem to be working. Moreover, they are comparatively inexpensive. Even when all renovation and social service costs are included, the supportive SROs cost a fifth of the cost of jailing someone and just over half the cost of housing someone in a shelter.[49]

Urban Solutions?

The last half-century has witnessed various pet nostrums for fighting urban blight and restoring vitality to the cities. Some of these have worked and some have not. The remedy during the 1950s and 1960s was public housing. During the 1970s it was urban homesteading, and more recently it has been urban revitalization or gentrification.

---

[45]Alice S. Baum and Donald W. Burnes, *A Nation in Denial: The Truth about the Homeless*, Westview, Boulder, CO, 1993.

[46]Melinda Henneberger, "Where the Beggars Meet the Begged," *New York Times*, January 16, 1994, p. 6E.

[47]David Wagner, *Checkerboard Square: Culture and Resistance in a Homeless Community*, Westview Press, Boulder, CO, 1993.

[48]Lynette Holloway, "With a New Purpose and Look, S.R.O.'s Make a Comeback," *New York Times*, November 10, 1996, p. 1, 44.

[49]Ibid., p. 44.

Box 7.3

Making a Difference

Understanding Being Homeless

John Coleman was the president of Haverford College when he spent 10 winter days living as a homeless man, spending his nights in shelters and on the streets of New York City. The following excerpt is from his January 27th diary entry.[a]

"Early this afternoon I went again to the restaurant where I had eaten five times before. I didn't recognize the man at the cash register.

" 'Get out,' he said.

" 'But I have money.'

" 'You heard me. Get out.' His voice was stronger.

" 'That man knows me,' I said, looking toward the owner in the back of the restaurant.

"The owner nodded, and the man at the register said, 'Okay, but sit in the back.'

"Tonight, after a repeat of the totally degrading dinner-line scene at East 3rd Street shelter, I signed up for Keener once again. No more Brooklyn for me.

"Sitting upstairs with the other Keener-bound men, I carelessly put my left foot on the rung of the chair in front of me, occupied by a young black.

" 'Get your foot off, yo.'

"I took it off. 'Sorry,' I said.

"But it was too late. I had broken a cardinal rule. I had violated the man's turf. As we stood in the stairwell waiting for the buses, he told a much bigger, much louder, much angrier friend what I had done.

"That man turned on me.

" 'Wait till we get you tonight, whitey. You stink. Bad. The worst I ever smelled. And when you put your foot on that chair, you spread your stink around. You better get yourself a shower as soon as we get there, but it won't save you later on. . . . And don't sit near me or him on the bus. You hear, whitey?'

"I didn't reply.

"The bombardment went on as we mounted the bus. No one spoke up in my defense. Three people waved me away when I tried to sit next to them. The next person, black and close to my age, made no objection when I sat beside him.

"The big man continued his tirade for a while, but he soon got interested in finding out from the driver how to go about getting a bus-driver's license. Perhaps he had come down from a high.

"I admit I was scared. I wrote my name, address, and office telephone number on a piece of paper and slipped it into my pocket. At least someone would know where to call if the threats were real. I knew I couldn't and wouldn't defend myself in this setting.

"I slept fitfully, I don't like lying with the sheet hiding my face."

[a]John R. Coleman, *"Diary of a Homeless Man," New York Magazine, February 21, 1983.*

Public Housing

Public housing began during the Depression of the 1930s and was a successful way of eliminating slums and housing the working poor. However, by 1970 the program had been redirected to the welfare poor. While earlier "projects" had held intact families, by the 1970s almost all the families were headed by single welfare mothers with no prospect of social mobility. The nation's 1.2 million public housing units (about 1.5 percent of the nation's housing stock) also were showing sharp physical deterioration, and "projects" came to be associated with welfare, crime, and drug abuse.

After decades of evading the issue, the Department of Housing and Urban Development (HUD) in 1993 acknowledged the failure of most public housing and began to demolish urban high-rise projects as rapidly as funds allowed. As of 2000, more than 75,000 of the worst units had been leveled. Among these were some of the country's most notoriously dangerous projects, such as the Cabrini-Green housing projects in Chicago. The goal had been to demolish 100,000 deteriorated units by the year 2000.[50]

---

[50]Department of Housing and Urban Development, *Moving Up to the American Dream: From Public Housing to Private Homeownership,* Government Printing Office, Washington, DC, July 1996, p. 4.

An idea that failed. One of three remaining thirteen-story buildings of Edward Scudder housing project in Baltimore were imploded in 1996. It is being replaced with a mixture of low-income, low-rise housing.

Michael Sypniewski/AP/Wide World Photos

To replace the widely discredited "projects," HUD now uses rent vouchers and is working with local programs to build new garden apartments, townhomes, and single-family houses. These units are then sold at a discount to public housing families and to low and moderate-income working families. The goal is to generate 25,000 new private homeowner families from former public housing residents. Public housing families who demonstrate an interest in becoming homeowners receive financial assistance such as grants or low-interest loans to lease-purchase or "rent-to-own" the homes. To protect those families moving into the new low-rise housing, residents who do not make their payments or who engage in criminal behavior are evicted.

The good news is that it appears that this is the most successful public housing program in 50 years. The down side is that far too few new units are being constructed or renovated. Because of limited Congressional funding, fewer new units can be restored than old units destroyed.

Urban Homesteading

urban homesteading
programs that provide for low-cost resale of abandoned city homes to those who will rehabilitate them.

In the 1970s urban homesteading gained attention as a solution to city housing problems. The term "homesteading" conjures up the image of the hardy Western pioneers who, under the 1862 Homesteading Act, were given 160 acres of Western land if they could stick it out for five years. **Urban homesteading** today consists of locally run programs that offer abandoned or foreclosed housing free or for a nominal amount, such as $10, to homesteaders who agree to rehabilitate the home.[51] The idea is that contemporary urban homesteaders will rebuild devastated city neighborhoods.

It sounds like an ideal program for reviving declining and abandoned neighborhoods, but the concept has some major practical pitfalls. The most serious is that most abandoned properties are economically beyond the point where they can be rehabilitated. Earlier "brownstone revival" programs in New York, or restoration programs elsewhere, almost always involved homes that had become run-down but were still occupied. Today, however, by the time the local government obtains an abandoned home, professional looters and vandals have usually stripped the building to its core.

Nor is urban homesteading anywhere near cost-free to homesteaders. In addition to their own hard work (sweat equity), homesteaders must obtain and pay back rehabilitation loans that run from $75,000 to $150,000. Thus, urban homesteading is definitely not the answer for the urban poor. It is particularly not the answer for the welfare poor, who require reasonable quality rental housing.

Also, once a house is rehabilitated, there still remains the question of the fate of the remainder of the neighborhood. Unless a substantial number of homes are simultaneously rehabilitated, the neighborhood may still be characterized by burned-out shells of buildings, high crime and violence, no stores, abysmal schools, and minimal public services. Thus, whole areas have to be rehabilitated. Well-run and well-financed urban homesteading programs can help older neighborhoods stabilize themselves or even revive. The reality, though, is that urban homesteading to date often has been more of a slogan than a program.

Gentrification

In the 1980s and 1990s, the period during which the federal government disengaged from the city, privately sponsored neighborhood revitalization or gentrification has been cited as the way to promote city revival. **Gentrification,** or **revitalization,** refers to the countermovement of mostly white middle-class homebuyers toward residences located in the older inner zones of the central city—specifically, the recycling of older declining neighborhoods from patterns of decay to patterns of prosperity. Gentrification especially occurs in inner-city neighborhoods of once-prosperous upper-middle-class housing, areas that frequently have architectural or historic merit. In larger cities well-located older working-class neighborhoods are also being revitalized. Such in-movement is significant because it challenges realtors' **trickle-down** theory of neighborhood change. The trickle-down model (based on the Burgess hypothesis discussed earlier) suggests that once a neighborhood begins to decline, it inevitably moves to less prestigious occupancy patterns. By decreeing that it is a bad investment to buy into declining neighborhoods, the model becomes a self-fulfilling prophesy.

As a result, for many years would-be gentrifiers were unable to get conventional mortgages because gentrification of older central-city neighborhoods was not supposed to occur. Experts held it as an article of faith that middle-class homebuyers would be interested only in newer city housing. Nor, excepting some historic-district programs, were federal, state, or municipal funds available to encourage the restoration of neighborhoods. Nonetheless, gentrification took place.

However, gentrification, for all the media attention, has encompassed only a limited number of central-city homes. As a consequence, gentrification has not pro-

gentrification
revitalization of central city housing and neighborhoods through the immigration of upper-middle class populations.

trickle-down
belief that housing quality and value decreases over time.

---

[51]For further details, see J. John Palen, Chapter 12, *The Urban World,* 5th ed., McGraw-Hill, New York, 1997.

duced the substantial displacement of poorer residents that once was feared.[52] Displacement of poorer residents far more commonly takes place from neighborhoods that are deteriorating than from neighborhoods that are upgrading.

There is a common belief that gentrifiers are dissatisfied young suburbanites who are engaging in a "back to the city" movement. This is a myth. Data from 1980 to the present shows that there has been no such movement.[53] In reality, most gentrifiers are "stayers" in the city rather than suburbanites moving back. Since urban gentrification only affects a few neighborhoods in any city, the importance of the gentrification movement lies not so much in its size but in its potential for shaping future housing trends.

Suburban Change

We think of ourselves as a nation of city dwellers. In reality, however, since 1970 more of us have lived in suburbs than anywhere else, and since 1997 an absolute majority of the population has lived in suburbs. The last census reported half again as many suburbanites as city residents (115 million suburbanites, 78 million in central cities, and 56 million in smaller places beyond metropolitan areas). Most of those reading this book have grown up in suburbs.

The dominant symbol of the urban twentieth century was the skyscraper. The dominant metropolitan symbol of the early twenty-first century is the suburban shopping mall. While downtown department stores have closed, there are now over 40,000 malls, ranging from small strip shopping centers to Canada's massive West Edmonton Mall with its 800 shops, 110 restaurants and places to eat, 19 movie theaters, a 355-room hotel, and the world's largest indoor amusement park with 47 rides and the world's largest indoor water park. The five-acre lagoon boasts a full-size replica of the *Santa Maria*, the world's largest wave machine, 22 water slides, and four 25 person submarines (more submarines than the Canadian Navy).

The suburbs now rule. (See Box 7.4.) They contain not only half again as many people as central cities, they also are home to most of the major shopping centers, restaurants, movies, and sports facilities. Jobs as well as people have moved to suburban zip codes, bringing congestion and urban problems. Two-thirds of the nation's metropolitan office space and two-thirds of all manufacturing jobs now are located in suburbs. The 1996 Olympics featured pictures of Atlanta's highrise skyline, but the reality is that Atlanta's suburbs hold twice the office space of the central city—and northern New Jersey now contains more office space than Manhattan. Today so-called **edge cities** are increasingly the dominant economic and population units in the metropolitan area. These new multinucleated outer suburban cities turn old definitions inside out. Economically and socially, edge cities now often dominate metropolitan areas, bordered inside by economically declining cities and outside by stagnant rural areas. With edge cities becoming the new downtowns, people accustomed to commuting now can live even further out.

For a quarter of a century, the most common daily commute has not been from suburb to city but from suburban home to suburban workplace. Indicative of the

edge cities
developed outer suburban areas that are becoming economically dominant over old downtowns.

[52]Michael Shill and Richard Nathan, *Revitalizing America's Cities: Neighborhood Reinvestment and Displacement,* SUNY Press, Albany, 1983; and J. John Palen and Bruce London (eds.), *Gentrification, Displacement, and Neighborhood Revitalization,* SUNY Press, Albany, 1984.

[53]J. John Palen and Bruce London, *Gentrification, Displacement, and Neighborhood Revitalization,* SUNY Press, Albany, 1984.

Box 7.4 # Ongoing Issues

Best Places to Live

Every year "Best Places to Live" lists emerge. Probably the list receiving the greatest attention is the annual ranking by *Money* magazine.[a] *Money* uses nine broad categories: economy, health, crime, housing, education, weather, transit, leisure, and arts to rank the 300 largest metropolitan areas in the United States. The weight given to each area differs yearly based on the concerns of a statistical sample of readers regarding 41 factors. This is the 1996 top ten and bottom ten urban places, plus the top five large cities and some other cities of interest. The magazine's choices may not be yours. New York or Chicago, for instance, would rate far higher for urbanites. Similarly, Punta Gorda is a rapidly growing city of 127,000 where the economy is strong and crime is low, but for those who want a cultural or night life beyond bingo or Little League, Punta Gorda is not the best choice.

Top Ten U.S. Cities	Bottom Ten U.S. Cities
1. Madison, Wisconsin	291. Alexandria, Louisiana
2. Punta Gorda, Florida	292. Waterbury, Connecticut
3. Rochester, Minnesota	293. Albany/Schenectady/Troy, New York
4. Fort Lauderdale, Florida	294. Mansfield, Ohio
5. Ann Arbor, Michigan	295. Springfield, Illinois
6. Fort Myers/Cape Coral, Florida	296. Lima, Ohio
7. Gainesville, Florida	297. Davenport, Iowa
8. Austin, Texas	298. Peoria, Illinois
9. Seattle, Washington	299. Yuba City, California
10. Lakeland, Florida	300. Rockford, Illinois

Five Best Large Metro Areas of Over a Million*	Ranking of Some Other Metro Areas of Note
1. Fort Lauderdale (1.4 million)	40. Los Angeles/Long Beach
2. Seattle (2.2 million)	128. Washington, D.C.
3. Tampa/St. Petersburg (2.2 million)	196. Chicago
4. Orlando (1.4 million)	231. New York City
5. San Francisco (1.6 million)	233. Philadelphia

*Metro areas here are central cities and their adjacent suburbs.
[a]"Best Places to Live in America: Our Tenth Annual Survey," *Money, July 1996, pp. 66–95.*

change is Sears, who in 1992 moved 5,000 employees out of the world's tallest building, the Sears Tower in Chicago, to suburban Hoffman Estates, 35 miles to the northwest beyond O'Hare Airport. Similarly, in the 1990s J.C. Penney moved its headquarters from New York City to Plano, Texas, north of Dallas.

We have also suburbanized social problems. While high rates of street crime, high welfare rates, and high levels of family disruption are thought of as city problems, suburban rates are climbing. There is a strong tendency to equate social problems with inner-city residence, but a full third of all poverty, for instance, is located in the suburbs. As previously noted, the social problems of alcoholism, drug usage, and racism are prevalent in the suburbs.

The twentieth century began as the age of the city and ended as the age of the suburb.[54] Whether you love suburbs or hate them, the twenty-first century will be a suburban century. Most of us already live in suburbs, work in suburbs, shop in suburbs, and find our recreation in suburbs. Suburbs also can anticipate becoming the prime location of American social problems.

Toward the Future

During the twenty-first century, urbanism, that is, urban values and lifestyles, will become even more dominant as the American way of life—regardless of where people live. Two major trends can be foreseen. The first is that, while during the twentieth century social problems were commonly associated with city life, during the twenty-first century social problems will have a far more dispersed pattern. Overall, suburbs not only will be the center of most manufacturing, retail trade, and entertainment, they also will be the loci of most social problems. This transformation is already occurring faster than most people realize. One-third of the nation's poor already are suburbanites, as are the majority of drug abusers.

The second trend is that, while problems become more uniform, the policies and programs dealing with these issues will become more local. Variation in ways of treating social problems will increase. Lines between cities and suburbs will become more blurred. As suburbs age and become more citylike the distinctions between economic and social problems in cities and in suburbs are likely to fade. Aging inner-ring suburbs are likely to be particularly heavily impacted. They will have to deal with city problems without city resources or experience. There is no magic wall that stops social problems at city boundaries.

It is one of the ironies of the new century that as our social problems are becoming more universal and national, our social policies and programs to deal with problems are devolving more to the local level. Approaches and standards of support are becoming not more uniform nationally but more different. Compared to even a decade ago, once national programs to address issues such as poverty and welfare have devolved into a wide range of different state programs. Some suburbs will cope far more successfully than others. Some suburbs, lacking the city's elaborate infrastructure, will be poorly equipped to deal with social problems. The consequence will be considerable local variation in policies and programs and, consequently, greater variation in successes and failures. The new century will witness some cities controlling their social problems, while some suburbs will see their rates of social problems accelerate.

Old assumptions and patterns no longer hold. During most of the twentieth century, it was assumed that there was a rough correlation between a city's size and its crime rate. The larger the place, generally, the higher the crime rate. However, such simplistic formulas no longer work. New York City, for instance, now has a far lower crime rate than the smaller city where the author of this text lives. As we move into the twenty-first century, broad sweeping generalizations are likely to become less and less useful. Rather than all becoming the same, during the new century, successful urban-suburban social problems solutions are likely to have more of a local than a national focus.

---

[54]J. John Palen, *The Suburbs,* McGraw-Hill, New York, 1995, p. 226.

Summary

Cities are a relatively new social invention, being only roughly 9,000 years old. Within the next decade, for the first time in history, more than half the world's population will live in urban places. The United States has a high rate of urbanization, with just over three-quarters of its population living in urban or suburban places.

- Functionalist theories, which dominated urban studies until the 1970s, stress that for cities to retain vitality the various city zones must have a functional purpose.

- Conflict theorists see the decline of the central city as a result not of market forces but of the conscious decision of economic elites to disinvest in the city. The "urban growth machine" ideology of urban business leaders encourages them to view cities not as places where people live and work but as a place where increasing the land values and keeping wages low creates a good business climate.

- Social interactionists focus on the social-psychological aspects of urban life. They note that Americans have always been ambivalent about cities and view them as associated with the breakdown of family and social relationships.

- The **Burgess concentric zonal model** describes how cities grew until the 1960s: from center to suburbs through a series of zones.

- Urbanization was seen by the Chicago School social theorists as producing a goal-oriented way of life called **urbanism.** Urbanism was characterized by personal alienation, social disorganization, and the various ills generally lumped together today under the label "crisis of the cities."

- The urban crisis model of the death of the city has dominated popular discussion about cities since the 1960s, and yet, despite all of their problems, cities are not about to disappear. They are switching their economic focus from manufacturing to service, adding white-collar jobs downtown while losing much of their blue-collar manufacturing. The result is a mismatch between jobs and the skills of inner-city entry-level workers.

- Probably the most crucial urban problems today are those of racial polarization and homelessness. Inner-city poor minorities are more economically and socially isolated than they were 20 years ago.

- Research estimates place the number of urban homeless in the 400,000 to 500,000 range. Many of the homeless have a range of problems, including mental illness and substance abuse. New single-room-occupancy (SRO) housing provides onsite drug and alcohol treatment and job counseling.

- Urban high-rise public housing programs have been a failure, and HUD is now destroying high-rise buildings as fast as funds permit. In addition to rent vouchers, HUD is joint-venture building some 25,000 low-rise lease-purchase units. Urban homesteading which offers abandoned homes for rehabilitation for as little as $1.00 has had only limited success.

- Urban gentrification has reversed the old Burgess hypothesis of housing trickling down in socioeconomic status. To date, the amount of gentrification or neighborhood revitalization has been limited. The "back to the city" movement is largely a myth.

- Today most of the population and economic growth is in the suburban edge cities, with more than half of all Americans now living in the suburbs.

Suburbs have at least as much alcoholism and drug abuse as cities and more white-collar crime.

- African American, Hispanic, and Asian American minorities now are suburbanizing at a faster rate than whites. In the suburbs the racial invasion-succession model has been replaced by that of parallel growth.

☞Key Review Terms

Burgess's concentric zonal hypothesis	outer or edge cities	urban ecology
gentrification	metropolitan area	urban growth machine
ghetto	parallel-growth model	urban homesteading
homelessness	suburbanization	urban infrastructure
invasion-succession model	trickle down theory	urbanism
	urban crisis	urbanism as a way of life

❓ Questions for Discussion

urbanization

1. Discuss American attitudes toward the city as shown in the media. What are your feelings about cities?
2. What is urbanism as a way of life? How has it affected our approach to social problems?
3. Discuss the "zoning out" of vice areas in a city. Is this a good idea? How successful have attempts been?
4. What is the urban crisis model? Is your local city in crisis?
5. Are ethnic and racial groups segregated in your local area? How are they segregated?
6. Who are the homeless today? Can anything be done to solve the problem?
7. What, if anything, is being done to provide housing for the poor in your community? What should be done?
8. Describe gentrification. Should it be encouraged or discouraged?
9. Discuss and critique the conflict approach to analyzing the city.

☛Suggested Resources

10. What is the major urban problem in your community? How is it being addressed?

Mark Abrahmason, *Urban Enclaves: Identity and Place in America*, St. Martin Press, New York, 1996. A readable examination and comparison of urban subcommunities ranging from Boston's Beacon Hill to Miami's Little Havana to The Castro District in San Francisco.

Herbert J. Gans, The *Levittowners,* Vintage, New York, 1967. An oldie but a goodie. The classic examination of the ways of life in the post World War II suburbs.

Paul A. Jargowsky, *Poverty and Place: Ghettos, Barrios, and the American City,* Russell Sage, New York, 1997. Excellent study of the status and causes of ghetto formation and the growing concentration of poverty.

John R. Logan and Harvey L. Moloch, *Urban Fortunes: The Political Economy of Place,* University of California Press, Berkeley, 1987. A much read analysis of what is happening to cities and suburbs as analyzed from a conflict perspective.

J. John Palen, *The Suburbs,* McGraw-Hill, New York, 1995. A comprehensive historical and sociological overview of the suburbanization of the United States and its consequences.

J. John Palen, *The Urban World,* fifth ed., McGraw-Hill, New York, 1997. The most widely used urban sociology text for the last two decades.

Internet Connection www.mhhe.com/palen

Saskia Sassen, *Cities in a World Economy,* second ed., Pine Forge, Thousand Oaks, CA, 2000. An examination of the new social formation of truly global cities in the twenty-first century.

1. A very useful site for those interested in studying the problems of urban life is The Urban Institute (*www.urban.org/*). It has comprehensive links to a broad variety of topics including homelessness, for example. Click on the "National Survey of Homelessness" a comprehensive report conducted by the Bureau of the Census for twelve federal agencies (*www.urban.org/ housing/homeless/homeless.html*), or just go to the report "Highlights."

   a. According to the report how many people in the United States are homeless?

   b Who are they? Start by finding the definition of a homeless **client.**

   c. What are the basic characteristics **of single homeless clients?**

   d. According to census estimates, what percentage of the homeless is found in the central cities; surburbia; and rural areas?

   e. What are the policy implications of this study?

2. Visit the website of the National League of Cities (*www.nlc.org/oldxdefault.htm*), an organization whose purpose is "to strengthen and promote cities as centers of opportunity, leadership, and governance." Examine this site.

   a. What resources does it have to achieve the stated purpose?

   b. What strategies has it developed to achieve its goals?

   c. What has it claimed to have done for its city-members?

   d. Overall, do you think that the National League of Cities has been an effective advocate for its constituency?

"I'm a dying breed. A laborer.
Strictly muscle work . . . pick
it up, put it down, pick it up,
put it down. We handle
between forty and fifty
thousand pounds of steel a
day. . . . You can't take pride
any more. You remember
when a guy could point to a
house he built, how many logs
he stacked. He built it good
and he was proud of it. I don't
think I could be proud if a
contractor built it for me. I
would be tempted to get in
there and kick the carpenter in
the ass and take the saw away
from him. 'Cause I would
have to be part of it you
know."

Studs Terkel, *Working*, Pantheon,
New York, 1974, p. xxxi.

The Economy and the World of Work

A Transformed Economy

American Dream
the belief that a growing economy will provide upward mobility and a better life for one's children.

Information Revolution
postindustrial economic system based on the production and exchange of knowledge and information rather than of goods.

economy
social institution that organizes the production, distribution, and consumption of goods and services.

The **American Dream** is that a growing economy will provide an ever better life for more and more workers. In a nation of unbounded opportunity, work supposedly provides the route to success. The American Dream always had exceptions—it never fully applied to minorities and women—but it has long been assumed by most Americans that growing the national economy will solve many of our social problems. This view is implied in the much repeated statement, originally made by President John Kennedy, that "A rising tide lifts all ships." Today, however, the dream of more-or-less automatic upward mobility for anyone has been taking a beating. Some ships are rising and some are sinking. The rich are definitely rising higher, but the poor are sinking further behind.

Economic conditions are rapidly changing. So much so that we are now undergoing an economic transformation every bit as revolutionary as the Industrial Revolution produced by the steam engine. Today, the United States is undergoing an **Information Revolution.** We are rapidly moving from the production of specific goods to the production of ideas. The twentieth-century economy was based on manufacturing. The twenty-first-century economy is primarily an idea and service economy.

The **economy** is the system by which necessary or desired goods and services are produced and distributed within a society. Our postindustrial semiconductor microchip-based economy is producing profound workplace changes. More people now work at computer screens than at manufacturing machines. Computer and literacy skills have replaced mechanical skills. The early twenty-first century continues the past decade's pattern of manufacturing production costs dropping (largely through the elimination of layers of production workers and middle-managers), while the speed with which goods can be manufactured increases. In contrast to 20 years ago, microchip-controlled robotics are now commonplace in manufacturing, and even country grocery stores use laser scanners and computerized registers. Even more impressive has been the radical transformation in the time required to transfer information. It is hard to imagine that just a decade ago email was only used by the Defense Department and academics at research universities, and before 1992 the World Wide Web as we know it didn't exist.

The downside of the Information Revolution is that wage inequality is increasing and job insecurity has become commonplace.[1] While professionals and managers make more, the typical high school graduate worker has seen his or her real income drop 20 percent during the past 20 years.

---

[1] Douglas S. Massey, "The Age of Extremes: Concentrated Affluence and Poverty in the Twenty-First Century," *Demography*, 33:4, 395, 1996.

A Global Information Age Economy

The twenty-first-century American economy with its streamlined corporation structure and flexible workforce is the worldwide economic success model. This success, however, has come at a price. What benefits corporations and stockholders is often less positive for workers. Part of America's international competitiveness is based on reduced wages for those who produce goods. To workers, terms such as "streamlining" and "flexibility" often mean stagnant wages or outright unemployment. Newspaper headlines regularly proclaim corporate mergers and the downsizing of both production and management positions. This translates into loss of jobs for both blue-collar and middle-management employees.

As firms become part of the global economic system, they commonly replace higher-paid American workers with low-wage Third World employees. A typical blue-collar worker who receives $19 an hour in wages and benefits in the United States can be replaced for $2.10 an hour in Mexico.[2] The average Nike worker in Indonesia makes under $2.00 a day. Even Levi Strauss, the firm that put America in jeans, closed its U.S. plants in 1999 and moved production overseas. Between 1990 and 1995 some 5 million American jobs went overseas.

The worldwide economy is now a reality. Goods we purchase today increasingly have non-North American origins. Location of manufacturing sites is increasingly diffuse. Even discovering what is manufactured in America becomes more difficult when a "Made in the USA" label can legally be applied to goods, such as sneakers, that have only a portion of their materials originating from and manufactured in the United States. Fabric for clothing often comes from one location, sewing and packaging from elsewhere. The 1998 Federal Trade Commission regulations, for example, specify that a product can be labeled "Made in the USA" if it is "substantially all" (by which they mean 75 percent of overall costs) domestic made.[3] Today Hondas and Volkswagens are assembled in the United States, while Chrysler is German owned. Sport-utility vehicles (SUVs) may be very American, but Jeeps are assembled in Canada, and most Ford Explorer's have engines that are manufactured in Germany and transmissions from France. International trade agreements, such as the North American Free Trade Association (NAFTA) or the European Common Market, mean that national governments no longer can control, or sometimes even regulate, economic activity within their borders.

Work and Society

Sociologists are interested not so much in the specific workings of the economy as in how work links us to the society. For many of us work is the prime basis for our social identity; it defines not just what we do but who we are. One of the first questions asked when meeting someone new is, "What do you do?" The job a person has, his or her occupation, helps us to place them socially as well as economically. Work, or the absence of work, ties into virtually all social institutions and social problems from the family to education to poverty to health care.

Thus, it is crucial to understand how the type of work we do, the workplaces in which we do it, and how certain types of jobs are transforming the world in which

---

[2]David Young, "Starting Over All at Once," *Chicago Tribune*, February 27, 1997, 5.1.
[3]John M. Broder, "Word for Word/Made in the U.S.A.," *New York Times*, May 18, 1997, p. E7.

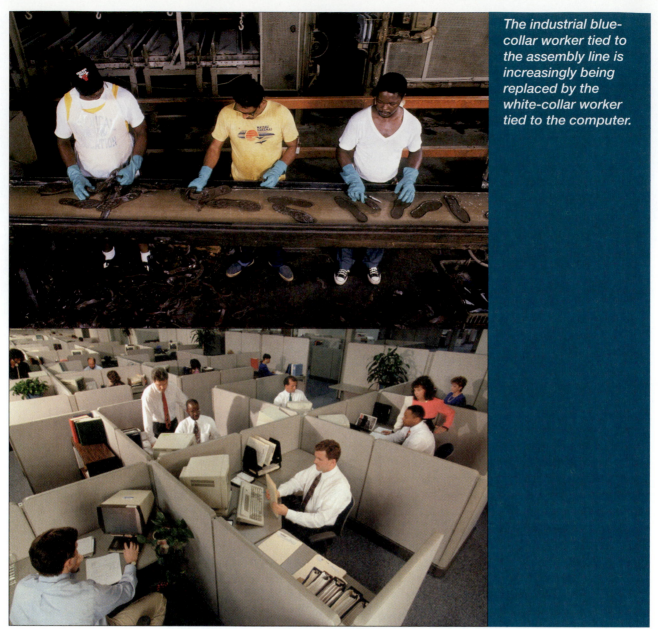

The industrial blue-collar worker tied to the assembly line is increasingly being replaced by the white-collar worker tied to the computer.

Top: © Henry Hornstein/Stock, Boston
Bottom: © Bill Lai/The Image Works

blue collar
work that involves manual labor, and often lower prestige.

white collar
desk jobs that do not involve actual production of goods.

we live. For example, a common assumption made by your parents' generation was that they would work much of their life for the same company or corporation. High school graduates could go right to work in an assembly plant, and if the plant was unionized they could expect that their job would both last their worklife and pay a living wage. Today, this is no longer realistic; no one expects to work for only one company. Changes have been especially severe for manufacturing workers. It is hard for us today to realize that until 1980 the average American urban worker was a **blue-collar worker,** that is, someone who produces goods, or whose work requires physical labor. As Figure 8.1 indicates, in 1960 some 70 percent of American workers were involved in production related work. Today, explosive changes in communicating and coordinating technologies mean most American workers are **white collar** (nonmanual labor workers whose job does not involve physical labor or the actual production of goods).

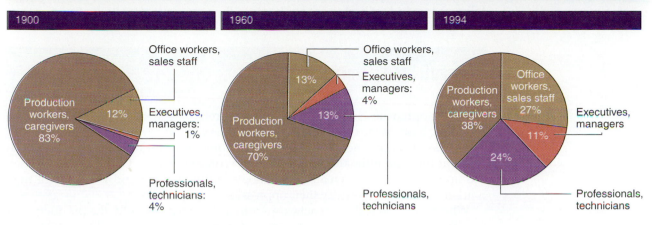

Figure 8.1 The Changing Workplace

1900

Office workers, sales staff

Production workers, caregivers 83%

12%

Executives, managers: 1%

Professionals, technicians: 4%

1960

Office workers, sales staff

Executives, managers: 4%

13%

Production workers, caregivers 70%

13%

Professionals, technicians

1994

Office workers, sales staff 27%

Production workers, caregivers 38%

11%

24%

Executives, managers

Professionals, technicians

Sources: Based on Census Bureau and Bureau of Labor Statistics data.

Sociological Perspectives

Functionalist Approaches

Functionalists focus on the integration of society and how goods and services can best be distributed to meet societal needs. They generally assume that the competitive free market is the best economic system for achieving societal economic goals. Some economic inequality is seen as a necessary incentive and as a way of allowing individuals to accumulate wealth, which they can then invest. Disorganization, or maladjustments of the economic system, or maldistribution of resources throws the system out of balance and causes economic disruptions. Functionalists would say that in America maldistributions are currently being caused by automation, computerization, and the flow of jobs to Third World nations where labor is cheaper.

Functionalists say economic domination by large multinational corporations can be dysfunctional for even the largest national economies. Decisions by multinationals dominate developing nations and can destabilize their national economies. Under such circumstances, with job and consumer goods decisions restricted, individual consumers have few choices and even less influence. Economic concentration of power in a few multinational corporations means that the cultural value of free enterprise is out of step with the economic reality of limited economic choices.

Although powerful multinational corporations distort the assumption of individual economic decisions, functionalists are generally unwilling to propose major changes to the economic system in order to deal with serious economic disruptions. Functionalists fear that major government intervention will cause new problems, and consequently they stress adaptation and adjustment. Disruptions are thought to be best resolved by the self-corrective operation of the free market or, in exceptional circumstances, through the intervention of the federal government. In order to solve problems such as the relocation not only of factories but of whole industries abroad, they propose government-sponsored worker reeducation and retraining programs and unemployment compensation programs. Heavy government involvement is sanctioned only at the time of general economic crisis. The goal is to keep the economic-social system in balance. Functionalists say capitalist systems adapt best to change because they are constantly undergoing change and innovation.

Conflict Approaches

Conflict approaches suggest that all societal relationships are determined by the economic base, or the means of production. Marxists, in particular, argue that other activities—legal, political, and so on—can sometimes influence economic activities, but they are ultimately controlled by economic forces. Conflict theorists say the upper classes even create an ideology (individualism and laissez faire free-market capitalism) to justify their oppression.

Where functionalist approaches are primarily concerned with the production of wealth, conflict approaches focus on its distribution. Consequently, conflict theorists focus less on how well the economy performs for the society at large, and more on which groups within the society benefit, and which lose, under the existing economic system. Thus, the major question is Whose interests are being advanced?

Competition, for a conflict theorist, doesn't benefit everyone, only those who are controlling the system. Because the economic system is run by those in power for their own benefit, the concentration of power and resources in the hands of a few is not a sign of a dysfunctional economic system; it is, rather, the normal state of affairs. Powerful corporations use their economic strength to advance their own interests at the cost of other groups and the nation. They use their size and power to gain political and economic advantage against the needs of workers.

From a conflict perspective, governments are largely controlled by a few economically powerful corporations. Trade policies and tax laws reflect corporate interests. Workers are thus exploited not as an exception but as a pattern. Against the controlling power of these corporations, workers can make gains only by developing a "class consciousness" and by organizing. Only through collective action that demonstrates power—be it at the ballot box, through strikes, or by outright class violence—will the economic situation of those without power be reversed.

Interactionist Approaches

Interactionist approaches do not examine the effects of economic changes on society as a whole, but rather are more social psychological, examining the effects of economic change on individuals and small groups and the central role of work to someone's identity. Interactionists examine how people are socialized into particular jobs and careers by parents, peers, schools, and the mass media. Parents, peers, and the media do this largely informally, while schools more formally socialize people for occupations. What we do defines who we are.

Interactionists also look at how major economic changes affect individuals. Factory closings, for example, commonly lead to unemployment. Being out of work can have severe social psychological as well as economic consequences for a worker; he or she can become depressed, disengaged from family, and withdrawn. In a society where one's worth is often measured by income, the absence of a paycheck can result in insecurity, mood swings, and even aggression. The world of work is so central that the loss of a job, and the resulting economic instability, is so personally destablizing it can even bring on mental illness. Interactionists may try to aid individuals in adjusting to macrolevel societal changes.

New Work Patterns

Over recent decades four major changes have taken place in the workforce. First, the economy is increasingly service oriented. Second, the educational level of the workforce has radically changed. Third, women now are a major component of the paid labor force. Fourth, there is a shift from full-time employment to temporary or part-time workers.

The Growing Information and Service Economy

At the beginning of the twentieth century, 4 out of 10 workers still were engaged in agriculture.[4] By contrast, at the end of the century less than 2 percent of all employed persons worked on farms. The first half of the twentieth century witnessed a massive population shift of people leaving farms to work in factories. By midcentury most workers were engaged in blue-collar manufacturing of products. Blue-collar jobs are now in decline. Fewer than 4 out of 10 workers today actually engage in production of goods, and the proportion of production workers will continue to decrease.

Not until 1980 did the census record more white-collar than blue-collar workers. Now we have a white-collar information- and service-based economy. Recent decades have witnessed computers, automation, and foreign competition restructuring the workforce. Where 100 years ago farming was the most common occupation, and where 50 years ago assembly line work was common, today employees are more likely to sit in front of computers. Since 1980, 9 out of 10 new jobs have been in the service sector.[5] Service jobs cover a wide range of positions—everything from minimum-wage jobs at McDonald's to New York stock traders whose yearly income begins at a quarter of a million dollars. However, on the average, service workers make only 70 percent of what factory workers make.

Higher Educational Expectations

Mass education is more recent than most Americans realize. At the beginning of the twentieth century, having a high school diploma placed a person among the educational elite. In 1900 only 6 percent of the population graduated from high school.[6] A high school diploma was rarer than a college degree is today. As recently as 1970, only slightly over half (55 percent) of the labor force had a high school education.[7] (See Chapter 9 for greater discussion.) By contrast, today only 13 percent of those under 30 have less than a high school education; 27 percent have at least a college degree.[8]

Today's college degree, however, no longer guarantees a job. It merely entitles the recipient to enter the ranks of those seeking employment. As the new century begins, those having only high school diplomas are marginally employable, and those possessing less than a high school education are virtually unemployable—at least at a living wage. Even the Army and Navy want you to have a high school diploma.

---

[4]U.S. Bureau of the Census, *Historical Statistics of the United States: Colonial Times to 1970, Part 1,* Government Printing Office, Washington, DC, 1975, p. 126.
[5]Robert F. Reich, "The REAL Economy," *Atlantic,* February 1991, pp. 35–52.
[6]U. S. Bureau of the Census, *Historical Statistics,* p. 379.
[7]Ibid., p. 380.
[8]U.S. Bureau of the Census, *Statistical Abstract of the United States, 1992,* Government Printing Office, Washington, DC, 1992.

At the upper end of the employment scale, a global professional elite of corporate executives, scientists, professionals, and even entertainers is now forming. Inequality is increasing within most countries, not just the United States. The income gap between the top fifth and the bottom fifth of the world's population has doubled since the 1960s. The split between those at the top and the bottom is particularly noticeable within the United States, the United Kingdom, China, and Russia.

Women in the Workplace

Today women are engaged in full-time employment in record numbers. Women now constitute roughly half of the labor force (46.2 percent in 1997).[9] Looking not at what proportion of the labor force is female but at what percentage of women work for pay, the data show that approximately 6 out of 10 women currently work for wages.[10] Poor women have always been in the labor force, but prior to the mid-1960s middle-class women generally did not work after marriage. From 1964 to 1997 the U.S. economy added almost 65 million new jobs. Some 40 million of those new jobs were filled by women and only 25 million by men. The pre-1980s pattern of stay-at-home wives is largely history. If you are a woman, the chances are 99 in 100 that you will spend part of your life working for pay, says the AFL-CIO.[11]

Historically, the lowest labor force participation has been among married women with children, but today women with children are far more likely to be working than were their mothers. A record three-quarters of all married women with children under age 18 now are in the paid labor force, and 38 percent of women with children work full-time.[12] These figures are not expected to increase much in the near future, because women are already heavily involved in the paid workforce.

The type of paid work women do also has changed. Traditionally, women were segregated into a few "pink collar" occupations, such as office work, school teaching, or nursing. Commonly such jobs were poorly paid. Now women are increasing their participation in higher-paid occupations. Bureau of Labor Statistics data show the proportion of managers who are women jumped from 19 percent in 1970 to 43 percent in 1995.[13] (See Table 8.1) Women's wages still remain below those of men, but the gap is slowly closing. According to Bureau of the Census tabulations, between 1980 and 1994 women's hourly wages as a percentage of men's increased from 64 percent to 79 percent.[14]

Why is women's pay lower than men's in an era when "equal pay for equal work" is the law? Part of the difference is due to women having more interrupted work histories and being more likely to move in and out of the labor force because of childbirth. However, the majority of the difference is due to job discrimination patterns that traditionally paid jobs performed by women less than jobs performed by men. Even within the 500 job categories used by the federal government, men and women still often do different jobs, and the professions or positions having a high proportion of females (pink-collar jobs) still pay less than those positions mostly occupied by males.

---

[9]Bureau of the Census and Bureau of Labor Statistics in *Information Please Almanac*, Houghton Mifflin, Boston, 1998.
[10]*Universal Almanac*, Andrews and McMeel, Kansas City, 1995, p. 266.
[11]Greg Edwards, "No Woman's Land: Despite Gains Women Are Still Underrepresented in Many Fields," *Richmond Times-Dispatch*, October 18, 1999, p. D22.
[12]Suzanne M. Bianchi and Daphne Spain, "Women, Work, and Family in America," *Population Bulletin*, 51:21, Population Reference Bureau, Washington, DC, December 1996.
[13]Ibid., p. 20.
[14]Ibid., p. 24.

Table 8.1 Woman's Share of Major Occupational Groups, 1970–1995

Occupational Group	Percent Female			
	1970	1980	1990	1995
Total labor force	38	43	45	46
Executives, managers	19	31	42	43
Professional, speciality	44	49	54	53
Technicians	34	44	46	51
Sales	41	49	49	50
Administrative support, including clerical	73	77	77	79
Private household	96	95	95	95
Protective service	7	12	16	16
Other service	61	63	63	65
Farming, forestry, fishing	9	15	16	20
Precision production, including craft	7	8	10	9
Machine operators	40	41	40	37
Transportation workers	4	8	10	9
Handlers, laborers	17	20	20	19

Note: The 1995 figures are based on the monthly Current Population Survey and are subject to greater sampling variability than the figures for 1970–1990, which are based on the decennial census.

Source: 1970, 1980, and 1990 Censuses, published tabulations; and U.S. Bureau of Labor Statistics, *Employment and Earnings* 43, no. 1: 1995, Table 11.

Douglas Healey/AP/Wide World Photos

Homemaking, long considered unpaid women's work, has been elevated by Martha Stewart, chairman and CEO of Martha Stewart Omnimedia, into a multi-million dollar business.

Box 8.1 Ongoing Issues

Women and Work

Suzanne Bianchi and Daphne Spain in their study "Women, Work, and Family in America" provide substantial statistical detail about the changes that have taken place in the work lives of American women over recent decades.[a] To quote the authors:

"The picture of women in the workplace is one of clear, albeit slow, progress toward equality with men. This bodes well for gender equality in the labor force. The more highly educated a woman, the more likely she is to work for pay, to work full-time when she is employed, and to be in a managerial or professional job where wages are higher.

". . . One factor that explains why women earn less than men is that they perform different work in the economy. . . . Even the 500 detailed occupational categories used in the decennial census may not fully capture the dissimilarity in the work that men and women do. Women are more likely than men to fill jobs in small firms in industries with labor-intensive levels of production and relatively low levels of unionization and profit. More women may be in managerial positions than before, but they are less likely than men to advance to top management, limited by the so-called glass ceiling. Moreover, the 500 occupational categories are aggregations of jobs. Women and men often cluster into different specialties within these categories.

". . . Lifelong socialization attracts men and women into different jobs. The occupational goals of boys tend to be more highly sex-typed than those of girls, and even preschoolers express sex-typed occupational differences. Men tend to place higher preference on status, power, money, and freedom from supervision. Men may also be more willing to take risks. Women more often value working with people, helping others, and creativity. Job choice may also reflect a preference for working with one's own gender.

". . . Women continue to earn less than men, both because they make different choices about schooling, jobs, and family—which results in women accumulating less human capital than men—and because women face greater constraints in a workforce still dominated by men."

[a]*Suzanne M. Bianchi and Daphne Spain, "Women, Work, and Family in America,"* Population Bulletin, 51:14–27, December 1996.

Part-Time Employment

Part-time or contingent employment is the newest workforce change. Part-time or "temp" employment has increased dramatically since 1980 because it serves an economy that stresses flexibility. Official figures grossly underestimate the actual number of temps. The Department of Labor conservatively puts the number at 6 million, while the Census Bureau reports that a 1997 Telecommute America survey puts the number at 11 million.[15] Some estimates go as high as 18 million. Temporary workers vary from low-skill, low-wage, seasonal workers to highly educated professionals such as the "gypsy faculty" that increasingly teach undergraduate university courses. Such "adjunct" faculty are not eligible for tenure and are paid on a low course-by-course basis.

Today, corporate usage of part-time employees does not usually reflect economic slowdowns but rather a move to increase profits by avoiding paying the benefits that come with full-time positions. Sometimes, employees are fired by the corporation and then hired back as independent contractors to do the same job—minus job security, health insurance, and retirement benefits. This pattern is

---

[15]U.S. Bureau of the Census, "Increase in At-Home Workers Reverses Earlier Trend," *Census Briefs,* Government Printing Office, Washington, DC, March 1998.

familiar to editors and other employees in the publishing business. Corporations will often go to considerable lengths to avoid hiring new full-time employees. General Motors assembly plants experienced major strikes in 1998, not because the workers wanted higher wages, but because the existing workers had been required for several years to work 6 days a week with heavy daily overtime. The workers were making excellent money, but they wanted some weekends without working so they could see their families. General Motors was willing to take strike losses of $10 million a day rather than hire new workers. Economically, it is cheaper for corporations to pay existing workers overtime rates rather than to provide health insurance and other benefits to new workers. Of course, not all temporary workers are seeking full-time employment; some people such as mothers with young children find flexible part-time work desirable.[16]

Consequences

Given the workforce changes described previously, it is not surprising that college students are apprehensive about their futures. Not to be anxious is to ignore economic reality. Even during periods of record business profits, there is limited job security; during downturns there is far less. This is a change. Until the 1990s, businesses making large profits generally hired, not fired, workers. Today downsizing is as likely to come from corporations that are prosperous and growing as those that are faltering. Now white-collar workers are as likely to be downsized as blue-collar workers. Instead of hiring full-time employees, firms in the United States increasingly hire part-time or independent contract white-collar employees who are not provided benefits.

This switch to part-time workers is also occurring at universities. Universities increasingly rely on adjunct instructors on short-term contracts to staff basic courses. Some of your courses, perhaps this one, are being taught by faculty members not holding tenure or a tenure-track appointment. Hiring tenure-track faculty members would mean both paying a living wage and providing full benefits. By contrast, "gypsy faculty" can be both poorly paid and heavily overworked.

Other Changes

The economy grew rapidly during the last half of the 1990s, but not all workers shared in the good times. High school educated workers have seen their real after-inflation incomes decline a full 20 percent over the past two decades. For such workers the future promises more pain and less gain. Nor are white-collar workers immune. In the 1980s the higher a person was in an organization, the lower the risk of being laid off; today being a manager provides little employment security. Job displacement has spread even to those previously sheltered from labor market turbulence.[17] Prosperity and a healthy corporate balance sheet often go hand-in-hand with downsizing.

After adjusting for inflation, median family incomes showed only a 0.2 percent per year increase from 1975 to 1995.[18] Not until 1997 did the wages of the average

---

[16]Chris Tilly, *Half a Job: Bad and Good Part-Time Jobs in a Changing Labor Market*, Temple University Press, Philadelphia, 1996.

[17]Thomas S. Moore, *The Disposable Work Force: Worker Displacement and Instability in America*, Aldine de Gruyter, Hawthorn, NY, 1996.

[18]Louis Uchitelle, "The Rehabilitation of Morning in America," *New York Times*, February 23, 1997, p. 1E.

Box 8.2 Making a Difference

Flextime at Xerox

Some corporations do start programs that help both workers and the corporation. Xerox Corporation, for example, allows flextime at their Dallas customer service center. The result is that work is done faster, absenteeism has dropped 30 percent, customer service has improved, and costs have gone down. How employees schedule their working hours is left up to them. According to Patricia Naxemetz, Xerox's human resource director:

"They were told. 'You've got to do these things. You come back and tell us what is the best way to get this done.' Instead of everybody must be here from 8am to 4pm, they worked out schedules where some people worked early and some stayed later. The result was that some people worked 7 to 3 and some started at 10 and left at 7. We had more coverage for more hours rather than nobody being there at 5:30 when a customer might call. They created their own schedules that required everybody to pull his or her own weight."[a]

Even at companies with flextime, however, it is still common that managers send negative signals that using family-friendly benefits such as workplace flexibility or a compressed workweek will not get you rewarded or moved up. Using flextime is still often viewed as not being committed to the company.

[a]Sherwood Ross, "Flextime Proves Profitable at Xerox," Reuters, October 25, 1997.

worker begin to outpace inflation. Declines in high-wage manufacturing jobs, falling levels of union membership with its wage-protection, and wage pressures from the globalization of the U.S. economy (i.e., moving jobs overseas) have eroded both wage rates and job security.

For corporations seeking to maximize profits in the new global economy, workers have become a disposable element. Unemployment is part of capitalism. The marketplace supposedly determines who works and who is fired. Karl Marx's nineteenth-century insight that capitalism required pools of surplus workers to depress wage rates has been updated with a vengeance by technology. Today, it is technology that is often used to suppress wages. It costs businesses less to automate operations and pay trained workers overtime than to train marginal workers. Those marginal workers who lack schooling, have limited abilities, or have poor work habits find themselves redundant except in times of unusual prosperity.

Unemployment during part of your work life is becoming a commonplace occurrence. University of Chicago NORC survey data indicate that even in times of prosperity 10 percent of American workers think they are likely to lose their jobs in the next year, double the percentage of 25 years ago.[19] Some 43 million jobs have been eliminated in the United States since 1979 (the first year such data were collected).[20] The good news is that more jobs have been created than destroyed, so that the total number of jobs in the country grew from 90 million to 117 million. The bad news is that the new jobs pay median wages of $382 a month less than did the old jobs.[21]

---

[19]National Opinion Research Center, *General Social Surveys, 1972–1994, Cumulative Codebook,* Roper Center for Public Opinion Research, Storrs, CT, 1994.

DILBERT reprinted by permission of United Features Syndicate.

The current situation is that:

- Roughly half again as many people are affected by layoffs each year (3 million) as are victims of violent crimes (2 million).
- One-third of all households have a family member who has lost a job.
- One in 10 adults acknowledges that a job loss has precipitated a family crisis.
- Layoffs are now as common during economic recovery as during recession.
- Workers with at least some college education make up the majority of those losing jobs.

Altered Job Concerns

Social problems textbooks written two decades ago spent considerable space emphasizing the dehumanizing aspects of blue-collar assembly line work. These texts stressed issues such as boredom, repetitive work, and the resulting worker alienation. It was assumed that good paying (if unexciting) jobs were available to all. Today, the repetitive blue-collar assembly line jobs of earlier decades are largely gone, as are the high union wages paid the workers. Workers today are less concerned with workplace boredom than with workplace survival.

Yesterday's factory worker who couldn't leave his or her production machine is today replaced by the white-collar worker sitting in a cubicle bound to the computer. The comic strip *Dilbert* mirrors contemporary white-collar concerns. In one strip the boss is tossing a temporary worker in the dumpster. When Dilbert says that using the dumpster seems inappropriate, the boss replies, "They're way too big to flush."[22] In another, his dimwitted boss tells Dilbert that he is about to become involved in all aspects of the company's production. Dilbert's immediate response is, "Dear Lord. You've fired all the secretaries."

Moonlighting

Sometimes working just one job doesn't cover the bills. And as college students know, one way of coping with inadequate income is to moonlight. The Department

---

[22]Scott Adams, *The Dilbert Principle*, Harper Business, New York, 1996.

Box 8.3 Ongoing Issues

Talking about Concrete

Blue-collar workers often feel marginalized in our increasingly professionally oriented society. Elliot Liebow neatly demonstrates this in his classic work, *Tally's Corner.*[a]

"Tally and I were in the Carry-out. It was summer, Tally's peak earning season as a cement finisher, a semiskilled job a cut or so above that of the unskilled laborer. . . .

" 'You know that boy came in last night? That Black Muslim? That's what I ought to be doing. I ought to be in his place.'

" 'What do you mean?'

" 'Dressed nice, going to [night] school, got a good job.'

" 'He's no better off than you, Tally. You make more than he does.'

" 'It's not the money. [Pause] It's position, I guess. He's got position. When he finishes school he gonna be a supervisor. People respect him. . . . Thinking about people with position and education gives me a feeling right here [pressing his fingers into the pit of his stomach].'

" 'You're educated, too. You have a skill, a trade. You're a cement finisher. You can make a building, pour a sidewalk.'

" 'That's different. Look, can anybody do what you're doing? Can anybody just come up and do your job? Well, in one week I can teach you cement finishing. You won't be as good as me 'cause you won't have the experience but you'll be a cement finisher. That's what I mean. Anybody can do what I'm doing and that's what gives me this feeling. [Long pause] Suppose . . . You remember at the courthouse, Changing Lonny's trial? You and the lawyer was talking in the hall? You remember? I just stood there listening. I didn't say a word. You know why? 'Cause I didn't even know what you was talking about. That's happened to me a lot.'

" 'Hell, you're nothing special. That happens to everybody. Nobody knows everything. One man is a doctor, so he talks about surgery. Another man is a teacher, so he talks about books. But doctors and teachers don't know anything about concrete. You're a cement finisher and that's your specialty.'

" 'Maybe so, but when was the last time you saw anybody standing around talking about concrete?' "

[a]*Elliot Liebow*, Tally's Corner, *Little, Brown, Boston, 1967, pp. 61, 62.*

of Labor reports that, while 20 years ago there were just over 4 million multiple jobholders, as of the late 1990s there were 8 million workers holding down two or more jobs.[23] This means at least 6.5 percent of the labor force carries a second, and in some cases a third, job (these figures are low since they don't count unreported off-the-books jobs).

As long-term hourly wages have declined, some workers hold multiple jobs as the only way to stay even. Workers with families have to run harder to stay in the same place. However, money isn't the only reason people moonlight. People carry multiple jobs for a variety of reasons; many need the money, some are trying out another career, and some enjoy working at different jobs.

Nonpaid Work

work
paid activity that provides a livelihood.

Work generally is defined as paid activity that provides a means of livelihood. Traditionally, though, much of society's most important work is not compensated financially. The most obvious examples of nonpaid valued work are work done around the house and the rearing of children. This is in spite of the high levels of

[23]Lawrence Misehl, Jared Berstein, and John Schmitt, *The State of Working America*, Economic Policy Institute, Washington, DC, 1996.

skills needed to raise children and the obvious need for the well-being of the society. It is an example of how much the ideology of paid work dominates our culture that we refer to those who care for home and children as "nonworking." Contemporary women often end up working two jobs, one in the labor force and one at home.

Society also is heavily dependent on nonpaid **volunteer work.** The society couldn't function without the volunteer services of the approximately 30 million persons, overwhelmingly female, who provide valuable nonpaid labor. Our culture tends to measure worth by a price tag, and thus to devalue any work, however important, that is unpaid.

Gender-role assumptions also influence our expectations regarding work. Traditionally, women cared for children and the house while males were expected to be in the paid labor force. Only half of this pattern has changed. Women are now heavily represented in the paid labor force, but contemporary American society does not readily accept men staying home as househusbands. Such violations of gender assumptions are often treated with humor or derision, by females as well as by males.

The Origin and Development of Economic Systems

How did we get to where we are today? A bit of background is necessary to understand the historical and social forces that have created our economic system, because systems of work have profoundly changed over the centuries.

The Agricultural Revolution

Economic systems have gone through a number of commonly recognized changes or stages. The first of these changes was the **agricultural revolution.** Nomadic hunting-and-gathering bands could not accumulate, store, or transport more goods than they could carry with them. Such bands were rarely larger than 35 persons, had a simple nuclear family system (husband, wife, and children), and no permanent leadership or status system. Fixed agriculture changed all this. About 6,000 years ago the plow was invented, allowing crops to be cultivated. Domesticated draft animals pulled the plow. The agricultural revolution, with its higher predictable yields, produced the first population explosion.

Settled agriculture also produced class differences because children born to parents with good land began life with major advantages. Settled agriculture encouraged extended family systems to emerge, while an agricultural surplus meant that for the first time some labor could be withdrawn from food production and applied to the production of other goods. Food surpluses allowed some people to cluster in communities. For the first time, not everyone had to live as a farmer or herder of animals. Trade and craft specialization could develop.

The Industrial Revolution

Some 250 years ago 98 percent of the world's population still worked in agriculture. Only a comparative handful of tradesmen and craftsmen were found in towns.[24]

---

[24]J. John Palen, *The Urban World*, 5th ed., McGraw-Hill, New York, 1997, p. 3.

This agriculturally based life was torn asunder by the **industrial revolution,** which began in England during the late 1700s. The industrial revolution represented a change from agriculture-based societies to societies primarily involved in manufacturing. A market economy replaced subsistence agriculture, economic rationality replaced tradition, and written contracts took the place of custom. Inventions to aid the processing of wool to cloth, such as the flying shuttle and the spinning jenny, were followed in 1776 by James Watt's first practical application of a steam engine to machinery, providing a virtually unlimited source of power. Machine power replaced the animate power of animals and men, first in manufacturing and then in transportation. The nineteenth century saw the development of the railway, and in the twentieth century the automobile and the airplane. For the first time in history, people could move faster than a running horse.

The use of steam-driven machinery in fixed locations led to the establishment of factories as centralized workplaces. Factory-based industrialization replaced cottage industry hand labor with machine-based mass production. Workers tending the machines did not have to master all aspects of a trade but only a few repetitive tasks. Ex-farmers working in the factories became wage laborers who sold their labor, often to absentee owners. The owners commonly valued and cared for their machines far more than the wage laborers who operated them for 10 or 12 hours a day. As industrialization spread, the proportion of farmers decreased. At the beginning of the twentieth century about 40 percent of American workers still were found on farms, and by the time of the nation's entry into World War II in 1941 only a quarter of all workers were agricultural. Today under 2 percent of Americans work on farms.

Capitalism

Industrialism spurred the development of capitalism as an economic system. **Capitalism** is an economic system in which the means of production and distribution of goods and services are privately owned. As a system, capitalism has three basic features. The first is the legitimation of *private ownership* of wealth-producing property. The second is pursuit of *personal profit* as a normal and socially desirable activity. The third is the reliance on *market competition* as the means of determining what should be produced and at what price it should sell. Adam Smith in his *The Wealth of Nations* (1776) maintained that a freely competitive economy regulates itself by the "invisible hand" of market forces.[25] Thus, the market forces of supply and demand ensure that successful capitalists will be those who produce the best goods at the lowest price.

The capitalistic assumption is that competition spurs invention and innovation. For this to work, though, there has to be minimum government interference, otherwise the market mechanisms will be upset and production and prices artificially distorted. Government, therefore, should adopt a policy of *laissez-faire,* that is, leave it alone. Competition and the desire for personal gain will ultimately benefit consumers by encouraging technological innovation and forcing down prices. Thus, from self-interest comes the greatest good for the greatest number. Various combinations of industrialism and capitalism have economically and socially dominated North American and Western European societies for two centuries.

---

[25]Adam Smith (1723–1790) was the founder of classical economic theory and is commonly considered to be the father of economics. His major work was *An Inquiry into the Nature and Causes of the Wealth of Nations,* (originally 1776), Modern Library, New York, 1937.

Socialism

Throughout most of the twentieth century there was intense economic and political competition between the industrial economic systems of capitalism and socialism. **Socialism** is an economic system in which the means of production and distribution are collectively owned. Whereas goods under capitalism are produced based on economic demand, under socialism the production of goods is supposed to be based on the economic needs of the general population. Thus, goods are produced for those in need regardless of whether or not they have the resources to afford them. Socialist economies (such as that of the old Soviet Union) thus reject the profit motive; the market economy of capitalism is replaced by a centrally controlled economy managed by the government. In such **command economies** production is decided by government decision rather than consumer demand. Government, not self-interest, directs the economy so that problems of unemployment, recession, and inflation are overcome. Also, with economic goals set by the collective interest of society, there is no need for commercial advertising.

Like pure capitalism, pure socialism is a rare creature. However, socialist-based economic systems, based on the writings of Karl Marx, were established in the Soviet Union, Eastern Europe, and China. Socialist states outlawed most private ownership of productive property on the grounds that private ownership leads to an economic elite and exploitation of workers. Socialist states (referred to as the Second World when compared to the capitalist First World and the developing Third World) failed to keep up with capitalist countries in providing income, goods, and services for their citizens. The fall of the socialist Eastern European governments in 1989, the collapse of the Soviet Union in 1992, and the practical abandonment of socialist economic policies in China (while keeping the socialist name) has meant that capitalistic economic systems are now dominant worldwide.

socialism
economic system where resources and means of production of goods and services are owned collectively.

command economy
a centrally directed economic system in which goods are produced based on government decision rather than market demand, the system of the Soviet Union prior to its collapse.

Mixed Economies

Western economies are a mixture of capitalistic and socialistic features. **Mixed economies** are essentially capitalistic systems with moderate-to-strong state regulation. The social goal is to achieve the economic efficiency of capitalism, while mitigating harsh social inequality and economic suffering with government regulations. Western European countries such as Germany, France, and Sweden have capitalistic economies. However, there is strong public support for government programs to modify and control the harsher aspects of unfettered capitalism.

In mixed economies such as found in Western Europe and Canada, citizens are protected by strong government programs providing unemployment benefits, health care, child care, elderly care, and housing. The United States is the most laissez-faire, or unregulated, of the developed industrial states. Only Japan has weaker government programs than the United States, but Japan has had a corporate tradition of retaining workers for life and not laying them off during poor economic times. Japan's long economic recession during the 1990s, however, began to modify this cultural tradition.

mixed economy
capitalist economic system whose inequalities are moderated by government policies, the economic system prevalent in Western Europe.

Corporate Welfare

The United States mixed economy is heavily tilted toward corporate welfare. While Congress has been reducing welfare benefits for individuals, it has been expanding its corporate welfare programs. Such taxpayer-supported programs are referred to as "economic development," "price supports," or "public-private partnerships," but what they amount to is major subsidies for some businesses or industries that are not offered to others. The conservative Cato Institute says the government spent $65 billion in 1996 on taxpayer welfare subsidies to businesses.[26] Others have far higher figures. According to a special report on corporate welfare prepared by *Time,* during the late 1990s, one of the most robust economic periods in the nation's history, the federal government alone rewarded corporations yearly with $125 billion in corporate welfare.[27] This sum is equivalent to all the income taxes paid by 60 million individuals or families, or the equivalent of two weeks pay from every working American.

Subsidy programs included the Advanced Technology Program, which gave $225 million to IBM, Dow Chemical, and Xerox for basic research and overhead costs, and the Market Access Program, which promotes overseas sales and gave $1 million to promote popcorn sales, $125,000 to promote frozen bovine semen, and $120,000 to promote alligator hides.[28] The subsidy programs for these corporate welfare queens appear secure, with Congress continually increasing funding for mining, ranching, and business subsidies.

In addition to federal moneys, state and local governments also provide generous subsidies, often to encourage firms to move into or stay in their area. In 1989 Illinois gave $240 million to Sears, Roebuck & Co. to keep 5,400 workers in the state at a cost of $44,000 for each job.[29] In 1993 Alabama gave $253 million to Mercedes-Benz to build an auto-assembly plant near Tuscaloosa, employing 1,500 workers at a subsidy of $169,000 for each job. In 1997 Pennsylvania gave $307 million to the Norwegian engineering firm Kvaerner to employ 950 people at the former Philadelphia Naval Shipyard. The subsidy works out to $232,000 for each job, a sum it will take 50 years for the state to earn back in state and local taxes.

Corporations

Over the last century and a half we have gone from a nation of small business owners to a nation where economic power is increasingly concentrated in a limited number of corporations. The corporation now is the most common form of large business ownership. Roughly a quarter of all business are incorporated.

corporation

a legally constructed organization whose existence, powers, and liabilities exist separate from those of its owners and employees.

A **corporation** is a legal organization with legal existence separate from that of its members. Legal incorporation confers a number of benefits. First, a corporation is essentially a legal "person." The corporation can do anything an individual can do. Second, the corporation is owned by its stockholders, but they have only "limited liability": They are not personally responsible for the legal transactions of the corporation beyond the amount they have invested in stock. Stockholders are thus shielded from lawsuits due to debts or defective products. Third, corporations can have thousands, or in a few cases even millions of stockholders, and can draw upon immense amounts of capital. (In practice the majority of corporate assets are held by a small economic elite.) Fourth, the day-to-day operation of the corporation is not managed by the owner-stockholders, but by professional managers

---

[26]James Glassman, "The Corporate Welfare Queens," *U.S. News & World Report,* May 19, 1997, p. 53.

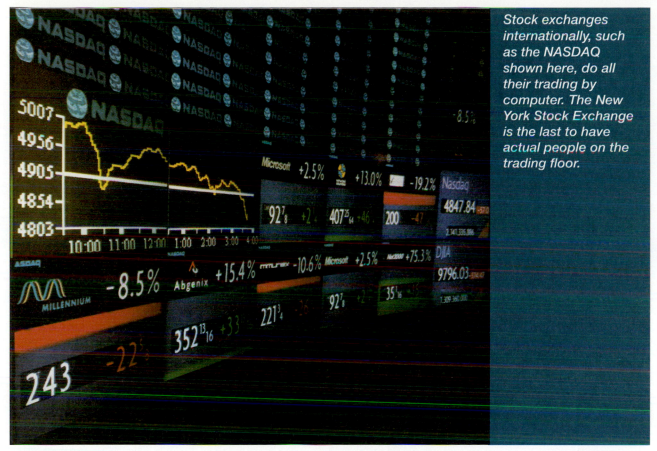

Stock exchanges internationally, such as the NASDAQ shown here, do all their trading by computer. The New York Stock Exchange is the last to have actual people on the trading floor.

Ed Bailey/AP/Wide World Photos

appointed by a board of directors. Thus, ownership is theoretically separate from operation of the corporation. In reality it doesn't quite operate this way because a limited number of top corporate executives often own substantial amounts of corporate stock, and stock purchase options rather than salary is the major source of their compensation. Finally, major corporations, because of their political power, receive special tax breaks and other economic subsidies from government that are not available to individuals or smaller businesses.

Concentrated Power

There are some four million corporations in the United States, but this number can be misleading because most are small and have limited economic, political, or social impact. A relatively few corporate giants dominate the nation's economy. Some 500 corporations account for three-quarters of the nation's gross national product, and among these 500 the largest 100 hold three-quarters of the nation's assets.[30] In fact in terms of gross national product *the top 10 American corporations had sales that were outdistanced only by the GNP of the major industrial nations of the United States, Japan, Germany, France, and the United Kingdom.* The largest of the American

---

[30]U.S. Bureau of the Census, *Statistical Abstract of the United States, 1994,* Government Printing Office, Washington, DC, 1994, pp. 558–559.

industrial corporations, General Motors, had a profit of $189 billion in 1999. GM's corporate budget exceeds that of all countries excepting the United States. As such it wields immense economic and political power.

The tremendous size of the largest corporations is further magnified and concentrated through **interlocking directorates,** whereby the members of one board of directors may also sit on several dozen other boards of directors. Over 90 percent of large American corporations have some interlocking directors with other corporations. For example, the Mellon Bank has interlocking directors with 33 other major corporations.[31] Interlocking boards make most of the nation's economic decisions. Because unions (which we will discuss presently) have been declining in number of members and power for two decades, there is no intervening force except government between workers and the power of corporations.

Conglomerates

A **conglomerate** is a corporation that is composed of many other corporations. For example, during much of the 1990s Pepsi Cola also had under its corporate umbrella KFC, Taco Bell, and Pizza Hut. Whichever of these fast food outlets you chose, you were filling the same corporate coffer. Phillip Morris during the 1990s owned not only tobacco brands, such as the world's best-seller, Marlboro, but also Miller Brewing and 10 percent of the food products sold in supermarkets. For protection from lawsuits, Philip Morris is now separating its tobacco and food interests. R.J. Reynolds tobacco company did the same a number of years back, creating RJR-Nabisco. Beatrice Foods owns over 50 other corporations, ranging from Samsonite luggage to Hunt's Foods to Orville Redenbacher popcorn. As of the late 1990s Paramount Viacom International owned not just Paramount Movie Studios, MTV, Showtime, Nickelodeon, and USA cable networks, but also Blockbuster Video stores, the publishing companies Prentice Hall, Simon & Schuster, and Macmillan, and the New York Knickerbockers basketball and New York Rangers hockey teams. Mergers take place so frequently that it is virtually certain these lists will be outdated by the time this book is published.

Even when product brand names differ, the corporate ownership is often the same. For example, over 4 out of 5 refrigerators sold in the United States are manufactured by only four appliance companies, and this degree of concentration is found in everything from lightbulbs to computers. Banking, which two decades ago was locally owned and managed, now is dominated by only a few megacorporations such as Citibank and Bank of America. Manufactured goods, clothing, and toys increasingly are purchased not from locally owned stores but from megaretailers such as Sears, Wal-Mart, and Kmart. Where mom-and-pop stores were once the rule, these three giants now employ over a million salespeople.

Multinational Corporations

Multinationals are conglomerates and huge corporations that have gone international. They have headquarters in one country but operate in many others. Multinationals span national boundaries to produce worldwide integrated systems of finance, production, and distribution. In pursuit of maximum profit, they view the world as one large marketplace, a global economy. Because of the effect of multinational corporations, it is becoming increasingly difficult to determine where a

interlocking directorate
pattern whereby many corporate board of directors members sit on numerous other boards of directors.

conglomerate
a large corporation composed of many smaller corporations.

multinationals
large corporation that operates in more than one nation, often with limited national control.

---

[31]Ralph M. Farris, *Corporate Networks and Corporate Control*, Greenwood, New York, 1991, p. 85.

Multinational businesses make economic decisions without regard to national considerations or boundaries. IBM, for example, manufactures computers for sale in the United States in Guadalajara, Mexico.

product was made. Autos made by General Motors or Ford now include so many components produced elsewhere that it increasingly is a stretch to call them American-made. Clothing bears labels from dozens of Third World countries. Products, whether made in America or elsewhere, show increasing conformity and standardization, sometimes known as "McDonaldization."[32]

Multinationals now account for almost a third of the gross world economy. The three largest U.S. multinationals are General Motors with 693,000 workers, Ford with 338,000 workers, and General Electric with 216,000 workers.[33] Multinationals commonly move their production facilities from high-wage nations (such as the United States) to low-wage nonunion Third World countries, where they can control and exploit both labor and natural resources. Corporations make decisions regarding raw materials, markets, and workers without regard to national boundaries, and thus domestic U.S. jobs have to compete with Third World wage scales. Nike, for instance, pays its Indonesian workers making sports shoes an *average* wage of $2.00 a day. Starting workers get less. (The post 1998 collapse of the Indonesian economy further dropped Indonesian workers' actual pay.)

One consequence of the global economy is that multinational corporations have fewer and fewer economic, political, or social loyalties to their nominal home nation. In our computerized world, corporate capital and information can be moved anywhere almost instantaneously. Corporate growth and profits are paramount to multinationals operating largely outside the control of nation-states. Employment in the multinational becomes a surrogate for citizenship in the nation.

Multinational corporations argue that they provide benefits to developing countries by introducing new capital and wages into their economies. Those who argue the issue from social welfare, nationalistic, or environmental perspectives maintain that multinationals show little concern either for their nominal home nation, from which they take jobs and tax revenues, or for the poorer countries they exploit to maximize corporate profits.

---

[32]George Ritzer, *The McDonaldization of Society*, New Century edition, Pine Forge, Thousand Oaks, CA, 2000.

Multinational corporations controlling vast economic resources are not always concerned with the impact of their behavior on various nations' populations. Nor are American multinationals especially responsive to the needs of American society. In many cases their decisions have created or intensified social problems in the United States. If transferring jobs to a nation with a low wage scale and no need to provide benefits would save money but deeply harm the American community where the factory is currently located, there is little doubt what the multinational corporation's response is likely to be.

By relocating outside the United States and other developed nations, corporations can often also avoid controls on pollution and restrictions on harming the environment. Unions and other critics of the NAFTA free-trade agreement with Mexico say that North American companies are increasingly moving their manufacturing operations to lower-wage, nonunion, and lower-tax Mexican facilities where there is little or no regulation of environmental pollution. Another example is that little corporate concern (other than for bad publicity) has been expressed about the policy of deliberately destroying Brazilian rain forests to obtain cattle-grazing land so the American fast food industry can have cheap beef for hamburgers.

Because economic globalization is based on an information-driven economy, globalization is also producing a new inequality among urban places.[34] Cities that are information centers prosper. Miami, for instance, is developing into a global information, banking, and trading center. It now has the fourth largest concentration of foreign banking offices in the United States, right behind New York, Los Angeles, and Chicago.[35] General Motors has moved its Latin American administrative headquarters from Brazil to Miami. Miami additionally has become an international trading city, largely due to the efforts of Cuban business people.[36]

Government Growth and Power

The Jeffersonian ideal as expressed by the nation's founding fathers was that government should remain small and with limited economic power. The assumption among those who had just fought a war for independence from British control and taxes was that big government inevitably becomes tyrannical government. Thus, except during wartime, American government remained small into the twentieth century. The federal government's role expanded greatly during the Depression crisis of the 1930s, when government programs such as the WPA (Works Progress Administration) and CCC (Civilian Conservation Corps) provided work on public projects for those who had no other source of employment. Many public works, such as public libraries and the development of our national parks, resulted from these programs.

Big Government

Massive expansion of the federal government accompanied World War II and the Cold War with the Soviet Union that followed. Prior to World War II federal

---

[34]Saskia Sassen, *Cities in a World Economy*, 2 ed., Pine Forge, Thousand Oaks, CA, 2000.
[35]Ibid.
[36]Alejandro Portes and Alex Stepick, *City on the Edge: The Transformation of Miami*, University of California Press, Berkeley, 1993.

expenditures accounted for just under 10 percent of the gross domestic product; from the 1970s through the 1990s that figure has hovered at over 20 percent.[37] In place of America's traditional small military, the Cold War saw the establishment of a permanent **military-industrial complex** in which there was a tight working relationship between senior military officers and the corporate defense industry.

Pentagon defense contracts built whole new government-dependent industrial sectors such as the aerospace industry. In fact, a common pattern for military officers is the so-called "revolving-door," in which military officers in charge of procurement contracts would retire and then immediately go to work for the defense industries to whom they previously had been giving and regulating contracts. A *New York Times* study done in the mid-1980s documented that one-fifth of the officers ranked major or higher and working at the Pentagon, immediately went to work for defense industry corporations upon military retirement.[38] The result was a strong convergence of military and business interests—and high defense expenditures.

Federal Downsizing

Defense expenditures have declined since the end of the Cold War in 1989, but many other expenses have not. People want low taxes but demand a wide range of social and other services, including regulating airline safety, building highways, running the national park systems, providing a social safety net of welfare programs, and providing Medicare and Social Security (Chapter 11 will discuss how these latter two now are our nation's major federal expenditure).

When discussing the size of the federal government, two facts have to be kept in mind: (1) the number of federal government employees has actually been declining for a number of years, and (2) federal government employees are declining as a proportion of the total labor force. In 1960 when Dwight Eisenhower turned over the presidency to John F. Kennedy, the federal government employed almost 4 percent of American workers. Today, federal employment constitutes only 2 percent of American workers. Also, the federal government now accounts for only 16 percent of all government workers; 84 percent of government workers now are found at the state and local level. Local government is where growth is taking place.

The Rise and Decline of Unions

For much of the twentieth century, labor unions were seen as the major counterweight to large corporations. A **labor union** is an association of workers organized for the purpose of advancing their compensation or conditions of work. Legislation passed during the Depression (Wagner Act, 1935) guaranteed workers the right to strike. Prior to that time employers had total control over wages and working conditions. Those who joined unions were commonly not only dismissed but also blacklisted so that they were not able to find employment elsewhere. During the 1940s and 1950s, unions were able to dramatically improve working conditions and wages, enabling many union members to join the middle class for the first

---

[37]U.S. Bureau of the Census, *Statistical Abstract of the United States, 1995,* Government Printing Office, Washington, DC, 1995, p. 333.
[38]J. H. Cushman, "Pentagon-to-Contractor Job Shift Is Profiled," *New York Times,* p. A1, A37.

time. Because of unions, wages went up, working conditions and safety improved, and union workers obtained benefits such as health insurance and retirement pensions.

Big Labor's Decline

At midcentury big labor was in its heyday, with union membership peaking at 27 percent of the labor force in 1953. The proportion of the labor force that is unionized fell to 14 percent in 1998.[39] In the private sector, union membership is just 11 percent. The drop in union membership occurred primarily because of the decline in heavy-manufacturing blue-collar jobs. Many industrial and manufacturing unionized jobs have been "exported" to developing countries with low wage scales. During the second half of the twentieth century, union membership among steelworkers, garment workers, and oil and chemical workers declined by half. The steelworkers alone lost over half a million union members in the last 25 years. Heavy manufacturing jobs remaining in the United States are being automated. The labor movement has had difficulty organizing service- and information-based firms, such as those associated with the computer industry. Technologically trained white-collar employees and office workers historically have been less responsive to union appeals, and most high-technology workers are not unionized.[40] In the postindustrial economy, white-collar workers, especially middle-class professionals, also are especially resistant to unionization. The greatest success today is in recruiting women and minorities who work in service industries.[41]

Additionally, in a tight labor market, workers often fear (with good reason) that they will lose their jobs if they push to unionize. When workers do unionize, management often threatens to close a plant and move to a low-wage area, often abroad. The result is both fewer elections and fewer voting to unionize. Today there are dramatically fewer strikes than in the period before 1980. In 1981 the air traffic controllers demanded a substantial wage increase and declared an illegal strike. They shut down the nation's airports, at considerable inconvenience to the public. President Ronald Reagan thus had widespread public support when he fired all the striking controllers who refused to return to work. President Reagan effectively broke the union.

Companies may even provoke a strike in order to break a union and lower wages and benefits. This happened in 1992, when union workers at Caterpillar Corporation went on strike only to discover that the corporation welcomed the strike as an excuse for replacing most of the workforce with cheaper nonunion workers. The striking workers eventually had to return on the corporation's terms. Moving corporation manufacturing plants from heavily unionized areas, or building new facilities only in antiunion "right to work" states (especially in the South), or in Mexico or other low-wage countries, has also weakened union strength.

Change in Unions

By the late 1990s, some unions were responding more effectively to changing conditions. Strikes are now used only as a last resort, and time lost to strikes is at an

[39]Michael Barone, "The Unions Go Public," *U.S. News & World Report,* October 4, 1999, p. 30.
[40]J. Gregg Robinson and Judith S. McIlwee, "Obstacles to Unionization in High-Tech Industries," *Work and Occupations,* 16:115–136, May 1989.
[41]D. W. Miller, "A Labor Activist Turned Scholar Helps Unions with Recruiting Woes," *Chronicle of Higher Education,* December 18, 1998, p. 15A.

Unions are no longer only for industrial workers. Unions increasingly are focusing their organizing activity on women and government workers. Here some 10,000 striking state workers demonstrate at the Oregon state capitol.

© Bette Lee/Impact Visuals

all-time low. Today's unions actively seek to recruit public sector white-collar workers and to recruit female manufacturing workers. Some 36 percent of government employees belong to labor unions.[42] While their numbers are down unions do retain political influence due to major election contributions and the ability to get out voters. However, they do not seem likely to exert as much power during the first half of the twenty-first century as they did during the last half of the twentieth century. Certainly, they are no longer an equal counterweight to business conglomerates or multinationals.

Dual Labor Markets

We tend to think of the workforce as people employed by companies. However, there is both a formal and an informal labor market. The **primary** or **formal labor market** includes those who are regularly employed by relatively stable companies or firms at a living wage or better. This includes traditional managerial, professional, and blue-collar workforce positions that provide relatively dependable

primary labor market
composed of those regularly employed in fixed positions by relatively stable firms paying fixed wages, same as formal labor market.

[42]**Universal Almanac,** Andrews and McMeel, Kansas City, 1995, p. 269.

income, benefits, and security. The **secondary or informal labor market,** in contrast, is composed of those whose employment is temporary, nonsecure, and poorly paid.

In developing nations the secondary labor market is sometimes larger than the primary labor market. More commonly the informal sector employs one-third to half of all urban workers and comprises those who are self-employed and those working for small marginal enterprises.[43] Informal or secondary-sector businesses usually lack access to credit, banks, or formally trained personnel. Such businesses also rarely comply with government safety regulations, minimum wage and benefit laws, or tax codes. Although it is difficult to get data on the secondary labor market in the United States, it appears to be growing. In the United States illegal immigrants are a part of the poorly paid and marginal secondary labor market. Female workers and minorities are overrepresented in the secondary labor market.

Toward the Future

Because we live in a society that values people by what they do for a living, the world of work will become even more important in defining who people are. As a consequence a prime question for the new century is how to provide meaningful work roles and work lives for all citizens. For many the "American Dream" of secure employment and upward mobility is slipping away. Where past generations hoped to do better than their parents, many of those now starting their work lives fear they will not do as well. For those without college degrees, this is likely to be the case. Education is increasingly the key to economic success and the twenty-first century will be especially hard on the marginally educated. If the twenty-first century is not to see the gulf widen between those who are generously compensated and those who are minimally paid, changes in wage and tax policies will have to be made. The current system favors the better-off and widens the nation's economic gap and its social division. If this continues, it may produce social upheavals and revolts similar to those seen in American cities during the late 1960s.

Current college students can anticipate work lives that differ significantly from those of their parents. First, the full-time work life of today's students will start later and end later. Because of advanced educational requirements, many will not begin full-time careers until they reach their mid-20s. Because they have a longer life expectancy, college-age cohorts also are likely to remain in the paid labor force longer than their parents. Second, both sexes will have much more common work-life experiences. Fewer jobs will be sex-typed, and the great majority of college-educated women will remain in the paid labor force after having children. A computer-driven society renders gender differences less and less relevant.

Third, telecommuting will become increasingly common. For those working at home, compensation will be based less on hours worked than on tasks completed. The question of how much time is spent on a project will have decreasing relevance. Those working at home without daily supervision will be judged and rewarded on the basis of goals met. The sharp twentieth-century distinctions between workday and home time will have less and less meaning in the twenty-first century.

---

[43]S. V. Sethuraman, "The Informal Urban Sector in Developing Countries: Employment, Poverty, and Environment," International Labour Organization, Geneva, 1981.

Finally, today's students can anticipate numerous job and even career changes. Being competent and a hard worker no longer guarantees not being "downsized," "separated," or "unassigned"(euphemisms for being fired). The idea of certain lifetime employment and retiring from a firm where one spent one's whole work life is an anachronism. In spite of a booming economy, there were more layoffs in 1998–1999 than at any time in the previous quarter-century. More varied and flexible work experiences will increasingly be the norm.

Summary

The American economy is undergoing profound changes. The internationalization of the economy, corporate mergers, and the downsizing of both production and management have changed the economic patterns of even two decades ago. While educated white-collar workers have generally done well, the average blue collar worker's income has declined by one fifth in the last 20 years. The old assumption that a growing economy automatically provides a growing general prosperity is increasingly being questioned.

- Functionalists look at the economy and focus on how goods and services can best be distributed to meet societal needs, believing that a competitive free market best does this job. They see work as meeting social as well as economic needs for the society. Thus, not having a job is a social as well as an economic problem.

- Conflict approaches focus on whose interests are being advanced, and whose are being hurt, by economic change. They see economic competition as benefiting only those who control the system.

- The interactionist approach is more social-psychological, looking at how economic changes affect individuals and small groups, such as how people interact and cope on an everyday basis.

- There are four major changes in the workforce and workplace: (1) the labor force that used to be agricultural and industrial is now oriented to providing services rather than producing goods, (2) educational levels have sharply risen, with over a quarter of the workforce now having at least a college degree, (3) women now make up almost half of the paid labor force, and (4) there's been a shift of workers from full-time employment with benefits to part-time work without benefits.

- The Western postindustrial service economy is the result of a long history of economic development, from the agricultural revolution resulting in a food surplus, to the industrial revolution replacing humans with machines. This resulted in factory-based industrialization and machine-based mass production.

- The economic system most associated with industrialization is capitalism, in which the means of production and distribution of goods is privately owned. Capitalism legitimizes private ownership of wealth-producing property, values the pursuit of personal profit, and states that market competition should determine what goods are produced.

- Socialism is an economic system in which the means of production and distribution are collectively owned. The market economy is replaced with a demand economy administered by the state, in which goods are produced based on the needs of the overall society, not on economic demand.

- Most economies today are actually mixed economies that combine free-enterprise economics with some government controls. Western Europe has more social controls, while America is more laissez faire.

- Over the past century and a half, America has been transformed from a nation of small business owners to a nation where economic power is concentrated in a few large corporations. Moreover, conglomerates composed of many corporations increasingly dominate the nation.

- The federal government expanded rapidly during World War II and continued to grow during the Cold War with the Soviet Union. Since the 1989 end of the Cold War, military expenditures have been declining as a proportion of the national budget. Contrary to the common myth, the federal government is actually declining in size, and proportionally is only half as large as it was in 1960.

- Unions are organizations in which workers band together to improve wages and working conditions. Union membership peaked in the 1950s, with members traditionally coming from blue-collar industries. White-collar workers are less responsive to unionization.

- The informal or secondary labor market in which wages are low, job tenure is uncertain, and benefits are nonexistent dominates much of the Third World and is increasingly found in American cities as well. Illegal immigrants in U.S. cities also constitute a secondary labor market.

☞Key Review Terms

agricultural revolution
American Dream
blue collar
capitalism
command economy
conglomerate
corporation
demand economy
economy

industrial revolution
informal labor market
Information Revolution
interlocking directorate
labor union
military-industrial complex
mixed economy
moonlighting

multinationals
postindustrial economy
primary labor market
secondary labor market
service economy
socialism
unions
white collar

? Questions for Discussion

1. Discuss the role of state government in your area. Include projects, taxes, regulations, and policies.

2. Discuss the changes in the U.S. economy since World War II. What has been the effect on workers?

3. It is said that the average worker may now expect not one but several careers in a lifetime because of changes in the workplace. What are the implications for you and your classmates?

4. How has the increased participation of women in the workforce changed the workplace? What are a woman's economic and social expectations in the workplace?

5. The text says that sometimes self-employed persons are those who have been downsized by a corporation and then hired back as independent contractors. Discuss the implications of this for your future worklife. How would you respond?

6. The President, all the ex-Presidents, and numerous public organizations have praised the role of volunteerism in America. Discuss the role of nonpaid work in American society.

7. What is capitalism? How does it differ from country to country? How is it practiced in America?

8. Discuss the role conglomerates and multinational corporations play in making economic and environmental policies in the United States.

9. Discuss the growth and power of the federal government. What did the Founding Fathers plan for and what have been the pressures for change?

10. What is the role of unions in the American economy? Why did they develop? What is their future?

☛Suggested Resources

G. William Domhoff, *Who Rules America? Power and Politics in the Year 2000*, third ed., Mayfield, Mountain View, CA, 1998. Domhoff argues that business interest groups form a tight knit corporate community that actively pushes its own interests over those of government, unions, or the public.

Barbara Reskin and Irene Padavic, *Women and Men at Work*, Pine Forge, Thousand Oaks CA, 1994. The gendered nature of the workplace and how it has changed, and how it hasn't.

Jeremy Rifkin, *The End of Work: The Decline of the Global Labor Force and the Dawn of the Post-Market Era*, Jeremy P. Thatcher/Putnam, New York, 1995. The title explains this view of the future as seen from a left-environmentalist perspective.

George Ritzer, *The McDonaldization of Society*, second ed., Pine Forge, Thousand Oaks, CA, 2000. A sociological best seller and favorite of students which readably discusses the international movement toward uniformity, predictability, and similarity in products and workforces.

David Vogel, *Fluctuating Fortunes: The Political Power of Business in America*, Princeton University Press, Princeton, NJ, 1996. Vogel is a proponent of the view that public interest pressure groups, government, and other institutions counter balance and prevent business domination.

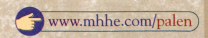
1. Americans have divided opinions about labor unions. For example, check the National Opinion Research Center's General Social Survey index: (*www.icpsr.umich.edu/GSS99/subject/s-index.htm*) Click "Labor Unions." Look at the variables, *POWER OF (UNPOWER), VALUE TO COUNTRY (UNION-SOK), and WORKERS NEED (STRNGUN)*. You will find that while 423 respondents surveyed between 1888 and 1991 felt that unions in the United States have too little power, 924 disagreed and felt unions either had enough or too much power. But when asked if unions were good for the country overall, 809 respondents replied that they were at least "fairly good," and 272 said that they were not good for the country.

   a. How did respondents reply to the item about workers needing trade unions to protect their interests (*STRNGUN*)?

   b. In your opinion, what accounts for the variation between these responses?

2. Visit the American Federation of Labor-Congress of Industrial Organizations (AFL-CIO) website (*www.aflcio.org/home.htm*).

a. What is this organization, what is its mission, and what are some of its member unions?

   b. Examine its home page. What items are on its "agenda"? What values does it reflect?

   Now go to The National Right to Work Legal Defense Foundation's site, (*www.nrtw.org/*).

   c. What is its mission?

   d. What are "right to work laws" and what states have enacted them?

   e. See if you can find a detailed list of supporters and contributors. What argument does this site make about the power of labor unions in the United States?

"I don't understand why I have to take courses in history, science, and social sciences. I'm planning to be a business major."

A freshman student's complaint to the author.

Education Under Stress

Education Today

College students usually think of attending high school as a universal experience and attending college as being relatively common, but until recently neither was. At the beginning of the twentieth century only 6 percent of the American population graduated from high school, and under 2 percent graduated from college.[1] Having a high school diploma marked one as part of the academic elite. In 1940, just before the United States entered World War II, over three-quarters of Americans 25 years or older had not graduated from high school. Not until the mid-1960s did half the labor force have a high school diploma. Today, by contrast, in the United States five-sixths of young people finish high school, half take at least some college courses, and almost a quarter graduate from college.[2]

As the nation has changed into a complex postindustrial urban society, so have the demands placed on our educational system. The main goal of a college education at the beginning of the twentieth century was to transfer classical learning to a small privileged elite. (The word "school" comes from the Greek "schola" or "leisure," because only the elite could afford the time for schooling.) The goal of twenty-first-century college education is much broader: providing both knowledge and job skills to a wide swath of the population. While at the beginning of the twentieth century the great majority of workers did manual labor on farms or in factories, our contemporary technologically driven economy requires a well-educated labor force. Today for example, it is expected that all job applicants have computer skills. Mass education has become a societal necessity, and a college degree has become a requirement for even applying for many jobs. While the industrial age emphasized standardization, the postindustrial world demands the ability to solve problems and think creatively.[3]

In this chapter we will focus on three issues regarding contemporary education: the quality of primary and secondary education in the United States, the changing cost and meaning of college education, and the future of affirmative action admissions. All three issues have policy implications, and all three will be considered in some detail.

---

[1]Bureau of the Census, *Historical Statistics of the United States, Colonial Times to 1970,* Washington, DC, 1975, p. 379.
[2]*Universal Almanac 1995,* Andrews and McMeel, Kansas City, 1995, p. 243.
[3]Jerald Hage and Charles H. Powers, *Post-Industrial Lives: Roles and Relationships in the 21st Century,* Sage, Newbury Park, CA, 1992.

Purposes of Education

Every society has a social heritage, or body of social knowledge and practices, that must be transmitted through social organizations. Education provides such cultural transmission. It also helps to shape the individual's personality to conform to the social framework of the culture. This molding of the social personality contributes to the integration of the individual into her or his society. All industrial and postindustrial societies, either formally or informally, organize their school systems in such a way that there will be a good "fit" between the goals of the individual and the needs of the society. Different societies vary in the societal goals they foster.

Asian societies, for example, generally put societal needs first. The technologically advanced nation of Singapore assigns college students to university programs and majors based on the government's assessment of societal needs rather than on the individual's desires. Whether a student goes into engineering, law, or sociology is largely out of his or her hands. Taiwan uses a matching system whereby students wanting admission to the more selective universities often must accept a major not of their choosing. American culture, by contrast, stresses the importance of individual decision making. American education endorses the belief that education must foremost serve the personal needs of self-development.

Sociological Perspectives

Functionalist Approaches

Education is viewed by functionalists as having three basic roles: (1) the social function of *transmitting the culture* from one generation to the next, (2) the social and personal function of *socializing and integrating individual members* into society, and (3) the personal function of *providing a channel for social mobility*. As expressed by the sociologist Émile Durkheim, the function of education is "to arouse and to develop in the child a certain number of physical, intellectual, and moral states which are demanded of him both by the political society as a whole and the special milieu for which he is specifically destined."[4]

In addition to these **manifest functions** (explicitly intended consequences), educational systems also have important **latent functions** (unintended or unspoken ones). One of these latent functions is to keep those who are under age, untrained, and unemployable out of the labor force as long as possible. Keeping young people in school holds down unemployment rates. Mandatory school attendance ages were legislated during the Depression as a means of keeping teenagers off the job market. (All state school attendance laws currently mandate school attendance to at least age 16.)

Today, parents expect primary schools to serve a custodial as well as an educational function. With both parents often in the labor force, primary schools

manifest function
intended and recognized consequence of social actions or policies.

latent function
unintended or unrecognized consequences of social actions or policies.

---

[4]Émile Durkheim, *Education and Sociology*, Choroid Fox (trans.), Free Press of Glencoe, Chicago, 1956, p. 71.

increasingly provide state-supported babysitting. Parents increasingly assume that it is the school's responsibility, not theirs, to care for the child during the workday. In addition, schools are expected to provide lunch and care for children taken ill. Any grade school teacher can relate stories of how parents become upset when called to pick up their child because the child is sick or because the school is closing early because of bad weather.

Attending college also has the latent function of keeping minimally skilled workers off the job market. If the nation's approximately 14 million college students were suddenly thrown onto the full-time labor market, our highly integrated economic system would be severely strained—perhaps beyond the breaking point. Keeping youths in college helps to control the flow of newcomers into the job market and often provides them with some useful preparation as well. Education also plays a "gatekeeper" role, channeling people toward some areas and away from others.

School reformers frequently are implicit functionalists insofar as they want to increase the effectiveness of the schools. They seek to create institutions where merit and work are rewarded, and where the young are socialized for economic productivity and mobility. Thus, racial integration of schools is seen by functionalists as necessary, not only as a moral imperative, but also as an economic necessity for reduced unemployment in a well-functioning economy. Functionalists generally advocate greater emphasis on core courses and the reorganization of schools to better reward good teaching. Community colleges are seen as highly functional, insofar as they explicitly seek to train students with new skills to meet the needs of a changing economy.

Education, however, does not always and automatically support the status quo. Higher education in particular can be a source of cultural disharmony and lead to dissension, deviance, and conflict. Today, as in the past, parents sometimes fear that colleges and universities may expose their young to the "wrong sort" of ideas and social behavior. Education is a means by which new ideas, information, and approaches are systematically introduced into the culture, thereby invariably transforming it.

Conflict Approaches

Those holding a conflict approach see the goal of education not as providing equal access and opportunity, but as perpetuating inequality and keeping the unequal status quo in force. Conflict theorists believe that the educational system is designed to meet the needs of the powerful and their children. Rather than providing a means of social mobility, the education system is seen as a mean of solidifying and perpetuating the existing order, and for providing employers with a trained labor pool.

Academic merit is defined in terms of upper-middle-class expectations. The culture and values taught by the schools are those of the white middle-class, a circumstance that prevents others from competing on an equal basis. This results in **cultural imperialism.** Schools socialize the young into stereotypes of the mainstream middle-class culture. In the conflict view, while systems of explicit and blatant racial, ethnic, and religious segregation have largely been abolished, the current system of racial and class divisions along urban-suburban lines accomplishes the same goals. That is, it keeps the poor and nonwhite at the bottom.

In addition to the official curriculum, conflict theorists say that schools also have a **hidden curriculum,** which is to transmit the often unspoken beliefs and values of the society (functionalists see this as a latent function of education). Conflict theorists view the middle-class hidden curriculum as a way of maintaining the cultural domination of those in power. This pattern of inequality starts in kindergarten, where the major emphasis is on teaching new students how to play the

cultural imperialism
assumption that middle class culture and values should dominate.

hidden curriculum
schools transmitting middle-class beliefs and values.

Middle and high schools sometimes devote more attention to sports and cheerleading than to improving academic performance. These cheerleaders are improving their skills by attending a summer cheerleading camp in Texas.

© Bob Daemmrich/The Image Works

student role.[5] The hidden curriculum rewards middle-class behaviors and values. Socialization includes teaching what the society considers appropriate gender, racial, and social-class behaviors. High school students from upper-middle-class professional families are expected to take college preparatory courses, while poor and working-class youth are tracked into vocational courses. Conflict theorists also support the view that the system is designed to subtly tell minorities that they are not really expected to stay and succeed, and that while they remain in school little other than attendance is expected of them. Furthermore, conflict theories note that while upper-middle-class males are socialized to be class leaders and achievers, females are socialized to stress attractiveness and popularity, to be cheerleaders and join the pep club.

Conflict theorists say the only way to change the status quo is to radically reorganize the schools so that the cultural beliefs and values of the middle class no longer dominate and all social and cultural beliefs are given equal value. Many conflict theorists would replace the current curriculum—heavily based on the Western European heritage of "dead white males"—with one giving major weight to works by Afrocentric, feminist, and Third World writers. However, most conflict theorists also believe it is impossible to radically reform the educational system until the controlling capitalistic economic system is reformed or replaced.

---

[5]Harry L. Gracey, "Learning the Student Role," in James M. Henslin, (ed.), *Down to Earth Sociology*, Free Press, New York, 1993, p. 383.

Interactionist Approaches

Rather than examining macrolevel effects, social interactionists are most concerned with how educational systems affect individuals and help them develop a self. For example, do schools socialize the poor to fail? Do they create a self-fulfilling prophecy? Do the rule-following and social conformity stressed in primary and secondary school systems foster the development of democratic values, or do they encourage authoritarian thinking? The answers aren't obvious.

Interactionists study questions such as How should schools deal with students who disrupt the learning of others? Should primary emphasis be placed on helping them, or on the learning of the other students? Do children who are living in disorganized families perform better in open learning environments which encourage self-learning? Or do such children learn better in school systems having a fixed curriculum and stressing the importance of discipline and civil behavior? The success of tightly organized inner-city schools, for example, is often attributed to their emphasis on discipline. But is this the best learning environment?

Interactionists see the socialization into new roles as a crucial element of the educational system. Labeling students as "good students" or "bad students" can often lead to a self-fulfilling prophecy, where students fulfill teachers' expectations. Much of the most important educational socialization, as college students are well aware, occurs outside the formal classroom. Fraternities and sororities seek to socialize their members in particular ways, but they are not alone in this. Different professions commonly have their own social norms. Universities not only provide art students, business students, and science students different information but also expose them to the values and norms of the particular postcollege world they hope to enter. Such informally taught anticipatory socialization provides the rules, dress codes, and behavior expectations within a field and is often crucial to success.

American Educational Results

At first glance America's educational record looks good. Officially, 99 percent of the population 14 years of age and over is literate. Moreover, some 86 percent of 25 to 29 year olds have completed high school.[6] A quarter of the population aged 25 to 29 have graduated from college. Today we spend twice as much on education as on defense, and the American university system is widely acknowledged to be the best in the world.

Now for the bad news. While virtually everyone may be literate as measured by years of school completed, **functional illiteracy**—that is, the inability to read and understand the language effectively at about a sixth-grade level—is still widespread. During the early 1970s, when the military draft was still in effect, one of every four men taking the Armed Forces qualifying test was judged functionally illiterate.[7] This means that they could not easily read a daily newspaper or instructions for operating machinery. Today, roughly one in eight adults in the United States still remains functionally illiterate. The problem is especially serious among immigrants and the poor. Half of those heads of households with incomes below the poverty level cannot read at an eighth-grade level.

functional illiteracy
inability to read and understand a language at roughly the sixth-grade level.

[6]U.S. Bureau of the Census, *Educational Attainment in the United States, March 1990 and 1991,* Current Population Reports, P20–462, 1992, p. 3.
[7]David Harman, "Keeping Up in America," *Wilson Quarterly,* Spring, 1986, p. 121.

In public education there is no uniformity of educational opportunity. Building condition, teacher quality, and equipment differ radically from school to school. Some schools lack even sufficient desks, while others have computers available for every student.

Top: © Bob Daemmrich/Stock, Boston
Bottom: PhotoDisc/Volume 41, Education 2

The most complete and accurate data on the current level of functional literacy in America comes from the Educational Testing Service's study of 26,000 persons chosen to represent a cross section of American adults. They found that, while almost everyone can read at a basic level, an estimated 90 million Americans over age 16 are not fully equipped for the literacy requirements of the workplace.[8] In practical terms this means they have difficulty calculating the difference between sale and regular prices; they cannot figure out a bus schedule or mentally compute the tip on a restaurant meal.

Moreover, those that are the worst off don't even know that they don't know. Of the 42 million American adults who fall in the bottom fifth in reading ability, 71 percent think they read very well. The reality is that such persons are largely excluded from skilled jobs. They almost certainly are outside the cybernet information networks that college students take for granted.

Educational Inequality

How to equalize educational opportunity remains perhaps the major educational problem. Public school systems, particularly those in large cities, have not been very successful with students who lack home preparation or strong family motivation. Inner-city primary and secondary schools are sometimes viewed even by

---

[8]Educational Testing Service, *Adult Literacy in America*, Department of Education, Washington, DC, 1993.

their teachers as little more than holding tanks, leaving nearly three-quarters of large-city school children reading below grade level. After decades of promises and programs, many inner-city schools still remain woefully deficient.

The educational reformer Jonathan Kozol says in *Savage Inequalities* that the nation maintains two separate and unequal school systems, one for poor minority inner-city children and another for the more affluent.[9] Poor children sometimes attend Third World condition schools with poorly qualified teachers, while there are well-equipped schools with good teachers only a bus ride away. The National Assessment of Educational Progress Tests indicate the average reading level of black 17-year-olds is about that of white 13-year-olds.[10] Twelve years of schooling in inner-city schools is not equivalent to 12 years in a high-income suburban system.[11] While federal and state governments have established a wide range of special education programs, inner-city schools remain the nation's problem schools. Their plight is analogous to that of Sisyphus, the cruel king of Corinth in Greek mythology, who was condemned eternally to push a rock uphill only to have it roll down again when he neared the top.

Declining Standards?

Middle-class schools also have problems. The good news is that the proportion of high school students taking core academic courses has increased from 13 percent in the mid 1980s to 47 percent today. The bad news is that the level of educational knowledge is not increasing. A high school diploma no longer guarantees that the student has mastered even minimal math, reading, and comprehension skills. To insure that all high school students graduate with at least basic reading and writing skills, many states now require students to obtain some form of "literacy passport" before receiving a high school diploma. To receive the passport, however, most states require only that twelfth-grade students be able to read at an eighth-grade level, and some states set the high school passing level even lower.

In an attempt to reverse declining standards, the nation's governors met in 1989 at the first educational summit and set educational goals for the year 2000. At the third educational summit meeting at the end of 1999, however, the governors confessed that none of the eight goals set by the governors 10 years earlier were yet within reach.[12] The 1998 National Assessment of Educational Progress indicated that only 1 percent of twelfth-graders reached the "advanced" stage in writing skills, while about a quarter were "proficient," and 22 percent failed to meet "basic" standards.[13]

Some educational experts believe that these problems are overstated and much of the discussion about failing schools is a near-myth.[14] Most observers, however, believe the problems are very real. The Third International Mathematics and Science Study, the largest and most thorough examination of what students know in mathematics and science, suggests there are serious problems with American schools. Some 500,000 students in 41 nations were tested. American

---

[9]Jonathan Kozol, *Savage Inequalities,* Crown, New York, 1991.

[10]"The Case for Tough Standards," *U.S. News and World Report,* April 1, 1996, p. 5.

[11]Kozol, *Savage Inequalities.*

[12]"Clinton, Governors Assess Efforts to Improve Education," *WashingtonPost.com,* October 1, 1999, p. 1.

[13]Ben Wildavsky, "Kids Don't Have the Write Stuff," *U.S. News and World Report,* October, 11, 1999, p. 28.

[14]Peter Schrag, "The Near-Myth of Our Failing Schools," *Atlantic Monthly,* October 1997, pp. 72–80.

eighth-graders ranked 28th in mathematics and 17th in science.[15] American high school students consistently score lower than students from other industrial nations.[16] This poor standing is attributed both to America's low academic expectations and to America's shorter school year. The average school year in the United States is 180 days, compared to 210 days in Germany and 244 days in Japan. Also, when in school American students spend less than half as much time studying core academic subjects such as science, English, math, and history as do students in Germany, France, or Japan.[17] American students think their schools are too easy and want to be challenged. Some 75 percent say they would study harder if schools gave them tougher tests and 74 percent say schools should not pass them to the next grade only when they have learned what's expected of them.[18]

Grade Inflation

While course expectations have been declining, **grade inflation,** where grades of "A" are routinely given in high school (and college) for work that would have received only a "B" or "C" a generation earlier, has become the norm. The College Board, sponsor of the SAT (Scholastic Assessment Test), announced in 1998 that, while students' grades are going up, students' knowledge and performance levels are declining. The number of students taking the SAT test who have an "A" grade average has increased dramatically over the past 10 years to 38 percent, but the SAT scores of those "A" students has declined an average of 12 percent.[19] By 1996 the average SAT scores had declined to where, in order to restore the SAT to its old norm of 1,000, the test had to be reconfigured, and all scores were raised by approximately 100 points.[20] Thus, a combined score of 1,000 today is equivalent to a score of 900 before 1996.

There is agreement that American primary and high school standards are low, but less on how to solve the problem.[21] One response is simply to do away with traditional grades. The state of Oregon is replacing all high school letter grades by statewide exams that test specific proficiencies. As of 2001, letter grades and grade point averages in Oregon high schools will be replaced by tests that measure having achieved certain necessary performance standards; the goal is to switch the focus from the students' grade to whether they actually know the subject.

Educational and business leaders often advocate establishing national standards for what students should know.[22] President Clinton proposed in 1998 establishing national standards of learning, but the Republican Congress strongly disagreed, feeling establishing national learning standards would interfere with the rights of local school boards.

Universities also are experiencing grade inflation and decreasing coursework requirements.[23] Students are usually unaware that many introductory course

grade inflation
common practice of giving higher grades for less work than in the past.

---

[15]"World Education League: Who's Top?" *The Economist,* March 29, 1997, p. 21.

[16]"U.S. Students Lag in Advanced Tests," *Associated Press,* March 21, 1996.

[17]National Commission on Education and Learning, *Prisoners of Time,* Government Printing Office, Washington, DC, 1994.

[18]"Challenge Me," Education Excellence Partnership, *New York Times,* Feb. 29, 2000, p. 9.

[19]"Grades, SAT Scores Show Disparity," *New York Times News Service,* September 2, 1998.

[20]Ben Gose, "Perfect Scores Are Not So Perfect with New SAT Scale," *Chronicle of Higher Education,* June 2, 1995, p. 34.

[21]Paul Ganon, "What Should Children Learn? *Atlantic,* December 1995, pp. 65–78.

[22]Albert Shanker, "A Major Accomplishment," *New York Times,* April 24, 1994.

[23]Diane Ravitch, *The Schools We Deserve: Reflections on the Educational Crisis of Our Time,* Basic Books, New York, 1985; and for an argument for raising standards, see William A. Henry III, *In Defense of Elitism,* Doubleday, New York, 1994.

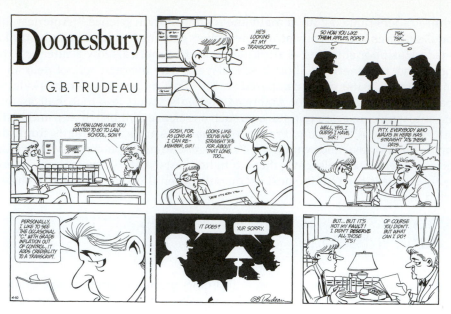

textbooks now are routinely "dumbed down" to a tenth-grade or lower reading level (this text hasn't been "dumbed down"). With high schools not teaching students basic skills, even prestigious colleges have been forced to run remedial programs. Over one-fourth of college freshmen require remedial mathematics, writing, or science courses. Some open-admission universities such as CCNY (City Colleges of New York) are now moving to raise standards and eliminating remedial courses. Students who are unprepared for regular college-level work must first take remedial courses offered by local community colleges.

Private and Parochial Schools

Some 45 million children attend U.S. public primary and secondary schools.[24] Another 5.7 million are enrolled in private schools. Private schools include some of the most exclusive (and expensive) schools in the nation. However, of the 11 percent of students in private schools, the great majority attend parochial schools. Most of these schools were originally founded to serve the children of Catholic European immigrants, but today city parochial schools commonly serve minority, and often non-Catholic, populations.

A growing body of research indicates that regardless of students' economic or social background, students generally learn more at urban parochial schools than at city public schools.[25] Why? Why are parochial schools generally more successful teaching disadvantaged inner-city students? It isn't money, because parochial schools commonly spend less than half as much per student as do public schools. Nor is it class size, because parochial schools usually have larger classes. Some

---

[24]U. S. Department of Education figures reported in the *Universal Almanac 1995,* Andrews and McMeel, Kansas City, 1995, p. 241.

[25]James Coleman, Thomas Hoffer, and Sally Kilgore, *Public and Private Schools: An Analysis of Public Schools and Beyond*, National Center for Educational Statistics, Washington, DC, 1981; and James Coleman and Thomas Hoffer, *Public and Private High Schools: The Impact of Communities*, Basic Books, New York, 1987.

suggest it is because the parochial schools take only the better behaved students. However, the counterargument is that, because parochial schools are believed to be stricter, parents who have youngsters with discipline problems send the youths to parochial school.

The answer seems to be that successful inner-city parochial and public schools *demand more* of their students. Unlike many inner-city schools, successful schools assume that all students can do good work and insist that they do so. Performance levels are not lowered, and dropping out of school is strongly discouraged. All students are expected to work hard and be successful. Parochial schools also insist that parents take an active role in the education of their children. This is a requirement that most local public schools cannot enforce.

Academic expectations and parental involvement have payoffs. Inner-city minority children attending parochial schools are four times more likely to graduate and three times more likely to go on to college than those in the local public schools. It is clear that inner-city schools can successfully motivate and educate students. The tragedy is that many inner city schools don't do so.

However, even among the worst school systems in the nation there are some signs of hope. In 1987 then Education Secretary William Bennett cited Chicago's system as being the nation's worst. It may not have been the worst large-city system, Detroit's and Washington, D.C.'s usually share that dubious honor, but it was in serious trouble. More recently, in 1999, William Bennett praised the Chicago system as, "a model of accountability and flexibility."[26] What changed things was a radical shake-up of the system. In desperation, the state legislature in 1995 gave Chicago Mayor Richard M. Daley control over the Chicago public schools, and he immediately installed Paul Vallas as school CEO. Vallas set achievement test goals, removed 36 principals, fired tenured teachers who were not performing, and sent poor-performing students to summer school. Chicago's attendance and test scores are still low by national standards, but they have risen dramatically since 1995.

Minority Educational Patterns

African American educational levels have increased sharply in recent decades. Census data document that when the United States entered World War II (1941) the median number of years of schooling for American black males was only 5.4 years, and barely 4 percent of black males had completed high school.[27] Today the Bureau of the Census reports that there is no longer any statistical difference between the high school graduation rates of young black and white adults aged 25–29.[28] All high school degrees, however, are not equal—average SAT scores for African Americans remain below those of whites. On the other hand, African American scores have risen 7 points over the last decade in spite of a major increase in the number of students taking the test.[29] White scores during the same period have declined slightly.

---

[26]Michael Barone, "Surprising School Reform," *U.S. News and World Report,* May 17, 1999, p. 30.

[27]U.S. Bureau of the Census, *Historical Statistics of the United States: Colonial Times to 1970,* Washington, DC, 1975, p. 380.

[28]U.S. Bureau of the Census, *Educational Attainment in the United States: March 1997, Current Population Reports,* P20–505, Washington, DC, 1998, p. 2.

[29]David Nakamura and Kenneth Cooper, "SAT Scores Steady in Washington Area," *Washington Post Online,* September 1, 1999.

Box 9.1 Making a Difference

The Coleman Reports

The Coleman Reports represent sociological research that has made a difference. Reaction to the reports also provides a study in how emotion and ideology can affect even scholars' acceptance of research. Being honest with one's data can have personal costs.

The first Coleman study was commissioned in the 1960s by the U.S. Office of Education to assess the impact of segregation and integration on school performance. Some questioned why it even was being done since "everyone knew" that segregated schools had unequal school resources (especially in the South) and lower expenditures produced lower results.

The research project was massive, involving some 600,000 students and 60,000 teachers in approximately 4,000 schools, and was designed by the late James Coleman, well known as the foremost mathematical sociologist of the time.[a] The 737 pages of the report—plus an additional 548 pages of statistical data released in 1966— documented that what "everyone knew" to be true was not so. Coleman had expected that when he compared schools attended by whites with those attended by African Americans, he would find that school resources made striking differences in student performance. The data showed otherwise. Per-pupil expenditure, number of books in the library, and quality of facilities made little difference in pupil performance.

Family background explained most of the variation in achievement levels, not differences between schools. What mattered most was support for education in the home, and this support was most common in the middle-class. Finding that the school itself was less important was deeply subversive since it ran contrary to almost all the popular educational myths.

Coleman also found that children from disadvantaged backgrounds did somewhat better in schools that were predominately middle-class than they did in schools that were solely lower-class. The beneficial effect came not from the racial composition, but from the better educational background and higher educational aspirations of middle-class students.

Because a high proportion of African Americans came from disadvantaged backgrounds, the report was widely interpreted as showing that equal educational opportunity required busing to achieve school integration. Coleman was hailed as a civil rights hero and school districts across the country, either voluntarily or under court order, began busing to achieve racial integration.

Coleman then did a follow-up study to examine the effects of busing on school performance. This second Coleman Report indicated that busing was having an effect opposite to that intended; racial isolation was being increased. Court-ordered busing orders in the 20 largest school systems in the country were self-defeating, according to Coleman, because busing resulted in whites either moving to white suburbs or putting their children in private schools. Coleman suggested that rather than busing students, major emphasis should be put on redrawing school lines to increase integration. In his view, it was essential to sharply increase the number of minorities living in integrated neighborhoods, particularly in the suburbs.

Coleman was moved by the data rather than doctrine, but his statements of fact were seen as statements of motive. At that time for a liberal scholar to say that busing didn't work was the academic equivalent of saying that the emperor had no clothes. Coleman was widely denounced and the then-president of the American Sociological Association even made an unprecedented personal attack. Referring to this era, Daniel Patrick Moynihan (a sociologist and, until retiring in 2001, the senior Senator from New York) says, "They tried to drum Jim out of the profession. They accused him of being a tool of conservatives who were trying to cut social spending. He was just trying to see the world as it was."[b]

By the 1990s it had become clear that Coleman's research was all too accurate, and that busing could not overcome neighborhood segregation. In 1993, James Coleman was overwhelmingly elected president of the American Sociological Association. He died in 1995.

[a] James Coleman et al., Equality of Educational Opportunity, U.S. Office of Education, Washington, DC, 1966.
[b] Jeffrey Toobin, "Pat 'n' Bill," New Yorker, February 8, 1999, p. 30.

Jackie Robinson Elementary School located in Long Beach, California, is one of numerous inner-city public schools that have improved academic performance, reduced social problems, and fostered school identification by requiring school uniforms.

© A. Ramey/Stock, Boston

College and African Americans

By the late 1970s, largely due to affirmative action programs, black and white high school graduates had an equal chance of going on to college. Then the 1980s saw black college rates slip while white rates continued to climb. The black decline is attributed to rapid increases in college costs and to sharp cutbacks in student aid during the Reagan years (1980–1988). Today, 40 percent of black high school graduates attend college compared to 45 percent of white high school graduates.[30] Some 17 percent of blacks aged 25 to 34 complete college, compared to 30 percent of whites.

African American college attendance and graduation rates increasingly reflect gender differences. Black females have college graduation rates that approach those of white males, but black male graduation rates are not showing similar increases. The United Negro College Fund reports that between 1976 and 1994 there was a 20 percent increase in bachelor's degrees for black men but a much larger 55 percent increase for black women.[31] African American men have high drop-out rates. As the new century begins African American women are twice as likely to receive bachelor's or master's degrees as African American men. And having a degree pays off. While African Americans with college degrees still make somewhat less than do whites with degrees, the gap is closing, and the census reports that African American college graduates now are as statistically likely as whites to hold executive, administrative, or managerial positions.[32]

---

[30] American Council of Education report based on Census and Education Department data, Associated Press release, February 10, 2000.

[31] "Black Women Fuel Advance," *Associated Press,* February 27, 1997.

[32] U.S. Bureau of the Census, *The Black Population in the United States: March 1994 and 1993, Current Population Reports,* P20–480, Washington D.C., 1995, p. 17.

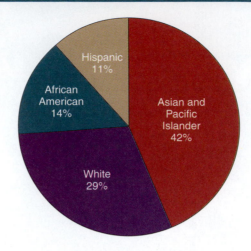

Figure 9.2 Percentage of Adults Ages 25 to 29 Who Had Attained a Bachelor's Degree or Higher in 1997

Hispanic 11%

African American 14%

Asian and Pacific Islander 42%

White 29%

Source: U.S. Census Bureau. Does not round to 100 percent due to 4 percent "Others."

Latino Patterns

Hispanic educational levels are lower than those of blacks and whites. Currently, just over half (53 percent) of Latinos 25 years of age and over have graduated from high school.[33] This is far below the mid-80 percent rates for blacks and whites. The Census reports that only 11 percent of Hispanics aged 25 to 29 have completed college.[34] Some Latinos come to school without a working knowledge of English, and immigrant parents with only grade school educational levels themselves have difficulty assisting their children in navigating the system. Primary and secondary schools have not developed enough programs to deal with at-risk Latino students.[35] However, the long-simmering dispute over bilingual education is moderating. A rough consensus seems to be emerging that initial teaching in the home language (Spanish or other) is beneficial to children when entering school, but the long-term educational and economic success of students requires their mastery of English.

While overall Latino educational levels are low Cuban Americans have high education levels. Cuban American families encourage education, and Cuban Americans are almost as likely as non-Hispanic whites to graduate from college. Within a few years Cuban American education rates will probably exceed national educational levels. (Refer to Chapter 4 for details.)

[33]U.S. Bureau of the Census, *Population Profile of the United States, 1995, Current Population Reports,* P23–189, Washington, DC, 1995, p. 46.

[34]U.S. Bureau of the Census, *Educational Attainments in the United States, Current Population Reports,* P20–505, 1998, p. 2.

[35]Harriet D. Romo and Toni Falbo, *Latino High School Graduation: Defying the Odds,* University of Texas Press, Austin, 1996.

Asians and Education

Asian Americans as a group are well educated. Nearly 9 out of 10 of those over 25 have completed high school, and almost half of young adults (25–29) have at least a college degree.[36] Asians today are twice as likely as whites to graduate from college.[37] Asians currently constitute the largest population groups at both Berkeley and UCLA. There is, however, great variation among Asian populations. Newer immigrant populations such as those from Laos do considerably poorer than established groups such as Japanese Americans.

The bottom line is that with Asians, as with whites, blacks, and Latinos, there is no "one size fits all" statement. Most ethnic and racial groups have relatively low high school and college graduation rates, but some groups, such as African American women, Cubans, and Asians, have higher graduation rates.

Changing Higher Education in America

While reading this section, keep two issues in mind. The first issue is that of *accessibility*, that is, who is deemed college material, and who isn't. The second issue is that of the growing *economic cost* of higher education. Recent decades have seen expanded accessibility to college and beyond, but the economic cost for those seeking a degree has accelerated far more rapidly.

Education for an Elite

The first colleges in America were founded to provide a proper moral and intellectual education for young gentlemen (higher education was thought unnecessary for women). Harvard and Yale were initially founded to train young men for the ministry, which by the time of the American Revolution had been broadened to providing a liberal arts background. Greek, Latin, mathematics, and the classics were stressed since a proper education was deemed to be one that taught a person how to think; it was *not* to be merely an accumulation of information. Colleges were organized to advance the Socratic ideal of developing the mind rather than providing technical or vocational training. The view that education involved a moral search for virtue, not the acquisition of skills, was brilliantly expressed by Cardinal Newman a century ago in *The Idea of a University*: "Knowledge is, not merely a means to something beyond it, or the preliminary of certain arts into which it naturally resolves, but an end sufficient to rest in and to pursue for its own sake; surely I am uttering no paradox, for I am stating what is both intelligible in itself, and has ever been the common judgement of philosophers and the ordinary feeling of mankind."[38]

The physical sites of American colleges were chosen to be removed from urban career opportunities. The ideal location was rural or in a small town—a location

---

[36]U.S. Bureau of the Census, *Educational Attainment in the United States: March 1997, Current Population Reports*, P20–505, p. 3.

[37]Robert Gardner, Bryan Robley, and Peter Smith, "Asian Americans: Growth, Change, and Diversity," *Population Bulletin*, 40, October 1995.

[38]John Henry Cardinal Newman, "Discourse V," *The Idea of a University: Defined and Illustrated*, Longmans, Green, London, 1901, p. 103. Some argue that universities today need to return from being employment agencies to equipping people to think. See Stanley Aronowitz, *The Knowledge Factory: Dismantling the Corporate University and Creating True Higher Learning* Beacon, Boston, 2000.

that was designed to provide students with a lack of distraction and a quiet, contemplative atmosphere in which to study properly. The Protestant religious affiliations of the colleges also assured that students would meet only those of similar religious background. When Catholic colleges were later established, they were similarly segregated to help ensure that Catholics "kept the faith." Catholics, like Protestants, stratified their colleges both academically and by social class. The Catholic elite, for example, went to Notre Dame, while working-class youth attended less prestigious institutions, often while living at home.

Colleges for females often were established near an equal social status male college. This was consciously done to facilitate marriage-oriented meetings between the daughters of the elite and the "right sort" of young men. Women's colleges, such as the female Ivy League "seven sisters," were even more social-class stratified than the men's schools.

Until the second half of the twentieth century, Ivy League colleges had informal religious and racial quotas. The number of Jews admitted to Harvard, Yale, and Princeton was commonly limited to 10 percent. Northwestern University, located next to the heavily Catholic city of Chicago, until the 1960s informally restricted the number of Catholics it admitted. Until the 1960s only a minority of private colleges admitted blacks, and those that accepted blacks would take only a few in each class.

The college students of earlier eras were socially privileged but not always intellectually gifted. Until midcentury elite colleges selected students at least as much on the basis of social background, ethnicity, race, and religion as on intelligence. Exceptional academic merit not only wasn't necessary, it was sometimes suspect as producing "unbalanced" students. Not until the mid-1950s did Harvard switch to using academic merit for entrance requirements. The change in admissions standards meant the average Harvard freshman in the class of 1952 would have ranked only in the *bottom tenth* of the class of 1960.[39]

Highly select colleges now admit largely on merit, but economic factors such as a parent being a potential donor still make a difference. Select colleges also confer major nonacademic benefits on students. A student who receives her bachelor's degree from Williams and then takes a law degree at Yale has been provided with a superior set of contacts and career opportunities—contacts and opportunities not available to even the best graduates of a local college.

State Universities

Morrell Act
federal act of 1862 establishing land grant colleges.

The initial broadening of college subjects and of students admitted occurred a century and a half ago with the establishment of state colleges and universities. State land-grant colleges are a product of the federal **Morrell Act** of 1862, which both opened up college to the middle-classes and began the American university emphasis on "practical" learning. The state university became the place where the middle class could send their children to be educated. Land-grant universities guaranteed admission to any young resident of the state who had a high school diploma and could manage the four-year tuition and costs of room and board. To meet middle-class needs, course offerings went beyond the traditional liberal arts curriculum to include career-oriented subjects such as engineering, business, agriculture, and teacher education. In this way, education expressly became a route to social mobility.

Great state universities such as Ohio State, the University of Illinois, the University of Wisconsin, and the University of Minnesota are land-grant institutions.

---

[39]Richard J. Herrnstein and Charles Murray, *The Bell Curve: Intelligence and Class Structure in American Life,* Free Press, New York, 1994, p. 30.

Box 9.2 Ongoing Issues

Are College Students Brighter?

Are genes more important than effort in determining success? The most hotly debated social science book during the 1990s, *The Bell Curve* made this claim. Written by the late Richard Herrnstein and the conservative social theorist Charles Murray, *The Bell Curve,* remained on the *New York Times* Best Sellers list for almost a year (in spite of its 845 page length).[a] The book provided grist for endless numbers of TV talk shows and magazine articles, and even President Clinton announced at a press conference that he disagreed with the authors' findings.

The main thesis of *The Bell Curve* is that American society is undergoing a transformation to a society that features an altered class structure dominated by a group the authors call the **cognitive elite,** who through self-selection at the time of college and marriage, are becoming increasingly concentrated in elite talent pools. Socially segregated on campus and later at work, the cognitive elite marry one another and thus have brighter children. While social-class factors still matter, inherited intelligence is becoming ascendent as a determinant of life chances. In the author's words, "Social class remains the vehicle of social life, but intelligence now pulls the train. . . . Modern societies identify the brightest youths with ever-increasing efficiency and then guide them into fairly narrow educational and occupational channels."[b]

The authors argue that, while intelligence is shaped by both heredity and environment, heredity plays the larger role, roughly 60 percent, and that it is almost impossible to nudge intelligence upward after the early years of life. Additionally, they state that low intelligence, independent of social, economic, or ethnic background, is highly correlated with most of our social problems. Thus, enrichment or compensatory programs can only fail since they cannot push a child above her or his genetic potential. Equality of opportunity merely accelerates the process by which the genetically advantaged move to the top and the dullards to the bottom. Similarly, affirmative action, they say, can influence these forces but cannot neutralize them. Although the reasoning is somewhat different, the conclusion is the same as that of the turn-of-the-century social Darwinists discussed in Chapter 2, that is, inequality is a result largely of genetic factors and cannot be changed by improving opportunities.

Reaction to *The Bell Curve* was strong and immediate. Critics said Herrnstein and Murray at best overstated, and at worst misrepresented, the data on race and IQ. Negative responses generally fell into one of two categories: concern over what trait IQ tests actually measure, and concern about the implications of the thesis. While scholars today generally accept that IQ tests show group differences, only some agree that IQ tests actually test general intelligence, and fewer still accept that the tests are not affected by environmental factors.[c] Also, most researchers on intelligence say that genetics accounts for roughly half the amount stated by Herrnstein and Murray. The belief that general intelligence (IQ) is largely innate, hereditary, and predetermined has largely been rejected by scholars since the 1920s.

Most researchers believe that environment has a profound effect on the development of cognitive ability and that inheritance and environment are interrelated and not causally independent. For example, the Committee on Psychological Tests and Assessments of the American Psychological Association says IQ is a measure of developed cognitive ability, not innate ability. Another problem with *The Bell Curve*, in addition to the argument that intelligence is immutable and unchangeable, is that the book's authors seem to confuse cognitive intelligence with social advantage or other factors, such as diligence or ambition. As William Raspberry points out, "It is a darn sight easier to be diligent and ambitious when you grow up with evidence that diligence pays off. . . . The 'crucial determining factor' in my view is opportunity, a term that embraces access, family resources and influence, non-family relationships, social environment and, still to a great degree, socioeconomic status, class, and race."[d]

Herrnstein's and Murray's critics don't suggest that intelligence doesn't matter but stress that it is impossible to consider cognitive abilities in isolation from social, racial, gender, and class factors. Still unanswered, though, are the long-run consequences to democracy of the social and educational segregation of a cognitive elite.

[a]*Richard J. Herrnstein and Charles Murray*, The Bell Curve: Intelligence and Class Structure in American Life, *Free Press, New York, 1994.*
[b]*Herrnstein and Murray,* The Bell Curve, *p. 269.*
[c]*See the 18 reviews of* The Bell Curve *in "Race and I.Q.,"* New Republic, *October 31, 1994, pp. 9–37.*
[d]*William Raspberry, "Is IQ Really Everything?"* Washington Post, *October 12, 1994, p. A23.*

Today, public universities educate 11.1 million of the 14.3 million higher education students.[40] Over the years many state colleges have grown from comparatively small places into megauniversities.

The GI Bill

GI Bill
federal legislation that paid for college education of World War II veterans.

The World War II **GI Bill** ranks as the twentieth century's most important education legislation, and it is generally considered the most effective federal program ever enacted. The GI Bill (officially *Public Law 346: The Serviceman's Readjustment Act of 1944*) made it possible for a whole generation of World War II veterans to pull themselves up by their combat boots to where they were the best-educated generation in U.S. history. The GI Bill moved the federal government into the direct support of college students' educations.

The GI Bill democratized attending college by providing funding to any veteran at any college where he or she could obtain admittance. (Remember, at that time college graduation was limited to 1 in 18 Americans.) The GI Bill paid up to $500 a year for tuition, books, and fees (tuition at the University of Michigan was $160 in 1946). Additionally veterans got a $65 monthly stipend ($90 if married) as long as they maintained their grades, enough to live on at that time. By the time the program ended in 1956, some 2.2 million veterans had graduated from college (including some 60,000 women and an estimated 70,000 African American veterans).[41] Some 3.5 million more went to technical schools. (Today's veteran's educational assistance program pays roughly a year's tuition and fees at a state university for every year served.)

Veterans in college broke the pattern of all college students being unmarried 17 to 22 year olds. The veterans not only were older and more serious, but also roughly half were married. Today the average college student is 26 years of age, and urban universities commonly have students in their 30s and 40s. Without the GI Bill, our modern technologically driven America would not exist. Moreover, the program more than paid for itself through higher taxes paid by program graduates. Estimates are that the U.S. Treasury received between two and eight times more in income taxes than was paid out in educational benefits. As noted by former President George Bush, "The GI Bill changed the lives of millions. . . . It changed the life of the nation."[42] The GI Bill also established the pattern of federal support for higher education. Programs such as Pell Grants that help support today's college students were introduced and enacted by senators and members of Congress who themselves went to college under the GI Bill.

Urban Universities and Community Colleges

Urban Universities. The Morrell Act and the GI Bill represent the two major changes in higher education prior to the mid-twentieth century. The development and expansion of urban-based universities and community colleges are the major developments during the last half of the twentieth century. New urban universities, mostly founded during the 1960s and 1970s, for the first time put institutions of higher education where most of the population was located. You no longer had to go away to

[40]Louis Menand, "Everybody Else's College Education," *New York Times Magazine*, April 20, 1997, p. 48.
[41]Edwin Kiester, Jr., "The G.I. Bill May Be the Best Deal Ever Made by Uncle Sam," *Smithsonian*, November 1994, p. 130.
[42]President George Bush, quoted in James Brady, "In Appreciation, the GI Bill," *Parade*, August 4, 1996, p. 4.

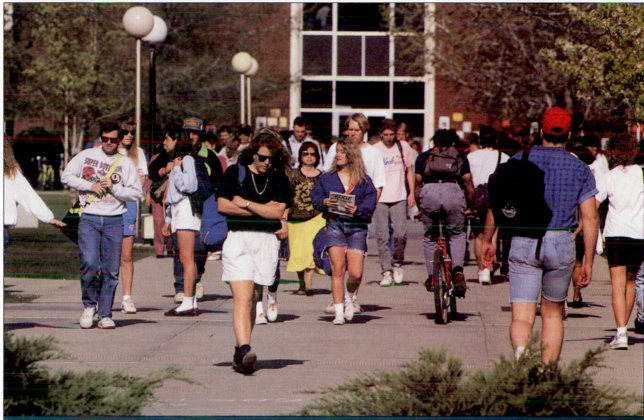

These urban university students could be anywhere in the country. In fact, they attend Boise State University in Boise, Idaho.

© David R. Frazier/Photo Researchers

get a college education but could live at home, keep your job, and even raise a family. Urban universities, with the majority of students coming from the local area, have grown rapidly during the last three decades. Such universities have an attraction for cosmopolitan-oriented faculty members who prefer living in cities with a wide range of amenities over living in small college towns. In the short period of three decades, urban or metropolitan universities have become major academic institutions.

Community Colleges The rise of community colleges represents the most recent major change in higher education. Community colleges now enroll more than one-third of all college students (35 percent) and 44 percent of all freshmen. Some 5.3 million students attend two-year public colleges.[43] Community colleges account for half of the growth in college students over the past twenty years. In addition to traditional subjects, these schools offer a wide range of practical career-oriented courses in occupations ranging from laboratory technician to hotel operator to flight controller. Community colleges thus meet vocational training needs not being filled by older institutions.

By bringing college courses directly to the students, community colleges offer educational opportunities to part-time students, married students, older students, and those who cannot afford to live away from home. Roughly 60 percent of community college students are the first in their family to go to college; for African

---

[43]Louis Menand, "Everybody Else's College Education," *New York Times Magazine,* April 20, 1997, p. 48.

Americans the figure is 80 percent. The success of the community colleges is often not recognized. Community colleges also provide a gateway into the middle class for ambitious immigrants or for those past "college age."

In terms of job security, occupational status, and earnings, community college students fall between high school graduates and those in four-year institutions. Functionalists are more likely to stress the role of the community college in providing economic opportunity, while those espousing a conflict orientation are more likely to suggest that these schools simply perpetuate social and educational inequality.

Some argue that the institutional and status separation between two- and four-year schools could be largely removed by transforming community colleges into branches of state universities.[44] States such as Wisconsin have this system, which considerably eases the transfer process and eliminates questions about accepting lower-division credits. Other states, such as North Carolina, automatically transfer community college credits to any state institution. In California one role of the community college system is to serve as a semiofficial feeder into the state university system.

Credentialism

Some 2,300 years ago Aristotle raised the issue of whether the goal of education should be the useful life, virtue, or higher knowledge. Aristotle came down for virtue, and defenders of the traditional liberal arts still believe it is blasphemy to measure a college education by jobs obtained or money earned. However, universities increasingly provide vocational training and certify the professional skills of their students, and the role of bestowing credentials is now dominant. Students now attend college expressly to be trained and certified as engineers, nurses, social workers, lawyers, schoolteachers, or accountants. To less-affluent students, "education for its own sake" appears to be an unaffordable luxury. However, it is worth noting that while those obtaining specific training obtain jobs faster and start at higher salaries after graduation, the long-term advantage remains with the liberal arts graduate, both in terms of lifetime income and achieving major management positions. In today's ever-changing skills and employment market, the long-term edge goes to those who have learned flexibility and how to ask new questions.

College Patterns for Women

Women are increasingly dominant on college campuses. Historically, women were more likely to graduate from high school than men (who were expected to go into the workforce), but there were more men at the college level. In 1960, for instance, men received 61 percent of the bachelor's degrees and 68 percent of all master's degrees. Now that has changed. The Department of Education reports that as of 1996 there were 8.4 million women and only 6.7 million men enrolled as undergraduates in college.[45] By 2007 the gender gap will be greater, with 9.2 million women and only 6.9 million men. The twenty-first century begins with women receiving 55 percent of bachelor's degrees and 57 percent of master's degrees. Some resident colleges, concerned that their sex ratio not go above 60 percent female, are already quietly practicing a form of de facto affirmative action in admissions in order to keep up their number of males.

---

[44]Kevin J. Dougherty, *The Contradictory College: The Conflicting Origins, Impacts, and Future of the Community College*, State University of New York Press, Albany, 1994.
[45]"Gender Gap Grows in Colleges," *New York Times*, December 6, 1998, p. A1.

Beyond college the historical advantage strongly favored males. In 1960 women received only 11 percent of all doctorates, 6 percent of the medical degrees, 4 percent of the MBAs, 2 percent of the law degrees, and 1 percent of the dentistry degrees. This has radically changed. American women now receive 44 percent of the doctorates awarded to Americans, 38 percent of medical degrees, 36 percent of MBAs, 42 percent of law degrees, and 34 percent of dentistry degrees.[46] Each year the proportion of females increases. Only a few fields continue to be sex-typed: Undergraduate women receive 16 percent of the engineering degrees but 78 percent of the education degrees.

Costs and Advantages of Higher Education

According to Congress's General Accounting Office, college costs have been increasing for two decades at more than double the increase in income levels.[47] Academically selective private colleges now cost over $30,000 a year for tuition, room, board, fees, and books. For example, in 1998 just tuition and fees at Yale were $23,780, and total costs were $30,830.[48] Notre Dame was a relative bargain at $26,550.[49] In reality many students at such schools pay much less. For example, 45 percent of the students at the University of Pennsylvania receive financial aid, and the average grant totals $13,485.[50]

Also, most colleges are nowhere near as expensive as Harvard, Yale, or Notre Dame. In 1997 the average state university tuition and fees ran $2,860. Recent tuition increases at public universities often reflect state policies of quietly transferring educational costs from all taxpayers to individual students. The assumption underlying this shift is that higher education is more of a private than a public good, and because students benefit, they should pay. The result is that during the 1990s, although state appropriations for universities increased, state appropriations for higher education per student substantially decreased. Many state universities are increasingly moving from being state supported to being state assisted.

From a students' perspective there is no question that higher education is rewarded economically, and the financial advantage of a college degree is increasing. In 1984, a college graduate could expect to have a median income level 39 percent higher than that of a high school graduate. The college graduate's median income advantage has now increased to 75 percent over a high school graduate and is still climbing. A college degree holds particular economic advantage for newcomers to the top echelons, such as women and minorities. For example, black males aged 25 to 34 who have completed college make 83 percent higher incomes than do black male high school graduates.[51]

Advanced degrees widen the income breach, with professional degrees (MD, law, MBA) providing the highest average incomes, doctoral degrees (PhD) next, and finally master's degrees. In dollar terms, a person with a bachelor's degree will earn $600,000 more over his or her lifetime than a person with only a high school diploma.[52] Having a master's degree boosts that to $800,000, and being a professional school graduate adds $1.3 million to lifetime income.

---

[46] All the figures in this section come from National Center for Education and Bureau of the Census statistics and can be found in Suzanne M. Bianchi and Daphne Spain, "Women, Work, and Family in America," *Population Bulletin*, 51:15–16, Population Reference Bureau, Washington, DC, December 1996.

[47] "Climbing Tuition Slows Pace, *Associated Press News Service*, August 26, 1996.

[48] *Chronicle of Higher Education*, October 16, 1998, pp. A58, A60.

[49] *U.S. News and World Report* data reported in *Notre Dame Magazine*, Winter, 1998–99, p. 22.

[50] Erik Larson, "Why Colleges Cost Too Much," *Time*, March 17, 1997, p. 54.

[51] Kimberly Crews, " A Look at Trends Shaping African Americans' Future," *Population Today*, February, 1996, p. 2.

[52] Terry W. Hartle, "The Spector of Budget Uncertainty," *Chronicle of Higher Education*, June 28, 1996, p. B2.

Education and Family

What contributes most to economic success? The classic study by Christopher Jencks suggested that it is not education itself but family background that contributes most to economic comfort.[53] In other words, getting ahead is much easier if you start ahead with educated and affluent parents. Other data show the same pattern. A U.S. Department of Education study done by the National Opinion Research Center at the University of Chicago followed 25,000 teenagers over six years.[54] The study tracked students from 1988, when they were eighth graders, until 1994, when many were college sophomores. It was found that family income counts more than race, ethnicity, sex, or even achievement test scores in determining future educational success. Students coming from more privileged backgrounds, whether black or white, do uniformly better than students coming from poorer families. Middle-class kids, regardless of race do well. The previously discussed Coleman Report had similar findings.

While education is, therefore, not a cure-all, it is second only to the family as the prime institution for socialization. By itself, education may not provide social mobility, but it does provide access to new opportunities— opportunities that those without an education will never have.

The Affirmative Action Debate

affirmative action

programs designed to compensate for past discrimination by offering special advantage and assistance to discriminated-against groups.

Affirmative action refers to government policies that are designed not merely to end discrimination but to actively recruit minorities and women to the point where their numbers, in the world of work reflect their proportions in the general population. Affirmative action programs are in effect at almost all universities, and few policies stir up as much controversy. Advocates of affirmative action argue passionately that forms of preference or positive discrimination are necessary to offset the effects of earlier exploitation and negative discrimination. They point out that affirmative action in the past meant preference for white males, and that preference for minorities and women is necessary to break this institutional pattern of discrimination. The question, they maintain, is not whether or not to discriminate but rather *for whose benefit* discrimination ought to be encouraged. Admission advantages are commonly given to the children of alumni and major donors, as well as to athletes. Advocates of affirmative action say it is necessary to balance the advantages long held by white males, and that more rather than less affirmative action is needed.[55] Compensation is necessary to undo past injustice in order to level the playing field. Supporters of affirmative action stress its positive accomplishments in producing a more multiracial society. They also stress that affirmative action has successfully created a substantial black middle and upper-middle class.[56]

Those opposed to affirmative action say that preference systems quickly turn into quotas, and preference systems violate the concept of equality of opportunity

[53]Christopher Jencks et al., *Inequality: A Reassessment of the Effects of Family and Schooling in America*, Basic Books, New York, 1972.

[54]William H. Honan, "Income Found to Predict Educational Level Better than Race," *New York Times*, national edition, June 17, 1996.

[55]Barbara Reskin, *The Realities of Affirmative Action in Employment*, American Sociological Association, Washington, DC, 1998.

[56]Derek Bok and Willian G. Bowen, *The Shape of the River: Long-Term Consequences of Considering Race in College and University Admissions*, Princeton University Press, Princeton, NJ, 1998.

The legality of race-based Affirmative Action admissions at all universities will probably be determined by the Supreme Court ruling on the University of Michigan case. Here students from Michigan demonstrate in support of retaining Affirmative Action programs.

© Najlah Feanny/Stock, Boston

and constitute illegal (reverse) discrimination. What is worse, they say, is that affirmative action programs do nothing to help those at the bottom; minority programs largely benefit the wealthy and middle-class minorities. They claim that affirmative action guidelines are implemented as quotas, and thus the term *affirmative action hire* has come to imply a lower level of competence. Shelby Steele argues that affirmative action heightens racial differences by lumping together all minorities as receiving affirmative action preference, even when minorities such as himself have won admission, jobs, or promotions solely on the basis of hard work or merit.[57] He says the result is white feelings of paternalism and increasing black feelings of victimization and self-doubt.

The media treat affirmative action attitudes as sharply dividing along racial and gender lines, but the reality is more complex. According to a *Washington Post*–ABC News Poll while, as expected, three out of four men oppose affirmative action programs, two out of three white women oppose affirmative action for women, and half of African Americans (48 percent) oppose preference programs for minorities.[58]

---

[57]Shelby Steele, *The Content of Our Character: A New Vision of Race in America*, St. Martin's Press, New York, 1990.

[58]Richard Morin and Sharon Warden, "Poll Says Americans Angry about Affirmative Action," *Washington Post*, March 24, 1995, pp. A1, A4.

California's Policies

California led the nation in adopting affirmative action and now is leading in abandoning the programs. In 1996 the state's voters passed Proposition 209 which prohibited giving preferences based on race, ethnicity, or gender. The legality of Proposition 209 was affirmed by the federal appeals court in 1997.[59] Washington State's voters passed an identical proposition in 1998. In a separate action, the Regents of the University of California voted to end all of their universities' racial preference programs. This had national importance because the California university system was the first university system in the country to adopt affirmative action criteria for both selecting students and hiring faculty. Also, with its eight campuses and 162,000 students, the California system is the largest in the country. (California enrolls one out of every 10 college students in the United States.)

The University of California's affirmative action guidelines, similar to most others, said that color-blindness in choosing applicants was not enough, and institutions must take positive action to overcome the prior effects of discrimination by affirmatively responding to members of previously disenfranchised and excluded populations. To do this, for decades California has used separate pools of white, Asian, Hispanic, and African American applicants, and then selected the top applicants from each category. This practice (known as norming) meant that, as of 1995, 40 percent of admissions at the Berkeley campus were made on academic merit criteria, and 60 percent were made using special criteria (special criteria in addition to race and ethnicity also included athletic admissions, band members, etc.).

Advocates of affirmative action admissions point out that all those admitted using special criteria had to meet basic admission standards. Opponents say that lower criteria are used; noting the average combined SAT score of black students admitted to Berkeley in 1995 was 288 points below the average for whites.[60] Current policies and regulations still allow choosing between a quarter and a half of all students using criteria other than grades and test scores as long as admission is not based solely on race or ethnic origin.

Supporters of affirmative action argue that without affirmative action university diversity will cease and Hispanic and African American enrollment will sharply drop.[61] In the first year (1998) after the University of California system eliminated race-based affirmative action, the picture was mixed. At the most selective campuses of Berkeley and UCLA, minority enrollments decreased sharply, white enrollments decreased slightly, and Asian enrollments increased.[62] However, other University of California campuses, such as Riverside, Santa Barbara, Irvine, and Santa Cruz, increased the number of black students enrolled.[63] This redistribution of minorities down to campuses such as Irvine and Riverside is known as **cascading.** That is, minorities not admitted to the highest-ranked schools cascade down to second-tier institutions. Advocates of affirmative action say cascading means minorities are being shut out of the best campuses. Supporters of Proposition 209 say minorities are better off because, instead of failing

cascading

enrolling in a good college where there is a higher likelihood of graduating, rather than at the most selective college.

---

[59]Associated Press, "Affirmative Action Vote Is Upheld," *Richmond Times-Dispatch,* April 9, 1997, p. A1.

[60]For discussion of test scores, see, Christopher Jencks and Meredith Phillips, (eds.), *The Black-White Test Score Gap,* Brookings Institution Press, Washington, DC, 1998.

[61]Kit Lively, "A Jolt for Sacramento," *Chronicle of Higher Education,* June 9, 1995, p. A25.

[62]James Ramage, "Berkeley and UCLA See Sharp Drop in Admission of Black and Hispanic Applicants," *Chronicle of Higher Education,* April 10, 1998, p. A43.

[63]Ethan Bronner, "Fewer Blacks, Hispanics to Enter University of California Next Spring," *New York Times on the Web,* May 21, 1998.

in the competition with whites and Asians with higher test scores and grade-point averages, minorities in less-pressure-cooker institutions do well and graduate. Reports suggest most minority students at University of California schools such as Irvine share this view.[64]

To prevent having university students largely coming from affluent top-performing high schools, and to provide an alternative to affirmative action, California now has borrowed an admissions policy from Texas. Under the new admission guidelines, the University of California guarantees admission to the top 4 percent of students in each high school in the state. This greatly helps blacks and Hispanics at inner-city and rural schools that send few students on to college. As put by the spokesperson for the UC system, "We believe that it will result in a student body that is more representative of the state's diverse population without sacrificing academic excellence."[65]

Court Rulings

The Supreme Court has been narrowing the grounds on which affirmative action is legal. In 1996 the 5th U.S. Circuit Court of Appeals declared, in *Hopwood v. State of Texas*, that the University of Texas Law School could no longer use different admission requirements for minority and white students.[66] The Supreme Court, by a vote of 7 to 2, upheld the Appellate Court ruling. While this Supreme Court decision to bar the use of race in student admissions only technically applies to the states of the 5th Circuit Court, the ruling leaves serious legal clouds over the future of university affirmative action programs everywhere. The Supreme Court's current position appears to be that it is illegal to use race, ethnicity, or gender to provide special benefits to any group, except if such use is narrowly targeted as a means of redressing a specific wrong. In practice this means that targeted affirmative action remains legal, but blanket use probably is illegal.

Future Affirmative Action?

While race-specific scholarships (and probably admissions) have been found by the courts to be illegal, scholarships or admission based on economic disadvantage are not. It is quite legal to give special scholarships to those from underrepresented areas, such as poorer rural or inner-city areas. While most Americans oppose quotas, they also feel that giving minorities an edge to help even the playing field is desirable, or at least acceptable. Most Americans support the idea of providing an additional boost to disadvantaged individuals.

Affirmative action programs are being reformulated so they are based on income rather than race; that is, they predominately benefit those who are most economically disadvantaged. The argument is that by targeting the poor, and eliminating preferences for affluent minorities, help will go to those most in need while ending much of the racial divisiveness over the program. Jesse Jackson, on the contrary, argues that all minorities, regardless of income level, deserve affirmative action, and even an affluent African American who graduates from Harvard may still

---

[64]Adam Cohen, "When the Field Is Level," *Time,* July 5, 1999, pp. 30–34.
[65]"Diversity Aim of 4% Plan at California Universities," *Associated Press News Service,* January 6, 1999.
[66]"Text of Appeals Court's Opinion on Affirmative Action in Admissions," *Chronicle of Higher Education,* March 29, 1996, p. A28.

face racial bias. He says, "Class does not offset the race problem."[67] Nonetheless, it appears that class-based, rather than strictly race-based, affirmative action programs are likely in the future.

Florida is an example of new programs. In 1999 Florida's governor, in order to head off a referendum that was certain to end all affirmative action programs, signed an executive order that wiped out race and ethnicity in university admissions and barred racial set-asides and quotas.[68] In its place the state now guarantees university admission to the top 20 percent of the high school seniors in each school and $20 million has been added to the state's financial aid budget to make it easier for poorer students to attend college. The new program has had a mixed review from black and Latino state legislators.

Toward the Future

Trying to foresee the future of American education requires making some assumptions. A linear projection from recent decades would suggest continuing grade inflation accompanied by weakening academic performance levels. On the other hand, the national concern over educational quality would suggest the opposite: that course requirements will become more rigorous and grading more reflective of actual achievement. There is some evidence of the latter: Urban public school systems such as Chicago are now refusing to give diplomas to students until they meet basic standards. University students, on the other hand, have become accustomed to grade inflation, and movement toward tighter standards will be difficult.

While the quality of public primary and secondary schools will remain problematic, the American university system will continue to be highly rated. So far self-governance has kept most institutions flexible enough to continually reform and rework themselves. During most of the twentieth century, university policies and practices were disproportionately influenced by a few selective private universities. The twenty-first century, by contrast, will be dominated by what occurs at public institutions, especially the larger research-based state universities. State universities are where most students will be educated and where much of the cutting-edge research will be done.

The early twenty-first century will witness a college degree becoming a basic job requirement. The proportion of the population with college degrees will continue to increase, and attending college will increasingly be open to all high school graduates. Approximately 60 percent of the higher education institutions in the United States have essentially open admissions, and the proportion of students they educate will increase. Twenty-first century student bodies will increasingly reflect the demographic profile of the general population.

Predicting what will happen to affirmative action programs is complicated. Government programs are always subject to political change, and court decisions have progressively narrowed the grounds for racially based programs. While no one can with certainty predict how the Supreme Court will rule, this narrowing pattern will most likely continue. Affirmative action probably will be reformulated from providing preference based on race to providing preference based primarily on economic need. Need-based programs will assist much of the same population as current affirmative action programs, but may be far less divisive politically and have wider popular support.

---

[67]Mark Johnson, "Some Say Poverty, Not Race, Is the Issue," *Media General News Service,* July 7, 1995.
[68]"Florida Governor Bars Affirmative Action," *Associated Press New Service,* November 10, 1999.

A continuing national problem will be how to equalize economically affluent and poorer school systems. In spite of state courts increasingly ruling in favor of equal economic support for all students, we still are moving toward a two-track educational system. Middle- and upper-middle-class children, often suburban, generally have access to quality public and private schools. This in turn leads to admission to selective universities. By contrast, working-class and poorer populations are often storaged during primary and secondary years in poorer-quality (often inner-city) schools. While both groups receive diplomas, the amount and quality of what they learn differs radically.

These same divisions increasingly are found in postsecondary institutions. The concern is that program and performance distinctions between highly selective and other colleges and universities will increase rather than decrease. This may increase elitism by explicitly shifting the hiring criteria from the general question, "Do you have a college degree?" to the more elitist question, "Where did you get your college degree?"

Summary

During the twentieth century, America's change from an agrarian to an urban society has placed huge pressure on the nation's educational systems.

- Functionalists say education serves the manifest function of transmitting the culture and socializing individuals into the society. Education also serves the latent function of keeping youths out of the labor market.

- Conflict theorists suggest that the educational system, rather than helping the poor and marginal get ahead, is designed to keep the children of the elite at the top.

- Interactionists take a more microlevel approach, focusing on how schools socialize students and the consequences for individuals.

- Three contemporary problems in education are: (1) the quality of primary and secondary education, (2) the changing nature of higher education, and (3) the issue of affirmative action.

- The first Coleman Report, which emphasized the role of the family and the advantages of racial integration, was well received. The second report, which suggested that busing without neighborhood integration was dysfunctional, was initially condemned.

- African Americans now have high school dropout rates similar to whites, but just over half of Hispanics graduate from high school. Virtually all Asians graduate from high school.

- Higher education in America has shifted from providing a liberal arts exposure for the elite to providing professional training and certification for the broad middle class.

- The Morrell Act of 1862 created state land grant universities while the post-World War II GI Bill provided the first opportunity for average Americans to obtain a college education.

- Community colleges and urban universities have helped to expand the numbers going to college.

- Affirmative action programs, now 30 years old, are undergoing major change. The Supreme Court in 1996 ruled against university affirmative action admission policies based on race. Affirmative action is likely to increasingly be based on economic need rather than race.

☞Key Review Terms

affirmative action

cascading

Coleman Report

community colleges

credentialism

cultural imperialism

functional illiteracy

GI Bill

grade inflation

hidden curriculum

illiteracy

latent function

liberal arts

manifest function

Morrell Act

urban universities

? Questions for Discussion

1. What is the purpose of education today? How have attitudes regarding the purpose of education changed? How has that affected educational institutions?

2. Discuss the concept of the hidden curriculum. What are some of the values and beliefs that have been transmitted to you?

3. The text states that perhaps 90 million Americans are functionally illiterate. How can this best be remedied? What are the consequences of functional illiteracy for society?

4. In many primary and secondary schools students can see a counselor, eat two meals a day, receive necessary medical care, and have after-school sports and other activities. Are these important functions of contemporary schools? Why or why not?

5. For a number of years religious schools have actively lobbied for tax support for their schools through the use of taxpayer-supported school vouchers. Would this damage public education? Would it be likely to improve or weaken urban schools?

6. Jonathan Kozol says the nation maintains two separate and unequal school systems. How can the quality of available education be equalized for all students? Will increased funding solve the problem or are other issues involved?

7. Discuss the findings of the two Coleman Reports and their impact on educational policy? Why did the second report stir up so much controversy?

8. Who went to college prior to World War II and who goes to college today? How has the GI Bill changed higher education?

9. Describe the development of urban universities and community colleges during the last 30 years. How has this affected who attends college?

10. The Supreme Court has narrowed the scope of affirmative action programs. What has affirmative action accomplished? What have been its limitations?

☞Suggested Resources

Stanley Aronowitz, *The Knowledge Factory: Dismantling the Corporate University and Creating True Higher Learning*, Beacon, Boston, 2000. An intellectual of the left who says universities should stop being employment agencies and go back to fostering intellectual growth. He advocates a common broad curriculum, and career-specific knowledge only during the second half of college.

Jeanne Ballantine, *The Sociology of Education: A Systematic Analysis*, third ed., Prentice Hall, Upper Saddle River, NJ, 1995. An overview of the theories, problems, and research questions raised by those concerned with the sociology of education.

Edward B. Fiske, *Smart Schools, Smart Kids: Why Do Some Schools Work?* Simon & Schuster, New York, 1992. How schools that are self managed and stress cooperation over competition achieve.

Jonathan Kozol, *Savage Inequalities: Children in America's Schools*, Crown, New York, 1991. Kozol provides a comparison of rich and poor schools, and the feel of trying to learn in dilapidated urban schools where students are warehoused.

James W. Loewen, *Lies My Teacher Told Me: Everything Your American History Text Got Wrong*, Touchstone, New York, 1995. A revisionist look at how history is taught in American schools.

Shelby Steele, *The Content of Our Character*, St. Martin, New York, 1990. Steel's much-quoted book argues that affirmative action hurts blacks more than it helps by undermining black self-help and creating self-doubt.

Internet Connection 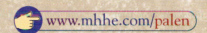 www.mhhe.com/palen

1. A good resource to begin with is the U.S. Department of Education's home page, (*www.ed.gov/index.html*). Here, you will find links to many useful sites including, The Digest of Educational Statistics, The Encyclopedia of Educational Statistics, and The National Library of Education. Click on "Nations Report Card (NAPE)." NAPE stands for the National Assessment of Educational Progress, a congressionally mandated project that has been monitoring the academic performance of fourth, eighth, and twelfth graders since 1969. Click on "Science" and then go to "Findings" (*www.nces. ed.gov/nationsreport card/science/sci_findings.asp*).

    a. What does NAPE have to say about the performance of U.S. students in the sciences?

    b. Check their performance in other subjects.

    c. Does NAPE make any provision for international comparisons of U.S. students with their counterparts in other nations?

2. Visit the website of the National Education Association (NEA), "America's oldest and largest organization committed to advancing the cause of public education" (*www.nea.org/*). Click on the "Issues" button.

    a. What is the NEA's position on Bilingual Education?

    b. What are the reasons that it gives for taking this position?

    c. What other issues that the NEA is currently concerning itself with?

    d. Would you consider this to be a liberal or conservative organization? Why?

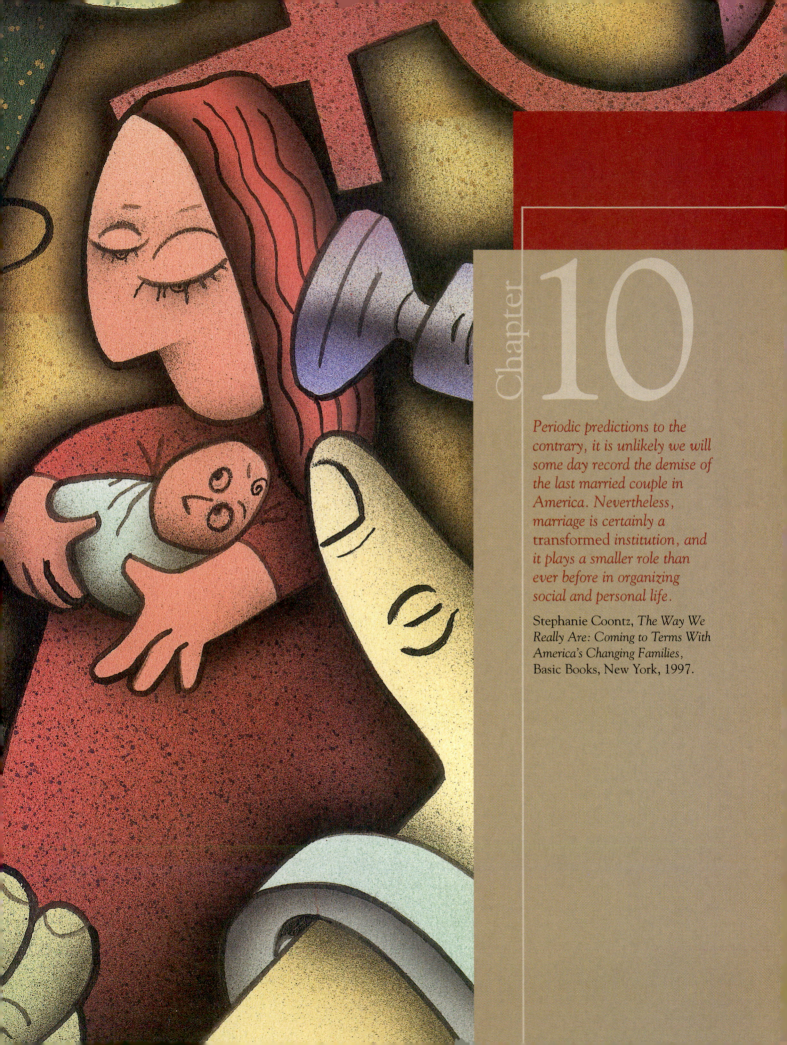

Chapter 10

Periodic predictions to the contrary, it is unlikely we will some day record the demise of the last married couple in America. Nevertheless, marriage is certainly a transformed institution, and it plays a smaller role than ever before in organizing social and personal life.

Stephanie Coontz, *The Way We Really Are: Coming to Terms With America's Changing Families,* Basic Books, New York, 1997.

Ties That Bind: The Changing Family

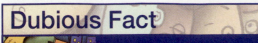

Dubious Fact

American divorce rates are high, but below the divorce rates of European nations such as Sweden.

In reality, America's divorce rate is the highest in the world and twice that of Western Europe.

The Contemporary Family

Everywhere one hears that the American family is in trouble. Popular media note the family's decline and predict its impending demise. Some see this loss of family influence as a sign of societal decadence. Others view the destruction as necessary to make way for the new family of tomorrow. Right-wing politicians seeking a "wedge" issue pontificate about the need for family values. Radical feminists, on the other hand, call for the destruction of the traditional family, accusing it of maintaining the values of a sexist, homophobic, and sexually repressed society.

What is certain is that the issue of family survival has moved from theoretical discussions among academics to public (and often bitter) debate. About the only thing everyone agrees upon is that contemporary families look less and less like the Brady Bunch. Whether or not the nuclear family of the mid-twentieth century was the norm, it is clear as the new century begins that the so-called traditional family of father, mother, and children is becoming scarcer. From 1970 to 1996 married-couple families declined sharply from 40 to only 26 percent of all households.[1] (Households include single householders and nonrelated persons living together.)

Current American divorce rates are far higher than those of previous generations. The number of divorced individuals nearly quadrupled between 1970 and the mid-1990s.[2] While American divorce rates are no longer increasing, they remain the highest of any industrial nation in the world. Children today have a greater chance of growing up in a family split by divorce than in any other period in American history. As recently as 1960 four-fifths of all American children were living with both their natural parents, but today's children have only a 50-50 chance of getting through childhood with both parents. Fatherless families now constitute one-quarter of all white families with children, two-thirds of black families with children, and over one-third of Hispanic families with children.[3] Daniel Patrick Moynihan observes that we "may be the first society in history where children are worse off than adults."[4]

Most academics writing on the family prior to the 1990s conceded that the American family, as a stable "till death do us part" bonding of two people, was undergoing dramatic transformation, but the idea of family disintegration was a myth.

---

[1] U.S. Bureau of the Census, *Household and Family Characteristics: March 1997, Current Population Reports*, P20–509, April 1998, p. 1.
[2] U.S. Bureau of the Census, *Marital Status and Living Arrangements, March 1993, Current Population Reports*, P20–478, Washington, DC, 1994.
[3] U.S. Bureau of the Census, *How We're Changing, Current Population Reports*, P23–170, Washington, DC, 1990.
[4] Quoted in David Popenoe, "A World Without Fathers," *Wilson Quarterly*, Spring, 1996, p. 12.

The conventional academic wisdom was that change was not equivalent to collapse, and that—far from disintegrating—the family was evolving into a new form or forms.[5] However, more recently scholars have come to question this view—noting a substantial decline over the last generation in the family as an institution.

The dispute is not so much over what has been occurring. Everyone agrees that the American family is undergoing stress: American divorce rates are the world's highest, and ever greater proportions of children are being raised in fatherless families. The dispute, rather, is over how these changes should be interpreted and what, if anything, should be done by government and other institutions to intervene.

Sociological Perspective

Functionalist Approaches

Functionalists generally hold that the family is the most important of all social institutions. It gives us our initial status, shapes who we are, and influences who we will become. Thus, some form of family is found in all societies since the family performs socialization and placement functions vital for the survival of society. Functionalists see the family losing many of its economic, religious, and social functions as a consequence of urban industrialization. Families have changed from the extended family of agricultural societies to the more flexible and mobile nuclear family of urban societies. The primary function of the married family has come to be providing social and emotional support to the partners. Thus, with other functions reduced or gone, when mutual love fades the reason for staying married also ends.

Functionalists argue that the high American divorce rates result in increasing family and social disorganization. The effects on children are said to be especially severe. While the idealized nuclear family of the 1950s and 1960s sitcoms existed more in myth than reality, functionalists see a strong need for a new egalitarian family form that has stability and is oriented toward responsibility for the needs of children. Functionalists call for a supportive pro-family ethos that sees the family as a necessary cornerstone of a civil society.

Conflict Approaches

From conflict perspectives, families are also important to society, but largely as a means of perpetuating social inequality and the power of dominant economic groups in the society. Conflict theorists are more likely to see the traditional husband-wife family as meeting the needs of a capitalistic economic system insofar as the creation of many small families leads to the maximum consumption of consumer goods.

The husband-wife family system is seen as perpetuating economic inequality through patterns of patriarchy and inherited wealth. Friedrich Engels, a century

---

[5]See S. M. Dornbusch and M. H. Strober, (eds.), *Feminism, Children, and New Families*, Guilford Press, New York, 1988; E. L. Kain, *The Myth of Family Decline*, D. C. Heath, Lexington, MA, 1990; and A. Skolnick, *Embattled Paradise: The New American Family in an Age of Uncertainty*, Basic Books, New York, 1991.

and a half ago, saw the family as a part of capitalism; promoting male domination and social inequality. Romantic love was seen as a myth used to perpetuate gender inequality. The very nature of the traditional family, with the wife taking her husband's name and men commonly earning more than women, is seen as working against equality, sexual freedom, and liberation of women. For the family to survive, it must become a totally voluntary unit stripped of all sexism and inequality. Women should be encouraged to enter the labor force and government should provide free day care and other child-care services.

From a conflict view, government acts in a repressive and reactionary manner when it seeks to define the family as a unit of one male and one female (as was done by the *1996 Defense of Family Act*). Rather, government should help end the exploitation of women by fostering the end of the traditional family. Family form will only change when people realize the existing husband-wife family does not serve their social and economic needs.

Interactionist Approaches

Interactionists approach the family by noting its importance in providing an intimate, loving, supportive, and stable environment for individuals in a contemporary society that provides few other supports. The type of family found in each society (the monogamous husband-wife family in our society) is seen as "natural" and is supported by the norms and values of the society. In our society the family's role in providing emotional support and the socialization of children is especially important. Patterns of early childhood socialization are seen as crucial in shaping the character of adults.

Social interactionists are interested in determining how different family forms influence the self-concept, personality, and behavior of family members, especially children. The negative social meanings attached to being divorced or remaining single have changed, as have the meanings of being the child of divorced parents or a single parent. Interactionists study how self concepts and changing social meanings influence family forms.

What Is a Family?

national family wars
term applied to dispute over how the family should be defined, and what family form is best for society.

The debate over the future of the family is sometimes referred to as the **national family wars.**[6] A basic element of the dispute is over what constitutes a family. The first heavy shots of the war were fired at the supposedly safe and dull 1980 White House Conference on Families. The Conference fell apart because its participants couldn't agree on whether the term *family* should be reserved for the traditional nuclear family of husband and wife, or whether marriage and family should also include gay and lesbian couples. There have been no attempts to hold another White House Conference since that time, but the dispute over what constitutes a family has escalated.

The issue is not only ideological and religious but also political and economic. For example, it involves major economic questions such as who is entitled to government and other benefits, such as health insurance, sick leave, or even death benefits. Should, for instance, a gay partner in a long-term relationship have primary

---

[6]On this issue see, "Sociologists Differ About Family Textbooks' Message," *Footnotes*, 25:7–10, American Sociological Association, January 1998.

Figure 10.1 Household Composition: 1970 to 1997

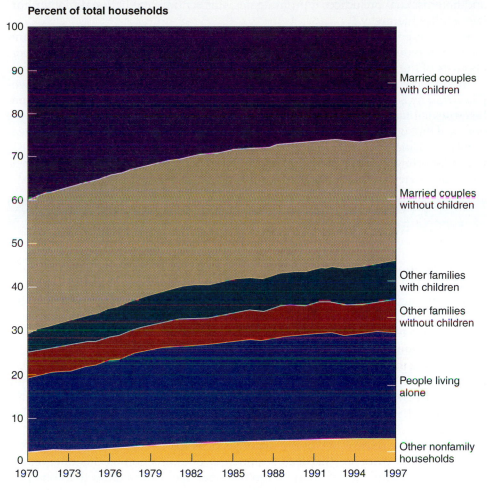

Percent of total households

Married couples with children

Married couples without children

Other families with children

Other families without children

People living alone

Other nonfamily households

Source: U.S. Bureau of the Census, *Current Population Surveys*

inheritance over children? Congress has even gotten involved in the issue, and there is now an official federal definition of a family. The *1996 Defense of Family Act* defined a family as a married unit of one man and one woman. The Bureau of the Census similarly defines a **family** as two or more people related by birth, marriage, or adoption and living together. A **household,** by contrast, consists of all the people, related or not, occupying a housing unit. A household can be family, nonfamily, or a single person.

In this chapter we will define the *family* as *a kinship unit of two or more people who live in the same household and are legally or biologically related to one another.* Thus, our definition does not automatically include two unrelated adults who live together, but it does include those adult single-sex units in which there are dependents. Where gay marriages are legal it also includes such units.

Family as a Repressive Institution

Those on the radical side of the family wars see the destruction of the traditional married two-parent family as necessary for society. In the words of the feminist sociologist Judith Stacey: "The family is not 'here to stay.' Nor should we wish it

family
kinship unit of two or more persons who live in the same household and who are legally or biologically related.

household
persons, related or not, who live in the same housing unit.

271

were. On the contrary I believe that all democratic people, whatever their kinship preferences, should work to hasten its demise. . . . And, along with the class, racial, and heterosexual prejudices it promulgates, this sentimental fictional plot authorizes gender hierarchy."[7]

From this perspective, the traditional male-female family must be abolished and the family redefined "to accommodate critiques made by feminists and gay liberationists of the gender and sexual oppression in that family form."[8]

In the view of those feminists sharing Stacey's social perspective, a stable two-parent family is not a solution but a serious social problem. New democratic and non-heterosexual family forms "expose the inequity and coercion that always lay at the vortex of the supposedly voluntary companionate marriage of the 'traditional nuclear family.' "[9] Holders of this view equate favoring traditional husband-wife families with supporting the physical abuse and the emotional suppression of women. In their view, the sooner that husband-wife families disappear, the better for society.

Family as Preserver of Social Stability

On the traditional side of the debate are sociologists such as David Popenoe who argue that the current high divorce rates represent real family decline and such decline has negative consequences for society.[10] Amitai Etzioni, president of the American Sociological Association during 1994–1995, stresses the importance of the family in teaching values and socializing children. Etzioni asserts,"Approximately half our children are not being properly socialized by their parents."[11] Those seeing the institution of the family as being in trouble take the position that families *cannot* come in any size or shape and still work well for children. They argue that research clearly documents that the decline in two-parent heterosexual families has been devastating for children, putting more and more of them at risk.

As Popenoe expresses it, "In my many years as a sociologist, I have found few other bodies of evidence that lean so much in one direction as this one: on the whole, two parents—a father and a mother—are better for a child than one parent."[12] Those holding this view say the data overwhelmingly indicate that children in two-parent families have greater emotional security, suffer less child abuse, get better school grades, have fewer psychological problems, and are less likely to be involved with the police. By putting personal individualism and fulfillment above family responsibilities, we have developed a society that is becoming increasingly less child-friendly. He says that there has been a markedly decreased willingness among Americans to invest time, money, and energy in both family life and the raising of children. Research indicates that even in two-parent families the amount of time children spend with their parents has been dropping.[13] Sharp declines in

---

[7]Judith Stacey, *Brave New Families: Stories of Domestic Upheaval in Late Twentieth-Century America,* Basic Books, New York, 1990, p. 269.

[8]Judith Stacey, "Good Riddance to 'The Family': A Response to David Popenoe," *Journal of Marriage and the Family,* 55:545, August 1993.

[9]Ibid., p. 546.

[10]David Popenoe, *Disturbing the Nest: Family Change and Decline in Modern Societies,* Aldine de Gruyter, New York, 1988.

[11]Amitai Etzioni, National Press Club Lecture, National Public Radio, June 11, 1993.

[12]David Popenoe, "A World without Fathers," *Wilson Quarterly,* Spring, 1996, p. 15.

[13]Harriet B. Presser, "Can We Make Time for Children? The Economy, Work Schedules, and Child Care," *Demography,* 26:523–543, 1989; and Steven Nock and P. W. Kingston, "Time with Children: The Impact of Couples' Work-Time Commitments," *Social Forces,* 67:59–85, 1988.

Changing societal attitudes toward family life often are reflected in TV shows. Families shown in today's TV series rarely have both parents. During the 1950s and early 1960s comedies like "Father Knows Best" projected a different image of the "ideal" middle-class family.

Culver Pictures

mothers' time with children has not been compensated by increases in fathers' time with children.

Academics arguing for a **new familism** maintain that the family is essential to children and to a well-ordered society, and society must become more child and family friendly. In so doing they say there should *not* be any attempt to reconstruct the mythic "Father Knows Best" families of the 1950s. To be successful today, families must have an even division of power and decision making between husband and wife and a firm understanding that both share a common (though not necessarily identical) commitment to working outside the home over the course of the marriage.[14] The characteristics of the traditional nuclear family that new familists say need to be saved at all costs are a sense of family obligation and the desire to put children first.

The family wars show no signs of becoming less heated. Norval Glenn in a 1997 report, *Closed Hearts, Closed Minds: The Textbook Story of Marriage,* contended that most marriage and family textbooks do not support marriage but have an anti-marriage and anti-family slant.[15] His charges brought forth a firestorm of criticism from family textbook authors. The report was denounced as part of a "vigorous, influential, campaign for neoconservative 'family values.'"[16] On the other hand, the well-know sociologist Alan Wolfe says: "I checked every marriage-and-family textbook displayed in an exhibit hall at a recent statewide meeting of sociologists I attended, and I found that his analysis was acute: Sociologists who write textbooks,

new familism

belief in the importance of two parent families, and that children have been hurt by recent family changes.

---

[14]David Popenoe, "A New Familism: Renewing Families," *Current,* February 1993, p. 39.
[15]Norval Glenn, "Closed Hearts, Closed Minds: The Textbook Story of Marriage," Institute of American Values, New York, September 1997.
[16]Judith Stacey, response to Norval Glenn's "Closed Hearts, Closed Minds" in "Sociologists Differ about Family Textbooks' Message," *Footnotes,* 26:10, American Sociological Association, January 1998.

Box 10.1 Ongoing Issues

The Way We Never Were

In her books, *The Way We Never Were: American Families and the Nostalgia Trap* and *The Way We Really Are: Coming to Terms with the America's Changing Families* Stephanie Coontz argues that working mothers are here to stay. In *The Way We Really Are* Coontz says:

"One of the most common misconceptions about modern marriage is the notion that coprovider families are a new invention in human history. In fact, today's dual-earner family represents a return to older norms, after a very short interlude that people mistakenly identify as 'traditional.'

. . . Proponents of the modified male breadwinner family believe that if we could drastically reduce the number of single-mother households, raise wages for men, and convince families to get by on a little less, we might be able to get wives to quit work during their child raising years. . . . But a return to the norm of male breadwinner families is simply not feasible for most Americans.

It is not just a dollars-and-cents issue. Most women would not give up the satisfactions of their jobs even if they could afford to quit. They consistently tell interviewers they like the social respect, self-esteem, and friendship networks they gain from the job, despite the stress they may face finding acceptable child care and negotiating household chores with their husbands. . . . Another reason women do not want to quit work is that they are not willing to surrender the increased leverage it gives them in the family. The simple truth is that women who do not earn income have much less decision-making power in marital relations than women who do."[a]

[a]*Stephanie Coontz*, The Way We Really Are: Coming to Terms with America's Changing Families, *Basic Books, New York, 1997.*

identify so strongly with feminists, racial minorities, and gays and lesbians that they are reluctant to endorse family forms that they believe oppressive to those groups."[17]

Family Forms

The Nuclear Family

The **nuclear family,** sometimes called the **conjugal family,** typically consists of a married couple and their dependent children—that is, two generations with no other family members living in the same home. It is the prevalent family type in industrial urban society; its greatest advantage is that it is flexible and mobile. The weakness or problem with the nuclear family is that the loss of either parent causes severe disruption. Until recently the American model for the nuclear family was a father in the paid labor force and a mother caring for the home and children. Today the model has both parents working outside the home. (See Chapter 8.)

Our image of a once stable and secure nuclear family may idealize a past that never was. As John Gillis points out, "Looking back from the 1990s, and preoccupied with rising divorce and illegitimacy rates, we perceive the 1950s as a rock of stability. But

---

[17]Alan Wolfe, "Scholarship on Family Values: Weighing Competing Claims," *Chronicle of Higher Education,* January 28, 1998, p. B7.

Extended families are not something of the past that have been eliminated from contemporary urban life. Family reunions are actually becoming more common. Shown here is the Garrett family of Atlantic City, New Jersey.

© Macia/Photo Researchers

that was a decade gripped by anxiety about family life, and especially by the threat posed by the new youth cultures."[18] Interestingly, in the 1950s the idealized version of the traditional family was the Depression-era family of the 1930s that stuck together through thick and thin. Each generation creates myths about earlier golden ages.

To say that the nuclear family is the predominant family form in urban settings is not to say that it is the sole one. Only one-quarter of all households in the country are now traditional two-parent families with children, a record low. The average nuclear family also is smaller than it has been at any time in the recorded past, partly because of lower birthrates. The first U.S. census in 1790 gave an average family size of about 6 people; by the beginning of the twentieth century, this figure was down to 4.8; by the 1990s, it had dropped to 3.1.[19]

An increasingly common type of American nuclear family is the **blended family.** A blended family is one in which one or both parents had previous marriages that produced children, and these children live in the same household along with any children resulting from the current union. In future generations blended families may become the norm.

blended family
family in which the marital partners were previously married and bring children from the earlier marriages.

The Extended Family

Extended families contain a nuclear core, to which are added additional family members and kin. Sometimes they extend laterally, including brothers, sisters, and even cousins. Sometimes they extend generationally, including not only parents and children but also grandparents and perhaps uncles and aunts. Frequently there is a combination of the two. In the United States extended families frequently

extended family
family unit containing additional family members beyond parents and children such as grandparents and parents, brothers and sisters.

---

[18]John R. Gillis, *A World of Their Own Making: Myth, Ritual, and the Quest for Family Values*, Basic Books, New York, 1996, p. 5.
[19]U.S. Bureau of the Census, *How We're Changing, Current Population Reports*, P23–170, Washington, DC, 1990, p. 1.

have been found among African Americans, with grandmothers and aunts playing a crucial role in providing economic and social support. Extended families have also been more prevalent among Native Americans and Asians than among European immigrants. Immigrants from Europe often left kin behind when they came to America.

Throughout history, extended families have been more commonly found in farming areas since they represent an effective division of labor in an agrarian world. While nuclear families are expected to be economically self-sufficient, the extended family commonly shares responsibilities and rewards. Marrying young and having numerous offspring provides new workers. In eras of high mortality rates, the extended family also provided a form of mutual insurance. If a father was disabled or killed in an accident or a mother died in childbirth (neither tragedy was particularly uncommon), other family members were present to support and rear the children. By sharing the inevitable risks, the death of a spouse does not mean the death of the family. The family, in this sense, has a life of its own apart from that of any individual member. In urban industrial societies, national governments now provide many of the welfare benefits (e.g., social security) previously provided by the extended family.

Effects of Urbanization

There is a general consensus that during the twentieth century the family's importance has declined in the nation's economic, educational, political, and religious life. This reflects the growth of formal institutions as our society has been transformed from one that was predominately rural to one that is overwhelmingly urban.

Loss of Functions

At the time of the nation's founding, the rural family was the basic economic unit of the nation. It was the worksite not just for the husband and wife but for the children as well. Today most parents leave home in the morning for a job totally separate from life at home. Children no longer work, but remain economic liabilities for twenty plus years. Just at the point when they begin making an economic contribution, they leave home. The U.S. Department of Agriculture estimates that raising the average middle-class child born in 1996 to age 17 will cost the parents $149,820.[20] For upper-middle-class parents the cost is a higher $218,400. College and maintenance costs beyond that age are additional. In a 1998 article *U.S. News and World Report* placed the total 1998 costs of raising a child at a far higher $1,455,581.[21]

While the modern family is no longer a production unit, it does remain the basic unit for consumption. Wives especially are expected to be skilled specialists in making purchases to supply the family's daily needs. However, as more family members enter the workforce and become financially independent, the family per se may become less important as a unit of consumption. In some cases, it already is being replaced by independent consumers. This is reflected in supermarkets, where foods are increasingly sold in individual rather than family portions.

---

[20]Bill Lohmann, "It Takes a Village—and $150,000," *Richmond Times-Dispatch,* December 31, 1997, p. D1.
[21]"The Cost of Children," *U.S. News and World Report,* March 30, 1998, p. 51.

In the past young people learned from the behavior of adults—sons emulated their fathers and daughters their mothers. Today, formal education, after the first few years of life, is no longer a family right or responsibility. Socialization from ages four or five onward is allocated, for the most part, to agencies and organizations outside of the family. Nursery schools, preschools, kindergartens, grade schools, high schools, trade schools, colleges, and professional schools all claim responsibility for education. Within a certain age range—usually six to sixteen—the state insists that it educate the child. Civil laws restrict parents from educating their children at home (except by following special home schooling requirements), insisting that education be done by accredited schools.

Specialization

Contemporary urban families specialize in providing socialization and emotional security. [22] In an urban society, where most relationships are impersonal, the family is the major source of emotional support. Couples today expect their relationships to provide deep bonds of love, intimacy, and affection—they expect to go on being in love, to be strongly compatible, and to resolve difficulties through open and honest communication. As a marriage grows more routine over time, these expectations are often not fully met. Thus, when ties of intimacy weaken or disappear, the reason for the marriage often also disappears. The importance of emotional security and support in the modern family is often the very factor that leads to divorce. Today female employment after marriage is routine and there are few of the traditional social or economic constraints to keep a couple together when they feel they are no longer in love. Consequently, when romantic love decreases, more and more people tend to agree that the marriage not only can, but probably should, be dissolved.

A family system based on love is far more volatile than broader-based systems since any threat to the emotional relationship between the married couple immediately threatens the marriage bond. The mythical nuclear family as portrayed on the early TV sitcoms is gone, and few want to revive it. But we have not yet learned how best to combine the stability of the intact nuclear family with the freedom of contemporary society.

Note that high divorce rates in themselves do not necessarily mean that the institution of the family is crumbling. One can argue that our high rate of divorce—and high rates of remarriage—testifies to the continuing importance of the family as the basic unit of emotional support in urban society. As will see later in the chapter, most divorced people remain strongly interested in establishing new emotional attachments and families once their old ties have been dissolved.

Effects on Children

Family breakdown often results in the loss to the child of the companionship and supervision of one of the parents. One-third of divorced fathers see their children only once a week, and another third see them not at all. Regardless of one's position on the future of the family, no one maintains that less parental attention paid to children strengthens a child's character, improves school performance, or discourages delinquency. Many single parents do an excellent job, but, as a group, children of such families have more problems than those in two-parent families.

---

[22]Talcott Parsons and Robert F. Bales, *Family Socialization and Interaction Processes*, Free Press of Glencoe, Chicago, 1955.

Without identifying the causes, government statistics document a strong correlation between living in a single-parent family and higher rates of adolescent delinquency, depression, dropping out of school, drug abuse, nonmarital pregnancy, and suicide.[23] Similarly, six different national data sets published in 1994 by Harvard University Press indicate that children growing up in single-parent households, whether the parents were never married, are separated, or are divorced, have twice the risk of dropping out of high school, being unemployed, or becoming a teenage parent.[24] Obviously, then, discussion of the family has a central place in a text on social problems.

One must be careful, of course, not to equate intact families with happy families. A violent home or one that is only an empty shell without love is hardly an ideal environment for raising children. But statistically, in a two-parent family a child has twice the chance of having at least one good parent.

Love, Mate Selection, and Marriage

To understand the problems facing the contemporary American family, it is useful to see how our family system differs from others. To begin with, it is axiomatic in contemporary American society that a couple should not even consider marriage unless they are in love.

The Importance of Romantic Love

Love is the key word in deciding to marry, in the marriage itself, and in evaluating the success of marriage. A couple meet, fall in love, and, unable to live without each other, marry and form a new family. Love is expected to conquer all. America has the highest rate of marriage of any industrialized nation. Currently some three-fifths of the total population is married.

Emphasis on a close emotional bond between potential spouses is historically only a few centuries old even in Western societies. Marriages often were arranged by parents, and selection was based on practical criteria such as economic considerations, family and political alliances, religious affiliation, and similarity of social status. The novels of Jane Austen give a clear picture of the importance of social position and money in making a "good" marriage. The pattern of arranged marriages persists in many societies today. In India, for example, upper-status males or females may pick their own careers, but—even in the twenty-first century —the Indian family has a major voice in choosing their spouses. Some societies believe that parents who already have experienced marriage can better choose good partners for their children than young people with no previous experience.

Americans tend to believe the United States has the best marriage system. However, lest we be too ethnocentric, we should remember that the United States has the highest divorce rate in the world. Most of the world views the American pattern of marriage and divorce not as a model to be copied but as a disaster to be avoided.

---

[23]U.S. Bureau of the Census, *U.S. Children and Their Families: Current Conditions and Recent Trends,* Washington, DC, 1989.
[24]Sara McLanahan and Gary Sandefur, *Growing Up with a Single Parent,* Harvard University Press, Cambridge, MA, 1994.

Controlling Love: American Mate Selection

Because romantic love is potentially disruptive, most cultures attempt to prevent socially undesirable marriages. The establishment of new families is felt to be too important to be left totally to chance or the whims of the young. Every society has norms to restrict marriage choices; American society is no exception.

There is less social control over the American dating-mating system than in the past, but there are still clear norms favoring marriage within the group (**endogamy**). Marriages that violate these norms are still often viewed as a "problem," both for the families involved and for the larger society. Societal norms also can be used as a means of predicting risks of divorce. Even where people are expected to marry for love, they are most definitely *not* expected to fall in love with just anyone. The norms for endogamy in North America focus on race, ethnicity, religion, socioeconomic status, and age.

endogamy
Custom of marrying within ones own group, often applied in terms of religion and social class.

Ethnicity Marriage endogamy within one's own ethnic group was virtually compulsory among first-generation immigrants to America, and it was expected to be the same in the second generation. With the passage of time, ethnic differences have become far less important as an impediment to marriage. However for today's new immigrant groups, ethnicity is an important factor in partner selection.[25] For those of European ancestry, a new general European ethnic group is being formed based on ancestry from anywhere in Europe.[26] (See Chapter 4 for discussion.)

Religion With ethnicity declining in importance, religion sometimes serves as the next bulwark against marriage outside the group. For most of the twentieth century America had a triple melting pot, with separate Catholic, Protestant, and Jewish marriage pools.[27] However, even these broad divisions are breaking down. The highest level of endogamy is now to be found in the relatively small Jewish population. Without in-marriage the Jewish population would cease to exist as a distinct group within a few generations. Marriages outside the Jewish group are most common among males who are not active religiously and interact socially outside the Jewish community.

Socioeconomic Status Love may be blind, but it is not expected to bypass the barriers of social status. One is expected to marry someone of roughly similar occupational level and educational background. The basic assumption is that such couples are most likely to have much in common and to share similar attitudes, values, and goals. The norms against cross-status marriages are strongest where there are large class and educational differences between spouses. Where differences do exist, it still remains more socially acceptable that the male have the higher economic or educational background. Historically, the term *husband* referred not to a married man but to one who had "husbanded" enough resources to marry.

Age Every society specifies "suitable" ages for marriage. In America, spouses are expected to be relatively close in age. The 1995 average age for first marriage

---

[25]Stanley Lieberson and Mary C. Waters, *From Many Strands: Ethnic and Racial Groups in Contemporary America*, Russell Sage, New York, 1988.

[26]Richard A. Alba, *Ethnic Identity: The Transformation of White America*, Yale University Press, New Haven, CT, 1990, p. 3.

[27]Ruby Jo Reeves Kennedy, "Single or Triple Melting Pot?" *American Journal of Sociology*, 49:331–339, January 1944.

Common ethnic background is becoming less important as a marriage criteria. Latino-Anglo weddings are now common. This wedding party is standing outside the Old Mission in San Juan Capistrano, California.

was 26.5 for males and 24.5 for females. These are the oldest average ages for first marriages in America's history. (It shocks today's student to learn that in the early 1960s most women had *completed* their childbearing by age 25.) Where ages do differ, the male is expected to be the older partner. Among those remarrying, there is a greater age difference between spouses.

Race Of all the endogamy rules, race has been the most persistent. Fifty years ago, interracial marriage was illegal in 28 southern and western states, and not until 1967 did the Supreme Court rule antimiscegenation laws (laws prohibiting crossracial marriage) unconstitutional. Even with legal sanctions removed, however, racial endogamy still remains a major factor in mate selection. While marriages between whites and Asians now are accepted as routine (so much so that most whites no longer even consider such marriages interracial), black-white marriages still meet disapproval from within both groups.

The strength of the norms against crossracial marriages can be seen in the fact that until the 1970s the proportion of black marriages that involved whites was less than 1 percent.[28] Since that time, interracial black-white marriages increased four

---

[28]David M. Heer, "The Prevalence of Black-White Marriage in the United States, 1960 and 1970," *Journal of Marriage and the Family,* 36, pp. 246–258, 1974.

times to 246,000 marriages a year, or about 2.2 percent of all marriages.[29] The most common interracial marriage is between a black male and a white female. Census data indicate that 6 percent of black men and 2 percent of black women have spouses who are not black. Outside the South, the percentage of black men marrying a white woman is over 10 percent, while under 2 percent of black women marry white men.[30]

The low interracial marriage rate for black females is showing signs of increasing. With the number of black women attending college double that of black men, some African American women feel they have little choice but to marry outside the race if they are to find a compatible mate.[31]

Overview Students are frequently unaware of the degree to which the factors of socioeconomic status, ethnicity, religion, and race have subtly influenced their lives. For instance, their family may have moved to a different school district in order to send adolescents to a "more appropriate" high school. Also, parents often urge children to attend a particular college, for more than academic reasons. The parents are aware that by controlling the college environment, they can partly control the marriage market for their children. As expressed by the director of public relations for a small Mormon college, "Families want kids to meet people with values similar to their own."[32] Peer pressures often do the rest. (At this small Mormon college 20 percent of the students married other students last year.) Students are also aware that attending a particular college or residing in a certain neighborhood enhances one's social opportunities. Only the workplace is a better place than college for meeting a potential partner.

Happiness and Marriage?

Jessie Bernard argues that every marriage is actually two different marriages: the man's marriage and the woman's marriage.[33] She states that women are less happy in marriages and have poorer mental health. Most sociology texts also take the view that women are less pleased with marriage.[34] However, this position is not supported by most research. Joan Aldous and Rodney Ganey reviewed 20 years of survey research on the question and discovered that women consistently describe themselves as both happier than men and happier in marriage.[35] This is even though married women possess less power and resources than married men.

Some have speculated that women aren't really happier, they just are more forthcoming with their feelings. Others suggest that it is easier for women, who are more interested in family and personal relationships, to achieve happiness than men, who measure self-worth in terms of career accomplishments. Data indicate that women's attitudes are becoming more like men's in that they are increasingly looking outside the home to their work lives as a measure of satisfaction, and this is producing a predictible decline in reported happiness. However, for whatever reason, women still consistently describe themselves as being happier than men describe themselves.

---

[29]Gabrielle Sandor, "The Other Americans," *American Demographics*, June 1994, pp. 36–42.
[30]Matthijs Kalmijn, "Trends in Black/White Intermarriage," *Social Forces*, 72:124, 1993.
[31]Steven A. Holmes, "Number of Black-White Couples Is Rising Sharply Study Says," *New York Times*, July 4, 1996, p. A1.
[32]"A Unique College Thrives," *Richmond Times-Dispatch*, February 7, 1999, p. C4.
[33]Jessie Bernard, *The Future of Marriage*, Yale University Press, New Haven, CT, 1982.
[34]Alan Wolfe, "Scholarship on Family Values: Weighing Competing Claims," *Chronicle of Higher Education*, January 23, 1998, p. B7.
[35]Joan Aldous and Rodney F. Ganey, *Journal of Family Issues*, forthcoming.

 **Box 10.2** **Making a Difference**

Back to the Future?

Popular readings are no substitute for research studies, but general readings often do tell us about people's concerns. Similarly, opinions sometimes differ as to whether those "making a difference" move us in a positive or negative direction. Such is the case with Danielle Crittenden's popular conservative take on marriage, *What Our Mothers Didn't Tell Us: Why Happiness Eludes the Modern Woman.*[a] Crittenden's solution for the modern marriage malaise is to reverse the current pattern of marrying later and to go back to the era of marrying young and having children immediately. She further recommends putting marriage ahead of career.

Crittenden points out that a typical woman will live 80 years, work 40 of them, but have young children for perhaps only 8 years. Despite the relatively short period with young children, she argues, women have convinced themselves they have no choice but to work full-time, while staying home with one's young children becomes "a perk of the rich, like yachting." According to her, the answer is not to delay marriage and childbearing but to marry early and promptly have children. This brings the satisfaction of spending time with your children, and also pre-

vents one from living "the introverted life of a teenager into middle age."

Crittenden says much modern angst results from not recognizing that women can have it all—but not all at once. She says that for a marriage to be successful men and women must make different compromises because they have the children, especially compromises regarding careers. The alternative is the current system, where weary women try to balance briefcase and baby and convince themselves that "quality time" with their children is a substitute for lots of time.

Crittenden's belief that women have distinctive desires to have and raise children, and that ignoring these desires causes unhappiness, directly contradicts the beliefs of most feminists. Feminists argue that Crittenden's assertion that women have unique needs for motherhood is socially reactionary and means turning back the clock. Crittenden replies that having a loving spouse and taking time to bring into the world life that is loved and will outlast us is an excellent trade-off for postponing a career.

[a]*Danielle Crittenden, What Our Mothers Didn't Tell Us: Why Happiness Eludes the Modern Woman, Simon & Schuster, New York, 1999.*

Compared to those who are single or divorced, married persons consistently report themselves as happier. This should not be surprising, because as a group married people are better off than those not married. Linda Waite's extensive research on the influences of family structure shows that married couples are stronger financially, have a higher standard of living, eat better, have better health, live longer, and even have more and better sex.[36]

Divorce—Cutting the Bond

As the opening sections of the chapter indicated, whether or not one considers divorce to be a social problem depends at least partially on one's theoretical perspective. Americans are both a marrying people and a divorcing people. As noted earlier, the divorce rate in the United States is the highest in the world, more than double that of most Western European nations and three times that

---

[36]Jeniffer Steinhauer, "Big Benefits in Marriage, Study Says," *New York Times,* April 10, 1995, p. A1.

There is a reason America has the world's highest divorce rate. A marriage system that places major emphasis on "self-fulfillment" and "being in love" provides little support when inevitable disagreements occur.

© Chris Andrews/Stock, Boston

of Japan. The commonly used figure is that half of all new marriages are likely to end in divorce, but after correcting for underreporting, Martin and Bumpass estimate that two-thirds of all first marriages are likely to end in divorce.[37] Others say this is a considerable overestimation and point out that, since divorce rates peaked in 1980, the divorce rate has been declining slightly. What is certain is that between 1970 and 1994, the number of divorced persons quadrupled from 4.3 million to almost 17 million.[38] This represents 9 percent of all those 18 and older.

Changes in Legal Codes

Legal codes traditionally have treated divorce as a social problem. Until 1966, New York State allowed divorce solely on grounds of adultery; in South Carolina, divorce was not legally possible before 1949. Such laws are no longer on the books, but one archaic practice that still remains in some states is to legally define divorce not as the breakdown of a relationship but as a legal proceeding in which one partner is guilty and the other innocent. No-fault divorce laws, which became common in the 1970s, were designed to move beyond the need for guilt and allow a marriage to be dissolved when one or both partners feel that the marriage can no

---

[37]Teresa C. Martin and Larry L. Bumpass, "Recent Trends in Marital Disruption," *Demography*, 26:36–51, 1989.

[38]U.S. Bureau of the Census, *Marital Status and Living Arrangements, March 1993, Current Population Reports*, P20–478, Washington, DC, 1994.

longer be sustained. While not preventing arguments over children and possessions, no-fault divorces seek to avoid the bitterness of requiring adversarial proceedings, to end matrimony without producing acrimony. Today, divorce can be obtained on the grounds of "irreconcilable differences" between the partners.

Another change in divorce law practice is that child support payments have become virtually universal, while alimony payments for nonworking spouses are becoming increasingly rare. (California's system, where some males have sued for alimony, and nonmarried live-in female companions have also sued for "palimony" is not typical of other states.) Some argue that divorce laws have now become a problem because obtaining a divorce has become too casual. Receiving an uncontested divorce takes less than six weeks in many states, and in some states neither partner has to go to court. In Minnesota, for instance, an uncontested divorce can be obtained through the mail.

Finally, keep in mind that divorce is a legal term, and that family breakups can be just as devastating (and just as nasty) for those who are not legally married. The courts currently are dealing with the difficult question as to who is a parent. When lesbian couples split, do both get custody rights? Some states say the nonbiological mom has no legal standing and thus no parental rights of custody.

Who Divorces?

Overall divorce rates fail to indicate that not all couples face the same risk of marital dissolution. The highest risk of divorce exists among those who marry young and are of lower socioeconomic status.

Age   The literature consistently shows that age is the single best predictor of divorce. Divorces are most common among those in their teens or early 20s—who, obviously, would have had to be even younger at the time they were first married. For the first five years of marriage, age when married is the strongest predictor of divorce.[39] Just over half of those divorcing are under 25 years of age. Teenage marriages are more likely to result in divorce than to survive.

Why is this? Those who marry young are less likely to have the maturity, experience, and competence necessary for marriage.[40] They also are more likely to start out with the wife already pregnant and thus face greater burdens, both financial and psychological. Age at marriage is also related to social-class level. Middle- and upper-status groups marry later and are more likely to be more mature emotionally as well as more secure financially.

The longer one is married, the greater the likelihood of remaining married. A third of all divorces are among those married less than five years, and almost two-thirds are couples married less than ten years. With Americans now marrying later, the divorce rate might be expected to decrease.

Poverty   Economic insecurity and financial problems also make divorce far more likely. Poor couples are about twice as likely to divorce as the nonpoor according to a survey of 33,000 persons interviewed three times a year for over two years by the Census Bureau.[41] The only exception to low income being tied to marriage dissolution is that couples were much more likely to break up if both

[39]Martin and Bumpass, "Recent Trends."
[40]A. Booth and J. N. Edwards, "Age at Marriage and Marital Instability," *Journal of Marriage and the Family,* 47:67–76, 1985.
[41]"Poverty as a Divorce Factor," *New York Times News Service,* January 15, 1993.

Figure 10.2 Children with Divorced and Never-Married Mothers, by Family Income (March 1995)

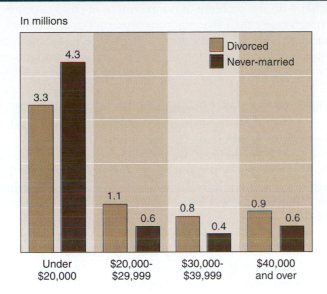

In millions

Legend: Divorced, Never-married

- Under $20,000: 3.3 (Divorced), 4.3 (Never-married)
- $20,000-$29,999: 1.1 (Divorced), 0.6 (Never-married)
- $30,000-$39,999: 0.8 (Divorced), 0.4 (Never-married)
- $40,000 and over: 0.9 (Divorced), 0.6 (Never-married)

Source: U.S. Department of Commerce; Bureau of the Census

poor parents worked full-time rather than if the mother worked only part-time. This higher rate may result from exceptional family financial need that requires both parents to work, or the difficulty of juggling two full-time jobs with the needs of children, or women who have a job feeling they can support themselves after divorce.

Social Class A reading of *People* might suggest that the upper classes have the highest rates of divorce. They don't. An upper-class divorce simply receives more publicity than does that of a factory worker. We may argue about whether or not money brings happiness, but, if divorce statistics are any measure, it would appear that money, at the very least, makes marriages more durable. Although divorce rates for all social classes have been converging, they are still inversely related to social class. In other words, divorce rates are highest among those at the bottom of the socioeconomic scale. If desertion—known as the poor man's divorce—is included, the lowest class has, by a large margin, the highest rate of marital dissolution.

The marriage stability enjoyed by the middle and upper classes is not surprising given their greater economic, social, and psychological resources. When crises occur, a middle- or upper-class couple is usually better prepared emotionally and financially to deal with them. Middle-class and more-affluent couples also know how to get necessary help—be it from relatives or marriage counselors—and even how to cope with problems such as alcoholism or mental illness. Additional advantages, such as household help and vacations away from the children, all help to reduce potential strain. Upper-middle-class married people with family problems can often compensate at least to some extent by throwing themselves into work or community activity. The job of a working-class man or woman, however, is unlikely to offer similar emotional or financial rewards.

Media images such as Ivana Trump with her multimillion dollar divorce settlement do not reflect reality for most divorced women. A severe problem facing most divorced women is a sharp decline in economic resources.[42] The average divorced woman loses about 30 percent of her predivorce family income (see Chapter 1 for a discussion of research on this topic). Recent "deadbeat dads" legislation has helped somewhat with the problem of nonpayment of child support. Men recover economically much faster than women from divorce, but remarriage for men with children often means added financial strain. Second wives are likely to see their income going toward child support for an earlier family—another source of family strain.

Gender

There are gender differences in both marriage and divorce rates. High-education and higher-income men are most likely to have lasting marriages. For women the pattern is different. The lowest divorce rates are among women having college degrees. The highest divorce rates are among those with very low educational levels, followed by those with postgraduate degrees. The longstanding pattern is that women holding advanced degrees are both more likely to remain single, or if married, are more likely to divorce.[43]

The high levels of singlehood and divorce among women with advanced degrees is usually attributed to three factors. First, graduate-level educated women are economically independent and more likely to choose not to marry. Second, women with advanced degrees often restrict their marriage interest to those males having equal or greater education. However, there are only a limited number of potential mates possessing these characteristics, especially since well-educated and successful men are likely to already be married. Third, if she is married there may be conflicts between a highly educated woman's career aspirations and her marriage. A woman with a successful career may be unwilling to sacrifice potential career advancement for marriage. If career and marriage conflict, she can afford to divorce.

Race and Ethnicity

Divorce patterns for whites and African Americans differ. Marital breakups are more than twice as common among African Americans as among whites, but the figures for both tend to fall into the same general pattern—in other words, the highest divorce rates exist among the young and those of low socioeconomic status. Still, even among women who attended college, divorce rates are over twice as high for blacks as for whites.[44] It has been speculated that some of this difference is due to the greater economic insecurity of black families and the relative economic independence of educated black women.

Divorce rates for Latinos are lower than those for non-Hispanic whites once other factors (age, education, etc.) are taken into account.[45] Asian American divorce rates also are lower than those for the white population.

Divorced One-Parent Homes

Twenty-five years ago, children who grew up in one-parent homes that had been split by divorce had a divorce rate 139 percent higher than those coming from two-parent families. Now the divorce rate of children of divorce is only 27 percent higher than the divorce rate of those

[42]Karen C. Holden and Pamela J. Smock, "The Economic Costs of Marital Dissolution: Why Do Women Bear Disproportionate Cost?" *Annual Review of Sociology*, 17:51–78, 1991.

[43]S. K. Houseknecht and J. B. Spanner, "Marital Disruption and Higher Education among Women in the U.S.," *Sociological Quarterly*, 21:375–390, 1980.

[44]Martin and Bumpass, "Recent Trends," p. 44.

[45]Parker W. Frisbie, "Variations in Patterns of Marital Instability among Hispanics," *Journal of Marriage and the Family*, 48:99–106, 1986.

coming from two-parent homes.[46] Children from intact two-parent families have an edge in that they are more likely to grow up with parents who have developed successful techniques for resolving problems and conflicts.

Why the High Divorce Rates?

Our knowledge of the demographic characteristics of divorce and those divorcing is far superior to our understanding of the causes of divorce. Thus, explanations for the high divorce rates of the recent decades are largely *ex post facto* (after the fact). Numerous factors are cited as causing high divorce: changes in the economic and social dependence of women, an increasing emphasis on self-fulfillment, declining moral standards, easy divorce laws, and changing economic conditions.

Past Patterns In the past physical strength and endurance were a criteria for many jobs. This encouraged a patriarchal family system in which males were in the labor force and women cared for the home and children. Today, males have lost their role as sole breadwinner; in the labor force separate male and female work spheres are disappearing. In our postindustrial knowledge-based economy, the greatest labor market growth currently is in areas such as health care, computer and data services, child care, and business services. Women dominate numerically in all these employment areas.

New Realities Social attitudes toward women's role in childrearing and making a home have changed. Contemporary attitudes often carry an implicit assumption that being a wife and mother is less praiseworthy than having a career. This is a long way from the common mid-twentieth-century belief that the care and raising of children was the most important social contribution any woman could make.

Social and religious attitudes toward divorce have also changed. Divorce is no longer considered a somewhat shameful breech of public decency; it is now accepted even by the most conservative religious denominations as a solution to personal conflicts. Legally, obtaining a divorce is also far simpler than at any time in the past. It may be personally or financially painful, but the procedure is now fairly routine.

Ideas about what partners are entitled to expect from a "good" marriage have also changed. Contemporary partners expect marriage to provide an intense and intimate relationship. Also, with more dual-career marriages, couples today may feel less committed to their marriage than were couples in earlier generations. Today, neither spouse need be dependent on the other for financial support. Nor do family responsibilities weigh as heavily as in the past. Staying married for the children's sake is less likely to be seen as a valid reason for maintaining a marriage that is no longer emotionally or sexually satisfying. This is particularly true if the couple does not have children. (Approximately 60 percent of divorces involve children.)

Marriage, in effect, is treated like another consumer good. When it doesn't seem to be working, you turn it in for a new model. Under such circumstances, it is reasonable to expect divorce rates to remain high.

---

[46]Nicholas Wolfinger, "Time Trends in the Intergenerational Transmission of Divorce," presentation at American Sociological Association Meeting, New York, August 20, 1996.

Remarriage: Second (or More) Chances

Any discussion of divorce must include the topic of remarriage, because Americans, who marry and divorce in record numbers, also rush to rewed. If divorce is seen as a social problem, remarriage is commonly seen as the solution. The American system of marriage, divorce, and remarriage has been referred to—only partly in jest—as a form of serial polygamy. Currently, over 40 percent of all marriages involve a spouse who has been previously married.[47] Roughly three out of four of those divorcing will remarry, with male remarriage rates being somewhat higher than female. Divorce rates seem to indicate disillusionment more with a particular relationship than with marriage and family living itself. The data suggest that spouses are seeking not so much to escape from marriage as to get more out of it. Remarriage can thus be viewed as a common solution for the problems of unhappy marriages and divorces.

Most divorced people remarry within three years—men somewhat sooner, women somewhat later. The most likely marriage partner for a divorced person is another divorced person, with the average age at remarriage being considerably higher than at first marriage (upper 30s for males, lower 30s for females). Because most divorces involve children, most second and later marriages necessarily create blended families.

Social custom favors the male in terms of the number of potential remarriage partners. A woman in her mid-30s is expected to seek a partner who is roughly the same age or somewhat older. This limits her choice of potential spouses largely to older divorced and single men. Women seeking partners thus outnumber the "available" men. For a man in his mid-30s or older, on the other hand, social custom allows greater latitude regarding the acceptable age of a potential mate. His pool of eligible females includes younger women, who are less likely to be already married.

Offsetting the man's selection advantage may be his less than ideal financial position. A divorced man who has children is paying child support, and he may also be paying alimony. For the economically successful man who marries a younger "trophy wife," this may not be a problem. However, in most cases a woman who marries a divorced man is likely to be, and to remain, a working wife. Many second marriages are quite successful, but overall second marriages are about twice as likely as first marriages to end in divorce, although the accuracy of the higher rates of divorce is questioned by some.[48]

Third and later marriages have high divorce rates. The often-divorced may repeat the same unsuccessful patterns. Those who are successfully married have learned—either through trial and error or from following the example of successful parents—how to cope with and overcome the inevitable marital strains. If a person has limited resources (economic and social) to bring to a first marriage, the chances are that there will be even fewer resources to bring to later ones. Finally, those who have been divorced know the legal routine and may be less reluctant to repeat the process.

In second or later marriages family relationships are far more complex than in a first marriage. In blended families each partner has to come to terms not only with the marriage partner but also with his or her former spouse, the partner's former spouse, and the children of the former marriages (both the husband's and the wife's). All these relationships carry a potential for conflict, and it takes maturity and judgment to satisfy everyone's needs and demands. When a remarrying couple both have children from previous marriages, there are additional causes for tension and anxiety.

---

[47]National Center for Health Statistics, *Monthly Vital Statistics Report,* 43, no. 12, July 14, 1995, Table 7.
[48]Martin and Bumpass, "Recent Trends," pp. 44–48.

However, in a situation as complex as repeat marriage, generalized statements—including those made here reflecting overall rates—can fail to reflect substantial and important variations. Later marriages in which the partners are reasonably secure psychologically and financially can closely approximate the "ideal" union. A second marriage can profit from the added maturity and experience gained by the partners.

Remaining Single: A Growing Option

Today, staying single is an increasingly common alternative to marriage. Discussing singles is a necessary part of any discussion of marriage. The proportion of singles in their early 30s tripled between 1970 and 1993.[49] It now includes 20 percent of the women and 30 percent of the men in their early 30s. Also, increasing numbers of couples live together without marrying. There now are 4.2 million unmarried-couple households, or 6 unmarried-couple households for every 100 married-couple households. Half of those living together eventually marry.

In the past, people who deliberately remained single were often viewed as socially irresponsible and a social problem. The colonial Puritan society of New England saw bachelors as slackers, both socially and economically, so they had to pay special "bachelor taxes" (e.g., 20 shillings a week in Hartford). Restraints on women were even tighter. In Puritan New England, they were labeled "ancient maids" if they were still unwed by the time they reached age 25. Those who did not marry were viewed as living "unnatural" lives. The stereotype was the prim and joyless old maid (often a schoolteacher) or the prissy busybody who criticized other people's lives instead of living her own. Countless novels, such as Jane Austen's *Pride and Prejudice* and Louisa May Alcott's *Little Women,* and plays, such as Tennessee Williams' *The Glass Menagerie,* have focused on the tragic consequences of failing to fulfill the social expectation of marrying. Scarlett O'Hara, the heroine in *Gone with the Wind* who is determined not be a spinster, reflected an attitude that prevailed until very recently.

Today women have a variety of educational opportunities and chances for self-fulfillment. The degree to which women in the future will choose alternatives to marriage can only be surmised. So far, marriage remains the American norm. The Bureau of the Census estimates that some 90 percent of white women, but fewer than three-quarters of black women, eventually will ever marry. (The latter figure is the result of a more limited number of "marriageable" black males.)

Same-Sex Unions

To some Americans, same-sex unions are a social problem. Tolerance of gays in the workplace and of gay lifestyles has not translated, thus far, into widespread acceptance of homosexual marriages. Only a few cities, such as San Francisco and Berkeley, allow same-sex marriages, and these unions are not recognized by the State of California. (In 2000 Vermont became the first—and only—state to legalize

---

[49]U.S. Bureau of the Census, *Current Population Reports,* P20–478.

gay and lesbian unions.[50] The Hawaiian Supreme Court rejected that state's gay marriage law in 1999. Denmark in 1989 became the first country to legalize same-sex marriage.) Congress, in 1996 passed and President Clinton signed the *Defense of Family Act,* which defines marriage as legally existing only in a heterosexual union of one male and one female.

Bans on same-sex marriages reflect religious and social values, but there also are economic considerations. Legally recognizing same-sex marriages makes gay or lesbian couples eligible for federal and state tax and retirement benefits, including health insurance and spousal and dependant support. Medical insurance benefits, for example, could not be denied a partner who had AIDS. Corporations increasingly provide such "partner" benefits. Opponents of same-sex marriages argue that taxpayers should not be forced to subsidize lifestyles of which they disapprove. On the other hand, advocates of gay marriage say they are entitled to the same economic benefits as heterosexual couples—the decision to marry belongs to the individual and not to the government or religious groups.[51]

There is also conflict about gays and lesbians as parents. All courts do not rule similarly, but in 1996 a Virginia court removed a child from the household of her lesbian mother and lover saying it was not a suitable home environment. The state appeals court upheld the ruling. (For further discussion of gay issues, see Chapter 15.)

Family-Associated Social Issues

In this section we examine a number of specific issues associated with contemporary American family life. The discussion is designed to provide some understanding of some of the most discussed challenges facing contemporary families.

One-Parent Families

As recently as 1960 three-quarters (73 percent) of all children lived with their two never-divorced natural parents. Today, children have a 50-50 chance of spending part of their childhood in a single-parent home. This is a consequence both of the doubling of the divorce rate and a doubling of the proportion of never-married mothers since 1980. Single parents now constitute a quarter of all white families and two-thirds of black families. Asian children are the most likely to be living in two-parent families (86 percent). Nine out of 10 single-parent families are headed by a woman.

There are major differences between families that have a single parent because of divorce and those with a never-married parent. Divorce often puts women in a precarious financial position, but by far the poorest families are those headed by unwed mothers, with 69 percent of the children of such families living in poverty.[52] Never-married mothers constitute 43 percent of recipients who have been on welfare for at least three of the last five years. By comparison, only 14 percent of divorced mothers are long-term welfare recipients.[53]

[50]"Gay Unions OKed by Vermont House," *New York Times,* April 19, 2000, p. A1.
[51]"Should Gay Marriage Be Legal?" *U.S. News and World Report,* June 3, 1996, p. 31.
[52]Bureau of the Census, "Children with Single Parents—How They Fare," *Census Brief,* 97–1, September 1997, p. 1.
[53]"Rise in Single Parenthood Reshaping America," *New York Times News Service,* October 5, 1992.

Out-of-Wedlock Births

The number and proportion of out-of-wedlock births rapidly increased during the 1980s and early 1990s and then began to decrease in the late 1990s. The Bureau of the Census reported that the early 1990s saw a dramatic 60 percent increase in unmarried women becoming mothers compared to a decade earlier.[54] While in 1960 only 5 percent of all births occurred outside of marriage, by the 1990s the proportion of out-of-wedlock births had gone up to 28 percent. This increase represents a remarkable social change in such a short period of time.

By ethnic group, the figures indicate that over a fifth (22 percent) of all white births, a third (33 percent) of Hispanic births, and two-thirds (68 percent) of black births now occur to never-married mothers. Before 1960, black and white marriage patterns were remarkably similar. In fact, until that point young black women were *more* likely than white women to be married.[55] Thus, the separation of marriage and childbearing is not a longstanding African-American pattern. As recently as 1960, 66 percent of all black women aged 30 to 34 were married. By 1990 the figure had dropped to 39 percent, and it is still falling.

Economics and Education

Economic changes can explain part of the increase in out-of-wedlock births. In urban areas having the highest proportions of unmarried mothers, there are few young men who are employed full-time. Without jobs young men are essentially unmarriageable. Marriage is still valued, but to those without jobs it is not a realistic possibility. As the social psychologist Kristin Moore puts it, "College educated people are not just able to get a better job, but to find a spouse and have their kids inside marriage and pass that along to the next generation. Marriage is another measure of who's able to make their lives work."[56]

While some middle-class unwed mothers are economically and educationally successful the great bulk of unwed mothers are not. Most unwed mothers come from economically disadvantaged families and are poorly educated. According to Census Bureau data, as of 1994 almost half (46 percent) of unwed mothers had not even graduated from high school.[57] Unwed motherhood is closely associated with long-term welfare dependency. According to the Congressional Budget Office, within five years of a baby's birth, 72 percent of white unwed mothers and 84 percent of black unwed mothers are on welfare.[58]

Whether unwed motherhood is viewed as a moral problem, an economic problem, or a health problem, or whether unwed mothers are regarded as the stereotyped victims of an outdated middle-class belief system, it is clear that most unwed mothers head educationally and economically marginal families. There also is overwhelming evidence that children of such families will be similarly deprived. The high level of out-of-wedlock births is disturbing to health and education officials because unwed mothers as a group are younger, poorer, less educated, and more dependent on welfare than other mothers. Children in the homes of unwed mothers have poorer academic grades and higher rates of school dropout, are more

---

[54]"Big Rise in Births out of Wedlock," *New York Times,* July 14, 1993, p. A1.
[55]Andrew Cherlin, *Marriage, Divorce, Remarriage,* Harvard University Press, Cambridge, MA, 1992.
[56]Margaret Usdansky, "Single Motherhood: Stereotypes vs. Statistics," *New York Times,* February 11, 1996, p. 4E.
[57]Margaret Usdansky, "Single Motherhood: Stereotypes vs. Statistics," *New York Times,* February 11, 1996, p. 4E.
[58]Congressional Budget Office, *Sources of Support for Adolescent Mothers,* Washington, DC, 1990.

likely to use drugs and alcohol, are more likely be delinquent, and are more likely to have out-of-wedlock children themselves.[59] Children in such families are two to three times more likely to be involved in premarital pregnancies and to come before the courts because of delinquency or crime. Such children account for a disproportionately high percentage of youths with social problems.

Family Violence

To those who think of the term "family" as a synonym for love, affection, and support, it comes as a shock to learn that the family is a major source of violence in American society. The most often cited study of domestic violence, done two decades ago by Straus, Gelles, and Steinmetz, found that one-sixth of 6,000 couples interviewed admitted to some violence during the past year, and one-quarter said that this violence had occurred sometime during their marriage.[60] The authors estimated the actual rate of violence to be twice that reported. However, the study used a very broad definition of violence; treating equally as a violent incident anything from a single push to a repeated pattern of beatings that caused serious injury. Straus estimates that approximately 6 percent of marriages involve serious violence such as punching, biting, kicking, or more.[61]

Egalitarian-type families are less likely to have physical abuse than families where power relationships are unequal. Abuse of a spouse, child, or elder is a case of the stronger taking advantage of the weaker. Men are most likely to abuse women, and women are most likely to abuse children. The limited data that do exist paint a bleak picture. Nationally, murders of spouses account for one-eighth of all murders; other types of family homicides, including parents killing children and children murdering parents, account for another eighth of all murders.

More requests for police response come from domestic disturbance calls than from any other source, and spouses sometimes turn their anger onto the police. According to FBI figures, domestic disturbances account for over one-quarter of all assaults on police. One-eighth of all police who die in the line of action die responding to a domestic disturbance call.

Spouse Abuse   As noted, the actual amount of domestic violence in the United States is not known, but it is substantial. Before the twentieth century a husband had a legal right to "chastise" or discipline his wife by physical force. Most people are not aware that the common phrase "rule of thumb" has a violent past. Under English common law, a husband could chastise his wife so long as the stick he used to beat her was no thicker than his thumb. Today, wife-beating is a criminal offense, and as the O. J. Simpson trial indicated, it is by no means limited to poor neighborhoods.

Dealing with the problem of domestic violence is often hampered by mistaken beliefs. One of the most common of these beliefs is the notion that violence is a form of abnormality involving only those who are sick, mentally ill, or alcoholic. Violence also occurs in so-called normal families. Ironically, some of today's domestic violence may take place because the family has become more and more a unit of intimacy and emotional support. Close intimacy can create hostility and conflict as well as love and affection. Problems of "getting on each other's nerves" may erupt

---

[59]Sara McLanahan and Karen Booth, "Mother Only Families," in Allan Booth (ed.), *Contemporary Families: Looking Forward, Looking Back,* National Council on Family Relations, Minneapolis, 1991, pp. 405–428.

[60]Murray A. Straus, Richard J. Gelles, and Suzanne K. Steinmetz, *Behind Closed Doors: Violence in the American Family,* Doubleday, New York, 1980.

[61]Murray A. Straus, "Physical Violence in American Families: Incidence Rates, Causes, and Trends," in Dean D. Knudsen and JoAnn L. Miller (eds.), *Abused and Battered: Social and Legal Responses to Family Violence,* Aldine de Gruyter, New York, 1991.

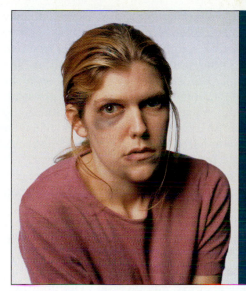

Domestic violence has a long American history. In spite of increasing public attention, social condemnation, and police intervention spouse abuse remains a serious problem.

PhotoDisc

into verbal and physical violence. Women sometimes stay in abusive relationships because they fear they will have no place to go, they are economically dependent, or they think the abuser will change his behavior.[62] The abusers rarely change. While husbands are more likely to beat up wives, wives are slightly more likely to murder their husbands. There are 60 million handguns in the United States, and it takes no special strength or skill to pull the trigger on a "Saturday night special."

Attempts to prohibit family violence by legislation have had little impact and will likely continue to be ineffective unless physical violence is also strongly condemned by the society. Legislation can, however, serve as a public statement of acceptable and unacceptable family behavior. An indication of changing societal values is the attention currently being given to wife and child abuse as major problems. Two decades ago an abused wife often had nowhere to turn. Today in most communities they can, at least, obtain information and support from crisis hotlines, while shelters provide refuge and physical safety for battered women.

Child Abuse   Child abuse is, in many ways, an even more difficult problem than spouse abuse since the child is in the weakest power position in the family. An infant cannot even communicate with outsiders. Those rare cases where a malnourished child is kept locked in an attic or backroom and systematically abused receive widespread publicity. Far more numerous are the cases where children suffer injuries not easily detected or where child abuse is not easily proven, such as the child who comes to school with bloody welts concealed under clothing.

Estimates of the number of abused children run as high as 1 million, but the actual number remains unknown. Evidence on whether child abuse is increasing or decreasing is contradictory. The decade old National Survey of Family Violence reported a 27 percent decline in wife beatings and a 47 percent decline in severe child abuse compared to survey findings of a decade earlier.[63] These surveys were based on parents' reports. On the other hand, the number of abuse cases reported to authorities has continued to climb. The hope is that the increase in the number of reported cases represents a greater awareness of child abuse, and thus a greater willingness to intervene.

Historically, outsiders have been unwilling to intervene in family matters. Barriers preventing aid to the abused include real concern for personal safety, fear of lawsuits, personal indecision about what is and what is not abuse, and general

[62]B. Strong and C. DeVault, *The Marriage and Family Experience,* West Publishing, St. Paul, MN, 1992.
[63]Richard L. Gelles and Murray A. Straus, *Intimate Violence,* Simon & Schuster, New York, 1988.

293

unwillingness to become involved. There is an American tendency to allow each family to run its own affairs and to discourage "meddling" by outsiders. Society traditionally has supported parents' right to physically discipline their children. Is the religiously conservative father who believes in the dictum "spare the rod and spoil the child" and physically punishes his 11-year-old son a child abuser or a strict disciplinarian? Even more difficult to deal with than physical abuse are situations in which a child is being verbally and emotionally abused by a parent.

Contrary to "commonsense" stereotypes, young boys are somewhat more likely to be physically abused than young girls. In part, this may be because boys are more likely to engage in behavior that is thought to merit "punishment." Also, it is still part of societal norms that hitting boys is more acceptable than hitting girls.[64] Contrary to stereotype, infants and young children are most often abused by their own mothers. Physical abuses, such as a mother deliberately scalding a child with hot water, violate our society's image of natural "mothering instincts." If at all possible, we prefer not to confront the reality of deliberate child injury by parents and frame them as "accidents."

Child abusers do not fit into easy stereotypes. As a group, they have difficulty handling stress, they are often in poor marital situations, and, most significantly, they come from families where abuse was present. "Parents Anonymous," a national self-help organization for abusing parents, has been relatively successful in improving the self-esteem, understanding, and behavior of abusing parents, but thus far the organization receives only limited referrals from doctors, hospitals, and community agencies. As awareness of the amount of child abuse increases and it becomes recognized that families can be helped, there may be decreases in child abuse.

Sexual Abuse The common assumption is that there is greater sexual abuse of young females. However, while girls report more abuse, experts think boys may be as likely to be victims.[65] Young females are most likely to be sexually abused within the family setting, often by a mother's boyfriend or a stepfather. Such sexual abuse sometimes involves rape and even pregnancy. Immature boys, on the other hand, are more likely to be victimized by male adults preying on children by offering pay or presents. Pedophiles targeting juveniles were often sexually abused themselves when they were children.

Toward the Future

One thing everyone seems to agree upon is that the contemporary family is more fragile than the family of a generation or two ago. Certainly, recent decades have been hard on the American family. While almost everyone agrees that the "Wonder Years" family of father leaving in the morning and mother staying home is history and shouldn't be brought back, but that is about as far as the agreement goes. There is severe disagreement about how to combine the best of the past with the opportunities of the present in a stable and secure family unit that values children. Some suggest that the whole idea of the family has to be abandoned.

The easiest prediction would be to suggest the continuation of the current pattern of fewer people marrying, later marriage, fewer children, high divorce rates, and high remarriage rates. More single adults, late marriage, and fewer children do seem to be the most likely pattern for the next decade. However, for those who get married there are some signs that their twenty-first-century families will differ somewhat from those of the end of the twentieth century.

[64]Richard J. Gelles, "Violence toward Children in the United States," *American Journal of Orthopsychiatry*, 48:580–592, 1978.
[65]C. C. Tower, *Understanding Child Abuse and Neglect*, Allyn and Bacon, Boston, 1989.

In the future the family as a social institution may become somewhat more stable, rather than less stable. While divorce rates remain high, they are down slightly from a decade ago. With couples marrying later and having children later, there is reason to think that families started during the new century will be economically and socially more stable. The proportion of children born to unwed mothers and especially to teenage unwed mothers is now declining. Stable gay and lesbian marriages may also become more the norm. Whether or not they are recognized legally, they will become more socially recognized.

A positive sign is that the egalitarian family is increasingly becoming the norm, and there is increasing social awareness of the needs of children. Government and business are finally beginning to adjust to meet the needs of working couples with children. Although change is coming far too slowly, more and more firms are promoting family leave and providing child-care facilities.

None of these developments portend major changes, but put together they suggest that the era of increasing family instability and rising divorce rates may be ending. During the new century the family as an institution will remain under stress, but discussions about the passing of the family may decrease. There are signs that, as a nation, we are finally discussing how to best strengthen contemporary families so they can provide emotional support, personal freedom, and proper care and nurture of the young.

Summary

Whether the American family is in a state of disintegration or transition is a matter of much dispute. What is clear is that marriage as a permanent bonding of two persons "till death do us part" has become less common. Current American divorce rates are both the highest in the nation's history and the highest for any nation where data are available.

- The typical American urban family is a nuclear, or conjugal, family consisting of a married couple and their dependent children. Blended families include children from previous marriages. Extended families include additional kin (grandparents, uncles, aunts, adult brothers and sisters, etc.).

- The contemporary urban nuclear family specializes in providing socialization and emotional security for family members with heavy demands of intimacy and emotional involvement. High rates of divorce and remarriage reflect the role of the family as the major unit of emotional support in urban society.

- In America, the norms of endogamy heavily encourage falling in love with someone of the same race, the same general ethnic background, the same religion, and the same educational and income level.

- Divorce is common in America. The rates are highest for those who marry young, who are poor, and higher for blacks than whites.

- Four out of five divorced Americans remarry. There are many variations in the success of second marriages.

- There are approximately six unmarried couples living together for every 100 married households. Living together in half of the cases results in legal union.

- Out-of-wedlock births have increased dramatically in recent decades; one-quarter of white children and two-thirds of black children are now born to unwed mothers.

- There is a considerable amount of family violence today. Men are more likely to abuse women, while women commit most child abuse. Boys are more likely than girls to suffer physical abuse and are as likely to suffer sexual abuse.

☞Key Review Terms

blended family

divorce

endogamy

egalitarian family

extended family

family

family violence

household

kinship

marriage

monogamy

national family wars

new familism

nuclear (conjugal) family

out-of-wedlock birth

patriarchal family

remarriage

romantic love

? Questions for Discussion

1. What is a family? Discuss the changing composition of the American family today.

2. What are the "national family wars?" Who are on the opposing sides and what are their positions? Where do you fall on the issue?

3. Discuss images of the family as presented on TV. How accurate are such images and how do they differ from TV images of a generation ago?

4. The text links urbanization and the loss of family functions. Discuss the changing functions of the family, such as time management, scheduling, transportation, etc.

5. The text states that the family still remains the major source of emotional support. Do you agree? How does this fit with America's ideas about romantic love?

6. Discuss American divorce rates. What are the effects of family dissolution on children?

7. Compare American patterns of mate selection with other systems. What are the advantages of the different systems?

8. What are the endogamy "rules" in our society? How do these norms work? Give examples from the lives of yourself and friends.

9. What groups in American society are most likely to stay married? Which are more likely to divorce? Why?

10. Discuss the changing attitudes toward remaining single. What factors have led to this change?

☞Suggested Resources

Stephanie Coontz, *The Way We Really Are: Coming to Terms with America's Families*, Basic Books, New York, 1997. The reality of contemporary and historical American families, and how this differs from our myths regarding the family.

William J. Goode, *World Changes in Divorce Patterns*, Yale, New Haven, CN, 1993. A demographer's examination of divorce trends in Asia, Africa, Latin America, and Europe.

Arlie Hochschild and Anne Machung, *The Second Shift: Working Parents and the Revolution at Home*, Avon, New York, 1990. An in-depth look at how dual-earner families cope with jobs and family responsibilities.

Harriette Pipes McAdoo, ed., *Family Ethnicity: Strength and Diversity*, Sage, Newbury Park, CA, 1993. A score of articles on family life among African American, Hispanic, Asian, Native American, and other American minorities.

Phyllis Moen, *Women's Two Roles: A Contemporary Dilemma*, Ashburn House, New York, 1992. The conflict between women's work roles and family roles and ways to resolve the conflicts.

David Popenoe and Jeane Bethke Elshtain, *Promises to Keep: Decline and Renewal of Marriage in America*, Rowman & Lettlefield, New York, 1996. The negative consequences for children resulting from the weakening of marriage.

Internet Connection 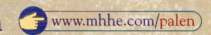 www.mhhe.com/palen

1. There are a number of sites with links to informative resources on the family. One is the University of Connecticut School of Family Studies, (*www.FamilyStudies.unconn.edu/*). Click on "Useful Links". Under "Family Policy" you will find a broad variety of sites including the conservative "Family Research Council" (*www.frc.org/home.html*); The National Network for Family Resiliency (*www.nnfr. org/home.html*); and "Find Law" (*www.findlaw.com/01topics/ 15family/index.html*).

   If you are interested in the status of same-sex marriage initiatives, this is a good site to visit. A very useful website (although somewhat dated) with links to a broad variety of family topics can be found at the University of Colorado, Department of Sociology (*www.socsci.colorado.edu/SOC/links.html*). Click on "WWW Resources for Sociologists" and then select "Family".

2. Dual worker and dual career families face formidable strains in coordinating the work activities of both spouses (or partners). Working couples with children face even greater challenges in maintaining a balanced family life. Check the Bureau of Labor Statistics website, (*www.stats.bls.gov/*), for information and news releases on family employment. A "Key Word Search" using "dual worker families" revealed several articles. One of them (*www.stats.bls.gov/news.release/famee.nws.htm*) reports that in 1998, "both parents were employed in 64 percent of married couple families with children under 18." Examine other news releases on this subject.

   Military families—families where at least one spouse is serving in the military—are especially subject to strains whenever a spouse is assigned to duties overseas for long periods of time. Even when the military spouse is at home, the rigors and demands of life in the service make it difficult for dual worker/career families. Most armed services have family support networks. The "Naval Services Family Line" (formerly "wife line") can be found at (*www.bupers.navy.mil/wifeline/wifeline1.html*). The Air Force's "Family Support Operations" website is (*www.afpc. randolph.af.mil/transition/default.htm*). The Army's "Community and Family Support Center" is located at (*www.armymwr.com/*). Briefly examine these sites.

   a. What kinds of information do they contain?
   b. Which one do you find to be most useful?

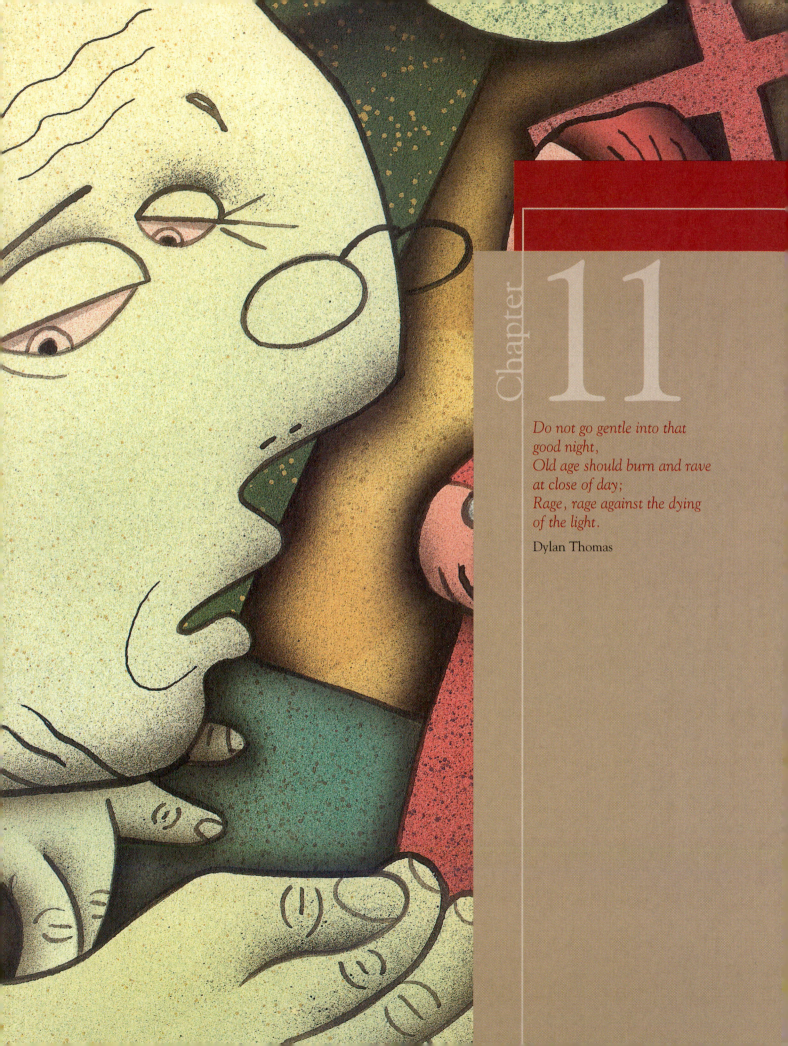

Chapter 11

Do not go gentle into that good night,
Old age should burn and rave at close of day;
Rage, rage against the dying of the light.

Dylan Thomas

Aging and Ageism

America Grows Older

While death has always been with us, aging as a social problem is new. The reason is that human societies of the past never had more than a small proportion of elderly people. Today, both the proportion and the absolute number of elderly worldwide stand at all-time highs. The same advances in public health and medicine that produced the population explosion (discussed in Chapter 6) have also, in a sense, "created" the problem of the aging. This chapter will discuss the situation in the United States, but the pattern is similar for all economically developed nations.

The graying of America is a social fact. By the year 2023 the United States will have the same proportion of persons aged 65 and over as is currently found in Florida (18.5 percent). By that time, there will be more people over 65 than under 18. Half the U.S. population now is over 36, and in a decade, half the population will be over 40 years old. Keep in mind that projections regarding the aging of the American population are not predictions but rather statements of what will occur. Those who will be the aged during our lifetime have already been born.

Some, like former Secretary of Commerce Peter Peterson, argue that the social and economic consequences of aging are fast becoming America's biggest problem.[1] It is a problem that was not anticipated. As recently as 1900, the United States had only slightly more than 3 million aged, representing just over 4 percent of the population. As the new century begins there are *35 million* Americans aged 65 and over, and the elderly represent 1 in 8 Americans. The elderly are the fastest growing segment of the American population, and the population over age 65 is increasing *twice* as fast as the population as a whole.

Additionally, more of the elderly are very old. As the century turned, there were approaching 70,000 persons in the United States over age 100, which is double the number 10 years ago. By the middle of the twenty-first century, there may be a million centenarians. The relatively vigorous and healthy "young old" (ages 65 to 74) will make up the majority of the elderly until about 2030.[2] After that, those 75 years of age and older will account for most of the elderly.

---

[1]Peter G. Peterson, *Gray Dawn: How the Coming Age Wave Will Transform America,* Random House, New York, 1999.

[2]Judith Treas, "Older Americans in the 1990s and Beyond," *Population Bulletin,* 50:6, May 1995.

Figure 11.1 Elderly Population: 1960 to 2050

(In millions)

Elderly (Aged 65 and Older)

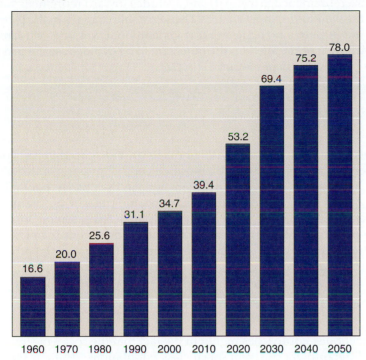

Oldest Old (Aged 85 and older)

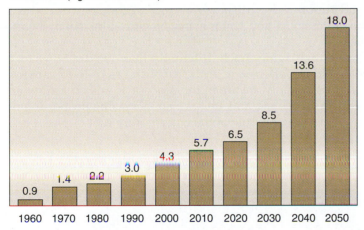

Source: U.S. Bureau of the Census.

Sociological Perspectives

Functionalist Approaches

Functionalist perspectives suggest that the role of the elderly in society is problematic. Family responsibilities of caring for the elderly have been increasingly transferred to government programs. Social programs such as Social Security and

Medicare have successfully reduced the proportion of aged living in poverty. However, in so doing the cost of the entitlement programs has become dysfunctional insofar as the programs have become the largest expenditures in the national budget and an increasing burden on the average worker. Functionalists suggest that attitudes toward retirement age (raise it) and attitudes toward retirement support (reduce it for the well-to-do) must change. Demographic changes in the proportion of elderly in the population suggest that if generational wars on one hand, or the reimpoverishment of the aged on the other, are to be avoided, social programs for the elderly need immediate reform.

Conflict Approaches

Conflict theorists see decreasing willingness to provide current levels of support for the elderly as an example of growing class conflict pitting comfortable generation Xers and middle-aged baby boomers against the elderly poor. The elderly are seen by them as an economic drain and income transfer programs as an unnecessary expense. For those taking a conflict perspective, seniors must band together as a political force to ensure their security and prevent Social Security and Medicare from suffering the cuts that are occurring to other social programs.

Interactionist Approaches

Social interactionist approaches highlight the fact that the social meaning of aging is defined differently for different social-class populations. Aging is no longer automatically associated with physical deterioration. For some, aging means being unneeded and out-of-touch with new workplace technology. For others, especially those in "the professions" and senior management, aging means increasing power and influence.

Socially we define aging much differently than we did 50 years ago. Today those 40 years old are often seen at the early stages of their career rather than the endpoint. Even legally we are in the process of raising retirement age from 65 to 70. As our society ages, and we have an increasing proportion of senior citizens, we are redefining the role of the elderly from that of passive retiree to active participant.

The Meaning of Aging

Aging is not a simple matter. There is not even an easy answer to the question of who is old and who is not. Aging can be viewed from physiological, social, or legal frameworks. In discussions of aging, the three frameworks are often confused.

Physiologically

Biological aging occurs at different times for different people. John Glenn completed his second space mission in 1998; he was 77 years old at the time. Former President George Bush went skydiving at age 72 and again at age 75. Jane Fonda has made exercise tapes in her 50s and 60s, and the model Cheryl Teigs is in her mid-50s. Harrison Ford and Robert Redford play romantic leads in their 60s. Not everyone ages the same biologically.

Generally speaking, workers involved in jobs that do not require heavy physical labor perform tasks as well as younger people at least until age 70. While some people seem old at 55, others seem to grow continually younger year by year. However, problems of loss of energy do become more common as one grows older, and after age 75 the biological aging process accelerates.

Socially

Social definitions of age are only loosely related to physical aging. A person's occupation often determines whether or not a person is socially defined as old. Michael Jordan retired as the old man of basketball at age 36. In national politics, on the other hand, people in their 30s are considered underaged youngsters. The Constitution says you must be at least 35 to serve as president. Some voters thought John F. Kennedy just too young at 42 to be running for that office. Many Americans thought President Clinton in his early 50s still not mature enough.

The age of entry into adulthood is growing later. World War II fighter and bomber pilots were in their early 20s, only a few pilots were over age 25. Today most airline passengers hearing that the pilot of their 747 is 21 years old would book another flight. Travelers are reassured to see that their 747 pilot has gray hair. Most of today's astronauts are in their 40s and many are in their 50s. Compared to earlier eras, we start careers later and end them later.

Social definitions of age differ according to social status. Lower-status groups both begin and end family and work life early. Factory workers commonly think of themselves as being of retirement age in their 50s. In the professions, on the other hand, it is usual to begin one's career in the early 30s, and to reach a career peak in the 50s and 60s. We expect corporate presidents, prominent lawyers, senators, and Supreme Court justices to be men and women of some years.

Legally

The elderly are legally defined by the U.S. Bureau of the Census and the Social Security Administration as those persons 65 years of age and over. This arbitrary chronological age has been legally enshrined as the age at which one retires, because when Social Security legislation came into effect in the 1930s, that was the designated eligibility age to receive full benefits. Sixty-five was the age chosen for retirement, not on grounds such as physical decline at that age, but because it happened to be the age used by the first modern social welfare system created in Germany in 1889. Perhaps Chancellor Otto Von Bismarck chose 65 because few workers lived to collect. When the United States chose age 65 in 1935 the average life expectancy was 62. Today the average life expectancy at birth is 76.

Age grading is based on legal chronological age, not on individual abilities or capabilities. For many of those reading this book, the most significant and recent age grading occurred at age 18 or possibly 21. Such legal age grading is based not on a person's actual level of maturity, but on reaching a chronological age. Similarly, retirement age is arbitrarily set at 65. Because government policies and programs for the elderly are based on legal definitions of age, they have practical impact whether or not all those who are legally old are declining physically, mentally, or in social power.

age grading
classifying people by age categories.

Attitudes Toward Aging

To grow old in American society is to confront a paradox. As Simone de Beauvoir observed, "Society has both the image of the white-haired and venerable sage rich in experience, and that of the old fool in his dotage, serving as a laughingstock for children. In any case, either by their virtue or by their degradation they stand outside humanity."[3]

In traditional societies of the past, the aged were often treated with respect and had clear roles as repositories of the society's accumulated wisdom and knowledge. As one grew older, one received greater privilege and honor as reflected in titles such as guru, elder, or senator. Whether the old were viewed as benign or tyrannical, they held both prestige and power.[4]

Today we are uncertain how to treat aging. Sometimes we treat it as an embarrassing circumstance, sometimes as an opportunity for self-fulfillment. Still, we worship at the shrine of youth, with much of the symbolic, ceremonial, and other practices common to organized religions. Billions of dollars are spent annually on cosmetics, clothing styles, dieting fads, and surgical procedures designed to maintain or restore youthful appearances. Couples pictured in advertisements show the male with a little silver around the temples, and his wife may have had a little unobtrusive "work" done, but they are constantly active. Television ads proclaim that the fountain of youth is attainable; women can remain forever young by using Oil of Olay, and men by using Grecian Formula or Just for Men hair coloring.

Even the American Association of Retired Persons has changed. Now the name is just AARP. *Modern Maturity*, AARP's magazine reflects the change. Until 1999 the magazine focused on a white-haired older generation; now the cover has pictures of sexy 50-somethings like Susan Sarandon and titles like, "Great Sex, What's Age Got to Do with it."

Ageism

ageism

prejudice and discrimination against the elderly.

Ageism is prejudice or discrimination against the elderly. It involves stereotyping or labeling the elderly as being out of date, rigid, set in their ways, grouchy, physically decrepit, and either senile or on their way to senility. A youth-oriented culture often regards the elderly as nonpersons or as an unwanted minority group.

Not having a positive role model of the aged, we sometimes fall back on treating older people as nonproductive dependents who are not entitled to full participation or rights in the society. Simone de Beauvoir notes, "It is not mere chance that makes families speak of a child who is 'extraordinary for his age' and also of an old man who is 'extraordinary for his age': the extraordinariness lies in their behaving like human beings when they are either not yet or no longer men."[5] Interestingly, the supposed "benefits" given the elderly—such as reduced bus fares, reduced admission to theaters, and special meal programs—are the same benefits that are given to children. It is worth noting that those singled out for special programs are generally seen as being unable to contribute an "adult" share to the society.

American society does not socialize people for growing older, so there is no clear cultural pattern to dictate how the elderly should be treated, or even addressed.

[3]Simone de Beauvoir, *The Coming of Age,* G. P. Putnam's Sons, New York, 1972, p. 4.
[4]David Hackett Fischer, *Growing Old in America,* Oxford University Press, New York, 1977.
[5]Simon de Beauvior, *Coming of Age,* p. 217.

Aging doesn't mean dropping out. With this 1999 cover featuring Susan Sarandon Modern Maturity, *published by AARP, deliberately set out to update its image and appeal to Baby Boomers.*

Photo of Susan Sarandon by Theo Westenberger. Cover reprinted by permission of Modern Maturity magazine and AARP.

The elderly are "senior citizens" or "golden agers." Who or what is a senior citizen? The name itself has an unintended air of condescension about it, suggesting that older citizens required a special label.

Graying Baby Boomers

A wave of elderly is coming. One in three Americans belongs to the large **baby boom** generation (born 1946–1964), and as this population becomes grayer, the nation ages with it. The baby boomers are already in their 50s and boomers will begin reaching age 65 in 2011. At midcentury, when many reading this will be retiring, there will be 80 million people 65 and over, and they will account for 1 in 5

baby boom
the dramatic rise in births following World War II until 1964.

Box 11.1 Making a Difference

D-Day Jump 50 Years Later

Not everyone in their 70s and 80s is ready to take to their rocking chairs. Some prefer to parachute out of planes. The Allies' invasion of Europe began on June 6, 1944, led by parachute jumps by the Airborne. On June 6, 1994, the fiftieth anniversary of D-Day, 33 veterans of the original jump strapped on their parachutes and repeated their historic jump into Normandy. The jumpers ranged in age from 67 to 83.

Some of the men had not jumped since World War II, some were still scared to death of jumping, but they did it to honor their fallen comrades. Until almost the last second, Pentagon officials opposed the jump. The Pentagon brass didn't fancy the idea of septuagenarians hurtling from the sky in the midst of the tightly scheduled events to commemorate the liberation of Europe; they wanted to substitute young reinactors.

The ex-paratroopers were adamant, however. The French, who view the World War II paratroopers as heroes, said they could jump from French planes. As one jumper said, "These men will sign any kind of waiver and even pay their own way over if they have

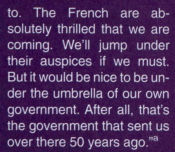

Former President George Bush at age 75 making a 12,500-foot parachute jump at the U.S. Army Yuma Proving Ground in Arizona. Bush jumped with the U.S. Army Golden Knights parachute team.

Mike Nelson/AP/Wide World Photos

to. The French are absolutely thrilled that we are coming. We'll jump under their auspices if we must. But it would be nice to be under the umbrella of our own government. After all, that's the government that sent us over there 50 years ago."[a]

Finally, the Pentagon gave in and said the elderly paratroopers could jump if each veteran proved his fitness by making three practice parachute jumps before coming. The ex-paratroopers jumped without a hitch. As one of the jumpers in his 70s remarked, "It won't replace sex, but it's the next best thing."[b]

[a] Ken Ringle, "Leaping Back into History," *Washington Post*, February 21, 1994, p. B11.F
[b] Ibid.

---

gerontology
study of aging and the aging process.

Americans.[6] Never before in history has any society had such a high proportion of elderly citizens. Not surprisingly, **gerontology,** the scientific study of aging is a rapidly developing field.

Other Countries

A rapidly aging population is not unique to the United States. Europe and Japan have even more rapidly aging populations; for example, in Japan a quarter of the population will be 65 and over by 2024, a circumstance that may put a huge brake

---

[6]Judith Treas, "U.S. Aging: 'Golden Oldies' Remain Vulnerable," *Population Today,* May 1995, p. 1.

306

Figure 11.2 Population Age Structure

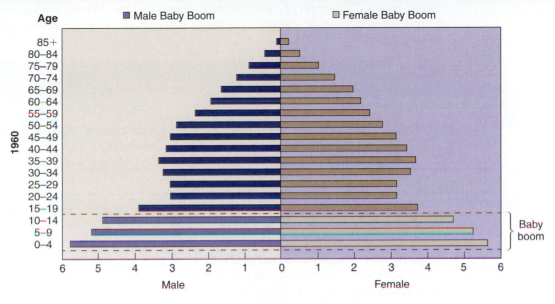

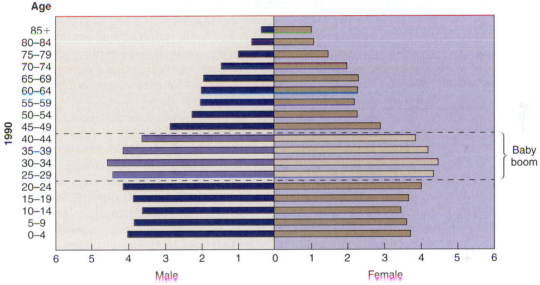

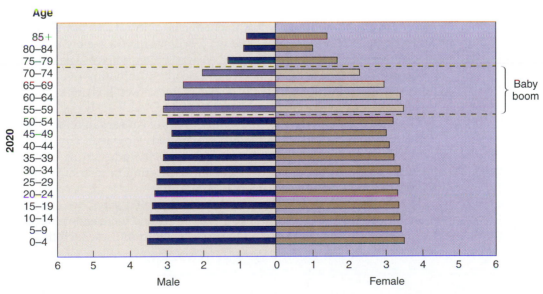

Source: U.S. Bureau of the Census.

on Japan's economic growth. Depending on which economic and demographic projections are used, Japanese social security payments as of 2024 will consume between 63 and 71 percent of Japan's total national income. Obviously, having aging populations has major economic, political, and social consequences for all developed nations.

The Consequences

The consequences of the graying of America are uncertain, but what is known is that the demographic shift to an older population structure will deeply affect the tax base, labor force, social services, public policies, and consumer purchases. With mandatory retirement now removed, will the elderly retire at ever later ages, thereby blocking the paths to promotion (or even retention) for younger workers? Or will a more mature trained workforce result in increased productivity?

Economic Consequences If more goods are produced who will buy them? Will an aging population purchase as many clothes, cars, and refrigerators as younger populations? If they do not, how can major industrial sectors maintain their prosperity? Will residential real estate markets wither with fewer people in the young family formation years, or will new markets develop especially to target the housing needs of the elderly? More retirement communities, particularly those having continuing care facilities, are likely to be built. Will an older population exhibit a reluctance to change or take speculative economic risks on new technologies? More funds should be available for investment, but will the elderly be willing to make capital investments in new ideas?

Virtually no aspect of American life—educational, economic, political, or recreational—will remain untouched by the aging of America. For example, older populations are often more reluctant to invest public tax monies in infrastructure and public schools; school bond issues increasingly encounter resistance from older taxpayers. However, retirement benefits depend on having well-educated successors who are able to pay the taxes to support Social Security and Medicare. Schools are an investment in one's retirement. It is reasonable to anticipate proportionately less money being spent on maternity wards and elementary schools, and more funds for nursing homes and programs for the elderly. Already, excluding interest on the national debt, half the federal budget goes to the elderly.

Social Consequences Socially, will a graying population remain vital and innovative, or will it be slow to change its cultural and political ideas, preferring to look back to the "good old days?" Will we have a society increasingly stratified along age lines? Will the gray society be an active society or dreary and colorless? Will it be a population of old people ruminating over old ideas in old houses? Most think not, but again, no one really knows. It is unlikely, however, that the diverse elderly population will act in unison.

Politically, the elderly tend to be more socially conservative, so some swing toward conservative positions might be expected. However, any political conservatism of the elderly most emphatically does *not* include cutting back governmental support for the aged. Political leaders attempting to restrict Social Security or Medicare benefits put their careers in jeopardy.

Medically, even in an era of ever-shorter hospital stays, we should anticipate more hospital facilities being built for the elderly and increasing emphasis on training programs for medical and other personnel to staff these facilities.

Japan's prominent woman's movement leader Fuki Kushida speaking at a press conference on her 100th birthday on February 17, 1999 about a forthcoming women's march. Ms. Kushida now has lived in three centuries.

Katsumi Kashara/AP/Wide World Photos

Even advertising, which has long glorified youth, is now beginning to adjust to a more mature population. Pepsi-Cola ads, which once featured the "Pepsi Generation" teenyboppers, now target an adult market with the slogan, "Act Young. Drink Pepsi." Levi Strauss, whose jeans became the symbol of the youth culture, now has an aging baby-boom clientele and is attempting to adjust to widening waist sizes with "relaxed fit" products. Movies with middle-aged lovers such as *The Bridges of Madison County,* with Clint Eastwood and Meryl Streep, are likely to increase.

The impact of an **aging population** will be felt on the nation's highways, where a sharp increase in elderly drivers will affect both the traffic flow and the accident rate. Will the young be tolerant of sharply increasing numbers of slow-moving older drivers with large autos and slow reflexes? Driving behind an older person going 40 mph on an expressway may produce more generational hostility than higher Social Security taxes.

aging population
the increasing average age of the nation's people.

Gender Differences in Longevity

America's elderly population is increasingly a female population. This is because there is one undisputed area of sexual inequality worldwide: Women almost everywhere outlive men. In America the average female outlives the average male by seven years (73 years for males compared to 79 years for females).[7] In order to ensure roughly equal numbers at time of mating, nature provides that some 105 boys are born for every 100 girls. Because of higher male mortality, by age 30 females already outnumber males.

---

[7]U.S. Bureau of the Census, *Statistical Abstract of the United States, 1999,* Government Printing Office, Washington, DC, 1999.

Research indicates that the mortality difference between the sexes is biological, not social: Women are built better to last longer. Even when factors such as occupation and lifestyle are controlled, women fare better.[8] Women's mortality from external causes—accidents, suicide, and homicide—is only one-third that of men, but even when deaths from violence and accidents are excluded, the age-adjusted death rate from natural causes for women is still only 60 percent of that for men.

The effects of female longevity are particularly noticeable when one looks at the elderly population. Today there are only 60 males for every 100 females among Americans aged 65 and older. Among those aged 85 and over, there are only 39 males per 100 females. Moreover, the surplus of females is growing larger. Soon there will be only one elderly male over 65 for every two elderly females.

Women's greater longevity means that social and economic programs for the elderly are mostly programs for older women. Women are more likely to outlive a spouse; thus while three out of four older males are living with their wives, only one-third of the women 65 and over live with their husbands. Socially, this means that elderly males are in great demand as companions if they can only manage to survive. Retirement communities for the elderly, such as the "Sun Cities" of Florida and the Southwest, tend to have heavily female populations. Couples move into the community, but higher male mortality rates soon produce a surplus of widows.

Problems of the Elderly

Massive increases in the number of elderly can conjure up the image of a population beset with chronic illnesses and dimming minds. However, the major problems of most old people are not biological but social. This is especially true of the young old under age 75.

Role Transitions

Retirement Retirement from work is a new social phenomenon. Through most of the millennia that humanity has occupied this globe, people ended their work life not by retiring but by dying. At the beginning of the twentieth century, two-thirds of all American men aged 65 and over were still working. At the end of the twentieth century only a quarter of the men and a tenth of the women aged 65 and over were employed.

There is no consensus among the elderly on what age is ideal for stopping work. There is a conflict of goals: whether to retire young and get some enjoyment out of life (while also giving a younger worker a chance) or to continue to work and retire later. Some older workers are fighting mandatory retirement. Others are battling just as vigorously for early retirement. It is worth noting that at General Motors, where the retirement age is 65, the average retirement age is 58. Only 2 percent of the blue-collar workers and 11 percent of the salaried employees at GM stay on to age 65. Most Americans retire as soon as they can afford to do so.

---

[8]Francis C. Madigan, "Are Sex Mortality Differentials Biologically Caused?" *Milbank Memorial Fund Quarterly*, 35:202–223, April 1957.

Problem or Promise? It seems paradoxical that some older workers fight for later retirement while others press for the opposite. However, this becomes easier to understand if we consider the different jobs these workers hold. When one's work defines one's social status, loss of work may be traumatic. Loss of an occupational role can mean the loss of social identity. Retirement can have an emotional impact similar to divorce.

On the other hand, those who do routine, dirty, or just plain dull tasks almost universally look forward to retirement. Assembly-line workers, coal miners, laundry workers, or even most office workers are unlikely to want to work any longer than necessary. In practice, most workers (male and female) retire early and begin receiving reduced Social Security payments when they are 62 years of age. Only about 30 percent of retired people report having difficulty with retirement. For those who have already established interests, "leisure-time" activities—such as building furniture, participating in a hobby, taking college courses, joining professional groups, or even being a Boy Scout leader—become their real work. For the retired who have money, retirement means the chance to do what they have always wanted.

Financial Problems

Thanks to Social Security and Medicare, which provides government health insurance for those over 65, poverty is no longer endemic in the older population. As recently as 1960, 35 percent of all persons aged 65 or over had incomes below the poverty level. By the late 1990s, this had been cut to 10 percent.[9] Among households with assets, those households headed by someone over 65 had an average net worth of $88,192 compared to the United States average of $36,623.[10] However, most of the net worth of older people consists of home ownership, so the figures overstate accessible assets. Still, whereas in 1970 the elderly were the poorest segment of the population, today, adjusting for factors such as household size, taxes, and noncash benefits such as health insurance, the elderly have a median per capita income two-thirds higher than that of the population as a whole.[11] Only about 5 percent of the elderly live in subsidized or public housing, and roughly 5 percent receive food stamps.

The general improvement in the status of the elderly, however, has not been equally shared. Some 28 percent of older African Americans and 21 percent of older Hispanics are below the poverty level.

Wealth Disparity The wealth (accumulated assets) of those approaching retirement age varies enormously. Among whites aged 51 to 61, the richest tenth hold 10 times as much wealth as the poorest tenth. In 1993, the richest tenth had $944,046 in assets per household while the poorest had $88,640.[12] (The figures seem high because, along with household wealth such as houses, real estate, stocks and bonds, the figures also include projected pension benefits and Social Security payments.)

For African Americans of the same ages, the figures are much lower; $495,851 for those in the highest tenth and $26,285 for those in the bottom tenth. Most "assets"

---

[9]National Institution on Aging, *Aging in the United States—Past, Present, and Future,* Bureau of Census, Washington D.C., July, 1997.

[10]U.S. Bureau of the Census, *Household Wealth and Asset Ownership: 1991, Current Population Reports,* P70–34, Washington, DC, 1994, Table 1.

[11]Lester C. Thurow, "The Birth of a Revolutionary Class," *New York Times Magazine,* May 19, 1996, p. 47.

[12]Data come from a 1995 study done by James P. Smith for the RAND Corporation (a nonprofit think tank), and are based on data collected by the University of Michigan Survey Research Institute.

of the poor consist of small pensions and Social Security. With fewer companies offering pensions it is clear that most Americans are not saving enough for their future retirement.

Generational Wars? With increasing numbers of elderly consuming ever-larger portions of the federal budget, are generational tensions going to assume the same importance as social class and race do now? Will class warfare in the twenty-first century come to be defined as the young against the old more than the rich against the poor? Are the elderly going to become increasingly protective of their benefit programs, while the young become increasingly resentful of paying higher taxes for programs from which they may never benefit?

Medicare

federal program financed from Society Security tax to provide health care for those 65 and older.

Medicare, which provides health care for the elderly, currently consumes 11 percent of the federal budget, and it is growing at 10 percent a year. By 2005 this program alone is projected to be 17 percent of the budget (by comparison, the military now takes 21 percent).[13]

Cost increases over the next decades are going to weigh more and more heavily on young and middle-aged workers. For several decades pundits have prophesied age wars as the resentment of younger workers increases, but so far there is little evidence of this. Partly this is because ties between the generations remain strong, and cutbacks affect one's own parents or grandparents. Self-interest also plays a part, for most workers understand that sharp cutbacks in government programs for the elderly will quickly translate into burdens shifted to younger family members.

Health and the Aging Process

Most elderly are hale and hearty, but health problems become both more serious and more numerous as we age. Older people are particularly affected by chronic or degenerative diseases such as arthritis, diabetes, and hypertension. Cancer and heart disease also strike the aged in disproportionate numbers. Most older persons report at least one chronic health problem.[14] However, most are not bedridden or in need of nursing care. Only 5 percent of the elderly are in nursing homes, and another 10 percent at most could use such care. The watershed age appears to be 75, with illness and disability problems beginning to take a major toll beyond that point.

Elderly people, not surprisingly, use more health services than younger people. The elderly average 11 doctor visits a year compared to 5 for other adults. The real difference, however, comes in hospital usage. For every 1,000 older persons there were 265 hospital usages, compared to 66 per 1,000 for those under 65.[15] Some 40 percent of all hospital beds are occupied by people 65 and over. This dramatically boosts the cost of elderly health care. Most seniors spend more than 15 percent of their income on medical care.[16] As the proportion of old elderly (75 and over) increases, there will necessarily be increasing problems of caring for the frail and incapacitated.[17]

---

[13]Robin Toner, "No Free Rides: Generational Push Has Not Come to Shove," *New York Times,* December 31, 1995, p. E-1.

[14]Judith Treas, "Older Americans in the 1990s and Beyond," *Population Bulletin,* 50, no. 2, May 1995, p. 32.

[15]National Center for Health Statistics, *Health and the United States, 1993,* Public Health Service, Hyattsville, MD, 1994, pp. 171, 180.

[16]Claudia Rhodes, "Aging America: Changing Responsibilities for Local Governments," *Public Management,* 71:2, 1989.

[17]Laura Katz Olson (ed.), *The Graying of the World: Who Will Care for the Frail Elderly,* Haworth, New York, 1994.

Box 11.2 Ongoing Issues

The Unwelcome Young

For some, retirement may mean a move to a retirement community, probably in the Sunbelt (some 3 in 10 Florida households are elderly[a]). Sun Cities designed for retirees often ban permanent residents under 18 years of age through age covenants written into deeds. This is done both for social reasons and to keep local property taxes low. While the Federal Fair Housing Act prohibits discrimination on the grounds of race, religion, sex, or family status, it does allow discrimination against children. This excerpt concerns the banning of a young boy from the nation's oldest retirement community of Youngstown, Arizona.

Bob and Peggy Jennings are standing in front of a model of their new home in the retirement community of Sun City Grand being built in Suprise, Arizona. They are two of the 23,500 retirees that move into Arizona every month.

Tricia McInroy/AP/Wide

"Fresh-faced and direct, 16-year-old Chaz Cope would seem to be the ideal poster boy for this Phoenix suburb of sunshine and orange trees. Instead, this retirement community sees him as human contraband. While Youngstown allows dogs, the City Council has voted unanimously to fine Chaz's grandparents $100 a day for illegally housing a child.

" 'All we wanted was permission for him to stay until he finished high school, only 16 months,' Lynne Rae Naab, the boy's grandmother said. . . . Chad moved here to escape physical abuse by his stepfather in another part of the state. . . . Last summer, when the Naabs first applied for a variance to the age ban, they had to pay $300 to file the application. Then town officials posted a sign on the lawn of their modest bungalow to inform neighbors that the Naabs intended to house a child.

"Leaders of retirement communities say they bar children to insure peace and quiet, and to avoid having to provide schools, which would mean higher taxes. 'Young people kind of like to hassle the old people,' said Lucille Retheford, the 75-year-old president of the Youngstown Historical Society. 'If we had young families in here, we would have to put in an elementary school, swings, sidewalks.' She estimated that with children around, new school taxes would double the average tax bill for houses here, now about $300 a year."[b]

[a] Bureau of the Census, "Housing of the Elderly," Statistical Brief, SB/94–33, January 1995, p. 1.

Medicare for those 65 and over has strict guidelines and payment limits. It does not cover long-term hospitalization for problems such as Alzheimer's disease, which affects millions and is becoming more common as overall age increases. Nursing home care averages $37,000 a year, so even substantial family assets can soon be depleted. While the poor can apply for Medicaid, the middle-class are squeezed by high long-term costs. Thus, while many seniors are living longer and more independent lives, some lack needed long-term care services. Old age is experienced much differently by different groups.[18]

---

[18]Eleanor Palo Stoller and Rose Campbell Gibson, *Worlds of Difference: Inequality in the Aging Experience,* Pine Forge, Thousand Oaks, CA, 1994.

Bill Graham/AP/Wide World Photos

A negative myth about older persons is that the elderly inevitably experience mental decline. In fact, research suggests that there is no necessary decline in mental ability with age. Rather, when and if such losses do occur, they are likely to be fairly dramatic. Alzheimer's disease, the leading cause of dementia in older persons, affects 3.8 million aged. The possibility of having Alzheimer's disease is less than 4 percent for the noninstitutionalized population aged 65 to 74, but reaches half (48 percent) for those 86 and older.[19] When precipitous mental deterioration occurs, death frequently shortly follows.

Urban Vulnerability

While the aged don't have the highest victimization rates, they fear crime more. Because of their age and physical weakness, the aged elderly, particularly those living in declining urban areas, fear burglary, assault, and robbery.[20] Swindlers and confidence men also prey on the elderly as easy marks who are unlikely to go to the authorities or act as reliable witnesses if a case ever gets to court.

A number of factors contribute to the vulnerability of older persons:

1. The poorer elderly live in public housing or apartments that are located in high crime-rate areas. Furthermore, many older people are sickly or weak and unable to protect themselves from assault.

2. Older people generally have fixed incomes. Thus, they are eager to take advantage of any proposition that promises to provide them with supplementary income, and they are inexperienced or gullible enough to fall for get-rich-quick schemes.

---

[19]Denis A. Evans et al., "Estimated Prevalence of Alzheimer's Disease in the United States," *Milbank Quarterly*, 68:274, Spring, 1990.
[20]Russell Ward, Mark LaGory, and Susan Sherman, "Fear of Crime among the Elderly as Person/Environment Interaction," *Sociological Quarterly*, 27:327–341, 1986.

3. Sometimes the elderly can be taken in by apparent friendliness shown them by strangers. They are not always aware of the many schemes to part them from their money, and confidence games work precisely because of this naivete.

4. Many old people become desperate because of illness, pain, or infirmity their doctors cannot help. They are willing to try almost anything promising relief from fear and pain.

Con artists operating outside the law, and "legitimate" businesses operating just inside its flexible boundaries, have long found the elderly a ready market for scams, questionable and overpriced goods, and unneeded services. Telemarketing scams have become increasingly prevalent in recent years. AARP estimates that there are 14,000 fraudulent telemarketing businesses operating nationwide.[21] Almost as bad, according to AARP readers, are the "Big Four" sweepstakes companies—American Family Publishers, Publishers Clearing House, Reader's Digest, and Time Inc.[22] Several state attorneys general are suing the "Big Four" for deceiving consumers into believing they have won big money or implying that purchasing products increases the chances of winning (it doesn't). In late 1999 the sweepstakes giant, Publishers Clearing House, settled a class-action lawsuit charging deceptive practices.[23] Class-action suits are pending against the remaining three.

Because of their health needs, elderly people more often get fleeced by alleged health aids and medical cures. Some quackeries, such as copper bracelets or belts to prevent rheumatism and other ailments, are unlikely to cause serious damage. However, over $1 billion a year is spent on unnecessary vitamin and food supplements, some of which are dangerous to elderly users, as well as harmful to the user's pocketbook.

Schemes featuring "revolutionary cures" directly prey on the fears and sometimes the physical pain of those suffering from diseases including cancer, arthritis, heart disease, and diabetes. The elderly person is persuaded that the machine, pills, or injections are a "miracle discovery" that will end pain and suffering. It is claimed that the treatment or device is not being used by medical doctors because of a plot by the medical profession to restrict new treatments. Since medical science cannot cure certain painful afflictions—arthritis, for example—the elderly victim is sometimes desperate enough to try any medication that holds out the hope of cure. Expensive pseudomedical quackery (such as supposed cancer-curing drugs) sometimes kill patients—not so much through the treatments themselves as through the patient's failure to receive legitimate medical attention while it might still be of some help.

Another area in which the elderly are particularly vulnerable is home repair schemes. Even though most such schemes are far older than their elderly victims, swindlers posing as city building inspectors still manage to deceive people. They begin by persuading older homeowners that their heating plants are dangerously defective or that their roof is about to collapse. Then the "inspector's" cohorts sell the victims unnecessary and high-priced furnaces or roof repairs. In some swindles, no work is ever done. The "contractors" demand payment in advance for "necessary" roofing or driveway repairs and then simply disappear with the money.

Finally, there are the confidence schemes that depend on persuading elderly victims to withdraw their savings from their bank. One venerable ploy is to call an elderly mark and claim to be an FBI agent or a bank representative. The victim is told that his or her help is needed to entrap a clever bank embezzler and is asked, with this end in mind, to withdraw funds for a 24-hour period. Once the funds have been withdrawn, the confidence artist may simply switch the envelope containing the money for another filled with wadded paper. An alternative maneuver

---

[21]"AARP Hits 'Phoney' Callers," *AARP Bulletin*, September 1996, p. 1.

[22]Patricia Barry, "Readers Narrate Sweepstake Woes," *AARP Bulletin*, September 1999, p. 4.

[23]Jane Bryant Quinn, "Sweepstakes Settlement Latest Surrender in an Ongoing War," *Washington Post Writers Group*, October 18, 1999.

is to offer to save the elderly person the trip back to the bank to return the funds and have a uniformed "bank messenger" pick up the money and give a worthless receipt.

Suburban Isolation

As noted in Chapter 7 we are now a suburban nation, and suburbs can present a special set of problems for the elderly. It had been assumed that as suburban "empty nesters" aged they would sell their large homes and return to city apartments or condominiums. However, the elderly are staying in their own homes, and as a consequence the suburbs are graying.[24] Among Americans aged 65 to 74, a quarter live alone, and half of those 75 and over live alone.[25]

Suburban elderly who own their own homes have some financial security.[26] However, living in a single-family home requires the physical ability to do maintenance and make repairs. It also may require going up and down stairs. Older suburbanites also are almost completely dependent on personal automobiles for shopping, getting a meal, or going anywhere. Even those without driver's licenses (because they can no longer pass the vision test) sometimes continue driving because they feel they have no choice. Without a car, they are isolated and cannot perform even routine daily tasks.

The Future of Social Security

Since its founding in 1935, Social Security administrators have used terms such as "insurance" "pension plan," "trust fund," and "earned income." All of these terms are misleading. Social Security is not a pension plan in which you lay away funds in your own account. Legally, Social Security or OASDI is a pay-as-you-go income-transfer program in which workers contribute funds to those already retired in the expectation that the same will one day be done for them. Benefits are paid from taxes levied on those currently working. The Supreme Court has continually ruled that Americans have no contractual right to Social Security. Thus the commitment is political, not legal. However, not to keep the commitment is politically unthinkable. Nonetheless, one poll indicated that more people under age 35 believe in UFOs than believe Social Security will be there when they retire.[27]

Social Security—officially Old Age, Survivors, Disability and Insurance (OASDI)—paid $337 billion in benefits to 43.4 million retirees, disabled, and surviving spouses and children. A retiree's spouse also receives a check for half the amount coming to the retiree, regardless of whether the spouse has been in the paid workforce. (Working spouses can take either what they themselves have earned or half their partner's amount, whichever is larger.)

Retired Americans feel they have earned their benefits and strongly resist any attempt to reform the system. Social Security is known among Washington politi-

Social Security
federal pension-like program that provides monthly payments to eligible elderly participants.

---

[24]Kevin M. Fitspatrick and John R. Logan, "The Aging of the Suburbs, 1960–1980," *American Sociological Review,* 50:106–117, 1985.
[25]U.S. Bureau of the Census, *Marital Status and Living Arrangements: March 1991, Current Population Reports,* P20–461, Washington, DC, 1992, p. 11.
[26]Michael Gutowski and Tracey Field, *The Graying of Suburbia,* Urban Institute, Washington, DC, 1979.
[27]George Church and Richard Lacayo, "Social Insecurity," *Time,* March 20, 1995, p. 24.

cians as the "third rail," touch it and you are dead. The problem is that if the system isn't modified it will go bankrupt when the 77 million baby boomers born between 1946 and 1964 begin retiring in 2011.

Social Security is the single largest federal expenditure. Together, Social Security, Medicare, and other programs for the elderly represent a full one-third of the national budget. Two-thirds of all workers already pay more in Social Security and Medicare taxes than in income taxes. This was not always the case. Until 1950 the maximum Social Security tax was only $30 a year, and in 1963 the maximum was $135 a year (as of 2000 the maximum was $4,724). Thus, many of the older elderly who currently receive Social Security payments have paid comparatively small amounts into the system. A person retiring in 1990 received more than they had contributed after being retired for 4 years. Today it takes 8 years after retirement, or age 73, before anyone retiring breaks even, and for those retiring in 2010 the break even point will come after 12 years, or at age 77.

Social Security is the nation's most effective antipoverty program. One in three seniors was poor in 1960; today it is 1 in 10. Two-thirds of Social Security recipients count on the program for at least half of their income. Poorer recipients get proportionally more than they paid into the system, but Social Security benefits still tend to perpetuate the existing status quo. For example, older minority workers who, because of job discrimination, were unable to earn decent wages when they were working often qualify for little more than minimum benefits. One-fourth of black males and one-fifth of black females draw only the minimum benefits. The system perpetuates the wage disparities of working years. The average 65-year-old worker who retired in 2000 was entitled to a payment of $804 a month, or $9,648 a year, while the maximum payment in 2000 was $1,433 a month or $17,196 a year.[28]

Future Problems

The current Social Security surplus is only a paper surplus because the Treasury Department has long "borrowed "the surplus funds to pay for ongoing government expenses and left a Treasury bond IOU. For example, in 1995 some $58 billion dollars were borrowed from the Social Security surplus and spent on other government programs. In 1999 the Republican Congress claimed to have balanced the budget without touching Social Security funds, but their own Congressional Budget Office said they took $17 billion from Social Security.[29] These IOUs, of course, eventually have to be paid out of monies raised by taxes when the IOU bonds have to be redeemed. The crunch will come when the baby boomers retire.

Social Security's companion program, Medicare, enacted in 1965, provides medical care and hospital coverage to the elderly, and has more severe financial troubles. Medicare costs were $176 billion in 1995, and $286 billion in 2000.[30] Medicare costs work out to more than $600 a year for every adult and child in the United States. To make the current Medicare program solvent for the next 75 years will require payroll tax increases of 175 percent or program cuts of 65 percent.[31] Congress in 1997 provided a series of patch-up changes to Medicare to allow it to remain solvent until 2007, and budget surpluses have extended that deadline.

Social Security and Medicare cost problems largely come from our success in raising life expectancy. In 1935 when the Social Security system was set up with an eligibility age of 65, life expectancy was 62. Today a male who has survived

---

[28]"Fact Sheet Social Security," Social Security Administration Website, January 2000.
[29]"Congress Makes a Deal," *New York Times on the Web*, November 16, 1999.
[30]Robert J. Samuelson, "Beneath Medicare Furor Lie Hard Facts," *Washington Post*, May 10, 1995.
[31]U.S. House of Representatives, Ways and Means Committee, *The 1994 Green Book*, Government Printing Office, Washington, DC, 1994, p. 182.

to age 65 can expect to live 15 more years, and a female another 19 years. This means that if a woman receives a payment of $1,000 a month she can expect to receive a total payment of $220,000, plus the yearly cost-of-living increases. If she has medical expenses, and most do, the average woman's cost will be $320,000, not counting the yearly cost-of-living increases. A surviving wife whose husband dies when she is in her 50s could expect to collect monthly payments for 30 years or more.

Not only are recipients collecting for more years, but the number of recipients is also growing proportionately faster than the number of workers contributing to the system. At the end of World War II, there were 35 wage earners for every recipient of Social Security benefits. By the 1960s there were seven workers paying taxes for every one collecting. Today, there are three workers paying taxes for every Social Security beneficiary. By the time most current college students retire, there will be only two workers per each retiree.

Proposed Solutions

Politicians fear to reform Social Security and Medicare because elderly voters (including those who oppose other public assistance) actively work against politicians who suggest modifying current benefits. Politicians know that the only alternatives that will preserve the system involve scaling back benefits, raising taxes, or raising the retirement age—or a combination of the above. Proposals to use the budget surplus for Social Security don't solve the system's problems, but simply postpone them. As the chairman of the 13-member Advisory Council on Social Security says, "If we stick to the plain old pay-as-you-go system, we will have to raise taxes or cut benefits."[32]

The reality is that balancing income and outlays could be done now through a couple of adjustments. The longer the adjustments are put off, the greater the cost. The first of the adjustments would be a more accurate formula for COLA (cost-of-living adjustment) increases. The economist Michael Boskin estimates that the Consumer Price Index overstates inflation by as much as two percentage points.[33] The more accepted figure by economists is that it overstates inflation by 1.1 percent.[34] If COLA was reduced by one point, this alone would eliminate approximately *two-thirds* of the projected Social Security deficiency. Senator (and sociologist) Daniel Patrick Moynihan has proposed such an adjustment (see Box 11.3).[35] The second change that most reformers also suggest is to gradually raise the age of retirement to 70 by the latter half of the twenty-first century. Given that people are living longer (some 10 million baby boomers are expected to live to at least 90 years of age), and that professional careers often aren't even begun until people are in their 30s, the work-till-70 pattern makes demographic sense.

Another disputed change that may occur is permitting the Social Security Administration to invest limited amounts of its funds in stocks. Since stocks historically pay more over the long run, it is argued that this change would put more money into the system. Conservatives' privatized version of this idea calls for allowing younger workers to put some amount of their Social Security payments

---

[32]Edward Gramlich, quoted in, "Where Candidates Fear to Tread," *Time,* April 1, 1996, p. 38.

[33]Quoted in Thomas Jones, "Social Security: Invaluable, Irreplaceable, and Fixable," *The Participant,* Teachers Insurance and Annuity Association, February 1996, p. 5.

[34]"Greenspan Again Asks Better CPI," *Associated Press News Service,* March 5, 1997.

[35]Daniel Patrick Moynihan, "How to Preserve the Safety Net," *U.S. News and World Report,* April 20, 1998, p. 25.

Box 11.3

Making a Difference

Preserving the Safety Net

Daniel Patrick Moynihan, who retired in 2001, was considered the most knowledgeable person in the U.S. Senate on Social Security. Here are excerpts of his thoughts:[a]

"There is now abroad a powerful set of distinguished academics and political activists who would turn the 60-year-old system of Social Security retirement, disability, and survivor's benefits over to a system that depends entirely on personal savings invested in the market. There are those who hold the belief—doctrinal in many ways—that the experience of stock market investors in a time of great economic growth can be easily applied to an entire population. Some adherents to this philosophy believe Social Security is a failed plan that perhaps should never have been put in place and now should be 'transitioned' out as the new term has it. They promise instead to make you a millionaire in the stock market.

"I don't think that will happen.

"The legislation I introduced with Sen. Bob Kerrey of Nebraska includes optional personal retirement accounts into which can be deposited up to 2 percent of wages. We can thus respond to the argument of the privatizers without compromising the basic structure of the Social Security program.

"The time to act is now, because we have a balanced federal budget for the first time in almost 30 years and because Social Security's problems become more difficult the longer we delay. . . . Under our bill, private accounts would complement Social Security, not replace it. Markets go up, but they also, frequently, go down. The best approach for Social Security in the 21st century is a three-tier system of the Social Security annuity, a private pension—which about half of Americans enjoy—and private savings. . . . Social Security, one of the great achievements of our government in this century, is ours to maintain. We can preserve it, and citizens ought not to think otherwise."

[a]Daniel Patrick Moynihan, "How to Preserve the Safety Net: Return to a 'Pay as You Go' System and Allow for Private Accounts," U.S. News and World Report, April 20, 1998, p. 25.

into private, individual Social Security investment accounts. Some variations also mandate that a portion be invested in "riskless" investments that earn less but are guaranteed to provide retirement benefits at roughly the poverty-level line.

The problem with individually managed accounts is that those who would do best are those who understand investment strategies and can stand some risk of capital—that is the rich and well-to-do. Also, how do you protect against naive investors putting their funds in highly speculative stocks? Historically, market movement is variable. All bull markets eventually run their course and turn downward. If workers are invested in stocks, what happens if at retirement time the market collapses, or even if there is a lengthy recession? The whole idea of Social Security is not to provide major retirement income, but to provide a basic safety net. The goal is a predictable and secure income, not one that fluctuates with market movements.

Without reforms, it is likely that Social Security will gradually evolve into a need-based program for the poor, rather than the current system of being an entitlement roughly based on the amount the worker has contributed. While turning Social Security into a need-based welfare program appeals to some, the political reality is that any move from an entitlement program will destroy Social Security's current broad base of support. If middle-class retirees are excluded from benefits they are unlikely to remain strong supporters of Social Security. Excluding all but the needy also sends the message that the government penalizes those prudent workers who save for their retirement.

The emotional response with which many older citizens regard any reform can be better understood if it is kept in mind that Social Security payments account for

40 percent of the income of the average elderly person.[36] Social Security is the "safety net" keeping tens of millions of Americans out of poverty. For low-income workers it is often their only source of retirement income. Were it not for Social Security and other government programs, the poverty rate for the elderly would be four times as high as at present and *over half* of all persons over 65 would be living in poverty. Social Security thus serves as social insurance and welfare for the elderly. Without it many elderly would sink into poverty.

Toward the Future

During the next half-century the proportion of aged in the population will increase, and they can be expected to become a more vocal and powerful political force. Those over age 65 already are the most likely to vote, and by 2030 almost a third of all voters will be over 65, and just under half will be age 55 and over. If the elderly and their lobbying organizations, such as the AARP, seek to move resources from programs for children to programs for the elderly, they will have the voting power to do so.

While older populations will lobby to hold current Social Security benefits, younger wage earners with families will, just as certainly, resist ever higher Social Security taxes. Increasing strain between the generations may be the consequence. Earmarking budget surpluses for Social Security does not solve the problem, but it does make solving it easier.

A number of predictions can be made with near certainty. The first prediction is that the elderly increasingly are rejecting the idea of policies and programs designed for them. Instead, they are demanding a role for themselves in the design and management of programs that affect their lives.

The second prediction is that the growing number of elderly women will have an increasing impact on the economy. Households headed by someone over 55 already control 56 percent of the nation's net worth. Some elderly women will remain pitifully poor, but many elderly women, as a consequence of both years in the workforce and of inheritance and insurance from spouses, will be well-to-do or wealthy. Such women, as major stockholders, will be able to influence corporate and government decision making and to make major political campaign contributions to politicians they support. The twenty-first century will increasingly see the elderly population include well-educated and sophisticated elderly women who have worked at managerial positions. If such women exert their economic influence, they will be a formidable power bloc.

The third prediction is that Social Security will not be abandoned. The program has become too important to the economy and to workers. Modifications, if made now, will keep the program solvent throughout most of the twenty-first century. Social Security is already moving in the direction of becoming more of an income transfer program. Current college students who obtain well-paying jobs will receive less in Social Security benefits than they pay in. On the other hand, those with good positions will benefit from government tax deferred retirement plans. Equally important, America's young adults will inherit from their parents some 3 trillion dollars. This is far far more than any generation in history. Thus, Social Security will need to play only a relatively small role in their total retirement resources.

---

[36]Social Security Administration, *Fast Facts and Figures about Social Security,* Government Printing Office, Washington, DC 1995, p. 4.

Summary

Today, increases in longevity are dramatically increasing the number and proportion of elderly. The population 65 and over is growing twice as fast as the population as a whole. In 1900 there were only slightly more than 3 million people over age 65; today the figure is 35 million and climbing. Thus, while death has always been with us, aging is a new social problem.

- Aging can be viewed from either a biological, social , or legal perspective, but in common practice the three are often confused.

- Biologically, or physiologically, people age at different rates.

- Socially, occupation defines whether or not one is "old." Professional people both start and end their working lives later.

- Legally, 65 has been the retirement age, but this is an arbitrary cut-off and can be expected to inch upward as people live longer.

- Whether a graying population will mean a swing toward social conservatism, less investment in the young, and a slowing of social change, or whether it will result in increasing social stability and a new burst of investment activity isn't known.

- Three out of five elderly are female. Thus, social and economic programs to provide for the elderly will increasingly be directed at and for older women.

- Forty years ago, the elderly were the poorest segment of the population, with over a third having incomes below the poverty line. Today, older citizens as a group are economically the most advantaged group in society.

- Crime is especially worrisome for the elderly, and they are preyed on by con artists.

- Suburban elderly, without public transportation, are dependent on their automobiles.

- Social Security and Medicare consume a third of the national budget. At the end of World War II there were 35 workers for every recipient. Today there are 3 workers per retiree.

- Politically, the elderly are an active voting constituency and increasingly they reject the idea of policies and programs being designed for them; instead, they are demanding the major role in designing programs that affect their lives.

☞ Key Review Terms

ageism	generational wars	physiological aging
age grading	gerontology	social aging
aging population	legal aging	Social Security
baby boom	Medicare	

? Questions for Discussion

1. Discuss the graying of America. What has caused this demographic change?

2. When does aging occur? What are the milestones for marking old age? What are the various ways of defining "old"?

3. What are American's attitudes toward aging? How will our attitudes toward aging change as the population ages?

4. Why is the baby boom generation important to the Social Security program? What is likely to occur with Social Security as the baby boomers retire?

5. Discuss some of the social, political, economic, and cultural changes that are already occurring or might occur because of an aging population.

6. What are the current differences in longevity rates for males and females? What are likely to be the social, economic, and political consequences of females living longer?

7. Retirement as a life stage is a relatively new development. When do Americans retire? What are the problems of retirement? What are the gains?

8. Thirty years ago the elderly had the highest proportion in poverty. How has this changed? What is the financial status of most elderly Americans?

9. Discuss the impact of an aging population on the health care system. What are the health concerns of the elderly? What health problems most affect them?

10. Discuss the financial status of Social Security. What is the future of this program for today's college students? What problems does it have and how can they be remedied? Why is this a political issue?

Suggested Resources

Karen A. Conner, *Aging America*, Prentice Hall, Englewood Cliffs, NJ 1992. A look at what an aging population will mean to the United States.

Peter B. Doeringer, ed., *Bridges to Retirement: Older Workers in a Changing Labor Market*, ILR Press, New York, 1990. Pieces on what is occurring and effects of retirement, including starting second careers.

Betty Friedan, *The Fountain of Age*, Simon & Schuster, New York, 1995. The woman who inspired the woman's movement confronts age not as a period of decline but as a time of adventure and possibilities.

Derek Humphrey, *Final Exit: The Practicalities of Self-Deliverance and Assisted Suicide for the Dying*, Hemlock Society, Eugene, OR, 1991. Support for and how-to-do-it for the aged who wish to end their lives. As more of the population ages this will increasingly become a social issue.

Elizabeth Kübler-Ross, *Questions and Answers on Death and Dying*, Macmillan, New York, 1987. The late Kübler-Ross, perhaps America's prime philosopher of dying, provides information on the process of dying.

Peter G. Peterson, *Gray Dawn: How the Coming Age Wave Will Transform America*, Random House, New York, 1999. A former Secretary of Commerce looks at the coming wave of aged, and how it needs to be prepared for now.

Internet Connection 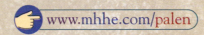 www.mhhe.com/palen

1. An excellent place to start gathering information about aging and gerontology is at a website maintained by The Department of Sociology at Trinity University (*www.trinity.edu/,mkearl/geron.html*). This site is very well-organized and provides links on a broad variety of subjects. Another exceptional resource is the American Society on Aging (*www.asaging.org/ASA_Home_New5.cfm*) Click on "Member Sites." Here, you will find links to many organizations ranging from "Gaycare" and "Gay and Lesbian Aging" to _____. Link to the American Association of Retired Persons (AARP), a very strong advocacy group for people 50 and over (whether they are retired or not). Click on "Issues" to see what this organization considers to be important for its constituency. Next, visit the site of the Gray Panthers (*www.gray panthers.org/*), a site that also has excellent links to related web resources. If you contrast the goals and objectives of this organization, established in 1970, to AARP, you will realize that older Americans, while a very diverse group of people, are still able to coalesce around core issues that affect them personally.

   a. What are some of these core issues?

2. If all the information available above appears overwhelming, you may want to begin with the basic facts. Visit the U.S. Census Home Page to obtain demographic data on aging (*www.census.gov/*). Click on "A" in "Subjects A-to-Z" and then select "Age." (You may also do an "Age Search" if you desire.) Under "Age" you will find a wide variety of reports. An excellent summary report can be found under "Elderly—Sixty-five Plus in the United States" (*www.census.gov/socdemo/www/agebrief.html*).

12

The Detroit News reported
that an 81-year-old woman
was attacked and beaten
while sleeping in her bed by a
youth seeking money for
drugs. The old woman fought
him off and survived. Just
another inner-city crime;
hardly something that merits
major media attention. The
old lady, however, was Rosa
Parks, "the mother of the civil
rights movement," who in
1999 was awarded the
Congressional Gold Medal.
In 1965 Rosa Parks refused
to give up her seat on a
Montgomery, Alabama, bus
to a white man and thus
began the modern civil rights
movement. To the young man
attacking her none of this
mattered; she was simply a
vulnerable old lady.

Crime and Violence

Crime in America: Perceptions and Reality

Chapter 1 posed the question: When is a social phenomenon a social problem? One answer was: when there is widespread belief that it is one. By this measure, crime, especially violent crime, is at or near the top of all social problems because opinion polls consistently rate crime as a major problem.[1] Until 1998 the majority of Americans polled said crime rates were increasing. They weren't.

The sense of pervasive crime is reinforced by daily news reports of random acts of violence. Drive-by shootings, carjackings, assaults upon joggers, and the murder of innocent youths while attending school (such as those in the 1999 Columbine High School killings) suggest a rising crime wave. The reality is that crime rates have been *decreasing* for a decade. National Crime Victimization Survey data show sharp declines in both property crimes and crimes against persons since 1992. FBI data place the U.S. murder rate at a 30-year low.[2] Some of the greatest declines have taken place in the nation's largest cities (populations over 1 million). In New York City, for example, the homicide rate decreased over two-thirds between 1991 and 1999, making New York today one of the nation's safer cities. In Los Angeles during the same period, the homicide rate dropped about half. Teenage homicides initially went against the trend, soaring 169 percent between 1984 and 1993, when the juvenile murder rate peaked. Since then, however, the juvenile murder rate has fallen more than 40 percent according to the Justice Department.[3] The amount of the drops in all categories of serious crime totally surprised experts. Nationwide, serious crimes declined 10 percent just during the first half of 1999.[4]

Still, this good news has to be put in perspective. Sharp drops in homicides and in violent crime rates have to be seen against the overall pattern of what is still a very violent society. After the decreases, there are still some 16,000 homicides a year. Each day about 70 people in the United States die as victims of homicide.[5] Five times more people die by handguns in one day in the United States than die of handguns in an entire year in England; in 1992 handguns killed only 13 English.[6] For that same year the United States had over 15,000 handgun

---

[1]Princeton Survey Research Associates, "Knight-Ridder Survey of American Attitudes," Knight-Ridder Newspapers, February 11, 1996.

[2]Associated Press, "Crime Drops in '97; Murders Are at 30-Year Low," *New York Times on the Web,* November 23, 1998.

[3]Michael Sniffen, "FBI: Crime down 5 Percent in the First Half of 1998," *Associated Press,* December 14, 1998.

[4]"Report: Serious Crime Falls in 1999," *Washington Post Online,* November 22, 1999.

[5]Landis MacKekkar and Machiko Yanagishita, *Homicide in the United States: Who's at Risk?* Population Reference Bureau, Washington, DC, 1995.

[6]Larry S. Stewart and Stephan P. Teret, *Guns—A Public Health Approach: Making Changes in Making Guns, Report of the Conference, May 23, 1995,* Association of Trial Lawyers of America and the Johns Hopkins Center for Gun Policy and Research, Baltimore, 1995, p. 3.

Figure 12.1 Crime Rates Fall

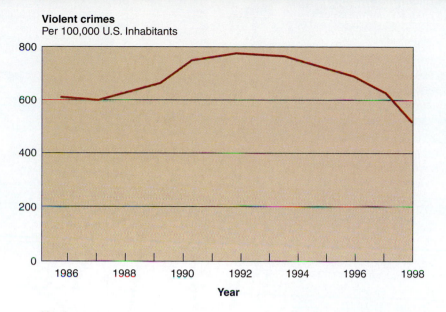

Violent crimes
Per 100,000 U.S. Inhabitants

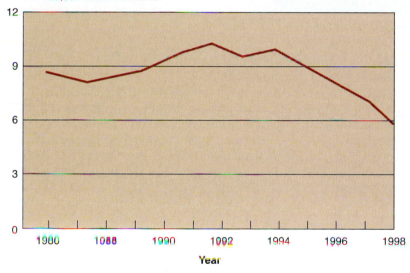

Murders
Per 100,000 U.S. Inhabitants

Source: FBI, Uniform Crime Report

deaths. Nor is England the exception; in Japan, with its 125 million people, there were only 38 murders by firearms in all of 1994.[7] Both Japan and England ban handguns.

There are, of course, cultural variations among the United States, Japan, and England. However, while Japan may be culturally different from the United States, the same argument cannot as easily be applied to Canada. In Canada, where handguns

[7]Nicholas Kristof, "Japan Says No to Crime: Tough Measures at a Price," *New York Times,* May 14, 1995, p. 8.

Violent crime doesn't only affect the poor. This LAPD evidence photo of the body of Nicole Brown Simpson and her bloodstained walkway was entered as evidence in the O. J. Simpson wrongful-death civil trial in 1996.

LAPD/AP/Wide World Photos

also are banned, there were 128 handgun deaths in 1994. The vastly higher U.S. figures are largely due not to cultural differences but to the ready availability of guns in the United States, where there are now more than 200 million guns.

Government estimates indicate that four out of five Americans will be a victim of violent crime at least once in their life. American children under age 15 are 12 times more likely to die by gunfire than their counterparts in the rest of the industrialized world.[8] Homicide by firearms now is the second leading cause of death (after unrelated injuries) for 15 to 24 year olds.[9] Homicide now surpasses accidents as the major cause of death of black males in their 20s.

Sociological Perspectives

Functionalist Approaches

Functionalists see society as a system of parts that interact to maintain the whole, and in contemporary urban society the rapid pace of social change has undermined traditional controls on personal behavior. Crime is functional for some in the society. Crime provides an alternative route to achieving the American value of

---

[8]Associated Press News Service, "Youth Murder, Suicide Surging: U.S. Tops the List in Gunfire Deaths," February 7, 1997.
[9]National Center for Health Statistics, *National Vital Statistics Report*, 47, no. 4, October 7, 1998, Tables 17–18.

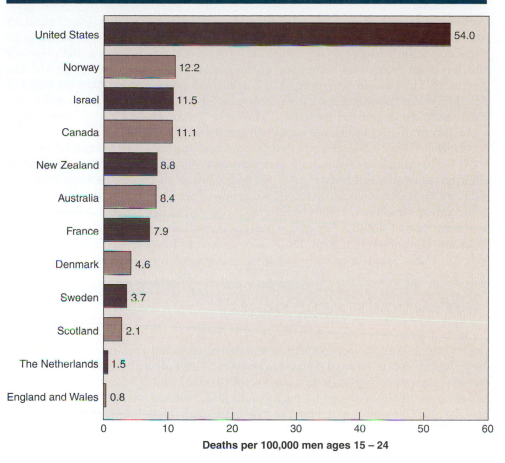

Figure 12.2 Firearm Injury Death Rates among Young Men in Selected Countries, 1992 to 1995

Country	Deaths per 100,000 men ages 15 – 24
United States	54.0
Norway	12.2
Israel	11.5
Canada	11.1
New Zealand	8.8
Australia	8.4
France	7.9
Denmark	4.6
Sweden	3.7
Scotland	2.1
The Netherlands	1.5
England and Wales	0.8

Source: National Center for Health Statistics, *Health United States 1996–97* and *Injury Chartbook*, 1997, p. 32.

financial success. Contemporary society values economic success, but class and race discrimination limit the access of some citizens to legitimate routes (e.g., higher education) for achieving this success. Robert Merton suggests that crime is an innovation through which illegal routes will be substituted when legal means of success are blocked.[10] Drug dealing and organized crime are ways of achieving the American goal of success. As Émile Durkheim suggested, deviance is normal for modern society.[11]

Functionalists suggest that the best way to reduce crime is to increase youth's social integration through connection and involvement with the traditional institutions of family, church, and school. If parents are not there for inner-city youths, other social institutions must take up the slack. Crime could also be reduced, functionalists say, through raising the cost of crime to perpetrators. To the extent that crime is a rational act, its commission can be reduced by making the likelihood of punishment more certain. This can be done partially by reorganizing the criminal justice system so that offenses are dealt with quickly and result in punishment.

---

[10]Robert K. Merton, *Social Theory and Social Structure*, Free Press of Glencoe, New York, 1957, pp. 131–192.
[11]Émile Durkheim, *The Division of Labor in Society*, Free Press, New York, 1964 (orig. publ. 1895).

Conflict Approaches

Advocates of conflict approaches stress that the definitions of what is a criminal act and who is a criminal reflect the interests of the powerful. Crime is what the poor do; respectable persons "make a mistake." Police and courts enforce the values of the dominant group. Law is the mechanism used by the powerful to control the less fortunate. Thus a holdup netting $150 is punished more severely than tax fraud of $50,000. While robbing a bank invariably gets a heavy sentence, a bank embezzlement may result only in probation. Similarly, "wars against drugs" are fought against central-city sellers, not suburban purchasers.

Conflict theory advocates say that insofar as crime is a consequence of inequality, it will continue to exist as long as exploitation and inequality continue. Conflict theorists generally hold that equality in treatment of all crimes, perhaps based on damage to society, would help reduce crime. Thus, someone who deliberately builds an automobile that kills hundreds of people but saves a few dollars in manufacturing costs would be treated at least as harshly as someone who accidentally kills another person in a fight. Drug laws also would be harshly applied to those who purchase drugs, regardless of the neighborhood in which they live.

Interactionist Approaches

Social interactionists view society as socially constructed and are concerned with how delinquent or criminal behavior comes to be socially learned and transmitted. Some social psychologists look more to child-rearing and the family environment; others stress the role played by peer groups and the local community. Interactionists are also concerned with how one becomes labeled a delinquent or a criminal.

Through differential association with those labeled as criminal, a youth becomes a gang member, thief, or drug dealer. Gangs not only promote a lifestyle emphasizing "easy money," they also teach members the techniques of crime. Many criminal skills have to be learned, and this is less likely to occur without exposure to groups possessing a criminal culture. Even relatively minor crimes, such as shoplifting, often take place when a young person is with peers.

Because delinquent or criminal behavior is often a consequence of socialization, an interactionist would say that preventing crime or reforming offenders requires removing offenders from the influence of groups that encourage criminal behavior. The socializing influence of family, church, school, and other positive groups must be maximized. To limit further criminal socialization, the justice system should never incarcerate a first offender with repeat offenders.

What Is a Crime?

crime
an activity that violates the criminal code.

Crime is a legal category, not a moral one. Crime is a violation of societal norms, but not all violations are crimes. For our purposes, a **crime** is an act that violates the criminal code and is punishable by the political authority of the state. Although crimes are generally acts that cause harm or injury to others, causing injury is not necessary for an act to be defined as criminal. Activities defined as immoral may or may not be defined as criminal. State variations in laws about what is illegal sexual behavior are a case in point; we are currently redefining what is or is not illegal in this area. In the past, acts regarded as immoral, such as abortion, homosexual acts, and the sale of pornography, were universally forbidden by law. Today, most of these laws have been taken off the books or are not enforced. Decriminalization is particularly likely to occur when previously defined criminal behavior (e.g., drinking alcohol during the 1920s) becomes widespread among people of the upper-middle and upper classes. Criminal law generally reflects the social and moral values of the society's dominant groups.

Criminal offenses are classified either as **felonies** (serious offenses usually punishable by a year or more in prison) or **misdemeanors** (less serious offenses with lesser penalties). Homicide, murder, assault, burglary, and rape are serious crimes, not only in our legal system, but according to every written legal code. (**Homicide** is the killing of a person. **Murder** is an illegal homicide committed with malice. **Assault** is an attack on a person with the intention of hurting or killing.) Beyond this commonly accepted core, however, there is considerable dispute among experts about what the "important" crimes are. As Gwynn Nettler puts it:

> The changing relationship between a people's moral beliefs and the criminal laws of their state allows criminologists to dispute the proper content of their discipline. . . . Thus the radical sociologist will want more attention paid to "crimes against the public interest" such as industrial pollution, racial and sexual discrimination, and dangerously misleading advertising. On the other hand, the conservative sociologist will want more attention paid to the "subversive crimes," such as the traffic in pornography and narcotics, and intrusion by the state upon the individual's religious, educational, and property rights.[12]

Generally we have been decriminalizing the so-called "crimes without victims" (such as homosexuality, prostitution, and drunkenness), while actions such as manufacturing and selling harmful products or polluting the seas, land, or atmosphere are being criminalized. Many of the "sharp" business practices of earlier decades, such as various types of stock manipulations, are now defined as criminal acts. Criminal law is not a static category.

felony
serious violation of the criminal code punishable by at least a prison term of a year.

misdemeanor
less serious violation of the criminal code that can be punished by less than a year in jail or a fine.

homocide
killing of a person.

murder
illegal homocide committed with malice.

assault
attack on a person intended to hurt or kill.

Delinquency

The Juvenile Court System

A crime is a violation of the law, but defining what constitutes **delinquency** is more difficult. Basically, a delinquent act is whatever a court defines as being a delinquent act. The juvenile court movement in effect "invented" delinquency.[13] Juvenile courts arose at the turn of the century from the moral reform movement's emphasis on saving wayward youth. (Juveniles are usually defined as those under 18 although for some crimes some states have lowered the age at which one is considered an adult.) Illinois established the first juvenile court in 1899; by the late 1920s such courts existed everywhere but Wyoming and Maine, where separate

delinquency
acts that would be criminal when committed by an adult plus activities defined by statute as punishable when committed by juveniles.

---

[12]Gwenn Nettler, *Explaining Crime*, McGraw-Hill, 1997, pp. 36–37.
[13]Anthony Platt, *The Child Savers: The Invention of Delinquency*, University of Chicago Press, Chicago, 1969.

These four youths are using a baseball bat, heavy sticks, and a gun to stop and carjack this auto.

PhotoDisc/Volume 25

juvenile laws weren't enacted until the 1950s. The emphasis of juvenile courts has been to rehabilitate and educate the offender. However, today there is pressure to stress punishment over rehabilitation and to have juveniles tried in adult courts for serious offenses.

The reformist goal of juvenile courts was to treat signs of deviance that might develop into criminality. One did not have to commit a crime to be judged delinquent; it was enough to be antisocial or to show signs of "potential criminality." A young boy could, under the 1905 Illinois statute, be adjudicated a delinquent for, among other things, being "incorrigible"; "knowingly associating with thieves, vicious, or immoral persons"; "growing up in idleness"; "frequenting a house of ill repute . . . or any saloon or dram shop where intoxicating liquors are sold"; "habitually wandering about any railroad yard or tracks, or jumping or attempting to jump into any moving train"; or "habitually using vile, obscene, vulgar, profane or indecent language."

The juvenile court acts thus created a whole new set of offenses that had not been previously subject to formal legal procedure. Juveniles, unlike adults, can be found delinquent for offenses against public values and morality. Alcohol consumption, for instance, is illegal for minors but legal for adults. As recently as the 1970s, roughly 40 percent of those found delinquent by the courts were not charged with committing any crime. Rather, they were so-called status offenders, who came before the court because they were alleged to be "unruly," "truant," or "incorrigible." Today, with more felony offenses by juveniles, states are less concerned about status offenses.

A juvenile's social class often makes a big difference in how authorities treat him or her. In a classic sociological study, William Chamblis examined how authorities label delinquent behavior by middle-class and lower-class teens attending the same high school.[14] He found that the higher-status boys, the "Saints," were involved in virtually every sort of delinquency and were constantly truant, openly cheated on tests, and drove recklessly and when drunk. They were rarely caught, however, and when caught were apologetic and respectful. Invariably, they were let off with warnings. The Saint's image was "good kids," and acts that violated that image were ignored by the police or explained as exceptions.

By contrast, the lower-class "Roughnecks" were expected to fail. Their actual behavior was similar to that of the Saints, but the Roughnecks were constantly monitored, and any slip was immediately punished. They didn't play the respectful "I'm sorry" role, as did the Saints. Rather, they tried to play tough with those in authority, and consequently were labeled as delinquents. Chambliss says that the societal reaction to the Roughnecks and the Saints helped lock them into patterns that reinforced the town's views of the two groups. Seven of the eight Saints went on to college and successful lives. Two of the Roughnecks got college football scholarships and ended up coaching high school football teams. The other five of the Roughnecks all ended up in prison (one for murder) or in marginal low-status positions. Both the Saints and Roughnecks had behaved similarly, but one group was expected to succeed and the other to fail.

Changing Juvenile Courts

Juvenile courts are designed to be flexible; making it easier for a youth to leave problem behavior behind without being labeled a criminal and carrying a criminal record. Rather than being "tried" for an offense—with prosecutor, defense lawyer, and jury—a juvenile is given an informal hearing in which, in theory, the basic issue is the well-being of the child. If the juvenile is to be a delinquent, the penalties are invariably far less severe than those for similar offenses committed by an adult. In practice, however, serious offenses may be referred to adult courts. Also, while juvenile court records are not commonly available to the public, certain government agencies do have access to juvenile records. Nationwide, juvenile courts handle about 1.4 million cases a year.

With more than half the serious crimes in the United States now committed by those under eighteen, and with more of these crimes being violent, both the concept and effectiveness of the juvenile court system is being challenged. Juveniles are increasingly being tried in adult courts for violent offenses, because juvenile courts were not designed to treat serious offenders or criminal gangs. Limited penalties are available to juvenile courts. As a 14-year-old New Haven youth, arrested for robbing and killing a Yale student, contemptuously put it to the prosecutor, "the most you're going to give me is two years." In Jonesboro, Arkansas, in 1998, 13-year-old Michael Johnson and 11-year-old Andrew Golden deliberately shot at school classmates, killing a teacher and 4 children. Under the then existing Arkansas law, the gravest penalty they could receive was being held in juvenile detention until they are age 18. Mass murders by youths, such as the 1999 Columbine High School killings at Littleton, Colorado, increase pressure for less emphasis on rehabilitation and more on punishment.

However, abandoning the juvenile court system means turning the clock back to the early nineteenth century when, under English common law, anyone seven or over could be imprisoned or hung. A recent case of stressing punishment regardless of young age was the 1999 Michigan criminal court trial and conviction of an 11-year-old for murder.[15] The preteenager was sentenced to a minimum of 25 years in prison.

---

[14]William Chambliss, "The Saints and the Roughnecks," *Society*, 2:24–31, 1973.
[15]"Youngster Sentenced for Murder," *New York Times on the Web*, November 16, 1999.

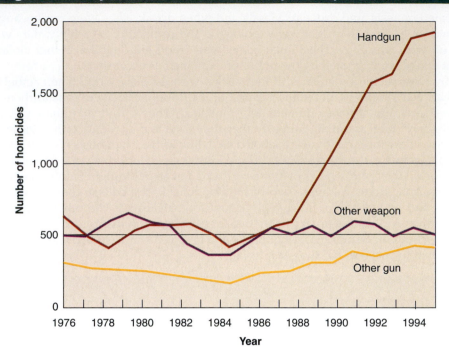

Figure 12.3 Juvenile Homicides by Weapon

Source: FBI, *Supplementary Homicide Reports.*

President Clinton and congressional Republicans, seeking votes and fearing that the increases in the population of 15–19-year-olds over the next decade will result in a surging wave of violent crime, made radical, if little noted, changes in the juvenile justice system in 1997. Under the *Juvenile Control Act of 1997*, those as young as 14 years of age now can be prosecuted in adult courts for violent crimes and serious drug offenses. Moreover, juvenile criminal records will no longer remain secret, but become public and permanent. Under the 1997 act, states that adopt these changes and put in strict mandatory punishments for even the first delinquent acts share $1.5 billion in crime-fighting funds.[16] No monies are provided by the act for crime prevention or rehabilitation.

Statistics on Crime

Uniform Crime Report

yearly report of crimes reported to the police and assembled by the FBI.

Politicians and public figures glibly quoting statistics about rising or falling crime rates usually appear unaware that crime statistics must be interpreted with care. The two major crime data sources are the **Uniform Crime Reports (UCR)** (sometimes referred to as the Uniform Crime Statistics [UCS]) published by the FBI, and

---

[16]Roburto Suro "White House, Hill GOP Offer Get-Tough Measures on Juvenile Crime," *Washington Post*, May 8, 1997, p. A4.

Table 12.1 Major Crimes Known to the Police, 1993 (UCR Part I Offenses)

Offense	Number	Rate per 100,000	Clearance Rate
Personal/Violence Crimes			
Murder	24,526	9.5	66%
Forcible rape	104,806	40.6	53
Robbery	659,757	255.8	24
Aggravated assault	1,135,099	440.1	56
Property Crimes			
Burglary	2,834,808	1,099.2	13
Larceny	7,820,909	3,032.4	20
Motor vehicle theft	1,561,047	605.3	14
Arson	82,348	—	15
U.S. total	14,140,952	5,482.9	21

Source: Federal Bureau of Investigation, *Crime in the United States, 1993* (Washington, DC: U.S. Government Printing Office, 1994).

the **National Crime Victimization Survey (NCVS)** published by the Bureau of Justice Statistics.

Uniform Crime Reports

The UCR is a collection of those crimes reported to the police, and thus does not fully reflect all crimes committed. The FBI does not collect the original data or even check their accuracy; it merely publishes the figures sent in by the nation's 11,000 local police agencies. The Uniform Crime Reports include eight major categories of crimes against persons and crimes against property: (1) murder and nonnegligent homicide, (2) forcible rape, (3) robbery (stealing by force), (4) aggravated assault (assault with intent to kill or do bodily harm), (5) burglary (breaking and entering with intent to commit a crime), (6) larceny (stealing without force or fraud), (7) auto theft, and (8) arson. These so-called Part I or **index offenses** cover street crime but not all serious crimes. For instance, the data exclude white-collar crimes (such as fraud and embezzlement), syndicate crimes (such as numbers rackets and loan sharking), and drug offenses.

Virtually all homicides are reported, but burglaries and larcenies often are not, because the victims feel it is futile to file a complaint, that "nothing will be done." This belief is sometimes justified. Most police departments, for example, don't actively pursue crimes such as bicycle theft. The major motivation to report a property crime often is that insurance won't pay claims for unreported thefts. What the Uniform Crime Reports does well is to indicate how rates of crime change over time.

index offenses
eight categories of street crimes against persons or property.

National Crime Victimization Survey

The National Crime Victimization Survey, run by the Justice Department, gets its data from interviews with roughly 80,000 people in 43,000 randomly selected households throughout the United States. Those interviewed are asked about

National Crime Victimization Survey
annual Justice Department survey of actual incidence of crime experienced by households.

crimes they have experienced in the previous six months. This is an accurate measure of the actual incidence of crime, reported and not reported. The NCVS findings indicate that only about a third of all crime is reported to the police (roughly half of all violent crime and only slightly more than a quarter of thefts).[17] Only one in five rapes is reported. About half of the violent crimes reported by those surveyed were committed by someone the victim knew.

Since 1992 the amount of crime reported by the National Crime Victimization Survey as well as the Uniform Crime Reports has been decreasing yearly across the country. In 1998 fewer Americans reported themselves victims of crimes than at any time in the 25-year history of the survey.[18] Rates continued to decrease through 2000.

Police Discretion

In many cases whether or not an act is reported as a crime involves police discretion in how they handle and report the situation. Are college students mooning passing cars, for instance, charged by the police with public indecency or simply told to go home? Before groups such as MADD (Mothers Against Drunk Driving) began campaigning against drunk driving, police officers often let upper-class members of the community off with a warning as long as someone else was in the car who could safely drive the person home. It is still not uncommon for prominent politicians or well-known people simply to be brought home in the police car. Needless to say, such discretionary treatment is rarely available to the less powerful.

Arrest records indicate that the poor and minorities commit more serious offenses. However, arrest and conviction data can be biased because those who are poor and members of minority groups are more likely to be arrested and convicted than others.[19] Higher-status groups have money and influence that can be used to avoid arrest or at least purchase good legal counsel. Thus, offense variations by social class are less than indicated by official statistics. Keep this in mind when reading the remainder of the chapter. Also keep in mind that when the public speaks of crime it almost always means street crime. White-collar crime, which is almost exclusively committed by "respectable" people, isn't included.

Spatial Distribution of Crime

Crime and the City

Crime and cities have long been linked. However, the belief that cities are inevitably the sites of murder and mayhem is not borne out by examining the historical record. In fact, until the 1960s, the general pattern of urban crime had been generally more downward rather than upward.[20] It is not cities or city life *per se* that causes crime,

[17]Sue Titus Reid, *Crime and Criminology*, 6th ed., Holt, Rinehart and Winston, 1991.
[18]New York Times News Service, "Crime at Lowest Level Since 1973," *New York Times,* December 28, 1998; New York Times News Service, "Serious Crime Dips 7% in U.S. , "*New York Times,* May 8, 2000.
[19]Delbert Elliot and Suzanne Ageton, "Reconciling Race and Class Differences in Self-Reporting and Official Estimates of Delinquency," *American Sociological Review,* 45:95–110, 1980.
[20]Theodore N. Ferdinand, "The Criminal Patterns of Boston Since 1849," *American Journal of Sociology,* 73:84–99, 1967; also see Fox Butterfield, "A History of Homicide Surprises the Experts: Decline in U.S. Before Recent Increase," *New York Times,* October 23, 1994, p. 16.

because American cities of the 1940s and 1950s had very low crime rates. In 1942, for example, there were only 44 murders in all of New York City.[21] That figure includes all domestic murders, street murders, and gangland hits. Movies set in New York during the 1930s and 1940s reflected this street safety, showing young couples after a night on the town, walking through Central Park after midnight. By 1960 the annual number of murders in the city had increased to 310, which was then thought to be an unbelievably high number. New York City's murder rate peaked at 2,262 in 1990 and dropped to 629 in 1998.

Patterns within Cities

For almost a century, sociologists have been studying the spatial distribution of criminal behavior within cities. The patterns are remarkably well documented and consistent. Within urban areas, crime rates follow the Burgess zonal pattern discussed in Chapter 7. That is, street crime is heavily concentrated in the older, inner parts of the city, with rates declining toward more peripheral areas.[22] "Delinquency areas" in sociological studies of the mid-twentieth century were associated with "social disorganization," as typified by high poverty and welfare rates, broken homes, low educational levels, and other social ills. The assumption was that where conventional social controls were weakened by conflicting traditions and social change, rates of delinquency would be high.[23] While later studies called some of these conclusions into question, they have confirmed this fairly regular pattern of decreasing street crime rates as one moves from the inner core of the central city to outer suburbs.

However, while it is important to know the spatial location of a phenomenon, this does not necessarily tell us the cause. As Ernest Van den Haag has expressed it: "The crime rate in slums is indeed higher than elsewhere; but so is the death rate in hospitals. Slums are no more 'causes' of crime than hospitals are of death; they are locations of crime, as hospitals are of death. Slums and hospitals attract people selectively; neither is the 'cause' of the condition (disease in hospitals, poverty in slums) that leads to the selective attraction."[24]

Concentration of crime in inner-city slum neighborhoods is a pattern that has remained unchanged over time, even though the ethnic and racial composition of the populations occupying the blighted areas has altered completely. Such consistency over time does not mean that the buildings or neighborhoods somehow create crime; rather, it suggests that different newcomer groups to the city have been subject to many of the same pressures. The rapid urbanization of rural populations—whether from Europe, the American South, Mexico, or Asia—often resulted in a breakdown of traditional patterns, including traditional means of social control, such as the family.

Crime in the Suburbs

Suburbs are not crime-free Edens. Although national crime rates are decreasing, that is not always true of suburbs.[25] During the 1980s violent crimes increased by

---

[21]J. John Palen, *The Suburbs*, McGraw-Hill, New York, 1995.

[22]Clifford R. Shaw and Henry D. McKay, *Delinquent Areas*, University of Chicago Press, Chicago, 1929.

[23]Clifford R. Shaw and Henry D. McKay, *Juvenile Delinquency and Urban Areas*, University of Chicago Press, Chicago, 1942.

[24]Ernest Van den Haag, "On Deterrence and the Death Penalty," *Ethics*, 78: 283, July 1968.

[25]Federal Bureau of Investigation, *Uniform Crime Statistics*, Government Printing Office, Washington, DC, 1998.

Suburbs aren't immune from crime. Two employees were killed and two badly wounded in an attack in this McDonald's in Hermitage, Tennessee, a suburb of Nashville.

Christopher Berkey/AP/Wide World Photos

14 percent in the cities but by 181 percent in the suburbs. During the 1990s suburban rates were more variable: some went up and some went down. The focus on rate increases, however, ignores the actual amount of crime, which may be relatively small. Suburban crime increases, if any, come from a much lower base, with suburban rates only about 28 percent of the crime rate in the nation's 52 largest cities. Also, suburban crime is often different in character from city crime. Suburban crime is overwhelmingly (87 percent) property crime; violent crime is more pervasive in the city. Burglary and theft account for four-fifths of all suburban index crimes. (The actual amount of unreported crime for offenses such as drug use and petty shoplifting may be much higher.) Suburbs having high automobile theft rates commonly have shopping centers and business parks. For a professional auto thief stealing a specific model for a "chop shop," there are few sites better than a large suburban parking lot.

Violent suburban crime tends to be centered in those suburbs having social and economic characteristics similar to those of large cities. Burglary and theft also are more common in low-income suburbs than in more affluent communities, where there is presumably more to steal. Well-to-do suburbs keep their crime rates down by restricting economic activity (e.g., no stores) and controlling the access of outsiders (e.g., the poor and minorities).[26] It is crucial to remember that the lower suburban crime rates apply only to so-called street crime. White-collar crimes are largely committed by "respectable" persons.

---

[26]See, for example, John M. Stahura and John J. Slone III, "Urban Stratification of Places, Routine Activities, and Suburban Crime Rates," *Social Forces*, 66:1102–1118, 1988.

Characteristics of Criminal Offenders

Crime rates differ considerably not only according to location but also according to age, gender, ethnicity, and race. The makeup of the population can affect crime rates strongly, regardless of other factors. A population with a median age of 42 can be expected to commit far less crime than a population with a median age of 22. We are speaking of differences in **rates**—that is, group differences—not the characteristics of a specific "criminal personality." Despite a century of writing and research on criminal personalities (and even the so-called research on body type and crime noted in Chapter 1), no scientifically reliable criminal personality measures have ever been developed.[27] Discussions of so-called "sociopathic personalities" invariably involve circular reasoning with someone defined as "sociopathic" because they have committed offenses, while it then is said they committed the offenses because they are sociopaths.

Keep in mind that only substantial and consistent variations in rates can be considered significant. The following data do not apply to white-collar offenses, which often show a much different pattern.

rates
differences among groups.

Gender

Crime remains one of the last bastions of male dominance. At the turn of the century, the arrest rate was roughly 50 males for 1 female. Today the ratio is five to one, with males accounting for 88 percent of those arrested for violent crimes and 74 percent of those for property crime.[28] Females are most often arrested for larceny and theft (such as shoplifting).

Today there are about 83,000 women in prison, about 6 percent of the nation's prisoners. However, while women are still a small percentage of all prisoners, women are being incarcerated for more serious offenses, and the number of women incarcerated in federal and state prisons is five times higher than in 1980. The historically lower incarceration rates among women may partially be seen as a result of their exclusion from full participation in the society. Increased crime among women may be a trade-off for increased opportunities. As Freda Adler stated in her classic study of female crime: "There is a tide in the affairs of women as well as men, and in the last decade it has been sweeping over the barriers which have protected male prerogatives and eroding the traditional differences which once nicely defined the gender roles."[29] Women are committing more violent crime and more white-collar crime. Women's incarceration rates for drug crimes are also up sharply. Between 1986 and 1998 the incarceration rate for drug offences for black women increased nearly twice as fast as for black men—828 percent over 429 percent.[30] Women, who work at low levels in drug organizations, are more likely to be caught.

While more women are being sent to prison, there still is a difference in the way male and female offenders are treated. Women are far less likely than men committing similar offenses to be arrested, prosecuted if arrested, convicted if prosecuted,

---

[27]Karl Schuessler and Donald Cressey, "Personality Characteristics of Criminals," *American Journal of Sociology*, 55:476–484, 1950; David Tennenbaum, "Research Studies of Personality and Criminality," *Journal of Criminal Justice*, 5:1–19, 1977.
[28]Federal Bureau of Investigation, *Uniform Crime Reports*, Government Printing Office, Washington, DC, 1993.
[29]Freda Adler, *Sisters in Crime: The Rise of the New Female Criminal*, McGraw-Hill, New York, 1975, p. 1.
[30]Tony Locy, "Like Mother, Like Daughter," *U.S. News and World Report*, October 4, 1999, p. 18.

Campuses occasionally are the site of violence. Jillian Robbins (in the plaid shirt) went on a random shooting spree on the Penn State University campus in 1996. Her rampage left one student dead and another seriously wounded.

Craig Houtz/AP/Wide World Photos

or imprisoned if convicted. This is especially the case if they are mothers. Women account for 20 percent of arrests, but make up only 6 percent of the prison population. This protective bias toward women is in part a reflection of the old common-law view that women, like children, should not be held fully culpable for their criminal acts. Women are more likely to be viewed as victims of circumstances or to be seen as striking back in response to family violence against them. Times are changing, but gender still remains the single best predictor of whether or not someone will engage in criminal behavior and of the penalty, if any, that he or she will receive for that behavior.

Age

Most street crime is committed by the young. Those under 25 account for half of all violent crime arrests and three-fifths of all property crime arrests. Thirty years ago juvenile crime was largely petty crime. Joyriding and vandalism still exist, but they have been joined by far more serious offenses. Homicides among juveniles sometimes result over disputes over minor matters such as a jacket, a pair of sneakers, or being "disrespected." A 1993 survey indicated that 35 percent of juveniles in detention and 10 percent of the general youth population in inner-city high schools believed "It is OK to shoot a person if that is what it takes to get what you want."[31] Curfew laws do not substantially reduce juvenile violence, because teen violence

---

[31]Ibid.

Table 12.2 Male-Female Involvement in Crime

UCR Index Crimes	Percentage of Arrests by Gender	
	Males	Females
Murder and nonnegligent manslaughter	90.6%	9.4%
Rape	98.7	1.3
Robbery	91.3	8.7
Aggravated assault	84.3	15.7
Burglary	90.1	9.9
Larceny-theft	67.3	32.7
Motor vehicle theft	88.2	11.8
Arson	85.3	14.7
Average, all major crimes	80.5	19.5

Source: Federal Bureau of Investigation, *Crime in the United States, 1993* (Washington, DC: U.S. Government Printing Office, 1994).

peaks during the after-school hours—not after midnight when curfews would be in effect.

Juvenile arrests increased 100 percent from 1983 to 1992. More frightening, the number of juvenile homicide offenders almost tripled from 1984 to 1994 and gun-related juvenile murders increased more than fourfold. The Office of Juvenile Justice and Delinquency Prevention predicted in 1995 that the juvenile arrest rate would double by 2010.[32] Fortunately, that isn't happening. Juvenile crime rates are decreasing. However, the amount of juvenile crime may increase early in the twenty-first century because the number of juveniles in the population will increase 31 percent by 2010.

As people age, they tend to become more law-abiding. Criminal activity peaks in the late teens and early 20s, and then declines. It isn't known whether this *maturing out* is a result of having greater responsibilities, such as a family, or simply a greater realization of the risks and costs. What is known is that maturing out is a phenomenon that occurs across white, African American, and Latino populations.[33] This suggests that "three strikes and you're out" programs are a waste when they confine large numbers of older inmates in their 50s, 60s, and 70s, who no longer pose a criminal threat.

While violent crimes are committed mostly by the young, white-collar crimes such as fraud, forgery, counterfeiting, and embezzlement—crimes that require trained skills—are committed mostly by older persons.

Ethnicity and Race

Crime traditionally has provided a path of upward mobility for disadvantaged groups who have been denied access to legitimate means of achieving success. Criminal activity provides an alternative route toward participation in the "American Dream."

---

[32]*Juvenile Offenders and Victims: A National Report,* Office of Juvenile Justice and Delinquency Prevention, Washington, DC, 1995.
[33]Mercer Sullivan, *Getting Paid,* Cornell University Press, Ithaca, NY, 1989.

Table 12.3 Arrest Rates by Race (per 1,000 persons), Selected Offenses, 1993

	Blacks	Whites
Murder	0.34	0.04
Rape	0.45	0.09
Robbery	3.00	0.28
Stolen property	1.82	0.37
Weapons	2.73	0.54
Drug abuse	11.70	2.68

Source: FBI, *Crime in the United States, 1993* (Washington, DC: U.S. Government Printing Office, 1994).

The ethnic and racial composition of those committing crime roughly reflects changes in the social, economic, and political position of minority groups in American society.

During the early twentieth century, for example, Yankees were replaced by the Irish and Jews, who in turn were succeeded by Italians, who are now being replaced by African Americans, Colombians, Mexicans, Jamaicans, Asians, and Russians.

Irish and Jewish Gangs A group that has high rates at one historic period may have low rates at another. A century ago the common stereotype was that the Irish would steal anything that was not nailed down, and at the beginning of the twentieth century, criminal street gangs were heavily Irish. Today the Irish are among the most law-abiding citizens.

Similarly, until they were displaced by Italians, Jewish mobs controlled organized crime on the east and west coasts. New York's 1930s Murder Incorporated was largely a Jewish organization. In Chicago in the 1920s Al Capone gained control of the city's rackets by eliminating the rival Irish-Jewish North Side gang run by Dian O'Banion and his lieutenants Hymie Weiss and Bugs Moran. The notorious 1927 St. Valentine's Day Massacre represented ethnic change, with Capone's Italian gang machine-gunning the remaining members of the Irish-Jewish Moran gang.

Although unique cultural factors operate within each group, the generalized pattern is that the highest crime and delinquency rates are concentrated in the newest and poorest groups in the metropolitan area. As newcomers are assimilated, there is movement toward the national norm. For historically low-crime groups such as Japanese Americans, this means crime rates going not down but up. Assimilated Japanese youth show higher delinquency rates than earlier Japanese populations, although these rates are still low.[34]

Black Crime Rates It is not race or ethnicity *per se* that causes crime, but the social norms, values, and opportunities of the environment.[35] Currently, African Americans are 12 percent of the population but account for 56 percent of those arrested for murder, somewhat under half those arrested for forcible rape, and half those arrested for violent crimes.[36] The Justice Department estimates that one-third (32.2 percent) of all black males aged 20 to 29 are either in jail or prison

---

[34]Harry H. L. Kitano, *Japanese Americans*, Prentice-Hall, Englewood Cliffs, NJ, 1976, pp. 143–150.
[35]Troy Duster, *Backdoor to Eugenics*, Routledge, London, 1990.
[36]William Julius Wilson, *The Truly Disadvantaged: The Inner City, the Underclass, and Public Policy*, University of Chicago Press, Chicago, 1987.

or on probation or parole.[37] More young black males are in prison than attending college. In California the black prison population is four times greater than the black college population. Police are more likely to monitor and arrest minorities. **Racial profiling** is a common police practice.

Black Victimization African Americans are much more likely than whites to be victims of both violent and property crimes. This is true even in suburbs.[38] Over 85 percent of the violent crimes committed by blacks involve black victims. Homicide data, which are the crime data least subject to manipulation, clearly show blacks more likely to be victims. Since 1989, more homicide victims have been black than white and the homicide rate for African American males is seven times that for whites. Young black males have become an endangered species. According to the National Center for Health Statistics, black against black homicide is the leading cause of death among black men aged 16 to 34. One out of every 21 young black men is murdered. In 1996 young black males aged 14 to 24 constituted just over 1 percent of the population, but this 1 percent accounted for 17 percent of the homicide victims and 30 percent of those convicted of committing murder.[39]

Robbery is the only violent street crime with a strong interracial component, with 45 percent of all robberies involving a black offender (almost always a young male) and a white victim (most frequently an older white male). Middle-class blacks have higher victimization rates than do whites of similar status; therefore, blacks often are more "hard line" against street crime than their less-victimized white counterparts. Black-on-black crime has real meaning for African American leaders since they, or their families, often have been victims. Reverend Jesse Jackson, who long has been active in the crusade against black-on-black crime, had his Washington, D.C., home burglarized in 1991, and eight months later his wife saw a man murdered while she was taking out the garbage. Two years later she saw three men murdered in a drug hit on their street. With sadness, the Reverend Jackson says, "There is nothing more painful for me at this stage of my life than to walk down the street and hear footsteps and start to think about robbery, and then to look around and see it is somebody white and feel relieved. How humiliating."[40]

African Americans have low involvement in white-collar crimes such as embezzlement, forgery, and price-fixing. The low involvement in white-collar crime reflects occupational discrimination, which has restricted black movement into positions where major funds are controlled.

Social Class

You might wonder why social class has not been stressed as one of the major characteristics associated with criminal behavior, especially since statistics indicate that prisoners are overwhelmingly drawn from the lower socioeconomic groups. The reason, as noted in the discussion of the Saints and Roughnecks, is that the link between crimes committed (not just arrests) and social class is not all that clear. There is a widespread assumption that "poverty causes crime." Representative John Conyers (D., Michigan), reflects this view when he says that crime "is the product of desperation brought on by joblessness, poverty, and community

---

[37]Washington Post News Service, "Black Offenders Up Sharply, Study Says," October 5, 1995.
[38]Richard Alba, John Logan, and Paul Bellair, "Living with Crime: The Implications of Racial/Ethnic Differences in Suburban Location," *Social Forces*, 73:395–434, 1994.
[39]James A. Fox, "The Calm before the Storm?" *Population Today*, 24:4, September 1996.
[40]"A New Civil Rights Frontier," *U.S. News and World Report*, January 17, 1994, p. 38.

disintegration."[41] However this common belief is not supported by data. First, the "poverty equals crime" thesis totally ignores white-collar and corporate crime. For decades criminologists have known that the most affluent may actually have a higher true crime rate than the lower classes.[42] Second, organized crime is not committed by members of the lower classes. Mobsters aren't poor. Third, most drug usage (but not most arrests) occurs among the middle class, not the poor. Fourth, there do not appear to be any differences among social classes in hidden crimes such as vice offenses. Finally, self-report studies of crime over a number of years reveal that middle- and upper-status youth report engaging in a large number of lesser offenses that were not detected or, if detected, did not lead to arrests. Thus, compared to lower-status groups, the middle class engage in more white-collar crime and drug crime, about the same amount of hidden crimes such as vice, but much less street crime. Thus, no simple association exists between overall crime and social class.[43]

Declining Crime, Community Policing, and Other Changes

For decades the common wisdom among criminologists, sociologists, and urban officials was that policing couldn't really prevent crime since its root causes—such as unemployment, drugs, family breakdown, and general urban social decay—were beyond police control. It was commonly believed that the best the police could do was to try to react rapidly to crimes. Thus, emphasis was placed on response techniques such as faster 911 response rates.

However, we now have discovered that we can prevent much crime from occurring and, thus, drop rates. There are a number of causes for the last decades' sharply decreasing crime rates. Demographers point to the effects of an aging population, because street crime is largely an activity of the young, and older populations commit fewer offenses. Also noted is the increasing number of criminals imprisoned and the longer prison sentences for repeat offenders. Repeat offenders can't commit crimes if they are taken off the streets. Police targeting their attention on confiscating illegal guns and on controlling gangs has also played a role. Local police departments in cities such as Richmond, Virginia, now routinely transfer all cases involving illegal firearms to the federal courts because federal law has an automatic mandatory five-year penalty for possessing an illegal firearm. The number of guns on the streets decreases once the word gets out that having a gun automatically gets you put away for five.

Another important change is the major shift in urban drug usage. Crack is out and heroin is in. Crack is a stimulant that makes users impulsive and violent. The crack epidemic hit inner-city neighborhoods in the mid-1980s much like a fever. Many of the crackheads that fueled the 1980s rise in homicides are now dead, in prison, or have outgrown the drug. The crack epidemic broke in the mid-1990s. Crack has been replaced by heroin, which is a depressant that mellows users out. Heroin users are addicted but not violent.

Also contributing to decreasing murder rates is the maturing of drug markets. Most drug-related killings are done by drug dealers, not drug users.[44] As the drug

---

[41]John Conyers, Jr. "We Can Fight Crime with Jobs," *Los Angeles Times Service,* January 18, 1997.

[42]Walter C. Reckless, The *Crime Problem,* Appleton Century Crofts, New York, 1967, pp. 110–112.

[43]Joseph J. Weis, "Social Class and Crime," in Michael Gottfredson and Travis Hisschi (eds.), *Positive Criminology,* Sage, Newbury Park, CA, 1987.

[44]Fox Butterfield, "Many Cities in U.S. Show Sharp Drop in Homicide Rate," *New York Times,* August 13, 1995, p. 18.

trade has been institutionalized, there has been decreasing warfare over territory, as dealers have secured their territorial boundaries. Gangs and drug rings now have established their turf. (The same phenomenon occurred during Prohibition, when gangs established their turf, ending the so-called beer wars.)

All the above factors contribute to the declining rates of urban violence, but there is a general consensus among police and criminologists (but not among all academics) that the largest contributor to dropping urban crime rates is community policing. Community policing strategies are based on the so-called Broken Window Theory first put forth in 1982 by James Q. Wilson and George Kelling.[45] Wilson and Kelling point out that the public's perception of public order plays a major role in preventing crime, and crime flourishes in an environment where there is a perception that no one cares about disorderly behavior. One broken window in an abandoned building soon leads to the breaking of other windows. Similarly, if petty offenses such as graffiti painting, aggressive panhandling, youths taking over parks, and public drinking are ignored, neighborhoods become fearful and eventually crime-ridden. In short, ignoring minor violations creates a disorderly environment that fosters more crime.

The broken window theory suggests that the best way to control crime is to prevent it before it occurs through community policing and zero tolerance. In contrast to the traditional view that effective policing should concentrate on serious offenses, community policing targets minor infractions. Rather than simply reacting to crimes and 911 calls, the police take an active role in *preventing* crimes. The assumption is that controlling minor offenses will prevent major ones. The police presence in the community should be collaborative and oriented toward serving local residences and businesses. This means getting officers out of their cars and onto the street.

The first large-scale application of the approach was in New York, where in the early 1990s it was adopted by Mayor Rudolph Giuliani and Police Commissioner Thomas Bratton. The New York police department, which had previously ignored minor offenses, began a major crackdown on so-called quality-of-life offenses—things like drinking beer in public, not paying subway fares, and public urination. This crackdown changed the culture on the streets. It turned out that many of those arrested for petty offenses, such as jumping turnstiles without paying their fare, were also doing the subway robberies and muggings. Often they were being sought on outstanding warrants for more serious crimes. Stopping someone for drinking an open beer on the street allows the offender's records to be checked by computer for other offenses. (Officially this is known as "police problem solving"; more commonly it is known as "beer and piss patrols.") Cracking down on previously ignored infractions such as public drinking and graffiti spraying also has led to increased resident and store-owner cooperation with police. With a higher risk of being stopped (and a mandatory federal five-year sentence for illegal weapons possession), fewer criminals carry guns. With fewer criminals carrying guns, there are fewer murders.

Community policing also brought modern technology to the street level. Computers are being used to track precinct crime patterns and to flood trouble spots with officers. By identifying a pattern early, an offender can be stopped after 3 crimes rather than after 30. Additionally, authority has been decentralized to precinct commanders, and the commissioner meets weekly with precinct captains, detectives, and others to chart where more cops should be deployed. Precinct commanders are no longer evaluated on how many crimes they clear, but on how few crimes occur in their area. Cities using such techniques have dropped their crime

[45]James Q. Wilson and George L. Kelling, "Broken Windows," *Atlantic Monthly*, March 1982, pp. 29–36; and James Q. Wilson, *Thinking about Crime*, Basic Books, New York, 1983.

Box 12.1 **Making a Difference**

Creating Safe Cities

Small cities have also had success in reducing crime. Charleston, South Carolina, has safe streets, crime rates half those of a decade ago, and only one person under 17 murdered from 1990 to 1995 (he was killed by an adult).[a] The reason in part is techniques introduced by Reuben Greenberg, the city's unorthodox police chief. Greenberg is a southerner, an African American, an Orthodox Jew, and has two master's degrees from the University of California, Berkeley.

Greenberg's methods are simple and old-fashioned. They include strengthening parental authority over teenagers, putting a curfew on teenagers, and getting cops on the street in high-crime areas. Open street drug sales were sharply curtailed, for example, by simply having uniformed police stand on the street next to known drug dealers, thus driving away their customers. After ACLU (American Civil Liberties Union) protests, the police moved down the street from the sellers, but the police also took photos of the license plates of those who stopped at suspected drug dealers.

A popular initiative in the Charleston black community is a curfew plan under which parents sign a form giving police permission to bring home their children found on the streets after midnight. Since parental consent is given, constitutional issues are avoided, as well as the perception that white kids are taken home while black kids go to jail. The result of this and other programs is a city where people feel safer and more in control of their community.

In Boston a combination of tough policing and active community programs focusing on gangs (often involving local churches) has helped drop Boston's homicides from 149 in 1990 to 43 in 1997. The 1995 shooting death of 16-year-old Cassius Love, who was caught in a dispute over a bicycle, led to African American clergy focusing on gangs and developing drop-in centers that provide sanctuary for those who want it. Violence prevention programs, going after violent drug gangs, and tough penalties for the possession of firearms also were implemented. Cassius became a symbol, and for 2 1/2 years there was not another juvenile homicide in Boston. By comparison, in Richmond, Virginia, a city having a population one-third that of Boston (and where this author lives), there were 32 juveniles slain in the same 2 1/2 year period.[b]

[a] Fox Butterfield, "Law and Order in Charleston under the Direction of a Berkeley Graduate," New York Times, April 28, 1996, p. 12.
[b] Frank Green, "Hail of Bullets Slows," Richmond Times-Dispatch, April 19, 1998, p. 1.

rates far below what was thought possible a decade ago. It turns out that smart policing can sharply reduce street crime.

Too aggressive policing by street crime units, though, can produce a backlash when it results in harassment of residents. Minorities, especially young males, are far more likely to be stopped on the street and questioned by the police. Stop-and-frisk laws succeed in getting guns off the street and reducing crime, but they also increase resentment against police in minority communities. Because poorer people of color live in high-crime areas, the stop-and-frisk programs often come to be perceived as primarily racial or ethnic harassment. In 1999 Amadou Diallo, an unarmed African immigrant in New York was killed by a fusillade of 41 bullets fired by four white officers who were seeking a serial rapist. The killing sparked widespread community outrage, and the four police officers were indicted for second-degree murder. A jury found them innocent. Without close supervision and clear rules of operation, street crime programs can turn into harassment or worse. The communities that most benefit from lower crime rates, thus, are often most opposed to heavy policing programs. To be successful, community policing must be perceived as fair and have the consent and approval of the local community. Without such support anticrime programs are seen as racist by residents.

White-Collar Crime

White-collar crime consists of illegal acts of a nonviolent nature committed by supposedly respectable persons, usually in line with their occupation. White-collar crime includes embezzlement, fraud, price-fixing, bribery, antitrust violations, and tax fraud. The term was first coined by Edwin Sutherland to expand the concept of crime beyond those acts more commonly committed by the lower classes.[46] Most white-collar crimes are related to the criminal's legitimate occupation and are committed during the ordinary course of business.[47] Whether this factor is essential to the definition of white-collar crime is a matter of disagreement. Tax fraud, for example, is not necessarily related to one's occupation. Index crimes, such as murder, rape, theft, and larceny, are not white-collar crimes even when they are committed by persons of upper-class status. Nor are professional con artists considered white-collar criminals.

White-collar crime constitutes the largest amount of unreported crime in the United States. It is far more expensive to the society than street crime. Overall yearly losses to white-collar crime are approximately $50 billion a year. Securities frauds perpetrated by Ivan Boesky and Michael Milken in the late 1980s not only cost hundreds of millions of dollars, they also seriously undermined confidence in the securities laws. Similarly, fraud and embezzlement by bankers caused the collapse of the savings and loan industry in the late 1980s and early 1990s. Total losses are estimated to have amounted to between $20 and $40 billion.[48] By comparison, the average bank robbery involves well under $5,000. (Bank fraud is also a federal offense, but the FBI has an informal policy of not becoming involved in prosecuting bank embezzlements of less than $30,000.) In spite of the economic and social cost, white-collar crimes continue to be treated leniently by the courts.

White-collar crime sometimes causes unintended deaths. Some even argue that negligent corporate actions by white-collar criminals kill more people each year than do street criminals.[49] Examples of such would be deaths caused by faulty building construction ("towering infernos"), violations of mine or factory safety laws, the production of unsafe drugs or chemicals, or the building of cars with known safety defects. For example, the Ford Motor Company knew that from 1971 to 1976 it produced dangerous Ford Pintos. Rear-ended at 30 miles per hour, the Pinto buckled like an accordion right up to the rear seat. Such crashes also ruptured the gas tank and jammed shut the doors. Over 500 persons were burned to death.[50] According to internal documents Ford continued to build the dangerous cars because their cost-benefit analysis indicated that at 180 burn deaths a year it would cost them less in lawsuits than it would to prevent the deaths by putting a $5.11 rubber bladder inside the gas tank.[51]

white-collar crime
crimes committed by those of respectable social position and related to their jobs.

---

[46]Edwin H. Sutherland, *White Collar Crime,* Holt, Rinehart and Winston, New York, 1960 (reprint).

[47]James W. Coleman, *The Criminal Elite: The Sociology of White-Collar Crime,* 2d ed., St. Martins Press, New York, 1989.

[48]Kitty Calavita and Henry Pontell, " 'Other Peoples Money' Revisited: Collective Embezzlement in the Savings and Loan Insurance Industries," *Social Problems,* 38:94–112, 1991.

[49]Jeffrey Reiman, *The Rich Get Richer and the Poor Get Prison: Ideology, Class, and Criminal Justice,* 3d ed., Macmillan, New York, 1990.

[50]Mark Dowie, "Pinto Madness," *Mother Jones,* 2, no. 7, September/October, 1977.

[51]Mark Dowie, "Pinto Madness," pp. 18–32.

Public Response

The lack of public response to white-collar crime can be explained by three factors.

First, white-collar crime is perceived as nonviolent, and it does not involve face-to-face contact. The victim is not an individual but usually a large, faceless organization, such as a bank, corporation, or government agency—the type of organizations the sociologist Max Weber defined as bureaucratic (large, impersonal, and dominated by formal rules and procedures).[52] Often there is latent public hostility toward bureaucratic organizations such as corporations, and the public may even applaud, quietly, a lowly employee who is clever enough to "stick it to the big guys."

Second, the costs of white-collar crimes are borne indirectly by society. Financial losses due to embezzlement, skimming off funds for illegal political contributions, or illegal polluting do not fall on particular individuals. The cost is camouflaged by being included with other costs in the form of higher taxes or higher prices for a company's products.

Third, white-collar offenders do not fit our stereotypes of what a criminal looks like or acts like. White-collar criminals are not gang members wearing gang colors; rather, they wear conservative business suits and appear to be pillars of the community. Invariably they are represented by highly qualified counsel. The crimes involve brain rather than brawn, such as financial manipulations that the average jury finds difficult to understand. When caught, white-collar crooks admit to having inadvertently committed "technical violations" without, of course, ever having intended to commit an outright crime. Both Ivan Boesky and Michael Milken came across to many as "legitimate businessmen."

Prosecution and Conviction

Most prosecutors prefer to avoid all but the most blatant cases of white-collar crime because there is usually no plaintiff, and cases are often complex and hard to prove to unsophisticated juries. There is little pressure from the public to take on such cases and "respectable" white-collar offenders are often major political contributors who can bring tremendous pressure to bear on overeager prosecutors. Moreover, in spite of the greater effort and care required to put a white-collar case together, the odds are stacked against actually winning it, thus hurting the prosecutor's conviction record. The chance that a bank robber will be convicted and imprisoned ranges from 83 to 89 percent. A bank embezzler, however, whose take is likely to be 20 to 30 times as much as that of the average bank robber, has only a 23 to 29 percent chance of conviction and imprisonment. The message is clear: Never steal less than a million dollars, and always do it from inside the organization.

Convicted white-collar criminals typically receive light sentences.[53] Both Boesky and Milken made over $500 million a year by fraud, both spent only minimal time in prison, both left prison millionaires, and both are still making millions as "economic advisors." Even when corporations receive huge fines for white-collar crime, the cost may be acceptable as a business expense to the corporation. In 1996, Archer Daniels Midland, the $13 billion a year agricultural products processor, pleaded guilty to price-fixing charges and agreed to pay a record $100 million in fines.[54] The stock market responded to the news by bidding up Archer Daniels stock to a record high. Stock analysts said the $100 million settlement was a small price to remove the question mark of further Justice Department action.

---

[52]Max Weber, *Theory of Social and Economic Organization,* Free Press, New York, 1964.
[53]James W. Coleman, *The Criminal Elite: The Sociology of White Collar Crime,* 3d ed., St. Martin's Press, 1994.
[54]"Archer Daniels to Pay $100 Million Fine," *Bloomberg Business News,* October 15, 1996.

Professional Crime

All social problems textbooks cover violent crime, and they usually add something on white-collar crime. Organized crime usually gets brief coverage at best, and professional criminals such as con artists are usually totally ignored. However, ignoring professional and organized crime presents a limited and biased picture of the range of crime and criminals. It unintentionally implies that crime is committed largely by the poor and minorities.

A Small Elite

As in legitimate enterprises, there are a limited number of highly trained and well-paid criminal specialists who are a professional elite. Criminal professionals include con artists, counterfeiters, check forgers, safecrackers, and more often today, experts at theft by computer. Professional crooks are freelancers and not part of any organization or syndicate (see next section). Career criminals are older since practice often improves their skills. Professional crooks abhor violence and look with disdain on common "snatch and grab" street criminals. Detectives also respect and appreciate the fact that professional crooks don't carry weapons. Professionals view getting caught occasionally as a business risk, and the professional handles the problem in a businesslike manner, often by paying off the officer or judge.

Con Artists

As the continued popularity of the movie *The Sting* indicates, there has always been in America a grudging respect for the professional con artist as a folk hero, especially when it is the rich and famous who get "taken." For example, the 1970s Home-Stake Oil swindle took in over $100 million from investors such as Liza Minnelli, Andy Williams, Bob Dylan, and Barbara Walters. The fraud was simply a new version of the **Ponzi scheme,** named after the infamous 1920 Boston investor who established the pyramid scheme that pays off one set of investors with money obtained from subsequent "marks." Ponzi offered a 50 percent profit in 45 days on the purchase of postal reply coupons that were supposed to appreciate greatly in value. Amazingly, some 40,000 people gave him a total of $15 million (or over $500 million in current dollars) before the scheme collapsed. Ponzi's original pyramid destroyed the life savings of many naive small investors, but the major expense faced today by wealthy people involved in get-rich-quick swindles is loss of face. The pain of the victims in the Home-Stake Oil swindle was soothed by our favor-the-rich tax laws, which allowed them to write off their Home-Stake losses as tax deductions.

A huge recent fraud was the 1997 collapse of the Canadian Bre-X Minerals Company. When Bre-X was launched on the Alberta Stock Exchange in 1989 it traded for pennies—until the firm announced a large gold find at their Indonesian mine site. Statements by Bre-X officers as to the size of the find kept growing: from 30 million ounces to 51 million to 71 million, and eventually 200 million ounces.[55] By 1996 Bre-X was one of the hottest stocks being traded and the

Ponzi scheme
an illegal pyramid scheme that pays off earlier investors with money from subsequent investors

---

[55]Kevin Whitlaw, "Fools Gold and Other Goodies from Canada," *U.S. News and World Report,* May 19, 1997, p. 50.

Box 12.2 Ongoing Issues

Scamming Sociologists

Many well-meaning sociologists were victimized by a con artist between 1995 and 1997. The scam worked like this. A well-educated man with a good knowledge of sociology phoned minority faculty members claiming to be Harry Edwards, the well-known African American sports sociologist at the University of California. The imposter sounded like Edwards and was very knowledgeable about sociology. He said his brother (or sometimes his nephew) C. K. (or sometimes Kevin) Edwards is in the mark's town for a job interview. The problem is that all of Kevin's credit cards are in his luggage, which didn't make it (or has been sent by the airline to Denver). Kevin is identified as being a heavy black male, and the supposed Harry Edwards says Kevin needs $200 (or $400) for clothes for his in-terview. He will sign a promissory note for the amount borrowed.

The imposter further states that he (Harry Edwards) will be arriving in the faculty member's town Sunday and will bring the cash to the door. For helping out his brother he promises to make a $1,000 donation to the department. Sometimes the bogus Edwards also offers the mark a pair of professional sports tickets.

This scam was good enough to get money from sociologists from at least 78 colleges. Sometimes several people in the same department were victimized. The fraud, or variations, took in everyone from new assistant professors to respected senior figures such as William Julius Wilson. The imposter was caught and, after a brief prison sentence, is now free.

market capitalization had soared to $4.5 billion. The company officers, meanwhile, were quietly selling their shares at huge profits. The bubble burst in 1997 when independent tests of gold samples from the mine site indicated that the original ore tests had been "salted" with outside gold. Share prices, which had been over $250, collapsed to nothing. From the outset the Bre-X gold site had been pure fraud.

Organized Crime

organized crime
criminal activity run in a systematic businesslike manner to provide illegal goods and services such as drugs, gambling, and prostitution.

If professional crooks are self-employed specialists, then organized crime represents a criminal corporate structure. **Organized crime** does not refer simply to a group of criminals working together but specifically to members of an hierarchically ordered syndicate. Organized crime is variously referred to as **The Organization, The Mafia, Cosa Nostra,** or in Chicago, **The Outfit.** While some of these names suggest Italian roots, organized crime is multiethnic, including Colombian drug cartels, Mexican syndicates, Asian triads, and the Russian mafia.

Syndicate or organized crime is big business; its income exceeds that of General Motors. Meyer Lansky, a New York crime syndicate boss of the midcentury, is reported to have boasted, "We're bigger than U.S. Steel." Organized crime does not pay taxes, but it does have considerable overhead expenses, such as payoffs to police and politicians. The Central Intelligence Agency estimates that up to half of organized crime's profits go to bribing and paying off various officials.[56] Front groups are used to contribute to individual politicians' Political Action Committees (PACs).

---

[56]John Dillen, "U.S. Probes Crime's Global Reach," *Christian Science Monitor,* April 22, 1994, p. 1.

Reputed New York mob boss John Gotti at his 1990 trial for ordering a revenge shooting of a union official. Unlike previous trials for racketeering and conspiracy where he was acquitted, Gotti was convicted this time.

Richard Drew/AP/Wide World Photos

Organized crime is rarely involved in one-time operations such as robbery. Instead, it functions as a business organization, providing continuing illegal products and services that the public demands, such as drugs, gambling, prostitution, and high-risk loans (loansharking). As a rule, those using the services of organized crime are also breaking the law. Syndicate violence is usually reserved for criminal competitors or internal syndicate members who get out of line.

For years illegal lotteries, known variously as "bookmaking," "numbers," or "policy," have been an organized crime standby. State lotteries have cut into organized crime's gambling operations, but for those in urban neighborhoods using local numbers runners, any winnings are totally tax free. While drugs and gambling remain organized crime's biggest money-makers, loansharking is also quite profitable. Loansharking is lending money at usurious rates to those individuals—perhaps small businesspeople such as restaurant operators—who for a variety of reasons cannot get credit elsewhere. The amount of interest charged is simply what the traffic will bear.

There is an old Chicago story—whether true or not—illustrating the process of wholesale loansharking. The story is that The Outfit boss gave a lavish Christmas party for his 10 lieutenants. After dinner, he had 10 large suitcases brought into the dining room and one placed before each guest. Each suitcase contained $1,000,000 in cash. The host simply said, "I want 1 percent a week for this. I don't care what you get, but I want 1 percent a week." No receipts were signed for the $10 million handed out. The boss's only problem was finding new lieutenants the next year to whom he could give suitcases.

Organized crime exists because it provides services that the public demands. If citizens don't want illegal liquor or drugs, government must allow legitimate alternatives. As Al Capone remarked about his illegal breweries during Prohibition, "It's a shame that the working man can't have a glass of beer after a long day's work. All I'm doing is providing a service." If pimp-run prostitution is to be reduced, legalizing prostitution (as in Canada and Western Europe) may be necessary. If loansharking is to be cut, other credit sources for high-risk loans have to be substituted. To repeat, organized crime flourishes by providing illegal services the public wants.

Investing in "Legitimate" Enterprises

Lucky Luciano is credited with the idea that criminally earned monies should be invested in legitimate businesses. For half a century organized crime has been involved in activities such as hard-core pornography clubs, porno shops, and making hard-core videos. Crime syndicates also invest in businesses, hotels, casinos, bars, and restaurants. Such covers provide legitimacy as well as offering a means of laundering funds and providing tax shelters.

Not surprisingly, "legitimate" syndicate businesses make handsome profits through the judicious combination of older syndicate methods and white-collar crime. The organization sees to it that competition from other businesses remains minimal and union "sweetheart contracts" ensure that their businesses have no union troubles. "Political contributions" are made to members of the city council or state representatives to make sure that lucrative municipal and state contracts will go to Organization-controlled firms.

Organized crime can be very inventive. Federal convictions in 1998 exposed an extortion scheme by the New York Gambino organization and what were thought to be minority-hiring civil rights groups. For three decades construction companies in New York have dealt with groups claiming to represent minority workers battling racial bias in the construction industry. It turns out that some of the best known of these groups, the United Construction Labor Coalitions, the Black and Latin Survival Coalition (BLES), and Brooklyn Fights Back had long been allies of the Gambino family in a shakedown scheme.[57] The "community coalitions" staged stormy protests that resulted in the coalition leaders being paid off by the construction firms with lucrative no-show jobs such as "community coordinators." At the same time, the Gambino family was also taking protection money from the contractors in order to supposedly reduce demands by the coalitions. What the contractors didn't know was that The Organization had helped set up the protests, and that the contractors were paying off both sides. No actual minority jobs were created.

Organized crime is far less effective today than in decades past, when the late J. Edgar Hoover even went on the record denying organized crime even existed. Today, the FBI devotes almost a quarter of its resources to combating organized crime. Successful prosecution of kingpins such as John Gotti have been aided by the use of conversation-monitoring technology, witness-protection programs, and new criminal-conspiracy laws.

The Criminal Justice System

The U.S. criminal justice system—police, courts, and correctional institutions—is rapidly expanding. Between 1980 and 1996 the number of prisoners in the United States shot up from 320,000 to 1.6 million.[58] It is now 1.8 million, giving us more people in prison than any other nation on earth. The prison population increase since 1980 is eightfold in California and Texas. In Texas, as of 2000, the system held 206,000 inmates or one of every 21 adults of both sexes.

Plea Bargaining

Currently, more than half of those convicted of a felony are not being sentenced to prison (partially because of prison overcrowding), and most convicted felons serve

---

[57]Selwyn Raab, "Minority-Hiring Groups Tied to Mob in Testimony," *New York Times*, January 16, 1999, pp. 19–21.
[58]The White House, *The National Drug Control Strategy, 1997*, Government Printing Office, Washington, DC, 1997, p. 18.

Box 12.3 Ongoing Issues

The Japanese Godfathers

Sensitive about losing face, the Japanese do not "export" the information that their "big seven" *yakuza* gangs are larger than the Mafia. Nearly 43,000 *yakuza* members are organized into seven major *gumi* and 20 to 30 lesser groups. Most of the gumis' income comes from drugs, prostitution, and gambling. The *yakuza* are also heavily invested in real estate and seriously aggravated Japan's 1990s banking crisis by insisting that all their bad loans resulting from the collapse of the Japanese real estate bubble be paid in full.[a] Many of the nearly $600 billion in bad loans were made to *keizai yakuza,* or economic gangsters, who use threats and violence to avoid foreclosures.[b] The "commission" that crime syndicates charge to clear bad property loans ranges from 30 to 40 percent.

Historically, the most powerful of the "big seven" gangs was Yamaguchi-gumi. The Yamaguchi-gumi alone number some 11,000 tightly organized gamblers, pimps, extortionists, and general hoodlums. Hideomi Oda, when director of the Yamaguchi-gumi syndicate, put it blandly: "The police have their own roles; we have ours. In the daytime the police protect the citizens, and at night I protect them."[c] Japanese gangs operate remarkably openly by Western standards. Yamaguchi-gumi even publishes its own magazine, complete with gang flag on the cover. Other touches that are uniquely Japanese are gang lodge uniforms worn during gang funeral parades, sponsored golf tournaments for members, and the use of formal calling cards with gang affiliation and specialties printed on the card. When Masahisa Takenaka, godfather of the Yamaguchi-gumi syndicate was murdered by a rival in 1985 over 1,000 dark-suited *yakuza* attended the funeral. Television crews in helicopters filmed the funeral while 400 police provided security.

Mob members in Japan often have wide public visibility. Rev. Hiroyuki Suzuki is shown here preaching outside Tokyo in 1999. Notice the severed tips of his little fingers, penalties for mob infractions. Suzuki has written a popular book with seven other former gangsters and has spoken at a White House prayer breakfast.

Atsushi Tsukada/AP/Wide World Photos

Organized crime, as in the United States, has a strong familistic orientation. In Japan's traditional hierarchical society, organized crime is a route to prestige open to economically deprived youth. As in the United States, organized crime offers an alternate illegitimate means of achieving social mobility to those who have internalized the success goals of the society but are denied the socially approved means of achieving these goals.[d] Members atone for a "mistake" by having the little finger removed at the first knuckle with a sword. For the next mistake, the finger is taken off at the second knuckle. Members are also elaborately tattooed as a symbol of lifetime fealty.

Similar to U.S. syndicates, Japanese organizations have invested heavily in legitimate front organizations, such as construction companies and longshoremen's "development associations." Japanese crime syndicates invest in legitimate enterprises abroad from ranches in Australia to gravel pits in Korea.

[a]*Sandara Sugawara, "Gangsters Aggravating Japanese Banking Crisis,"* Washington Post, *December 15, 1995, p. A1.*
[b]*David E. Kaplan, "Yakuza Inc.,"* U.S. News and World Report, *April 13, 1998, p. 46.*
[c]*Donald Kirk, "Crime, Politics, and Finger Chopping,"* New York Times Magazine, *December 12, 1976, p. 61.*
[d]*For discussion of this concept, see Robert K. Merton,* Social Theory and Social Structure, *Free Press of Glencoe, New York, 1957, pp. 131–192.*

less than half their sentence. The average murderer released from a state prison has served only 5.9 years. According to Department of Justice figures, for every 100 felony arrests brought by the police for prosecution, 49 are carried forward to trial and 45 of these are settled by plea bargains. Of the remaining four that go to trial, three will be found guilty and one acquitted. Of the total 48 convicted by plea bargaining or trial, 11 are sentenced to incarceration for a year or more.[59]

To clear court dockets—and improve conviction records—90 percent of serious crimes are settled by "plea bargaining." **Plea bargaining** is a system whereby a defendant waives his or her right to a trial and pleads guilty to a lesser offense agreed upon in advance. Also known as "copping a plea," this allows a defendant to escape the possibility of a heavier penalty. This compromise keeps the system working, but the terms of the deal between the prosecutor and defense attorney depend on a number of factors, including how busy the district attorney's office is at the moment, the strength of the prosecutor's case, and whether the D.A. is running for political office.

Plea bargaining is going to remain an integral part of the criminal justice system because there is no real alternative. If 80 percent of cases were settled by plea bargaining instead of the current 90 percent, the number of cases brought to trial would double. Court systems, already overloaded in many communities, would collapse under such an increased load. Without plea bargaining, the cost of the criminal justice system would be prohibitive. Plea bargaining meets the needs of courts, prosecutors, and defendants. Whether it also meets the requirements of justice is a separate question.

Prisons

Prisons generally hold those convicted of felonies punishable with sentences of a year or more; jails hold those sentenced to less than a year. In spite of crime rates falling, more prisons are being built. California spends $4 billion a year to operate the nation's largest prison system, and the state has built 21 prisons since 1984—and just one university campus. Over the last decade California's pay for prison guards has doubled to a 1999 average of $51,000 a year. By comparison, a new assistant professor in the state's university system averaged only $41,000.[60] There is no relationship between a state's prison expenditures and its crime rate. New York, for example, during the 1990s had a much larger drop in homicides than California, despite the fact that California locks up nine times as many people.

Crowding prisons with nonviolent offenders is not only costly but has two serious side effects. The first is that nonviolent offenders take up space better devoted to violent criminals. The second is that prison, rather than reforming, often converts misfits into long-term criminals. Oregon is experimenting with alternatives to prison for nonviolent offenders. Oregon has increased penalties for violent criminals, but decreased prison time for thieves and other nonviolent offenders. Violent offenders now make up two-thirds of Oregon's prison population as compared to a third in 1986.[61] Oregon, unlike California or Texas, is transferring money

[59]Barbara Boland and Ronald Stones, *The Prosecution of Felony Arrests,* Bureau of Justice Statistics, Department of Justice, Washington, DC, 1986.
[60]Timothy Egan, "Nation's War on Crack Retreats, Still Taking Prisoners," *New York Times,* February 28, 1999, p. 20.
[61]Bob Evans, "Oregon Tries Lesser Penalties," *Richmond Times Dispatch,* September 14, 1994, p. A4.

out of its corrections budget and into education, counseling, and alternative probationary programs. Because the cost of maintaining a prisoner is roughly $22,000 a year, decreasing the prison population means major tax savings.

Goals of Imprisonment

The "official" goals of the prison system are (1) punishment or retribution, (2) restraint, (3) deterrence, and (4) rehabilitation. Of these four goals, prisons have been by far the most successful in punishment or retribution.

Punishment In traditional cultures, retribution long followed the Old Testament law of "an eye for an eye." Such practices are still found in Saudi Arabia, where the punishment for repeated thefts is amputation of the offending hand. In colonial America offenders were flogged, branded, put in stocks, or otherwise singled out for public humiliation. Hawthorne's classic tale *The Scarlet Letter* illustrates how public humiliation was used in early America.

Prisons were not widely used in the United States until the early nineteenth century. The initial impetus for imprisonment came from the Pennsylvania Quakers, who viewed crimes not only as violations of the civil code but also as offenses against God. Criminals, the Quakers believed, needed time in isolation to contemplate their sins and repent. Although few other states apart from Pennsylvania adopted this concept of total solitary confinement, we still refer to prisons as *penitentiaries* (places for doing penance).

That prisons succeed in punishing people is beyond question. Alabama, Arizona, and Florida even brought back chain gangs in 1995. (They have since given up chain gangs as a result of a court settlement, and cost reasons.)

Restraint To a degree, prisons have been successful at preventing or restraining people from harming others. Incarceration protects society by keeping convicted felons off of the street for at least part of their criminal careers, thus preventing them from committing more crimes. If prisons fail to convince the criminal to "go and sin no more," they at least take some violent repeaters out of circulation. The extent of the protection is evidenced by the estimate that 65 percent of those imprisoned are recidivists, or repeaters. (This, of course, also argues the failure of prisons to rehabilitate or deter.)

Deterrence Prisons have been less successful at deterrence—that is, influencing offenders to "go straight" (specific deterrence) or persuading potential criminals to remain within the law (general deterrence). The two-thirds of prison inmates who are repeaters certainly have not been deterred by their previous penitentiary experience. The degree to which the larger public is deterred from criminal acts by fear of punishment is unknown. Evidence about whether punishment does indeed deter crime is fragmentary, but statistical data (going back a number of years) suggest that it does act as a deterrent to some degree.[62]

The threat of punishment is an effective deterrent only where there is some premeditation before a crime is committed. Certainty of punishment has a significant deterrent effect on upper-status white-collar criminals. On the other hand, impulsive

---

[62]Jack Gibbs, "Crime, Punishment, and Deterrence," *Southwestern Social Science Quarterly*, March 1968, pp. 315–530.

crimes, such as a murder of passion, are unlikely to be deterred by knowledge of the level of punishment. Sociologists and criminologists agree that *certainty* of punishment is much more important than its severity.

Rehabilitation Throughout much of the twentieth century, rehabilitation was widely regarded as the most important function of imprisonment. Convicts in prison are supposed to learn a trade and become useful, law-abiding citizens. Unfortunately, the trade is often something like making license plates, and the convict who enters prison illiterate is likely to leave the same way. Authorities generally agree that there is no clear proof that rehabilitation treatment decreases crime. This does not mean that rehabilitation cannot be effective but only that it frequently is not effective as currently practiced. The problem is that no one—criminologists, judges, or prison officials—knows any certain technique for rehabilitating criminals.

Quick-Fix Solutions

"Quick-fix" solutions, as we saw in Chapter 1, often create more difficulties than they solve. One of these quick-fixes is "three strikes and you're out" laws mandating life in prison for a third conviction. Mandatory life in prison for a third felony conviction (whatever the offense) means that criminals with two convictions never plea bargain to a felony. The result is that, instead of only 10 percent of such cases going to court, 100 percent do so—a result that has dramatically crowded court calendars in states such as California that implemented three-strike laws.

Another consequence of the law is that prosecutors often drop cases where they feel the penalty for conviction outweighs the crime. Three-strikes laws also may increase the number of murders because someone with two convictions may be less inclined to leave a witness if he or she knows that a third conviction means life imprisonment. Three-strikes laws also are extremely costly. The Rand Corporation (one of the nation's premier think tanks) estimates that the additional annual cost to California taxpayers of actually enforcing its three-strikes law would be $5.5 billion—or a yearly cost of $350 per taxpayer.[63] In 1996 the California Supreme Court restricted the use of the law. As of 2000 of the 23 states that had adopted three-strikes laws only a handful (mostly California and Georgia) have put more than a half-dozen people permanently behind bars.

Elderly Inmates

John Bedarka, an 86-year-old in frail health clutching a walker, is in prison at Laurel Highlands in Pennsylvania for shooting his wife's lover 30 years ago. Inmates like him are an unanticipated consequence of mandatory life sentences. There now are 125,000 state and federal inmates over age 50. The National Criminal Justice Commission reports the cost of maintaining a state inmate over 55 is $69,000 a year, or three times the cost of imprisoning the typical adult inmate.[64] Worse, a number of states, such as Florida and California, have had to give early release to

---

[63]"Crime and Punishment," *U.S. News and World Report*, July 3, 1995, p. 24.
[64]National Criminal Justice Commission, *The Real War on Crime*, Harper Perennial, New York, 1996.

younger, and potentially far more dangerous, prisoners because of court orders to reduce prison crowding.

Is there any reason to keep a wheelchair-bound 70-year-old diabetic in prison? Or an old man with Alzheimer's disease who doesn't even know who he is? Rather than turning prisons into geriatric nursing homes, a cheaper alternative would be to incarcerate nondangerous geriatric residents in secured nursing homes.

Certainty of Punishment

Certainty of punishment for the guilty is the crucial element that is missing from our present criminal justice system. Research consistently indicates that the greatest deterrence to crime is not the severity of the sentence but simply the certainty of having to face some kind of punishment. Harsher sentences have little or no effect on a criminal who recognizes that the odds are overwhelmingly against his or her ever being sentenced to prison. The current emphasis on heavier punishment diverts attention and priorities away from structural reforms in society that might help to deter crime.

Toward the Future

What is the prognosis for the future? While fear of crime remains high, the reality is that the situation in most localities is much improved from a decade ago. American crime rates remain high in comparison to most of the world, but in recent years there have been fewer murders, rapes, muggings, and car thefts.

There has been no magic cure, but we have learned that community policing that focuses on preventing rather than reacting to crimes can help citizens to feel more in control and can reduce overall crime rates. Locking away the truly violent offenders for longer periods also contributes to lower crime rates.

Youth crime will be the real challenge for the next decade. With the number of teenagers increasing in the early years of the century, there will be more young people at risk. If we become complacent, we could be blind-sided by a new youth crime wave. On the criminal justice side, it is likely that juveniles committing felonies will increasingly come before criminal courts. Whether the courts and prisons can effectively deal with young offenders is doubtful.

The political response to crime during the last decade and a half has focused heavily on increasing punishment levels. With penalties already at record high levels, this trend may slacken somewhat. Declining fear of crime may also lead to increasing concern paid to rehabilitation experiments. Such increased national concern with rehabilitation will come not from any widespread movement for prison reform but rather because the cost of incarcerating prisoners takes a large share of state government budgets. As yearly costs rise beyond the current $22,000 a year average, the pressure will build to find less expensive (and hopefully more humane) alternatives. Nonviolent offenders may be increasingly sentenced to remain at home (and at work), while being electronically monitored by sophisticated monitoring devices.

If crime rates continue to decrease, the fear of crime should begin to abate. Under such circumstances, a real national discussion on how to prevent crime might emerge, a discussion that is not driven simply by fear.

Summary

Crime is defined not as a moral category but rather as actions that violate the criminal code. Current U.S. crime rates actually are going down, but crime is still viewed by urban residents as the nation's most serious social problem. Crime statistics must be used with care, however, because all crimes committed are not reported, and the Uniform Crime Reports do not include entire categories of crime, such as white-collar offenses. National Crime Victim Surveys often provide better data. Only a third of all crimes and half of violent offenses are reported to the police.

- Functionalists see much crime as a consequence of the breakdown of traditional institutional constraints on behavior.

- Conflict theorists stress that what is criminal and what is not is determined by the powerful: What the poor do is a crime and what "respectable" people do is "make mistakes."

- Social interactionists focus on how delinquent and criminal behavior come to be socially learned and transmitted.

- Large cities have higher crime rates than smaller municipalities, with rates within metropolitan areas highest for inner-city areas.

- Crime rates vary dramatically according to the sex, age, race, and ethnicity of those involved.

- White-collar crimes, such as embezzlement and price fixing, cost the nation more than street crime, yet they are often viewed by the public and courts as relatively minor or "technical" violations.

- Professional criminals, including con artists, counterfeiters, safecrackers, and specialized thieves, are the elite, freelance specialists of the criminal world. They rarely engage in violent crime.

- Organized crime represents the corporate approach to crime by providing illegal services for a relatively fixed clientele. Organized crime is heavily involved in gambling, drugs, prostitution, and loansharking.

- Ninety percent of all serious crimes are resolved not by trials but by plea bargaining.

- America's prison population proportionally is the highest on earth. The rate of incarceration is five times that of 1980 and still growing.

- The goals of prison are punishment, restraint, deterrence, and rehabilitation, yet they've only been successful at the first two.

☞Key Review Terms

crime
criminal justice system
delinquency
deterrence
felony
misdemeanor
National Crime Victim
Survey

organized crime
plea bargaining
Ponzi scheme
prison
professional crime
punishment
rehabilitation
restraint

street crime
Uniform Crime Report
white-collar crime

? Questions for Discussion

1. Discuss popular and media perceptions of crime in America. How does this differ from the picture presented in this chapter?

2. What is occurring with violent crime rates in America? What is the situation in your community? Who is most likely to be the victim of a violent crime?

3. What is a delinquent act? Compare the adult and juvenile justice systems. Why do they differ? How should the juvenile court system be reformed?

4. We are constantly bombarded with crime statistics. How accurate are they and how are they collected? What are the two major national sources of statistics on crime? Which is better and why?

6. Discuss and compare how a functionalist and a conflict theorist would view street crime and white-collar crime. Which position comes closest to your views and why?

7. What personal characteristics are most associated with criminal behavior? Discuss the role played by gender, age, race, and socioeconomic position. How do these differ by type of crime?

8. How effective are policing efforts in large cities such as New York? How have policing techniques changed in the last decade? Have such changes been effective? Why?

9. What type of offenses fall under the heading of "white-collar crime?" Who commits these crimes, and what are the differences in prosecution, conviction, and sentencing when compared with street crime?

10. Discuss organized crime in America and how it functions. What are the criminal activities in which it engages and who becomes a member? Is organized crime unique to the United States? How have the police and court systems dealt with organized crime? Is that changing?

☞ Suggested Resources

James W. Coleman, *The Criminal Elite: The Sociology of White Collar Crime*, third ed., St. Martin Press, New York, 1994. A detailed examination of white-collar crime and why it is treated differently than street crime.

Victor Hassine, *Life Without Parole: Living in Prison Today*, Roxbury, Los Angeles, 1996. A convicted murderer gives the feeling of the violence and hopelessness that surrounds him in prison.

Joy James, ed., *States of Confinements: Policing, Detention, and Prisons*, St. Martins Press, New York, 2000. A collection of articles dealing with the prison system, and especially its incarceration of minorities.

Martin Sanchez-Jankowski, *Islands in the Street: Gangs and American Urban Society*, University of California Press, Berkeley, 1991. An award winning study of Latino gangs in Los Angeles and the important role of fighting as a means of establishing status.

Geni Sikes, *8 Ball Chicks: The Violent World of Girl Gangsters*, Anchor, New York, 1997. An eight-year participant observation study of violent female street gangs.

Wayne S. Wooden, *Renegade Kids, Suburban Outlaws: From Youth Culture to Delinquency*, Wadsworth, Belmont, CA, 1995. Rebellious suburban teenagers who join deviant groups from skinheads to cults.

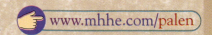
1. Begin gathering information about crime in the United States by visiting the following government websites: The FBI Home Page (*www.fbi.gov/ucr.htm*). Here, you'll find the most recent compilation of crime statistics under the Uniform Crime Reporting (UCR) system as well as links to other valuable sources of information. Another important site is the U.S. Department of Justice home page, (*www.usdoj.gov/index.html*). Click "Fugitives and Missing Persons" and you will be taken to a site that lists everybody from the FBI's "Ten Most Wanted" to "Deadbeat Parents." A third important federal resource is the U.S. Department of Justice, Federal Bureau of Prisons website (*www.bop.gov/*). Also, an independently maintained (although somewhat dated) website with many excellent links is the Blue Leprecon's Corrections Directory (*www.tiac.net/users/leprecon/blue.htm*).

2. Gather information on the debate over Capital Punishment. Visit the Derechos Human Rights website at (*www.derechos.org/*). Click on "Site Map" and then click on "Death Penalty" for a comprehensive list of national and international sites. Next, link to the ACLU's website on the death penalty (*www.aclu.org/issues/death/hmdp.html*).

   a. What are the major reasons given for opposing the death penalty? Pro-Death Penalty.com (*www.prodeathpenalty.com/*) is a site that supports the death penalty. Select "Death Penalty Links" and you will find links to sites that are either Pro Death Penalty or Anti Death Penalty.

   b. What percentage of the U.S. population favors the death penalty? See if you can find out through the National Opinion Research Center (*www.norc.uchicago.edu/homepage.htm*) General Social Survey. (You may have to revisit Chapter 1 of this text to refresh your memory on how to do this).

Chapter 13

His name is Frankie. He's walking up Vine Street toward 13th Street with his head down, and he isn't really walking—he's shuffling and his head is down because he's looking for a dry cigarette butt. It rained last night and the goddamn butts are wet and even if you put them in a little paper bag, it takes too long to dry them out so you can get a smoke. And those sons-of-bitches that smoke filters should drop dead right now, because you spot a big one and when you bend over to pick it up it's a Salem or a Kent. And what he wouldn't give for a drink. A drink of wine or squeeze of witch hazel or anything! If it only had alcohol in it!

Leonard Blumberg, Thomas E. Shipley, Jr., and Irving W. Shandler, *Skid Row and Its Alternatives,* Temple University Press, Philadelphia, 1973, pp. 30–32.

Substance Abuse: Legal and Otherwise

outline

Drugs as a Way of Life

Cramming for an exam, your roommate lights another cigarette and pours another cup of coffee. Writing an overdue term paper, you pop a pep pill to stay awake. Finishing several hours later, you both relax by having a beer. Two hours later, unable to fall asleep, you take a Sominex and an aspirin.

Extent of Usage

America has become a giant drugstore, where "better living through chemistry" seems to have become a national slogan. We accept that most people cannot get through a normal day without taking drugs of some sort. If you doubt this, go through your living quarters and count the number of drugs you find. Include all prescription and nonprescription "medicines," such as sedatives, tranquilizers, stimulants, and narcotic and alcoholic based cough syrups. Because alcohol is a drug, include beer and alcoholic beverages in your total. Be sure not to overlook the pack of cigarettes with its addictive nicotine. Then include milder drugs, such as caffeine in coffee or tea. All the above are legal drugs.

Name the problem, and there is a drug to solve it. Drugs are the answer to outbursts of temper, lack of energy, inability to sleep, constipation, and diarrhea. Psychoactive (mood-altering) drugs promise even more by providing shortcuts to self-awareness, inner peace, and euphoria, or by simply allowing one to forget or ignore all the complex and messy problems that come with being alive. There is Ritalin for hyperactive children and Prozac for everyone else. We even expect to cure drug problems with drugs (e.g., heroin dependence with methadone or buprenorphine). While reading this chapter, keep in mind that, while using drugs to solve problems or to make us feel better is imbedded in our culture, society makes sharp distinctions between using what are defined as legal drugs and those prohibited as illegal.

Social Definitions of Drugs

In the first chapter we discussed C. Wright Mills's distinction between private troubles and public issues. Drug abuse falls into the second category because it harms society and the problem can be resolved only with collective action. Today drug abuse is closely associated with crime. According to the National Institutes of Justice, the percentage of arrestees testing positive for illicit drug use ranged from 51 percent in San Jose to 80 percent in Chicago (based on urine samples of male arrestees in 23 cities).[1] In New York City, where three-

---

[1]Office of National Drug Control Policy, *Drug Data Summary,* Government Printing Office, Washington, DC, April 1999, p. 2.

364

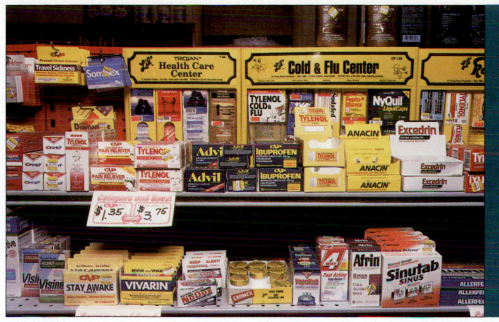

© Eastcott-Momatiuk/The Image Works

fourths test positive, drug abuse is estimated to cost the city $20 billion a year. Nationally, the Bureau of Justice Statistics reports that 60 percent of prison inmates report being under the influence of drugs or alcohol at the time of the offense that got them incarcerated.[2] Drug abuse also contributes to spouse and child abuse, is heavily implicated (through contaminated needles) in sexually transmitted diseases such as AIDS, and undergirds much street violence. Drug abuse is also remarkably expensive. Each year drugs and alcohol trigger some $75 billion in health care costs, including treating drug dealers' gunshot wounds, terminal AIDS patients, and crack babies in $2,000-a-day neonatal wards.[3] Government spending on the war on drugs increased from roughly $1 billion in 1980 to $17.7 billion in 2000.[4] The lion's share of these billions go to law enforcement and the criminal justice system. Funds for treatment are perpetually in short supply.

When discussing drug usage, keep in mind that social definitions (or even medical definitions) of drugs are not always consistent from a scientific point of view. We do not define a drug as legal or illegal on the basis of medical criteria, such as the degree to which it affects the mind, endangers the user's health, or is habituating. Long-established social custom is more important. For example, alcohol use is accepted by our culture, yet alcohol has greater mind-altering potential than marijuana, an illegal drug. In terms of health risk, alcohol is far more deadly than heroin. According to the highest estimates, heroin addiction affects 600,000 people. This is a large number, but nowhere near the minimum of 9 million Americans who are alcoholics. Yearly, some 35,000 Americans die of cirrhosis of the liver, a condition mostly caused by excessive drinking.

When officials or the media speak of **drug abuse,** they invariably are referring to the illegal use of hallucinogens, stimulants, and depressants. The major "drug problem" in North America is not one of young people becoming addicted to illegal drugs (**addiction** is dependence on a drug to the point where cessation of use

drug abuse
use of a chemical substance to the degree that physical, psychological, and social harm results.

addiction
habitual use of drugs or alcohol to the extent that stopping causes physiological as well as psychological trauma.

[2]Ibid.
[3]Joseph A. Califano Jr., "It's Drugs, Stupid," *New York Times Magazine,* January 29, 1995, p. 38.
[4]J. Horgan, "A Kinder War," *Scientific American,* 24:26, July 1993; and Office of National Drug Control Policy, *Drug Data Summary,* p. 5.

causes severe physical or psychological trauma). The largest problem is the over-use and abuse of legal drugs, such as tranquilizers, pep pills, alcohol, and tobacco. Which drugs are defined as a problem depends on a society's customs, norms, morals, common practices, and laws. This means that our "drug problem" definitions are *primarily social* and only secondarily medical or legal.

Sociological Perspectives

Functionalist Approaches

Functionalists don't attempt to explain individual drug use. Rather, they look at how macrolevel changes in society might affect drug usage patterns. To some functionalists, drug usage is seen as a response to pressures and contradictions of urban industrial society that weaken social norms. Increased drug abuse is seen as a reflection of the breakdown of traditional social institutions of family, church, and community. Rules and values become unclear, causing social strain, which in turn leads to drug and alcohol abuse.

Others see heavy drug and alcohol abuse among the poor and minorities as a form of retreatism in which using drugs reflects rejection of both the socially approved goal of success and the socially approved means of achieving the goal. Rather than fighting an unequal fight, the retreatist "turns on and drops out." Drugs give relief from stress or a grim social environment. This can also be the case for suburban adolescents. Other functionalists see the sale of illegal drugs as a means for those economically excluded to achieve the American cultural value of quick economic success.

To most functionalists, drug interdiction and police programs don't deal with basic causes. Drug abuse, like other antisocial behavior, can best be reduced by strengthening traditional institutions of social control. Because it is recognized that this may not occur, as a minimum, policing and court policies have to be made more fair and uniform.

Conflict Approaches

Similarly to functionalists, conflict theory advocates focus on drug usage largely as a consequence of other social problems reflecting inequality, such as unemployment and racism. Conflict approach advocates suggest that the existing power structure determines which drugs are legal and which are not. Alcohol use, supported by the large and politically powerful alcohol industry, is legal while marijuana use is not. Thus, the war on drugs ignores alcohol abuse, while concentrating on street drugs used by the poor.

Authorities are far more likely to enforce drug policies against the poor and minorities than against the powerful. Thus, the penalties for using an inner-city drug such as 5 grams of crack cocaine are the same as for 500 grams of powdered cocaine, the suburban version. Although most drug users are middle-class whites, most of those arrested for drug offenses are African American males. This in turn can lead to conspiracy theories. Black Muslims, for example, see drug use in inner-city areas as the result of a direct policy by whites to addict, and thus control, minorities.

Culver Pictures

Interactionist Approaches

Social interactionist advocates note that much drug usage is a learned behavior. Drug use occurs as part of a socialization process. Youths learn from peers which drugs are "in" and which are not, how to use different drugs, and where to buy them. They also learn how to interpret and label drug effects (e.g., dizziness, disorientation, or mood swings) in a positive fashion. Interactionists are interested in how a drug user comes to internalize the definition of him- or herself as a drug user, and how that leads to further drug use.

To interactionists the drug subculture plays a crucial role in socializing individuals into drug usage. Thus, to change drug usage it is necessary not just to arrest people but to change the culture surrounding drugs. Interactionists point out that drug legislation reflects more the social customs of the society than the pharmacological effects of the drugs. Morphine and heroin, for instance, are pharmacologically similar, but the former is viewed as being proper when used medically while the latter is not. There also are age and ethnic group differences regarding which drugs are acceptable and which are not. Most baby boomers, for instance, grew up in a youth culture that saw the use of marijuana as socially acceptable. Later generations did not.

Alcohol: Uses and Abuses

We begin with alcohol, because it is the most widely used drug. The yearly American adult consumption of alcohol is about 2 gallons of liquor, 33 gallons of beer, and 3 gallons of wine.[5] The actual consumption of the average drinker is higher

---

[5]U.S. Bureau of the Census, *Statistical Abstract of the United States 1994*, Washington, DC, 1994, Table 211.

367

since one-quarter of adult Americans don't drink. Alcohol was brought to America in 1607 by the Jamestown colonists, and its use has been part of American life ever since. The Pilgrim fathers weren't quite as sober as they have been pictured. When they set sail from England for the New World, the Pilgrims carried some 42 tons of beer and 10,000 gallons of wine along with their 14 tons of fresh water. As the Massachusetts Bay Colony developed, the rum trade became a boon to shipping and the production of alcoholic beverages became the colony's third largest industry.

From the earliest contact, Europeans used alcohol to manipulate Native Americans. It is said that Henry Hudson offered gin to the natives living on an island at which he stopped. According to one version, the Indians named the island Manahachtanienk, or "the place where we all got drunk."[6] The island's name was later shortened to Manhattan. For centuries after, alcohol was used to induce Native Americans to sign unfavorable treaties.

"Wets" versus "Drys"

By the last half of the nineteenth century, the pattern of almost universal drinking had changed into a clear division between "wets" and "drys." Prohibitionists or "drys" came heavily from members of the more conservative Protestant churches; many lived in small towns. Those described as "wets," by contrast, were usually city dwellers. The slur "rum, Romanism, and rebellion"—damning drinking, Catholicism, and anarchy all in one phrase—neatly pulled together the antiurban prejudices of provincial Protestant America. As a popular nineteenth century writer warned: "The city has become a serious menace to our civilization. . . . It has a particular attraction for the immigrant. . . . Because our cities are so largely foreign, Romanism finds in them its chief strength. For the same reason the saloon, together with the intemperance and the liquor power it represents, is multiplied in the City."[7]

Prohibition and After

Prohibition of producing or selling alcoholic beverages was ratified as the Eighteenth Amendment in January 1919, and the Volstead Act was passed by Congress to enforce it. Herbert Hoover called Prohibition "the noble experiment." Others, particularly in the cities, had less flattering terms. Once official morality had been served by the passage of the Volstead Act, the nation did not dry up but rather went on a binge. Prohibition suddenly made drinking seem all the more attractive because it was forbidden. To quench America's thirst, gangsters such as Al Capone organized mobs to control the illegal liquor trade; politicians and police were commonly bribed to look the other way. Capone claimed to be providing a public service by giving the working man his glass of beer. Prohibition gave organized crime its start. (See Chapter 12 for a discussion of organized crime.) Since the 1933 repeal of Prohibition the control, and in some states the sale, of alcoholic beverages has been a state function.

---

[6]Joel Fort, *Alcohol, Our Biggest Drug Problem*, McGraw-Hill, New York, 1973.
[7]Josiah Strong, *Our Country*, Baker and Taylor, New York, 1891, chap. 11.

Movies made during Prohibition demonstrated that the legal banning of liquor often was taken as a sign for everyone to go on a nationwide bender. Saloons were closed, only to be replaced with speakeasys.

Culver Pictures

Drinking Patterns

Alcohol sales in the United States now stand at about $40 billion per year.[8] General alcoholic consumption has been *declining* since 1981. Still, the National Household Survey on Drug Abuse indicated that 98 million people said they had had a drink within the last month.[9] Possibly the decline is due to greater awareness of health risks and the greater emphasis on "health and fitness." However, the number of heavy drinkers has remained constant at about 10 million. Men are more likely than women to drink (58 percent to 44 percent), but the gap between the sexes is narrowing.[10] As with tobacco, decreases among males are partially being compensated for by increases among females. Young people drink more than the middle-aged, whites drink more than blacks (with Hispanics in the middle). Those with college degrees and higher incomes drink more, and are more likely to drink, than those with lower educational and income levels.

According to the Gallup poll, one in four Americans admit to sometimes drinking more than they should. The National Institute on Drug Abuse indicates that 5 percent of the adult population consumes five or more drinks at a time at least five times a year.[11] About one-tenth of the American population has a drinking problem, and this 10 percent accounts for half of all the alcohol consumed.[12]

---

[8]James D. Wright and Joel A. Devine, *Drugs as a Social Problem*, Harper Collins, New York, 1994, p. 3.
[9]*The Universal Almanac 1995*, Andrews and McMeel, Kansas City, 1994, p. 225.
[10]Bureau of the Census, *Statistical Abstract of the United States 1993*, Washington, DC, 1993, p. 137.
[11]Wright and Devine, *Drugs as a Social Problem*, p. 4
[12]National Institute on Drug Abuse, *National Household Survey on Drug Abuse: Main Findings, 1990*, Washington, DC, 1991.

Binge drinking has become a major college problem. This "Kegs & Eggs" party only ends when the beer runs out.

© Andrew Lichtenstein/The Image Works

Student Drinking

Alcohol kills more people under age 21 than cocaine, heroin, and marijuana combined. One-third of high school students report binge drinking (5 or more drinks at a time for a male, 4 or more for a female) in the previous three weeks.[13] A 2000 Harvard School of Public Health survey of 14,000 students at 119 colleges identified 43 percent of college students as binge drinkers.[14] Some 22.7 percent of all students are "frequent" binge drinkers, consuming an average of 18 drinks a week. Those most likely to binge drink are white and male and live in a fraternity house. Those least likely to be binge drinkers are black or Asian, over age 24, or married.

A nationwide survey of nearly 37,000 students at 66 four-year colleges and universities found that better students drink less. *A* students consume a little more than three drinks a week, *B* students consume three and a half drinks a week, *C* students have almost five drinks, and *F* students have nine drinks.[15] Colleges and universities are responding to binge drinking by students both by instituting antidrinking programs and increasingly by banning alcohol at any campus-related location or event. (Also see the section on the prevention of alcohol abuse.)

Another study at the University of North Carolina suggests reports of college binge drinking may be exaggerated.[16] Instead of using questionnaires, the researchers gave 1,790 student Breathalyzer tests during prime party hours (10 pm

---

[13]Lloyd Johnson, Patrick O'Malley, and Jerald Bachman, *Drug Use among High School Seniors, College Students, and Young Adults, 1975–1990,* National Institutes of Drug Abuse, Washington, DC, 1991, Figure 10.1.

[14]"Binge Drinking Up, But So Is Abstinence: More Heavy Drinkers in College," *Associated Press News Service,* March 15, 2000.

[15]C. A. Presley, P. W. Meilman, J. R. Cashin, and R. Lyerla, *Alcohol and Drugs on American College Campuses: Use, Consequences, and Perceptions of the Campus Environment,* Vol. 3, 1991–1993, Core Institute, Carbondale, IL, 1996.

[16]"A New Study Suggests That Most Students Are Not Heavy Drinkers," *Chronicle of Higher Education,* September 3, 1999, p. A80.

to 3 am). On the traditional party nights of Thursday, Friday, and Saturday, 66 percent of the students had no detectable traces of alcohol in their blood. On other nights the proportion was 86 percent.

Effects of Alcohol

Alcohol usage in and of itself is not necessarily a problem (except for pregnant women). For decades, the well-known Harvard studies and numerous follow-ups have shown that moderate drinking—about one drink a day—lowers the risk of heart disease. The 1995 Harvard study of more than 85,000 female nurses indicated that women who drank moderately had a 12 percent lower chance of death from all causes than those who did not drink, and a 26 percent lower risk than those who drank heavily.[17] Although there is evidence that women's bodies are more vulnerable to the toxic effects of alcohol, women who drink moderately consistently do better than nondrinkers on physical function tests. Both men and women who drink moderately also get less depressed under stress.[18]

Although commonly used as a stimulant, alcohol is a **depressant** that suppresses the central nervous system and reduces psychomotor coordination. Its preeminent worldwide position as the drug of choice is directly related to its social usefulness as a relaxant; it makes people loosen up, reducing their usual inhibitions and restraint. Its role in reducing tension and worry has been recognized for at least as long as there have been records of any kind. Alcohol differs from most other psychoactive substances in that its use by adults is legal. Taken in moderate amounts, its use is not only socially tolerated but sometimes even expected (normative).

Alcohol impairs both muscular coordination and mental judgment. Until recently a level of 0.1 percent alcohol in the bloodstream—roughly four mixed drinks in two hours—was legally defined as drunkenness in most states. In 1998 the federal government set the level at 0.08, and it is quickly becoming the new legal definition nationally. Because the effects of alcohol do not disappear until the body uses or excretes the alcohol, other drugs cannot counteract it. The common practice of drinking coffee after a long party can only wake a drinker up; it cannot restore either muscle response or reaction time.

Alcohol is responsible for about 22 percent of all auto fatalities, down from 30 percent a decade ago. Much of the decline is attributed to campaigns against drunk driving by MADD (Mothers Against Drunk Drivers). The practice of partying groups having a designated driver is only a little more than a decade old. Public toleration of drunk driving has dramatically decreased, and all but a handful of states now have mandatory jail sentences for a second (and increasingly for a first) DUI (driving under the influence) conviction.

The body builds up a dependence on alcohol, and withdrawal sickness, the abstinence syndrome, can occur. During withdrawal, an alcoholic will be nauseated and nervous; within 12 to 24 hours, convulsions, hallucinations, and delirium tremens will occur. Alcohol delirium tremens (also know as "the DTs," "the shakes," or "the fits") is physiologically more severe and causes more deaths than withdrawal from heroin. Because alcohol provides calories but has no other food value, alcoholics frequently have health problems from not eating properly.

depressants
drugs that slow the response of the central nervous system and reduce alertness and coordination.

---

[17]"Alcohol Consumption and Mortality among Women," *New England Journal of Medicine*, May 11, 1995.
[18]Judy Foreman, "A Mixed Drink on Alcohol Risks for Women," *Boston Globe*, January 11, 1996, p. E1.

Table 13-1 The Effects of Alcohol Consumption

Amount of Distilled Spirits Consumed in Two Hours (fl oz)	Percent Alcohol in Blood	Typical Effects
3	0.05	Loosening of judgment, thought, and restraint; release of tension; carefree sensation.
4.5	0.08	Tensions and inhibitions of everyday life lessened.
6	0.10	Voluntary motor action affected; hand and arm movements, walking, and speech clumsy.
10	0.20	Severe motor impairment; staggering; loud, incoherent speech; emotional instability (extreme drunkenness); 100 times greater traffic risk.
14	0.30	Deeper areas of brain affected; parts affecting stimulus response and understanding confused, stuporous.
18	0.40	Deep sleep; inability to take voluntary action (equivalent of surgical anesthesia).
22	0.50	Coma; anesthesia of centers controlling breathing and heartbeat; death.

Psychoactive Drugs

psychoactive drugs
drugs that are used to alter mood and provide euphoria rather than for improving medical condition.

Psychoactive drugs are substances that affect the functioning of the brain by producing euphoria, intoxication, relaxation, and stimulation, as well as those that depress pain and increase general feelings of well-being. Not included in our discussion are drugs used to prevent or treat disease, to compensate for missing body chemicals, or to prevent pregnancy. We concentrate on psychoactive drugs because they are socially perceived as having the greatest potential for causing negative consequences, both personal and social. Along with alcohol, this list includes narcotics, psychedelics, amphetamines, and sedatives.

Drugs that are *perceived* to produce the greatest physiological and psychological damage and dependency are viewed most harshly. Although the term addiction is still commonly used, the World Health Organization (WHO) back in 1969 suggested that a more precise description would be **physical and psychological dependence.**[19]

Social beliefs about which drugs are "dangerous" have changed radically over time. Tobacco (nicotine) and coffee (caffeine) have at times been forbidden drugs. In past centuries Russia, Iran, Turkey, and parts of Germany have punished smoking with the death penalty. (In Russia a bit over two centuries ago, tobacco smokers could be punished by having their noses cut off or split.) Today, all but the most rabid antismoking campaigners might find these penalties a bit extreme.

---

[19]"Expert Committee on Drug Dependence," *World Health Organization Technical Report Series*, No. 40, Geneva, 1969.

Past Patterns

Abuse and misuse of drugs is not new. In Homer's ancient Greek epic, *The Odyssey*, the valiant Ulysses, on his homeward journey from the Trojan Wars nearly lost his crewmen in the land of the Lotus Eaters. Once the men had eaten the narcotic lotus blossoms, they lost their will to do anything but sit and dream away their lives.

At the beginning of the twentieth century there was proportionately more drug addiction than there is today. Morphine commonly was used in patent medicines; it was even an ingredient in calming syrups used to stop babies from crying. Medicines with cocaine remedies (such as an antidote for toothache pain or a cure for hay fever) were as much a part of everyday life as aspirin and decongestants are today.[20] Middle-class women daily took patent medicines and "tonics" containing laudanum for menstrual cramps, depression, and "female disorders." Laudanum is an old name for opium. Morphine could be picked up at the local drug store. The 1902 Sears-Roebuck catalogue listed guaranteed triple-strength opium for 45 cents for a 2-ounce vial sent by prepaid U.S. mail.[21] Until 1906 Coca-Cola included trace amounts of coke (thus its name), possibly contributing to its early popularity.

Opiate and cocaine use at the beginning of the century was not yet regarded as dangerous and degenerate. It was simply a bad habit, like cigarette smoking is today. Popular literature reflected this view. In the Sherlock Holmes episodes, Dr. Watson did not approve of Holmes's habit of shooting a 7 percent solution of cocaine, but he did not regard Holmes as a degenerate drug fiend either. Ironically, when heroin was first developed in 1898, this more powerful and concentrated derivative of morphine was thought to be nonaddictive and thus touted as a substitute for opiates. Bayer Drugs sold both aspirin for fever and heroin as a cough suppressant. (Heroin is still occasionally prescribed in Great Britain for severe coughs.)

Criminalization of Drug Usage

In the United States the 1914 Harrison Narcotics Act criminalized drug usage and restricted the possession of opiates. (The act misidentified cocaine as an opiate.) The purpose of the act was to end opiate addiction by law, just as the Eighteenth Amendment, a few years later, was supposed to end drunkenness and alcoholism. It is conservatively estimated that in 1914 there were between 141,000 and 269,000 opiate addicts.[22] Because the Harrison Act was ostensibly a tax act, its enforcement became the responsibility of the Narcotics Bureau of the U.S. Treasury Department. The Narcotics Bureau criminally prosecuted those doctors who continued to prescribe opiates for addicted patients.

The Supreme Court ruled in 1925 that doctors could legally prescribe drugs for addicted patients, but by then the Narcotics Bureau had convinced the public that drug addicts were both moral degenerates and dangerous criminals. Addiction had been turned into a criminal rather than a medical problem. Creating a new social category of "degenerate drug addicts" was easy to do because the general public knew virtually nothing firsthand about the effects of various drugs, and scientific research was practically nonexistent. In such circumstances, the statements of a federal agency were likely to go unchallenged.

---

[20]David F. Musto, "America's First Cocaine Epidemic," *Wilson Quarterly*, Summer 1989, pp. 59–64.
[21]*Sears-Roebuck Catalogue*, 1902, p. 451.
[22]Charles E. Terry and Mildred Peliens, *The Opium Problem*, Bureau of Social Hygiene, New York, 1928.

In 1937 marijuana was added to the list of dangerous narcotics, even though it is not a narcotic. Harry J. Anslinger, head of the Federal Bureau of Narcotics in 1937 feared that his budget was about to be slashed.[23] In response he stirred up a major campaign against marijuana, a drug virtually unknown except to Mexican Americans and jazz musicians. The public was fed a publicity campaign of marijuana smokers as sex crazed "dope fiends" whose "next step" was invariably heroin, and who were out to corrupt American youth. The camp movie *Reefer Madness*, describing how marijuana turns youths into sex fiends, was produced with Bureau of Narcotics aid. The public was sold Anslinger's view that the "parasitic drug addict is a tremendous burden on the community."[24] Congress responded to the whipped-up public outcry by outlawing marijuana—and Anslinger's budget was increased to deal with the newly defined scourge.

Addictive Personality?

For most of the twentieth century the existence of an "addictive personality type" was a standard ingredient in introductory psychology texts. Profiles of addictive personalities usually focus either on criminal street addicts, or addicted members of the music and entertainment industry. "Respectable" users are ignored. However, if drug use is looked at by occupation, doctors, dentists, and nurses top the list. Such a picture is, of course, at variance with the stereotypical view of who is a drug addict. Statements regarding typical addictive personality types—or for that matter a typical alcoholic personality—should be taken with extreme skepticism. They mostly reflect cultural biases.

Edwin Schur has noted how popular views of drug addiction automatically result in us defining the addict as a criminal and a member of the drug subculture:

> It is noteworthy that although the physician-addict and the subcultural-type addict are addicted in precisely the same physiological sense, their self-images are likely to be strikingly different. Both may recognize themselves as addicts, yet the physician is most unlikely to consider himself a criminal. On the other hand, the addict who is driven to underworld connections and to crime in order to support his habit cannot help but begin to feel that he is an enemy of society (or at least that society is his enemy). A self-fulfilling prophecy cycle is set in motion from which it is very difficult for such an addict to extricate himself.[25]

Types of Drugs and Drug Dependence

The effects of a particular psychoactive drug depend upon many factors, including the user's personality, physical condition, emotional state, and attitude, the social setting, and the size and recency of the dose. While the *general* response to each drug is known, the *particular* response of different individuals may vary widely. What the user "knows," or expects, from a given drug is also important; this affects the user's interpretation of, and response to, the experience. Anyone attending a college party knows that the same amount of alcohol may make one person loud, outgoing, and antagonistic, while another becomes quiet, morose, and withdrawn.

---

[23]Donald Dickson, "Bureaucracy and Morality: An Organizational Perspective on a Moral Crusade," *Social Problems*, 16:146–156, Fall 1968.

[24]Harry J. Anslinger and W. F. Tompkins, *The Traffic in Narcotics*, Funk & Wagnalls, New York, 1953, p. 170.

[25]Edwin M. Schur, *Crimes without Victims*, Prentice Hall, Englewood Cliffs, NJ, 1965, p. 145.

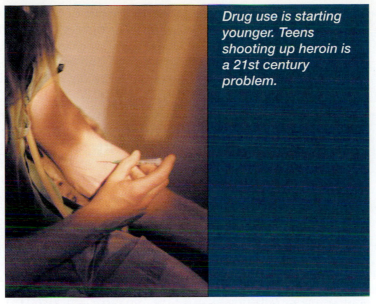

Drug use is starting younger. Teens shooting up heroin is a 21st century problem.

© Doug Menuez/PhotoDisc

The effects of specific psychoactive substances are never as neatly predictable in reality as pharmaceutical charts would make them seem.

There is no universally used system of classifying drugs. Some authorities divide psychoactive drugs into depressants, stimulants, and hallucinogens; some use the World Health Organization's scheme; others distinguish between legal and illegal substances; and still others prefer to rank substances on the basis of the supposed seriousness of their effects. We will divide the drugs into depressants, stimulants, and hallucinogens.

Depressants

Opiates   Opiates, like alcohol, are depressants and can produce feelings of tranquility and drowsiness. True opiates are derivatives of the opium plant and have medical applications as painkillers. There are also synthetic opiates, such as methadone and Demerol. Opiates, (opium, morphine, codeine, heroin) which are sometimes referred to as narcotics, do not affect motor responses as much as does alcohol (see Table 13.1), but they are extremely addictive and require regular and increasing dosage in order to prevent withdrawal symptoms.

Drug usage follows fads. In the 1970s the stimulant cocaine was the cocktail of choice for the chic, and heroin was for dead enders. Now the pattern has reversed, and high-grade heroin has caught on as the new glamour drug on both the east and west coasts of the United States. The new high-grade heroin is also much more potent. According to the Justice Department, while in the 1980s the average bag of heroin was only 4 percent pure, today it is 60 to 70 percent pure.[26] Today's heroin, also called "smack" or "junk," is so powerful that it can be smoked rather than injected, something that previously put off many middle-class drug users.

Today's heroin now comes largely from Colombia rather than Asia and is so pure that injecting it can stop the heart. The federal Drug Abuse Warning Network has

[26]Trip Gabriel, "Heroin Finds a New Market along Cutting Edge of Style," *New York Times*, May 8, 1994, p. 22.

reported increases in emergency room heroin overdose cases.[27] Affluent users often think they can control heroin usage like they did cocaine, but they soon develop a drug tolerance that requires ever larger doses to achieve the same effect. Despite the new purity, many eventually upgrade from smoking and snorting to injecting.[28] The death of rocker Kurt Cobain was caused by the purer heroin.

Sedatives
Sedatives, such as the barbiturates (pentobarbital, secobarbital) and their milder cousins, tranquilizers and sleeping pills, have a depressant effect on the central nervous system. Heavy use can produce euphoria. Because the overall effects are similar to those of alcohol, they can be thought of as **solid alcohol.** Use of the drugs produces tolerance and a requirement for ever heavier doses. In small doses, barbiturates, known as "barbs," "downers," and "yellow jackets," can reduce tension and provide a release from anxiety. Very heavy doses can depress respiratory and cardiovascular functions to the point where death results. Combined with other drugs or alcohol they are synergistic and cause an effect called *potentiation,* that is, they produce a magnified effect. The rock star Janis Joplin died as a result of mixing downers with alcohol, as did the comic John Belushi.

Barbiturates are highly addictive, and they must be taken in ever larger doses if euphoria is to follow consistently. Barbiturate withdrawal should be attempted only under medical control, because it is a far more dangerous process than withdrawal from heroin. Sedative tranquilizers such as Valium, Librium, and Equanil act to reduce depression and slow down response rates; therefore they are widely used in treating mental depression (see Chapter 14).

> **solid alcohol**
> *sedatives having a depressant effect.*

Rohypnol
Rohypnol is known as the "date rape" drug. It is a tranquilizer in the same drug class as Valium but is 10 times more potent. It is illegal in the United States but is legally available in Mexico and Europe. It produces a drunken state and can be bought on the street for between $1 and $8. Rohypnol—also called "Ruth," "roofies," "roopies," "R-2," or "rope"—is tasteless and odorless. It comes as a small white pill that can be ground into a powder, which is commonly taken in a drink. It is used as a rape drug because, in addition to a drunken state, it produces lack of judgment and amnesia for up to 24 hours. Some deaths have occurred as a result of the combination of Rohypnol with other drugs, especially alcohol.

Stimulants

Stimulants have the opposite effect of depressants; they act to increase the activity of the central nervous system. About half the stimulants legally manufactured in the United States end up in the illegal drug trade.[29]

Methamphetamines
Methamphetamines used to be known as "speed." Today "meth," "crank," or "ice" are the more common terms. Meth is a manmade stimulant used to produce alertness, to heighten sensitivity, and to decrease fatigue. Truck drivers have long used speed to stay alert on long hauls. Today's meth is ten times stronger than that used during the 1960s and early 1970s. Methamphetamines have a reputation as the poor man's cocaine. Crank use is widespread in Los Angeles, the southwest, and the midwest. A solid form of meth known as "ice" is primarily found in Hawaii and the West Coast. While the use of

---

[27]Tim Johnson, "Colombian Drug Floods U.S., *Richmond Times-Dispatch,* September 4, 1996, p. A14.
[28]Trip Gabriel, "Heroin Finds New Market," p. 32.
[29]Marc Schuckit, *Drug and Alcohol Abuse,* 3d ed., Plenum, New York, 1989.

crack cocaine is associated with urban minorities, the use of crank is identified with rural, and increasingly suburban, whites and Hispanics.

Meth can be smoked, snorted, or injected. Meth freaks say that an initial heavy injection produces a rush similar to orgasm and a feeling of well-being and alertness. It also produces an unrealistic sense of self-confidence and power. A heavy dosage can bring on paranoia, known as amphetamine paranoia. Meth freaks become nervous, impulsive, paranoid and sometimes violent. Insomnia is common. After being up for perhaps days, they "crash." Meth is highly addictive. Heavy speed usage, especially among males, is often associated with violent crime.[30]

Cocaine As noted earlier, drug taking often has a strong element of fad. Cocaine, an alkaloid derived from the coca leaf, went from gutter to glitter in the 1970s and early 1980s. It was the drug of choice for upper-class users. Until the mid-1980s, when the price dropped radically, the cost of cocaine made it an expensive indulgence. Biologically, cocaine stimulates the central nervous system in a way similar to amphetamines; it intensifies sexual highs and boosts the ego. Cocaine appealed to the upper class partly because its rush or surge can be achieved without the help of a needle (although the mythical Sherlock Holmes and other serious users did and do inject it) and because many cocaine users thought it was not addictive. It is extremely addicting. The brief intense high is followed by depression and the intense craving for another "hit."

Cocaine had a good press a hundred years ago. Sigmund Freud described it as a source of "exhilaration and lasting euphoria" that allowed "intensive mental or physical work (to be) performed without fatigue. It is as though the need for food and sleep were completely banished."[31] Freud later revised his opinion of this "harmless" drug. The side effects are serious. Heavy or chronic consumption can cause liver damage, manic states, paranoid psychotic states, and severe depression.

Crack, a highly addictive, smokable form of cocaine, which appeared in the mid-1980s, is sold in inexpensive chunks called "rocks." Crack usage has been associated with inner-city minority populations. Crack is a dangerous drug because feelings of euphoria are quickly followed by irrationality, intense downs, and cravings for the drug. Continued usage results in irritability, delusions, paranoia, and heart and lung failure. Crack use is strongly associated with crime and street violence. In cities crack usage is declining as heroin use increases.

There exists a major inconsistency in the legal penalties for selling powdered cocaine, used mostly by whites, and crack cocaine, used mostly by minorities.[32] Because of its association with violence, federal law requires a five-year minimum sentence for anyone caught selling 5 or more grams of crack, but it takes selling 500 grams of powdered cocaine to get the same sentence. Harsh crack laws discriminate against heavy-user groups such as African Americans. Police target poor neighborhoods for drug enforcement, and African Americans account for 90 percent of those convicted in federal court of distributing crack. The 1997 report by the judges on the U.S. Sentencing Commission stated, "Although research and public policy may support somewhat higher penalties for crack than for powdered cocaine, a 100-to-1 quantity ratio cannot be justified."[33] Nonetheless, Congress continues to reject lowering the penalties for selling crack. Congresspersons know that if they vote to lower the penalties for distribution of crack cocaine, their vote will be used by opponents in attack ads during the next election campaign.

---

[30]Paul J. Goldstein, et al., "Volume of Cocaine Use and Violence: A Comparison between Men and Women," *Journal of Drug Issues*, 21:345–367, Spring 1991.

[31]Quoted in Ann Crittenden and Michael Ruby, "Cocaine: The Champagne of Drugs," *New York Times Magazine*, September 1, 1974, p. 14.

[32]Michael Tonry, *Malign Neglect*, Oxford University Press, New York, 1995.

[33]Associated Press, "Higher Penalties for Crack Questioned," *Washington Post*, April 30, 1997, p. A2.

Hallucinogens or Psychedelics

Psychedelics or hallucinogens distort reality but are difficult to classify since they can affect one person one way and another person another way.

LSD and PCP The best-known psychedelics are LSD (lysergic acid diethylamide) and PCP (phrencyclidine). Hallucinogens distort reality and increase one's sensitivity to stimuli, but the way this is felt varies sharply from individual to individual. The lack of predictability combined with wide mood swings probably accounts for the relatively limited use of psychedelics despite the ease with which they can be produced. Some LSD "trips" have been described as extremely beautiful; others have been described as totally terrifying. Bad trips can lead to panic and horror, particularly in suggestible persons. In rare instances, they have resulted in suicide. However, probably the most feared problem for psychedelic users is the possibility of "flashbacks" that can occur months after usage. Because psychedelics' chances of a bad trip are so unpredictable, "acid heads" came to be seen by the late 1970s as "crazies." Now younger generations, largely unaware of the bad experiences of the baby-boom drug culture of the 1960s and 1970s, are beginning to again experiment with hallucinogens.

One of the most dangerous drugs is PCP, known on the street as "angel dust" or "killer weed." Developed in the 1950s as an anesthetic, PCP was banned after tests showed erratic side effects. Small dosages of the drug produce a highlike drunkenness (with feelings ranging from euphoria to depression), hallucinations, and sudden rage. Angel dust distorts reality so grossly and the effects are so unpredictable that users call it "heaven and hell." During the 1980s, PCP was supplanted on the streets by crack cocaine. Now, PCP is back.

The PCP that is now being produced in small labs is a liquid rather than the powder variety. (Liquid PCP has different names in different parts of the country; in the midwest it is commonly referred to as "wet" or "water.") Cigarettes are sometimes dipped in PCP that is cut with other liquids. Often the liquids used to cut the PCP, and to increase the effect, are more deadly than the drug itself. PCP is cut on the street with formaldehyde or ammonia. Even brake fluid is used. All can kill or brain-damage the user.

MDMA Known as "Ecstasy" or "ADAM," MDMA is a synthetic mind-altering drug that is popular at "raves" and is also used by gay populations and college students. Regular use produces blurred vision, nausea, confusion, depression, sleep problems, and severe anxiety. Ecstasy's use is growing.

Inhalants Not really fitting any of the usual categories are common products used as inhalants, primarily by adolescent males. Common inhalants are butane found in cigarette lighters, propane found in air fresheners, chlorofluorocarbons available in Freon, trichloroethane, spot removers, and other household products. Inhalant abuse causes severe intoxication and brain damage. Deaths occur due to overdosing and heart attacks.

Marijuana

Cannabis, including hashish and marijuana, does not easily fit in the standard categories of narcotic, depressant, stimulant, or hallucinogen. Marijuana is typically smoked in hand-rolled "joints" or in pipes and is the most commonly used illegal

Table 13.2 1998 Monitoring the Future Study: Drug Use among High School Seniors

Drug	Ever Used	Past Year	Past Month
Marijuana	49.1%	37.5%	22.8%
Cocaine	9.3	5.7	2.4
Crack	4.4	2.5	1.0
Stimulants	16.4	10.1	4.6
LSD	12.6	7.6	3.2
PCP	3.9	2.1	1.0
Heroin	2.0	1.0	0.5

Source: *Monitoring the Future Study*, University of Michigan.

drug. A third of Americans over age 25 have smoked it at some time, but only 3 percent are current users. According to the National Survey of Drug Abuse, as of 1998 there were 11 million marijuana users in the United States, compared to 1.5 million users of powdered cocaine and 600,000 crack users.[34] Marijuana may be the nation's number one cash crop, with roughly 100,000 commercial growers and over a million persons growing pot for their own use. During the 1960s and 1970s drug usage was a symbol of youth protest, and by 1980 over half of all teens reported using an illicit drug, usually marijuana. Since then drug use has declined.[35]

Until the last decade the physiological effects of marijuana were generally rather mild. Some effects—such as increased sensory perception and relaxation—depended partly on the user's expectations. One had to learn how to identify and experience the mild hallucinogenic effect.[36] Today's marijuana crops are many times more potent and produce far stronger effects. While most early health scare warnings about marijuana turned out to be overexaggerations, the new higher potencies do have definite effects.

A recent Harvard study of college students indicates that a residual effect among regular users makes it difficult for them to perform simple tasks.[37] Studies done at UCLA indicate daily smoking of one to three joints produces approximately the same lung damage and cancer risk as smoking five times as many cigarettes. Marijuana smoke is deliberately inhaled into the lungs, and its ingredients are more damaging than tobacco.[38]

Marijuana usage for medical reasons is gaining professional support. The National Institutes of Health has determined that research into its medical uses is justified, and a 1999 report of the Federal Institute of Medicine concluded that the chemicals in marijuana ease anxiety and pain, reduce nausea and vomiting, and

---

[34]Timothy Egan, "The War on Crack Retreats, Still Taking Prisoners," *New York Times*, February 28, 1999, p. 20.
[35]University of Michigan, *Monitoring the Future Study*, funded by National Institutes of Drug Abuse, 1999, Table 1a, MTFweb@isr.umich.edu.
[36]Howard S. Becker, *The Outsiders*, Free Press, New York, 1963.
[37]"Heavy Pot Use Hurts Thinking," *Associated Press News Service*, February 21, 1996.
[38]Eric Schlosser, "Reefer Madness," *Atlantic Monthly*, August 1994, pp. 45–63.

can help people undergoing chemotherapy or those with AIDS.[39] The Institute also found, despite claims to the contrary, no evidence that pot is a "gateway drug" to the use of other illegal drugs. Most heavy drug use starts with underage use of tobacco and alcohol.

A major negative effect of marijuana use is the legal consequences of its use. While enforcement is erratic, marijuana use has not been decriminalized except in a few locations. It is estimated that 15,000 inmates of the federal prison system are incarcerated primarily for a marijuana offense.[40] Legalization efforts are concentrated in western states. Voters in Alaska, Arizona, California, Colorado, Nevada, Oregon, and Washington have all approved measures for medical marijuana usage or decriminalization.

Tobacco

The 1964 Surgeon General's report positively linked smoking and cancer, and health warnings have been required on cigarette packages since 1966. Nonetheless, roughly one out of four Americans 18 and over still smokes. The average smoker begins smoking at age 14. The greatest growth in numbers of new smokers has been among teens. Between 1991 and 1995 the proportion of teens who had smoked within the past 30 days went from 28 percent to 35 percent.[41] Young black males, who in the past had low smoking rates, show especially steep increases. The Center for Disease Control (CDC) found that nationwide some 5.3 million youth under 18 years of age will suffer premature death from smoking-related diseases such as lung cancer and heart disease.[42] The estimates are that one-third of today's young smokers will die from smoking's consequences. In the United States, tobacco each year kills more people than guns, alcohol, automobile accidents, and AIDS combined.

Worldwide the figures are even worse. The World Health Organization (WHO) says that 1.1 billion people smoke, and they expect that half will die from smoking-related causes.[43] A joint study by the Harvard School of Public Health and the WHO estimates that the current 3 million smoking-related deaths a year can be expected to increase to 8.4 million tobacco-related deaths every year by 2020.[44] This means that tobacco-related disease will be the world's largest killer, causing almost 1 in every 10 deaths.

Changing Attitudes

In late 1999 Philip Morris for the first time acknowledged that scientific evidence shows that smoking causes lung cancer and other deadly diseases.[45] The tobacco industry had long maintained that nicotine is not an addictive drug and cigarettes

---

[39]"Medical Role for Pot Is Seen," *New York Times,* March 18, 1999, p. 1.
[40]Eric Schlosser, "Reefer Madness," p. 46.
[41]"Teen Smoking Rate Rises to Nearly 35%," *Washington Post News Service,* May 24, 1996.
[42]Chip Jones, "Smoking Losses Outlined," *Richmond Times-Dispatch,* November 8, 1996, p. A1.
[43]"WHO Issues New Warning on Smoking Death Rates," *Washington Post News Service,* May 24, 1996.
[44]David Brown, "In Changing Face of Illness, an Optimistic Prognosis Emerges," *Washington Post,* September 16, 1996, p. A3.
[45]"Company Changes Stance: Philip Morris No Longer Disputes Link to Diseases," *New York Times News Service,* October 13, 1999.

are not a drug delivery system. Today tobacco use among the young is increasingly viewed as a "gateway drug" whose usage leads to other drugs. However, federal anti-smoking policies suffered a major setback in 2000 when the Supreme Court ruled 5-4 that the Food and Drug Administration (FDA) lacked the authority to regulate tobacco, including the sale of cigarettes to minors.[46]

Twenty years ago smoking was considered both socially acceptable and sophisticated. Today, cigarette smoking is banned from most offices, public places, and private homes. Smokers feel they have been ostracized and demonized, treated as virtual social lepers. An indication of how much attitudes have changed is that the Motorola Corporation has not only banned all smoking in their buildings, but said any employee who is caught smoking more than three times anywhere on their property would be dismissed, even if they were smoking in their own car while leaving the parking lot. (The corporation later rescinded the threat to fire those who smoke in their cars.)

Legal Settlements

Federal and state governments have sued tobacco companies to recover the costs of medical treatment for tobacco users. In order to avoid state-by-state litigation, the tobacco industry in 1998 struck a historic $248 billion deal (the actual amount paid out over 25 years will be a lower $206 billion).[47] In return the states agreed to stop all state litigation and to make the companies immune from further state suits. Additionally, the tobacco companies agreed to take down 50,000 cigarette billboards and cease sponsoring sporting events. Also banned are well-known logos such as Joe Camel and the Marlboro Man.

The tobacco industry, however, is far from out of business. It has the nation's largest and best-financed lobby in Washington and remains the largest contributor to members of Congress.[48] During the 1990s the largest tobacco contribution made to any legislator in Washington went to Republican Congressman Thomas Bliley, Jr., representing Richmond, Virginia. Congressman Bliley until he retired in 2001 was the Chairman of the House Commerce Committee, which oversees tobacco regulation. The Congressman rejected "any more legislation regarding tobacco" and refused to hold any hearings on the question.[49]

In 1999 the federal government initiated its own lawsuit against the tobacco industry under the organized crime Racketeer Influenced and Corrupt Organizations Act (RICO). This action is opposed by the states as threatening their settlement with the tobacco companies. The federal government contends that selling cigarettes that cause cancer is an illegal conspiracy and criminal enterprise.[50] The cigarette companies respond that the health risks of smoking have long been known and no one has been misled. Because the federal government has been warning consumers of the dangers of cigarettes since 1964, and because the government also continues to collect massive taxes on cigarettes, the federal government may have a hard time convincing the courts that the government was misled by the tobacco industry about the health risks of smoking.

---

[46]"Supreme Court Rules F.D.A. Does Not Have Authority to Regulate Tobacco," *New York Times on the Web*, March 21, 2000.

[47]"Historic Deal Reached," *Richmond Times-Dispatch*, June 21, 1997, p. A1.

[48]"How Do They Live with Themselves," *New York Times Magazine*, March 20, 1994, p. 37.

[49]Chip Jones, "Philip Morris Center of a Storm," *Richmond Times-Dispatch*, p. A12.

[50]"The Feds Sue Tobacco Firms for Health Costs," *U.S. News and World Report*, October 4, 1999, p. 29.

Marijuana seized during a raid in the Sacramento San Joaquin Delta. Even if the borders could be sealed marijuana can still be grown in the United States. Some claim that marijuana currently is the most valuable cash crop grown on the West Coast.

Ray Chavez/AP/Wide World Photos

Declining Drug Usage?

Political clamor over illegal drug usage might make one think that taking drugs is at an all-time high. Actually, illegal drug usage *declined* about half during the 1980s and 1990s. Even with recent increased usage among teenagers, drug usage is half the 1979 peak of 25 million persons. The current level of drug usage has fallen to 12 to 13 million persons, largely because of declining drug usage among the middle class.

Baby-boomer parents who used drugs themselves have difficulty talking to their children about avoiding drugs and are more likely to expect their children to use drugs. The first national survey to simultaneously ask parents and their children about drugs (done by Columbia University's Center on Addiction and Drug Abuse) found that 62 percent of the parents who had been regular users of marijuana as teenagers expected their teenagers to try illegal drugs, while only 29 percent of the parents who had never used drugs thought their children would use drugs.[51] Moreover, 83 percent of the nonuser parents thought a teen under age 16 smoking marijuana was a crisis, but only 58 percent of the parents who had used drugs were similarly alarmed.

Drug laws and the vigor with which they are enforced reflect social norms and beliefs more than the actual medical or psychological effects of a particular drug. The image of the drug addict as a lower-class nonwhite, or as a marginal person of any kind, took a real beating during the 1960s, when middle-class youth began to "turn on and drop out." Marijuana usage, in particular, became associated with the middle-class youth movement. Today, declining middle-class drug use has led to decreasing middle-class tolerance of drug usage by the poor. However, contrary to the popular stereotypes, the average drug user today is white, not black; middle class, not poor; and lives in the suburbs, not the central city core.

---

[51]"Parent's Drug Views Disturbing," *Associated Press News Service*, September 10, 1996.

Table 13.3 Estimated Arrests for Drug Offenses

Year	Total Arrests	Sale/ Manufacturing	Possession	Percent of All Arrests
1988	1,155,200	316,525	838,675	8.4%
1989	1,361,700	441,191	920,509	9.5
1990	1,089,500	344,282	745,218	7.7
1991	1,010,000	337,340	672,660	7.1
1992	1,066,400	338,049	728,351	7.6
1993	1,126,300	334,511	791,789	8.0
1994	1,351,400	360,824	990,576	9.2
1995	1,476,100	367,549	1,108,551	9.8
1996	1,506,200	375,044	1,131,156	9.9
1997	1,583,600	324,638	1,258,962	10.4

Source: Federal Bureau of Investigation.

Drug Policies

Like other social problems, the question of psychoactive drugs and their control involves a series of trade-offs. While anti-drug-use programs have had some effect, attempts to cut off drug shipments from South America and Mexico have not been successful. The availability of drugs can only be restricted somewhat by vigorous police and court action. The question that is raised by some is whether it is worth all the effort. The Drug Enforcement Administration and U.S. Customs for 20 years have estimated that they seize only 10 percent of what is smuggled into the country. Some 70 percent of the cocaine, most of the marijuana, and a quarter of the heroin in the United States flow across the Mexican-U.S. border.[52] Because the border can't be sealed, and it costs about $25,000 in prison costs for each of the roughly 400,000 persons serving drug offenses, the question is whether such expenses are worth it. Moreover, it has led to tremendous corruption in Mexico. Drug cartels have virtually bought the Mexican police force and justice system, spending $500 million a year just on bribery of Mexican officials, or roughly double the budget of the Mexican federal attorney general's office and the federal police.[53]

The FBI reports that 10.4 percent of all arrests in the United States now are for drug law violations.[54] The United States currently has more people behind bars for drug offenses than are in prison for all crimes in England, France, Germany, and Japan combined. According to Barry McCaffrey, the four-star general heading the Office of National Drug Control Policy, "We have a failed social policy and it has to be reevaluated. Otherwise, we are going to bankrupt ourselves. Because we

---

[52]Linda Robinson, "An Inferno Next Door," *U.S. News and World Report*, January 24, 1997, pp. 38–39.
[53]Sebastian Rotella, *Twilight on the Line: Underworlds and Politics at the U.S.-Mexican Border*, W.W. Norton, New York, 1998.
[54]U.S. Department of Justice, *Substance Abuse and Treatment of State and Federal Prisoners, 1997*, NCJ-172871, January 1999.

can't incarcerate our way out of this problem."[55] He maintains that treating rather than incarcerating people could save $5 billion a year.

Others advocate shifting back to the attitude that preceded the passage of the Harrison Act in 1914: that is, treating drug use as socially disapproved but not as a criminal act. Drug usage would thus have essentially the same status as cigarette smoking. Those taking this position suggest that drug usage may be one of those social problems where the supposed "cure"—in this case, defining drug use as a criminal act—produces consequences for society that may be more harmful and costly than the original problem. Decriminalizing drug usage has conservative as well as liberal support. The conservative financier George Soros argues that all drug legislation should be abandoned as causing the society more harm than good.[56] The well-known conservative writer William Buckley, Jr., also has called for the legalization of drugs, arguing that the war on drugs has made a mockery of antidrug laws and increased violent crime in pursuit of illegal drug profits.[57] On the other side, William Bennett, former federal drug program czar, argues that expanding access to drugs would result in soaring drug use and abuse.[58]

Alcoholism

Abuse of alcohol and abuse of drugs are treated differently by most Americans. Drug usage commonly is viewed as a sign of moral failure, but alcoholism is commonly referred to as a "disease." This reflects a change from the older belief that alcoholism is the result of moral weakness and lack of character. Churches, except some fundamentalist groups, no longer preach that alcoholism is a sin against God and society. Alcoholics are more likely to be viewed as people needing help than as public sinners. The legal system has also changed. Public drunks are no longer dumped in the local jail's drunk tank.

Alcoholism as a Disease

alcoholic
drinking to the point where it injures health, earning a living, and social relationships.

An **alcoholic** is commonly defined as one whose drinking produces serious personal, social, or health consequences, such as marital problems, occupational difficulties, accidents, or arrests.[59] An alcoholic thus is unable to choose whether he or she will drink or not and is unable consistently to choose whether or not to stop.[60] Note that while we call alcoholism a disease, alcoholism is defined socially, not medically. Someone is an alcoholic when drinking seriously disrupts his or her life: when it interferes with holding a job or it disrupts family or social life.

Defining alcoholism as a disease has many advantages. Professionals working in rehabilitation find it easier to communicate with the public when they can use the trappings and language of the medical environment. The disease concept also helps to engender a more acceptable self-image among alcoholics, who can see themselves as the victims of illness rather than as moral failures. The disease con-

---

[55]Quoted in Timothy Egan, "The War on Crack Retreats, Still Taking Prisoners," *New York Times*, February 28, 1999, p. 20.
[56]George Soros, "The Drug War Cannot Be Won," *Washington Post*, February 2, 1997, p. C1.
[57]William Buckley, Jr., "Time to End Stupid Drug Policy," *Richmond Times-Dispatch*, February 9, 1996, p. A17.
[58]William Bennett, "The Legalization Debate," *Business Today*, Fall 1990, p. 50.
[59]Marc A. Schuckit, *Drug and Alcohol Abuse*, 3d ed., Plenum, New York, 1989.
[60]Mark Keller and Mairi McCormick, *A Dictionary of Words about Alcohol*, Rutgers Center of Alcohol Studies, New Brunswick, NJ, 1968, p. 12.

Box 13.1 Ongoing Issues

An Open Drug Border

Discussions about interdicting drugs coming into the United States and seizing drugs at the source often seem to sidestep unpleasant realities. Today, the NAFTA free-trade agreements and, more importantly, the all-but-total breakdown of law enforcement in northern Mexico all but guarantees free movement of drugs into the United States. The Mexican police and army are often on the payroll of violent drug cartels. In December 1999 the Mexican Attorney General announced that mass graves of persons killed in the last few years by the Juarez drug cartel were located.[a] Twenty-two Americans were among those whose bodies were found.

Honest Mexican officials who fight drugs and corruption in border cities often are violently killed. Holdin Gutierrez, a 29-year-old prosecutor in Tijuana, and the eighth Mexican law enforcement official murdered in Tijuana, is a case in point.[b] Gutierrez angered drug lords by prosecuting a corrupt police official who had shot a police commander trying to arrest the brother of a Tijuana drug overlord. He also had investigated the murder of a police chief who refused a $100,000 bribe from traffickers and who had made enemies in the federal police by weighing and record-

ing the amount of captured drugs he turned over to them—an action that made the routine reselling of the drugs by the federal police more complicated. Gutierrez was pulled from his car at his condo and shot 120 times by four men carrying AK-47s. The killers then drove back and forth several times over Gutierrez's dead body. They have not been caught.

For political reasons, it is virtually impossible not to yearly recertify Mexico as "fully cooperating" in the war against drugs. The reality is that corruption has reached so deeply into Mexican society that President Ernesto Zedillo has declared drug trafficking that country's number 1 security threat. In 1997, Gen. Jose de Jesus Gutierrez Rebollo, the head of Mexican antidrug policy, was caught taking a large bribe from a drug cartel. Meanwhile, drug cartels continue to ship tons of drugs northward from Tijuana and Juarez.

[a]Associated Press, "IDs Sought for 100 in Mexican Graves," New York Times on the Web, December 1, 1999.
[b]Linda Robinson, "An Inferno Next Door: Mexico's Drug Gangs Buy the Officials they Can—and Kill Those They Can't," U.S. News and World Report, February 24, 1997, p. 36.

---

cept also gives the alcoholic a socially acceptable reason for refusing drinks at social gatherings.

Alcoholism as a Social Behavioral Disorder

Treating alcoholism as a disease removes the stigma of moral degeneracy, but it does create problems of its own. This is because little about alcoholism fits the usual medical definition of disease. As a disease, alcoholism has the unique characteristics of having no agreed-upon cause, no agreed-upon medical treatment, and no known cure. As noted previously, alcoholism is commonly defined as the use of alcoholic beverages to an extent that exceeds community standards and interferes with physical health, social relations, and economic functioning. The old saying that an alcoholic is one who drinks to live and lives to drink is essentially accurate, but it is a rather loose definition of disease. The American Medical Association definition of alcoholism as a disease complex which has physiological, psychological, and sociological components sounds more impressive but is, if anything, less exact.

Alcoholism is increasingly being defined as a *social behavioral disorder*. Alcoholism is treated as primarily a social and behavioral problem rather than as a biological-medical one. Physicians, not surprisingly, find alcoholics difficult and uncooperative patients. Promises of reform made when sober rarely lead anywhere but back to booze. When drunk, alcoholic patients may be abusive and surly. It is no wonder that physicians feel uncomfortable about treating alcoholism. Physicians are asked to apply a treatment that does not exist, to a disease that has not been defined, to a patient that does not want to be treated. Physicians commonly refer alcoholics to community rehabilitation centers, Alcoholics Anonymous, or—if the alcoholic's funds permit—private residential clinics.

Treatment of Alcoholics

Many alcoholic treatment programs have solid recovery rates. A number of significant social factors contribute to the success with which alcoholism, as opposed to drug abuse, can be treated. First, alcoholism most commonly occurs later in a person's life than does drug abuse. In practical terms, this means that alcoholics usually have jobs and established roots in the community. When they get in trouble, there is often someone and someplace to turn to. Families, friends, and frequently employers support the alcoholic's efforts to get treatment and to go "on the wagon."

Second, alcoholism has become a respectable "disease." In middle-class society, alcoholism in no way carries the moral stigma attached to drug addiction. The fact that almost everyone has a family member, relative, or friend who is an alcoholic helps to make the public more understanding.

Finally, alcoholics, unlike users of hard drugs, are not publicly branded as degenerates or felons who are a menace to the community. Alcoholics—unless they drive—are not usually considered dangerous, while drug users have a far less savory reputation. Middle-class society brands the drug addict as a social outcast but is more tolerant of the alcoholic.

Alcoholics Anonymous

AA is by far the best-known organization devoted to the rehabilitation of alcoholics. In fact, some lay people mistakenly believe AA offers the only useful treatment program for alcoholics (we discuss other programs in the next section). The organization, founded in 1935, has changed in the background characteristics of its members. Initially it was a fellowship of down-and-out men whose drinking had led them to "hit bottom." Today the organization is not only for down-and-out older males. It claims some 2 million United States and Canadian members, including young people, women, and minorities. The association, which is made up entirely of recovering alcoholics (who sometimes are also addicted to other drugs), holds weekly therapy meetings at which members tell how alcohol had ruined their lives and how AA helped give them hope.

A limitation of AA is the implicit belief that alcoholics have to "bottom out" before AA or anyone else can really reach or help them. Indirectly, this belief—along with the conviction that an alcoholic can never take even one drink without falling—leads to the impression that AA can help only those who have touched bottom. In a 1997 cover story, *U.S. News and World Report* claimed that AA prevents more people from recovering by insisting on its way being the only way, since "by calling abstinence the only cure, we insure that the nation's $100 billion alcohol problem won't be solved."[61]

AA refuses to allow research on its programs or members, so they have no actual hard data on what works best for whom. Research that has been done on drunk

---

drivers randomly assigned to AA or other programs has found no difference in effectiveness. Spokespersons for AA are, of course, those for whom the program has worked. Those whom it has not helped are unlikely to be noted or quoted. Also, contrary to AA assertions, controlled drinking programs do work for many people.

Business Programs

Some of the highest success rates in alcoholism treatment have come from programs run by businesses for their employees, sometimes run in conjunction with Alcoholics Anonymous. Business administrators, for hard-headed dollars-and-cents reasons, have made efforts to salvage workers in whom they have an investment. DuPont for over 40 years has had a program for middle- and upper-level executives. Major airlines also have successful programs, although for obvious reasons they do not publicize the fact that some of their pilots are in AA. While a politician can proclaim to the world that he is a reformed alcoholic, few airline passengers would be reassured if their pilot made such an announcement. A major force in getting companies to establish programs for ordinary workers has been the United Auto Workers (UAW) union.

The threat of being fired can propel someone with a drinking problem into a treatment program. (Alcohol abusers are more likely to be employed than are drug abusers.)[62] Alternatively, an alcoholic employee is simply informed that he or she might benefit from the program. When the employee protests that he or she is not an alcoholic, it is suggested that he or she prove it to themselves by not drinking for a fixed time period, such as two weeks or a month. Usually the employee signs up for treatment within a few days.

Prevention of Alcohol and Drug Abuse

The best treatment for alcohol and drug abuse is prevention. Unfortunately, many school-run alcohol and drug programs still use the one-shot "don't let this happen to you" approach, complete with horror stories. Some educators still use the old trick of dropping a worm in a glass of alcohol, suggesting that the worm's reaction (it shrivels up and dies) is like that of alcohol on a drinker's brain. A more honest approach would stress that alcohol, while it has some health advantages when used moderately by adults, creates major problems when abused. College anti-drinking campaigns sometimes feature graphic ads such as a disoriented drunk student wearing vomit and urine stained clothes. The goal is to scare students sober and suggest that drunks look like fools. However, most ads now use the "social norms" strategy, which plays up statistics showing most students drink responsibly or not at all.[63] Young students are more likely to resist pressures from others to get drunk if they realize most other students don't drink heavily.

Alcohol is treated both legally and socially differently from other psychoactive substances. Alcohol use is socially acceptable, while even minimal drug use can result in imprisonment. Young people note this basic inconsistency, but they often fail to realize that our attitudes toward alcohol reflect long-established cultural patterns. Parents who, drink in hand, condemn getting high on drugs are not deliberately blind to their own drug habits. They are simply reflecting their cultural conditioning, which has taught them that alcohol and drugs are separate and distinct categories.

---

[62]Wright and Devine, *Drugs as a Social Problem*, p. 20.
[63]Loe Reisberg, "When Do Scare Tactics Become Health Terrorism?" *Chronicle of Higher Education,* September 3, 1999, p. A79.

Box 13.2 Making a Difference

The British and Heroin

The major alternative to the American approach of punitive legal drug-control policies is the British health system of both drug control and drug maintenance. The British never fully removed the question of drugs from the medical area. In practice, the British police ignore marijuana for personal use, but arrest for cocaine and heroin use. Sentencing for drug possession is usually to rehab centers for first offenses. British addiction is not associated with crime and violence as is the case in the United States.

The idea of dealing with drug use medically rather than legally produces strong emotion on both sides of the Atlantic. Tony Blair's Socialist government, not wanting to appear soft on drug usage, in 2000 officially rejected proposals to decriminalizing most drug use. However, British practice is moving in that direction. The underlying philosophy that guides the emerging British approach is that the interests of treatment and prevention are best served by regarding addicts as patients, by wooing them rather than coercing them into treatment, and by keeping addic-

tion above ground rather than by driving it into the criminal underworld, and supporting criminal drug cartels. The British approach is to separate drugs and crime. Data from British prisons, and from Scotland Yard indicate that the British find no relationship between criminal activity and addiction to hard drugs. At the same time, New York addicts are thought to account for over half of New York's property crime.

However, there are no easily transferred answers for North America. The size and uncontrolled nature of American drug use, plus its close association with crime, have convinced most experts that the British system would not work in the United States. We don't know whether a heroin maintenance program would reduce crime, or whether it would simply subsidize and encourage the growth of the addict population (methadone treatment programs have had limited success). However, what Britain can teach North America is that greater flexibility in treatment can help drug users and reduce drug-related crime.

Toward the Future

Predicting what the future will bring in terms of substance abuse has always been hazardous. What will happen in the next decade depends not only on public attitudes and fads but also on drug availability and federal drug policies. Different substances have different prognoses. Alcohol consumption will probably remain high among the college aged but continue its slowly declining usage among the population in general. Hard liquor consumption will probably continue its decline. Beer consumption will likely continue its more moderate decline as nonjuvenile drinkers continue to shift from tossing-down standard brands to savoring more complex (and expensive) microbrews. Wine consumption, by contrast, will probably increase. Alcohol treatment programs, especially when aided by medications to decrease alcohol craving, will become even more effective.

Public toleration of tobacco smoking will almost certainly continue to decrease. As a result, smoking will be banned in virtually all public settings. It may become common for both health and life insurance companies to charge smokers sharply higher premiums. However, in spite of increased general public disapproval, anti-smoking campaigns, and rising cigarette prices, the number of smokers will not fall dramatically. The adult population of smokers may decline from one-quarter to roughly one-fifth, but this 20 percent will remain hard-core smokers.

Predicting what will occur regarding other drug usage is more complex. The good news is that, if present trends continue, crack cocaine usage will radically drop and with it the erratic, violent, and criminal behavior associated with its usage. The bad news is that methamphetamine abuse may not show similar declines. Also, because meth can be produced in simple local labs, its spread is largely unaffected by border

Charles Bennett/AP/Wide World Photos

drug interdiction programs. Heroin use is likely to increase. Although drug inter-diction programs are both expensive and largely ineffective, stopping only 10 per-cent of illegal drugs, the programs are politically popular and thus likely to grow. Libertarians arguing for legalizing drugs, as was done with alcohol, are likely to re-main a vocal minority.

The next decade is likely to see the public increasingly making distinctions be-tween what they consider to be socially serious and less serious drugs. Marijuana use for medical purposes is already legal according to state law (but not federal law) in most western states. In western states local prosecutors have become less interested in dealing with cases of individual use, and this pattern probably will spread. Thus, even without a change in legal status, private marijuana use is likely to join the cate-gory of personal behavior state laws that are only irregularly enforced. Public atti-tudes, and enforcement, against other drugs are unlikely to see a similar change. Illicit drug use will continue to be seen as different in kind from alcohol use. In the United States drug use will continue to be viewed more as a legal than a medical problem.

Summary

America is a drug-using society where abuse of alcohol and drugs has moved from being a private problem to a public issue. Most drug use involves legal substances such as alcohol. Laws regarding the use of psychoactive substances reflect a primarily social definition of the problem rather than scientific or medical definitions.

- America has historically attempted to solve problems of alcohol and drug abuse through legislation. However, neither the Harrison Narcotics Act (1914) criminalizing the use of opiates nor the Volstead Act (1920) enforcing Prohibition were successful in achieving their goals.

- Psychoactive drugs affect the functioning of the brain, producing euphoria, intoxication, relaxation, and stimulation. They can be classified as depressants (alcohol, opiates, and sedatives) or stimulants (metamphetamines, cocaine, and psychedelics).

- Alcohol remains the most widely used drug, but overall consumption has been decreasing since 1981. Alcoholism is slowly moving from being defined as a disease to being seen as a social behavioral disorder.

- Marijuana, the most commonly used illegal drug, is in a separate category.

- In 1995 nicotine was declared a drug, over the fierce opposition of the tobacco industry. In 1998 the tobacco industry reached a historic $206 billion settlement with the states.

- Usually more important than the actual clinical effects of a drug is the social perception of effects (e.g., alcohol, a depressant, is socially viewed as a stimulant). Social norms and beliefs regarding the use of chemical substances are currently undergoing a major transition.

- Because legal prohibition of both alcohol and drugs has proved ineffective, the question is increasingly being raised as to whether current enforcement practices, with their high financial costs and problems of police corruption, are worth the effort.

- Treatment programs vary in their success; Alcoholics Anonymous, which is based on group support, has been reasonably successful, and yet drug treatment programs, for reasons not wholly understood, have been less successful.

☞Key Review Terms

addiction	depressants	psychoactive drugs
alcoholism	drug abuse	psychedelic drugs
Alcoholics Anonymous	marijuana	social behavioral disorder
cocaine	methamphetamines	stimulants
crack	opiates	

? Questions for Discussion

1. What is the major drug problem in the United States today? Do we define the problem mostly medically, legally, or socially? Explain.

2. What drugs are defined in the United States as most dangerous? What criteria have been used historically to define drugs as dangerous?

3. Is alcoholic consumption in America a new problem? What are current consumption patterns?

4. Discuss the American criminalization of drug usage and its consequences. Should American drug policies be changed? How and why?

5. Discuss the concept of the addicted personality. Where do our stereotypes of drug users and alcoholics come from? How are they changing?

6. Discuss marijuana's listing as a dangerous narcotic. Should marijuana be legalized for medical usage? Should marijuana laws be repealed? Explain your position.

7. How do depressants affect the body? What are the three most used depressants?

8. What are the physiological effects of stimulants? What are the three most used stimulants?

9. Discuss tobacco usage in America. Should government regulation of tobacco smoking be increased or not? Explain your position.

10. How do British and American methods of dealing with drug usage differ? Would the British system work in the United States? Why or why not?

☞ Suggested Resources

Ronald L. Akers, *Drugs, Alcohol, and Society: Social Structure, Process, and Policy*, Wadsworth, Belmont, California, 1992. The use of drugs and alcohol as examined from three different perspectives.

David J. Hanson, *Preventing Alcohol Abuse: Alcohol, Culture, and Control*, Praeger, Westport, CT, 1995. The author's review of worldwide data on alcohol abuse and his suggestions as to policy reforms.

Public Health Service, *Trends in the Incidence of Drug Use in the United States, 1919–1992*, U.S. Department of Health and Human Services, Rockville, MD, 1996. Data on trends in drug and alcohol use in the United States during the twentieth century.

Paul B. Stares, *Global Habitat: The Drug Problem in a Borderless World*, Brookings, Washington, D.C., 1996. The nature and extent of the global drug problem and what can be done to control drugs.

William Weir, *In the Shadow of the Dope Fiend: America's War on Drugs*, Archon Books, North Haven, CT, 1995. A look at current drug attitudes and policies in America, and the history of America's drug crusades.

Larry C. White, *Merchants of Death: The American Tobacco Industry*, Beach Tree Books/Morrow, New York, 1988. Although somewhat dated by recent events it provides a good look at how the tobacco industry lied and misled the public about the effects of smoking.

Internet Connection 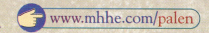 www.mhhe.com/palen

1. An excellent resource on drug use in the United States is National Institutes of Health; National Institute on Drug Abuse (NIDA), (*www.nida. nih.gov/NIDAHomel.html*). This site contains a wealth of statistics and many links to other web sites. A search engine is available on the site. To examine statistics on marijuana use type in "marijuana" and you'll be sent to a site with nearly 200 pages of information on the subject.
   a. According to NIDA how prevalent is marijuana use?
   b. What are the long-term effects of usage?

Now visit the site of the National Organization for the Reform of Marijuana Laws (NORML) (*www.norml.org/home.shtml*).

   c. What arguments does it make for legalizing marijuana? Click on the "Principles of Responsible Marijuana Use." Now visit the site of "Americans for Responsible Alcohol Access" (*www.araa.org/*).
   d. What is the purpose of this organization? Do you see any parallels between "responsible alcohol use" and "responsible marijuana use"?
   e. What are the pluses and minuses of legalizing marijuana in the United States?
2. Social problems often result in the creation of advocacy groups. Examine the websites of three such groups: Mothers Against Drunk Driving (*www.madd.org/*); Alcoholics Anonymous (*www.alcoholics-anonymous. org/*); Action on Smoking and Health (ASH) (*www.ash.org/*).
   a. What similarities and differences can you detect between these organizations?
   b. Examine their histories by selecting their "About" buttons. Is there a general pattern to the emergence of organizations like these?

I am now the most miserable man living. If what I feel were equally distributed to the whole human family, there would not be one cheerful face on earth. Whether I shall be better I cannot tell. I awfully forebode I shall not. To remain as I am is impossible, I must die or get better.

Abraham Lincoln, 23 January 1841 (20 years before he became President of the United States)

Problems of the Health System and Mental Disorders

Dubious Fact

The United States has the best health care system in the world.

Based on both infant mortality rates and life expectancy, the United States health care system falls behind 16 Western European nations, Japan, Taiwan, and Singapore.

Health and Illness

health
state of physical, mental, and social well-being.

Health is not just the absence of illness and infirmity. It is defined by the World Health Organization as *a state of complete physical, mental, and social well-being.* The importance of this definition is that it stresses the importance not just of a person's physical conditions but of social well-being and mental state as well.

Health care problems affect all the world's nations, but the problems of developing countries are most likely to be high infant mortality, infectious diseases, and poor sanitary conditions. In the developed nations the problems are more likely to be those of aging, such as heart disease and cancer. Differences in life expectancy between developed and developing countries largely reflect the higher infant and child mortality rates in developing nations. The United States is unique among developed nations in having a largely private system of providing medical services. Thus, the United States has the special problem of how to provide equal access to health care for all its citizens.

Contemporary Americans are the healthiest generation ever. At the beginning of the twentieth century, life expectancy at birth in the United States was only 49

Just getting medical services has become a problem. Crowded waiting rooms have become an American way of life.

© Yvonne Hemsey/Liaison Agency

years.[1] Currently it is 76 years. Most of the increase in life expectancy can be traced to sharp declines in infant mortality and in deaths due to contagious or infectious diseases. Moreover, at the beginning of the twentieth century most workers labored 60 hours a week, often under unhealthy and dangerous conditions. Today, the average worker works 35 hours a week under far safer conditions. The major cause of death today is chronic disease, such as heart disease or cancer. In the area of mental illness, it is harder to make precise comparisons with the past because data for earlier periods are often not available. However, there now are effective drug and other treatments for mental problems. Conditions such as depression, which were once considered simply something that had to be lived with, are now treatable.

Sociological Perspectives

Functionalist Approaches

Functionalists examine how health and illness affect social life and how the health care system operates as a social institution. Does it operate to keep members healthy? How effective and economical is it in meeting its own goals? Illness is viewed as dysfunctional insofar as it makes it difficult for individuals to carry out their socially assigned roles. Functionalists see the current patchwork mixture of private and government programs as a consequence of the rapid changes in the amount and effectiveness of medical technology. Whereas early in the twentieth century technology was largely limited to what a physician could carry for a home visit in his or her black bag, today knowledge has exploded to where there is a wide range of health care specialists and often expensive treatments. The assumption of health care as a fundamental human right conflicts with treating quality health care as a consumer commodity to be sold to the highest bidder.

To functionalists, the current American health care system is complex, disorganized, expensive, and inefficient. The goal of making profits interferes with providing health care to the broad population. Functionalists say health care as a social institution needs to be reformed to bring the sometimes conflicting goals of profit and service into functional balance. There is, however, considerable disagreement as to how this should be accomplished. There is no consensus whether we should go more in the direction of a market-driven system or whether we should move toward a "single-payer" government system such as that found in Canada. The former is often seen as allowing too many people needing care remain unserved, while the latter is often perceived (by Americans) as creating a bureaucratic nightmare. The current system of purchasing health-insurance-based HMOs (Health Maintenance Organizations) is often accused of combining the worst of both alternatives.

---

[1]Richard T. Gill, Nathan Glazer, Stephan A. Thernstrom, *Our Changing Population*, Prentice Hall, Englewood Cliffs, NJ, 1992, p. 22.

Conflict Approaches

Those using a conflict approach view health care as a scarce societal resource where the best care goes to the wealthy and powerful. There is a close relationship between health care and social inequality. Medical resources, like all scarce resources, go to those who can afford them rather that to those who most need them. The problem, conflict theorists say, is that the capitalist system turns medical care into a for-profit corporate enterprise. Doctors, hospitals, and especially the pharmaceutical industry are part of billion dollar corporations. The emphasis is more on profits than on service. Reflecting physicians' dissatisfaction with HMOs overriding doctor's medical decisions regarding appropriate treatment and drugs, the American Medical Association (AMA) in 1999 reversed its long-standing opposition to physicians forming unions.

According to conflict theorists, the system is based on power, and the present health care system most benefits the well-to-do and males. You get what you can pay for. For example, three-quarters of all surgery is elective rather than medical emergency. Surgery may have more to do with financial status and insurance than with the medical condition of the patient. More attention and medical resources are put toward prolonging the lives of a few affluent persons than to federal programs such as WIC (Women, Infants, and Children), which provide nutrition and prenatal care for poor women in order to reduce infant mortality rates. Powerful interests set up health care "reforms" such as "managed care" not as a way of improving medical care but as a means of restricting services and increasing profits.

From a conflict perspective as long as health care remains a business, many health services will be sold at prices only the wealthy and well-to-do can afford. Only government can ensure that health care will be available to all. And only through demonstrating power by politically organizing can low-power groups gain the medical benefits now available to the affluent. Universal health insurance will never become a reality as long as business profits determine the level of national health care.

Interactionist Approaches

Interactionist perspectives look less to the macro institutional level and more to the micro small group or personal level, where social meanings are learned through social interaction and then attached to health or various illnesses. Having a mental disorder often puts a person in a different social as well as medical category than having an infection. We define illness and mental illness socially. For example, a few decades ago epileptics were defined as dangerous. Thus, some states prohibited them from having a driver's license or even marrying.

Our lifestyles and health habits, as well as our ideas of health and illness, are socially defined and thus have changed over time. Some deprived groups today may still see living with disease and illness as normal states. For the middle-class, on the other hand, the social situation sometimes defines whether we are "well" or "sick." How busy we are, whether we are going on a trip, or whether we are trying to avoid a chore may define whether we see ourselves as healthy or ill.

Interactionists also examine how social beliefs define medical situations. Stigmatizing and blaming-the-victim scenarios can occur that have nothing to do with the illness itself. For example, those with HIV/AIDS are often stigmatized socially just because they are infected rather than because of the actual physical condition of the individual.

Problems of the Health Care System

Quality

Overall, the American system of health care provides good general medical care and excellent care for serious medical problems. However, the level of health care a person receives is closely tied to ability to pay. Access to quality health care is based to varying degrees on income, race, and where one lives. Historically in the United States, the well-to-do have gotten better care than the poor, whites have gotten better care than blacks, males have gotten more attention than females, and those in suburban areas have received better care than those living in rural areas or the inner city.

Almost half of those with incomes over $35,000 rate American health care as excellent (48 percent), while only a quarter (26 percent) of those with incomes under $10,000 do so.[2] There are clear differences by race, with black infant mortality rates being about double those of whites and whites having a life expectancy about seven years longer than blacks.

The American health care system provides the best care in the world to those who can afford it, and America leads the world in adopting new medical technology. For example, internal organs are now routinely examined without surgery. CAT scans (Computerized Axial Tomography), which use X-rays to take 3-D image pictures of the patient's body, MRI (Magnetic Resonance Imaging), which uses a combination of a strong magnetic field and radio waves to view 3-D images of the brain and other soft tissue, and Thermographic Imaging, which uses an infrared camera to make a heat map to detect cancers, are now quite commonly used in American hospitals but not in Canadian or Western European hospitals. Ultrasound or sonography imaging is also commonly used to examine in vitro the fetuses of pregnant women over age 35.

Because drug and biomedical technology industries are profit driven, they constantly pressure physicians to introduce new drugs and technologies. Less attention is given to preventive measures that may save more lives in ways that are less spectacular and less profitable but more cost effective. The best and cheapest method of treating health problems is to prevent them. For example, providing expectant mothers with adequate nutrition, encouraging exercise, and teaching the dangers of smoking and drinking while pregnant can do much to reduce infant mortality. Canada's provinces, for instance, provide basic medical and dental care to all. The Canadian system, like European health care systems, focuses on providing good general preventive and medical care for the bulk of the population. The trade-off is that they do less well in providing rapid access to the latest equipment or cutting-edge technologies to treat rarer problems. There also are waiting lists for specialized services and operations. Canadian physicians, while well compensated by local standards, make considerably less than their U.S. counterparts. Because of this, Canada is experiencing an exodus of physicians, especially young researchers, to the United States.[3]

---

[2]National Center for Health Statistics, *Current Estimates from the National Health Interview Survey, 1994,* Series 10, no. 193, Government Printing Office, Washington, DC, 1995.
[3]"Canadian Doctors Take Their Talents South," *Globe and Mail,* July 11, 1998, pp. 1, 8–9.

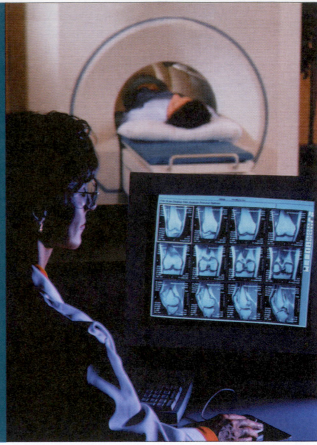

A strength of American medical care is its widespread use of technology. MRI machines are now routinely used by U.S. hospitals to view soft tissue. MRI machines are not as common in Canada and Europe.

Corbis CD

National Health Care Comparisons

A common measure of how well a nation provides for its citizens is the quality of its health care system. The oft repeated claim that "the United States health care system is the best in the world" is not supported by the data.[4] Overall, international data indicate that the American health system is good by global standards. In terms of providing for average citizens, however, it is behind other developed nations, especially those in Western Europe. One measure of the quality of health care is life expectancy, which closely correlates with the level of health care. As the twentieth century ended, life expectancy ranged internationally from a low of only 36 years in Malawi to a high of 80 years in Japan.[5] The United States average of 76 years puts it slightly below the 77-year average for all Western European nations.[6]

Demographers generally consider the infant mortality rate (number of deaths of infants under one year of age per 1,000 births) to be the best single measure of a nation's health status. As Table 14.1 showing international infant mortality rates indicates that the United States is far from being the world leader in healthy infants. The U.S. rate of 7 deaths per 1,000 births is over a third higher than Western Eu-

[4]Andrew L. Shapiro, *We're Number One*, Vintage, New York, 1992.
[5]*1998 World Population Data Sheet*, Population Reference Bureau, Washington, D.C., 1998.
[6]Ibid.

Table 14.1 Highest and Lowest World Infant Mortality Rates, 1999*

Lowest 12 Rates		Highest 12 Rates	
Iceland	2.6	Malawi	137
Singapore	3.3	Sierra Leone	136
Sweden	3.6	Guinea-Bissau	136
Japan	3.7	Guinea	134
Norway	4.1	Mozambique	134
Finland	4.2	Gambia	130
Luxembourg	4.2	Ethopia	128
Austria	4.8	Somolia	126
Slovenia	4.8	Angola	125
Switzerland	4.8	Niger	123
Germany	4.9	Mali	123
France	5.0	Equatorial Guinea	117
United States	**7.0**		

*Infant deaths per 1,000 live births.

Source: Population Reference Bureau, *1999 World Population Data Sheet.*

rope's average of 5 per 1,000.[7] Infant mortality rates reflect the health status of women before and during pregnancy. Nationally, black infant mortality rates are roughly twice as high as those for whites.[8] The highest infant mortality rates in the United States are found in the nation's capital, where black infant mortality rates were 25.5 per 1,000 in 1994.[9] This high level reflects poverty, poor prenatal care, and bad prenatal health habits, such as smoking, drinking alcohol, and using illegal drugs. For a nation with America's resources, such high rates are a disgrace.

Costs

The costs of the American health care system are by far the highest of any nation. The United States now spends over *$1 trillion* a year on health care, and the price is growing. This averages to about $4,000 per person each year for health care. By comparison, Canada spends half as much and Great Britain a third as much.[10] The Department of Health and Human Services estimates that health expenditures consumed 18.1 percent of the nation's gross domestic product (GDP) in 2000.[11] That is *far* more than is spent by any other nation (Canada spends 10 percent, Germany 8.5 percent, and Great Britain 6.6 percent). America today spends over double the GDP percentage on health care that we spent as recently as 1970.[12] If such a large

---

[7] *1999 World Population Data Sheet*, Population Research Bureau, Washington, DC, 1999.
[8] Gill, Glazer, and Thernstrom, *Our Changing Population*, p. 31.
[9] National Center for Health Statistics, *Health, United States, 1993*, Government Printing Office, Washington, DC, 1993.
[10] U.S. Bureau of the Census, *Statistical Abstract of the United States: 1999*, Washington, DC, 1999.
[11] "National Expenditures for Health Care, 1961–91," *Universal Almanac, 1995*, Andrews and McMeel, Kansas City, 1994, p. 212.
[12] Ibid.

portion of the nation's funds are spent on health care, that means less for everything else. Currently, insurance companies pay about a third of the health care bill, individuals directly pay about a quarter, and government taxes pay the rest.

Have the sharp increases in health care costs during the past quarter century produced comparable increases in the quality of the nation's health care? Here the record is far more mixed. New medical technologies often benefit a limited number of patients but contribute a great deal to America's high medical costs. Expensive malpractice insurance also has driven up physicians' and hospitals' costs. This affects the services offered. For example, few new family medicine physicians offer obstetrical services, because yearly OB insurance costs commonly run tens of thousands of dollars a year. Unless a physician delivers many babies, the cost is prohibitive. Fear of being sued also affects medical procedures. For example, largely due to legal concerns some one-third of all births are now Cesarean section deliveries.

Further driving up health care costs is the American belief that every health or medical problem has a cure. The respected Consumers Union organization estimates that the United States wastes $200 billion a year on unnecessary medical procedures and administrative overlap and waste.[13] Yearly over half a million hysterectomies are performed and approaching half a million coronary bypass operations. There are medical concerns, however, that many, if not most, of these procedures are more financially, legally, and convenience driven rather than medically required. Joseph Califano, former Secretary of Health, Education, and Welfare, estimates that between 60 percent and 80 percent of those submitting to coronary bypass operations obtained results no better than they would have obtained with less intrusive and expensive beta blockers and other drugs.[14]

Ability to Pay

We tend to think of health issues largely as medical questions, but they are at least equally economic and social questions. Health care reflects not just a society's technology but also its level of social inequality. Worldwide, poverty is still a major cause of health problems, and in the United States, while the poor don't starve to death, they do have twice the infant mortality rate and, as adults, are over a third more likely to die from cancer, almost half again as likely to die from heart disease, and 150 percent as likely to die from diabetes. As Table 14.2 indicates, poor children fare particularly badly in America. Overall, poorer people are more likely to have health problems, less likely to use health care services, and more likely to engage in poor health practices such as smoking or eating fatty foods. In America who gets what services is determined by more than just medical need; health care is purchased just like other consumer goods.

The United States is the only industrialized nation to have a largely private, rather than government-based or government-supported, health care system. What this means is that in the United States people are responsible for their own health care. Health care is based primarily on ability to pay, either privately or with the assistance of insurance. Nearly 1 in 5 working-age adults lacks health care.[15] The figure is 1 in 3 for those with incomes under $35,000. In other Western nations, by contrast, it has long been assumed that access to health care should be based on an individual's medical need rather than on personal income or social class. Good health care is seen as a personal right essential to both personal and national welfare.

---

[13]"The $200 Billion Bottom Line," *Consumer Reports*, July 1992, p. 436.

[14]Joseph A. Califano, Jr., *America's Health Care Revolution: Who Lives? Who Dies? Who Pays?* Random House, New York, 1986, pp. 83–84.

[15]"Nearly 1 in 5 Said to Lack Health Coverage," *Scripps Howard New Service*, September 2, 1999; the article is based on a 1999 Princeton Survey Research Association survey of 5,000 Americans aged 18 to 64.

Table 14.2 The Penalties of Poverty for Poor Children

Outcome	Poor Children's Risk Relative to Nonpoor Children
Health	
Death in childhood	1.5 to 3 times more likely
Stunted growth	2.7 times more likely
Iron deficiency in preschool years	3 to 4 times more likely
Partial or complete deafness	1.5 to 2 times more likely
Partial or complete blindness	1.2 to 1.8 times more likely
Serious physical or mental disabilities	About 2 times more likely
Fatal accidental injuries	2 to 3 times more likely
Pneumonia	1.6 times more likely
Education	
Average IQ score at age 5	9 points lower
Average achievement scores at age 3 and above	11 to 25 percentiles lower
Learning disabilities	1.3 times more likely
Placement in special education	2 or 3 percentage points more likely
Below usual grade for child's age	2 percentage points more likely for each year of childhood spent in poverty
Dropping out between ages 16 and 24	2 times more likely than middle-income youths; 11 times more likely than wealthy youths

Source: Children's Defense Fund, *The State of America's Children: Yearbook 1998*, Children's Defense Fund, Washington, DC, 1998, p. xiv.

American low-wage workers not only are less likely to have employer-paid health insurance, but the insurance they do have is unlikely to cover other than a part of health care expenses. Because of rising health insurance costs, fewer employers offer health insurance to their workers. The Census Bureau reports that some 44 million Americans are without *any* health insurance.[16] This is 13 million more than a decade ago. Young adults aged 18–24, those with lower levels of education, and Hispanics are more likely to lack health insurance. One-third of Latinos don't have health insurance. Excepting Hawaii, no state requires that workers be offered employer-paid health insurance.

The largest uninsured, and undercared for, group is not the welfare poor, who at least have free access to care (if not always quality care), but the so-called working poor (see Chapter 2). Because under current law trauma hospitals must treat all emergency room patients, hospitals make up for the cost of treating those without insurance by doubling or tripling the charges to those with insurance or who will pay. The result is a medical system in which neither physicians, hospitals, nor patients are really happy. The group that most profits from the current system is the wealthy, who can buy premium access and premium services.

---

[16]"One in Six Lacks Health Insurance," *Associated Press*, October 4, 1999.

Box 14.1 Making a Difference

A Black Doctor

Debbie Phoenix-Davis practices medicine in Savannah, Georgia, and is a pioneer in minority and indigent medicine.[a] In Savannah more than 50 percent of the residents are black, but only 6 percent of the physicians are black. Nationally the figure is only 4 percent. Having risen from the Savannah projects, Dr. Davis understands the special concerns of poor blacks, the flaws in their diets, and the financial problems that often make health care a low priority. Because Dr. Davis came from the neighborhood, she is trusted and listened to in ways other physicians might not be.

Dr. Louis Sullivan, president of Morehouse School of Medicine, who was Secretary of Health and Human Services under former President Bush, puts it this way, "It's knowing what questions to ask. It's knowing that if you prescribe a $50 medicine, the patient might not have the funds. And it is trust, communication, things that affect compliance. Coming back to the doctor when they should. Taking medicine when they should."[b]

The Westside Urban Health Center, where Dr. Davis works, is subsidized with federal and local government funds. This allows them to charge only $12 a visit, and nothing to those who don't have the $12. Part of Dr. Davis's success with patients is that, in spite of pressures to see ever more patients, she takes time in the examining room to chat about family members, and even say a prayer, because Dr. Davis is also an ordained Pentecostal minister. Her practice demonstrates the rapport that can develop when doctor and patients share the same experiences.

[a]Peter L. Kilborn, "Filling Special Needs of Minority Patients," New York Times, *February 14, 1999, p. 16.*
[b]*Ibid.*

Government Programs

There are three large populations in the United States that receive federal government supported health care. These are the elderly, the welfare poor, and those in the armed forces. Americans aged 65 and over receive most (but not all) of their health care from **Medicare.** Medicare covers major costs, which must be supplemented with a Medicare supplement insurance policy or private funds. Two contradictory major issues currently face Medicare. The first issue is that Medicare will face major financial problems as the baby boomers begin retiring in 2011 (see Chapter 11). The second issue is that increases in prescription drug costs have produced strong pressure from seniors to include subsidized prescription-drug coverage, with a modest user premium, under Medicare. This would require funding from tax revenues. Legislation to provide prescription drug coverage under Medicare was proposed by the Clinton administration in 1999, but it was opposed by the Republican-dominated Congress on the grounds that it would cost too much.[17] As of now there is no prescription drug coverage.

The second population receiving government paid care is the welfare poor, who receive **Medicaid.** Medicaid covers the medical costs of those receiving public assistance, but it does not usually cover the working poor. Medicaid is supported by both federal and state funding. The difference between Medicare and Medicaid is that Medicare provides for all elderly regardless of income, while Medicaid programs are for the poor regardless of age. Finally, the third population receiving government health care is the military (and their families) and some veterans who use military medical facilities. Also members of Congress (including those who vote against such programs for others) are essentially covered by socialized medicine.

Medicare
federal program financed from Social Security tax to providing health care for those 65 and older.

Medicaid
federal program financed from tax revenue designed to pay medical costs for those unable to afford any health care.

[17]Walt Duka, "Drugs Stir Up Medicare Debate," *AARP Bulletin,* September 1999, p. 1.

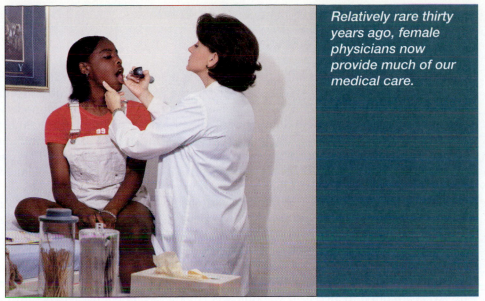

Relatively rare thirty years ago, female physicians now provide much of our medical care.

© David Buffington/PhotoDisc

Women's Health Care

Women live 10 percent longer than men (7 years) and use medical services twice as often as men. Male cultural values say to tough it out, a factor that probably contributes to higher male mortality rates. Males also engage in more coronary-prone activities, such as aggressive behavior. They are also more likely to engage in activities hazardous to health, such as heavy drinking, drugs, and smoking (although men's smoking is decreasing and women's increasing).

Medical research historically has focused on males, and, until recently, the health care system was largely male dominated and oriented toward men's health issues. Feminists see health care as another area in which women's needs remain subordinated to men's needs.[18] Times, however, are changing. Over a third of new physicians are women, and the great majority of new gynecologists are women. Increasing attention is being paid to women's health issues. Research on breast cancer, for example, is now a major national health priority. Everything, including approaches to delivering babies, is changing. While most births still are attended by a physician, birthing by nurse midwives is increasingly common, especially in university communities.

Health concerns over predominately women's disorders, such as anorexia and bulimia, have now received widespread attention, and research as to the underlying social and physical causes is accelerating. That 95 percent of eating disorders occur in women reflects the emphasis that our society places on women being thin. The Duchess of Windsor's offhand comment: "A woman can never be too rich or too thin," has become the accepted view of physical attractiveness. Interaction between social and health factors results in some women dieting to a point where their health is endangered.

---

[18] Alison M. Jaggar and Paula S. Rothenberg (eds.), *Feminist Frameworks*, 3d ed., McGraw-Hill, New York, 1993.

AIDS Impact

AIDS
acquired immunodeficiency syndrome, major sexually-transmitted infection killing 2.6 million yearly.

No discussion of American health care would be complete without including **AIDS** (acquired immunodeficiency syndrome). AIDS is the most explosive global health threat. Worldwide in 1995, 17.6 million persons were HIV (human immunodeficiency virus) infected and 1.5 million persons died.[19] Today the figures are almost twice as high. Some 33.6 million are infected.[20] Worldwide in 1999 some 2.6 million people died of AIDS.[21] About half of those contracting HIV become infected before they turn 25 and they typically die of AIDS before their 35th birthday. In the United States, AIDS is now the leading killer of young adults age 25 to 44, surpassing even accidents.[22] Some 35 of every 100,000 young adults die of AIDS compared to 32 per 100,000 from accidents. AIDS destroys the mind as well as the body. A quarter of the AIDS population will develop cognitive dysfunction and two-thirds will develop neuropsychiatric problems.[23]

As bad as the medical consequences of AIDS are, the social consequences of AIDS are often as hard to bear as being infected. In the United States those with AIDS are often treated as social outcasts. Treated as lepers were in centuries past, AIDS victims are feared as being infectious and unclean. For those non-symptomatic HIV-positive persons, who don't yet have any physical problems, the greatest difficulty often is the reaction of others. People negatively react to HIV-positive persons emotionally rather than logically. This is bad enough when it happens to HIV-positive adults, but it can be devastating for children. HIV-positive children may be shunned, with parents going so far as to pull their children out of classes where an HIV-positive child, or a child with active AIDS, is present. Again, as the sociological dictum says, situations that are believed to be real are real in their consequences.

AIDS is sometimes compared to the Black Death plague that swept through Europe in the middle of the fourteenth century, but the comparison is not really a good one. In the first place, the Black Death wiped out a full third of Europe's population in half a decade. (In today's terms that would mean 2 billion deaths in five years.) Second, no known preventive measures could be taken against the plague, whereas we know that the HIV virus is spread primarily through unprotected sexual contact and secondarily through drug users sharing contaminated needles. AIDS can't be cured, but it can be prevented through safe-sex practices, such as limiting the number of sexual partners and using condoms, and by not engaging in drug use.

North American Patterns

The first reported case of AIDS in the United States was in 1981. Between 1981 and 1995, some 440,000 U.S. cases of AIDS were reported to the Centers for Disease Control. By 1995 AIDS was causing 53,000 deaths yearly in North America.[24] The yearly death toll is now down, but in the two decades since 1981 more than 250,000

[19]"Women, Children, and AIDS," *Population Today,* April 1995, p. 3.

[20]Joint United Nations Programme on HIV/AIDS, "AIDS Epidemic Update: December 1999," *UNAIDS,* December 1999.

[21]Ibid.

[22]Lawrence Altman, "AIDS Is Now the Leading Killer of Americans from 25 to 44," *New York Times,* January 31, 1995, p. A1.

[23]National Mental Health Association, *MHIC: Mental Illness and the Family: Mental Health Statistics,* 1997, www.nmha.org.

[24]"Status of the HIV/AIDS Pandemic as of January 1995," Global AIDS Policy Coalition, Harvard School of Public Health, 1995.

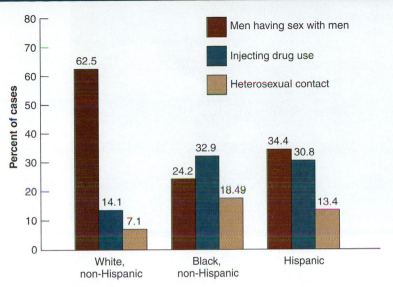

Figure 14.1 AIDS Cases by Race, Hispanic Origin, and Method of Transmission, 1996

Legend:
- Men having sex with men
- Injecting drug use
- Heterosexual contact

Y-axis: Percent of cases

White, non-Hispanic: 62.5, 14.1, 7.1
Black, non-Hispanic: 24.2, 32.9, 18.49
Hispanic: 34.4, 30.8, 13.4

Source: Centers for Disease Control.

have died in America from AIDS-related causes. (A person infected with AIDS doesn't die from AIDS but succumbs to other diseases because the immune system has been destroyed and cannot fight off infections.) Some 1 million Americans are HIV positive but have not yet developed AIDS. Those who are HIV positive may not develop AIDS for a decade, but once AIDS develops the person usually dies within two to three years unless they are on a very expensive "AIDS cocktail" including **protease inhibitors.**

Protease inhibitors are not a cure, but they can dramatically reduce the amount of immunodeficiency virus (HIV) in a patient's bloodstream. In the United States protease inhibitors have been widely used since 1997, and they have brought major relief. Protease inhibitors provide AIDS patients additional years of relatively healthy life. The use of protease inhibitors and "safe sex" programs in North America decreased the number of new AIDS cases, especially during the late 1990s. The annual death rate fell from 59 per 100 people with AIDS in 1987 to 4 deaths per 100 people in 1998.[25] Vaccines are being tested, but none has yet proven successful.

The decline in AIDS death rates, however, has started to level off, and there are signs of new infections. Centers for Disease Control researchers are concerned that unsafe sex is increasing among young gay males who mistakenly believe that if they get AIDS it can be controlled by protease inhibitors. While in North America and Europe the AIDS epidemic now has stabilized among gay men, AIDS researchers are concerned that a second wave of new infections will occur among younger men if they fail to take safe-sex precautions.

In North America thus far, little HIV infection is passed heterosexually. The great majority of HIV infection in North America is transmitted by homosexual sexual activity, and, as a result, gay men currently account for five out of six AIDS deaths. In North America the second largest cause of HIV infection is intravenous drug use, which has grown from roughly 10 percent to about 20 percent of the HIV infections. Women now constitute 18 percent of the AIDS cases among adults and adolescents.[26] According to the Centers for Disease Control, half of the U.S. women

protease inhibitors
complex and expensive "AIDS cocktail" drugs that inhibit AIDS development.

[25]"AIDS Deaths Dip Starts to Level Off," *Washington Post News Service,* August 31, 1999.
[26]*Chronicle of Higher Education,* March 10, 1995, p. A7.

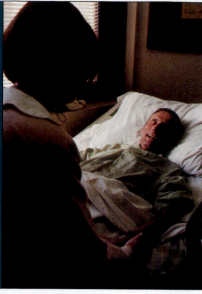

AIDS deaths are declining somewhat in the United States, but increasing worldwide. This New York AIDS patient is talking to a social worker about plans for his burial.

© J. Griffin/The Image Works

who contract AIDS are intravenous drug users, and most of the remainder are women who have had sex with IV drug users or bisexual men.[27] For women, heterosexual contact with an infected partner is becoming more important for HIV transmission.[28] However, so far heterosexual transfer has been common only among Haitian immigrants.

There is fear that heterosexual transmission will increase in the United States unless sexually active people always practice safe sex, and most importantly, restrict all their sexual activity to proven HIV-safe partners. Within the medical community, there is particular concern about AIDS now spreading more rapidly in the African American community. Black physicians are concerned that AIDS is often cast in the black community as primarily a white gay disease, and that many young African American males view condom use as a threat to their manhood. The result is substantially increased risk. According to the Centers for Disease Control African Americans now account for 33 percent of all new AIDS cases (Hispanics account for 18 percent, Asians 1 percent).[29]

Third World Patterns

Throughout the world, HIV is increasingly being passed heterosexually. There are 73 women infected for every 100 males. A third of the world AIDS deaths occur in women. However, in sub-Saharan Africa, where AIDS transmission is primarily through heterosexual contact, women make up the greatest number of victims; there are 110 infected women for every 100 infected men. As of 2000 there were 11.2 million AIDS orphans who had lost their mother before reaching the age of 15.[30]

---

[27]"HIV/AIDS Surveillance Report," Centers for Disease Control, Atlanta, 1992.
[28]Lawrence Altman, "AIDS Is Now the Leading Killer of Americans from 25 to 44," *New York Times*, January 31, 1995, p. A1.
[29]"Minority AIDS News Worsens," *Associated Press News Service*, January 14, 2000.
[30]Joint United Nations Programme on HIV/AIDS, "AIDS Epidemic Update: December 1999," *UNAIDS*, December 1999.

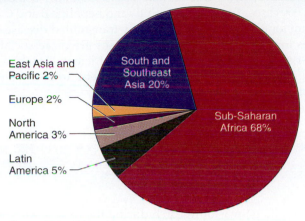

Figure 14.2 Regional Distribution of People with HIV/AIDS

East Asia and Pacific 2%

Europe 2%

North America 3%

Latin America 5%

South and Southeast Asia 20%

Sub-Saharan Africa 68%

Source: United Nations.

AIDS is spreading at far different rates in different world regions.[31] New HIV cases are declining (although at a slow rate) in North America, and the number of new HIV cases has reached a plateau in Europe (except in Eastern Europe). The infection is still at epidemic levels in Africa, however, and Asian HIV incidence is rising sharply. As of 2000 some 95 percent of those who are HIV positive live in the developing world. As Figure 14.2 indicates, over two-thirds of those with HIV/AIDS live in Africa and another 20 percent live in Asia. An increasing proportion of the world's new infections now occur in Southeast Asia.[32] The World Health Organization (WHO) estimates that some 10 million people in Asia are infected with the HIV virus and can be expected to eventually die from AIDS-related causes.[33]

Sub-Saharan Africa has disastrously high HIV/AIDS levels with 23.3 million people infected. In the 29 African countries hardest hit by AIDS, the average life expectancy is now seven years less than it would be without AIDS.[34] Many villages have been virtually wiped out, and four out of five hospital beds in Sub-Saharan Africa are occupied by patients suffering from AIDS-related diseases. Over a quarter of the population of Zambia is HIV positive, and the figure is probably higher in Uganda. In Kenya, where rates are rapidly increasing, it is now assumed that all prostitutes are infected. Because protease inhibitors, which are extremely expensive, are not even available in most of Africa (and most of Asia) and condom use is rare, HIV rates can be expected to continue to increase.

Other Sexually Transmitted Diseases

It should be noted that while HIV/AIDS is the most serious sexually transmitted disease, it is far from the only one. The federal Centers for Disease Control reports that

[31]"Status of the HIV/AIDS Pandemic as of January 1995," Global AIDS Policy Coalition, Harvard School of Public Health, 1995.

[32]"Women, Children, and AIDS," *Population Today*, April 1995, p. 3.

[33]Philippe Debeusscher, "AIDS Cases Up 60% in a Year, Asia to Overtake Africa: WHO," *Jakarta Post*, July 4, 1994, p. 7.

[34]Carl Haub, "UN Projections Assume Fertility Decline, Mortality Increase," *Population Today*, vol. 26, no. 12, December 1998, p. 2.

chlamydia, with 478,000 cases yearly, is the nation's most reported sexually transmitted infectious disease.[35] Chlamydia is a symptomless infection striking mostly women that can cause infertility and pregnancy complications. Gonorrhea is the second most common sexually transmitted disease, with 393,000 cases. HIV/AIDS is third, with 72,000 cases. These, plus syphilis and hepatitis B and C (which destroy the liver), account for 87 percent of the sexually transmitted disease cases.

The remedies for sexually transmitted diseases are more social than medical. Changing high-risk sexual behaviors is far more efficient, is far cheaper, and saves more lives than attempts at "after the fact" treatment. In every sense, sexual diseases are "social diseases."

Mental Disorders

One of the most exciting areas of research during the new century is in the area of mental health. Mental disorders ranging from temporary depression to serious incapacity affect a quarter of the American population every year.[36] The National Institute of Mental Health estimates that every year some 51 million Americans suffer from a mental disorder, although only about 8 million seek treatment.[37] Persons with serious mental illnesses approach 5 million. Some 20 million Americans suffer from depression, major and minor. Nearly half of all American adults will have a mental illness at least once in their lifetime, though most will not seek treatment.[38] One out of every 12 Americans will receive treatment at some time for mental disorders. This means huge social and economic costs for the society. The total economic costs exceed $150 billion.[39] If any other problem was so widespread, it would be the focus of immense national concern; massive programs would be mounted to provide both cure and care.

Problems Defining Mental Disorders

mental disorder and mental illness

not coping with or responding rationally to the circumstances of everyday life.

Experts disagree on how to define mental illness. The terms **mental disorder** and **mental illness** are commonly used interchangeably, although the term *mental illness* is more often used to refer to those being treated by mental health practitioners, programs, or institutions. From a sociological perspective, the focus is not so much on psychiatric definitions or treatment modalities *per se*, but on how and why certain types of behaviors come to be defined or labeled as mental disorders. In other words, sociologists focus less on why people become mentally ill and more on what the reaction to those so defined tells us about our society.

Even in our "enlightened" era, those with mental problems or disturbances are frequently seen as strange, different, and potentially dangerous. Although we no longer believe the mentally ill are possessed by the devil nor do we drill holes in skulls of the mentally disturbed to release evil spirits, social attitudes have not progressed as much as we like to think. Even today, many people still choose to pretend that the problem doesn't affect them personally. For example, a parent

[35]"The Nation's Most Common Infections Are Sexual," *New York Times*, October 20, 1996, p. 28.
[36]Ronald C. Kessler, et al., "Lifetime and 12 Month Prevalence of DSM-III-R Psychiatric Disorders in the United States," *Archives of General Psychiatry*, 51:8–27, January 1994.
[37]National Mental Health Association, *MHIC: Mental Health and the Family: Mental Health Statistics*, 1997, www.nmha.org.
[38]Robert Pear, "Mental Illness Often Ignored, U.S. Declares," *New York Times News Service*, Dec. 14, 1999.
[39]National Mental Health Association, *MHIC: Mental Illness and the Family.*

might approve of tax appropriations for community mental health services while refusing to recognize emotional problems in her or his own spouse or child.

Search for Cures

Until very recently little was known medically about mental illness. **Schizophrenia,** for instance, is now viewed as a brain disease, but it has been blamed on everything from demonic possession to bad parenting to the person being willful. The hallmark of the disease is disordered thinking and distorted perceptions of reality, but the interplay between genetic and environmental social factors remains unclear. Searches for genetic or biochemical variation in people with severe mental disorders, especially schizophrenia and **bipolar (manic-depressive) disorders,** and normal populations is beginning to produce results. For example, for those who suffer from auditory or visual hallucinations, new drug therapies such as clozapine offer the first real breakthroughs in decades.

While there long has been some evidence that schizophrenia runs in families and is genetically linked, it still is not clear whether schizophrenia is inherited directly, or whether there is a genetic predisposition that is triggered by stress, isolation, low social status, or other social factors.[40] Current genetic studies concentrate on chromosomes 6 and 13, but evidence is still unconfirmed.[41] An eight-year multimillion dollar NIH (National Institutes of Health) study confirmed the location of a specific gene that contributes to the risk of schizophrenia in those having the same vulnerable gene on chromosome 6.[42] The evidence demonstrating that genetics is linked to mental disorders also shows that genetics is only part of the answer. Studies of identical twins, who share the same genetic structure, generally show that if one twin becomes schizophrenic, the chances of the other twin following suit are somewhat less than fifty-fifty. If genetic structure were the entire explanation there should be no difference between identical twins.

The large majority of people with schizophrenia show substantial improvement when treated with **antipsychotic drugs.** The first of the new "atypical antipsychotics," clozapine (Clozaril), has been shown to be the most effective, but unfortunately also has the possibility of severe side effects.[43] Newer antipsychotic drugs such as risperidone (Risperdal) and olanzapine (Zyprexa) are better tolerated, but may not treat the illness as well.

schizophrenia
the most diagnosed mental illness involving withdrawal and a break with reality.

bipolar (manic-depressive) disorders
mental illness involving extreme elation or more commonly, depression.

antipsychotic drugs
drugs that reduce symptoms of mental illness.

Stigma

Regardless of whether mental illness has a genetic base or social base, what most interests sociologists is how people react to, label, and set apart people identified as having mental problems. Since there are no universally agreed upon objective measures as to whether or not someone is mentally ill, the labeling is largely socially determined. The label "mentally ill" still has such negative consequences in American society that a person's life is far more affected by being socially identified as mentally ill than being clinically so defined.

For example, in 1972 Senator Thomas Eagleton was forced to withdraw from running for Vice President of the United States when it was discovered that he had

---

[40]I. I. Gottesman and James Shields, *Schizophrenia and Genetics: A Twin Study Vantage Point,* Academic Press, New York, 1972.
[41]National Institute of Mental Health, *Schizophrenia,* Government Printing Office, Washington, DC, June 1999, p. 6.
[42]See particularly the research of Kenneth S. Kendler et al., in *Nature Genetics,* November 1995.
[43]National Institute of Mental Health, *Schizophrenia,* p. 7.

sought treatment for depression. In terms of social consequences, the greatest stigma is attached not to having a problem but to *seeking treatment.* In contemporary America, seeking psychiatric treatment is still not fully acceptable for those people occupying positions of influence, authority, and power. A stigma, or mark of shame, is attached to seeking help for mental problems. Socially, people feel more at ease with a reformed alcoholic than with someone receiving treatment for a mental disorder. How would the American public today respond to learning that someone whose finger might be on the nuclear trigger has been treated for schizophrenia or bipolar disorder?

Definitions of Mental Disorder

Popular Usage

psychosis
serious mental illness that involves a sharp break with reality and prevents day-to-day operation.

neurosis
mental disability that produces anxiety but does not prevent day-to-day operation.

It is hard to treat someone without accurate diagnosis. Traditionally, distinction was made between **psychoses,** which involve a fairly sharp break from reality, and the **neuroses,** which involve anxiety that impairs functioning but usually not so severely that hospitalization is required. While these terms are no longer used clinically by psychiatrists, they are still commonly used, so we will note them here. Neurotic symptoms usually involve anxiety and sometimes depression. Severely neurotic behavior may also be compulsive, as when someone must always get out of bed using the same foot first, put their clothes on in the same manner, line books up very precisely, or walk only on one side of the street. Such disorders can cause discomfort and anxiety, but they are not usually disabling. A person who is in constant fear of being diagnosed with cancer or having a heart attack may still appear to function reasonably well in society. Those suffering from neurosis are not incapacitated or dangerous. Even without treatment, they are able to get by, but at a considerable price in mental anguish.

Psychosis differs from neurosis largely on the basis of ability to function. Whereas the neurotic is able to manage ongoing, everyday situations, the psychotic is not. Psychotics may have great difficulty in coping with external reality, and in some cases they may not be able to tell what is and what is not external. (Their private fantasies may seem to exist "out there.") A person who is psychotic may reside entirely in his or her own mental world. Breaks with reality may or may not be accompanied by occasionally bizarre behavior.

Clinical Definitions

For 50 years the American Psychiatric Association (APA) has used a classification of mental disorders which it has substantially revised over the years. The APA's 1994 fourth revised *Diagnostic and Statistical Manual of Mental Disorders,* referred to as *DSM-IV-R,* now includes 15 categories of major mental disorders:[44]

1. Disorders of infancy, childhood, or adolescence (e.g., mental retardation)
2. Delirium, dementia, and cognitive disorders (e.g., organic brain damage)

---

[44]American Psychiatric Association, *Diagnostic and Statistical Manual of Disorders IV,* revised, American Psychiatric Association, Washington, DC, 1994.

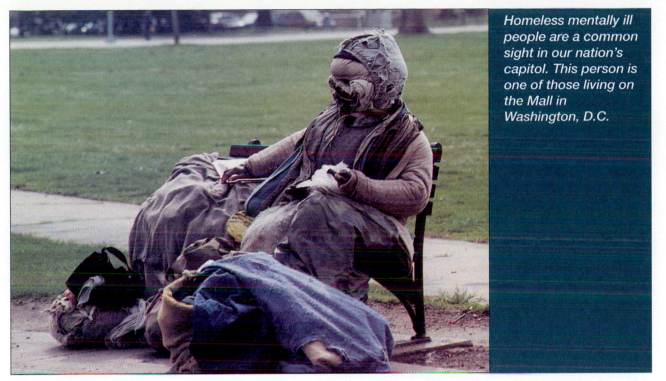

Homeless mentally ill people are a common sight in our nation's capitol. This person is one of those living on the Mall in Washington, D.C.

3. Substance-related disorders (e.g., alcohol and drug abuse)

4. Schizophrenic and other psychotic disorders (e.g., withdrawal from social contacts)

5. Mood disorders (e.g., depression or mood swings)

6. Anxiety disorders (e.g., phobias or panic attacks)

7. Somatoform disorders (e.g., psychological problems that manifest themselves as disease symptoms)

8. Factitious disorders (e.g., feigning mental problems)

9. Dissociative disorders (e.g., multiple personalities)

10. Sexual and gender identity problems (e.g., transsexualism or exhibitionism)

11. Eating disorders (e.g., anorexia and bulimia)

12. Sleep disorders (e.g., insomnia)

13. Impulse control disorders (e.g., kleptomania, impulse gambling, or pyromania)

14. Adjustment disorders (e.g., inability to adjust to stress)

15. Personality disorders (e.g., paranoid and antisocial personalities)

The most likely mental disorder to be suffered by a patient during the past year is *anxiety*.[45] This means not just an occasional anxiety attack but prolonged and severe anxiety. Anxiety disorders affect just over a quarter of all adult Americans over their lifetime. The second most common disorder during the past year (and the most common by a small margin over a lifetime) is *substance abuse* from alcohol or drugs. The third most common is *mood disorders*, primarily severe depression. This affects almost one-fifth of the adult population sometime in their life.

---

[45]Ronald C. Kessler et al., "Lifetime and 12-Month Prevalence of DSM-III-R Psychiatric Disorders in the United States," *Archives of General Psychiatry*, 51:8–19, January 1994.

This list, however, is not as objective as it might seem. Politics and lobbying play a role in defining what is or is not listed as a mental disorder. As one example, because of gay protests, the APA in 1974 voted 5,854 to 3,810 to redefine homosexuality not as a "psychiatric disorder" but rather as a "sexually oriented disturbance." Deciding essentially by a show of hands whether or not a given behavior is or is not an illness is hardly a scientific approach. However, as Chapter 13 noted, the criteria for defining alcoholism as a disease are equally arbitrary.

Models of Mental Disorders

The Medical Model

medical model
defines a disorder as an "illness" that can be treated medically.

Mental difficulties can be viewed from a number of different perspectives. The **medical model** treats psychological disorders as "illnesses" similar to physical disorders. The medical model describes mental problems as a form of "illness" and the afflicted person as a "patient" who is treated by "doctors" in a "hospital" or "clinic." The discovery of genetic linkages to mental illness suggests that the medical perspective has validity.

Socially, the medical model has the advantage of moving mental illness from being seen as madness or possession to being viewed as a treatable medical condition. But in spite of its wide acceptance by professionals and lay people alike, the medical model has several serious weaknesses. A major difficulty is that the illness categories are not clear-cut. There are no clear medical criteria for telling just when someone crosses the line into mental illness or when they are considered cured. In diagnosing bipolar personality or schizophrenia, for instance, the medical model applies more by analogy than on the basis of scientific evidence. There are not precise symptoms that result in uniform diagnoses.

In an innovative and now classic study, David Rosenhan, a psychiatrist, attempted to find out whether the medical staffs in several of the nation's best mental hospitals could distinguish completely sane people from those with psychiatric problems.[46] Accordingly, Rosenhan arranged to have eight normal volunteers admitted to 12 different mental hospitals. To gain entrance to the hospitals, the volunteers reported that they thought they heard voices saying a single word, such as "empty" or "hollow." Except for their names, all background statements they gave about their lives were true. Once inside the hospital, they immediately stopped hearing the voices and acted in a completely normal way.

Other patients knew the volunteers weren't ill, and they suspected that the pseudopatients were journalists, professors, or others who were checking on the hospital. However, not a single staff person—doctor, nurse, or other professional—ever expressed any doubt that the pseudopatients were mentally ill. The staff even viewed the note-taking of the pseudopatients as evidence of pathology.

The pseudopatients were confined an average of 19 days, the range being from 7 to 52 days. All were released as schizophrenics "in remission." In an equally innovative follow-up study, a cooperating mental hospital was told that over the next three months pseudopatients would attempt to gain admission. Although no actual pseudopatients were ever sent, the hospital judged 41 patients to be pseudopatients. Obviously, even experts have problems in defining mental disorders, particularly where marginal cases are concerned.

---

[46]David Rosenhan, "On Being Sane in Insane Places," *Science*, 173:250–258, 1973.

There is also ambiguity regarding treatment. The treatment modalities used by psychiatrists are determined more by their training in a particular psychiatric tradition than by the patient's symptoms. For bipolar disorder, one psychiatrist might employ extensive psychotherapy; a second, group therapy; a third might prescribe drugs; and a fourth might recommend electroshock. Some psychiatrists might try one after another. Any of these treatments might help, or all might fail. Whether or not they work, there is little scientific evidence to explain why a particular approach is used in a particular instance.

Thus, the medical model as applied to mental disorders has the same strengths and limitations as does the concept of "alcoholism as a disease." The major advantage of the medical model is that, by calling mental disorders illnesses, those who are so diagnosed are entitled to treatment. However, once patients accept the definition of themselves as mentally ill, they are, in effect, let off the hook regarding responsibility for past and perhaps future actions. Supposedly, they cannot help what they are doing because they are "ill." The medical model thus offers convenient rationalizations for both medical personnel and patients.

Social Deviation

While psychiatrists apply clinical criteria for determining mental illness, most sociologists use **social deviation** as the criterion. Lacking any clear or precise methods of deciding who is or is not in need of treatment, society crudely applies ad hoc rules. In this way sociologists refer to mental illness as being **socially constructed.** As put by one authority, "It appears that there is no clear-cut criterion of what constitutes a psychiatric case. Whether a person is regarded as in need of medical treatment is clearly a function of his behavior and the attitude of his fellows in society."[47] The psychiatrist Dr. Karl Menninger once noted, "Insanity is a question of public opinion."[48] Was Joan of Arc a saint or a delusional psychotic? Today people who claim they hear voices are considered in the latter category. Insanity is at least as much a social and legal question as a clinical one.

Broadly speaking, we define people as mentally ill when they appear incapable of responding rationally to the circumstances of everyday life. The behavior may be one of extreme withdrawal, excitability, or irrationality. It is not as much the behavior itself as its **inappropriateness to the circumstances.** Uncontrollable weeping, for instance, may be an appropriate response in a person who has just learned of a child's accidental death, but it would not be appropriate behavior for a college professor in the middle of a lecture. Even with behaviors generally conceded to be abnormal, such as auditory hallucinations (hearing voices), there are no clear guidelines as to what constitutes illness or insanity. A person who "speaks in tongues" at church at 11:00 am on Sunday morning is judged by some to be blessed by God. However, if the same person began speaking in tongues at a business meeting at 11:00 on Monday morning, the social judgment would be somewhat different. What is socially acceptable (or even approved of) in one context is aberrant or delusional behavior in another.

The line between sanity and mental illness is socially and culturally drawn; it is subjective rather than objective. Mental illness can be seen as *behavior that lies beyond the social limits of eccentricity.* A person is considered mentally disturbed only after other explanations for his or her erratic or inappropriate behavior have been found inadequate. Thus, mental illness is in many ways a **residual category** for behaviors that cannot be explained otherwise. The behavioral breach also has to be viewed as serious. Seriousness in this context is the distance between a person's actions and the

social deviation
behavior that substantially differs from the expected norm.

socially constructed
socially created and defined.

residual category
catch-all category for unexplained behaviors.

[47]George M. Corstairs, "The Social Limits of Eccentricity: An English Study," in Marion Opler (ed.), *Culture and Mental Health,* Macmillan, New York, 1959, p. 377.
[48]*Time,* October 20, 1975, p. 57.

norms and folkways of the society. Thus, the disheveled old man who argues with himself every day while sitting on the same park bench is probably simply a local character—as is the obese woman who lives with her 10 cats in the deteriorating house that always has its shades drawn. However, if either of the above people were to decide one warm summer day to walk downtown without bothering to clothe themselves, they would probably be committed for psychiatric observation and treatment. They would have exceeded the bounds of what our society generally regards as "normal" behavior.

Another of the ad hoc rules used to decide on someone's sanity is whether or not those already certified as mentally ill exhibit similar behavior. For example, a person who goes into catatonic trances from time to time—as the seriously mentally ill are known to do—is readily labeled as being mentally ill.

Residual Deviance and Labeling Theory

labeling theory
theory holding that branding someone as a deviant encourages further deviant behavior. Society responds to labels more than actions, i.e., someone seeking mental health care is mentally ill.

Probably the major challenge to the medical model of mental disorder has been offered by **labeling theory.** Contemporary labeling theory owes much to Edwin Lemert's distinction between primary and secondary deviance.[49] **Primary deviance** exists when one commits socially deviant acts but is still accepted as a responsible member of the society. **Secondary or residual deviance** exists when one joins a deviant subculture and is more or less officially labeled as a deviant.

Labeling or societal-reaction theory as it applies to mental disorders has been developed thoroughly by Thomas Scheff. According to Scheff, society has all sorts of social conventions which all of us occasionally violate without consequences. However, when actions are labeled as mental disorders, and the person engaging in residual deviance accepts that definition of his or her actions, then labeling takes place. Mental illness is playing the socially defined role of a person who is mentally ill, a set a behavioral rules for "acting crazy." Scheff says, "Most mental disorders can be considered to be a social role."[50]

primary deviance
initial deviance that does not result in being labeled deviant.

Though he does not reject psychiatric and psychological explanations in their totality, Scheff believes that once people have been labeled mentally ill, others come to expect them to play the role of a "crazy" person—to represent what Scheff refers to as the "social institution of insanity."

secondary or residual deviance
adoption of the role of a deviant by someone who has been publicly labeled as a deviant.

Criticisms of Labeling Theory

Once labeling has occurred, is it irreversible? Not necessarily. They have simply chosen not to conform. The notion that "there is no turning back" after secondary or residual deviance is also questionable. Hospitalized mental patients, upon their release, often manage to avoid rehospitalization and thus reinforcement of the mental illness role. One study indicates that over two-thirds of hospital patients who were followed up seven years after their release had not been rehospitalized.[51] Labeling is far from an automatic process.

---

[49]Edwin M. Lemert, *Social Pathology*, McGraw-Hill, New York, 1951.
[50]Thomas Scheff, *Being Mentally ILL, A Sociological Theory*, Aldine, Chicago, 1966; and Thomas Scheff, *Labeling Madness*, Prentice-Hall, Englewood Cliffs, NJ, 1975.
[51]Walter Gove, "Societal Reaction as an Explanation of Mental Illness: An Evaluation," *American Sociological Review*, 35:873–884, October 1970.

Critics of labeling theory point out that a label is not applied arbitrarily. Usually it is only after a problem has existed for a long term that someone finally is labeled mentally ill. Labeling theory does not explain deviance that precedes the application of the label. The labeling itself merely marks a point along a sequence; it does not initiate the sequence. Defining a person as ill often expedites effective professional treatment. Today such treatment does not mean being locked up in an institution where one's deviant role is reinforced. Today, symptoms are rapidly brought under control and the person returned to the community. Being labeled as mentally ill is a result of both the individual's behaviors and the label being attached.[52]

The "Myth of Mental Illness"

Perhaps the most controversial approach to mental illness is associated with the psychiatrist Thomas Szasz. He questions whether mental illness even exists.[53] Szasz has been arguing for years that mental illness is a **myth** or a fictitious construct. Szasz does not argue that there is no such thing as serious mental disorders. Instead, he maintains that it is both misleading and dangerous to call these behavior disorders "diseases of the mind."[54] Although commonly called mental illnesses, these disorders, Szasz claims, are simply *problems of adjusting to life*. "Human relations are inherently fraught with conflict," and becoming mentally ill is a way of avoiding unpleasant reality and having to deal with real problems. In short, mental illness is nothing more than a myth that hides and makes more palatable the moral conflicts in human relations. Szasz's views have become popular with the political far right, because he argues that laws often destroy citizen's rights to liberty. For example, he says a person has the right to believe that he or she is God without interference from the state, which insists that such people be "cured." Szasz pushes his argument to the extreme of denying not only a physiological basis for mental disorders but the existence of mental illness itself.

myth
nonfactual beliefs that have social consequences

A Note on Mental Illness and Mental Incapacity

Occasionally people confuse mental illness with lack of mental capacity. Limited mental capacity is a mental disorder, but not a mental illness. Those who are mentally ill are not necessarily mentally slow, and vice versa. The following story makes this point.

> A man was driving past the mental asylum grounds when he had a flat tire. He jacked up the car and was putting on the spare tire when he inadvertently knocked the nuts that anchor the wheel down a sewer. As he stood there wondering how he could attach the wheel to the bolts without the nuts an inmate of the asylum came up to the fence. Immediately sizing up the situation the inmate said, "All you have to do is take one nut off of each of the other three wheels and use them." The driver profusely thanked the inmate for his advice and asked him, "How did you ever think of such a solution?" The inmate replied haughtily, "I may be crazy, but I'm not stupid."

[52]A. C. Schull, "Deviance and Social Control," in Neil J. Smelser, (ed.), *The Handbook of Sociology*, Sage, Newbury Park, CA, 1988.
[53]Thomas Szasz, *The Myth of Mental Illness*, rev. ed., Harper & Row, New York, 1974; and "Mental Illness is Still a Myth," *Society*, May/June, 1994, pp. 34–39.
[54]Thomas S. Szasz, *Cruel Compassion: Psychiatric Control of Society's Unwanted*, Wiley, New York, 1994.

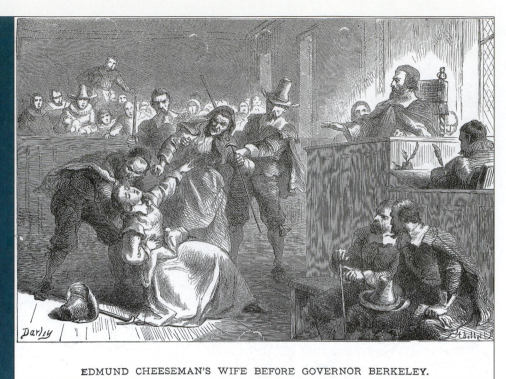

The 1692 Salem, Massachusetts witch trials resulted in the death of some twenty-two women. Here Edmund Cheeseman's wife accuses an old woman of witchcraft.

EDMUND CHEESEMAN'S WIFE BEFORE GOVERNOR BERKELEY.

Culver Pictures

Historical Treatments

Recent decades have seen huge advances in the treatment of mental disorders. As recently as the 1950s, the remote wards of many state mental hospitals were so-called snake pits, in which long-term patients were treated as vegetables, many being put in straitjackets or chained to their beds if they acted up or did not behave properly. The major function of asylums was to provide custodial care. Since then the populations of mental hospitals have decreased sharply, largely because drugs have facilitated the control and treatment of symptoms.

Mental Illness as Possession

Throughout much of Western history, mental disorders were viewed as signs of God's displeasure. Even worse, it was sometimes believed that the victims of madness had made a pact with the devil. In the latter case, the rite of exorcism would be used to drive out the devil; if this did not work, flogging or even burning at the stake was the next step. "Not all accused of being witches and sorcerers were mentally sick, but almost all mentally sick were considered witches, or sorcerers, or bewitched."[55]

Salem, Massachusetts, in 1692 was seized with witch-hunting hysteria. On the basis of charges made by young girls, 22 women were actually executed or died in prison as a result of the Salem witch trials, and some 150 persons were imprisoned for witchcraft and another 200 accused.[56] Only when the charges of witchcraft be-

---

[55]G. Zilboorg and G. W. Henry, *A History of Medical Psychology,* W. W. Norton, New York, 1941, p. 153.
[56]Kai T. Erikson, *Wayward Puritans,* Wiley, New York, 1966, pp. 149–152.

Box 14.2 Ongoing Issues

Treatment of Witches

The **Malleus Maleficarum,** the handbook of the witch courts written by two Dominican monks of the fifteenth century, provided for centuries a guide to identifying, examining, and sentencing witches. The devil, said the monks, seeks to lure women into sin by sending an incubus (male evil spirit) forth to co-habit with the human and to spread the devil's evil on earth. The incubi were allegedly able to assume human form for their carnal purpose.[a] Once the pact was sealed, the powers of the witch were limitless. Witches could cause a man to have "evil love" for a woman or a woman for a man. They could bring about bodily diseases and cause death. They could cause the death or disease of animals, the drying up of milk cows, and the failure of crops.

There are assurances all through the *Malleus Maleficarum* that women are inferior by nature, vice-ridden, impure, and vicious—and the tools of Satan. Sorcery courts justified their actions on the biblical injunction, "Thou shalt not suffer a witch to live" (Exodus 22:18). The courts insisted on confession—and because confession brought death, various means of torture were often found necessary. Torture of witches was described as a means of driving the demon from the subject's body until he

came forth to announce his defeat by the tormentors. To drive out the demon and force a confession, various instruments of torture were used, such as the Spanish boot, which crushed the bones of the foot, the rack or the "Catherine's Wheel," on which the body was stretched and torn, and many other imaginative devices conceived by sadistic minds. One handy device was the witches' collar, an iron collar with a metal tongue that went into the mouth and had a number of sharp prongs which pierced the palate, the tongue, and the inside of the mouth. This device was inserted and the witch was then tied to a post for 24 hours before being asked to confess. Between the fifteenth and seventeenth centuries, Catholics and Protestants competed with each other to see how many witches they could burn at the stake. Between them they killed a minimum of 100,000 and perhaps as many as 500,000 women as witches.

[a]*Brian P. Levack*, The Witch-Hunt in Early Modern Europe, *Longman, Reading, MA, 1995; Elinor Lander Horwitz*, Madness, Magic, and Medicine: The Treatment and Mistreatment of the Mentally Ill, *Lippincott, Philadelphia, 1977; and Marvin Harris*, Cows, Pigs, Wars, and Witches: The Riddles of Culture, *Random House, New York, 1974.*

gan to reach those in high places—for example, the governor's wife—was the hysteria suppressed. Nor is the belief in demonic possession simply an artifact of less-enlightened times. As movies such as *The Exorcist* show, there is still widespread interest in demonic possession.

Asylums and Other Reforms

The first American mental hospital was founded in Philadelphia with the assistance of Benjamin Franklin. Franklin was concerned about the growing number of "lunatics" who "are going at large and are a terror to their neighbors, who are daily apprehensive of the violences they might commit."[57] The inmates in mental hospitals were chained up like animals, and the attendants were called keepers.

A great forward step in asylum reform was made during the French Revolution (1793), when Phillippe Pinel, a French physician chosen to head the Paris Mental Institution, freed mental inmates from their chains. Pinel emphasized "moral treatment," which essentially meant treating inmates as sick people rather than as dangerous and deranged animals. Asylums, according to his thinking, were to be

---

[57]Quoted in Erik Eckholm, "Changing Visions of Madness in America," *New York Times News Service,* November 20, 1994.

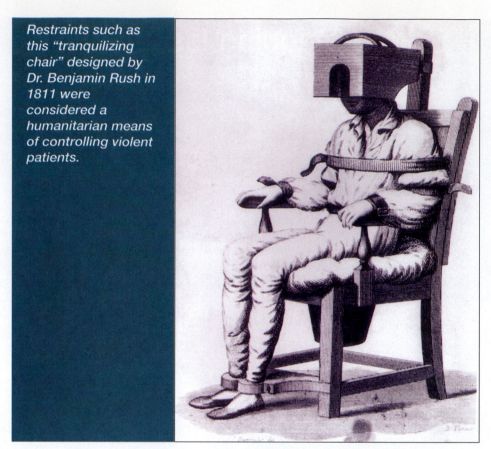

Restraints such as this "tranquilizing chair" designed by Dr. Benjamin Rush in 1811 were considered a humanitarian means of controlling violent patients.

National Library of Medicine

places of asylum or refuge from outside pressures. State-supported asylums in the United States owe much to the reforming zeal of Dorothea Dix, who lobbied strongly for such facilities during the early nineteenth century.

Despite these and other reform efforts, such as those of ex-mental-patient Clifford Beers around the turn of the twentieth century, the basic concept of insane asylums remained not treatment but confinement for the potentially dangerous. In sociological terms, the manifest (intended) function was treatment, but the latent (secondary) function was keeping "crazy" people off the streets. Even a superficial look at most older mental hospitals impresses one with their prisonlike quality. Thick stone walls, barred windows, and high surrounding walls all proclaim the function of protecting society from those who are dangerous. These institutions were designed to meet society's perceived need to be protected from "raving maniacs."

Total Institutions

total institutions
places that cut persons off from society in order to reform or remake them.

Inside the walls of the asylum, the inmate traditionally is stripped not only of his or her clothing but also of any contact with the world outside. The sociologist Erving Goffman referred to places where one is cut off from society for appreciable periods of time and required to lead a regimented life as **total institutions.**[58]

---

[58]Erving Goffman, *Asylums: Essays on the Social Situation of Mental Patients and Other Inmates,* Doubleday, Garden City, NY, 1961.

Early Psychiatry in America

Benjamin Rush, the most famous physician in the early United States, was the first American psychiatrist. Rush, a Philadelphia Quaker and signer of the Declaration of Independence, was a man of liberal principles, broad education, and a friend and correspondent of Thomas Jefferson.

Rush was a reformer, but today many of his methods sound harsh. He bled his patients to an extraordinary degree, and since he disapproved entirely of any restraint—chaining, whipping, or even "mad-shirts" or straitjackets—he invented his own methods of keeping control. He invented a "tranquilizing chair" in which unruly patients were restrained for long periods of time. The chair, which held arms, legs, body, and head in a state of total immobility, was intended to heal through lowering the pulse and relaxing the muscles.[a]

Rush believed that absolute control over patients was necessary—and that this control was best established by inspiring the patients with fear of the doctor's authority. The kindly Quaker did not think it unseemly to subject patients to sudden dunkings by means of trapdoors over tubs or even to threaten to kill someone who needed a bit of terrorizing. He reported the case of a woman he cured after he threatened to drown her.

[a]*Elinor Lander Horwitz*, Madness, Magic, and Medicine: The Treatment and Mistreatment of the Mentally Ill, *Lippincott, Philadelphia, 1977.*

Total institutions—such as mental hospitals, prisons, some military training establishments, or even monasteries —attempt to control the inmates completely and to remake their lives. (In monasteries there is, of course, the major difference that the inmates are volunteers. In such institutions, the major control mechanism is fear of expulsion.) Regimentation and uniformity, rather than individuality, are the goals.

In the case of the mental institution, long confinement tends to make people lose their capacity to respond in an adult fashion; it actually undermines their ability to cope with the outside world. Goffman pointed out that in mental hospitals an act of assertiveness or rebellion on the part of the patient is taken not as a sign of self-confidence and maturity but as a symptom of sickness.[59] Not to accept the staff definition of the situation is to "act out" or be "difficult." The "good" patient, from the staff's point of view, is one who is docile, undemanding, and obedient. This is a form of resocialization, with the goal of remaking the person. The military basic training or boot camp's goal is to convert civilians into soldiers or sailors who will automatically follow orders.

Deinstitutionalization

Mental hospitals reached a peak patient population of almost 600,000 in 1955. At that date there were more people held in mental institutions than being treated in all other types of hospitals combined. Today, there are less than a tenth as many long-term patients. Declining commitments signify not a decline in the number of mental disorders but rather a change in treatment policies. Today, we dump schizophrenics not into hospitals but on the street. Only those of demonstrated danger to themselves or others remain institutionalized.

---

[59]Ibid.

As with the other social problems we have discussed, deinstitutionalization invariably involves tradeoffs. Involuntary institutional commitment has to be weighed against the person's civil rights. The negative consequence of reducing involuntary commitments is that large numbers of people in need are left without a secure place to go. Theoretically, community mental-health clinics and welfare departments are supposed to look after them, but this only sometimes occurs. Also what if they will not apply for welfare or attend a clinic? What happens to the marginally competent or disturbed who are incapable of handling their own affairs yet who have no supportive families? At least one-third of the homeless living on the streets are mentally disturbed (see Chapter 7). What should be done about the old lady who spends her days mumbling to herself and picking through downtown refuse cans? What if the old lady also sleeps in the park and refuses to take her medication or doesn't apply for welfare? What is society's responsibility to such people?

There is no easy answer to such questions in a society that values personal freedom. The mental commitment law reforms of recent decades were not designed to cut off those in need from treatment, but that is often the result. As a society we deal with marginal people by ignoring and abandoning them. We have no effective way of caring for those who, while not dangerous, are not capable of handling their own affairs. Unless they raise a fuss, we pretend they do not exist.

Urban Life and Mental Illness

That most social problems are more pronounced in urban areas is sometimes attributed to social and personal disorganization and the absence of stable long-term relationships. Mental disorders, however, *do not* appear to be more prevalent in urban places. Early twentieth-century data showing higher rates of mental disturbance in urban areas were in part the result of the availability of hospitals in urban locations and in part the result of better record-keeping in cities. People with mental disorders may also tend to drift toward cities. Extremely homogeneous, tightly knit, and supportive rural communities do not seem to have lower rates of mental disturbance than large urban locations. The classic study by Joseph Eaton and Robert Weil is of mental health among the Hutterites, a conservative and fundamentalist Anabaptist group living in tightly structured agricultural communities in the Dakotas, Montana, and western Canada.[60] Eaton and Weil found that the rural Hutterites had rates of serious mental illness about equal to the rate of hospitalization in New York State. Rather than being institutionalized, however, the mentally disturbed Hutterites were cared for within the community.

Leo Srole argues that the big city is a healthier accommodation to the human condition than the small town. Using data from the National Center for Health Statistics, Srole compared people living in rural areas and cities of under 50,000 population with people living in cities of 50,000 or more. Interviews were conducted with 6,700 people nationally, and psychological distress scores were created based on 12 symptoms, including sleeping difficulties, the feeling that "everyone is against me," the complaint that "worries get me down physically," and the fear of a nervous breakdown. Srole found that rural areas had 20 percent higher symptom scores (showing psychological distress) than urban areas.[61]

---

[60] Joseph W. Eaton and Robert J. Weil, *Culture and Mental Disorders*, Free Press, Glencoe, IL, 1955.
[61] Leo Srole, paper delivered at American Psychiatric Association Meetings, Toronto, May 2, 1977.

Social Class and Mental Illness

Serious mental disorders are most prevalent in lower-class populations.[62] This fact has remained consistent for half a century. Probably the most quoted study of the relationship between mental disorders and social class on the individual level is that conducted by A. B. Hollingshead and Frederick Redlich of almost all the psychiatric patients in New Haven, Connecticut.[63] Not only were records obtained for 98 percent of all patients undergoing mental treatment in the city of New Haven, including those in public hospitals, clinics, and private nursing homes, but also included were patients undergoing private therapy, both locally, in nearby states, and in New York City. The 1,565 patients were divided into five classes on the basis of occupation, education, and area of residence; they were then compared to a 5 percent random sample of the city population. When compared with the total population, the lowest class had almost twice as high a rate of psychosis as would be expected. Not only was the prevalence of mental disorders highest in the lowest class, but disorders decreased with each increase in social-class level.

Drift Hypothesis

One hypothesis advanced to explain the higher rate of mental disorders in the lower social strata is the **drift hypothesis,** which suggests that those suffering mental disorders have difficulty in coping with everyday problems of work and life, and thus tend to drift down to lower socioeconomic positions.[64] According to this hypothesis, the low social position of many of the mentally disturbed is not a cause but a consequence of their mental difficulties.

drift hypothesis
those with mental disorders drift toward lower socioeconomic status.

Hollingshead and Redlich's research found little skidding among patients when their status was compared with that of their parents.[65] The midtown Manhattan study, on the other hand, found that the most serious problems existed among downwardly mobile sons.[66] It is unclear whether mental illness is a consequence either of downward mobility or of blocked aspirations. One could argue that rather than promoting downward mobility, mental illness makes it impossible to advance. Certainly emotional distress and hospitalization are not associated with upward mobility.[67]

Social Environment

A second explanation for the prevalence of mental disorders in lower socioeconomic groups is that mental disorders reflect the stressful social environment of

---

[62]A. B. Hollingshead and Frederick Redlich, *Social Class and Mental Illness,* Wiley, New York, 1958; William Rushing, "Two Patterns in the Relationship between Social and Mental Hospitalization," *American Sociological Review,* 34:533–541, 1969; and Leo Srole, Thomas Langer, Stanley Michael, Marvin Opler, and Thomas Rennie, *Mental Health in the Metropolis: The Midtown Manhattan Study,* McGraw-Hill, New York, 1962.
[63]A. B. Hollingshead and Frederick Redlich, *Social Class and Mental Illness.*
[64]John W. Fox, "Social Class, Mental Illness, and Social Mobility: The Social Selection-Drift Hypothesis for Serious Mental Illness," *Journal of Health and Social Behavior,* 31:344–353, December 1990.
[65]Hollingshead and Redlich, *Social Class and Mental Disorder.*
[66]Thomas S. Langer and Stanley T. Michael, *Life Stress and Mental Health,* Free Press, New York, 1963.
[67]Renee Fox, *The Sociology of Medicine,* Prentice Hall, Englewood Cliffs, NJ, 1989.

those less well off. Middle-class people, in this view, have more resources for dealing with mental anxieties, as well as greater sophistication in recognizing them; they are more likely to recognize the existence of problems and know where to get help. Lower-status people muddle along longer before seeking aid. When they do finally get professional help, they are more likely to have serious symptoms. The hypothesis of mental illness being tied to stressful environments appears reasonable, but scientific support is still only indirect. The assumptions on which it rests, such as that lower-class life is more stressful than that of the middle class, remain to be proved.[68]

Social Power

A third explanation of the social-class differences in mental illness is that these are not real differences but only a reflection of the social power and prestige of higher-status groups. Advocates of this conflict-theory position argue that aberrant behaviors are judged far more leniently when they come from an upper-class as opposed to a lower-class person. This view is embodied in the old saying, "The poor are crazy, the rich are eccentric." There is no question that the well-to-do have both legal and monetary resources to fight procedures such as involuntary commitment. If they are committed, upper-status patients receive better care and more attention from psychiatrists, who prefer working with them on the grounds that they are "more cooperative."

But in spite of these differences, the evidence suggests that because the poor underutilize both inpatient and outpatient facilities, the rates of lower-class mental disorders are probably understated. Real differences in rates of mental disorder by class are probably substantially greater than those suggested by the official figures.

Other Factors

A number of other variables show a relationship with mental disorder. Age is one factor. As a group, the aged are the most likely to be hospitalized, especially in public hospitals. This reflects the higher incidence of organic disorders in the older population and probably their greater isolation from meaningful roles in the society. However, if the number of new cases rather than the number of those confined at any one time is the criterion—that is, *incidence* rather than *prevalence*—then the rates are highest for the young adult and middle-aged groups (ages 18–44). Schizophrenia, for instance, is primarily a disorder of young adults.

Race does *not* appear to be related to mental disorders when socioeconomic status is taken into account. Gender on the other hand does make a difference. Women experience much higher levels of depression. This is especially true of women who are working and who are single parents.[69] Men, by contrast, have higher levels of substance abuse and personality disorders. Rates for schizophrenia appear to be roughly equal for both sexes.

[68]Walter R. Gove and Patrick Howell, "Individual Resources and Mental Hospitalization," *American Sociological Review,* 39:86–100, February 1974.
[69]W. C. Cockerham, "Medical Sociology," in Neil J. Smelzer, (ed.), *Handbook of Sociology,* Sage, Newbury Park, CA, 1988.

Marital status may be more relevant than gender for mental disorder. Whatever the reason, married people have the lowest rates of diagnosed and treated mental disorders. Durkheim noted a century ago in his pioneer research on suicide that the married have lower rates of serious mental and emotional problems than the unmarried or divorced.[70] Contemporary research shows the same pattern.[71] Those not married generally have higher rates of mental disorder, and by far the highest rates are among the no-longer married: the divorced, separated, and widowed.

While these findings are consistent and predictable, there is less agreement about what they mean. The problem is one of causation: Does marriage, for example, help "protect" people against mental problems, or do those who marry have fewer mental problems to begin with? Because marriage is the result of a selection process, do those who never marry or who eventually divorce have a higher proportion of pre-existing problems? Are these problems at least partly responsible for their inability to establish lasting relationships? In one view, those who stay married are among the most stable and well-adjusted people in our society. The opposing view is that, in a society where being married is taken as the norm, the single person is exposed to stresses and pressures that are not felt by the married. The predictability of married life acts to insulate and protect partners from stress.

Toward the Future

The American health care system provides cutting-edge treatment for disease and illness. However, it does far less well in providing routine medical care to those who are not wealthy or are not covered by good health insurance plans. The major medical problem of the new century is not curing disease but making known medical techniques, care, and medicines available to all citizens. The prognosis for this occurring is very guarded.

Attempts to reform the American jerry-built health system thus far have been no more than marginally successful. The Clinton administration's 1994 attempt to totally reform payment for health care totally failed. Reform was defeated by the political ineptness of the administration, combined with an exceptionally well-funded lobbying effort by opponents of reform in the insurance and health care industries.

Proposals for rationalizing the medical system by moving toward a "single-provider" insurance plan probably have little practical chance of implementation. Such a change would radically cut down on paperwork and save at least $100 billion every year. However, health insurance companies that profit from the current confusion of plans and limits on services argue that single-provider systems interfere with competition and free choice of medical care. That such free choice is only available to those who can afford it is not mentioned.

For the immediate future America's health care system will continue to differ from the single-provider systems used by virtually every other developed nation. The American system will remain one designed for, and providing for, those who can afford to pay the costs. In America, medical care will remain not a right but a consumer good to be purchased like any other.

---

[70]Emile Durkheim, *Suicide,* John Spaulding and George Simpson (trans.), Free Press, Glencoe, IL, 1951.
[71]Lee N. Robins and Darrel A. Regier, *Psychiatric Disorders in America,* Free Press, New York, 1991.

Women's health issues will receive increasing attention during the next decade. National Institutes of Health research dollars are increasing dramatically for these issues. Perhaps equally important is that the number of women physicians interested in women's health issues is growing. AIDS is not going away as a major health problem. The incidence of new AIDS cases is growing worldwide but decreasing in the United States. There are indications that with public education Asian rates of infection will slow, but sub-Saharan African HIV/AIDS rates show no similar signs of improvement. Whether U.S. AIDS victim numbers again begin to grow depends not so much on new treatment drugs as on convincing high-risk young males that practicing safe sex is still essential. The prevention of AIDS remains substantially a social rather than a medical problem.

Understanding of, and sympathy for, mental disorders is increasing, and major advances are being made in chemotherapy treatment. Widespread adoption of the medical model to explain and treat mental disorders has led to a sharply increasing reliance on drug-based treatments. During the next decade the use of mental hospitals, especially as treatment sites, will continue to decline. Community mental health organizations and facilities will increasingly emphasize the use of chemotherapies. This will be done more for budget than for treatment reasons. With budgets tight, drugs are seen as more cost effective than using psychologists and social workers.

Within the next decade new chemotherapy treatments are likely to further change our ideas about the nature of mental illness. Some researchers are increasingly concerned that the focus on genetic factors will convince the public that social factors and life conditions don't matter in mental disorders, that all life's problems can be solved with the right pill or medication.

Summary

Health is not just a medical question but also a social and economic one. The United States spends 14 percent of its Gross Domestic Product on health care, which is far in excess of what any other country spends. While the American health care system provides excellent care for those who can afford it, it is far less successful in providing adequate care for the lower portion of the population. Some 40 million Americans lack any form of health insurance, and the working poor receive the least health care.

- Functionalists look at how the health care system fails to meet its own goals.

- Conflict theorists focus on health care as a scarce resource that is distributed according to social power.

- Social interactionists look more to the effects at the individual level. An example is when social labels are attached to various illnesses.

- Being labeled mentally ill in American society has more force than meeting the clinical definition. Labeling occurs when someone is judged incapable of coping with or responding rationally to the pressures of everyday life.

- Although the terms *neurosis* and *psychosis* are still popularly used, professionals now use the 15 categories of the *Diagnostic and Statistical Manual of Mental Disorders* (DSM-IV).

- Most people don't define mental illness clinically, but in terms of social deviation from expected "normal" behavior.

- The asylums, or total institutions, of the early 1900s attempted to cure the patient by totally controlling inmates' lives. Today, because of the high value placed on personal freedom, people are rarely confined to institutions. However, this leaves the marginally competent wandering the city without protection or services.

- Medical models treat mental disorders as "illnesses" that must be treated by doctors in a medical setting. Labeling theory emphasizes, on the other hand, the degree to which patients play social roles because they are labeled.

- Sociologists are not as much concerned with how people become mentally disturbed as with the social consequences to the individual of being so labeled; sometimes a person learns to play the expected role of a "crazy" person.

- Mental disorders appear to be much more prevalent among lower-class populations and are found equally in both urban and rural areas. Possible causes for the higher incidence among the poor are the stressful lives of the poor, the chance of those with mental illness drifting down to lower strata, or the social class differences are reflecting differences in social power.

- While many mental disorders may have a genetic or organic basis, social situations also influence who becomes mentally ill and the consequences of being so labeled.

☞Key Review Terms

AIDS	Medicaid	residual category
antipsychotic drugs	Medicare	secondary (residual)
bipolar	mental disorders	deviance
clinical definitions	myth of mental illness	schizophrenia
drift-down hypothesis	neurosis	socialized medicine
DSM-IV-R	prevalence	social deviation
HIV	psychosis	stigma
incidence	primary deviance	
Malleus Maleficarum	protease inhibitors	

? Questions for Discussion

1. Analyze the statement "American health care is the best in the world" using all available data.

2. What are the strengths of the American health care system? What are its weaknesses?

3. How does the American health care system differ from that of Canada and the nations of Western Europe?

4. Discuss the AIDS epidemic worldwide. What are the social consequences of the disease?

5. How does the incidence and treatment of AIDS differ in the United States from the African and Asian patterns?

6. How prevalent is mental illness in the United States? What is the focus of sociologists studying mental disorders?

7. Describe the difference between mental illness and mental incapacity. How are they linked?

8. Discuss the statement "Insanity is a social or legal question more than a medical one."

9. What is labeling theory? Explains the strengths and criticisms of its use when discussing mental illness.

10. What are the demographic and social-class characteristics of the mentally ill? What hypotheses are used to explain these differences?

☛Suggested Resources

Arnold Birenbaum, *Putting Health Care on the National Agenda*, Praeger, Westport, CT, 1993. How to deal with American health care delivery problems, and especially rising costs.

Erving Goffman, *Asylums: Essays on the Social Situation of Mental Patients and Other Inmates*, Doubleday, Garden City, NY, 1961. An excellent participant–observation study of mental patients in St. Elizabeth's in Washington, and how much of what the staff does is to control rather than help patients.

Gerald N. Grob, *The Mad Among Us: A History of the Care of America's Mentally Ill*, Free Press, New York, 1994. How we have treated our mentally ill over the centuries.

David Mechanic, *Inescapable Decisions: The Imperatives of Health Reform*, Transaction, New Brunswick, NJ, 1994. A sociologist long-involved in the field recommends how to best reform the damaged American health care system.

William A. Rushing, *The AIDS Epidemic: Social Dimensions of an Infectious Disease*, Westview, Boulder, CO, 1995. A sociologists examination of the social consequences of AIDS.

Rose Weitz, *Life with Aids*, Rutgers, New Brunswick, NJ, 1991. All aspects of living with AIDS as seen from the viewpoint of the victims.

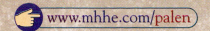
1. The World Health Organization (*www.who.org/*) of the United Nations is a primary resource on international health issues. Click on "Reports" and you'll be taken to a site that contains the "World Health Report Series." Click on "1999 World Health Report" and then again on "Full Report" to examine the table of contents. Scroll down to Chapter 5, ("Combating the Tobacco Epidemic").

    a. What are the worldwide trends on tobacco usage?

    b. Go back to the ASH site from Chapter 13 (*www.ash.org/*). Were any of these trends addressed in this site?

    For information on health issues in the United States, visit The National Institutes of Health (*www.nih.gov/index.html*). This site contains information on everything from "poison ivy" to "xerostomia." (What is xerostomia?) Click on "Institutes and Offices" for a wide variety of sites on specific health issues and subjects. For example, if you select the National Institute of Mental Health (NIMH), you will have access to the Surgeon General's Full Report on Mental Health. Another site, "The National Institute of Environmental Health Studies" (NIEHS) is devoted to research on environmental factors promoting human illness. For example, to learn about the dangers of asbestos, click on "NIEHS Web Search" and enter the word, "asbestos."

    c. What dangers do materials like asbestos, chromium, and mercury pose to people?

    d. Do you feel that sites like NIEHS serve a useful purpose to U.S. citizens or are they a waste of the taxpayers money? Explain.

2. Information available on the web about AIDS is overwhelming. Begin with a visit to AEGIS (*www.aegis.com/*) (the largest HIV/AIDS website in the world with links to all major AIDS/HIV sites). It is updated hourly. Click on "The Basics" and then go to "HIV Statistics." You will be taken to The National Institute of Allergy and Infectious Diseases fact sheet on HIV/AIDS statistics (*www.niaid.nih.gov/factsheets/aidsstat.htm*). Examine the fact sheet.

    a. What are the most recent demographic trends in HIV/AIDS?

    b. According to what you can find on this site, how close is medical science to finding a cure for HIV/AIDS?

"Beverly?"

"Yes?"

"I've heard you use the words, 'a good whore' several times. Apparently, you mean something very specific?"

"Well, sure. To begin with, the good whore is a girl who solves your problems and don't create them. The good whore makes it easy for the management, which is why you don't see us hire what all you men seem to want, the teenage, virgin-looking cutie-pies. They may look wonderful on TV but they can be a pain here in a house. The Lolitas just don't make good whores."

"Why?"

"Well, for example, they keep putting their own feeling into it too much, their own pride. Suppose a man comes in and he's a little drunk and bragging. Well, a young girl will get irritated and show it. The older girl takes it as it comes, makes him feel like the president.

Gabriel R. Vogliotti, *The Girls of Nevada*, Citadel Press, Secaucus, NJ, 1975, pp. 166–167.

Society and Sexuality

Sociological Perspectives

People often assume that sexual behavior is genetically programmed, but research has demonstrated that even the sexual behavior of rhesus monkeys is learned, not genetic.[1] Adult male monkeys raised in isolation have no idea how to perform sexually and are terrified of females monkeys who do. Human sexual behavior is learned behavior, occurs within a particular sociocultural system, and is strongly influenced by the norms, values, and attitudes of those within the group. Human sexuality is socially rooted and controlled by social factors, including age, gender, ethnicity, marital status, and socioeconomic status.

Functionalist Approaches

Functionalists suggest that marriage exists because it is functional for society insofar as it produces social stability (see Chapter 10). The institution of marriage ensures that a specific male can be assigned the responsibility for children that might result. Society (and its laws) is concerned not with whether a child is conceived in wedlock but with whether it is born in wedlock. Socially, identifying the biological father is less important than assigning paternity within a family unit. This preserves the kinship system.

Functionalists say prostitution continues to exist because it also is functional for society. St. Augustine (354–430 CE) argued that prostitution had the function of protecting "good" women and stabilizing the family. Suppress prostitution, he warned, and capricious lusts will overthrow society. St. Thomas Aquinas likewise gave a functional argument for permitting prostitution on the grounds that it protected the virtue of "good" women.

The classic sociological argument stressing the social function of prostitution has been articulated by Kingsley Davis.[2] Davis maintains that every society has ways of controlling the sex drive to insure that children resulting from intercourse will be property nurtured. This is accomplished primarily by limiting sexual activity to partners in marriage—that is, to those who constitute family units and are willing to raise their children and assume responsibility for them. By providing sexual gratification free of any obligation but the immediate fee for service, prostitution constitutes a threat to the survival of the family and is therefore universally condemned. Paradoxically, these same characteristics—easy sex, often of an unconventional type, provided impersonally—also make prostitution functional for society by providing a relief valve for gratifying sexual impulses without jeopardizing the family unit or producing unwanted children.

---

[1]Harry Harlow and Margaret K. Harlow, "Social Deprivation in Monkeys," *Scientific American,* 207: 137–147, 1962.

[2]Kingsley Davis, "The Sociology of Prostitution," *American Sociological Review,* 2:744–755, 1947; and Kingsley Davis, "Prostitution," in Robert K. Merton and Robert A. Nisbet (eds.), *Contemporary Social Problems,* Harcourt, Brace & World, New York, 1961, pp. 275–276.

Sex saturates growing up in America. A thirteen-year-old boy in his bedroom with numerous pinup wall posters.

© James Carroll/Stock, Boston

In short, attempts to tie sexual activity to social requirements, especially to tie it to the durable relation of marriage, keeps prostitution alive. It is analogous to the black market, which is the illegal but inevitable response to official attempts to exert full control on an economy. Pornography is similarly seen as dysfunctional insofar as it encourages nonmarital sexual activity, and thus could be a threat to the family.

Conflict Approaches

Marxian and feminist conflict approaches view both sexual regulations and marriage as a form of structured inequality designed to keep men dominant and women subservient (see Chapter 10). Traditional male-female relationships are seen as a means of subordinating women and maintaining patriarchy. Forms that differ from the norm, such as homosexuality, are declared criminal. Sexual minorities are oppressed just as are racial or ethnic minorities.

Conflict theorists see historical prostitution as a direct consequence of economic systems that oppressed and exploited poor women. Prostitution was sometimes necessary as a means of survival. Today, prostitution continues to reflect gender and class biases in that the sex workers most likely to be arrested and prosecuted are lower-class female streetwalkers. Higher-status call girls and call boys are far less likely to be harassed.

Homosexuals similarly suffer because society defines allowable sexual activity as occurring only between a man and a woman. Other sexual activity is defined as illicit and possibly criminal. Established and powerful societal institutions such as churches are seen as imposing their values through legislation and the courts. Only through organized opposition can sexual minorities gain their rights by repealing all laws restricting sexual activities between consenting adults.

Interactionist Approaches

Interactionist perspectives stress how we learn socially to express ourselves sexually and how the meanings are socially constructed. In discussing both prostitution and homosexuality, interactionists stress the process of self-identification and self-labeling. Once labeling takes place, the person affected may become part of a subculture which provides both an identity and a social life. Urban gay communities, for example, are often socially well integrated—even to the point of having gay Yellow Pages phone books. Prostitutes, male and female, are also often tied both economically and socially into "the life."

Interactionists are concerned with how groups become stigmatized and with the consequences that stigma has for group members. Prostitutes, for example, have difficulty leaving "the life." Another area of interest to interactionists is how social attitudes change. Attitudes toward homosexuality, for example, have been undergoing rapid social change.

Interactionist approaches can also be used to examine the degree to which our society has become sex saturated and the consequences that has for many people, especially the young. Media portrayals of "normal" sex life, for example, can set unreasonable expectations and do not correspond with actual data. However, the movie, TV, and magazine image of sexuality is better known than actual facts to most adolescents. One goal of interactionists is more accurate and realistic portrayals of sexual behavior.

Changing Views of Sexuality

Influences of Victorian Morality

Victorian morality
social code supporting public prudery and double standard where males are allowed greater sexual freedom than females.

double standard
assumption that society allows for sexual activity in men, while women are held to stricter standards.

Every society controls the sexual behavior of its members, but there is a wide range of differences in what is considered proper or improper. Contemporary American sexual attitudes and customs are still partially influenced by the **Victorian morality** of a century ago. Victorian morality all but banished sexuality from respectable relationships and stressed modesty to the point of extreme prudery. In Philadelphia, for instance, men and women could not even visit art galleries together for fear that their modesty would be offended by the classical statues. (Plaster fig leaves were added to these works to minimize their offensiveness.) In polite conversation such simple anatomical terms as leg or breast were taboo; ladies had limbs and bosoms. Even the legs of tables had to be covered by modestly long tablecloths.

A basic tenet of the Victorian social code was the **double standard,** the assumption that males have strong sexual appetites while women—decent women, that is—do not. In Victorian times it was socially accepted that most men occasionally had to give way to their "animal natures." Covert premarital or extramarital sex by men was tolerated as a necessary evil, given the male's more pressing sexual urges. Prostitutes, or lower-class women, it was tacitly agreed, provided the proper outlets for urges too base to be imposed on wives. Thus women were categorized as virtuous women versus whores and the double standard implicitly allowed men to be sexually active but expected middle-class women to remain virginal until marriage. This double standard demanding chastity and fidelity from women but not men dates back millennia. In ancient Greece, the orator and statesman Demosthenes was succinct on this subject: "Man has the Hetaerae [educated courtesans] for erotic enjoyments, concubines for daily use, and wives of equal rank to bring up children and to be faithful housewives."[3]

At the opening of the twentieth century, proper women were not expected to experience desire. In his *History of Prostitution* (1855), Dr. William W. Sanger, a New York physician of wide experience, suggested that some horrid immorality will result if the two parties even in a legal union are equally passionate. He wrote:

> But it must be repeated and most decidedly, that without these or some other equally stimulating cause (such as destitution, drink, or seduction and abandonment), the full force of sexual desire is seldom known to a virtuous woman. In the male sex, nature has provided a more susceptible organization than in the females, apparently with the beneficent design of repressing those evils which must result from mutual appetite equally felt by both.[4]

The respected English physician, Sir William Acton, made the same point in *The Functions and Disorders of the Reproductive Organs* (1857), a work that enjoyed many editions. He states that married couples should not indulge in coitus more often than once in every 7 to 10 days because any more was thought to be unhealthy and dangerous to life. Today, despite the widespread acceptance of sexual equality, both sexes often hold the sexual conduct of women to stricter standards than those applied to men. Ira Reiss has suggested that society exerts this greater control over female sexuality because the female role is more essential to family integrity than that of the male.[5] If this is so, the hypothesis would be that as long as marriage and family roles remain important, women will be expected to be somewhat more circumspect in expressing their sexuality.

The Kinsey Reports

The post World War II **Kinsey Reports** were the first large-scale studies of sexual behavior. *Sexual Behavior in the Human Male* was published in 1948, and *Sexual Behavior in the Human Female* followed five years later.[6] The revelation of the study was Kinsey's documentation of the great amount of "nonapproved" premarital and extramarital sexual behavior that occurred among ordinary Americans. Of the 5,300 white males Kinsey's researchers interviewed, 83 percent had engaged in premarital intercourse and about half had extramarital intercourse.

Kinsey also documented wide differences in sexual behavior in terms of educational level. For example, 98 percent of men with only a grade school education had engaged in premarital sex; for those with some college the figure was 68 percent. These facts were viewed with alarm by moralists, but they could still be rationalized by the double standard, that is, "boys will be boys" who need to "sow their wild oats." More shocking to most Americans were the figures on females, which suggested that about half of American women were not virgins by the time they married, and about a quarter had extramarital affairs. Kinsey's figures permanently laid to rest the belief that women were basically uninterested in sex.

Serious questions have been raised regarding the reliability of Kinsey's findings, particularly his use of paid volunteer respondents rather than a random sample. Also, serious errors occurred in Kinsey's data on homosexuality because he deliberately mixed in interviews taken at gay bars and in prisons with his general sample. The American Statistical Association concluded that although the study had flaws it

Kinsey report
first major study of American sexual behavior.

---

[3]Hans Licht, *Sexual Life in Ancient Greece,* Barnes & Noble, New York, 1953, p. 399.
[4]Milton Rugoff, *Prudery and Passion,* Putnam, New York, 1971, pp. 46–47.
[5]Ira Reiss, *Family Systems in America,* 2d ed., Dryden Press, Hinsdale, IL, 1976, p. 184.
[6]A. C. Kinsey, W. B. Pomeroy, and C. E. Martin, *Sexual Behavior in the Human Male,* W. B. Saunders Company, Philadelphia, 1948; and P. H. Gebhard, *Sexual Behavior in the Human Female,* W. B. Saunders Company, Philadelphia, 1953.

was nonetheless superior to all previous studies of American sexual behavior.[7] One problem pointed out by sociologists was Kinsey's tendency to rely on counting frequency of behavior rather than attempting to assess in any manner the *quality* of the behavior as perceived by the participants. This emphasis on external counting probably reflected Kinsey's training in zoology, which ignored the assessment of subjective feelings.

Masters and Johnson

Carrying physiological research on sex to its ultimate limits, Masters and Johnson observed and recorded the responses of 694 men and women who were paid to perform coitus, masturbate, and perform other sexual acts.[8] They even used a plastic, electrically powered penis through which a camera could film changes in the interior of the vagina during sexual excitement. Masters and Johnson discovered that the orgasmic cycles of males and females are not only similar, but occur at the same repeated intervals of 0.8 seconds. It was also discovered that—contrary to the Victorian myth of limited sexual potential—women have, theoretically, an almost limitless capacity for multiple orgasms.

Masters' and Johnson's data have been questioned because of the laboratory conditions under which intercourse occurred. Their research also raised major questions regarding the ethics of their research and the scientific propriety of wiring up paid volunteers to perform sex acts under observation. Criticism was also directed at Masters and Johnson for using female "surrogates"—paid sex partners—to aid males with sex problems. To some this is little more than prostitution under the guise of science.

Even some who are committed to freedom of research are dismayed by the treatment of intercourse as nothing more than a mechanistic biological function, where the goal of a relationship becomes the perfect orgasm. They say what is being forgotten is that intercourse should also involve emotional involvement, that it should include an element of playfulness and fun, and that it serves to express feelings within an ongoing relationship. These human elements are diminished or lost if the culture emphasizes only "technique" and "performance."

The National Health and Social Life Survey

Since the Kinsey Report, much has changed: the introduction of the birth control pill in the early 1960s, the Sexual Revolution of the late 1960s and 1970s, and the AIDS crisis of the 1980s and 1990s. Nonetheless, not until the 1990s was there a comprehensive, nationwide, scientifically reliable study of contemporary sexuality. The National Health and Social Life (NHSL) Survey conducted by the respected University of Chicago-based National Opinion Research Center (NORC) obtained its data from 90-minute face-to-face interviews and questionnaires administered in 1992 to 3,432 men and women aged 18 to 59 in a randomly selected national probability sample of households across the country. The response rate of 80 percent was very good for this type of interview. The report of the study runs 718 pages and revises many of our myths about sexual behavior.[9]

---

[7] William G. Cochran et al., *Statistical Problems of the Kinsey Report on Sexual Behavior in the Human Male*, American Statistical Association, Washington, DC, 1954, p. 39.
[8] William H. Masters and Virginia E. Johnson, *Human Sexual Response*, Little Brown, Boston, 1966; and William H. Masters and Virginia E. Johnson, *Human Sexual Inadequacy*, Little Brown, Boston, 1970.
[9] Edward O. Laumann, John H. Gannon, Robert T. Mitchel, and Stuart Michaels, *The Social Organization of Sexuality: Sexual Practices in the United States*, University of Chicago Press, Chicago, 1994.

The NHSL survey indicates that, contrary to the media image, most Americans today are sexually monogamous; over the previous year, 83 percent reported one or zero sex partners. Over a lifetime the average man reported six partners and the average woman two. While young people now have sex earlier, in the 1960s people had more sexual partners and casual sex than they currently do. Young people now are more careful with sex.

The NHSL study shows that in terms of sexual frequency there are three groups: one-third have sex twice a week or more, one-third a few times a month, and one-third a few times a year or not at all. Adultery also is far from the rule. Almost three-quarters of American men and 85 percent of American women say they never have been unfaithful to their spouses. Over the past year 94 percent have been faithful. This flies in the face of the media portrayal of widespread promiscuity, but it should not really have come as a surprise. As John Gannon, one of the coauthors of the study expresses it, "Good sense should have told us that most people don't have the time and energy to manage an affair, have a family, *and* the Long Island Railroad."[10]

Interestingly, the data clearly indicate that married couples, not singles, have the most sex and are most likely to have orgasm when they do. While almost 40 percent of the married persons have sex twice a week, only a quarter of singles do so. In sharp contradiction to popular stereotypes, married women who are religious not only have the most sex, but are most likely to reach orgasm. Jewish women have the most sex partners (34 percent have 10 or more), Catholic women have the most frequent intercourse, but fundamentalist Protestant women are the most likely to achieve orgasm every time (34 percent).[11]

The most important findings, though, have less to do with sex itself than with whom Americans choose for sexual partners. Simply put, very little sexual mating takes place with those who are not part of our social groups. **Homogamy,** or "like marrying like," is the most common pattern. Partners most often meet partners in common settings, such as work, and most often are introduced by friends or family members. Only 13 percent of short-term sexual relationships and only 4 percent of marriages result from meeting someone in a bar, on vacation, through personals, or bumping into someone to whom you were not introduced.[12] Laumann notes: "The cultural image of 'I saw her across a crowded room and lurched after her' is a cultural myth."[13] If you do see someone across the room, it is likely to be in a social setting where you know most of the people. Ninety percent of sexual relationships take place between people having a similar ethnic background, and 84 percent between those of a similar educational background.

Nor do Americans jump into bed as fast as sometimes is suggested. Only 10 percent of marriages result from a situation where the couple has had sex within the first month after meeting. Even in short-term relationships, only 37 percent had sex within the first month.[14] Overall, Americans apparently talk more than they act.

> **homogamy**
> *marrying within one's group.*

Homosexuality: Attitudes and Practices

Homosexuality is sexual orientation toward, and sexual activity with, members of the same sex. The most common term for male homosexuals is **gays;** and for female

> **homosexuality**
> *sexual activity with members of one's own sex.*

> **gay**
> *a homosexual, generally male.*

---

[10]John Gannon, quoted in Suzanne Fields, "At Last, America's Sexual Freeze Frames Rate a PG-13," *Richmond Times-Dispatch,* October 14, 1994, p. A23.
[11]Laumann et al., *The Social Organization of Sexuality.*
[12]Kim A. McDonald, "Correlations Add New Detail to Sex Study," *Chronicle of Higher Education,* March 3, 1995, p. A8.
[13]Ellen K. Coughlin, "The Sex Lives of Americans," *Chronicle of Higher Education,* October 12, 1994, p. A8.
[14]Laumann et al., *The Social Organization of Sexuality.*

homosexuals, **lesbians** (from the inhabitants of the Greek island of Lesbos). Although recently there have been substantial changes in social attitudes, homosexuality is still stigmatized in American society.[15] Ancient Athens and Rome tolerated homosexuality, but Judeo-Christian moral codes do not.[16] Historically, Western civilization has treated homosexuality with derision, contempt, or sharp humor. **Homophobia** or negative and hostile attitudes toward gays and lesbians has a longstanding Western cultural tradition. This has been true despite the suspected or known homosexuality of major literary and artistic figures, including Michelangelo, Christopher Marlowe, Pyotr Tchaikovsky, Walt Whitman, Marcel Proust, and Oscar Wilde.

Until very recently, Western legal codes followed religious proscriptions in making sodomy a crime as well as a sin. Today the legal codes of most Western European countries now permit homosexual acts between consenting adults, but in the United States laws against such behavior remain on the books (though they are rarely enforced). In 1986 the U.S. Supreme Court found the Georgia consensual sodomy law constitutional (*Bowers v. Hardwick*), ruling that anal-genital acts, even among consenting adults, can legally be punished by states as criminal acts.[17]

Homosexuality was automatic grounds for dismissal from the military until 1994. Under the "Don't Ask, Don't Tell" policy, homosexuality is not a reason for dismissal unless a person is discovered engaging in homosexual behavior or the person publically announces that she or he is homosexual.

Changing Times

Recent decades have seen a substantial shift in societal attitudes toward homosexuality. Cities such as New York, San Francisco, Washington, and Toronto now have equal-rights ordinances covering homosexuals. In 1996, Mayor Willie Brown of San Francisco presided over a marriage ceremony for over a hundred gay and lesbian couples. (Because they are legal only by San Francisco ordinance, not by California law, these gay marriages are symbolic rather than legal.) There is still considerable opposition to recognizing gay unions. Disney World's policy recognizing gay unions has received official condemnation from Southern Baptists, and in 2000 California voted against recognizing gay marriages.

Being gay no longer bans one from federal government employment. (Homosexuals were long viewed as potential security risks because they could be blackmailed. They were banned in the State Department by custom, and legally banned from working for the CIA or FBI.) The Clinton administration, in fulfillment of a campaign promise, established an office to actively recruit gays for government jobs. Similarly, major corporations—such as IBM, AT&T, Bank of America, and TV networks—for years have declared themselves equal-opportunity employers in terms of sexual preference.

The general population has grown more accepting of homosexual lifestyles. A *New York Times*/CBS News poll indicated that 78 percent of adults say homosexuals should have "equal rights in terms of job opportunities."[18] (In the 1970s, only 56 percent thought gays and lesbians should have equal job opportunities.) Polls on gay rights show the general pattern to be one of more toleration, but still dis-

---

[15]J. N. Katz, *The Invention of Heterosexuality*, Dutton, New York, 1995.

[16]Otto Kiefer, *Sexual Life in Rome*, Dutton, New York, 1935.

[17]Lisa Keen and Suzanne Boldberg, *Strangers to the Law: Gay People on Trial*, University of Michigan Press, Ann Arbor, 1998.

[18]Jeffrey Schnalz, "Poll Finds an Even Split on Homosexuality's Cause," *New York Times*, March 5, 1993, p. 1.

Gay and lesbian Pride Parades are now an annual sight in most American cities. These police officers are marching in the 1999 New York Gay Pride Parade.

approving.[19] Only 42 percent support laws to ensure equal rights for homosexuals, 36 percent say homosexuality should be considered an acceptable lifestyle, and only 34 percent would permit their child to play at the home of a friend having a homosexual parent. Alan Wolfe's in-depth study of suburban Americans found that the only area where suburban Americans have qualms about toleration is on the question of homosexuality.[20] So does Congress. In 1999 Congress held up all of President Clinton's federal appointments for almost a year because he appointed an open gay as Ambassador to Luxembourg.

For decades, gay activist groups have pushed to amend the 1964 Civil Rights Act by adding "affectional or sexual preference," but this amendment is given little chance of passing Congress in the foreseeable future. Conservative attitudes also prevail regarding the raising of children in homosexual home environments. Only the District of Columbia has a law that sexual orientation alone cannot be used as a factor in determining custody or visitation. In some 30 states homosexuality is sufficient reason to limit a parent's rights, while in 20 states courts can keep homosexual parents from children only where some harm to the child can be proven. Usually such laws are not applied, but they are on the books. The Virginia Court of Appeals in 1994 ruled in the nationally discussed Sharon Bottoms case that her child could not be taken from her just because she was living with her lesbian lover. Nonetheless, a 1996 court ruling found her lifestyle made her an unfit mother and granted the grandmother permanent custody.

Size and Distribution of the Gay Population

Ten percent is usually the figure used by the general press to estimate the size of the gay population. The 10 percent figure appeals both to the homophobic, who see homosexuality as a threat, and to gays seeking comfort in numbers. However, research data over a 50-year period have shown consistently that the actual proportion

---

[19]Richard Berke, "Chasing the Polls on Gay Rights," *New York Times*, August 2, 1998, p. wk3.
[20]Alan Wolfe, *One Nation, After All*, Viking, New York, 1998.

predominantly or exclusively gay is about 2 to 5 percent across societies, with about half as many lesbians as male homosexuals.[21] The figures from the 1992 National Health and Social Life NORC study indicate that 2.8 percent of men, and 1.4 percent of women identify themselves as homosexual.[22] Some 6.2 percent of all the males, and 4.4 percent of all the women interviewed said they are at least somewhat attracted to those of the same gender.

Why the persistence of the 10 percent figure? It originally came from an overestimate presented by Kinsey in his 1948 report on sexual behavior in the human male.

First, Kinsey did not use random-sample techniques but, rather, obtained his data from paid volunteers. A number of his male respondents were recruited directly from gay groups and gay bars; these interviews were not treated separately but were combined with other male interviews. Second, Kinsey also combined interviews from prison populations (where homosexuality was common) with the general population data. Finally, Kinsey labeled an extremely wide variety of behaviors homosexual, including some that did not involve explicitly sexual activities. For example, the label "homosexual behavior" was applied to 12-year-old boys dropping their pants on a dare and to "mooning" pranks by college boys. Kinsey originally reported that a full 37 percent of males had to some degree been homosexual for at least three years after age 15. Paul Gebhard, one of Kinsey's coauthors at the Institute for Sex Research, says that Kinsey's figures on homosexuality were in error and should not have been published. In spite of its repudiation by its own authors, Kinsey's data on homosexuality have been widely quoted for half a century—providing a classic example of how erroneous data, constantly repeated, becomes entrenched in popular consciousness.

Ironically, the geographic concentration of the gay population in certain neighborhoods in larger cities, such as New York, Washington, San Francisco, and Los Angeles means that the 10 percent figure may actually represent the social reality for these highly visible locations. Additionally, the higher proportion and visibility of gays in the art, entertainment, and literary worlds tends to inflate the perceived numbers in the general population.

Perspectives on Homosexuality

Before the twentieth century, homosexuals were commonly viewed as morally depraved individuals. During the twentieth century the psychiatric approach developed, which regarded homosexuality as a form of mental illness that could be treated by psychiatric intervention. This position was endorsed by the American Psychiatric Association. Then, in 1974, as the result of major gay protests and lobbying, the American Psychiatric Association voted 5,854 to 3,810 to redefine homosexuality not as a "psychiatric disorder" but rather as a "sexually oriented disturbance" (see Chapter 14).

As a result the homosexuality-as-mental-illness viewpoint was largely replaced by the viewpoint that homosexuality is a way of life or a sexual preference.[23] Homosexuals argued that homosexuality was largely a question of sexual choice. Today, within the gay community, the sexual preference perspective is increasingly being supplanted by the position that homosexuality is a genetic orientation. Those holding this view say homosexuality represents not a lifestyle choice but a predetermined biological orientation. Advocates of this view use the term *sexual orientation* rather than *sexual preference*.

Advocates for the genetic orientation and lifestyle positions often speak with certainty, but the reality is that the question is still scientifically open. An early (1952)

[21]Frederick L. Whitam and Robin M. Mathy, *Male Homosexuality in Four Societies: Brazil, Guatemala, the Philippines, and the United States,* Praeger, New York, 1985.
[22]Laumann et al., *The Social Organization of Sexuality.*
[23]Barry M. Dank, "Coming Out in the Gay World," *Psychiatry,* 34:195, May 1971.

much quoted study of identical twins (who share the same genetic heredity) indicated that if one male twin was gay so was the other.[24] However, no one else has ever been able to duplicate these findings and they have been scientifically discredited.

Research in 1993 analyzing pairs of brothers who are gay found a distinct patterning along a segment of the X chromosome inherited from their mothers in two-thirds of the cases.[25] No similar pattern has been found for lesbian sisters. This would suggest, at least for some males, that there is some genetic component. However, the molecular biologist who headed these studies says social influences play the leading role in determining homosexuality. As he states it, "From twin studies, we already know that half or more of the variability in sexual orientation is not inherited."[26] Moreover, research directed at replicating these studies, published in *Science* in 1999, failed to find any evidence of a "gay gene" on the X chromosome.[27] For the moment, the genetic basis for homosexuality remains uncertain.

The uncertainty of the scientific research is matched in the opinions held by the general population, which is almost evenly split between those who say homosexuality is a choice and those who say it is biologically predetermined.[28] From a sociological perspective, however, the exact role played by genetics is not significant. What is important is whether or not people *believe* the differences are a matter of environment or of biology. For example, only 32 percent of those who think homosexuality is a choice say homosexual relations between consenting adults should be legal, but some 62 percent of those who believe it is biological think so.[29] Thus a person's views about whether or not homosexuality is inherited affect his or her attitudes toward homosexuals. Beliefs shape differences in attitudes and behavior.

Gender Patterns

There is evidence that gay males, as compared to heterosexual males, report themselves as being more sensitive, having more artistic interests, being more likely to avoid fights, being called "sissies," and being more effeminate than their peers during their childhoods.[30] Similarly, lesbian women generally report themselves as having more masculine-type interests and behaviors than heterosexual women.[31] How much of this is social patterning, and how much is genetic is unknown. Certainly stereotypical images of the effeminate gay male and the "butch" lesbian are common.

Coming Out

The social act of publically acknowledging one's gay or lesbian orientation is know as **coming out.** For reasons of social pressure, many homosexuals remain "in the closet." They may fear occupational problems or may be married and have children.

> **coming out**
> *publicly identifying oneself as a homosexual and accepting the homosexual role.*

---

[24]F. J. Kallaman, "Comparative Twin Study on the Genetic Aspects of Male Homosexuality," *Journal of Mental and Nervous Diseases*, 115:283–298, 1952.

[25]Dean Hammer of the National Cancer Institute, quoted in "New Evidence of a 'Gay Gene,' " *Time,* November 13, 1995, p. 95.

[26]Ibid.

[27]"A 'Gay Gene'? Perhaps Not," *Chronicle of Higher Education,* April 30, 1999, p. A21.

[28]Jeffery Schnalz, "Poll Finds an Even Split on Homosexuality's Cause," *New York Times,* March 5, 1993, p. 1.

[29]Ibid.

[30]J. M. Baily and K. J. Zucker, "Childhood Sex-Typed Behavior and Sexual Orientation: A Conceptual Analysis and Quantitative Review," *Developmental Psychology,* 31:43–55, 1995.

[31]Ibid.

Although coming out may be a gradual process, the final break with straight society is often traumatic: once this step has been taken, it is difficult to turn back. Most reluctant to come out are those who have engaged in homosexual relations for many years while assuming a public heterosexual identity. They fear damage to their career or social standing. Gays who resist coming out are sometimes derided by overt gays as being "closet queens."[32]

Establishing a public identity as a homosexual is an example of the social transition from what sociologists refer to as movement from primary to secondary deviance (deviance here meaning deviance from the norm). Once a person comes out, he or she is gay in the eyes of society and responded to as such. Persons with homosexual tendencies may think of themselves as not "really" gay. Coming out, however, signifies a clear change of self-identity and a new societal label. Coming out also is associated by both gays and straights with being in certain occupations and living in gay neighborhoods. But this is only true of some homosexuals. As a gay living in Omaha puts it, "Things are so closeted that even gay people don't realize that gay people are just like everyone else."[33]

Gay Communities

Gays, like other minorities, have their own communities or ghettos. San Francisco has two major gay ghettos, one around Castro Street and the other in the area around Polk Street.[34] Both areas are crowded with clothing stores, bookshops, grocery stores, theaters, and restaurants run by and for gays; both areas also contain their share of the 80 or so gay bars in the city. New York has its downtown Manhattan West Side gay community. Even staid cities such as Milwaukee and Omaha have openly gay communities. Gay bars usually have a clear gay identity, and even in the era of AIDS these establishments often serve as short-term sexual meeting places. In many cities gay and lesbian communities even have their own Yellow Pages directories to gay businesses. There even is a predominantly gay religious denomination, the Metropolitan Community Church.

Situational Homosexuality

situational or deprivational homosexuality

homosexuality due to the absence of heterosexual partners.

For some, homosexuality is a consequence not of preference but of availability. **Situational or deprivational homosexuality** involves people who are heterosexual but are deprived of sexual contact with the opposite sex. This is most prevalent in total institutions such as prisons. The exploitative homosexuality of prisons is one of the greatest complaints against such institutions. It is estimated that over one-fourth of male prisoners engage in some homosexual behavior, while perhaps half the females in confinement do so.[35] In the United States, only the state of Mississippi permits conjugal visits to married prisoners.

Male homosexual relationships in prison are likely to be exploitative, while women prisoners often have affectional bonds and often form family groupings.[36] Most female inmates view homosexuality as a temporary necessity.[37] Male prison-

---

[32]Laud Humphreys, *Tearoom Trade: Impersonal Sex in Public Places,* Aldine, Chicago, 1970.
[33]Ibid.
[34]For a discussion of gay and lesbian communities in San Francisco's Castro and Mission Districts, see Chapter 7 of Mark Abrahamson, *Urban Enclaves: Identity and Place in America,* St. Martin's, New York, 1996.
[35]Rose Giallombardo, *Society of Women: A Study of a Women's Prison,* Wiley, New York, 1966.
[36]John H. Gagnon and William Simon, *Sexual Conduct,* Aldine, Chicago, 1973, p. 254.
[37]Rose Giallombardo, *Society of Women.*

A mature couple celebrate a lesbian marriage ceremony.

© Rick Gerharter/Impact Visuals

ers who engage in homosexual behavior generally fall into one of three highly stereotyped roles: the "queen" or "fag," the "punk," and the "wolf."[38] Queens are self-identified homosexuals who exaggerate supposed female characteristics including makeup and flirtatious walking. Punks are low-status inmates who perform sexual acts for personal favors such as cigarettes or money. When new inmates accept cigarettes or favors from others, they are often told to pay back the favors with sex; they must then either fight the aggressor or become a low-status punk. The wolf, on the other hand, is viewed as a real man in spite of his homosexual activity because his sex is impersonal and often violent. He rapes other inmates and may run a number of punks as prostitutes. Upon release from confinement, the majority of both male and female prisoners return to heterosexual activity.

Lesbian Populations

Lesbianism is about half as prevalent as male homosexuality, but science doesn't know why the gender difference exists. Reappraisals of the data gathered by both Kinsey and the NORC study indicate that about 1.5 percent of American females are homosexual. The percentage is highest among single women: Only a fraction of 1 percent of married women are homosexual or bisexual.

The major difference between male and female homosexuality is in the number of sexual relationships. Prior to the AIDS epidemic, about half of white gay men had over 500 sexual partners in a lifetime, and 28 percent had over 1,000 partners.[39]

---

[38]George L. Kirkham, "Homosexuality in Prison," in James M. Heslin (ed.), *Studies in the Sociology of Sex,* Appleton, New York, 1971, pp. 325–349.
[39]Alan P. Bell and Martin S. Weinberg, *Homosexuality: A Study of Diversity among Men and Women,* Simon & Schuster, New York, 1978.

By contrast, relationships between female homosexuals are often long-term. Female homosexual as well as heterosexual relationships reflect the societal expectation that women should not engage in sex unless they are in love. The popular assumption is that lesbians imitate the traditional relationship between straight married couples, with one partner assuming the "male" role and the other the "femme" role. Most often, gay men behave like men, women like women.[40] Lesbian couples are often less conspicuous than gay male couples, and less identified with overtly gay or lesbian communities. While all big cities have lesbian bars, they are generally less conspicuous than male gay bars.[41] Overt discrimination against lesbians, such as being dismissed from the Armed Forces, often surfaces only when their sexual identity becomes a public issue.

Prostitution

prostitution

promiscuous sexual activity for money.

Prostitution is promiscuous, paid sexual activity. As such, it probably deserves its reputation as "the world's oldest profession." Today, the sex trade appears to be undergoing two apparently conflicting trends. On one hand, it often is more blatant, with open solicitation by streetwalkers in the central business districts of most large cities and widespread advertising of escort services. At the same time, the actual use of prostitutes is declining.

Kinsey's data indicated that 50 years ago 69 percent of men had relations with prostitutes, and one in six visited them more than a few times a year for a period of over five years.[42] Studies done since then indicate that while premarital sexual activity has increased, the use of prostitutes has radically declined. For instance, Morton Hunt's 1974 study indicated that only 3 percent of males below age 25 had been with a prostitute during the previous year.[43] Other data show similar declines.[44]

Estimates as to the number of female prostitutes in the U.S. run from 80,000 to roughly half a million.[45] The precise number of sex workers in the United States is unknown, particularly given the number of part-timers (see Box 15.1). (While we mostly use the female pronoun when discussing prostitution, keep in mind that roughly a third of sex workers are male.) In 1992, 57,000 females and 31,000 males were arrested for prostitution.[46] Yearly changes in rates largely reflect changes in law enforcement.[47] Prostitution is a billion dollar a year business in the United States.

---

[40]Martha R. Folkwes, "Single Worlds and Homosexual Lifestyles," in Alice S. Rossi (ed.), *Sexuality across the Life Course,* University of Chicago Press, Chicago, 1994, pp. 151–184.

[41]Lettia A. Piplau and Hortensia Amaro, "Understanding Lesbian Relationships," in William Paul et al. (eds.), *Homosexuality: Social Psychological and Biological Issues,* Sage, Beverly Hills, CA, 1982, pp. 233–247.

[42]Kinsey, Pomeroy, and Martin, *Sexual Behavior in the Human Male,* p. 597.

[43]Morton Hunt, *Sexual Behavior in the 1970s,* Playboy Press, Chicago, 1974.

[44]Laumann et al., *The Social Organization of Sexuality.*

[45]J. J. Potterat, D. E. Woodhouse, J. B. Muth, and S. Q. Muth, "Estimating the Prevalence and Career Longevity of Prostitute Women," *Journal of Sexual Research,* 27:233–243, 1990; and Helen Reynolds, *The Economics of Prostitution,* Charles C. Thomas Publishers, Springfield, IL, 1986.

[46]Federal Bureau of Investigation, *Uniform Crime Reports for the United States,* Washington, DC, 1993.

[47]Marshall B. Clinard and Robert F. Meier, *Sociology of Deviant Behavior,* 7th ed., Holt, Rinehart and Winston, Fort Worth, 1989.

Views on Prostitution

Traditionally prostitutes have been viewed as (1) helpless, exploited victims, (2) exploiters and potentially dangerous criminals, and (3) nonconventional working girls. Sometimes they are even heroines. Dostoyevsky's heroine Sonya in *Crime and Punishment* gives her body as a prostitute in order to feed her family, while her heart remains pure. The reality was, and is, that many prostitutes are victims. The history of urban America produced all too many stories of poor immigrant girls being imprisoned in houses of prostitution. These abuses motivated the White Slave Traffic Act of 1910, commonly known as the Mann Act, which was designed to end the transport of girls across state lines for prostitution. Today, the exploitation of prostitutes still exists. Pimps often recruit their girls from groups of underage runaways who gather on the street. Taking virtually all the money the girl gets from her "tricks" and preventing her from leaving his "stable" with threats of violence and actual beatings, these girls fit the picture of the prostitute as victim.

Contrasting to the view that prostitutes are victims is the second view: that prostitutes are tough, hard-boiled women who exploit the Johns for all they are worth. (Customers are called "Johns" because in the past whenever a male was arrested his name was officially listed as "John Doe.") This exploitation may even include blackmail and occasionally violence, when a mark, after being brought to a room, is beaten and robbed by the prostitute's pimp. Few Johns want to go to the police and explain just how they were beaten and lost their money.

The third view sees prostitutes as sex workers who provide a necessary social service. Movies such as *Pretty Woman* portray the "happy hooker" as a working girl who is at heart far more honest than other people. The sex worker is simply making a business of pleasure, and her activities provide her customers with necessary psychotherapy. Far from being a homewrecker, she helps to save marriages. The prostitute as a romanticized figure is well-known to fiction. In novels and opera, the fallen heroine usually dies, a victim of consumption (tuberculosis), pneumonia, or some similar disease that allows her to waste away (e.g., Violetta in *La Traviata*) while all repent her loss. In today's *Pretty Woman* version of the fable, she marries the John and becomes wealthy.

Becoming a Prostitute

Knowledge of who becomes a prostitute and why is extremely sketchy. Research samples tend to be small; one often-quoted study of streetwalkers included 15 respondents, while another study on call girls had only 25 respondents.[48] Moreover, there is no way of determining how representative are those few who have been interviewed.

Street prostitutes overwhelmingly come from lower-income backgrounds and most come from broken homes. There often is an absence of warmth between the girl and her parents, particularly the father. Many of those who become prostitutes were sexually abused as children.[49] Many also have come before the courts for juvenile delinquency.[50] Women who later become prostitutes often are social isolates, had no

---

[48]Normal Jackman, Richard O'Toole, and Gilbert Geis, "The Self-Image of the Prostitute," *Sociological Quarterly,* 4:150–161, April 1963; and Harold Greenwald, *The Call Girl,* Ballantine, New York, 1958.
[49]Mimi H. Silbert and Ayala M. Pines "Early Sexual Exploitation as an Influence in Prostitution," *Social Work,* 28:285–289, July–August, 1983.
[50]Ronald L. Simons and Les B. Whitbeck, " Sexual Abuse as a Precursor to Prostitution and Victimization among Adolescent and Adult Homeless Women," *Journal of Family Issues,* 12:361–379, September 1991.

close friends during adolescence and dropped out of school. While many prostitutes have held other jobs, these have generally been low-skill, low-paying positions (e.g., salesclerk, nurse's aide, waitress). Often they drifted from casual sex to sex for money or drugs. Teenagers are most likely to drift into "the life" because they lack alternatives that pay well, being too young and unskilled for other kinds of paid work.

Expensive call girls, on the other hand, are more likely to be attracted by the possibility of big money and fast living. Call girls as they age often retire to marry or take up another career; but while they are working, the living is good. Call girls can make over $100,000 a year tax free. In the words of one call girl:

> "I got to the point where I was living in a fairy-tale. I was telling myself. 'Well, you just need the money and then you'll get out of this and get back to a career or something. . . you're not like the other girls who make a life out of this,' " said Miriam, a call girl who works the traveling-business-executive circuit in Philadelphia and New York.
>
> "After about a year, I got to the stage where I was able to admit openly to myself that I liked it. I don't know, it has a style to it; a zing that I really enjoy. You're moving with really classy people. Some girls hate the marks they service. I don't. I can really get into the give-and-take of the situation. I like the sex and I like the personal contact. It's not just an assembly line with me. A couple months ago, one guy took me on a five-day trip to Puerto Rico. O.K., it was a business arrangement, but it was also great fun and we both enjoyed it."[51]

Social Hierarchy of Prostitution

Sex workers are frequently lumped together in a single category, but there are four major subgroupings. These reflect not only fees charged but also mode of operation, type of customers, and how the prostitute entered her line of work.

Call Girls   Call girls represent the *creme de la creme* of the profession. Generally they are in their early 20s, dress tastefully, and live at "respectable" apartment addresses. They are also more likely to come from middle-class backgrounds.[52] Call girls are so named because appointments for their services are almost always made by phone. Some call girls work as independents, but most get referrals from escort services, pimps, or madams. Evidence at the 1995 trial of Heidi Fleiss, the Hollywood madam, showed, for example, that the actor Charlie Sheen had ordered call girls 27 times and paid them more than $50,000. And this figure excluded the expected large tips.

Bar Girls   Well below the call girls are the bar girls or hustlers who work out of bars, hotel lounges, and similar locations. While still somewhat selective as to clients, they charge less and turn more tricks in a night than do call girls, who may spend the entire evening or even go on trips with a client. In some cases bar girls may have been call girls before they began to fade or before they got involved with drugs.

House Girls   Brothels still exist but they are declining in number. A prostitute working as a house girl in a place such as the legal Mustang Ranch in Nevada is,

[51]Freda Adler, *Sisters in Crime: The Rise of the New Female Criminal,* McGraw-Hill, New York, 1976, p. 76.
[52]C. Edgley, "Commercial Sex, Pornography, Prostitution, and Advertising," in K. McKinnley and S. Sprecher (eds.), *Human Sexuality: The Social and Interpersonal Context,* Ablex Publishing, Norwood, NJ, 1989, pp. 370–424.

A legal prostitute named Sweet Leif strikes a pose outside the Moonlight Bunnyranch bordello near Carson City, Nevada. Prostitution had been declining but legal bordellos reported a twenty percent increase in trade after Viagra was introduced.

K.M. Cannon//AP/Wide World Photos

in effect, an employee of the madam or pimp who runs the house. In some cases the madam "turns out" or trains the novice in the tricks of hustling—particularly in how to get more money from the John.[53] Generally, the prostitute keeps half or less of the fee paid by the client. The tip is solely hers. In urban areas brothels often bill themselves as "massage parlors" or "gentlemen's clubs."

Streetwalkers The most common prostitutes are streetwalkers who solicit customers directly. The prostitute rights organization COYOTE (Call Off Your Old Tired Ethics) estimates that only 10 to 20 percent of prostitutes work on the street. A streetwalker uses the customer's car or takes the John to a cheap hotel. In any case, she is back out on the street in less than half an hour.

Streetwalkers tend to be either older prostitutes who are over the hill, addicts, or young runaways. Most adolescent prostitutes are streetwalkers, sometimes only 14 or 15 years of age.[54] Most streetwalkers, particularly young teenage runaways, are exploited by a pimp who protects them from harassment by other pimps. Streetwalkers not only make the least money but are also the most likely to be arrested by vice-squad police. Even the famous, who can afford call girls, sometimes get caught with streetwalkers. Actor Hugh Grant was caught literally with his

---

[53]Barbara Sherman Heyl, "The Madame as Teacher: The Training of House Prostitutes," *Social Problems*, 24:545–555, June 1977.
[54]D. K. Weisberg, *Children of the Night: A Study of Adolescent Prostitution*, Lexington Books, Lexington, MA, 1985.

pants down with a $65 hooker in a parked car just off Hollywood Boulevard. Unlike more expensive and discreet call girls, streetwalkers are regarded as a public nuisance.

Regulation of Prostitution

There have been many attempts to suppress the sex trade in the United States. Early in the twentieth century every American city of note had its red-light district near (but not in) the central business district. Here were congregated the city's brothels, gambling dens, and more notorious saloons that catered to "sports" looking for some action. Societies for the suppression of vice eventually shut down most of the brothels, but prostitution, rather than being abolished, simply transformed into the call girl in her high-rise apartment.

Legalized prostitution exists in most of Europe (German law, for example, requires every large city to establish at least one prostitution zone), and sex workers commonly are tested for AIDS and other sexually transmitted diseases. Prostitution, but not pimping, is legal in Canada. In the United States, prostitution is legal only in Nevada, and there, only in counties with populations under 200,000. (This keeps prostitution from being visible in "family" resorts such as Las Vegas, Reno, and Lake Tahoe.) Prostitutes at legal brothels must get weekly medical examinations, and the brothels pay business taxes, while the sex workers participate in Social Security and other government programs.

Elsewhere in the United States, prostitution is illegal, but it is commonly "semitolerated" within restricted zones. Some municipalities attempt to restrict commercialized vice to a specific geographical area, a modern reinvention of the traditional red-light district. Brothels advertise under the guise of escort services in phone directories and newspaper classified ads.

Debate continues about whether prostitution should be decriminalized as a "victimless crime."[55] When a pimp is involved and there is coercion, it is hard to call prostitution victimless. Police response to prostitution is highly selective, with almost all attention directed toward suppressing visible, lower-status streetwalkers. At the street level, police–prostitute relationships often involve the use of decoys and the "survival of the fastest." As long as prostitutes do not become a public nuisance, the general public would probably prefer to see police departments spending their time and effort in dealing with muggings, rapes, and other street crimes rather than attempting to stamp out voluntary sexual activities.

Male Prostitution

Male prostitutes are called **hustlers** and their clients are **scores**. Hustlers may be either gay or heterosexual. Similarly, their clientele includes heterosexual, bisexual, and homosexual men, as well as some women. In some cities, male hustlers are almost as familiar as their female counterparts; the Los Angeles vice squad, for example, reports that 40 percent of the prostitutes arrested in Hollywood are males. Like their female counterparts, male streetwalkers hang out on corners, hustlers size up "tricks" in bars that cater to their trade, and call boys work out of apartments. There are also male houses of prostitution.

About 15 percent of the men who use male prostitutes pick them up on the street. The majority use bars, make contacts through friends, or answer ads placed in gay newspapers. Houses of male prostitution commonly bill themselves as modeling agencies. Homosexual films involving young boys are a staple of the hard-core porno movie industry.

In spite of the AIDS epidemic, male prostitution continues to flourish. The rate of HIV infection for gay male prostitutes is estimated to be one in two.[56] A pattern of denial leads some prostitutes not to protect neither themselves nor their clients.

hustlers
male prostitute.

scores
prostitute's client.

Pornography

The conventional definition of **pornography** is that it is written or visual material designed to produce sexual excitement. Supreme Court Justice Potter Stewart provided a good working definition of pornography when he stated, "I know it when I see it." Some 95 percent of Americans believe that the sale of hard-core pornographic materials should be banned or at least forbidden to be sold to those under age 18. But there is less consensus on what constitutes pornographic materials.

Public concern about pornography, interestingly enough, exceeds concern about prostitution, perhaps because pornography is more visible. The strongest opposition to pornography focuses on films and magazines; pornographic books with no pictures receive less attention. Practically, we classify pornography as being either "hard-core" (X-rated) or "soft-core" (R-rated).

pornography
depicting sexual behavior designed to sexually excite the viewer.

---

[55]Linda M. Rio, "Psychological and Sociological Research and the Decriminalization or Legalization of Prostitution," *Archives of Sexual Behavior*, 20:205–218, 1991.
[56]J. Boles and K. W. Elifson, "Sexual Identity and HIV: The Male Prostitute," *Journal of Sex Research*, 31:39–46, 1994.

Pornography is not a recent invention. Much Greek and Roman literature ranges from ribald to raunchy, while *Penthouse* and *Playboy* are relatively mild compared to the ancient Indian *Kama Sutra*. The *Kama Sutra* long had the reputation of being a thinking person's dirty picture book. Today, the fight against pornography is often based as much on its perceived role as a public nuisance as on the argument that it is disgusting or a sign of moral decay. In 1976 the Supreme Court ruled that it was constitutional for municipalities to restrict pornographic theaters and bookstores to nonresidential neighborhoods partly on the grounds that the widespread display of pornography was a public nuisance.

Legal Regulation of Pornography

Until 1957 the legal test of obscenity was based on the Hicklen test of 1868, which was to ask "whether the tendency of the matter charged as obscenity is to deprave and corrupt those whose minds are open to such immoral influences, and into whose hands a publication of this sort might fall."[57] In the United States, it was prohibited to mail or import into the country books ruled obscene by the Postmaster General. Under this rigid standard, James Joyce's literary classic *Ulysses* was defined as obscene and legally barred from this country until 1933. In the 1957 Roth decision, the Supreme Court ruled that material can legally be defined as obscene only if "the material taken as a whole appeals to prurient interest" and is "utterly without redeeming social value," and it violates "contemporary community values." In 1973 the Supreme Court dropped the "redeeming social value" criterion entirely and said that "community values" meant local community values. This means that what is obscene in California may or may not be obscene in Tennessee.

In 1967 Congress declared the problem of pornography "a matter of national concern" and a presidential Commission on Obscenity and Pornography was appointed. The Commission's findings and recommendations were published in 1970. President Richard Nixon immediately disowned the report because it concluded that data showed *no* clear relationship between exposure to pornographic materials and deviant sexual behavior, criminality, delinquency, or emotional disorders. Moreover, the majority of the Commission took the position that the government should not legislate morality and that pornography *per se* was not as great a problem to a democratic society as was censorship. The Commission recommended that adults be given full freedom, free of censorship, to read or view sexually explicit material if they chose to do so. The majority report stated: "The Commission recommends that federal, state, and local legislation prohibiting the sale, exhibition, or distribution of sexual materials to consenting adults should be repealed."[58]

A minority of the Commission took strong exception to this viewpoint, believing that the majority report was pro-pornography and biased when it assumed that pornography has no detrimental effects on the society. The statement by two of the Commission members indicates the extent of the opposition: "The Commission's majority report is a Magna Carta for the pornographer. It is slanted and biased in favor of protecting the business of obscenity and pornography, which the Commission was mandated by the Congress to regulate."[59]

---

[57]Cited in *The Report of the Commission on Obscenity and Pornography*, Government Printing Office, Washington, DC, 1970.

[58]*The Report of the Commission on Obscenity and Pornography*, Washington DC, 1970.

[59]Morton A. Hill and Winfrey C. Link, "A Minority Statement in Response to the Report of the Commission on Obscenity and Pornography," in Robert J. Antonio and George Ritzer, *Social Problems: Values and Interests in Conflict*, Allyn and Bacon, Boston, 1975, p. 207.

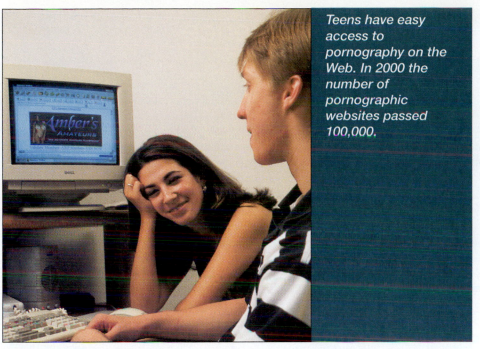

Teens have easy access to pornography on the Web. In 2000 the number of pornographic websites passed 100,000.

© Bob Daemmrich/Stock, Boston

Responding to concerns of the religious right, President Ronald Reagan appointed a second commission to examine the effects of pornography. The Meese Commission, named after the then Attorney General was derided by many for its obvious political connections. The Commission, however, did make the point that there is a real distinction between pornography and violent pornography. The Meese Commission found "a causal relationship between exposure to sexually violent materials and an increase in aggressive behavior directed toward women."[60] In other words, sexual activity (even if degrading) does not promote sexual violence, but violent pornography does indeed encourage real-life violence against women. Thus, while X-rated sex videos may be degrading, they have little effect on violence. On the other hand, the so-called "slasher" movies do increase violence against women.

The Commission based its finding in part on research by Edward Donnerstein and his colleagues, which indicated that men who watched sexually violent films, when compared to those viewing nonviolent pornographic films, were more likely to be sexually aroused, to view rape as acceptable, and to say they would rape if they could get away with it.[61] This association between sexual violence and violent pornography has been criticized as being based on hypothetical (and artificial) laboratory experiments that cannot predict what will occur in the real world. Another unanswered question is whether viewing the films has any lasting impact, or whether the effects fade after a few minutes. Most data indicate that real rapists actually have had less, not more, contact with pornography than others in their adolescent or adult years.[62]

---

[60]Meese Commission, *Final Report of the Attorney General's Commission on Pornography,* Department of Justice, Washington, DC, 1986, p. 39.
[61]Edward Donnerstein, Daniel Lintz, and Steven Penrod, *The Question of Pornography: Research Findings and Policy Implications,* Free Press, New York, 1987.
[62]Berl Kutchinsky, "Pornography and Rape: Theory and Practice?" *International Journal of Law and Psychiatry,* 14:47–64, 1991.

Box 15.2 | Making a Difference

The Antipornography Movement

Arguments for banning sexually related materials come from the political left as well as the religious right. The feminist lawyer Catherine MacKinnon has argued that speech and pictures that oppress women should not enjoy free speech legal rights.[a] This view is supported by the feminist writer Andrea Dworkin, who says, "The whole purpose of pornography is to hurt women."[b] MacKinnon and Dworkin lobby for banning all written and pictorial pornography. Working in cooperation with organizations on the religious right, they drafted a law in Minnesota that would have banned all sexual coercion, defined as any sexually explicit material that subordinates women through pictures or words. According to the statute, anything that portrays women unequally is subordination.

Opponents pointed out that this would ban not only *Playboy* (coercion under the statute would still exist even if the written consent of models had been obtained) but also Homer's *Iliad*, James Joyce's *Ulysses*, and D. H. Lawrence's novels. The statute was thrown out by the Court of Appeals—and its unconstitutionality affirmed by the Supreme Court—as a clear attempt at suppression of free speech and thus a violation of the First Amendment.

Commenting on the Court's opinion MacKinnon stated: "In Andrea Dworkin's and my approach to freedom of speech, we don't limit ourselves to the traditional equality areas. Women haven't been permitted to address the ways in which we are distinctively subordinated. And the inequality interests at stake for women, for people of color, for all people who are subjected to inequality on the basis of sex or race, or sexual orientation in particular—those are the interests that the First Amendment as it has been interpreted has not taken into account."[c]

Feminists such as Nadine Strossen, however, defend sexual erotica, arguing that censoring sexual expression does women more harm than good by undermining their equality and their freedom to make decisions. Some people feel that pornography must be controlled, not because it excites people sexually but because it has a destructive effect on the moral framework on which society depends for its very survival. Irving Kristol has argued, for example, that because it debases human relationships—particularly by degrading women into mere objects—pornography is a nihilistic annulment of civilization.[d] He argues that sex becomes obscene when it sinks to the level of mere exploitation. Others argue that pornography turns sex into work by removing all romance or even human feeling. Courts have yet to settle where the line exists between First Amendment free-speech rights and limits on portraying sex and violence.

[a]*Catherine A. MacKinnon, Only Words, Harvard University Press, Cambridge, MA, 1993.*
[b]*Quoted in Philip Elmer-Dewitt, "Cyberporn," Time, July 3, 1995, p. 43.*
[c]*Catherine MacKinnon and Floy Abrams, moderated by Anthony Lewis, "The First Amendment, Under Fire from the Left," New York Times Magazine, March 13, 1994, p. 71.*
[d]*Irving Kristol, "Pornography, Obscenity, and the Case for Censorship," New York Times Magazine, March 28, 1971.*

Cyberporn

The newest venue for pornography is the Internet, something well-known to college students long before it was discovered by Congress. A 1995 study of so-called cyberporn by Martin Rimm, a Carnegie-Mellon student researcher, found that trading sexually explicit imagery constituted the largest single recreational use of computers, and that of the Internet newsgroups where pictures were stored, 84 percent were pornographic. Moreover, the biggest demand was not for hard-core sex pictures but for pedophilia, bondage, sadomasochism, and sex with animals.[63] The research methodology Rimm used has been strongly criticized as being sloppy.[64] However, no one doubts that there is considerable on-line pornography, nor is there any legal way of controlling access for adults.

---

[63]Philip Elmer-Dewitt, "Cyberporn," *Time*, July 3, 1995, pp. 38–45.
[64]Thomas J. DeLougry, "Researcher Who Studied On-Line Pornography Gets Invitation from Congress, Criticism from Scholars," *Chronicle of Higher Education*, July 21, 1995, p. A19.

Toward the Future

Sex sells in America. Everything from toothpaste to autos is sold using sex, and the sexual saturation of the culture is unlikely to decrease in the near future. What might occur, though, is that discussions of sex become more factual and matter-of-fact. One positive trend is that over the next decade the different gender treatment of sexual activities is likely to decrease. The double standard is being replaced by a single standard.

During the next decade, homosexuality will continue to lose its stigma, and public acceptance of homosexuals will increase. Gay communities will continue to grow in size and political influence. Politicians increasingly openly court the gay vote. The one area where change is not occurring is in the general public's acceptance of gay marriage. There is not only strong religious and social opposition, but the issue is more complicated than it might first seem. For example, in a same-sex union would the surviving partner automatically have spousal inheritance rights? What if this meant nothing for surviving children and biological heirs? Society at large has not started dealing with such issues.

Prostitution is "the world's oldest profession" and is likely to continue. However, the number of female prostitutes has been declining for decades, and there appears to be no reason for the decline not to continue. Male prostitution does not seem to be undergoing a similar decline. During the next decade, attention paid to sex workers will become less frequent, not because of a changing moral climate, but because of the rising cost of police enforcement and the fear of AIDS.

Pornography is more available than ever with the expansion of sex websites and cable and satellite sex stations. Paradoxically, this very overexposure may lead to pornography's lessening social impact. Pornography may lose its mystery and become just sex. When Denmark legalized pornography a couple of decades ago, there was a huge expansion of sex shops in Copenhagen. Now they are virtually all gone. It is possible that saturation will produce the same effect in the United States. Sex may truly become an adult activity.

Summary

The traditional Western view of sexuality upheld a double standard for men and women, which posited that men were promiscuous by nature and women chaste. The postwar Kinsey reports on human sexual behavior empirically demonstrated the distance between official morality and actual behavior, thus contributing to a new sexual openness among Americans. The 1992 National Health and Social Life Survey, however, revealed that most Americans are sexually monogamous, married couples have the most sex, and most adults have more limited sex lives than current media portrayals would suggest.

- Homosexuality is shedding much of its traditional stigma, but homosexual acts are still a crime in most U.S. states.

- Kinsey's widely accepted statement that 10 percent of the U.S. male population is homosexual is inaccurate; the actual figure falls in the 3 to 5 percent range, with the lesbian percentage approximately half as large.

- Homosexuality, long viewed as a mental illness, is increasingly being viewed as a life choice or as a genetically determined sexual orientation.

- Gay communities are increasingly found in most cities, with gay bars playing a pivotal role as sexual meeting places and centers of social and emotional support.
- Prostitution, "the world's oldest profession" and long viewed as a social problem, is growing less common while at the same time becoming more visible.
- There is a clear social hierarchy of sex workers from call girls to bar girls to those in houses and massage parlors to streetwalkers.
- Streetwalkers are most likely to be harassed and arrested by authorities and are also most likely to be underage and under the control of a pimp who controls them economically, sexually, and socially.
- Streetwalkers were often sexually abused by their fathers, were misfits in school, and drifted from casual sex into sex for money or drugs. Because prostitution fills a social need, it will probably continue to exist with or without legal sanction.
- Contemporary opposition to pornography often centers on its nuisance to the public as much as on its corruption of the young.
- The Commission on Obscenity and Pornography found no clear relationship between exposure to pornography and deviant sexual behavior.
- The 1988 Meese Commission found a strong relationship between violent pornography and sex crimes.
- Cyberporn is the newest means of distributing and viewing pornography, and much of this Internet pornography features sexually deviant material.

☞ Key Review Terms

bar girl	homogamy	Presidential Commission
call girl	homophobia	on Pornography and
closet queens	homosexuality	Obscenity
coming out	house girl	pornography
cyberporn	Kinsey reports	prostitution
double standard	learned behavior	situational homosexuality
gays	lesbians	streetwalker
heterosexual	Meese Commission	Victorian morality

? Questions for Discussion

1. Discuss the influence of "Victorian morality" on contemporary American sexual attitudes and beliefs.
2. Discuss the methodological problems of the Kinsey reports. How did the 1992 National Health and Social Life Survey overcome these difficulties?
3. How have social attitudes toward homosexuality changed? Use data to support your position.
4. Discuss the different sociological consequences of viewing homosexuality as a way of life and viewing it as a genetic orientation.

5. What proportion of the population is gay? Why do commonly used figures differ from the scientific ones?

6. Describe the major differences in the size and characteristics of the gay and lesbian populations. Sociologically how would you explain these differences?

7. Describe the social hierarchy of prostitution. How would a functionalist explain the social and demographic pattern?

8. Should prostitution be decriminalized and legalized? Explain your position using sociological data and arguments.

9. What is pornography? What are the opposing feminist views on suppression of pornography versus free speech?

10. What were the findings of the 1967 Presidential Commission on Obscenity and Pornography and the 1986 Meese Commission? How were their views similar and how were they different?

☛Suggested Resources

Cecil Greek and William Thompson, *Porn Wars: The Battle Over Pornography in England and America,* Aldine de Gruyter, New York, 1995. The attempt to suppress pornography by what the authors call "moral entrepreneurs"; that is, politicians, preachers, and anti-free speech feminists.

Daniel Harris, *The Rise and Fall of Gay Culture,* Hyperion, New York, 1997. How the gay culture formed in response to straight hostility and violence, and how gay culture is now changing.

Brian McNaught, *Gay Issues in the Workplace,* St. Martin's, New York, 1993. An examination of the difficulties gays and lesbians face in work situations.

Robert T. Michael, John A. Gannon, Edward O. Laumann and Gina Kolata, *Sex in America: A Definitive Survey,* Little Brown, Boston, 1994. Probably the best single source of information on people's sex lives in America. The popular version based on the NORC National Health and Social Life Survey.

Randy Shilts, *Conduct Unbecoming: Lesbians and Gays in the U.S. Military, Vietnam to the Persian Gulf,* St. Martin's, New York, 1993. Stories of what it was like to be gay in the military before "Don't Ask, Don't Tell."

Dorf Zillman and Jennings Bryant, eds., *Pornography: Research Advances and Policy Considerations,* Erlbaum, Hillsdale, NJ, 1989. Professional research from a Surgeon General's workshop on pornography and its effects.

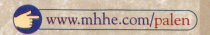

1. Should prostitution be legalized? There are two websites that you should visit to gather information to help form an educated opinion. Start with the Prostitute's Education Network *(www.bayswan. org/penet.html)* Examine this site closely as it contains a wealth of information.

   a. What is the significance of discarding the term "prostitute" for "sex worker"?

   b. What are the key objectives that advocates of legalized prostitution want to achieve for all sex workers?

   c. Read one sex worker's account of her employment at the Nevada Brothels. What does she conclude about them?

   d. Next, visit a site that opposes legalized prostitution, the Prostitution Research and Education website, *(www.prostitutionresearch.com/).* Examine the articles it has posted and be sure to read the interview with Melissa Farley. Why does she oppose using the term "sex worker"? Why does she oppose legalized prostitution?

   e. Now go to the web page of the National Organization for Women *(www.now.org/index.html).* What stand does it take on legalized prostitution? (Hint: This one's hard to find—Do a search under "sex workers.")

   f. Finally, what is your opinion—Should prostitution be legalized? State the reasons for your answer. (Realize, at this point, that you have been looking at the issues from the individual's perspective. Where would you go to gather data about the effects of "sex work" at the societal level?)

2. Search the web for gay, lesbian, and bisexual advocacy groups. List those that you were able to find. Group them by their stated objectives.

   a. Is there much overlap in what they set out to achieve?

   b. Can you find any sites that are specifically anti-gay? On what grounds do they base their objections to gay, lesbian, and bisexual lifestyles?

Chapter 16

In the settlement and civilization of the country, bread more than timber or beauty was wanted; and in the blindness of hunger, the early settlers, claiming Heaven as their guide, regarded God's trees as only a larger kind of pernicious weeds, extremely hard to get rid of.
    . . . Lovers of their country, bewailing its baldness, are now crying aloud, "Save what is left of the forests!" Clearing has surely gone far enough; soon timber will be scarce, and not a grove will be left to rest or pray in. [1]

Written over 100 years ago by John Muir, America's greatest early conservationist.

The Environment:
War and Terrorism

[1]John Muir, "American Forests," *Atlantic Monthly*, 80:146–147, August 1897.

Introduction—The Environment

This final chapter discusses two social problems that are likely to be among the most serious during the twenty-first century: the environment and war and terrorism. The chapter will also offer some speculation on what we can expect regarding social problems in general during the early decades of the twenty-first century.

In contemporary America, we tend to assume that problems of any sort (health, social, political) have a technological solution. Environmental problems in particular are treated as if technological solutions can provide the answer. However, no simple technological fix exists. Environmental problems aren't the result of "natural" occurrences happening on their own. Rather, they are the result of particular human actions affecting the ecosystem. (The **ecosystem** is the complex relationship of all living organisms and their natural and social environment.) Sociologists contribute to the environmental discussion by pointing out how specific economic, cultural, and political choices affect the ecosystem.[2] Solutions to environmental problems depend upon our social beliefs, attitudes, behaviors, and values, which color how we perceive problems and what is thought possible to do about them. Thus, the purpose of this chapter is not so much to list a series of environmental problems as to remind us that such problems are the consequence of social choices and social behaviors.

ecosystem
community of interdependent organisms and their environment.

Historical Pattern

Europeans first settling North America looked upon nature as a resource to be exploited rather than as an environment to be protected. Colonists came seeking to dominate what they saw as a wilderness. They saw nature as something to be tamed, controlled, and mastered. New England Puritans saw themselves as God's chosen people with a mandate to tame and clear the wilderness and in its place build their theologically based "city upon a hill." They were the first American land developers.

To European town-oriented settlers the natural environment of the New World was strange and hostile and in need of being "civilized." Fear of the wilderness environment was expressed in a 1620 letter to England by William Bradford, the leader of the Pilgrims (a Puritan sect):

> They had now no friends to welcome them nor inns to entertain or refresh their weather beaten bodies, no houses or much less townes to repaire too, to seeke for succoure. . . .

---

[2]Edward Crenshaw and J. Craig Jenkins, "Social Structure and Global Climate Change: Sociological Propositions Regarding the Greenhouse Effect," *Sociological Focus*, 29:341–358, October 1996.

Americans traditionally have viewed the environment as something to be exploited. This open pit copper mine is in New Mexico. Similar open pit mines scar the landscapes of Arizona, Montana, and Utah.

© Jess Alford/PhotoDisc

> Besids, what could they see but a hidious and desolate wilderness, full of wild beastst and wild men? and what multitudes ther might be of them they knew not.[3]

Note that the colonists saw both Native American Indians and wild beasts as part of the environment. Native Americans saw themselves the same way, living in harmony with nature as opposed to trying to control nature. This unfortunately meant that the Indians were treated by the colonists as just another environmental problem that had to be overcome before the lands could be cleared and towns built. In the colonist's plans, there was no niche for either Native Americans or nature.

Only comparatively recently have we begun to realize that in spite of all our technology we are part of the ecological web. Still, we often continue to behave as if we were not subject to the laws of nature, laying waste to the ecosystem on which we depend. We continue to pollute the waters with organic and chemical wastes; we fill the air with carbon monoxide, ozone, hydrocarbons, and particulates; and we continue to clear the remaining virgin forests and to poison the land on which we depend with toxic wastes and agribusiness chemicals. We prefer not to hear that ecological changes such as global warming are the consequence of both our population growth and our social organizational decisions. We resist the fact that the problem is us.

Sociological Perspectives

Functionalist Approaches

Functionalists suggest that our approach to the environment reflects the belief in industrial societies that nature is a resource to be used. The previous section notes how European settlers in North America took it as their right and duty to clear the forests, dam the rivers, and build great cities. Western industrial societies also put

---

[3]William T. Davis (ed.), *Bradford's History of Plymouth Plantation,* Scribner, New York, 1908, p. 96.

459

a heavy value on the production and accumulation of goods (needed or not), which causes waste and pollution and exhausts resources.

Functionalists see the environmental crisis as an inevitable by-product of industrial society. This is one of the dysfunctions of modernity. Improvements in standards of living often have environmental costs. To functionalists, these dysfunctions need to be controlled and reduced through pollution control and more environmentally friendly manufacturing. They see such control coming primarily from government regulations and secondarily through cost-effective manufacturing efficiencies. One side effect of pollution is the birth of new companies who profit by cleaning up the environment.

Most functionalists want continued economic growth and do not believe that growth itself is the problem. Rather, the problem is the type of growth. The assumption that more goods are needed for more of the world's peoples is accepted. Thus, the emphasis is on cleaning up the environment and using resources more efficiently, not on changing fundamental societal values. Conservation is stressed. For example, recycling is stressed as a source of raw materials for new manufacturing goods.

Conflict Approaches

Adherents of the conflict approach say that environmental problems are the inevitable result of a social system that encourages individuals and companies to seek wealth and power at the cost of social inequality. During the nineteenth and twentieth century, large corporations raped the land and exploited their workers in the pursuit of ever-larger profits. Destructive technologies, such as strip mining of whole hillsides, continue because exploitation of the environment brings quick and massive profits. The capitalistic profit motive stresses making a profit regardless of environmental damage.

Corporations use their wealth and political power to prevent effective environmental regulations and controls. Major corporate polluters use political action committee (PAC) monies to buy off state and federal legislators. Internationally, multinational corporations exploit and destroy rain forests and other natural environments worldwide in the search for profits without responsibility. Social conflict approaches, whether Marxist or otherwise, raise the question of who benefits from pollution.

One criticism of conflict approaches is that they focus only on problems and do not acknowledge that there has been increased protection of the environment, such as North America's cleaner waters. Nor is there evidence that socialist societies have been any better at protecting the environment. Russia and China are among the world's worst polluters. The most polluted place on earth is the Russian city of Dzerzhinsk, for years Russia's main chemical-weapons production site.[4]

Interactionist Approaches

Interactionists suggest that much of the environmental crisis is due to our attitudes, beliefs, and values. Our view of humankind's place in the ecosystem makes a difference in setting our environmental goals. To the early Puritans, stewardship meant clearing the woods, planting fields, eliminating Indians, and building towns. To Hindus in India, following one's religious and social values and beliefs

---

[4]Michael Specter, "The Most Tainted Place on Earth," *New York Times Magazine,* February 8, 1998, p. 49.

means allowing cows to roam city streets and forbids their killing for food or other purposes. Values matter and have consequences. Corporations, recognizing this, and knowing the symbolic importance of labels, try to redefine their corporate image through **greenwashing,** which suggests that the corporation is environmentally responsible and its products are "environmentally friendly."

Values fundamentally shape our view of the world, and we set appropriate goals and behaviors based upon our worldview. Americans generally are socialized to view the world through individualistic eyes. Thus, the first question we usually ask is whether or not something is good for our personal happiness. Only secondarily are we socialized to think of the common good. We think riding a high-powered all-terrain vehicle through a national forest is great fun; we don't consider that it destroys the environment for others. To resolve the environmental crisis, we must resocialize ourselves to think of the common good, the larger community. Interactionists say that we must teach the next generation that the goal of life is not to conquer and subdue nature but to do the least possible damage and live in harmony with nature.

Major Factors in Environmental Issues

During the twentieth century, rapid population growth and dynamic technological changes combined to cause both rapid destruction of the natural environment and dramatically accelerating levels of pollution. We are creating levels of environmental stress unknown in previous eras.

Population

In Chapter 6 it was noted that it took millions of years to get the world's population to 1.6 billion by the beginning of the twentieth century, but by the beginning of the twenty-first century the population had exploded to 6 billion people. Additional people dramatically increases strain on the natural environment. Currently, the world is adding 86 million more people every year and almost all of this population growth is happening in developing countries.

In this chapter the concern is not with population growth itself but with the impact of growth on the environment. Even if we can feed, clothe, educate, and employ such large numbers, it is certain that adding more people will radically increase environmental pressures and problems. Just during the past 10 years some 600,000 square miles of forest have been cut, most of it for living space and fuel.[5] Continuing space and fuel demands, plus the demand for forest products, will likely lead to the destruction of the remaining rain forests. Billions more people result in far more sewage and chemical waste, sharp increases in the numbers of trucks and autos, and thus dramatically more pollution. This pollution in turn will accelerate both global warming and the depletion of the ozone layer. Continuing population growth inevitably means major ecological damage. The degree of population growth, however, is largely a social question because technologies for controlling rapid growth exist.

---

[5]Werner Fornos, "Myopic Majority's Roadblock Mentality," *Popline,* November–December 1995, p. 2.

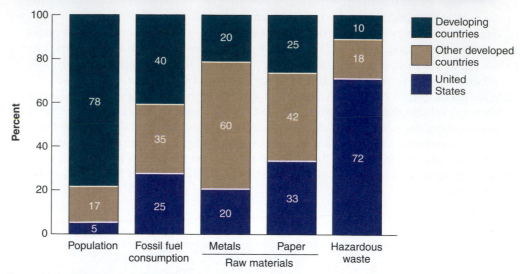

Figure 16.1 Share of Population, Resource Consumption, and Waste Production

Source: National Resources Defense Council.

Technology

Until the late eighteenth century **Industrial Revolution** all power, other than water and wind power, was generated by people or animals. The world population was far smaller and, because people depended on muscle power such as horse-drawn plows, human impact on the environment was limited. The Industrial Revolution with its use of fossil fuels, especially coal to power steam engines, changed everything. Now people could use coal- or oil-powered machinery to reshape the earth, and fossil fuel burning machinery first polluted the atmosphere. Widespread use of oil- or gasoline-burning internal combustion engines during the twentieth century dramatically accelerated this pollution.

At the beginning of the twenty-first century, developed nations make up only 23 percent of the world's population, while consuming roughly 70 percent of the world's energy. Developed countries, therefore, produce the majority of the globe's pollution. However, most of the heavily polluted locations are in developing nations. Developing countries often lack the funds to police or control industrial pollution. Poorer nations are now industrializing using "dirty" technologies, and the most polluted places on earth are the urban areas in developing countries. Cities in the developing world commonly have contaminated drinking water, few sanitary sewers, and no pollution controls of any sort on industry or vehicles. Virtually all the vehicles in Africa, and the vast majority of those in Asia and Latin America, still lack pollution controls and burn leaded fuel. Lead-polluting vehicles foul the air and poison young children, but they are cheaper to build and operate. Just breathing the air in some developing nations' cities is often dangerous to health, especially for children and the elderly.

In Mexico City, the world's largest city, pollution emergencies were in force for half the days in 1998 and 1999. Mexico City's air pollution—very high particulate and carbon monoxide levels—results from the absence of any pollution controls on vehicles and from industrial pollution, burning garbage, and airborne fecal matter. Just breathing the air is equivalent to smoking two packs of cigarettes daily. The air is literally poisoning its youth, and the Mexican capital remains one of the most

AP/Wide World Photos

dangerous places on the planet to take a breath. Sometimes nations deliberately increase pollution levels for economic reasons. Brazil, for example, has actively courted polluting industries as a road to faster development. Shanghai, China, deliberately switched its utilities from burning oil to dirtier soft coal so that the oil could be exported for cash. During Beijing's winter, smog commonly blocks the sun until afternoon. China's water pollution is also serious. In one instance some 26 million pounds of fish were killed in the Huai river when factories dumped a deadly mix of ammonia, nitrogen compounds, and highly toxic phenols.[6]

Citizen attitudes make a difference in environmental control. Residents in Third World countries may believe that they are powerless to affect issues such as pollution, and thus resign themselves to toxic smog and water pollution. As put by the Mexican sociologist Jose Luis Lezama, "The citizens and the government share in

[6]Patrick Tyler, "A Tide of Pollution Threatens China's Prosperity," *New York Times,* September 24, 1994, p. 3.

Box 16.1 Ongoing Issues

Unintended Consequences

Environmental actions, like other actions, sometimes have unintended consequences. Perhaps the classic case of what can go wrong is the World Health Organization's (WHO) early attempts to kill malaria-bearing mosquitoes in Borneo. The World Health Organization sprayed insecticides to kill the mosquitoes, and it largely did. But spraying didn't kill the roaches, who survived even heavy insecticide concentrations. However, the geckoes (lizards) that ate the roaches weren't as hardy. The insecticide they ingested from the roaches affected their nervous system so that they became less agile and fell victim to cats. The insecticide in the geckoes then began killing off the cats. Rats then started moving in from the Borneo forests, bringing with them the threat of plague.

The WHO solution was to parachute cats from planes into the villages to catch or drive away the rats, which they did. But the thatch roofs of houses began falling in. The geckoes, it turned out, had been eating caterpillars, and without geckoes the caterpillars had been feasting upon the thatching of the roofs.

The moral is that you have to think through all the consequences when you fool with mother nature.

---

the will to minimize the problem. Since the possibilities for change are so slight, the best solution is to ignore it. Mexicans have other problems. They see pollution as a luxury problem."[7]

Industrial countries have their own serious problems. They have discovered that toxic messes created by industrial and military development are far easier to create than eliminate. For instance, in America the atomic and chemical technological innovations of the Cold War include chemicals so deadly that less than a drop on the skin will kill. Destroying such chemicals and restoring contaminated land have proven far harder than expected. Cleaning up the toxic and radioactive legacy of the Cold War costs $6 billion a year and is expected to last over 50 years.[8]

Technological advances also have often unintended negative by-products and consequences. So-called "clean" industries sometimes have heavy hidden environmental costs. The computer industry, for instance, is commonly spoken of as a "clean" industry. However, the chemicals used in the chipmaking process are highly toxic. The State of California Bureau of Labor Statistics and Research found that the "systemic poisoning" rate was three to four times higher in the semiconductor industry than in all manufacturing. In California's Silicon Valley at least 18 of the 29 federal Superfund sites—the nation's most polluted sites—are tied to the chip industry.[9] In the early 1990s industry-sponsored studies showed a 40 percent higher rate of miscarriages among female workers exposed to ethylene-based ethers (EGE) used in making computer chips. These EGEs have now been phased out.

Cultural Lag

cultural lag
condition in which one part of the culture changes before others causing disruption, usually technological change precedes social.

Different parts of the culture change at different speeds. Half a century ago William Ogburn suggested that technological changes in a society often occur faster than social changes.[10] He referred to this disequilibrium as **cultural lag.** Taken to its ex-

[7]Julia Preston, "Mexico City's Air: A Fatal Case of Fatalism," *New York Times,* February 14, 1999, p. 3.
[8]Keith Schneider, "Toxic Messes: Easier Made than Undone," *New York Times,* October 2, 1994, p. 5.
[9]Julie Schmit, "Dirty Secrets: Exposing the Dark Side of a 'Clean' Industry," *USA Today,* January 12, 1998, p. 1B.
[10]William F. Ogburn, *Social Change,* Viking, New York, 1950.

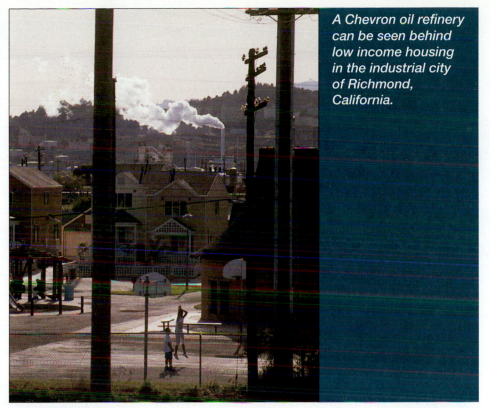

A Chevron oil refinery can be seen behind low income housing in the industrial city of Richmond, California.

treme this becomes a form of technological determinism, but there is no question that rapid technological changes can be socially disruptive. For instance, not until decades after leaded gasoline and auto pollution clearly had been identified as major health threats did the United States, in the 1970s, mandate auto pollution controls and lead-free gasoline. Since then the mean blood level of Americans has declined 75 perecent.[11] Leaded gas, which is known to cause lead poisoning, is still sold in developing countries. Social institutions and governments slowly respond to technologically induced problems.

Environmental Racism

Environmental racism refers to a deliberate pattern whereby toxic-producing plants and toxic waste dumps are placed in the communities of poor people, often people of color. It refers to policies or actions that disadvantage specific racial groups.[12] Certainly, the wealthy never live near steel mills, refineries, or waste dumps. None of these are found on Manhattan's East Side, Chicago's North Shore or Los Angeles' Bel Air. However, polluting industries and environmentally hazardous sites can easily be seen along the highways going through Newark, New Jersey. Similarly, the tollway south from Chicago takes one through the pollution of Gary, Indiana.

That the poor and people of color are unequally subjected to environmental burdens is beyond dispute. However, the term "environmental racism," suggests a deliberate plan on the part of powerful interests, which is not usually the case. Poor

environmental racism
deliberately placing environmental hazards in minority neighborhoods.

---

[11]Jamie Lincoln Kitman, "The Secret History of Lead," *The Nation*, March 20, 2000, www.thenation.com
[12]R. D. Bullard, *Dumping in Dixie: Race, Class, and Environmental Quality*, Westview Press, Boulder, 1990, p. 1.

Figure 16.2 Number of People per Vehicle, Selected Countries

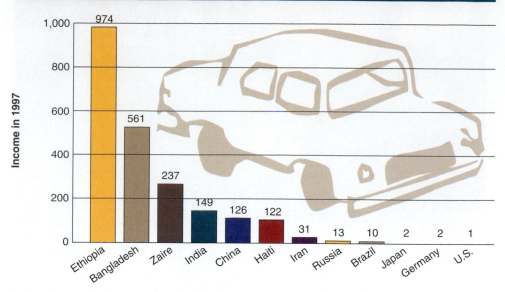

Source: Automobile Manufacturers Association.

people lived in homes near the polluting steel mills in Gary not because they were forced to move there by the mill owners but because the housing costs were low and the housing was close to work. That the poor live in the worst housing and worst neighborhoods is a truism worldwide. There is clear economic discrimination. However, there is less evidence that there is a deliberate and conscious policy of environmental racism.[13]

Air Pollution

sick building syndrome

airtight buildings which produce physical ills.

The atmosphere, like the earth's waters, will eventually clean itself if given the chance. Currently it is not getting that opportunity because we are overstressing the atmosphere. All urban areas in the United States have high levels of carbon monoxide, almost half of which comes from automobiles and trucks. In fact, in the United States there are as many trucks and automobiles as there are people. Sometimes our technology itself causes problems. Energy-efficient air-tight buildings occasionally develop **sick building syndrome,** which produces headaches, eye, nose, and throat irritation, and sometimes dizziness and nausea.[14]

Toxic Emissions

Utility plants and factories burning fossil fuels (oil and coal) emit huge amounts of toxic emissions of hydrochloric acid, hydrogen fluoride, and sulfuric acid. About

[13]Tracy Yandley and Dudley Burton, "Reexamining Environmental Justice: A Statistical Analysis of Historical Hazardous Waste Landfill Setting in Metropolitan Texas," *Social Science Quarterly,* 77:477–492, September 1996.

[14]Wendy Lindauer, *Sick Building Syndrome,* Environmental Health Center, February 1999, www.nsc.org.

four-fifths of these go into the air, and the remaining one-fifth goes into the soil and water. The combination of pollutants often has **synergistic effects,** whereby the interaction of pollutants has a more severe effect than the single effect of each.

Not until 1999 did the U.S. Environmental Protection Agency require that utility companies report toxic emissions. In Virginia, where the author lives, the two largest electric utilities, Virginia Power and American Electric Power, reported releasing more than *18 million pounds of toxic chemicals* into the environment during the previous year. Hydrochloric acid was the most common emission. Among its toxic emissions, Virginia Power included almost 6,000 pounds of deadly mercury. It was pointed out by industry representatives that these figures represented no new emissions or changes in the way the utility plants were operated. It was also pointed out that all these toxic releases were legal under current laws. According to the spokesman for Virginia Power, "People associate big numbers with a problem, but there is no problem here."[15]

Global Warming

Mention global warming and you are certain to get a debate. Controlling global warming through reducing greenhouse gases is as much a social as a scientific issue. Utility executives and ideological conservatives are likely to suggest that global warming is largely science fiction, while environmentalists and liberals are more likely to hold as an article of faith that the earth is warming. The debate is bitter because the cost of reducing air pollution in high-energy-consumption countries such as the United States and Canada will be steep. Because the North American economies are built upon energy availability, heavy carbon taxes could force energy prices to soar and economic growth to slow.

The scientific evidence has convinced most climatologists that the **greenhouse effect,** the global warming of the earth due to burning fossil fuels, is real and that it will continue and probably accelerate during the twenty-first century. Certainly, we have had some hot years recently. Climatologists say that the twentieth century was the warmest century of the millennium. According to the National Oceanic and Atmospheric Administration 9 of the last 11 years have been the hottest in the 119 years since records were first kept.[16] The winter of 2000 was the warmest in U.S. history.[17] Records were also broken in 1997, 1998 and 1999. During the twentieth century the burning of fossil fuels and other human activity not only increased carbon dioxide levels but also raised the concentration of methane in the atmosphere and introduced chlorofluorocarbons into it—two other greenhouse gases.

Limiting greenhouse gas emissions is the most pressing environmental issue facing governments of the industrialized world. To resolve this global crisis, the United Nations held international conferences on climate change in Rio de Janeiro in 1992, Berlin in 1995, and Kyoto in 1997. The Kyoto Conference committed developed nations to reduce their emissions according to strict timetables. The Kyoto Conference set the legally binding deadline of 2000 to reduce emissions to 1990 levels. The United States was the only major developed nation that refused to make any legal commitment. The United States rationale was that no timetables for controlling emissions were applied to developing nations, and most growth in energy usage over the next 20 years will occur in the developing world.

Both the United States and Canada failed by a large margin to meet the 2000 standards. By contrast, most European nations met or came close to the 2000 timetable. However, this was due less to European energy conservation than to an

---

[15]Greg Edwards, "VA Utilities among Biggest Polluters," *Richmond Times-Dispatch,* June 5, 1999, p. A1.
[16]Kim A. McDonald, "Debate over Global Warming Heats up Meeting of Climatologists," *Chronicle of Higher Education,* February 5, 1999, p. A17.
[17]"Winter of 2000 Warmest in History of U.S." *CBS News,* March 9, 2000.

economic slowdown in Europe during the 1990s and to increasingly heavy European reliance on nuclear power rather than fossil fuels. For safety reasons, nuclear power is being phased out in North America.

Renewable Resources

Renewable resources are energy resources that do not come from fossil fuels and are replaceable. Optimistic estimates of past decades as to the economic feasibility and adoption of renewable solar energy and other resources have not been borne out. Early twenty-first-century North America evidences some limited power generation using solar, wind, and water power, but nothing has been done to substantially reduce the dependence on fossil fuels. There are some positive signs. Solar heating systems, for example, are a cost-effective method of heating buildings and water, but initial installation costs remain high. There also have been some remarkably inventive uses of waste products fueling power plants. Some enclosed cattle feed lots are recovering enough methane gas from the cattle to power their entire operation. Nonetheless, the sad reality is that there is not yet widespread use of cost-effective alternatives to fossil fuels. If greenhouse gas emissions continue to escalate, however, finding alternatives to fossil fuels will become essential.

Water Pollution

Water is an irreplaceable resource, but for years we gave little thought to water pollution. After all, two-thirds of the globe is covered with water, and water cleanses itself. However, 97.5 percent of the earth's water supply is ocean saltwater. Most of the remaining 2.5 percent of the earth's water is imprisoned in glaciers and ice caps. Only 0.7 percent of the earth's water is in lakes, rivers, swamps, and aquifers. We have long used waterways as convenient waste removal sites. We dump garbage into the ocean or a convenient river and let those downstream worry about it. This is not new. A Boston municipal ordinance of 1666, for instance, ordered that "all garbidge, bests entrails & c" were to be dumped from the drawbridge into Mill Creek.[18] In the early twentieth century cities in northern Wisconsin advertised nationally their advantages as sites for paper mills because there were available streams into which the heavy industrial wastes from the mills could be dumped.

Algae Blooms

Harmful **algae blooms** (HAB) occur when algae photosynthesize and multiply rapidly by converting dissolved nutrients and sunlight. Algae blooms can prove lethal to fish when they deplete the oxygen the fish need to survive. Toxins from poisonous algae can contaminate planktonic communities. Red tides and pfiesteria, whose toxins can rip a hole through the skin of a fish, are multiplying at far

---

[18]Carl Bridenbaugh, *Cities in the Wilderness*, Capricorn, Putnam, New York, 1964, p. 18.

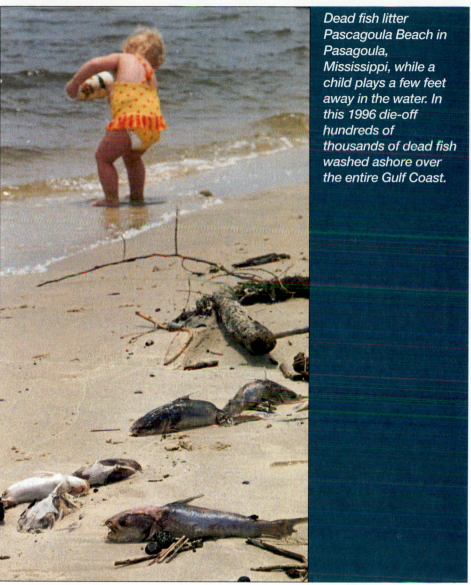

Dead fish litter Pascagoula Beach in Pasagoula, Mississippi, while a child plays a few feet away in the water. In this 1996 die-off hundreds of thousands of dead fish washed ashore over the entire Gulf Coast.

William Cogin/AP/Wide World Photos

faster levels.[19] An algae bloom along the Texas coast in 1997 killed 14 million fish, and in Alaska red tides have become so common that the entire coastline is now closed to shellfishing.[20]

Nitrate and phosphate fertilizers used by farmers, homeowners, and golf courses contribute heavily to creating algae blooms. So do human and animal waste runoffs. Research links outbreaks of pfsteria in North Carolina's coastal waters to spillage of hog wastes from open lagoons (basically cesspools) into rivers and then into the ocean. North Carolina's 10 million hogs produce more waste than all the people in California and New York combined.[21]

Algae blooms can poison even the largest bodies of water. By the 1970s the shallowest of the Great Lakes, Lake Erie, was well on the way to becoming a dead lake. Its bottom at some points was covered by a mass of dead algae over 100 feet deep,

---

[19]Dick Russell, "Underwater Epidemic," *Amicus Journal,* Spring, 1998, pp. 28–33.
[20]Kim A. McDonald, "Scientists Explore Rise in 'Red Tides' of Harmful Algae," *Chronicle of Higher Education,* March 6, 1998, p. A15.
[21]Russell, "Underwater Epidemic," p. 30.

Box 16.2 Making a Difference

Screaming Bird

Sometimes it takes real courage to argue for the environment. After the 1989 *Exxon Valdez* oil spill that covered the Alaskan coastline with crude oil, Exxon paid a $1 billion settlement. Dune Lankard, a member of the Eyak Indian tribe, proposed that the funds be used to buy development rights for forest land that could then be saved for hunting, fishing, and tourism.[a] This would mean foregoing immediate profits from logging.

His fellow Eyak Corporation board members thought he was crazy, called him a "tree hugger," and voted him down 8 to 1. Believing in his cause, he gave up his fishing and began lobbying native Alaskans. His argument was: "Indigenous people have thousands of years of being preservationists. We need to become stewards of the land again."[b] He was voted off the Eyak Corporation board and sued, but he wouldn't give up. Gradually his lobbying gained converts, and by 1998 some 700,000 acres of coastal habitat were protected. As an extra bonus, this produced a $380 million windfall to native corporations. The chief of the Eyak renamed Dune "Janachakih," which translates as "little bird that screams real loud and won't shut up."

[a]David S. Jackson, "Scream of the Little Bird," Time, December 14, 1998, p. 70.
[b]Ibid.

and the bottom no longer supported any oxygen-dependent life. The lake had become "too thick to drink, and too thin to plow." The fish remaining in the lake were unfit for eating, being heavily contaminated with DDT, PBCs, and mercury.

But the process of decline is not inevitable. Federal clean air and clean water legislation and regulations have returned Lake Erie to life. While the Environmental Protection Agency lists one of every three American rivers as not being in good condition, this is actually an improvement. In the United States once-polluted rivers, lakes, and streams have been cleared of industrial waste and are far cleaner than 30 years ago. Even New York's Hudson River, which was given up for dead, now abounds with life. The federal government is increasingly requiring buffer zones along waterways to limit chemical runoffs. Water will clean itself if given the opportunity.

Elsewhere around the globe, especially in Russia and developing nations, the situation is not as favorable. The tragedy is that we have come to *expect* that rivers, lakes and waterways worldwide will be polluted. We are surprised when they are not.

Overfishing

Oceans provide most of the world's seafood, but they also are dumping grounds for everything from urban garbage, to human waste products, to waste oil, to nuclear wastes. Not only are the oceans being polluted but they also are being overfished. Overefficient factory ships virtually vacuum the ocean floor which has resulted in the closing of major fishing grounds off the Georges Bank of Newfoundland and southern New England waters. Once inexhaustible cod and ground fish have been driven to the brink of extinction. (See Chapter 6 for further discussion.)

Coastal Shelf Pollution

All the ocean shellfish and most of the fish are found on the ocean shelf extending out from coastlines. Unfortunately, the ocean shelf also is where most ocean pollution occurs. Pollution from the land, including viruses from human waste, have resulted in previously unknown bacteria and viruses killing marine life. Some 10 percent of the world's coral has already died and another 30 percent is threatened. Studies demonstrate that vast colonies of human virus migrate into Florida's coastal waters from the 1.6 million septic tanks in the state.[22] It is not something the Chamber of Commerce advertises, but nearly a quarter of the people using Florida's marine beaches develop ear infections, sore throats, respiratory, or gastrointestinal disease.

Social Consequences

In the twenty-first century water, land, and air pollution are more *social* than physical or technological problems. Scientifically we know what needs to be done and technically we know how to do it. What we lack is the moral and financial commitment. While everyone professes to be in favor of clean air and water, this commitment is often limited. Clean water, for instance, may be viewed as less important than jobs. For example, for decades Reserve Mining Company dumped known cancer-causing fibers into Lake Superior. Even though the local water system was contaminated and known to be dangerous to health, local inhabitants preferred to continue toxic dumping rather than lose jobs. They feared that if pollution controls were required the company would carry out its threat to close the plant.

It turns out that the jobs versus environment dichotomy is a bogus choice. If environmental regulations did cause financial harm—the argument often heard from those trying to loosen environmental controls—then the states with the strongest protections should have the weakest economies. However, the opposite is the case. States having the strongest economies also tend to have environmental controls and healthy environments. Clean air and water attract high-tech companies offering decent wages. States such as Vermont, New Hampshire, Oregon, Washington, and California have both strong regulations and economies. One the other hand, states such as Mississippi, Alabama, Arkansas, and West Virginia have among the poorest environmental records and the poorest economies. New businesses are less attracted to states with environmental problems and that do not have clean air and water.

Complicating the question of pollution control is that many costs of pollution are indirect. For example, a person living in Birmingham, Alabama, who sees the paint on his new car fade after a couple of years may not relate the fading to air pollution. The pollution itself may be indirect, because areas producing pollution often ship it elsewhere. We have already discussed how waste is dumped in rivers for those downstream to deal with it. We also have known for decades that the acid rain killing the forests in the Blue Ridge Mountains and in forests in New England and eastern Canada comes largely from power plants in Ohio and the Midwest. Switching away from burning cheap pollution-producing fuels would raise Midwest power prices. Thus, tall smokestacks are used to pump the pollutants into the atmosphere so they come down on the East Coast.

---

[22]"As Oceans Warm, Problems from Viruses and Bacteria Mount," *New York Times,* January 24, 1999, p. 15.

Who is to pay pollution costs and *how* they are to be paid are the basis of much of the current environmental debate. Are the costs to be paid directly by the polluting industries and their customers in the form of higher prices? Or should the costs be borne generally and indirectly by the entire population through pollution damage or higher taxes?

Eco-Terrorism

eco-terrorism
destroying, often by arson, property owned by those judged to be harming animals or the environment.

Not everyone is willing to use only legal means to save the environment. Several radical environmental organizations have turned to **eco-terrorism,** using arson as a means of stopping developers. In 1998 a group called the Earth Liberation Front took responsibility for seven arson fires and bombs on Vail Mountain in Colorado, causing over $12 million in damages, destroying among other things three lodge buildings and four ski lifts. The group says the ski lifts will interfere with attempts to reintroduce the lynx into the region. In a letter to the news media, the Earth Liberation Front said, "Putting profits ahead of Colorado's wildlife will not be tolerated. This action is just a warning. We will be back if this greedy corporation continues to trespass into wild and unroaded areas."[23] Similar tactics have been used to stop logging. The spokeswoman for the Animal Liberation Front said that her group has allied itself with the Environmental Liberation Front and the two groups have declared war on all companies that desecrate the Earth.[24] She said that they get their information on how to build bombs and other devices from the Internet.

Introduction—War and Terrorism

war
organized armed conflict among nations.

War is organized armed conflict. The history of the world is in good part the history of wars. Western literature has its beginnings with Homer's accounts of the Trojan War. Norman Cousin's much-quoted estimate is that since 3600 B.C., or for the last 5,600 years, there have been only 292 years of general peace in the known world.[25] Whether this is precisely accurate is not as important as the implication that war is a normal state of events. Warfare certainly has been frequent in the history of the United States. In addition to roughly a dozen declared and undeclared wars up until World War II, the President had sent troops abroad, without the approval of Congress, some 163 times.[26]

terrorism
acts of violence used as a political strategy.

There continues to be much dispute over the definition of terrorism, but **terrorism** always includes using violence for political ends against nonmilitary or civilian populations. In all cases, it is violence by political, religious, ethnic, or racial zealots to obtain political ends.

---

[23]Steve Paulson, "Blazes Mark Ominous Step in Eco-Terror," *Associated Press,* October 24, 1998.
[24]Ibid.
[25]Quoted in Francis A. Beer, *Peace against War: The Ecology of International Violence,* Freeman, San Francisco, 1981, p. 20.
[26]R. Leckie, *The Wars of America,* HarperCollins, New York, 1992.

Sociological Perspectives

Functional Approaches

War has been the historic method for nations to resolve conflicting interests and goals. While not supporting war, most functionalists would argue that war is used by societies for resolving disputes that cannot be resolved otherwise. War and conflict thus are seen by functionalists as the more-or-less inevitable consequence of conflicting interests between nation-states. Only when the international system is reorganized to give international organizations the power to resolve disputes and impose solutions will warfare cease. In addition to war's tremendous human and economic costs, it is also socially dysfunctional when it drags on too long, as was the case of the Vietnam War.

Political systems within nations are also dysfunctional insofar as they promote great inequality in access to resources and power. If groups within the society see themselves as unable to achieve their goals through legitimate means, they may turn to violence. When there is no legitimate means of political change for dispossessed economic or ethnic populations, the consequence may be violence and internal revolutionary warfare. Internal reforms and open access to power through nonviolent means can prevent internal political, ethnic, racial, or religious violence.

Functionalists generally argue that the best way of preventing war is through reorganizing international relations so that an international system, such as the United Nations or World Court, can resolve national conflicts and preserve world order.

Conflict Approaches

Conflict theory advocates see war as detrimental to most people but beneficial to those corporations and major political powers who can force their economic system on those less powerful. War, or the preparations for eventual war, benefits the military-industrial complex of powerful military, business, and government interests. An arms race is good for defense industries. Warfare is the consequence of the struggle of nation-states for political and economic dominance over others.

War between capitalist developed nations occurs because they form alliances that conflict with other developed-nation alliances over which group will have worldwide dominance and be able to exploit the natural resources and labor of poor less-developed countries. War is a way for capitalist countries to control the flow of cheap labor and raw materials.

Conflict theorists often make a distinction between just and unjust wars and revolutions. Those that eliminate the oppression of the capitalists in power are just. Internal revolutions are a means by which the exploited can overthrow the local elites who are the lackeys of exploiting capitalist states.

Conflict theory adherents, like functionalists, also see the importance of international organizations, but they especially stress the need for international organizations to eliminate economic oppression by the strong and to distribute resources equally according to need. Revolutionary violence, including terrorism, is justified by some if it produces greater equality among peoples. Only when oppressive political systems are removed and there is economic justice can conflict be eliminated.

Interactionist Approaches

Interactionists see war partially as a result of the way we are socialized. We are taught that our nation is good and virtuous and that the other side is aggressive and the "evil empire." Cultures can legitimate violence as an acceptable way of dealing with problems, both domestic and external. We can be socialized to view backing down or compromising as "unmanly."

The mass media are used to socialize people for international conflict, and war can be used to produce social cohesion. During wartime, leaders use patriotic symbols, slogans, and songs to bring unity and solidarity to a people. The German bombing of London during World War II actually unified the English behind the war effort, as the Allied bombing of Germany unified the Germans. For individuals, war may bring the psychological advantage of "all being in it together." It also allows people to put aside difficult personal decisions, such as divorce, for "the good of the war effort."

War reinforces stereotypes about one's own nation and about the enemy. Because we are fighting to save civilization and the enemy is evil, anything we do to bring them down is justified and honorable. Some cultures, such as that of early-twentieth-century Prussian Germans, have been accused of glorifying war by emphasizing the cultural virtues of personal military honor and aggressiveness toward outsiders. Similarly, some radical political and religious groups define as martyrs terrorist bombers who blow themselves up while killing others.

Interactionists generally say that, to limit warfare, cultures have to socialize their members to put a higher value on nonaggression and cooperation. We should advocate and teach discussion and compromise as a means of settling disputes. Rather than people thinking of themselves first as members of a particular nation-state or ethnic group, children must be socialized to first think of all people as sharing a common humanity.

War

Technology

War and technology have been closely linked throughout history. War has driven the development of new technologies; bronze spears and knives, the horse as military transport, the war chariot, iron weapons, the crossbow, the English longbow, gunpowder, atomic weapons, and computer-guided weapons were all created to serve warfare. Technologies used in warfare have been getting deadlier and deadlier. A **military-industrial complex,** the close tying together of government, military, and weapons production industries, can be traced back at least to ancient Egypt.

military-industrial complex
tight association and job movement among the military, defense industries, and the federal government, warned against as a threat to democracy by President Dwight Eisenhower in his Farewell Address.

Scale of Warfare

War has always been deadly, but until the French Revolutionary and Napoleonic Wars (1789–1815) wars were commonly fought by professional soldiers and rarely involved more than 10,000 persons in a battle. War rarely affected the general citizenry except by way of taxes. The last century has been labeled the Century of Total War. Using very conservative estimates, World War I (1914–1918) caused 8.6 million military deaths.[27] World War II (1939–1945) was even more deadly, causing at least 16 million military deaths. Russia alone lost 6 million soldiers. At least another 20 million civilian deaths are attributed to World War II, making the total 36 million at a very minimum.

Nuclear War

During the **Cold War** (1946–1989) the overriding fear was of **nuclear war** breaking out between Russia and the United States. The scale of any nuclear war would be almost beyond comprehension. A single hydrogen bomb exploded over a major city could kill half a million people outright and seriously injure hundreds of thousands more. Toxic and biological weapons are equally deadly. Although banned by international treaty, at least a dozen nations are developing toxins or biological weapons. Some 20 nations have chemical weapons.[28]

Today the fear is not that major nuclear powers such as the United States, Russia, or China will go to war with one another, but rather that nuclear proliferation is spreading. **Nuclear proliferation** is the spread of nuclear weapons to more nations, often nations that are less stable politically or have fewer controls over the use of nuclear weapons. The Nuclear Nonproliferation Treaty pledges signers not to permit the spread of nuclear weapons to countries not already possessing weapons of mass destruction. However, some nations possessing nuclear weapons, such as India, Pakistan, and Israel, have refused to sign the treaty. Others, trying to develop nuclear weapons, such as North Korea, Iraq, and Iran, ignore its provisions. China has provided information on building nuclear weapons to Pakistan. Iraq and Iran have actively sought to buy or steal nuclear weapon technology. India and Pakistan both boast of having nuclear weapons with which they continue to threaten each other.

Nuclear weapons have not been used in war since 1945. Recent wars, such as Desert Storm in 1991 and NATO's war against Serbian genocide in Kosovo in 1999, have been wars with limited aims. They have not involved armed conflict between the major powers, and both have been short conflicts with few U.S. casualties. They are not total wars. Rather, they are current examples of the view of warfare given by Karl von Clausewitz, the nineteenth-century Prussian military general and philosopher. Clausewitz postulated that war is simply the extension of politics by other means.[29] In other words, war should only be resorted to when the ends to be obtained by warfare can't be obtained by other means and the costs are moderate. War should be used not as a means of total domination or extermination but as an arm of political policy.

Cold War
economic and political struggle between the West and Soviet systems which ended with the 1989 collapse of communism.

nuclear war
warfare using nuclear weapons.

nuclear proliferation
spread of nuclear weapons to additional nations.

Terrorism

For the United States the early twenty-first century is more likely to see terrorism than outright war. Terrorism can be used either against the state or by the state. Terrorism is used semi-officially by some nations. Libya has been implicated in placing the bomb in Pan Am 103, which exploded over Lockerbie, Scotland, in 1988. In 2000 the State Department listed Cuba, Libya, North Korea, Sudan, Iran, and Iraq as nations violating international law by supporting terrorism. Terrorism is also used by aggrieved religious, ethnic, and political groups who cannot see, or refuse

---

[27]*1995 Information Please Almanac,* Houghton Mifflin, Boston, 1995, p. 391.
[28]K. C. Bailey, *Doomsday Weapons in the Hands of Many,* University of Illinois Press, Urbana, 1991.
[29]Karl von Clausewitz, *On War,* Anatol Papoport (ed. and trans.), Viking, New York, 1983.

Terrorists often target civilians in order to maximize casualities. Volunteers are helping carry a U.S. Embassy office worker over the rubble of a collapsed building next to the embassy in Nairobi after Muslim terrorists set off bombs minutes apart in both Nairobi, Kenya, and Dar es Salaam, Tanzania, in 1998. Some 130 people, including 15 Americans, were killed instantly, and over 2,200 people were injured. Most of those killed and injured were simply bystanders.

to see, any other alternative to influencing change. The 1998 bombing of U.S. embassies, which killed and injured hundreds of civilians near U.S. embassies in Nairobi, Kenya, and Dar es Saalaam, Tanzania, is an example.

Revolutionary Terrorism

revolutionary terrorism

anti-government terrorism designed to change the government.

Revolutionary terrorism seeks to overthrow, or at bare minimum determine the policies of, the existing government.[30] Most terrorists are political extremists seeking political change (IRA bombings in Northern Ireland) or expressing anger and retaliating against a government (the 1995 bombing of the Oklahoma City federal building by Timothy McVeigh and Terry Nichols, apparently as a reprisal for earlier FBI actions at Waco, Texas). But revolutionary terrorism may seek religious change (Afghan Islamic terrorism against other Muslims), revenge against other groups (Libyan-sponsored bombing in 1988 of Pan Am flight 103 over Lockerbie), or even terrorism for profit (Colombian narco-terrorism).

---

[30]Peter Sederberg, *Terrorist Myths: Illusion, Rhetoric, and Reality*, Prentice-Hall, Englewood Cliffs, NJ, 1989.

A Serbian police officer stands in front of slain ethnic Albanian KLA (Kosovo Liberation Army) members and residents in the Kosovo village of Rogovo after Serb police stormed the village in January 1999. International verifiers reported 23 ethnic Albanians were killed here. NATO eventually intervened to stop the genocide against ethnic Albanians.

Srdjan Illc/AP/Wide World Photos

Terrorists usually see themselves being at the forefront of a political, religious, ethnic, or racial struggle. They also see themselves as unfairly isolated from sources of power. Terrorists who hold political and religious views similar to one's own are commonly labeled "freedom fighters." Thus, whether you label someone a terrorist or a freedom fighter depends on your position. Revolutionary terrorists, with some exceptions such as the IRA targeting British military installations in Northern Ireland and Muslim radicals bombing U.S. airbases in Saudi Arabia, overwhelmingly avoid military targets. Rather, they strike only "soft" civilian targets. Even in the above noted Saudi truck bombings, the attack was not upon the military airbase itself but upon dependent-housing areas.

On occasion terrorist victims are prominent people singled out for assassination, but usually they are just helpless victims who were in the wrong place at the wrong time. In the United States the two most deadly terrorist attacks during the 1990s were the 1993 bombing of the World Trade Center in New York by Islamic extremists and the 1995 bombing and killing of 186 civilians working in the Federal Building in Oklahoma City. The bombers, Timothy McVeigh and Terry Nichols, are not foreign radicals, but native-born right-wing political extremists who saw themselves striking a blow against a tyrannical government. Terrorists often are not the wild-eyed fanatics or crazed killers one might expect. Research on militant terrorists shows they are articulate individuals to whom terrorism is a rational choice.[31] The chilling fact is that those who choose to murder innocent civilians may appear otherwise quite normal.

Until the 1990s, terrorist factions commonly were political groups directed by militant organizations. They would issue lengthy communiques explaining their actions and their political agendas. They justified and took credit for their acts and often used hostage taking and other acts to obtain "the oxygen of publicity." Twenty-first-century terrorists, by contrast, are more likely to belong to small subcultural groups with less coherent, or even comprehensible, ideological, political, or religious agendas. They range from the Islamic fanatics of the Iran-influenced Hezbollah to movements such as the Japanese Aum Shinri Kyo religious sect that carried out the 1995 nerve-gas attack on the Tokyo subway. Compared to the larger and known terrorist groups of the

---

[31]Bruce Hoffman, *Inside Terrorism*, Victor Gollancz, London, 1998.

past, such subcultural groups are harder for intelligence agencies to penetrate. Terrorism has become both more lethal and more anonymous and unpredictable. Democratic governments have particular difficulty tracking down potential terrorists because they cannot use "strongarm" tactics. Governments have to balance between preserving order and not abridging civil rights. This is not always easy to do.

Contemporary right-wing fringe groups and militias in the United States commonly have white-supremacist ideologies. Race-centered fringe groups are often identified with so-called "Christian Identity" churches and movements. Included here would be groups such as Aryan Nation, The Covenant, the Sword and Arm of the Lord, the White Patriot Party, and the Posse Comitatus.

State Terrorism

state terrorism
government use of terrorist means against its own people.

Terrorism can be directed by the state as well as by disaffected groups outside the government. **State terrorism** is terrorism used to support government aims. The best-known examples of state terrorism in the first half of the twentieth century are Joseph Stalin's and Adolf Hitler's use of murderous purges and terror to subdue opponents, both real and imagined.

The most lethal state terrorism during the second half of the twentieth century was carried out by the Pol Pot Communist regime in Cambodia. In the late 1970s Pot's Khmer Rouge party systematically murdered 4 million Cambodians. A closer to home example of state terrorism would be the 1970s "official" terrorism by military officers in Argentina and Chile. Those holding left-wing or liberal positions were systematically murdered by the military. More recently there is Slobodan Milosevic's 1999 attempt to use murder, rape, and terror as part of a government policy to ethnically cleanse Kosovo of all ethnic Albanians. Those of Albanian background were to be forced out or eliminated.

State terrorism, of course, means that citizens have no government agencies to defend or protect them. The military and the police do not protect citizens but are themselves the terrorists.

Current Status

As this is written, none of the major world powers are warring. And, in spite of terrorist attacks such as the bombing of the federal building in Oklahoma City, state-sponsored and revolutionary terrorism is at a level below that of a decade ago. This trend toward declining terrorist attacks will not necessarily continue as a long-range pattern.

The favorable news is that long-standing conflicts, such as those between Palestinians and Israelis in the Middle East and that between Protestant Unionists and Catholic Republicans in Northern Ireland, are apparently finally being resolved. Further, rogue states such as Libya and Iraq that have been known to sponsor external terrorism are finding that such acts increasingly are counterproductive, isolating them from other world nations. Similarly, the international community is increasingly intolerant of internal terrorism against one's own people. The 1999 NATO bombing of Serbia in reaction to ethnic cleansing in Kosovo marked an international turning point in this regard. The head of the Serbian government, Slobodan Milosevic, was indicted by the World Court as a war criminal. Similarly, in 1999 Indonesian gangs opposed to the independence vote in East Timor were suppressed by an international force under United Nations authority. World opinion no longer allows state sovereignty automatically to protect a nation practicing terrorism or ethnic cleansing against its own people.

The less favorable news is that with the United States now being the sole superpower, America becomes the prime target for all those groups and individuals unhappy with the status quo. Some of these disaffected groups and individuals may transfer their anger into terrorism.

Conclusion—The Twenty-First Century

None of us have crystal balls, so all prognostications about the future, including those by scholars, are fraught with uncertainty. The record of prophecy regarding technological change is particularly bad.[32] At the opening of the twentieth century, few experts saw the automobile other than as a rich person's plaything, and it has become a cliché that after World War II the head of IBM estimated that the United States had a market for no more than 5 mainframe computers.

This does not mean, however, that all is chance or that nothing can be said about the near future. Some things about the social problems discussed in this text can be predicted, particularly when social trends appear well established and likely to continue. It is certain, for instance, that during the next few decades our reliance on technology will continue to accelerate.

The early twenty-first century may very well see substantial progress made in addressing social problems. Social problems texts, by listing one problem issue after another, can create the pessimistic impression that nothing can be done. That is not the case. Projecting current patterns into the next decade shows some clear positive patterns, as well as trends that are more negative. For example, it is evident that pollution is a major social problem, but compared to a quarter of a century ago America's air and water both are cleaner. Similarly, there is less international war and terrorism than 30 years ago when American soldiers were dying in the Vietnam War.

Projecting for the next decade using the template of current patterns enables us to make a number of forecasts. Remember, though, that the following forecasts reflect projections from current patterns, and in some cases are the author's professional opinion. All projections should be treated with a dose of caution.

Among the projections based on current patterns would be the prediction that economic inequality between the haves and the have-nots will increase during the next decade. Economic inequalities will increasingly reflect differences in educational levels. While socioeconomic status will become increasingly important, race will continue to be a major defining factor in American life, affecting both personal behavior and government policies. Affirmative Action, as official government policy, will likely fade from the scene. New and renamed programs will be implemented to accomplish the same goals. Such programs based on income rather than race are likely to increase in number. While ethnicity will probably remain a divisive issue, gender will probably become less so. Gender inequality will still exist but will decrease as women increasingly move into policy-making positions and older generations of males unaccustomed to gender equality pass from the scene.

The population explosion will continue in developing countries. By contrast, the populations of European nations will in many cases actually decline. The population of Japan also will decline. In the United States population growth will become dependent upon immigration and the children born to immigrants.

---

[32]Edward Tenner, *Why Things Bite Back*, Knopf, New York, 1996.

If we project current education patterns into the near future, we would expect less of a gap in the number of years people spend in school. At the same time the quality of education received may increasingly reflect social-class factors. A countertrend is that many states are trying to raise the educational level of marginal primary and secondary schools. Increasing emphasis is likely to be placed by states on achieving specific skill levels as a condition for high school graduation. The semiracist assumption that disadvantaged groups cannot meet general performance standards is increasingly being challenged. The abandonment of social promotion (already the policy in states such as Illinois and Texas) may result in the education of the poor and of minorities being taken seriously. At the college level the new century may see some tightening of academic standards and a reversal of the recent decades' pattern of increasing grade inflation.

The common assumption during the late twentieth century was that high divorce rates were an inevitable consequence of women in the workforce and gender equality. American divorce rates are now the highest in the world, but there are some indications that divorce rates are reversing somewhat and may actually decline during the next decade. Couples are marrying later, and egalitarian families are increasingly becoming the norm. Also, out-of-wedlock births, which increased rapidly from the 1960s to the mid-1990s, have begun to show signs of decline. Declining rates should continue in the early twenty-first century. Rates of teenage pregnancy also will continue their late 1990s decline. Moreover, the more general use of efficient contraception and the widespread availability of post-intercourse pills suggests that the abortion issue will fade from the national radar as a divisive social and political issue.

As the nation's population grows older, a major social revolution will take place. Perceptions of age and aging are rapidly changing, and as the baby boomers approach traditional retirement age this change will accelerate. Social age based on activity level will become increasingly more important, while simple chronological age will become less significant. Politically, older populations will become an even more potent force.

On the less positive side, despite user complaints, the health system will still largely be controlled by bureaucratic rather than medical norms. However, this will be done more subtly than during the last decade. Overall, the health care system will increasingly favor those having liberal health insurance plans over those who are not covered. As doctors increasingly become employees and hospitals become branches of national chains, the providing of charity medical and hospital care will increasingly become a thing of the past. Care of the less advantaged will fall almost entirely on government programs. On the positive side, the pharmacological bringing of mental illness under control will become an increasing reality.

During the first decade of the twenty-first century urban life should exhibit somewhat less social deviance than experienced during the late twentieth century. Crime rates, which exploded from the 1960s to the 1990s, have dropped since 1992. If present trends continue, crime levels will continue to decrease slowly in the early twenty-first century, perhaps falling to the low crime levels of the 1950s and early 1960s. This decline will be due partly to the aging of the general population, partly to more effective policing, and partly to the unemployed becoming part of the legitimate job market.

Substance abuse, on the other hand, will show no general decline. It will remain a substantial problem. What will change is the kind of illicit drugs used. Crack cocaine use will continue to decline significantly, while ecstasy and heroin use will increase.

Finally, the free-wheeling sexual revolution of the 1970s will increasingly become a legend of the past. Safe sex has become the norm, and relatively conservative sexual behaviors regarding numbers of sexual partners will continue. Some of

Predictions of the future often look a bit silly to later generations. This is a view of the city of the future as envisioned less than a hundred years ago.

Culver Pictures

this will be driven by changing social norms and some by the fear of sexually transmitted diseases. AIDS will remain a serious, but controllable, problem in developed nations. In developing nations it will be the major killer of young adults.

All of the previous projections and predictions are quite plausible, and most of them will probably be close to the mark. However, not all will be. One thing we know with certainty about contemporary social problems is that the past is not always a clear predictor of the future. Unfortunately, clichés such as "The only certainty is change" are useless as views of the future because they tell us nothing about what will change or when change will occur. Fortunately, social scientists can provide some indications as to what is likely to change and what is not. However, even the best social scientists sometimes become so familiar with the established shibboleths and beliefs that they fail to recognize when a pattern is changing. Social scientists, like others, can become wedded to old ideas and patterns. For example, social problems texts published in the mid-1990s all had chapters on crime explaining why urban crime rates would "inevitably" remain high. All these texts have had to be rewritten. Similarly, social scientists did not foresee the late 1990s sharp declines in welfare dependency and more ex-welfare recipients holding jobs. These changes were said by some to be impossible. Yet between 1994 and 2000, welfare case loads dropped by half. Some still insist that the declines are largely a result of forcing the needy off welfare rather than a real change in social behaviors.

An examination of the various projections described previously suggests that the first years of the new century will differ interestingly from the last decades of the old century. The last part of the twentieth century was a period of intense and rapid social change. The decades from the mid-1960s to the 1990s were very rough-and-tumble ones for American society. Old social patterns collapsed, and viable new ones did not always emerge. Some of the changes, such as those in race and gender relations, were long overdue. Other changes, such as increasing economic inequality, a rising tide of violence, and increases in drug usage, contributed to a far less civil society.

The slowness of positive changes and the rapidity of negative ones created an atmosphere of relative pessimism regarding the possibility of managing social change.

Overall, the picture for the early twenty-first century is more one of guarded optimism. While the next decade is unlikely to see any social problems eliminated, several may become less serious threats to the maintenance of a civil and equal society. The difficult task is to make policy changes without creating new problems. For instance, street crime can be substantially reduced by community policing, but overbearing enforcement creates community resentment. Welfare dependency can be reduced and former recipients helped and encouraged to find jobs, but a safety net for the truly needy must be maintained. If those newly entering the labor force cannot obtain living-wage jobs, their wages have to be subsidized.

We may even see the pace of social change, as opposed to technological change, slow a bit. This in no way suggests that social change is going to cease, just that the pace of change may be more measured. Among other factors, the United States population is growing older. More mature populations are usually more socially stable. If a period of relatively greater social calm does materialize, social scientists will have less need to be constantly in a reactive mode. They will have the opportunity to place more emphasis on examining possible solutions to social problems. And some of these new approaches will be successful.

Finally, students should always keep in mind that the nature of the policies proposed to resolve social problems invariably reflects social ideologies about the nature of human nature. The dispute over gun control is an example. Those politically and socially liberal press for more gun control, especially over handguns and assault weapons. Those on the political and social right don't want restraints put on what they can do with their property. School slaughters such as the 13 people killed at Columbine High School in Littleton, Colorado, highlight these policy differences. Liberals see the problem as one of youths having easy access to guns, while conservatives are more likely to blame violent messages in popular culture and a breakdown of religious-moral authority. As informed citizens, future policy choices are yours to make. Remember, if you do not make the choices, others will make them for you.

Summary

The serious problems of the environment and of war and terrorism are mainly social problems. Environmental problems are the result not of natural occurrences but of specific human actions.

- Functional approaches see the environmental crisis as an inevitable dysfunction or consequence of an industrial society that puts primary emphasis on economic growth.
- Conflict approaches stress how major industrial powers invariably pollute because that is the cheapest way to maximize profits.
- Interactionist approaches note that Americans are socialized to view the world in terms of individual benefits. Resocialization stressing the common good is necessary.
- The major factors accelerating environmental destruction have been population growth and technology.
- *Cultural lag* refers to the social disequilibrium that occurs when technology changes faster in a society than social changes.

- *Environmental racism* refers to a deliberate pattern where toxic wastes and other pollutants are placed in the neighborhoods of poor people of color.
- Global warming based on the burning of fossil fuels producing a greenhouse effect is a much debated scientific issue. Political and economic conservatives are more likely to say global warming is a myth, while political and economic liberals (and an increasing amount of scientific data) are more likely to say it is a reality.
- Renewable resources such as solar, wind, and water power have not yet proven to be economically feasible on the large scale. However, they may be the only real alternative.
- Jobs versus environment arguments have little scientific backing. States with strong environmental regulations have the strongest economies. Clean air and water attract high-tech companies.
- In cleaning up the environment, a major question is *Who* is going to pay the costs? Will the costs be paid by polluting industries directly through higher product costs, or will the costs be paid indirectly through higher taxes paid by the general population?
- Both the level of military technology and the scale of warfare have made war much more deadly to the general population than in the past.
- The Cold War (1946–1989) led to massive expansion of the military-industrial complex, the close tying together of the military, the government, and weapons industries.
- Functionalists see war as the last resort for resolving conflicts that cannot be resolved otherwise.
- Conflict adherents see arms races and war as profiting military-industrial complexes.
- Interactionists stress that cultural patterns shape the idealization of war. Interactionists emphasize socializing people to put a higher social value on cooperation, nonaggression, and compromise.
- Terrorism uses violence for political ends against civilian populations. Revolutionary terrorism seeks to overthrow the existing social order, while state terrorism is the application of terror to support government aims.

☞Key Review Terms

algae bloom	greenwashing	revolutionary terrorism
Cold War	Industrial Revolution	sick building syndrome
cultural lag	Information Revolution	state terrorism
ecosystem	military-industrial complex	synergistic effect
environmental racism	nuclear proliferation	terrorism
global warming	pollution	
greenhouse effect	renewable resources	

? Questions for Discussion

1. Discuss the functionalist, conflict, and interactionist approaches toward the environment. Which of these positions do you favor? Why?

2. Explain the effects of population growth on the environment. What is the interaction between population and technology?

3. What is the cultural lag hypothesis? How does it apply to environmental issues?

4. Define global warming. What are the contrasting political and social issues? What group holds which position?

5. What are renewable resources and what is their future? How successful have we been in developing them to date?

6. If two-thirds of the globe is covered with water, why is water pollution an environmental problem?

7. Is pollution a social problem? Why or why not?

8. Discuss the relationship between war and technology. Are there ever positive social outcomes to war?

9. Compare functionalist, conflict, and interactionist approaches to war. Which approach do you find the most useful? Why?

10. Define and compare revolutionary and state terrorism. Which is the most dangerous to the world? Why?

☞ Suggested Resources

Karl von Clausewitz, *On War*, Anatol Papoport, ed. and trans. Viking, New York, 1983. This is the classic work read by every student of war on the use of war as a tool of national policy.

Murray Fesbach and Alfred Friendly, *Ecoside in the USSR: Health and Nature Under Siege*, Basic Books, New York, 1992. Fesbach is an expert on Russia and Russian data and this is a horrible but accurate depiction of the massive environmental damage done by the Soviet Union prior to its collapse in 1992.

David Helvarg, *The War Against the Greens*, Sierra Book Club, San Francisco, 1994. The book details attempts by polluters and corporate interests to roll back environmental protection laws as being bad for business.

Michael Howard, George J. Andreapoulos, and Mark R. Shulman, eds. *The Laws of War: Constraints on Warfare in the Western World*, Yale, New Haven, CT, 1995. How from ancient to modern times how warfare has been limited and controlled including the medieval religious restraints placed on waging war.

John Keegan, *The Book of War*, Viking, New York, 1999; and *The First World War*, Knopf, New York, 1999. The most respected, and most readable, contemporary historian of war provides an understanding of the true nature and horror of war.

Jeffrey D. Simon, *The Terrorist Trap: America's Experience with Terrorism*, Indiana University Press, Bloomington, 1994. How terrorism affects the United States and what we can and can't do to respond to terrorism.

Internet Connection   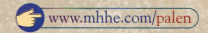 www.mhhe.com/palen

1. The desiccation of the Aral Sea is one of the greatest human-caused ecological disasters of the twentieth century. Visit the following websites to gather information about the Aral Sea: People and the Planet's Site on the Aral Sea (*www.oneworld.org/patp/pap_aral.html*); Visualizing Earth's website on the Aral Sea (*www.visearth.ucsd.edu/VisE_Int/aralsea/index.html*); and The Aral Sea Home Page (*www.dfd.dlr.de/app/land/aralsee/index.html*).

   a. What social policy decisions caused this disaster?

   b. List the social, health, and environmental consequences of these decisions.

   c. Search the web to see what remedial actions are being planned. List the sites and describe what measures will be taken to restore the Aral Sea.

2. Search the web on the subject of terrorism with an emphasis on potential terrorist attacks on the United States.

   a. List at least five sites that you feel are most comprehensive and informative on this subject. What trends do they forecast for this country?

   b. What are the most feared terrorist groups in the near future?

   c. What resources does the United States have available to monitor world terrorism?

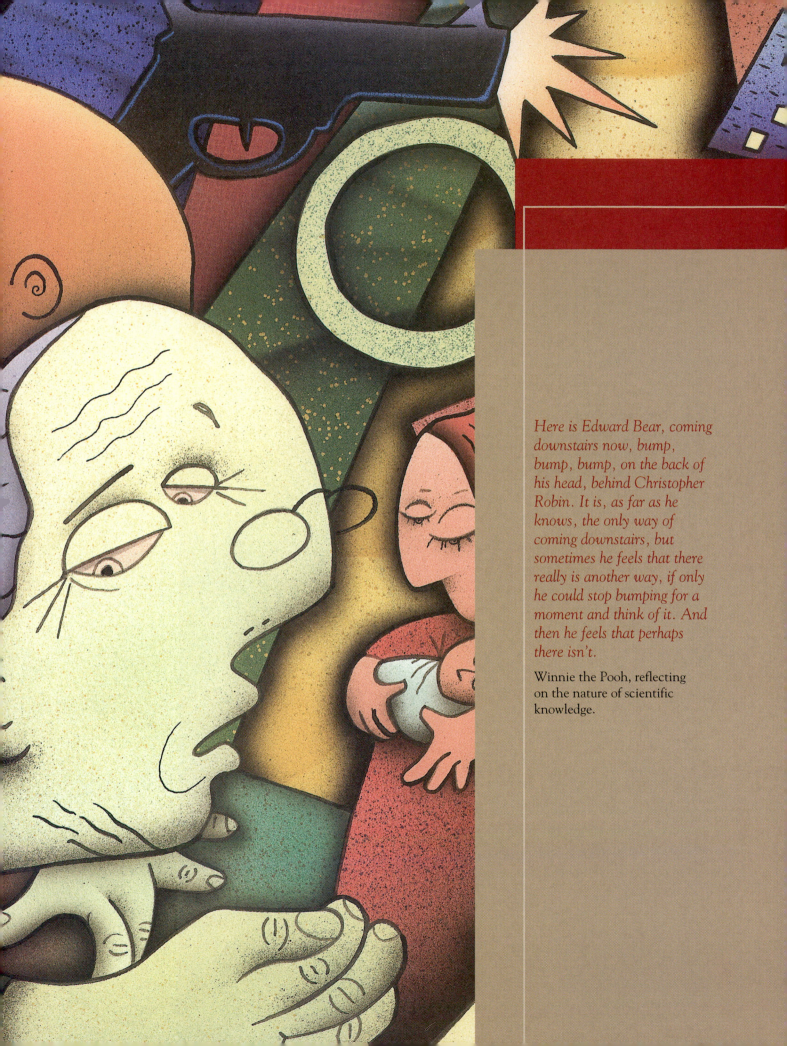

Here is Edward Bear, coming downstairs now, bump, bump, bump, on the back of his head, behind Christopher Robin. It is, as far as he knows, the only way of coming downstairs, but sometimes he feels that there really is another way, if only he could stop bumping for a moment and think of it. And then he feels that perhaps there isn't.

Winnie the Pooh, reflecting on the nature of scientific knowledge.

Methodological Appendix

Sociological Research

The brief overview that follows is not designed to be comprehensive. To fully discuss research methods would take far more space than is available in this Appendix. The purpose of this overview is to expose you to some of the basic concerns and issues that guide social research.

Science is not so much a subject matter, such as physics, astronomy, psychology, or sociology, or body of knowledge as it is a methodology of principles, rules, and procedures that guide scientific investigation. Science is a method of uncovering information in a systematic, consistent, reviewable, and replicable manner. That is, *science is a means by which we find out what we know and how we know it*.[1] Science provides an effective and reliable method of seeking and checking information.

Science in general, and social science in particular, cannot answer philosophical or theological questions as to the "why" of life. Science can only examine questions upon which empirical or observed information can be gathered. Social science, however, can test the consequences of beliefs that are held by members of a society. For example, sociological research cannot say anything as a science about whether God exists; it can, however, test how having a belief in God affects social behavior.

While raw data or facts are essential for science, data alone are not enough. Facts do not speak for themselves. To be scientifically useful, facts must be organized in a way that enables us to explain or predict. The goal of scientific study is to systematically organize data so that regular patterns, or generalizations, emerge. Science is concerned with generalizing and with general patterns and rates. Rather than ask why a particular crime was committed, sociologists ask why rates of crime vary by group, by area, and by social characteristics. For example sociologists may ask not why Jim Jones committed a robbery but why robberies are most frequently committed by those who have certain characteristics, such as being young and male.

Sociology shares with the other social sciences some special difficulties conducting certain types of research because human beings are the subject matter and humans can be difficult to study. There are limits on what sort of information sociologists can licitly gather and on the methods they use to gather this data. Sociologists, for example, cannot encourage or provoke criminal behavior in order to observe its consequences. Nor can people be put at physical or psychological risk.

The social sciences also must address questions of interpreting meaning. While elements or chemicals have no "volition"—the ability to know and respond—humans attach meanings to their acts. Sociology and the other social and behavioral sciences must deal with complex, malleable, and changing human beings.

Hawthorne effect
contamination of an experiment by subjects' behavior being changed by their awareness of their being studied.

If experimental or observational research is being done on human subjects, we must ask how the presence of a researcher might affect findings. Humans (such as college students in psychology experiments) may behave differently when they know that they are being studied. Since the 1930s social researchers have been aware of the **Hawthorne Effect** (named after the Western Electric Plant where it was first documented by researchers), whereby the presence of "outsiders" changes the behavior of those being observed. Researchers have had to learn how to control for such contamination of results. There is also the difficulty of generalizing from potentially atypical subpopulations (such as freshman college students) to the population at large.

---

[1]See, for example, Chava Frankfort-Nachmias and David Nachmias, *Research Methods in the Social Sciences*, St. Martin's, New York, 1992.

Finally, it is not ethical to perform certain types of social experiments on humans, such as experiments that might emotionally damage participants. Detailed government regulations now protect the rights of human subjects in federally sponsored research. For example, Stanley Milgram's famous experiment at Yale—in which he tested obedience to authority by having participants supposedly administer painful and potentially lethal shocks to another participant—can no longer be replicated.[2] Such experiments were very useful in telling us just how easily subordinates can be influenced to carry out actions, even against their own judgment. However, because of the potential mental and emotional harm to participants, such experiments are no longer acceptable. Fortunately, most sociological research can be carried out by statistically manipulating, rather than by physically manipulating, variables.

Almost a century of social research has demonstrated that the scientific method can be applied to examining social behavior and problems. That is, on the basis of research we can make generalizations that apply to similar cases and situations. This text covers some of these sociological research findings which have been examined, discussed, and debated. This in turn enables us both to explain why something happens and to make some projections as to the likelihood of it occurring again. While much remains to be done, we enter the new millennium with a substantial understanding of social behavior.

Research Terminology

Hypotheses

Research begins by systematically laying out what question or questions are to be examined. Using previous research or theories as a guide, the investigator states a proposition about what the research expects to discover. This proposition is referred to as a "hypothesis." Specifically, a **hypothesis** is a tentative answer to a research problem, expressed in the form of a relationship between variables.[3] The hypothesis is used to guide research and is based on an understanding of what previous research on the topic has produced. Two examples of hypotheses are:

hypothesis
posited but unverified relationship between variables.

- Exposure to pornographic material increases sex crimes.
- Increasing poverty leads to increasing rates of crime, so the poor commit the most crime.

(Both of these hypotheses are widely held by the general populace, but neither is supported by research data.)

Variables

variable
characteristic that can change or differ from case to case.

Variables are concepts or characteristics that can change from time to time or case to case. Variables measure the attributes, activities, behaviors, and attitudes

---

[2]Stanley Milgram, *Obedience to Authority: An Experimental View*, Harper & Row, New York, 1973.
[3]Frankfort-Nachmias and Nachmias, *Research Methods*, p. 552.

and beliefs of the people and societies we study. Variables used by sociologists include age, gender, education, occupation, race, income, and other attributes that vary from person to person. The data may come from person-to-person interviews, questions on surveys, information from governments or other organizations, or from observations by the researcher. While we use variables to measure attributes, it is essential to remember that we are studying human behavior and beliefs—we are not merely measuring the variables.

When doing research, we seek correlations, or relationships, using three types of variables: independent variables, dependent variables, and control variables.

Independent Variables

independent variable
a variable that causes change in another (dependent) variable.

Independent Variables Independent variables are the variables that result in or are connected with changes in other variables. The independent variable is used to "predict" or explain the dependent variable; it is the "cause" of a particular behavior or opinion. For example, in research on racism we may try to "explain" attitudes and behaviors defined as racist. The independent variable might be a person's residence in a particular area of the country, age, religious beliefs, or level of education. In an example in the text, we examined research attempting to explain increases in levels of unemployment (the dependent variable) for inner-city residents. The independent variables include the relocation of manufacturing jobs out of inner-city areas, low educational levels of potential workers, and poor attitudes toward work. Note that the independent variable can change or vary. The dependent variable is a result; that is, it is what happens when you change or manipulate the independent variable.

Independent variables are not selected on a random basis. Because science is cumulative, variables are selected on the basis of previous research which suggests that certain independent variables have predictive ability.

Dependent Variables

dependent variable
a variable that is changed by another (independent) variable.

Dependent Variables Dependent variables represent those behaviors that are connected to or are influenced by independent variables. Variation in the dependent variable is what we are trying to explain or measure. In a strict sense, dependent variables are the "effects"—behaviors, opinions, and so on—or results of the independent variables. A research study that examines racial issues, for example, may want to ask under what circumstances landlords do or do not discriminate. The dependent variable would be whether the landlord does or does not offer to rent an apartment to minority as well as to white couples. A variable seen as independent in one study may be treated as a dependent variable in another. For instance, the variable "social class" is treated as an independent variable in some studies and as a dependent variable in others.

Control Variables

control variable
holding all variables except one constant in order to see effect of the one variable.

spurious relationship
a meaningless correlation.

Control Variables Control variables are used to ensure that the correlation between the independent variable and the dependent variable is causal and not the result of some other factor or factors. Sometimes, in our normal everyday routine, we experience something (a dependent variable) and immediately assume we know the "cause" (independent variable) of what happened. Yet sometimes, we are profoundly mistaken. This mistake is due to a **spurious relationship**—one in which a correlation (measure of the strength of a relationship between two variables) is found, but this correlation doesn't tell us anything useful. Merely looking at the relationship of one dependent and one or more independent variables is insufficient for understanding what really is happening. The following hypothetical example, while somewhat simplistic, helps explain this importance.

There exists a strong positive correlation between the sales of ice cream (independent variable) and the number of rapes committed (dependent variable). If we were to look only at this relationship, we might be tempted to conclude that consuming ice cream causes an increase in rape. Obviously there is a serious flaw

490

in this interpretation. We have come across a spurious relationship. In order to control for possible spurious relationships, we add control variables. In the case of our example, we need only include the control variable "time of year." We then find that (1) ice cream sales are higher in summer (because of the heat) and that (2) the number of rapes increases during the summer (because more people are out and about). Although this example may be simplistic, spurious relationships are a very real problem for all research. It is particularly important that the relationship not be spurious when researching social problems, because "scientific findings" are often used in debates over public policy. Many examples exist in which the populace and politicians have all too quickly latched on to an explanation about the causes of racism, discrimination, violence, or other social problems, only to have subsequent research reveal these "causes" to be spurious.

Correlation

Correlation is the measure of the strength of a relationship between variables. It refers to the extent to which, as one variable changes, another variable changes. One typical correlation is that of height and weight in children. As a child gets taller, weight usually increases. Thus, you could say that there is a strong correlation between height and weight. In the sciences, perfect correlations are exceptionally rare. (Usually expressed as 1.00, a perfect correlation indicates that one variable perfectly predicts another.) Rather, scientists discuss the strength of various correlations between variables, or how "strong" those relationships are. It is important to remember that correlation is not causation (one variable does not *cause* another), but a high correlation indicates a strong statistical relationship.

Correlations can be positive or negative. A **positive correlation** is where the relationship between the variables changes in the same direction. For instance, research has found a strong positive correlation between education and income: As educational level increases, income increases. Education and income thus "move" in the same direction. A positive correlation is also found when the relationship shows two variables both decrease together. For example, a positive correlation is found between studying and grades: As the amount of time studying decreases, exam grades also decrease. Again, although the result may be unwanted, this represents a "positive" correlation.

Negative correlations are those relationships where an increase in an independent variable results in a decrease in the dependent variable. For example, in the area of race relations, an increase in the amount of contact between whites and blacks (independent variable) results in a decrease in antiblack and antiwhite attitudes (the dependent variable).

> **correlation**
> *measure of strength of a relationship between two or more variables that systematically change together.*

> **positive correlation**
> *relationship between variables changes systematically in the same direction.*

> **negative correlations**
> *relationship between variables changes systematically in the opposite direction.*

Characteristics of Research

Validity and Reliability

> **validity**
> *extent to which a measure measures what it is intended to measure.*

When your research variable actually measures what you want it to measure, it has **validity.** For example, the SAT test was reputed for decades to measure innate scholastic aptitude or ability. Thus, the test score was a variable that supposedly indicated scholastic aptitude. It became clear, however, that the tests were not measuring innate academic ability or aptitude, but rather the tests were measuring exposure to middle-class schools and values and the achievement of certain knowledge and skills. Therefore, the test's administrators changed the "A" in SAT from "aptitude" to "achievement" and it is now generally accepted that the SAT test is reasonably valid as a measure of exposure to academic opportunities and knowledge. It is far less valid in measuring intellectual aptitude or ability.

If you repeat the same study several times and you get the same result, the research measure is said to have **reliability.** That is, the data are consistent. SAT scores, for example, would have little reliability as a measure of performance if every time you took the test you had a widely different score. Some disputes over the use of SAT scores reflect concerns over the reliability or consistency of test results.

reliability
consistency in measurement over several repetitions.

Replication

Reliability in science is usually determined by **replication** or repeating. A finding is reliable if others repeat the research and get similar results.

What makes sociology a "science" is not the subject matter but the means by which information is obtained. When a sociologist presents scientific findings, she or he is not operating by fiat. Rather, the sociologist has gathered and presented the information in a manner that other sociologists recognize. This means the data have been collected in a systematic fashion and analyzed using procedures that have been agreed upon. The findings are then published in recognized sociological journals. Other sociologists can critically examine the data and the findings because they know what was done and how it was done. If they wish, they can replicate—that is redo—the analysis to ensure its accuracy and reliability. Keep in mind that a measurement can have high reliability but low validity, or high validity but low reliability. One does not ensure the other.

replication
other researchers repeating the research.

Probability

Science by its very nature deals not in certainty but in levels of **probability** or predictability. All science is based on probability. Sometimes the **correlations** or relationships are so high that nonscientists treat them as a given. For example, it is said that water boils at 212 degrees Fahrenheit, and "normal" body temperature is 98.6 degrees Fahrenheit. However, these statements are based on certain assumptions. The boiling water, for example, is assumed to be at sea level. Water boils at lower temperatures at higher elevations. Any cook living in the high altitude of Denver knows that directions for baking have to be modified to consider the variable of altitude.

Also the "normal" 98.6 degree body temperature is simply an approximated average. Some persons run higher and some lower. This average doesn't precisely apply to women between ages 15 and 50. Women of childbearing age show monthly temperature variations, experiencing a slightly lower temperature during the first half of their menstrual cycle followed by a slight elevation in body temperature at the time of ovulation. Women often use this temperature variation to help when they seek to become pregnant. In spite of the fact that 98.6 is not "normal" for all persons or at all times we continue to use 98.6 as "normal" because for the practical purpose of detecting a fever this "average" is close enough.

Because social science research involves humans who are self-aware and who can change and modify their behavior, levels of probability are generally somewhat lower than in the physical sciences. However, this isn't always the case.

probability
the likelihood or predictability of an event occurring.

correlation
measure of strength of a relationship between two or more variables that systematically change together.

Within sociology, generally high levels of probability are found in the more quantitative areas, such as demography. For example, we can safely say that all economically developed countries have low birthrates.

Research Methodologies

Quantitative Methods

Studies relying on statistical analysis for their interpretation of social problems and conditions are referred to as **quantitative** research. The most widely used method of quantitative data collection in social science is the survey. A **survey** is a study that uses a sample from a larger population in order to test variables' distribution and interactions. To ensure that the sample represents an entire population, **random sampling** is often used. Random sampling means using a sample in which each part of the population has an equal chance of being selected, for example, a telephone sample of both listed and unlisted numbers in which every twentieth number is called. Surveys commonly use **questionnaires,** a printed research instrument on which the subject is asked a series of written questions. Questionnaires can be administered any number of ways, including to a class at school or through the mail. An alternative to a printed questionnaire is an **interview,** a series of questions administered face-to-face to the respondent. Findings from quantitative survey studies are among the best-known social science research.

Data originally collected for U.S. Census information and government reports are another major source of quantitative data. We see quantitative data sets presented in newspapers, in magazines, and on the nightly news every day. Any findings that use statistics are quantitative data. Sociologists like quantitative data because of the ability to control statistically for extraneous variables and the possibility of replicating the research. Quantitative studies are most useful for examining macrolevel, or structural, changes within society. Quantitative studies are used by different various theoretical orientations, including the functionalist and conflict perspectives.

Qualitative Methods

Qualitative studies rely on researchers' observations rather than on quantitative data. This approach allows the researcher to better "get inside" and develop insights about the phenomenon being observed. **Participant observation,** that is, direct systematic observation of the social group being studied, is one method by which an observer attempts to test hypotheses. Qualitative research focuses on how small groups or individuals interact, with less emphasis placed on quantifying (or counting) such interactions. This is not to say that no counting is taking place (nor does quantitative research necessarily ignore interpersonal interactions). Rather, qualitative analysis centers principally on examining people within their personal milieu. Thus it is more likely to be used by those with an interactionist perspective. A qualitative study might involve, for instance, being a participant observer in a juvenile gang for a period of two years. As Jerome Kirk and Marc Miller explain: "Qualitative research is a particular tradition in social sciences

quantitative studies
research based on numerical data and statistical analysis.

survey
selecting a sample from a larger population.

random sample
a sample chosen in such a way as every member of the population being sampled has an equal chance of being selected.

questionnaire
prepared written questions.

interview
face to face asking set questions.

qualitative studies
research based on observational rather than numerical data.

participant observation
method in which the researcher participates in the activities of the group under study.

493

that depends fundamentally on watching people in their own territory and interacting with them in their own language, on their own terms."[4]

Qualitative research is a particular mainstay for those using the interactionist and labeling perspectives. Qualitative research can be described as the attempt to substantiate the existence (or nonexistence) of "something." Quantitative research can be described as the enumeration of the degree or extent to which this condition identified by the qualitative research exists. High quality research is done using a range of qualitative and quantitative methodologies.

Data Sources

As mentioned in the discussion of variables, sociologists get information from a wide variety of sources. In qualitative studies, research is a hands-on experience, in which the sociologist directly observes the phenomenon in question. Going into the field and directly observing how people interact, deal with problems, and live their lives constitutes the primary data collection process. For others, data collection is an activity largely based on quantitative surveys and experiments. Most Americans have had some exposure to survey research, because we have been a subject of either phone surveys or mail surveys. Some of these have been nonscientific product surveys of marginal quality. Sociologists frequently use scientific survey research to examine social problems because surveys are useful in obtaining detailed information on attitudes and opinions about various issues.

An important source of information for many sociologists is government data and reports. Much of what we know about the extent of poverty, women in the labor force, changes in population and many other issues is taken from information gathered by the government. All branches of government collect information. Some sources include the decennial Census, Current Population Survey, and a number of other ongoing data collection efforts, such as employment data. In addition a number of educational and private organizations can be useful sources of information about social problems. Historical research, utilizing library documents, diaries, and the like as sources of information is also useful in examining social problems.

Although data from sociological research comes from a wide variety of sources, the underlying theme throughout all good research is that it is systematic and that it can be reexamined by others in the discipline to ensure accuracy and reliability.

Putting Research Together

Drawing together the material above it is clear that research involves a number of activities. Here is a list of steps that researchers go through in developing sound research.

First, you must develop a good research question. Based on your readings and examination of previous research (often through library research) you determine what others have learned. Based on this research, you create a good *testable* hypothesis.

Second, now that you have a research question (or questions) and hypotheses based on them, what resources do you need to carry out the project? How much staff, time, money, and equipment? Beginning researchers often underestimate the resources required. Established researchers commonly submit research proposals

---

[4]Jerome Kirk and Marc L. Miller, *Reliability and Validity in Qualitative Research,* Sage Publications, 1986, p. 9.

for project funding to government or private funding sources, such as the National Science Foundation, the National Institutes of Health, or the Ford Foundation. Different agencies and foundations focus on different issues; that is, some focus on homelessness whereas others may specialize in health issues. If you are to be the sole researcher and you are providing resources such as money and time, you have to make sure the project is not too ambitious and is tailored to your resources.

Third, what research methods will you use? Will it be participant observation, a specially created survey, or a secondary analysis of existing data sources such as the census? If you are examining juvenile crime, are you focusing on the structure of a particular gang or are you interested in how the rate of gang violence is changing? The methodology used will depend upon both the question being asked and the resources you have available. In considering the method and type of data collection, you also have to be sensitive to ethical concerns. For example, if you are observing gang members, what do you do if during your research you see a crime occurring? Or if you are conducting a class survey on crimes, how do you assure respondents' anonymity? What if the police want to examine your research notes? Researchers have actually been jailed for refusing to surrender such information.

Fourth, how do you plan to record your data? Are you recording data in a manner that can confirm or reject your hypotheses? If you are carrying out participant observation and keeping a diary of daily activities, how do you plan to organize your impressions? Are you putting information into preset categories? With survey data what checks do you have to prevent errors in coding. On what basis do you collapse categories where you have insignificant cases?

Fifth, how do you interpret your findings? Which hypotheses are confirmed and which are rejected by the data? How do your findings fit with what others have discovered?

Sixth, writing up your conclusions and presenting them to others is your final step. In preparing your final report you should note not only how your study advances what is known and supports or rejects existing theoretical models, but also any specific problems with your research. Finally, by presenting your finding either through a presentation at a professional meeting or through publication in a professional journal, you allow others to share in your information. It also allows others to critique, replicate, and build upon your work.

If you do the above you will have a scientific research project. Readers will know not only your results, but also how you arrived at your findings.

☞Key Review Terms

control variable	interview	survey
correlation	negative correlation	qualitative methodology
dependent variable	positive correlation	quantitative methodology
Hawthorne Effect	probability	questionnaire
hypothesis	reliability	random sampling
independent variable	science	validity

Glossary

absolute poverty absence of basic necessities of food, clothing, shelter, education, and health care.

addiction habitual use of drugs or alcohol to the extent that stopping causes physiological as well as psychological trauma.

affirmative action programs designed to compensate for past discrimination by offering special advantage and assistance to discriminated-against groups.

age grading classifying people by age categories.

ageism prejudice and discrimination against the elderly.

aging population the increasing average age of the nation's people.

agricultural revolution the invention of fixed agriculture some 6,000 years ago led to predictable yields and a population explosion. It also produced social class differences.

AIDS acquired immunodeficiency syndrome, major sexually-transmitted infection killing 2.6 million yearly.

algae blooms rapid algae growth polluting lakes and rivers.

alcoholic drinking to the point where it injures health, earning a living, and social relationships.

American dream the belief that a growing economy will provide upward mobility and a better life for one's children.

anorexia nervosa a condition in which a person diets and sometimes exercises compulsively in an effort to be thin, regardless of her measured weight.

antipsychotic drugs drugs that reduce symptoms of mental illness.

apartheid legally mandated racial separation.

assault attack on a person intended to hurt or kill.

assimilation process by which a minority takes on the values of the dominant group and ceases to be a distinct entity.

baby boom the dramatic rise in births following World War II until 1964.

behavioral assimilation taking on the outward characteristics of the majority society, e.g., food, dress, behavior.

bipolar (manic-depressive) disorders mental illness involving extreme elation or more commonly, depression.

blended family family in which the marital partners were previously married and bring children from the earlier marriages.

blue-collar work that involves manual labor, and often lower prestige.

bulimia nervosa a condition in which a person alternately engages in bingeing and purging, often with the aid of laxatives or other drugs and usually in secret.

capitalism economic system based on markets in which most wealth and means of production are held by corporations and private individuals, rather than by the government.

cascading enrolling in a good college where there is a higher likelihood of graduating, rather than at the most selective college.

Cold War economic and political struggle between the West and Soviet systems which ended with the 1989 collapse of communism.

coming out publicly identifying oneself as a homosexual and accepting the homosexual role.

command economy a centrally directed economic system in which goods are produced based on government decision rather than market demand, the system of the Soviet Union prior to its collapse.

concentric zonal hypothesis theory of urban growth developed by Ernest Burgess suggesting that cities grow from the center to periphery through a series of concentric zones having distinct social and housing features.

conflict approaches theoretical models of society that focus on struggle, competition, and change.

conglomerate a large corporation composed of many smaller corporations.

conspicious consumption consumption designed to show ones status or position rather than consumption for actual use.

corporation a legally constructed organization whose existence, powers, and liabilities exist separate from those of its owners and employees.

correlation measure of strength of a relationship between two or more variables that systematically change together.

crime an activity that violates the criminal code.

cultural imperialism assumption that middle class culture and values should dominate.

cultural lag condition in which one part of the culture changes before others causing disruption, usually technological change precedes social.

cultural pluralism belief advocating that each group keep its distinct cultural characteristics, similar to multiculturalism.

cyclical unemployment unemployment tied to the rise and fall of the business cycle.

deferred gratification putting off short-term rewards for long-range goals.

deindustrialization shutting down of factories due to movement from a manufacturing to a service economy.

delinquency acts that would be criminal when committed by an adult plus activities defined by statute as punishable when committed by juveniles.

demographic transition the movement of a country from high birth rates and death rates to low birth and death rates through the decline of death rates followed by the decline of birth rates, usually attributed to economic development.

depressants drugs that slow the response of the central nervous system and reduce alertness and coordination.

discrimination inequality of treatment, often based on minority group membership.

double standard assumption that society allows for sexual activity in men, while women are held to stricter standards.

drift hypothesis those with mental disorders drift toward lower socioeconomic status.

drug abuse use of a chemical substance to the degree that physical, psychological, and social harm results.

economy social institution that organizes the production, distribution, and consumption of goods and services.

ecosystem community of interdependent organisms and their environment.

eco-terrorism destroying, often by arson, property owned by those judged to be harming animals or the environment.

edge cities developed outer suburban areas that are becoming economically dominant over old downtowns.

endogamy Custom of marrying within ones own group, often applied in terms of religion and social class.

environmental racism deliberately placing environmental hazards in minority neighborhoods.

ethnic group body of people seeing itself and seen by others as possessing a distinct culture.

ethnicity shared cultural heritage.

evil-causes-evil fallacy belief that if an act is bad it is caused by evil circumstances.

extended family family unit containing additional family members beyond parents and children such as grandparents and parents, brothers and sisters.

family kinship unit of two or more persons who live in the same household and who are legally or biologically related.

felony serious violation of the criminal code punishable by at least a prison term of a year.

feminism advocates the equal treatment of women and men in society.

feminist theory a theoretical approach for understanding society that focuses on the role of gender and the unequal treatment of women.

feminization of poverty the increasing trend for the poor in America to be single, deserted, and divorced women and their children.

field study research done in real-life settings; participant observation is one variant.

first wave immigrants coming to the U.S. between 1820 and 1880, largely from the British Isles, Ireland, and Germany.

functionalist approaches theories that view society as an integrated whole where the parts of the society have functions, or practices and patterns, that act to maintain society.

functional illiteracy inability to read and understand a language at roughly the sixth-grade level.

gay a homosexual, generally male.

gender refers to both identity and statuses ascribed to men and women based on sociocultural distinctions.

gendered social order the principle that gender roles are built into social institutions, as well as relationships between women and men in society.

gentrification revitalization of central city housing and neighborhoods through the immigration of upper-middle class populations.

gerontology study of aging and the aging process.

GI Bill federal legislation that paid for college education of World War II veterans.

glass ceiling barriers to women's upward mobility through the highest levels in organizations.

greenhouse effect global warming due to the burning of fossil fuels.

green revolution Recent dramatic improvements in agricultural yields—especially in developing countries—due to the use of new genetically-engineered seeds.

greenwashing corporations giving products environmentally positive names and advertising in order to suggest that the product is environmentally friendly.

grade inflation common practice of giving higher grades for less work than in the past.

health state of physical, mental, and social well-being.

hidden curriculum schools transmitting middle-class beliefs and values.

homelessness poor urban residents who live full-time on the street.

homocide killing of a person.

homogamy marrying within one's group.

homophobia holding negative attitudes towards homosexuality.

homosexuality sexual activity with members of one's own sex.

household persons, related or not, who live in the same housing unit.

hustlers male prostitute.

hyperghettoization extreme racial segregation of very poorest inner city residents.

index offenses eight categories of street crimes against persons or property.

Industrial Revolution basic change in the production of goods in Western societies owing the application of mechanical power leading to the factory system, beginning in the late eighteenth century.

inequality disparity in status or resources.

Information revolution postindustrial economic system based on the production and exchange of knowledge and information rather than of goods **institutional racism** discrimination practices that are built into the social structure.

institutional racism discrimination practices that are built into the social structure.

interactionist approaches theories that focus on how people in society define themselves and their social relationships, and respond to social interactions.

interlocking directorate pattern whereby many corporate board of directors members sit on numerous other boards of directors.

invasion-succession process by which one activity or population displaces another in an ecological area.

Kinsey report first major study of American sexual behavior.

labeling theory theory holding that branding someone as a deviant encourages further deviant behavior. Society responds to labels more than actions, i.e., someone seeking mental health care is mentally ill.

labor union worker organization that seeks to improve wages and working conditions.

latent function unintended or unrecognized consequences of social actions or policies.

lesbian female homosexual.

manifest function intended and recognized consequence of social actions or policies.

Marxist theory the explaining of a society's political and social behavior based upon its economic system.

Medicaid federal program financed from tax revenue designed to pay medical costs for those unable to afford any health care.

medical model defines a disorder as an "illness" that can be treated medically.

Medicare federal program financed from Social Security tax to providing health care for those 65 and older.

melting pot model belief that all ethnic groups upon coming to America should become part of one common American heritage.

mental disorder and mental illness not coping with or responding rationally to the circumstances of everyday life.

middle-class squeeze the fear of the middle class that their position is worsening and their children will not do as well.

military-industrial complex Tight association and job movement among the military, defense industries, and the federal government, warned against as a threat to democracy by President Dwight Eisenhower in his Farewell Address.

minority groups category of people treated negatively because of appearance or cultural differences.

misdemeanor less serious violation of the criminal code that can be punished by less than a year in jail or a fine.

mixed economy capitalist economic system whose inequalities are moderated by government policies, the economic system prevalent in Western Europe.

Morrell Act federal act of 1862 establishing land grant colleges.

multiculturalism belief in the equality of all cultures and the value of diversity, similar to cultural pluralism.

multinationals large corporation that operates in more than one nation, often with limited national control.

murder illegal homicide committed with malice.

myth nonfactual beliefs that have social consequences.

National Crime Victimization Survey annual Justice Department survey of actual incidence of crime experienced by households.

national family wars term applied to dispute over how the family should be defined, and what family form is best for society.

neurosis mental disability that produces anxiety but does not prevent day-to-day operation.

new familism belief in the importance of two parent families, and that children have been hurt by recent family changes.

nuclear (or conjugal) family family unit composed of parents (or parent) and children.

nuclear proliferation spread of nuclear weapons to additional nations.

nuclear war warfare using nuclear weapons.

organized crime criminal activity run in a systematic businesslike manner to provide illegal goods and services such as drugs, gambling, and prostitution.

parallel-growth model simultaneous suburban growth of white and black populations, as opposed to invasion-succession.

participant observation method in which the researcher participates in the activities of the group under study.

patriarchy a system in which men are ascribed a disproportionate share of power and authority.

plea bargaining a defendant pleading guilty to lesser charges and lesser penalty in return for a guilty plea.

Ponzi scheme an illegal pyramid scheme that pays off earlier investors with money from subsequent investors.

pornography depicting sexual behavior designed to sexually excite the viewer.

prejudice rigid predisposed negative opinion toward a group that is unaffected by any contrary evidence.

primary deviance initial deviance that does not result in being labeled deviant.

primary labor market composed of those regularly employed in fixed positions by relatively stable firms paying fixed wages, same as formal labor market.

prostitution promiscuous sexual activity for money.

protease inhibitors complex and expensive "AIDS cocktail" drugs that inhibit AIDS development.

psychoactive drugs drugs that are used to alter mood and provide euphoria rather than for improving medical condition.

psychosis serious mental illness that involves a sharp break with reality and prevents day-to-day operation.

qualitative studies research based on observational rather than numerical data.

quantitative studies research based on numerical data and statistical analysis.

racial profiling stopping suspects based on their racial or ethnic characteristic.

race a group that is assumed to share common genetic traits that society sees as socially significant.

rape sexual intercourse forced either by psychological coercion or physical force

rates differences among groups.

redlining pattern of banks and financial institutions refusing to make any loans in inner-city areas defined as high risk.

redneck poor rural or working-class southern whites, often used in a derogatory sense.

relative poverty feeling poor based on having less than others in the society, the emphasis is on inequality rather than an absolute level of need.

renewable resources energy resources such as wind and water which do not come from fossil fuels.

residual category catch-all category for unexplained behaviors.

restrictive covenants attachments to property deeds, especially those specifying ethnic-racial groups to whom the property cannot be transferred.

revolutionary terrorism anti-government terrorism designed to change the government.

schizophrenia the most diagnosed mental illness involving withdrawal and a break with reality.

scores prostitute's client.

secondary labor market composed of those working for oneself or small businesses whose employment is poorly paid and nonsecure, also called the informal labor market. Includes a third to a half of all workers in developing countries.

secondary or residual deviance adoption of the role of a deviant by someone who has been publicly labeled as a deviant.

second shift the burden of housework which continues to fall primarily to women even when they work outside the home.

second wave European immigrants to the U.S. between 1880 and 1920s, predominately from Southern and Eastern Europe, e.g., Slavs, Russians, Poles, Italians, Greeks.

sexism the integrated cultural and social systems through which the disadvantages of gender are constructed, perpetuated, and enforced.

sexual harassment unwelcome verbal or physical conduct of a sexual nature which affects the recipient's work conditions or contributes to a hostile environment.

sick building syndrome airtight buildings which produce physical ills.

situational or deprivational homosexuality homosexuality due to the absence of heterosexual partners.

Social Darwinism application of the "survival of the fittest" concept to social life in society.

social deviation behavior that substantially differs from the expected norm.

socialism economic system where resources and means of production of goods and services are owned collectively.

social labeling assigning group characteristics.

socially constructed socially created and defined.

Social Security federal pension-like program that provides monthly payments to eligible elderly participants.

sociological imagination allows us to develop a broad perspective as to how social norms and behaviors affect our lives.

sociological perspective focus on seeking general overall patterns rather than individual examples.

solid alcohol sedative having a depressant effect.

state terrorism government use of terrorist means against its own people.

steering showing home buyers only homes in neighborhoods of their racial group.

stereotype attributing fixed characteristics, usually negative, to all members of a group.

structural assimilation full acceptance by the majority population, usually represented by intermarriage.

structural mobility changes in socioeconomic status due to changes in the structure of the economy.

structural unemployment unemployment due to long-term changes in the economic system.

synergistic effects combined effects are more severe than adding individual effects.

terrorism acts of violence used as a political strategy.

theory a statement that organizes and relates facts in a way that explains the relationships among them.

third wave current immigrants coming largely from Latin America and Asia.

Thomas theorem situations defined as real are real in their consequences.

total institutions placed that cut persons off from society in order to reform or remake them.

trickle-down belief that housing quality decreases over time.

underclass the long-term poor who are in practice excluded from the social and economic life of society.

Uniform Crime Report yearly report of crimes reported to the police and assembled by the FBI.

urbanism behavioral aspects of urban life, the characteristics of urban life produced by city living.

urbanism as a way of life supposed consequences of urban living such as economic goal orientation and decreasing importance given to personal interaction and neighborhood values.

urbanization process of urban growth through the concentration of population in metropolitan places.

urban homesteading programs that provide for low-cost resale of abandoned city homes to those who will rehabilitate them.

variable characteristic that can change or differ from case to case.

Victorian morality social code supporting public prudery and double standard where males are allowed greater sexual freedom than females.

volunteer work unpaid community or charity work.

war organized armed conflict among nations.

wealth the value of a person's total economic assets including real estate, stocks and bonds, and other assets as well as money.

white collar desk jobs that do not involve actual production of goods.

white-collar crime crimes committed by those of respectable social position and related to their jobs.

white ethnic usually refers to working-class second- and third-generation Americans of eastern and southern European ancestry.

work paid activity that provides a livelihood.

Index

B

Baby boom (1946–1964), 152
  generation, 305–306
Bahr, Howard M., 192n
Bailey, K. C., 475n
Baily, J. M., 439n
Bales, Robert F., 277n
Baltzell, E. Digby, 37n
Banfield, Edward, 51, 52
Bank of America, 436
Barcus, Francis Earle, 121n
Bar girls, 444
Barone, Michael, 247n
Barrickman, P. J., 121n
Baum, Alice S., 194n
Bean, Fran D., 95n
Becker, Howard S., 379n
Beer, Francis A., 472n
Beers, Clifford, 418
Behavioral assimilation, 89
Bell, Alan P., 441n
Bellair, Paul, 343n
The Bell Curve: Intelligence and Class Structure in American Life (Herrnstein and Murray), 8, 31
Bengtson, Vern L., 117n, 129n
Bennett, William, 384n
Benson, V., 44n
Berger, Peter, 6n
Berke, Richard, 437n
Bernard, Jesse, 281
Berrios, Jerry, 101n
Berstein, Jared, 218n
Bianchi, Suzanne, 21, 212n
Binion, V., 121n
Biology
  and gender differentiation, 117–119
  and race, 63
Bipolar, 409
Black; *See* African Americans
Black victimization, 343
Blaming the victim, 52
Blaming the Victim (Ryan), 52
Blaming the victim response, 52
Blended families, 275
Blue collar workers, 208
Blum, Deborah, 120n
Blum, Robert W., 126n
Blyth, Dale A., 126n
Bogue, Donald J., 192n
Bok, Derek, 258n
Boland, Barbara, 354n
Boldberg, Suzanne, 436
Bolduc, D., 120n
Boles, J., 447
Booth, A., 284n
Borjas, Georg J., 170n, 171n
Bowan, William G., 258n
Bowers v. Hardwick, 436
Bradford, William, 458
Branigin, William, 168n
Bridenbaugh, Carl, 468n
Brimlow, Peter, 167
Brinkerhoff, David, 120n
Broken window theory, 345
Brown, David, 380n
Brown, Lester R., 156, 158
Browning of America, 66
Brownmiller, Susan, 137
Buckley, William Jr., 384n
Bulimia nervosa, 120, 128
Bullard, R. D., 465n
Bumpass, Larry, 283n, 284n, 286n, 288n
Burgess, Ernest W., 182
Burgess concentric-zonal model, 182, 183, 337
Burnes, Donald W., 194n
Burt, Cyril, 21
Burton, Dudley, 466n
Bush, George, 254
Bush, George W., 39
Butterfield, Fox, 346

C

Calavita, Kitty, 347n
Calhoun, Thomas C., 135n
Califano, Joseph A., Jr., 365n, 400n
California, educational policies, 260–261
Call girls, 444
Cancio, A. Silvia, 78n
Capitalism, 220
Cashin, J. R., 370n
Castells, Manuel, 181n
Caucasoid, 62, 63
Caudill, Harry M., 51n
Census Bureau, U. S., 48
Chamblis, William, 332–333
Cherlin, Andrew, 291n
Chicago, University of , National Opinion Research Center, 20, 434
Chicago school of sociology, 180, 182
Child abuse, 293–294
Child rearing and gender, 120–121
Children
  and poverty, 47–48
  and single parent families, 277–278
Chiswick, Barry, 171n
Church, George, 316n
Cities
  best places to live, 199
  and crime, 336–337
  future of, 186–188
  racial divisions in, 189–190
  and safety, 346
Civil Rights Act, 437
Clark, C., 121n
Clayton, Horace, 73n
Clinard, Marshall B., 180n, 442n
Clitoridectomy, 119
Close, Ellis, 77n
Closet queens, 440
Coastal shelf pollution, 470–471
Cobain, Kurt, 376
Cobb, Jonathan, 110n
Cobb, N. J., 121n
Cocaine, 377
Cochran, William G., 434n
Cockerham, W. C., 422n
Cofer, Judith Ortiz, 120n
Cohen, Carl I., 192n
Cold war, 475
Coleman, James W., 246, 248, 347n, 348n
Coleman, John R., 195